America's International Relations Since World War I

Wesley M. Bagby

New York • Oxford
Oxford University Press
1999

D0420390

To Dad

Oxford University Press

Oxford New York
Athens Auckland Bangkok Bogotá Buenos Aires Calcutta
Cape Town Chennai Dar es Salaam Delhi Florence Hong Kong Istanbul
Karachi Kuala Lumpur Madrid Melbourne Mexico City Mumbai
Nairobi Paris São Paulo Singapore Taipei Tokyo Toronto Warsaw

and associated companies in
Berlin Ibadan

Published by Oxford University Press, Inc.
198 Madison Avenue, New York, New York 10016
http://www.oup-usa.org

Library of Congress Cataloging-in-Publication Data

Bagby, Wesley Marvin, 1922–
    America's international relations since World War I / Wesley M.
  Bagby.
      p.   cm.
    Includes bibliographical references and index.
    ISBN 0–19–512388–3 (cloth). — ISBN 0–19–512389–1 (pbk.)
    1. United States—Foreign relations—20th century.   I. Title
E744.B34   1999   98–16039
327.73'09'04—dc21   CIP

9 8 7 6 5 4 3 2 1

Printed in the United States of America
on acid-free paper.

Contents

Preface

This history of U.S. international relations since America's entry into World War I draws on the work of many scholars. Excellent studies of U.S. foreign relations have multiplied in recent years and what merits this book possesses rests on them.

This account is primarily a diplomatic history, but it makes references also to military, cultural, and economic factors and to developments abroad as needed to make intergovernmental relations intelligible. It also gives attention to domestic factors that affect foreign policy, the evolution of ideas, the special problems encountered by democracies in foreign relations, and long-term trends in relative national power.

Any organizational scheme solves some problems while creating others. If one writes of America's relations with many areas of the world, some jumping around geographically or chronologically is inevitable. Basically, this book is organized chronologically by presidential administrations, and topically within presidencies. One advantage of this plan is that it facilitates appreciation of the impact of personality, bureaucracy, and domestic politics on foreign policy. To minimize the problems it creates, exceptions are made; such as considering the 1923–1933 Republican administrations, and the Nixon-Ford administrations as units, and treat in one place subjects such as Reagan-Bush relations with Nicaragua. In addition, chapter subheads are made comparable so that one who wishes to examine the Vietnam War chronologically, for example, can do so by reading the relevant subheads in sequential chapters.

I have also sought to avoid polemics, to minimize imputations of good or evil intent, and to remain mindful of the imperfect international system within which humans of varying degrees of enlightenment seek to cope.

I thank my mentors for their contributions, and my students for their stimulus and challenge. A number of colleagues and students, too many to mention, all of them, have made much appreciated contributions to the manuscript. Particularly noteworthy were those of Professors Jack Hammersmith, Arthur Link, and Dennis Wainstock and also of Wesley Bagby, Jr., Janice Bagby, Steve Bagby, Mary Heironimus, Mike Shane, Karla Miller, and Todd Stoops. The maps were crafted by Debbie Benson. I hope that readers find this a useful introduction to the fascinating field of U.S. foreign relations.

Morgantown, WV
July, 1998   W. M. B.

Introduction: Elements of the System

U.S. foreign policy is more intelligible when leading characteristics of the international environment are held in mind. Some of these aspects seem so obvious as to scarcely require mentioning until one remembers that occasionally in the past framers of the U.S. foreign policy, and the American people to their detriment, appear to have lost sight of some of them.

For more than a hundred years after the War of 1812 Americans concerned themselves primarily with the conquest of the continent, while giving slight heed to developments in Europe or Asia. As a result, four generations of Americans acquired little experience in old-world international politics. Not surprisingly, many of them, however sophisticated they might have been on internal politics, appeared to Europeans to be uninformed and naive on world politics. The effect of this inexperience was magnified by the growth of democracy and the consequent impact of public opinion on policy. "When foreign affairs were ruled by autocracies or oligarchies," wrote former Secretary of State Elihu Root, "the danger of war was in sinister purposes. When foreign affairs are ruled by democracies the danger of war will be in mistaken beliefs. It is essential, Root added, to educate the people on relations among nations.

As technological developments brought distant parts of the world closer together, rising international trade and security interests drew the United States deeper into world politics. Also, economic, environmental, and health problems became increasingly global in their causes and effects. With the advent of nuclear weapons, national survival became even more dependent on well-informed conduct of foreign affairs.

Ungoverned International Competition

In the late nineteenth century, empires seemed to be the most powerful political organizations, but after World War I, and especially after World War II, most empires broke up into independent states; between 1945 and 1974, sixty-five new nations appeared. By 1998, members of the United Nations numbered 185.

In area, nations range from Russia's 17 million square kilometers to Liechtenstein's 160 square kilometers. China's population is more than a billion, while Andorra's is fifty three thousand. The United States had a 1996 gross national product (GNP) of $28,000 per capita (person), while Ethiopia produced only $500 per capita.

The most important characteristic of the international system, or lack of system, is that each nation is "sovereign," which means that it recognizes no superior authority, is free from external control, and determines its own policies. No higher governing authority exists. So-called international law is little more than a set of customs and standards, with no world police to enforce it. Thus, international relations are conducted in a state of anarchy, the condition of society in which there is no law or supreme power.

Consequently, international relations remain in a condition in which only armed strength and determination to be independent enable nations to survive. Under these circumstances, a high value is put on the willingness of citizens to defend their nation. Patriots teach that it is wrong to put any other loyalty above loyalty to the nation and that any action is justified if it contributes to national survival. This makes international relations basically amoral.

Consequently nations are dangerous to each other and find it necessary to arm themselves and stand guard as if every other nation were a potential enemy. They must behave much as men did in lawless frontier towns that had no sheriffs and where all men, some greedy and unscrupulous, carried guns.

In these circumstances, all nations are necessarily obsessed with protecting their national security. This leads them to favor measures that give them control of more territory, vital trade routes and waterways, and access to vital natural resources such as oil, and also measures that weaken actual or potential enemies and ensure friendly or subservient governments in nearby countries. However, to the degree that they succeed in so bolstering their security, they undermine the security of other nations.

Sometimes two or more nations form an alliance, thereby suspending hostilities between themselves in order to combine against another nation or coalition that they regard as more threatening to them than they are to each other. Thus, the cause of an alliance is the menace of a powerful common enemy. If the mutual enemy is defeated, the alliance usually dissolves.

What makes a nation powerful? A large territory is an asset, but the second largest nation, Canada, is not a great power, and neither is the fifth largest, Brazil. (See Fig. I.1.) A large population can be an asset, but those with the largest populations, China and India, are not the greatest powers. Other assets are secure access to the sea and to natural resources, an educated and patriotic citizenry, defensible borders, weak neighbors, able leaders, internal social justice, allies, strong armed forces, and large industries.

Economic production is more closely related than any other single factor to modern national power. It gives nations the wealth with which to improve education and technology and to produce expensive modern weapons. In 1996 the nation with the largest GDP (gross domestic product), the United States, was the world's greatest power, and the one with the second largest, China, ranked second. Following them in size of GDP were Japan, Germany, India, France, Britain, Italy, Brazil, and Mexico.

Area in Millions of Square Kilometers		Population in Millions 1996	
Russia	17.0	China	1,210
China	9.3	India	952
Canada	9.2	United States	266
United States	9.2	Indonesia	207
Brazil	8.5	Brazil	163
Australia	7.6	Russia	148
India	3.0	Pakistan	129
Argentina	2.7	Japan	125
Algeria	2.4	Bangladesh	123
Sudan	2.4	Nigeria	104
Zaire	2.3	Mexico	96
Saudi Arabia	2.0	Germany	84
Mexico	1.9	Philippines	74
Indonesia	1.8	Vietnam	74
Libya	1.8	Iran	66
Iran	1.6	Turkey	62

Gross National Product in 1996 In Billions of U.S. Dollars	
United States	$7,433
China	4,047
Japan	2,945
Germany	1,729
India	1,493
France	1,256
United Kingdom	1,173
Italy	1,141
Brazil	1,023
Mexico	714
Indonesia	652
Canada	641
Russia	619
Spain	600
South Korea	596
Thailand	402

Figure I.1 The Sixteen Largest Nations in Area, Population, and Production. World Bank, *World Development Indicators 1998.*

In their propaganda, nations usually describe their foreign policies in terms of ideals (religion, humanitarianism, social justice, democracy, peace), but, in practice, they usually subordinate ideology when the national interest (military security, territory, natural resources, markets) so requires. However, ideology sometimes influences foreign policy and may, in the short run, override the national interest. Nevertheless, in World War II the United States, a leading champion of democracy, allied itself with Communist Russia; after the war, it allied itself with repressive dictatorships. Also, a common ideology did not prevent the Soviet Union and Communist China from becoming enemies. Furthermore, clashes of national interests often underlie international conficts that on the surface may appear to be clashes of ideologies.

Diplomats

Nations have developed elaborate procedures for managing their relations with each other. Each country maintains a special department of goverment, usually called the foreign office (in America the State Department), to supervise international affairs. Each nation stations its diplomats in other countries. The highest-ranking diplomat is an ambassador, and the next in rank is a minister. In other major cities, nations maintain consuls, who concern themselves primarily with business opportunities and the safety of their citizens abroad. A diplomat's residence and offices, called an embassy or legation, is treated as if it were the territory of the diplomat's home country and is off-limits to the laws and the police of the host country.

The chief functions of an ambassador or minister are to deliver and receive messages and to gather information. He or she is assisted by a staff of experts who include defense, political, economic, and public affairs attaches and members of the U.S. Defense, Treasury, and Commerce Departments, as well as undercover CIA agents. Staff members sometimes number a thousand or more. Attaches gather all the information they can through personal observation, conversations with government officials and citizens, and the study of newspapers, government documents, and other publications. This kind of open spying is expected by all countries. But diplomats caught attempting to discover official secrets by illegal means may be expelled.

Most illegal searches for secret information are conducted by separate secret intelligence agencies. Most nations maintain one or more secret service organizations, which are sometimes larger than the regular diplomatic service. In addition to spying, they sometimes carry on warlike undercover operations. The best known of U.S. secret service organizations is the Central Intelligence Agency (CIA).

Behind diplomacy, of course, lies the threat of war. Often a request from one goverment to another carries the unspoken threat of retaliation, and perhaps war, if the request is refused.

Causes of War

Among primitive groups, war was generally regarded as an acceptable means of settling intergroup conflicts. Despite its destructiveness, it was generally considered not shameful but glorious. Successful warriors were acclaimed as heroes and rewarded with positions of leadership.

Increasingly, however, with the advance of civilization, more people came to look on war as a social problem that humankind should seek to eliminate. They saw it as destructive not only of life and property but also of the higher moral and spiritual values of a society. The development of nuclear weapons deepened the conviction that war was no longer a feasible means of achieving national objectives. "Mankind must put an end to war," said President John F. Kennedy, "or war will put an end to mankind."

In early times, the causes of war were probably simpler than they are today. An increase in the population of a tribe of hunters might cause the tribe to encroach on the hunting grounds of others. Or one group might raid another to rob food, clothing, tools, and other goods or to take captives to serve as slaves. In somewhat more sophisticated form, such motives persist in modern times. However, as civilizations developed, the causes of war grew more complex.

In modern times, imperialism, excessively narrow nationalism, war propaganda, militarism, ideological disputes, and the absence of other means of resolving conflicts have all contributed to causing international war.

IMPERIALISM

A nation that conquers and extends its rule over another nation thereby becomes an empire; the policy of pursuing this kind of expansion is called imperialism. Ancient motives for imperialism were to rob and enslave. Later motives were to secure and protect opportunities for merchants, missionaries, and investors. After the industrial revolution, a powerful new motive arose from the growing dependence that some industrializing nations developed on foreign food, raw materials, and markets. After England, France, Germany, Japan, and Italy industrialized, they found it profitable to exchange manufactured goods for food from abroad, and the imported food allowed their populations to grow beyond the capacity of their own farms to feed. Thus, they became increasingly dependent on food and raw materials, such as cotton and fuels, purchased abroad with receipts from foreign sales of manufactured goods. A trade stoppage could cause their economies to collapse, their wealth and power to vanish, and many of their people to starve. Consequently, they built navies to guard trade routes and sometimes landed troops to seize areas that produced essential food and raw materials.

Imperialism produced three types of wars: the conquest of less developed areas by industrialized nations, fighting between industrialized nations for possession of colonies, and revolts by colonies for independence. By 1900, most less developed areas were dominated by Europeans, whose competition for control of these areas was one cause of both world wars. After Europeans weakened themselves in destructive wars and lost their monopolies of manufactured goods, they became less able to resist the demands of colonies for independence.

EXCESSIVELY NARROW NATIONALISM

Another cause of war arises from aspects of modern nationalism. Nationalism's promotion of a sense of brotherhood within nations produced enormous benefits through improved cooperation, and it became the strongest political loyalty of most people. More people will sacrifice money and lives for their nation than for any other cause. However, the insistence by nationalists that any act is morally right if performed for the nation makes relations between nations potentially amoral. Furthermore, nationalists, however reasonable on other matters, tend to be irrational on any dispute that affects their nation's wealth and power. Frequently attributing the worst possible motives to foreign rivals, they reject compromise and insist on the destruction of enemies. These attitudes add to the difficulty of peacefully resolving international disputes.

WAR PROPAGANDA

International hostility gives rise to a type of propaganda that contributes to causing war. Modern wars require the participation not only of armed forces but also of civilian populations to mobilize economic resources and produce war materials. This necessitates wide popular support, which is often mobilized in advance of hostilities. Through centuries of experience, leaders have perfected arguments that have proved effective in arousing popular support for war. They include four somewhat overlapping points:

1. the enemy commits atrocities,
2. the enemy is the enemy of God,
3. the enemy seeks to conquer the world, and
4. the enemy's victory would mean the end of civilization.

Both sides have made these charges in almost all wars. An effect of this propaganda is to dehumanize the enemy and make him appear to be demonic. Many people accept war propaganda as true and sometimes demand that their leaders act as if it were true. Thus, people sometimes favor wars that they would oppose if they were not misinformed.

MILITARISM

A fourth major contributor to war is militarism, the policy of building up strong armed forces and relying on them as the primary means of achieving international objectives. Even when they wish to avoid war, militarists tend to regard armed force as the most effective means of solving international conflicts and to distrust diplomatic efforts to reduce international tensions as likely to lower spending for the military. Their policies are sometimes supported by the industries and regions that benefit from high military spending. Arming has long been the most popular means of preserving peace. Each nation feels that its enemies are likely to attack if they believe they can win. Consequently, each nation believes that the best way to prevent war is to make its military forces so powerful as to convince any aggressor that an attack would meet defeat.

However, the frequent failure of large-scale arming to preserve peace suggests that this theory has flaws. It assumes that other nations will recognize that one arms only for peace. Actually, military preparations that one nation intends only for defense appear to others to be designed for aggression or intimidation. Each responds by increasing its own armament. The ensuing arms race can raise tension and hostility to the point where even a small incident can trigger a war. Thus, unrestrained search for security through armament can unintentionally draw nations into war.

IDEOLOGICAL CONFLICT

A fifth basic cause of international war is the clash of opposing ideologies. People differ on the most desirable way of organizing society. Russia long advocated communism, some Europeans practice socialism, many developing countries have military dictatorships, Iran pursues Islamic fundamentalism, and the United States upholds democracy and free enterprise. Why should this cause war?

Within every country, advocates of different systems struggle with each other for power. Some Americans want their country to adopt communism or a military dictatorship, while even during the Cold War many Russians preferred free enterprise. Russia's Communist rulers feared that replacement of communism by free enterprise anywhere increased the danger that they themselves might be overthrown. Similarly, American leaders feared that a Communist takeover of any nation anywhere magnified the threat of a Communist seizure of America. Conversely, adoption of their ideology by another country made them feel more secure.

Usually, an ideology constitutes a defense of the right of a particular class to rule. For example, under communism the economy is controlled by persons who claim to rule in the interest of workers. Under free enterprise, the economy is controlled by the middle class, of which businessmen are the leading component. A conflict between nations with different ideologies adds the element of a clash of class interests, thereby intensifying fear and hatred. Thus, when the national interests of two nations already conflict, ideological differences add to the danger of war.

LACK OF AN ALTERNATIVE

An even more basic cause of modern war is the lack of other means of resolving major international problems. The institutions that society has developed to settle conflicts and promote justice inside nations, such as laws, judges, and elections, have not been extended to relations between nations. Each nation surrounds itself with military, immigration, and economic walls. Meanwhile, nations change in different ways and at different rates. Those that grow more rapidly in population or industry than others may need more land or markets. As a consequence, even if all boundary and other disputes between countries could be settled with perfect fairness, in twenty years that settlement might no longer be just. Because no nation surrenders territory or other advantage unless forced to do so, no means exists for bringing about redistribution peaceably. A needy nation, therefore, must choose between permanently submitting to injustice or going to war. Consequently, until nations develop a peaceful means of readjusting international political arrangements to correspond to changing social and economic conditions, aggressive war may be inevitable.

The Balance of Power

Many national leaders and some political scientists believe that the best available hope of preserving peace lies in maintaining a balance of power. This means such an equal distribution of war-making ability that no one state or group of states could dominate or conquer the others. In practice, this may require forming alliances among the weaker nations to restrain more powerful nations.

As a means of preserving peace, however, a balance of power has demonstrated shortcomings. It tends to be unstable. The theory assumes that national governments have accurate information and sound judgment and that no nation will attack another equally as powerful. In some instances, however, nations that have proved to be weaker have started wars. Also, if the theory were valid, one would expect wars to occur more frequently in areas that had no balance of power. But in the Western Hemisphere, where no nation or combination of nations could match U.S. power, no major multinational war has occurred in more than a century. Meanwhile, Europe, where conditions approximated a balance of power, has had history's most destructive wars.

However, it can be shrewd strategy for nations to promote a balance of power among potential enemies. For example, England long sought to maintain a balance of power in Europe to minimize the danger that any one nation there could become sufficiently powerful to defeat Britian. Also, twentieth-century America has sought to prevent the domination of either Europe or Asia by a single power.

World Trade

Nations trade with each other on an enormous scale. In 1996 they exchanged goods and services valued at $6.8 trillion (an amount equivalent to 76 percent of all goods and services produced in America that year). It is enormously profitable for them to do so. International trade makes possible geographic specialization, the concentration by each area on producing what it produces best to exchange for other goods that foreign areas produce better. The result is more total wealth than could be produced if they did not specialize. Nations have fought wars to enlarge and keep open opportunities to trade.

Nevertheless, most nations also restrict international trade. Producers within each country resent importation of competing foreign goods that cut into their own sales or profits, and demand tariffs or import quotas to exclude them. Many governments yield to such pressures by powerful special interests. Also, because of the threat of war, each country seeks to become as self-sufficient as possible in production of essential goods.

The United States is the world's leading trading nation, followed by Japan and Germany. Chief U.S. exports are machinery, motor vehicles, electrical apparatus, and wheat, and chief imports are machinery and petroleum. In 1990 America's leading trading partners were Canada, Japan, Mexico, Germany, Taiwan, South Korea, France, the Netherlands, and China. In 1995, America's merchandise exports totaled $585 billion, about 18 percent of all the goods it produced.

Population Problems

The world's population is soaring. The number of people did not reach 1 billion until the early 1800s. It doubled to 2 billion by 1930 and doubled again within forty-five years to 4 billion in 1975. In 1996, it totalled 6.8 billion.

This population explosion was caused, not by a rise in the birth rate, but by a drop in the death rate brought about by improved diets and medical advances. It began in Europe, but today most of the growth is occurring in less developed nations, particularly in Africa, South Asia, Latin America, and Oceania, whose share of the world's population is expected to rise from 66 percent in 1950 to 78 percent by 2000.

Some scientists, sometimes called neo-Malthusians, fear that mankind is approaching a terrible Malthusian crisis, with uncontrollable population growth reaching a point where it will produce unbearable air and water pollution, depletion of natural resources, physical and mental illness, social tensions, revolution, war, and mass starvation.

Other scientists, although agreeing that the danger is alarming, add that it should be seen in perspective. They maintain that the predicted dread crisis is actually the normal state of humans and other species whose populations usually press against the available food supply to be limited by starvation. In some countries in Africa, and in Bangladesh, that situation persists. What is new, they say, is that science and technology have so greatly increased food-producing possibilities as to enable many world areas to escape the Malthusian crisis. America and Western Europe have food surpluses, and other areas, once characterized by endemic starvation, including China and India, have become self-sufficient in food.

Also, the world's birth rate is falling. As nations became industrialized and urbanized, their families have fewer children. Among white Europeans, in Europe and elsewhere, the birth rate has dropped below replacement levels. Part of the explanation is economic. Rural parents need children to do farm work and to care for them in their old age, while urban families find children to be an economic burden. Also, by 1990 the governments of nearly all of the people in less developed countries had begun birth- reduction programs. By raising the age of permitted marriages and limiting families to one child each,

China achieved a substantial reduction in births. India's birth rate fell from 41 per thousand in 1971 to about 36 per thousand in 1996. Overall, the world's birth rate dropped from 34 in 1965 to 23 in 1996, while the annual rate of population growth declined from 2 percent to 1.4 percent. In 1992 the World Bank predicted that population would level off in 2150 at 11.6 billion.

The Gap Between Rich and Poor Nations

The gap in living standards between rich and poor nations is great and widening. In a recent year, according to the World Bank, the richest twenty-seven countries, located mostly in the Northern Hemisphere, contained only 25 percent of the world's population, but received 80 percent of its income. In 1991 the richest 20 percent of nations enjoyed 85 percent of the world's production and the bottom 20 percent only 1.4 percent. According to former World Bank president Robert McNamara, a billion people lived in "absolute poverty . . . characterized by malnutrition, illiteracy, and disease." In 1991, the relief organization CARE reported that each night more than 800 million people, mostly in the less developed countries of the Southern Hemisphere, went to sleep hungry.

Much of the aid extended by rich nations to less developed nations was in the form of loans. By 1995 the debts of less developed nations to rich countries totalled $2 trillion.

In 1967, seventy-seven developing countries agreed on a statement of what they needed for economic development. They asked the rich countries to devote 1 percent of their GNPs to helping them. They also called for international agreement to maintain reasonable prices for their exports of cocoa, sugar, vegetable oils, bananas, rubber, sisal, and tungsten, and to place no new tariffs or other restrictions on these products. Many economists doubted that these measures would suffice to give developing nations satisfactory economic growth. The social and political systems in many of them retarded growth. Where a small number of individuals held nearly all of the wealth, the average person had too little purchasing power to provide a mass market sufficient to support mass production. Most of the poorer nations contained small wealthy classes who exported much of their capital to invest in advanced countries. Many of them were controlled by their military forces, which absorbed excessive sums. Giving money to less-developed countries did not improve production, the World Council of Churches concluded, where "ruling groups monopolize the product of their economy."

In 1974 the UN secretary general called "the continued existence of stark poverty among two-thirds of the world's population" "the single most devastating indictment of our current world civilization." In 1980, a commission chaired by former West German Chancellor Willy Brandt concluded that reshaping worldwide North-South relations was "the greatest challenge to mankind for the remainder of this century."

Basic U.S. Foreign Policies

Every nation has goals and interests that it seeks to win or defend, such as improving security, promoting trade, and, perhaps, expanding the national territory. Major foreign policies that America has followed for considerable periods in the past include: (1) isolationism, (2) expansionism, (3) championing democracy, (4) promoting trade, (5) maintaining supremacy in the Western Hemisphere, (6) preserving a balance of power, (7) opposing socialism, (8) seeking collective security, and (9) promoting peaceful settlement of disputes.

ISOLATIONISM

After winning independence, America's leaders advocated a policy of isolation. At that time two great powers, France and England, were struggling for world supremacy. The United States was still small and might have been defeated by either of them. Seeking to preserve America's freedom of action and believing that the United States should fight only in defense of its own national interest, the founding fathers advised against alliance with either empire.

President George Washington and most other isolationists did not want America to avoid all contacts with other parts of the world. On the contrary, they sought expanded trade and cultural relations. They wanted isolation only from Europe's wars.

Twentieth-century isolationists maintained that war was so destructive that a nation should fight only when forced to do so to defend its life, and they insisted that America's vital interests were not intolerably endangered by political changes outside the Western Hemisphere. Even the conquest of all Europe or Asia by a hostile aggressive power, they maintained, would not mortally endanger the United States because it could easily repulse any military force that could be sent into the Western Hemisphere.

America followed a policy of isolationism through much of its history. The Monroe Doctrine (1823), which warned Europe against further conquests in the Western Hemisphere, also promised that America would not intervene in Europe. In 1917, however, the United States for the first time entered a war largely to affect the outcome of events in Europe. After 1939, reversing isolationism, America assumed a major continuing role in world politics. The development of atomic weapons and intercontinental missiles weakened the argument that an isolated United States could be secure.

EXPANSIONISM

Self-aggrandizement seems to be characteristic of all life. Most people want their nation to grow in wealth and power, and normally national governments take advantage of opportunities to do so. The newly independent United States was a country of 3 million people that extended only to the Mississippi River. But with lands to the west and south thinly occupied and weakly defended by

Native Americans and the declining Spanish empire, most Americans were easily convinced that their "manifest destiny" was to take additional territory. In less than a century, they advanced westward to the Rio Grande and the Pacific, an expansion seldom matched in speed and extent. Unlike the expansion of many nations, it proved to be enduring partly because, under Thomas Jefferson's influence, America gave whites in the new territories equal citizenship and thereby enlisted their loyalty and support.

CHAMPIONING DEMOCRACY

For most of America's history, it has sought to promote the growth of democracy abroad. The American Revolution brought not only independence but more democracy and equality. Transferring power from appointed governors to elected legislatures, Americans gave more men the right to vote, abolished titles of nobility, separated church and state, and seized and divided the estates of the king's supporters. As the first large-scale republic, and one with "leveling" tendencies, the United States was regarded as a menace by the kings and nobles who then governed most of the world. Aware of their hostility, Americans feared that they would form a coalition to destroy the United States. In 1823, when Europe's monarchs threatened to join together to suppress revolutions in Latin America, President James Monroe announced that the United States would oppose any attempt by them to extend their undemocratic system in the Western Hemisphere. Also, delighted by popular revolts against kings in Europe, Americans gave such revolts at least moral support.

In 1853, to demonstrate America's republican principles, the State Department ordered U.S. diplomats to dress in plain business suits instead of the aristocratic finery worn by Europe's diplomats. When a European diplomat asked the U.S. minister to Berlin why U.S. diplomats "all dressed in black, like so many undertakers," the minister replied that Americans represented "the burial of monarchy." He was a good prophet, and eventually most monarchies were overthrown.

In 1917 President Woodrow Wilson announced that the United States was entering World War I to "make the world safe for democracy;" and, in his 1918 victory proclamation, he declared it America's "fortunate duty to assist . . . in the establishment of just democracy throughout the world."

Championship of freedom and democracy won friends for the United States among common people throughout the world. Later, when America grew wealthy, other policies sometimes took precedence. Concern for the safety of foreign investments, for example, sometimes caused Washington to support some friendly feudalistic oligarchies and military dictators.

PROMOTING TRADE

Early America produced food and raw materials and exchanged them with Europe for manufactured goods. Americans insisted that international law gave them the right to trade freely with all countries, even those at war. Defense of "freedom of the seas" was one of the reasons that America fought England in 1812 and Germany in 1917.

However, after the United States became a major naval power, it became more interested in maximizing the effectiveness of its naval weapons. During both World War I and World War II, the U.S. Navy blocked trade by neutral nations with America's enemies.

By the end of the nineteenth century, European nations and Japan had seized parts of China and divided much of the remainder of it into "spheres of influence" for possible future annexation. Fearful that these nations would exclude U.S. trade, America in 1899 formally proposed that they not discriminate in their spheres of influence against the trade of other nations, a demand known as the "Open Door Policy."

Overriding ideological anti-imperialism, America's interest in trade helped cause the United States, for a time, to become imperialistic. Many Americans feared that they might eventually need colonies to provide a market large enough to keep their growing industry in full production. Some were also motivated by desire for naval bases, an impulse to civilize and Christianize "backward" peoples, and an expectation of profits. After 1867 the United States annexed Midway, part of Samoa, and all of the Hawaiian Islands. Defeating Spain in 1898, America took Spain's empire, including Puerto Rico, the Philippines, and Guam, and assumed control over Cuba.

Acquisition of empire led the United States to build a larger navy to defend it. It also involved America more closely in the international politics of East Asia and added to the difficulty of remaining isolated from the wars of Asia and Europe. In the 1940s, America freed parts of this empire but retained other parts.

MAINTAINING SUPREMACY IN THE WESTERN HEMISPHERE

The United States insisted that Latin America was within its sphere of influence. The Monroe Doctrine ordered Europeans to refrain from acquiring new colonies or extending their political system in the Western Hemisphere. In 1895 President Grover Cleveland proclaimed that the United States was "practically sovereign" over South America, and in 1904 President Theodore Roosevelt asserted that the United States had a right to send troops into Latin American countries that did not pay their debts or preserve order. The United States annexed Puerto Rico, purchased the Virgin Islands, and made Cuba, Panama, the Dominican Republic, Nicaragua, and Haiti "protectorates" by securing the right to station troops on their soil and to control their foreign policy and finances.

PRESERVING A BALANCE OF POWER

For centuries England sought to preserve a balance of power in Europe. If Europe were ever conquered by one nation and thus united, it would be more powerful than England. Seeking to prevent this, England regularly opposed aggression by the strongest European nation and supported the independence of weaker ones.

The division of Europe into a number of mutually hostile nations was also to America's advantage. By requiring European nations to keep most of their military forces standing guard against each other, such a division left fewer forces available for possible use against the United States. This weakened their resistance to U.S. expansion and to the maintenance of the Monroe Doctrine. One of America's reasons for entering World War I and World War II was fear that if Germany conquered all of Europe, it might endanger the United States.

Americans were not always aware that they were defending a balance of power and seldom described their policy as such. Tending to regard such "power politics" as unworthy, even immoral, they preferred to describe their policy as defense of humanity or ideals. Fearing, almost instinctively, that Europe's most powerful nation sought "world domination," Americans depicted it as a threat to peace and America's ideals. Americans usually regarded the strongest nations of Europe and Asia as their leading enemies.

OPPOSING SOCIALISM

In the twentieth century, Americans frequently described their foreign policy in terms of opposition to socialism. They opposed the "National Socialism" of Italy and Germany and, particularly, the Marxist-Leninist form of socialism called communism. Both were accompanied by undemocratic rule, state control of the economy, and obstacles to the free flow of U.S. trade and investments. U.S. hostility was heightened by fear that Germany and Russia were aggressively seeking to conquer all of Europe and then the world.

The story of the implementation of this policy is told in later chapters.

SEEKING COLLECTIVE SECURITY

Formation of permanent alliances came late for the United States. The North Atlantic Treaty Organization (NATO), founded in 1949, was America's first peacetime alliance. By the 1980s, however, the United States had alliances with forty-eight nations, gave aid to many more, and maintained military forces on bases throughout the world. The reversal of isolationism seemed to be complete.

PROMOTING PEACEFUL
SETTLEMENT OF DISPUTES

Americans have long been leaders in developing means for peaceful settlement of international disputes. The United States was a leader in submitting disputes to arbitration. President Wilson drew up the plan for the League of Nations. America helped found the United Nations, was the first nation to join it, referred important disputes for its consideration, and paid much of the costs of

UN emergency troops sent to separate combatants. However, the United States resisted attempts to strengthen the UN through charter amendment.

Who Makes Foreign Policy?

Who decides which policy to follow and what actions to take regarding particular international situations? The answer is the president. The constitution gives him the power to appoint ambassadors, to negotiate treaties, and to conduct foreign relations. He is the nation's foreign policy leader and commander of its armed forces, and there are few restrictions on his power to conduct foreign affairs.

The president is assisted by the Department of State. As late as 1940 it employed fewer than two thousand people, but by 1980 had expanded to fourteen thousand. Between 1940 and 1997, its annual spending mounted from $24 million to $5.4 billion. Its chief functions are to gather information, to advise the president, and to supervise the eight thousand Foreign Service officials stationed abroad.

After the president's cabinet grew too large for efficient discussion of foreign policy issues, President Harry Truman, in 1947, secured the establishment of a subcabinet on foreign affairs called the National Security Council. Its members are the president, the vice president, the secretary of state, the secretary of defense, and the president's national security adviser. Others, including military chiefs and the head of the Central Intelligence Agency, usually attend its meetings. The National Security Council developed its own staff and functions, which tend to overlap those of the State Department. It oversees the CIA and, during the Reagan administration, sponsored secret military supply operations.

The CIA was formed in 1947 to consolidate several different military intelligence (spying) agencies and to replace the Office of Strategic Services, which had conducted secret warfare against World War II enemies. It operates under the general supervision of the National Security Council. The numbers of its personnel and the size of its budget are not divulged (but in 1995 it requested $3.1 billion), and its director has considerable latitude in hiring and firing personnel and spending its funds. In addition to gathering information, it conducts secret warfare against U.S. enemies such as the 1954 invasion of Guatamala, the 1961 Bay of Pigs invasion of Cuba, and ensuing attempts to assassinate Cuba's Fidel Castro. Foreigners accuse it of interfering in the internal affairs of many countries. It is barred by law from operations within the United States but has been caught violating that ban.

The largest agency involved in the conduct of America's international relations is the Department of Defense. In 1992 it had 1.2 million men and women in uniform and, in addition, employed more civilians than any other government department. Furthermore, more than 8 million Americans, 10 percent of the labor force, were employed in supplying it with goods and services. Admiral Hyman Rickover charged that the Defense Department had become "the most influential of all the executive departments" and had acquired "an equal status with the Department of State" in advising the president on foreign problems involving possible use of force.

The large numbers of persons who handle foreign relations are under the president's command.

The Constitution's framers intended the Senate to play a larger role than it does in foreign policy formulation. The Constitution directs the president to make treaties with its advice and consent. In practice, however, he gives the Senate information, but seldom seeks its advice. One-third plus one of the Senate can block a treaty, but the president can bypass the Senate by making similar arrangements through executive agreements. Thus, senators who disagree with him are forced to resort to appeals to public opinion as a means of changing his foreign policy.

The House of Representatives plays an even smaller role in foreign policy formulation. The most important of its powers is its share in the control of funds, which enables Congress to raise or reduce the size of the armed forces or to refuse to provide money to carry out presidential commitments. Sometimes it can legislate specific actions, such as penalizing foreign companies that do business with Cuba. Also, according to the Constitution, the approval of both houses is required before the president can wage a war, but, in practice, the president can order troops into battle, leaving Congress with little choice but to support them.

The president's powers in foreign policy are as unrestricted as those of the leaders of any other industrialized nation. This is welcomed by many who want to see America play a more active role in world affairs. They argue that the Senate's role is mostly negative, and that only the president can conduct a strong positive policy. Others argue that allowing the president unchecked control is dangerous, because if he is misinformed or ill he could make tragic mistakes.

Of course, the president can control foreign affairs only within the limits of what public opinion will support or tolerate. In order to fight a war effectively, for example, he needs strong popular support. Therefore, he is reluctant to embark on foreign policy courses for which popular support is lacking. This gives considerable importance to the special interests, organizations, publications, and individuals who influence public opinion on foreign policy.

Perhaps the most consistently effective pressure on makers of foreign policy, at least in relations with less developed countries, is that exerted by the corporations that trade and invest abroad. Poorly informed on foreign affairs, most Americans tend to support the president in whatever course of action he takes. Many corporations, on the other hand, are intensely concerned, and they have the economic and political clout to help defeat or reelect politicians. Consequently, their wishes frequently, though not always, prevail.

Also, most military officers spend more years in government service than any president or cabinet officer. This gives them opportunities to develop policies and exert long-term influence. They often have many backers in Congress and industry and among the people. Not until after World War II did America maintain a large military force in peacetime, and only in this period was a large part of U.S. industry engaged in producing war materials. President Dwight D. Eisenhower warned that what he called a "military-industrial complex" was gaining great influence over U.S. policy.

A number of groups, such as the Foreign Policy Association, the American Association for the United Nations, and the World Federalists, educate the public on foreign policy. Patriotic societies like the American Legion and the Daughters of the American Revolution insist that the United States remain armed and vigilant. Other groups, including Americans for Democratic Action, the John Birch Society, the National Association of Manufacturers, and the AFL-CIO sometimes demand particular courses of action. Newspapers, such as the *New York Times, Washington Post*, and *Christian Science Monitor*, news magazines, columnists, television news programs, books, and college students can influence policies. Also, churches express their views on international issues.

Twentieth-century developments have magnified the already great consequences of success or failure in the conduct of international relations. The economic welfare of nations is increasingly dependent on developments in the world economy. Worsening environmental problems are worldwide in origins and consequences, diseases sweep across national borders, and the population explosion affects all. Also, the quantum leap in the power of weapons seems to threaten not only unprecedented destruction of property and life, but also the survival of civilization and human life on the planet. The situation urgently demands that international relations be conducted with caution, skill, and wisdom, supported by enlightened public opinion. In H. G. Wells's phrase, humankind seems to be in a race between education and disaster.

1 The United States Enters World War I

The Outbreak of War in Europe

On June 28, 1914, a Serbian nationalist ran up to the carriage of Archduke Francis Ferdinand, heir to the Hapsburg throne, and shot him and his wife. This murder set in motion a chain of events that drew Europe into a world war and the United States into a new era in its foreign relations.

Europeans had contructed great national states which, by virtue of their political, economic, and intellectual development, made Europe the world's chief center of power. However, Europe's major nations had grouped themselves into two main opposing alliances—the Central Powers, composed of Germany, Austria-Hungary, and Italy, versus the Triple Alliance of Great Britain, France, and Russia. The intensity of their rivalry made Europe a powder keg that a small spark could ignite.

The assassination occurred in Sarejevo, the capital of Bosnia, the Slav-inhabited province that Austria-Hungary had annexed in 1909. That annexation had greatly distressed Serbia, the small adjoining Slavic nation that had itself hoped to annex Bosnia. Serbia retaliated by promoting revolution by Bosnians and other national minorities within the Austria-Hungarian empire. With nationalism on the rise, such revolutions might shatter the empire.

The crown prince of Austria-Hungary, Francis Ferdinand, favored giving more self-government to Bosnian Slavs, a policy that could have reduced Bosnian discontent and thus the likelihood that they would revolt and join Serbia. Enraged Austrians suspected, with good reason, that officials in the Serbian government had conspired with the assassin, and they resolved to punish Serbia and to suppress Serbia's promotion of revolutions. Unfortunately, it proved to be impossible to confine this conflict to Austria-Hungary and Serbia.

German and Austrian aspirations to expand east through the Balkans clashed with Russia's desire to control the Dardanelles, the outlet from Russia to the Mediterranean. Also, as the largest Slavic nation, Russia had inherited the historic Slavic struggle against German advances into eastern Europe. Embittered by Austria's annexation, in 1909, of Slavic Bosnia, Moscow had resolved to allow no further extension of Austrian rule over Balkan Slavs.

The great European powers were packed closely together, mostly on the vast European plain where few geographical barriers obstructed the advance of armies. Within days they could mobilize (call reserve forces into active service) and attack. The first nation to mobilize might quickly inflict fatal damage on one who hesitated. The situation resembled a standoff between hostile groups of gunmen in a Wild West saloon. If one started to draw his pistol, all must go for their guns.

Some Frenchmen welcomed the prospect of a general war. In the 1870 Franco-Prussian War, Germany had wrested from France the provinces of Alsace and Lorraine. Regarding them as rightfully part of France, the French government made their recovery its chief foreign policy goal. Because Germany was stronger, France could regain them only in a war in which it received help from Russia and Britain. On July 20–23, 1914, French President Raymond Poincare visited Moscow and urged the Russians to defend Serbia.

Germany's military commanders had long feared that France and Russia might launch coordinated invasions, forcing Germany to fight simultaneously on two fronts. To meet this danger, they had developed the Von Schlieffen Plan to quickly throw most of their army at France in an effort to defeat it before sprawling Russia could fully mobilize. Of course, this would not work if Germany allowed either Russia or France to get a headstart on mobilization.

Austria invaded Serbia on July 28, whereupon the Russian tsar ordered mobilization. On July 29, the Germans urged him to cancel the order. At first he did; then, after a few hours, he yielded to arguments by his military commanders that Russia could not afford the risk. On July 30, France began mobilization. On July 31, the Germans issued ultimatums to both France and Russia to stop mobilizing. When they refused, Germany, on August 1, declared war on Russia and, on August 3, on France. On August 4, Britain entered the war. Later, Japan fought on the side of the Allies, and Turkey entered on the side of the Central Powers. Thus, the assassination of the archduke ignited world war.

The question of responsibility for bringing on the ruinous tragedy has been much debated. Partisans of both sides insist that they were forced to act to defend themselves against aggressive foes. In the 1919 peace treaty, the victorious Allies would compel Germany to confess that the war was "imposed on them by the aggression of Germany and her allies." But historian Sidney Fay concluded that this verdict was "historically unsound," and historian Harry Elmer Barnes wrote that "responsibility for the World War falls upon Serbia, France, and Russia." Most historians, however, apportion the blame, in varying measures, among the Central Powers and the Allies. One historian concluded that the greatest effort to prevent the Austrian-Serbian war from spreading into a general conflagration was made by England, followed in order by Germany and Russia. The debate continues.

Europe's chief industrial center was separated from its markets and sources of raw materials by national boundaries, including tariff walls. Germany had the largest population of any European country other than Russia, and German industrial production had surpassed British production. This enhanced Germany's power but also created within Germany the pressures felt by industrial centers to make secure their access to foreign food, raw materials, and markets. Such pressures had influenced the British to conquer a far-flung empire. Thus, Germany seemed to be terribly threatening to its neighbors.

Also, war was such a regular feature of the international system that almost no one believed that it could be permanently avoided. The question was on what terms it would be fought. In 1914, many European leaders on both sides preferred immediate war to developments that could tilt the balance of power against them and thereby force them to fight later on less favorable terms. The ensuing war proved that the opposing alliances were of approximately equal strength— a "balance of power" that many expected to preserve peace. This balance was disrupted by an assassin's bullet.

Wilson's Administration of Foreign Affairs

When World War I began in August 1914, President Woodrow Wilson had been in office for a year and a half. He was a Southerner, a Calvinist, and a leader of the American progressive movement. Highly educated, he held a Ph.D. in political science and history, and had been a political science professor, president of Princeton University, and governor of New Jersey, but he had little training or experience in international relations. "It would be the supreme irony of history," he told a friend shortly after his 1912 election, "if my administration should turn out to be primarily concerned with foreign affairs."

Despite, or perhaps because of, his inexperience, Wilson soon developed strong views on foreign affairs. Lacking extensive information on foreign lands, he tended to base his evaluation of international problems on broad generalizations, often with a moral content. The principles he proclaimed have often been called "Wilsonian idealism." A Christian moralist, he opposed imperialism , and he championed human rights, respect for law, self-determination, world peace, and the worldwide spread of democracy, free enterprise, and free trade. Americans, he told businessmen, had a mission "to carry liberty and justice and the principles of humanity" wherever they went among the world's people and to "convert them to the principles of America." Some have called his diplomacy "missionary diplomacy."

To the post of secretary of state, Wilson named William Jennings Bryan, a former Nebraska lawyer, congressman, and three-time Democratic party nominee for president (see Fig. 1.1). Of benevolent countenance and rural background, Bryan had run in 1900 as an anti-imperialist and was a favorite speaker at meetings of peace groups. His moral standards led him to ban alcoholic beverages at diplomatic functions, which some sophisticates ridiculed as "grape-juice diplomacy," and his devotion to negotiating "conciliation" treaties reinforced an impression that he was less sophisticated than Wilson in foreign affairs. Later, however, some historians rated him as realistic as Wilson on the issues on which they disagreed.

Wilson received much advice on foreign affairs from his closest friend and adviser, Edward M. House, a wealthy Texan who had helped him get the 1912 Democratic presidential nomination. In 1914 and 1915, Wilson sent House to Europe as his confidential agent. He later made him a member of the U.S. peace

Figure 1.1 Secretary of State William Jennings Bryan, Secretary of the Navy Josephus Daniels, and President Woodrow Wilson. At far right is young Assistant Secretary of the Navy Franklin D. Roosevelt. National Archives.

delegation and consulted him so much that Bryan complained that House was the real secretary of state.

Americans Take Sides

After a January 1914 mission to Europe, House reported to Wilson that Europe was plagued by "militarism run stark mad" and that, "whenever England consents, France and Russia will close in on Germany and Austria." Nevertheless, the news of the outbreak of world war was received in America with stunned disbelief. Not well informed on Europe's international politics, many Americans had hoped that humans had become too civilized, and weapons had become too horribly destructive, to allow another major war. Shortly before Austria invaded Serbia, America's ambassador to Germany reported that the crisis would be peaceably resolved, and only one vice consul in Hungary warned that world war was imminent. Later, Wilson expressed a widespread view when he said: "With the objects and causes of the war we are not concerned. The obscure foundations from which its stupendous flood has burst forth we are not interested to search for or explore."

Most Americans were glad to be a safe distance from the war and hoped to stay out. A poll of newspaper editors showed that a large majority favored neutrality. Even former President Theodore Roosevelt said that "it would be folly to jump into the gulf ourselves."

Going beyond the customary proclamation of neutrality, Wilson asked Americans to be "neutral in fact as well as in name," which would require them to be "impartial in thought as well as in action," and to avoid any "transaction that might be construed as a preference of one party." Nevertheless, from the outset, many Americans favored one side or the other.

Some Americans sympathized with Germany and its allies, Austria-Hungary, Turkey, and Bulgaria. Eleven million Americans were of German or Austria-Hungarian birth or parentage. Also, Irish-Americans hated the British, who had conquered Ireland, while Jewish- and Scandinavian-Americans disliked Russia. Some Americans had studied in German universities, then widely regarded as the world's best, and admired Germany's social legislation and city government. Furthermore, many liberals, including leaders of the Social Gospel movement, believed that Germany was fighting a defensive war.

From the first, however, a much larger number of Americans favored the Allies. Most Americans traced their ancestry to England, France, Russia, Belgium, or other Allied countries, and America shared a common language and literature with England. Many U.S. scholars had studied in British universities, and wealthy Americans had ties, sometimes by marriage, to British aristocrats. Also, in the prewar period, the British had made concessions to the United States, including withdrawing British warships from the Caribbean and yielding on an Alaska boundary dispute, which had improved British-American relations. Furthermore, many Americans admired French culture and romanticized France's aid to the American Revolution; when U.S. troops arrived in France, they laid a wreath on Lafayette's grave with the words: "Lafayette, we are here."

Prewar relations with Germany were not as cordial. Germany seemed to be less democratic and more militaristic, and antimilitarism was then a component of America's democratic tradition. Also, like America, a latecomer in the scramble for imperial possessions, Germany seemed to be more aggressive in promoting its trade and other interests in less developed areas. This gave many Americans the impression that Germany was America's most active competitor for markets and influence in Asia, the Pacific Islands, and the Caribbean.

The kind of news about the war that reached Americans persuaded many that Germany and Austria were aggressors. The Austrians had invaded Serbia, a much smaller country, and a few days later, Germany had invaded little Belgium. Austria and Germany had struck first, and few Americans were aware of any reason for their attacks. Furthermore, the cable from Europe to America, over which came the bulk of news dispatches, ran through London, giving British censors and propagandists an edge in promoting their point of view.

Allied propaganda found receptive ears in the United States. Many Americans were indignant when the Germans executed a British nurse as a spy and were appalled by British accounts of German atrocities in Belgium. With skill and discretion, and with the aid of prominent Americans, the British worked to implant in U.S. minds an image of the Germans as cruel and brutal militarists, "Huns," who sought to conquer Europe and the world and to destroy freedom, democracy, and civilization itself.

In contrast, German propaganda seemed clumsy. It emphasized the evils of the British empire, which, it charged, oppressed and exploited peoples throughout the world. It attacked England's illegal blockade, particularly the food blockade, and depicted Russians as brutal oppressors of Jews and seekers of despotic world power. However, it won few converts, perhaps because most Americans were predisposed to accept British propaganda.

Most U.S. government leaders were pro-Ally. All members of the president's cabinet, except Secretary of State Bryan, strongly favored the Allies. Secretary of the Treasury William Gibbs McAdoo wanted to encourage U.S. banks to give them loans. "Germany must not be permitted to win or even to break even," said State Department Counselor Robert Lansing. Ambassador to London Walter Hines Page even helped Britain write answers to U.S. protests. The president, also, was far from neutral. An admirer of England's government and of nearly all things British, Wilson, in early 1915, said that the Allies were "standing with their backs to the wall fighting wild beasts" and that America should do nothing "to hinder or embarrass them in the prosecution of the war." He told the British ambassador that a German victory would "be fatal to our form of government and American ideals." England, he said later, was "fighting our fight."

Economic factors also drew the United States closer to the Allies. So complete was the British navy's control of the seas that it quickly cut U.S. exports to Germany from $169 million to only $2 million annually. Meanwhile, between 1914 and 1916, annual U.S. sales to the Allies quadrupled from $824 million to $3.2 billion, which lifted the U.S. economy out of a recession. The price farmers got for wheat tripled, the production of steel rose from 40 to 75 million tons annually, and the stock market soared.

The Allies had invested large sums in America, and they paid for their wartime purchases by selling $1.5 billion of their U.S. stocks and bonds. They also shipped $1 billion in gold to America. As their resources diminished, however, they redoubled their efforts to secure credit and loans.

Bryan warned that extending credit would be highly unneutral. Money, he told Wilson, was the worst form of contraband (war supplies) because it could command everything else. Furthermore, he warned, bankers who made loans would seek Allied victory to ensure repayment and would use their influence with newspapers to sway public opinion. Nevertheless, it was customary for warring nations to get credit in neutral nations and, in October 1914, Wilson approved of credit sales and, in September 1915, he told banks they could make loans. By April 1917, private loans by Americans to the Allies totaled $2.3 billion.

The enormous flow of supplies, including weapons, to Germany's enemies severely hurt Germany, and the Berlin government attempted to slow the flow. Its agents in America, numbering perhaps three thousand, sought information about ship sailings and attempted to foster strikes in munitions factories. A number of German diplomats suspected of such activities were ordered to leave the country.

The Controversy over Allied Violations of Freedom of the Seas

Historically, the United States had championed freedom of the seas—freedom to trade with all nations in both peace and war. Americans recognized that all belligerents had the right to blockade enemies during war, but held that they could legally stop neutral ships only after establishing an "effective" blockade, which required stationing their warships so closely around an enemy's port that no merchant ship could enter it without coming within range of their guns. Even then, Americans insisted, the blockader could seize only contraband, which Americans defined as arms and ammunition. Historically, Britain had insisted on greater latitude to use its navy against its enemies. International law on the subject had long been debated and was not yet clearly established. The closest the nations had come to agreement was the 1909 Declaration of London, proposed by a conference of England, the United States, Japan, and the leading European naval powers, but World War I erupted before enough nations had ratified it to put it into effect. The declaration proposed broad protection for the rights of neutral nations to continue trade during a war. When Wilson proposed that both sides abide by its terms, Germany and Austria agreed, but Britain refused.

The British never officially declared a blockade, but they nevertheless enforced one that violated the rules of the London Declaration. Stopping neutral ships anywhere on the high seas, they forced them to enter British ports to be searched. The London Declaration defined contraband as arms and ammunition, plus a few goods that could be used for either war or peaceable purposes, but strictly excluded wool, cotton, certain ores, and food. However, the British steadily expanded their list of contraband to include all commodities, including food. Of course, a food blockade hits civilians, especially the poor, the old, the young, and the friends of the blockader. The British also seized goods bound for neutral Denmark and Holland, from which they might reach Germany. They laid explosive mines in international waters, flew American flags on their ships, censored U.S. mail, and blacklisted (forbade all business relations with) U.S. companies that did business with the Central Powers.

America's State Department protested against Britain's illegal blockade, particularly its March 1915 announcement that it would seize neutral ships bound for Denmark or Holland. But Wilson did not protest the mining of the North Sea nor the seizure of German assets from U.S. mail bags. After Bryan resigned, (discussed later in this chapter), Robert Lansing, the new secretary of state, followed a policy of stretching out negotiations with Britain and thereby postponing a showdown. Because a U.S. threat to stop selling supplies to England probably would have sufficed to force England to change its policy, Wilson appeared to be acquiescing in British violations of long-claimed U.S. rights. To the Germans, America appeared to be almost a partner in the Allied economic strangulation of Germany.

The Controversy with Germany

The Germans protested against America's failure to insist that Britain respect the rights of neutrals and the law of the sea. To them, the food blockade seemed particularly atrocious. Calling Britain's conduct of the war "barbarous," German General Erich Ludendorff charged that "the blockade was only possible if the United States agreed to it." A German-language newspaper published in America commented that "ten thousand German widows, ten thousand orphans, ten thousand graves bear the legend: 'Made in America.'"

A bitter dispute with Germany soon erupted over submarine warfare. Britain's fleet bottled up the smaller German surface navy in the Baltic Sea, but German submarines could slip past the blockading force to attack merchant ships. The submarine was not new—one had been used in the American Revolution—but it had not yet been employed on a large scale in war, and international agreements on naval combat had not yet fully taken it into account. The German submarine fleet, which numbered only twenty-one ships at the beginning of the war, peaked at 127 in October 1917. These submarines were small, slow, and fragile. According to international rules, an enemy freighter must be stopped and its crew removed before it could be sunk. At first, German subs allowed crews to get off in lifeboats, which they sometimes towed toward shore (most pre-1917 sinkings were by surfaced submarines), but this practice stopped after the British armed their freighters with cannons and also ordered them to ram submarines.

On February 4, 1915, the German government announced that the waters surrounding Britain and Ireland were a war zone in which submarines would attack enemy freighters without warning. They were taking this step, they insisted, in retaliation for England's illegal food blockade, and they offered to abide by international law if England would. They said they would try to avoid firing on neutral ships, but, because Britain flew neutral flags, they urged neutrals to keep their ships out of the war zone.

Bryan wanted to demand that both sides obey international law and, meanwhile, keep U.S. ships out of the war zone. The only demand Wilson made on Britain, however, was that it stop flying the American flag. To Germany, he sent a stiff note saying that he was "reluctant to believe" that Germans would commit such an "indefensible violation of neutral rights" as sinking merchant ships without warning and that he would hold them to "strict accountability" for any loss of U.S. ships or lives.

However, Americans made a compromise proposal—that the British allow shipments of food to be distributed to German civilians by U.S. agents, and that both sides stop submarine attacks on civilian ships, flying neutral flags, or mining the open sea. On March 1, 1915, the Germans replied that they would agree if allowed to import civilian-use raw materials, but the British rejected Wilson's plan altogether.

On March 28, 1915, an American on the British passenger ship *Falaba* was killed when German submarines sunk it. Not yet ready to challenge Germany's right to use the new weapon, Wilson made no protest. On May 1, 1915, a U.S. ship in a British convoy (a group of merchant ships escorted by warships) was hit by a German torpedo, killing three Americans. Expressing regret, Berlin promised "full recompense," and the German kaiser and Chancellor Theobald von Bethmann-Hollweg ordered German submarines to avoid sinking neutral ships. No more U.S. ships were hit for nearly two years.

The controversy with Germany then shifted to the issue of whether the Germans had the right to sink British ships on which Americans were traveling. Bryan wanted to stop Americans from traveling on belligerent ships, or at least to notify them that they did so at their own risk, but Wilson took a different course.

The question was complicated when the British ordered their passenger liners, as well as freighters, to carry munitions and to ram submarines. By May 1915, they had sunk five German submarines by ramming. According to the German government and some experts on international law, these practices converted such passenger ships into warships. And, customarily, neutrals did not allow belligerent warships to enter their ports.

On May 7, 1915, a German submarine torpedoed the *Lusitania*, a large British passenger liner. On its way to New York, it had stopped in Canada, where it took on passengers and munitions, including 4.2 million rifle bullets. When it called at New York, the Germans ran newspaper advertisements warning that, by carrying ammunition, it had made itself a war target, and advising Americans not to sail on it. Assured by its captain that it was too fast to be sunk by submarines, 197 Americans, including the playboy Alfred Vanderbilt, took passage.

When King George asked U.S. Ambassador Page what Washington would do if the Germans sank the *Lusitania*, Page replied that America would immediately declare war. Normally, British ships approached the Irish coast at a high rate of speed and in a zigzag course to evade submarines. The *Lusitania* approached slowly on a straight course. Maneuvering into her path, a German submarine fired its one remaining torpedo. It set off a tremendous explosion, and the great ship sank in eighteen minutes with the loss of 1,198 lives, including 128 Americans.

The sinking of the *Lusitania* had a tremendous impact on U.S. public opinion. The *Nation* called it "wholesale murder," and the *New York Times* branded the Germans "savages." Many Americans, including Colonel House, wanted to declare war at once. Seeking to cool the war sentiment, Wilson said that peace was "the healing and elevating influence," and one could be "too proud to fight." He was, snorted Theodore Roosevelt, surrounded by "flubdubs, mollycoddles, and flapdoodle pacifists."

Secretary of State Bryan, insisting that relying on passengers to protect a contraband-carrying ship from attack was "like putting women and children in front of an army," wanted Wilson to warn Americans against traveling on munitions-carrying ships, and to demand that Britain stop shipping arms on passenger liners. Wilson did not agree.

The note Wilson sent to Germany on May 15 was harsh. Clearly, he said, submarines could not be used against unarmed passenger ships without "inevitable violation of many sacred principles of justice and humanity," and he insisted that the right of Americans to travel on the high seas was indisputable. He demanded that Germany pay reparations and permit no recurrence. The Germans replied that they regretted the loss of American lives but that the *Lusitania* was armed and carried ammunition, so that its sinking was "just self-defense."

In a second note, Wilson denied that the ship carried explosives and insisted that its sinking violated the "rights of humanity." Bryan objected. Enforcing U.S. rights solely against Germany, he said, was unneutral and would lead to war. Rather than sign it, he resigned, which the *New York World* called "unspeakable treachery." Wilson replaced him as secretary of state with Robert Lansing, an advocate of entering the war in support of England.

In a third note, Wilson told the Germans that America would regard the sinking of another passenger liner as "deliberately unfriendly," which in diplomatic language was a threat of war. Changing their position, the Germans asked that the dispute be submitted to arbitration, and they offered to pay an indemnity. Secretly, on June 6, they had already ordered submarine commanders to sink no more passenger liners.

On August 19, 1915, a German submarine commander, disobeying orders, sank a British passenger ship, the *Arabic*, killing two Americans. Lansing warned that unless Germany stopped sinking passenger ships, America would "certainly declare war." To mollify U.S. anger, the German ambassador to Washington, Johann von Bernstorff, promised that no more passenger liners would be sunk. This *"Arabic* pledge," said the U.S. chief justice, was the "greatest victory for American diplomacy in a generation." Public demand for war abated.

In January 1916, after Wilson accepted that Americans had the right to travel on Allied ships even if they were armed, a number of congressmen who suspected that Wilson sought to enter the war introduced the Gore-Mclemore Resolution to bar Americans from traveling on armed belligerent ships. (By March 1917, German torpedoes had killed three Americans on U.S. ships and about 190 on Allied vessels). The Senate Foreign Relations Committee backed it unanimously, but, insisting that giving up any American right would destroy the "whole fine fabric of international law" and America's "independent position among the nations," Wilson persuaded Congress to defeat it.

On March 24, 1916, the Germans mistakenly torpedoed another passenger ship, an unarmed channel packet, the *Sussex*, killing eighty persons and wounding four Americans. In profile, it resembled a British minelayer, and, at first, the Germans denied that they had sunk a passenger vessel.

On April 18, before a joint session of Congress, Wilson extended U.S. protection to British freighters. Submarine warfare, he declared, was incompatible with humanity, neutral rights, and "the sacred immunities of non-combatants." Unless Germany immediately halted unwarned submarine attacks on both passenger and freight-carrying vessels, he said, America would break diplomatic relations, a move generally regarded as preliminary to war.

The Germans protested that America was discriminating, that the British blockade was starving women and children, and that Germany had repeatedly offered to abide by international law if the British would do so. Nevertheless, in May 1916, in what became known as the *Sussex* pledge, the Germans promised that they would stop sinking enemy merchant ships without warning. This was a great victory for U.S. diplomacy, and it largely protected Britain from Germany's most effective weapon.

The Germans expressed the hope that, having forced Germany to abide by international law, the United States would insist that Britain also respect U.S. rights, and warned that, otherwise, Germany might have to reconsider her pledge. In reply, Wilson warned that Germany's promise must not be contingent on America's relations with any other nation. Injury to property, he added in September 1916, could be repaid, but loss of life was irreparable.

Thus, while, in effect, acquiescing in the illegal Allied economic strangulation of Germany, Wilson had given Germany what amounted to an ultimatum: either cease unrestricted submarine warfare or face war with the United States. This ultimatum limited Wilson's subsequent freedom of action. If Germany were to renew submarine warfare, he would be forced to either back down or go to war. This predicament seemed to stimulate his desire to arrange a peace settlement to avert being drawn into war.

Preparedness

Meanwhile, a great debate raged in America on the issue of whether America should enter the war. Interventionists, including Theodore Roosevelt, General Leonard Wood, Elihu Root, Robert Lansing, Henry L. Stimson, and the *New York Tribune*, insisted that only complete Allied victory could save America, democracy, and civilization.

Antiwar forces, including liberals Jane Addams, House Majority Leader Claude Kitchen, Senator Robert M. LaFollette, and William Jennings Bryan, argued that the British and the French were as brutal as the Germans. He was not swayed by atrocity reports, said Bryan, because war itself was atrocity. Furthermore, these critics charged, bankers and munitions makers sought war for selfish reasons, and going to war would militarize America and destroy America's progressive reform movement.

An immediate issue was whether America should significantly enlarge its armed forces. Advocates of arming ("preparedness") including Roosevelt and Wood, argued that weakness invited insult that would eventually compel America to fight, while military strength would cause others to respect America's rights. They formed the National Security League which soon enrolled, among others, twenty-two state governors. They also had the support of veterans' organizations and of many wealthy Republicans associated with industrial and banking interests.

Opponents of preparedness included the Women's Peace Party, the peace churches, labor unions, and farm organizations. They argued that preparing for war would arouse a war spirit, provoke German countermoves, and take the country closer to war.

Wilson shared many of the views of opponents of preparedness, and he also feared the effects of war on the reform movement. "To fight you must be brutal and ruthless," he told a friend, "and the spirit of ruthless brutality will enter into every fiber of the national life, infecting Congress, the courts, the policeman on the beat, the man in the street." America, he maintained, already had enough arms for defense.

However, as Wilson's controversy with Germany intensified, he changed his mind. Perhaps he felt that having larger armed forces would help back up his demands. In speeches made in January and February 1916, he called for military readiness, forceful assertion of U.S. rights, and "incomparably the greatest navy in the world." His preparedness speeches received enthusiastic applause.

Congress responded with large military appropriations. The June 1916 National Defense Act provided for enlarging the army from 90,000 to 200,000 and for compulsory military training in high schools and colleges. In August 1916, Congress approved construction of five new battle cruisers and numerous smaller warships. In September, it put U.S. merchant ships under federal control and authorized the government to build and operate merchant vessels. To finance armament, new taxes were enacted, which Progressives and peace advocates, who wanted to take the profits out of war, succeeded in placing mostly on upper-income groups—doubling the income tax, imposing a new inheritance tax, and adding taxes on munitions manufacturers.

Efforts for Peace

Meanwhile, Wilson vigorously sought to mediate an end to the war. In December 1915, at the suggestion of England's Foreign Minister, Sir Edward Grey, Wilson had sent House to Europe to ascertain if opposing leaders were ready for peace based on justice, disarmament, and a league of nations. For nearly three months, House visited Britain, France, and Germany. Exceeding his instructions, House told the French that if the war went against the Allies, America would enter the war. On February 22, 1916, in the House-Grey Memorandum, with Wilson's approval, House made Britain an offer. He said that, when the Allies decided that conditions were favorable, Wilson would propose that the two sides enter a peace conference. If Germany refused, House stated, America would probably declare war on Germany. If Germany attended but refused to accept terms favorable to the Allies, America would probably enter the war.

Although this proposal put America in the Allied camp and seemed to guarantee an Allied victory, the British never notified America that the time was ripe for a peace conference. Apparently believing that America would sooner or later enter the war anyway and thereby ensure Germany's total defeat, the British fought on for what they believed to be the difference between what America considered favorable terms and what the British wanted.

In a May 1916 speech, Wilson promised that if the two sides would negotiate a peace, America would help guarantee "territorial integrity and political independence" in Europe. Apparently this meant protection of the Allies against any future German aggression. But Grey insisted that the time was not yet ripe for negotiations.

Wilson showed some impatience when the Allies, despite his guarantee of terms favorable to them, refused to cooperate with his peace plans. Also, German concessions on submarine warfare allowed his attention to shift to disagreements with the Allies. Wilson was offended by the brutality of British suppression, in April 1916, of an Irish rebellion. Then, in July, when they blacklisted American companies, Wilson was furious—"I am, I must admit, about at the end of my patience with Great Britain." Wilson told House that continuance of the illegal Allied blockade was "altogether indefensible" and that he was considering cutting loans and exports to the Allies.

Meanwhile, the election of 1916 neared. Rejecting Theodore Roosevelt, who had bolted the party in 1912, the Republicans nominated Supreme Court justice and former governor of New York Charles Evans Hughes. Their platform denounced Wilson for failing to protect U.S. rights, and called for more military spending.

The Democrats renominated Wilson with only one dissenting vote. The platform praised his conduct of foreign affairs and called for reasonable preparedness. Endorsing Wilson, Bryan said that the president did not want to go to war, and another nominator reiterated the theme that Wilson had handled crises so skillfully that "we didn't go to war." The main Democratic campaign slogan became "He Kept Us Out of War."

In the campaign, Wilson charged that the election of Hughes would take America into the war. Hughes said that he would have broken diplomatic relations after Germany sank the *Lusitania*. The fact that Theodore Roosevelt campaigned for Hughes added to an impression that he was more prowar than Wilson. Wilson won a narrow victory, 9.1 million votes to Hughes's 8.5 million. It seemed to be an endorsement of his program of domestic reform and international peace.

Conscious of the danger that Germany might renew submarine warfare ("any little German lieutenant can put us into war"), Wilson redoubled his efforts to arrange a negotiated peace. Civilians in the German government welcomed his initiatives—generals and admirals were pressing for renewed submarine warfare, which German civilians feared would draw America into the war. In October, Chancellor Bethmann-Hollweg had urged Wilson to call a peace conference, but British Prime Minister Lloyd George said that Britain would not "tolerate" U.S. mediation. Impatient at Wilson's delay, the Germans, on December 12, invited the Allies to a peace conference.

On December 18, 1916, Wilson sent a note to both sides. Both, he said, claimed to be fighting for the same objects. Perhaps, he said, their war aims were similar enough to permit a compromise peace. Therefore, he requested that each specify exactly what it required for peace and security.

When the Allies received Wilson's note, they were offended; England's King George V wept. The Germans, fearing that Wilson sought to get Germany to state its peace terms in order to denounce them and ask Congress for war, replied that they would reveal their terms at a peace conference. After delay, the Allies replied that the Central Powers must pay indemnities, restore past conquests (Alsace-Lorraine), give self-government to subject peoples (which might mean dissolution of the Austria-Hungary and Turkish empires), and surrender Polish-inhabited regions to a new independent Poland. Disappointed, Wilson considered Allied demand to be far too extensive to permit a negotiated peace.

In a remarkable speech on January 22, 1917, known as his "peace without victory" speech, Wilson told the Senate that it would be better if neither side won the war. Victory, he said, would produce an unjust peace, a "victor's peace imposed upon the vanquished—at an intolerable sacrifice," and would leave bitter resentment, upon which peace would rest "only as upon quicksand." Consequently, "only peace between equals" could last. He then outlined the kind of terms he favored: self-determination, freedom of the seas, an international league for peace, and disarmament.

Wilson had always opposed a German victory. Now he was expressing opposition to Allied victory. Justice would be better served, he told the cabinet on February 2, "if the war ended in a draw." German Ambassador Bernstorff reported that, disillusioned with the Allies, Wilson had for the first time become neutral.

Entry into the War

Two months after expressing his desire for a peace without victory, Wilson asked Congress to declare war on Germany. What changed his mind?

The major development was Germany's resumption of submarine warfare. Efforts by German civilians to arrange a peace conference failed. Meanwhile, the collapse of Russia's armies enabled German generals to transfer troops to France for a great offensive that they hoped would win the war. Chances of success would be enhanced if they could use submarines to cut France's supply lines. When civilians warned that submarine sinkings would bring America into the war, military leaders answered that America was already furnishing supplies to help the Allies kill Germans, and an admiral promised victory before a single U.S. soldier could reach France. On January 31, 1917, the Germans unleashed their submarines to sink all ships in the designated war zone around the British Isles. This act, reported Bernstorff, turned Wilson into "an embittered enemy."

On February 3, Wilson broke diplomatic relations but did not ask for war. The Germans sank two American ships in February, but after warnings and with no loss of life. Wilson armed U.S. merchant ships and ordered them to shoot submarines on sight. The Germans could no longer give warnings.

On February 25, the British gave Wilson a note (which they had intercepted) from the German foreign secretary, Arthur Zimmermann, to the German ambassador to Mexico. Germany would try to avoid war with America, Zimmerman wrote, but, if war occurred, the ambassador should seek an alliance with Mexico with a promise to help Mexico recover territories taken by the United States. According to Secretary of State Lansing, this Zimmermann note, which Wilson released to the press, aroused more anti-German sentiment than resumption of submarine warfare.

A revolution in Russia, on March 15, 1917, overthrew the tsar and gave power to democratic groups in the Duma (parliament). It also had a great effect on U.S. opinion. For a time it appeared that all of the principal Allied countries were democracies, in contrast to the undemocratic Central Powers.

Between March 16 and March 18, the Germans sank three U.S. ships, with the loss of fifteen lives. A March 20 cabinet meeting approved Wilson's decision to ask for war. On April 2, 1917, Wilson delivered his war message to Congress.

The Germans, said Wilson, had "thrust" war on America by their submarines' wanton destruction of life and "warfare against mankind." America's quarrel, he said, was not with the German people, for whom Americans felt "sympathy and friendship," but with Germany's autocratic government. America, he said, fought for peace and justice, for the liberation of the world's peoples, "the German peoples included," and "the privilege of men everywhere to choose their way of life and of obedience. The world must be made safe for democracy." America sought peace "planted upon the tested foundations of political liberty," and "a universal dominion of right by such a concert of free peoples as shall bring peace and safety to all nations and make the world itself at last free." America, he insisted, had "no selfish ends to serve" but was "privileged to spend her blood and her might for the principles that gave her birth and happiness and the peace which she has treasured."

Wilson's eloquent speech received great applause. Only six senators voted against war. In the House, fifty members, including the first woman congressman, Jennette Rankin, voted nay, while 373 voted for war. Wilson signed the war declaration on April 6. In late 1917, America also declared war on Austria-Hungary, but it did not declare war on Bulgaria or Turkey.

The causes of U.S. entry into the war have been much debated by historians, who find evidence to support different conclusions. Some, like Wilson, emphasizing German aggression and submarine warfare, conclude that America fought because it was attacked. Later "revisionists" point to the role of munitions makers, bankers, British propagandists, and presidential deception in influencing Americans to go to war. While interventionists argue that U.S. entry proved that modern conditions make isolation impossible, other historians maintain that the war was unnecessary.

Others even see it as an aggressive expansion of America's role in the world. They quote Wilson's statements that he favored the "righteous conquest of foreign markets," that America had a "moral obligation . . . to free the course of our commerce and our finance," and "let us build a navy bigger than [Britain's] and do what we please." The historian Thomas G. Patterson concluded that America entered "because expansionist American leaders were finally willing to fight in order to implant in the Old World the best principles and goods America had to offer."

What conclusions does the evidence indicate? The most obvious cause was unrestricted submarine warfare. Germany's resumption of submarine warfare prompted Wilson to sever diplomatic relations, and its sinking of U.S. ships, killing Americans, prompted Wilson's request for war. Thus, America fought because it was attacked.

This answer, however, must be seen in context. At the time, it appears, Germany's leaders wanted to avoid war with America. Also, Wilson's interpretation of U.S. rights, including the right of Americans to lend immunity to belligerent ships on which they traveled, would later seem exaggerated. Furthermore, in 1919 Wilson concluded that America would have entered the war even if the Germans had not used submarine warfare.

Thus, although the U-boats were the precipitating factor, they were not the only cause of U.S. entry. Also influencing Americans to side with the Allies were the sympathies many felt for their countries of origin, growing economic ties, the financial interest of bankers and industrialists, and the effectiveness of Allied propaganda in giving Americans a distorted view of the war.

Also contributing to U.S. entry into the war was a growing conviction among America's intellectuals and leaders that America could not, and should not, continue to avoid a major role in international affairs. Convinced of the superiority of their economic, political, and ethical culture, many Americans had long believed that the United States was destined to save the world and that it was high time to abandon selfish isolationism and assume an active world role. Wilson's "peace without victory" speech and his other wartime speeches were permeated with this sentiment. He believed that it was vitally important for him to be present in the postwar peace conference to promote a new world order of democracy and free trade.

Furthermore, legalisms, sentiments, and idealism aside, it can be argued that entry into the war was in America's national interest. Germany was Europe's second most populous nation and its greatest industrial producer. Regardless of the origins of the war, a German victory might so increase Germany's preeminence as to destroy the balance of power in Europe. The division of Europe into mutually hostile camps had contributed to U.S. security. A unified Europe would be more menacing. One finds few references to balance of power in the contemporary debate, but many Americans feared that a German victory would make the world less safe. This was expressed, not as reasoned political theory, but as fear that a victorious Germany might continue to expand, endanger democracy, and seek to conquer the world. Fears of the consequences of German victory may have underlain the unneutrality that took America so close to war that "any little German lieutenant" could precipitate its entry.

2 World War and Peace Settlement

America's Military Contribution

The Allies enthusiastically celebrated America's entrance into the war. It meant fresh infusions of supplies and loans, huge naval reinforcements, and, possibly, troops. They expected it to break the military deadlock and ensure victory.

The United States did not sign a formal treaty of alliance. Instead, America became an "associated" power and thus avoided entanglement in any agreements the Allies had already negotiated among themselves.

The U.S. Navy quickly moved into action. Already much enlarged, it grew to a total of two thousand vessels and 533,000 men. As it protected convoys and hunted submarines, Allied shipping losses dropped from 880,000 tons in April 1917 to less than 200,000 tons per month after April 1918. Although America had denounced Britain's blockade of Germany as illegal, the U.S. Navy joined in enforcing it. Seizing neutral ships, Americans mined the high seas and enforced the food blockade. This was a heavy blow to the doctrine of freedom of the seas.

Many Americans assumed that U.S. participation in the war would be limited to naval action and provision of supplies, but the Allies rushed delegations to America to plead for troops. In April 1917, America had only 310,000 troops, but it quickly enlisted and drafted many more. By the war's end, its armed forces peaked at 4.8 million, including 400,000 blacks.

Americans sent an Expeditionary Force to Europe under the command of General John J. Pershing. Pershing insisted that these troops fight as separate U.S. units on a separate sector of the front. Not until October 1917 did Americans suffer battle deaths. By the end of the war, 2 million U.S. troops were in France, where they held 21 percent of the front. They played a key role in stopping Germany's spring 1918 offensive, and spearheaded the September Allied counteroffensive that forced Germany to surrender. America's intervention probably averted a German victory in France and enabled the Allies to score a crushing triumph.

Fifty-three thousand Americans died in battle, and another sixty-two thousand died of disease. These losses were light, however, when compared to the number of Europeans killed: 14.8 million persons, including 3.7 million Russians, 2.6 million Germans, and 1.4 million Frenchmen.

Uneasy Alliance with Japan

The wartime ally with which America experienced the most friction was Japan. It had been long gathering.

After 1854, when U.S. Admiral Matthew Perry had forced a reluctant Japan to open itself to commerce, it had appeared to many Japanese that the world was being conquered by Europeans. Japan could preserve its independence, its leaders concluded, only if it adopted the features of Western cultures that gave whites such irresistible force. Importing Western weapons, they adopted Western-style military organization, a Western-style constitution, and modern industrial technology. As had happened earlier in England, manufacturing provided quantities of low-cost goods that Japan could trade for foreign raw materials and food, which allowed its population to soar far above the number Japan's own farms could feed. These developments made the country ever more dependent on foreign trade. As the British had reacted to similar circumstances, the Japanese built a navy to protect trade and sought to secure foreign areas that produced essential raw materials and food.

Defeating China in 1895, Japan acquired Taiwan and expanded its influence in Korea. In 1905 it defeated Russia, strengthened its hold on Korea, and moved military forces into southern Manchuria. Japan also joined European nations in securing control of areas of then-underdeveloped and disorganized China.

In 1914, Japan declared war on Germany. In January 1915, with Europe enmeshed in war, it secretly presented China with twenty-one demands, which insisted that the Chinese recognize Japan's control of Korea, Manchuria, Outer Mongolia, and Shantung, appoint Japanese advisers, and allow the Japanese to share in the control of police and army arsenals. If China made these concessions, it would be putting itself largely under Japanese control.

Hoping for foreign support against Japan, China leaked these demands. Secretary of State William Jennings Bryan, in May 1915, sent Japan a note asserting that America would not recognize any agreement that impaired its rights in China, China's political or territorial integrity, or the Open Door (the freedom of all nations to trade with China).

Japan shelved most of its political and military demands, but China conceded most of the others. Japan also won British and French agreement to assign to it, as its share of war booty, the German islands in the Pacific and the German sphere of influence on China's Shantung Peninsula.

In 1917, a distinguished Japanese diplomat, Viscount Ishii Kikujiro, visited America in an effort to secure U.S. agreement to the concept that Japan had "paramount interests" in China and therefore more rights than other nations to intervene there. Secretary of State Robert Lansing wanted to demand that Japan reaffirm respect for the Open Door and for China's territorial integrity, but Wilson, eager to keep Japan in the war and to secure its entry into a new international organization, made a considerable concession. The November 1917 Lansing-Ishii Agreement conceded that, because "territorial propinquity creates special relations between countries," Japan had "special interests in China." Although Tokyo promised not to take advantage of the war to acquire privileges that impaired the rights of others, this was a major diplomatic victory for Japan.

Wartime Relations with Russia

The fighting in World War I went badly for Russia. At the outset of the war, its armies drove into Prussia, but were decisively defeated, and a counteroffensive took German armies deeply into the Russian empire, including Poland and the Baltic states. A 1915 British naval expedition to open a supply route through the Dardanelles, the passageway between the Mediterranean Sea and the Black Sea, was defeated by the Turks. A 1916 Russian offensive failed, with heavy losses. Russia's economy and the tsar's government crumbled under the strain.

In March 1917, striking workers and mutinous soldiers forced the tsar to abdicate. At first, government power was assumed by Russia's parliament, the Duma, led by Alexander Kerensky. Seeking to continue the war, Kerensky organized a July offensive, but it collapsed, and army discipline deteriorated. A revolt by a general failed but nonetheless fatally wounded the Kerensky regime.

The Communist Bolsheviks, led by Vladimir I. Lenin, organizing workers, soldiers, and peasants, seized control of the government in November 1917. Opposed to the war, Lenin surrendered to the Germans and, in March 1918, signed the Treaty of Brest-Litovsk, in which he bought peace at the price of 1.3 million square miles of territory, including Poland, Finland, and the Ukraine, containing 62 million people, Russia's best farm lands, and a third of its factories. However, anti-Communists, called "Whites," formed armies and, with foreign support, advanced on Moscow to overthrow the "Reds." Thus, the disastrous war with Germany was followed by a civil war.

Many in the Allied countries were extremely hostile to the new Communist government because it had surrendered to Germany and because it was Communist and sought world revolution. French Marshall Ferdinand Foch, commander of Allied armies, and Winston Churchill, Britain's secretary of state for war, recommended that, after defeating Germany, Allied forces continue marching east to destroy the Bolsheviks.

The British, French, and Japanese sent troops into Russia. Their stated purposes were to prevent arms from falling into the hands of Germans, to preserve an eastern fighting front, and to rescue 40,000 Czech soldiers who, refusing to surrender to the Germans or to turn over their arms to the Communists, were withdrawing across the Trans-Siberian Railway to fight elsewhere. Secretly, the Allies also hoped to overthrow the Communist regime, an effort for which Wilson predicted failure. "Trying to stop a revolutionary movement with armies," he said, was "like using a broom to hold back an ocean"—it could be stopped, he said, only by removing its causes.

Although resisting Allied proposals for a larger intervention, Wilson, in June 1918, ordered five thousand U.S. troops to Archangel and Murmansk and, in July, sent ten thousand troops to Siberia. He directed them to guard storehouses and port facilities but not to intervene in Russia's civil war. Nevertheless, while not directly entering the fighting, Allied troops operated in ways, such as helping Czechs control the Trans-Siberian Railway and securing rear areas, that aided White armies. Also, U.S. troops remained after Germany's surrender, in November 1918, removed the original justification for their presence, and they cooperated with the Allies who supported Admiral A. V. Kolchak's White army in its futile attempts to overthrow the Reds. The Communists regarded them as part of a foreign coalition that sought to suppress their revolution.

In February 1919, during the Versailles peace conference, Wilson sent the young William C. Bullitt to Russia to meet Lenin, who offered to accept a cease-fire, negotiate with White armies, and pay the tsar's debts if the Allies would recognize his government and withdraw their troops. However, the reaction of the U.S. press and of Allied leaders was unfavorable, and Wilson did not follow up on Bullitt's mission. The last U.S. troops were not withdrawn from Russia until 1920.

Although Russia had been one of the victorious Allies, its Communist revolution and its surrender to the Germans made it an international outcast. It was not invited to the peace conference, and it lost more territory from World War I than any of the defeated enemy powers. The peace conference awarded independence to Finland, Estonia, Latvia, and Lithuania. Russia also lost territories to Poland and Romania.

Wilson's Peace Program

A major component of the pre-war Progressive Movement in America, and of similar reform movements in Europe and Asia, was the effort to promote international peace. Important peace groups appeared in America, including the American Peace Society, the World Peace Foundation, and the Carnegie Endowment for International Peace. In 1915, former President William Howard Taft, Harvard University President A. Lawrence Lowell, and others organized the League to Enforce Peace, which called for compulsory arbitration of legal disputes. By World War I, a consensus seemed to have emerged on the need for open diplomacy, democratic control of foreign policy, freedom of the seas, disarmament, and self-determination (allowing people to vote on which country they wished to belong). Most of this program was endorsed by Wilson in his January 1917 "peace without victory" speech and in his April request for a declaration of war.

In November 1917, after the Bolsheviks (Communists) seized control of the Russian government, they found in its files secret treaties in which the Allies had agreed on what each country would take from Germany. To support their charge that the war resulted from capitalist greed, the Communists published these agreements. The treaties returned Alsace-Lorraine to France and also gave it the Saar from Germany, and parts of Turkey. To further weaken Germany, the Rhineland (the part of Germany west of the Rhine River, which contained 5 million persons), would be made independent. Britain would acquire German colonies, plus Iran and Iraq from Turkey. Russia would achieve its age-old ambition to control the Dardanelles. Italy would acquire colonies, plus territories from Austria-Hungary. Japan's share would be Germany's Pacific islands and Germany's sphere of influence in China.

Wilson was appalled by the greed of these treaties. Their publication confronted him with a dilemma. He hesitated to demand that the Allies repudiate them for fear of disrupting Allied wartime unity and thereby enabling Germany to escape defeat. He did suggest that the Allies prepare a common reply to the Bolshevik charges, but they refused. Therefore, he adopted a strategy of pretending that the secret treaties were Communist propaganda, meanwhile proclaiming America's peace program publicly in the hope of overriding the secret treaties and counteracting Lenin's charge that the war was a war of capitalist greed.

In a speech to Congress, on January 8, 1918, Wilson, repeating that America's fight was not with the German people but only with their "military masters," outlined his peace program in fourteen points. Point one demanded an end to secret treaties in favor of "open covenants of peace, openly arrived at." Point two promised absolute freedom of the seas, in war as well as in peace. The third called for removal of tariffs and other trade discrimination. The fourth advocated disarmament "to the lowest point consistent with domestic safety." Point five promised an "absolutely impartial adjustment of all colonial claims" in the best interest of subject peoples. Point six called on the nations to withdraw their troops from Russia and to allow that country to determine its own political development. Points seven through thirteen demanded settlement of territorial disputes according to the principles of self-determination, including formation of an independent Poland and autonomy for the peoples in the Austria-Hungarian and Turkish empires. In point fourteen he proposed "a general association of nations" to guarantee "independence and territorial integrity to great and small states alike."

Wilson's fourteen point peace program was greeted with enthusiasm in America and abroad, and it raised popular morale in the Allied countries. Many copies were dropped in Germany, where it undermined support for continuing the war. It was a tremendous propaganda success.

Armistice Negotiations

By late summer 1918, it was becoming clear that Germany had lost the war. Its great spring drive had stalled, and U.S. troops, pouring into France, were spearheading an attack that forced German armies to retreat. Germany's allies were surrendering: Bulgaria in September, Turkey in October. Also, the food blockade was causing starvation in German-controlled areas. In September, General Ludendorff told the government that it should make peace quickly before the military front completely collapsed. On October 1, the kaiser made Prince Max of Baden, a liberal advocate of peace, chancellor, and on October 3, Max cabled Wilson that Germany was ready to surrender if the peace terms would be the Fourteen Points. His offer was not accepted by the Allies for more than five weeks, during which time tens of thousands died. What caused the delay?

First, Wilson sought revolution in Germany. Did Prince Max speak for the German people, he asked, or merely for the despotic German government? A democratic Germany, he suggested, would get more favorable peace terms. Hardly needing this encouragement, German civilians launched an uprising, the kaiser fled to Holland, and Social Democrats, who had opposed the war, took control.

Second, Wilson needed to get Allied agreement to accept German surrender on the basis of the Fourteen Points. When they refused, he threatened to make a separate peace with Germany and cut supplies to the Allies. Still, Britain rejected freedom of the seas, and both England and France insisted that Germany pay reparations. After Wilson agreed to delete freedom of the seas and add reparations, the amended Fourteen Points became the surrender terms, a commitment by the Allies to Germany.

Wilson also insisted that the military provisions of the cease-fire must weaken Germany to the point that it could not change its mind and renew the war. This meant acceptance of complete defeat. British generals advocated mild armistice terms so as to stop the killing as quickly as possible. Pershing wanted to continue fighting until the Allies had destroyed Germany's armies and conquered its territory. The French proposed that Germany be allowed to surrender, but on conditions so severe as to remove all possibility that it could renew the war. Adopting the French position, the Allies required the Germans to surrender their navy, completely withdraw from France and Belgium, and allow Allied troops to occupy German territory to the Rhine River, and also bridgeheads east of the Rhine. Fighting finally stopped on November 11, 1918, ending the four-year war that had taken the lives of 8 million soldiers and 20 million civilians.

In Allied countries, the news was greeted with wild enthusiasm. "Everything for which America fought has been accomplished," Wilson announced. "It will now be our fortunate duty to assist . . . in the establishment of just democracy throughout the world."

Obstacles to a Just Peace

A week later, Wilson announced that he would personally attend the peace conference as head of the U.S. peace commission. Because no previous president had gone abroad as head of a negotiating team, this announcement caused a sensation. Wilson said that his presence was needed to persuade the Allies to accept terms in conformity with his Fourteen Points. However, some of Wilson's contemporary critics, and also later historians, argued that he might have exerted greater influence if he had remained in Washington.

Wilson's choice of the other members of the peace commission provoked more criticism. He named Secretary of State Robert Lansing, Colonel House, General Tasker H. Bliss, and a career diplomat, Henry White, to the commission. All were Democrats, except White, who was not a leader of the Republican party. Thus, Wilson passed over leading Republicans who had supported his program, including Taft, Elihu Root, and Hughes. He appointed no senator, and he did not consult the Senate Foreign Relations Committee. Basically, the peace commission consisted of Wilson and his aides. The credit, or blame, for the peace settlement would not be shared.

Wilson and the peace delegation sailed on board the *George Washington* on December 4, 1918. He would be out of the country for nearly six months. He took with him a large group of scholars and researchers known as the "Inquiry," who had been working on a peace program for more than a year. "Tell me what's right," he instructed them, but some of them complained that it was difficult to get their ideas through to the busy president.

Landing in Europe more than a month prior to the January 18 opening of the peace conference, Wilson made a tour of England and Italy. As the nation whose entry had enabled the Allies to win, the champion of unselfish war aims, the proponent of international organization, and the only nation with sufficient economic resources to help restore Europe's economy, America enjoyed enormous prestige. Wherever the president went, the people greeted him with tremendous enthusiasm. For a time he seemed to be the moral leader of the world.

It would not be easy, however, to secure a peace treaty in conformity with the Fourteen Points. Serious obstacles to a just peace existed. Nearly everyone professed to favor justice, but different nations had different concepts of what would be just. Most hailed the victory as an opportunity to satisfy long-held ambitions for more territory and colonies. Americans, said Wilson, "would be the only disinterested people at the peace conference." Also, four years of killing and being killed amid a flood of propaganda had aroused so much hatred that many sought revenge. Europe was in the grip, wrote one historian, of a "savage war psychosis."

In America, a congressional election came a few days before the armistice, and Democratic congressmen implored Wilson to help them win reelection. Yielding, Wilson, in October 1918, urged the people to demonstrate support for his peace program by electing Democratic congressmen to make him America's "unembarrassed spokesman" abroad. When he thus used his peace program against Republicans, they replied with attacks on it. America should demand not the Fourteen Points, said Roosevelt, but unconditional surrender. The Republicans won the election, gaining a majority in both House and Senate, and Roosevelt called this result an emphatic rejection of Wilson's leadership.

England also held an election in 1918. Although Prime Minister David Lloyd George was receptive to Wilson's idealism, he pandered to the public's hatred of Germans and promised to "hang the kaiser" and make Germany pay for the war. He won overwhelmingly. Later, many Englishmen would express shame at the level on which this election was conducted.

In France, Premier Georges Clemenceau made no pretense of seeking a fair peace. Saying "my war aim is to conquer," he won a smashing three-to-one vote of confidence in the Chamber of Deputies. Thus, all three democratic elections seemed to express public desire for vengeance, which boded ill for the Fourteen Points.

Another serious obstacle was the existence of the secret treaties in which the Allies had agreed on what they would take from the Central Powers. Wilson hoped that their subsequent agreement to allow Germany to surrender on the basis of the Fourteen Points had canceled the secret treaties, but at the peace conference the Allies often cooperated to implement those treaties instead of the Fourteen Points.

A third obstacle to a just peace was the general perception of a need to get a treaty signed quickly. Europe was in turmoil. National economies were in shambles, with widespread unemployment and hunger. The empires of eastern Europe were fragmenting into new nations which were fighting over boundaries, while within nations hostile armed factions battled for control. Over all loomed the menace of communism: Russia had gone Communist, Hungary came under a Communist government for a time, and the red flag was flying over many city halls in Italy and Germany. It seemed essential to make peace quickly to restore stability.

The Paris Peace Conference and the Treaty of Versailles

Seventy delegates from twenty-eight nations assembled in Paris on January 18, 1919. Strictly speaking, it was not a peace conference, because the enemy was not present, but a preliminary meeting of the Allies to agree on what terms they would demand of the Central Powers.

Seventy was too large a group for efficient discussion of complex problems, and most decisions were arrived at in meetings of the Big Four—Wilson, Lloyd George, Clemenceau, and Premier Vittoria Orlando of Italy. From March to June, they met 145 times. Because Orlando walked out for a time to protest decisions regarding Italy, much of the work was done by Wilson, Lloyd George, and Clemenceau—three men in a room deciding the fate of the world (see Fig. 2.1). One of their first decisions was to exclude reporters, in disregard of the "openly arrived at" provision of the first of the Fourteen Points.

They were an oddly assorted group. Lloyd George and Clemenceau wondered how the moralistic Wilson, whom they regarded as more suited to the clergy than to politics, had come to head a nation. But they soon discovered that he could be a tough negotiator. The British prime minister found Wilson to be an "extraordinary compound" of "the noble visionary, the implacable and unscrupulous partisan, the exalted idealist, and the man of rather petty personal rancor." Lloyd George, a handsome and personable orator who had led Britain's prewar reform movement, had some sympathy with Wilson's idealism and gave him some support against French demands. A liberal in his youth,

Figure 2.1 The "Big Three" at the 1919 Versailles Peace Conference—British Prime Minister David Lloyd George, French Premier Georges Clemenceau, and President Woodrow Wilson. National Archives.

Clemenceau had grown old (he was seventy-seven) and cynical, and his disposition was not improved by a skin ailment that required him to wear gloves. Impatient at Wilson's Fourteen Points, he exclaimed: "God Almighty only had ten!" Lloyd George thought he was Napoleon, said Clemenceau, "but Wilson thinks he's Jesus Christ."

Wilson scored a notable success when, early in the conference, he won agreement that a league of nations would be among the first matters considered and would be incorporated as an integral part of the treaty. Made chairman of the commission to prepare a constitution for the new league, he, after intense work, presented his plan on February 14.

The League Covenant provided that all nations at war with Germany would be members and that each, regardless of size or power, would have one vote in the League's largest body, the Assembly. The Assembly, by two-thirds vote, would decide economic and social matters, including health and labor issues, and would elect four of the nine members of the League Council. The Council would handle political matters, particularly those involving war and peace. Five nations—Britain, America, France, Italy, and Japan—would be permanent members, and four others would be elected for short terms by the Assembly. No important measure could be adopted without the unanimous vote of the big five, which empowered any of them to veto any Council action on any dispute that did not directly involve them.

Associated with the League would be a Permanent Court of International Justice, an International Labor Organization, and a number of specialized international organizations, some of which, like the International Postal Union, had already existed for years. The League would be headquartered at Geneva, Switzerland.

The treaty provided for the League to supervise disarmament and the former German colonies. No treaty would be considered binding until registered with the League, which also might recommend that treaties be modified.

How would the League prevent war? The Covenant provided that, whenever a dispute arose that threatened to erupt into war, the nations involved would have to submit it to the League Council. If either nation accepted the Council's decision, the other could not legally go to war. Of course, this did not outlaw all war. If the Council was unable to reach a decision, or if neither nation accepted its decision, a war was legal. Also, if attacked, a nation was entitled to fight in self-defense.

In addition, Article X of the Covenant made the League a military alliance. Each member undertook "to preserve as against external aggression the territorial integrity and existing political independence of all the members of the League." The nations pledged to do so through imposing economic sanctions or taking joint military action against an aggressor.

In his Fourteen Points, Wilson had insisted that territorial disputes be settled by "self-determination," a vote by the inhabitants of the disputed area. To most liberals, this seemed to be both democratic and idealistic. Critics, however, pointed out that America had not applied this principle to American Indians, the southern Confederacy, or the Philippines. Also, cynics said, it would serve to further fragment Europe to the benefit of America's relative power position.

France, which had great fear of its more powerful neighbor, sought to so weaken Germany that it could never launch a new war to recover its losses. In addition to Alsace-Lorraine, Clemenceau sought to annex the coal-rich Saar basin and to make the Rhineland a separate buffer state. He further insisted that Germany surrender all of its colonies, disarm, and pay huge sums in reparations.

Indignantly threatening to walk out of the conference, Wilson protested that such harsh treatment would violate the Fourteen Points, increase Germany's vulnerability to communism, and plant the seeds of future wars: "Our greatest error would be to give her powerful reasons for wishing one day to take revenge." With support from Lloyd George, who was influenced by Britain's historic policy of preventing any nation, including France, from dominating Europe, Wilson forced some compromises. France got Alsace-Lorraine, but only a fifteen-year occupation of the Saar, after which that region's people would be allowed to vote on whether to be governed by France or Germany. France was also allowed to occupy the Rhineland for fifteen years, and Germans were permanently barred from placing any troops or fortifications in the Rhineland, but it remained German territory.

To compensate France for getting less than it demanded, Britain and America agreed to sign a treaty of alliance with France promising to come to its rescue if it were attacked by Germany. The U.S. Senate would reject this treaty.

Although the Fourteen Points called for a "fair and absolutely impartial adjustment of colonial claims," the Allies took all of Germany's colonies. Britain, South Africa, and France split Germany's African holdings, while Japan got Germany's Pacific islands north of the equator. England and France took parts of the Middle East from Turkey. Wilson succeeded in designating most former enemy colonies "mandates," with the implication that they would be held only temporarily under League supervision until they could be prepared for self-government. Nevertheless, they became, in effect, colonies, except that the holding powers submitted annual reports on them to the League.

Wilson had much conflict with Japan. The Japanese wanted the conference to adopt a statement that all races were equal, but the British felt that this would undermine the rationale for their empire, and Wilson knew that it would be unpopular in America's South. Wilson conceded Germany's Pacific islands to Japan but wanted one of them, Yap, for a U.S. cable station. To avert a Japanese walkout from the conference, he reluctantly agreed to transfer Germany's sphere of influence in China to Japan. Bitterly disappointed, Chinese students in Peking launched a huge protest, the May Fourth Movement, and China refused to sign the Versailles Treaty.

Wilson agreed that Italy might take South Tyrol, which contained 200,000 Austrians, to give it a defensible border but, convinced that Italy's demand for Fiume was unjustified, he appealed to the Italian people to repudiate Orlando's demand for it. Orlando withdrew from the conference in protest, but returned after receiving overwhelming endorsement by Italy's parliament. The Italians failed to get Fiume at the conference, but seized it in 1922.

The Poles had not had an independent state since 1795, when Poland was partitioned by Russia, Prussia, and Austria. In line with the principle of self-determination, the Fourteen Points called for an independent Poland. To provide it with an outlet to the sea, Poland was given a corridor through Germany that contained many Germans and that separated East Prussia from the rest of Germany; Hitler's effort to recover it would set off World War II.

The Fourteen Points called for self-government for the minority peoples within the Austria-Hungarian and Turkish empires, but not for dissolution of those empires. Nevertheless, they were dissolved. Of Turkey's possessions, England got Iraq, Trans-Jordan, and Palestine; France got Syria and Lebanon. New nations, Czechoslovakia, Hungary, and Yugoslavia, were formed from former Austria-Hungarian territory, leaving a small Austria. To give Czechoslovakia a defensible border, it was given the mountainous Sudetenland which was home to 3 million Germans.

In all, Germany lost 13 percent of its European territory, containing more than 6 million people, a tenth of its prewar population. (See Fig. 2.2.)

The surrender terms specified that the Germans must pay reparations for damages to civilians and their property. At the conference, however, Wilson yielded to French and British demands to include pensions for veterans and widows, thereby doubling the total (as determined in 1921 by a Reparations Commission) to $33 billion.

Figure 2.2 German and Russian Territorial Losses in World War I.

The treaty restricted the German army to a maximum of 100,000 men and forbade the army to have military airplanes, submarines, tanks, or heavy artillery. To justify the treaty's severity, Germany was forced to sign, in Article 231, a confession that it was guilty of forcing war on the Allies.

After agreeing on the terms they would demand, the Allies called in the Germans and presented them with the treaty. Denying that Germany was solely responsible for the war, the Germans condemned its harshness. The Allies made only a few minor concessions. Meanwhile, to maintain pressure on Germany, they continued the food blockade while thousands of Germans starved. The Germans signed, "yielding to superior force, and without renouncing our view of the unheard-of injustices of the peace conditions."

The Treaty of Versailles was a victor's peace rather than a victory of idealism, more in the spirit of the secret treaties than of the Fourteen Points. Nevertheless, Wilson's efforts made it somewhat more moderate than it otherwise might have been. His chief victory was to so interweave the League into the treaty that the Allies must join it to collect their booty. He consoled himself with the thought that the League might later correct some of the treaty's injustices.

Defeat of the Treaty

By February 1919, when Wilson made a month-long trip home to attend to government business, opposition to U.S. membership in the League was rising. "America is the hope of the world," he said, and it was America's purpose to make people free. When he invited the Senate Foreign Relations Committee to the White House, two members declined. There was little meeting of minds— "I feel as if I had been wandering with Alice in Wonderland," said Senator Frank Brandegee, "and had tea with the Mad Hatter." Before Wilson sailed again for Paris, Senator Henry Cabot Lodge, chairman of the Foreign Relations Committee, secured the signatures of thirty-nine senators, six more than needed to defeat the treaty, on a statement opposing U.S. membership in the League. Defiantly, Wilson said that the League would be so intertwined with the treaty that the United States could not ratify the treaty without joining it.

However, back in Paris, Wilson secured modifications to the Covenant to meet some of the senator's objections. He made the right of a nation to withdraw from the League, and to refuse to administer a mandate, more explicit, and he excluded from League jurisdiction U.S. tariffs, immigration laws, and the Monroe Doctrine.

After he returned to America, Wilson submitted the treaty to the Senate on July 10, 1919. U.S. isolation had ended, he said, America was a world power, and the world relied on America for moral leadership. At this time, it appeared that most Americans favored the League. A survey of 1,377 newspapers found that 710 favored it unconditionally, and only 181 opposed it. Thirty-two state legislatures, thirty-three governors, and many clergy and senators endorsed it.

However, several groups strongly objected. The war was followed by a postwar reaction that brought a slump in idealism. Also, isolationists feared that the League might unnecessarily draw America into Asian and European wars, while nationalists feared that it might require Americans to defend empires and otherwise restrict America's freedom to act independently in its own self-interest. "Are you willing to put your soldiers and your sailors at the disposition of other nations?" asked Lodge, and Senator William E. Borah called it a step toward "sterilization of nationalism."

Unexpectedly, many liberal idealists and internationalists also opposed the League. They regarded the Versailles Treaty as unjustly harsh, and they saw the League as an organization of victors designed to perpetuate its injustices. The *Nation* magazine called the treaty one of "vengeance" and an "international crime." It was, said the *New Republic*, an "inhuman monster." Senator George Norris said it was an instrument for perpetuating big power domination, and Senator Robert LaFollette called it an "imperialist club."

Furthermore, the treaty became a football in the contest between political parties for control of the government. By his decision to go to Paris personally, and by his exclusion of any senator or leading Republican from the peace commission, Wilson had monopolized credit for the treaty for himself and the Democratic party. It was widely assumed that he intended to run for a third term on the grounds that his leadership was needed to inaugurate the League. Senate approval of the treaty might so enhance his already exalted reputation as to make him unbeatable at the polls. Apparently, in order to avoid defeat in the coming election, Republicans must either force Wilson to share credit for the League by making him accept enough Republican-sponsored changes to convert it from a Wilson league to a bipartisan league or, if Wilson refused, to discredit and defeat it.

Wilson sought to mobilize public support of the League. Although exhausted from the strenuous work at the peace conference, he, against his doctor's advice, embarked on an eight thousand-mile cross-country speaking tour. He drew large and enthusiastic audiences, but, following him, the anti-League senators Borah and Hiram Johnson also drew large crowds. On September 25, Wilson's tour reached an emotional climax at Pueblo, Colorado, where a huge crowd greeted him with a ten-minute standing ovation, but that night he was so exhausted that his doctor insisted that he cancel the remainder of the tour. Back in Washington, he walked unaided from the train, but on October 2 he was found unconscious on the White House floor.

Wilson had suffered a massive coronary thrombosis (a stroke) that destroyed part of this brain and left him partially paralyzed. For weeks, totally incapacitated, he was seen only by his wife and physician, and he did not meet with his cabinet for more than seven months. He partly recovered—pictures show him looking well, and visitors found him mentally sharp—but some thought that he had undergone personality changes that made him more uncompromising. He fired Secretary of State Lansing for holding cabinet meetings in his absence and failing to fully back him on the League. He also severed relations with his old friend, Colonel House, after House advised him to compromise.

After the Senate Foreign Relations Committee completed its deliberations, the Senate began debate on the treaty. Only a small group of senators, the "irreconcilables," totally opposed U.S. membership. Most were willing to join if certain changes were made. Lodge proposed fourteen reservations that would further restrict the League's authority to question U.S. policies concerning imports, immigration, drugs, and the Monroe Doctrine; withhold U.S. consent to giving Shantung to the Japanese; reject being bound by a vote decided by Britain's six votes; and reject membership in the International Labor Organization. His most important reservation stated that, without specific congressional approval in each case, the United States would assume no obligation under Article X to defend other members of the League—largely annulling the League's role as a defensive alliance.

Maintaining that the Lodge reservations would "nullify" the League, Wilson urged Democratic senators to vote against them. Although more than two-thirds of the senators favored U.S. membership, when the treaty came to a vote on November 19 it failed to get a majority, either with or without the Lodge reservations.

Arguing that joining the League with the Lodge reservations was better than not joining at all, many of Wilson's closest friends and political associates, and the French and British governments, urged the president to compromise, but he refused. Lodge also rejected compromise. On January 9, 1920, Wilson announced that the forthcoming presidential election should be conducted as a "great and solemn referendum" on the issue. Some cynics pointed out that this would make Wilson the most logical Democratic candidate. Many others considered his position a tragic error.

Under great popular pressure to compromise, the treaty was brought up for another vote on March 19, 1920. This time, with the Lodge reservations, it got a large majority, 49–35, but this was still short of the two-thirds majority needed for ratification. At Wilson's urging, about half of the Democratic senators voted against approval with the Lodge reservations.

The League figured prominently in the 1920 presidential campaign. Nominating Senator Warren G. Harding of Ohio, who had voted for approval with the Lodge reservations, the Republicans adopted a platform that condemned the "Wilson league." They blurred the issue, however, by declaring in favor of an "international association" providing "instant and general international conference whenever peace shall be threatened."

In the Democratic convention, Wilson's devoted followers, aware that Wilson was partially incapacitated, sadly rejected his efforts to win renomination. Instead, the convention nominated Governor James M. Cox of Ohio, who was not of Wilson's wing of the party and who had not taken part in the flight over the treaty. However, Cox visited Wilson and became a vigorous and eloquent champion of U.S. membership in the League.

Harding straddled the issue. In every speech, he both strongly denounced "Wilson's League" and advocated U.S. membership in an "association of nations." He did this so successfully that he got endorsements from both Senator Hiram W, Johnson, the most vigorous opponent of the League, and William Howard Taft, one of the League's foremost champions.

By this time Wilson had lost his former popularity. Many considered him to be too unyielding and too autocratic—his biographer, Arthur Link, wrote that Wilson had conducted foreign affairs as if he were a divine-right monarch. Also many feared that Cox, if elected, would continue Wilson's policy and reject the compromises necessary to get Senate approval. Cox insisted that he would compromise, but those statements were not well reported in the mostly Republican press.

Harding won a smashing victory, getting 16 million votes to Cox's 9 million. Of course, this was not a clear vote on the League issue—no American election can be a referendum on a single question, particularly a foreign policy issue. After the election, Harding finally clarified his position by saying that "the League is deceased." In July 1921, Congress passed a joint resolution declaring peace with the Central Powers. Thus, America returned to its traditional policy of noninvolvement in the international affairs of Europe.

In later years, the question of whether America should have joined the League would be much debated. Many League advocates argued that, by rejecting its own creation, the United States had lost the best chance of preventing international war. If America had been a member, they maintained, it could have stiffened League resistance to the Axis aggressors at an early stage when that aggression could have been stopped without war. By the late 1930s, 70 percent of Americans believed that staying out of the League was a mistake.

Others, however, argued that the League lacked adequate procedures for peaceably altering the international status quo to provide justice in a changing world. Therefore, they maintained, it was essentially an organization of victors designed to guarantee continued possession of the fruits of victory and failed to provide a reasonable alternative to war.

However, the principal lesson the American people would draw from the experience was simply that the united States should join an international peace organization.

America's intervention in World War I had mixed consequences. This major departure from isolationism, and deep involvement in European politics, had not produced as many benefits as some had hoped. A war fought in the name of democracy had been won, but victory had not made the world safe for democracy. Instead, from the war and its aftermath would arise communism in Russia, fascism in Italy, and Nazism in Germany. The war to end war produced a treaty of conquest that set the stage for World War II. However, the devastation of European nations, and the stimulation of U.S. industrial and financial growth, had increased America's relative world power. How would that power be employed?

3 Foreign Relations in the 1920s

The United States as a Major Power

Before World War I, America had acquired a larger combination of the basic elements of national power—population, industrial production, education, and internal unity—than any other nation. However, the superiority of U.S. power was not generally recognized, at home or abroad, because of the nation's small military force, its low level of exports, and its disinclination to participate in political contests outside of the Western Hemisphere.

World War I brought an additional shift of economic power to America. Other leading nations—Germany, England, France, Russia, and Italy—were weakened as the fighting destroyed factories and transportation, depressed industrial and agricultural production, and took them deeply into debt. In contrast, U.S. industrial and agricultural production greatly expanded, Americans made huge profits, and America climbed out of international debt to become a creditor nation.

By World War I, the United States had a sizable empire. Its noncontiguous possessions included Alaska, Hawaii, Midway, Wake Island, Guam, Samoa, the Philippines, Puerto Rico, and the Virgin Islands. America also exercised protectorates (a large measure of military and financial control) over Cuba, Panama, the Dominican Republic, Nicaragua, and Haiti. This empire was protected by a navy that ranked second or third in the world.

Because America rejected membership in the League and alliances with non–Western Hemisphere nations, some contemporaries and historians called America's policy in the 1920s "isolationist." To some extent, this was accurate, but it must be seen in perspective. Certainly, a nation that maintained a far-flung empire was not a hermit nation. Also, not even the "isolationism" of George Washington and Thomas Jefferson contemplated severing economic and cultural relations with the rest of the world; but envisioned only abstention from Europe's wars. In the nineteenth century, some Englishmen had called British foreign policy "splendid isolation," by which they meant that Britain could defend its worldwide interests singlehandedly without the assistance of allies. America's rejection of the League was partly an expression of such independent nationalism, of a determination to retain freedom to act in its own self-interest, regardless of the wishes of its allies. Also, although disengaging somewhat from European political affairs, the United States played an active and expanding role in the international economy. In addition, it remained active in the international politics of the Western Hemisphere and East Asia.

Administration of Foreign Policy in the Republican Era

The Republican party controlled the White House for twelve years, from 1921 to 1933, under three presidents: Warren G. Harding (1921–1923), Calvin Coolidge (1923–1929), and Herbert Hoover (1929–1933). The personnel of these administrations overlapped (Hoover was in the government for the entire twelve years, and Secretary of the Treasury Andrew Mellon served all three presidents), and their foreign policies showed considerable continuity.

Harding had little background or interest in world affairs. In his 1920 campaign, he preached a gospel of America first: "Think of America first, prosper America first." He delegated much foreign policy authority. Once he told a reporter to address questions to the secretary of state because "I don't know anything about this European stuff."

However, Harding appointed the able Charles Evans Hughes as secretary of state. A former law professor, governor of New York, Supreme Court justice, and Republican nominee for president, Hughes proved to be one of the ablest secretaries of state in the nation's history. After Harding's death, Coolidge retained Hughes in his post until March 1925. Hughes was followed in office by Frank Kellogg, a lawyer and former U.S. senator and ambassador to Britain, who served as secretary of state from 1925 to 1929.

Herbert Hoover (1929–1933) was well qualified in foreign affairs. As a mining engineer, he had served for years abroad, in Latin America, China, and Russia. Retiring at age forty-six, he devoted the remainder of his life to public service, and as Wilson's relief administrator in Europe he gained a reputation as a humanitarian. As secretary of commerce, he championed free enterprise and individualism and energetically promoted U.S. business interests abroad. As president, he announced that the primary object of his foreign policy was peace: "We have no hates; we wish no further possessions; we harbor no military threats" but wish only to "advance the cause of peace."

Hoover's secretary of state, Henry L. Stimson, was of a different stripe. An aristocratic friend of Theodore Roosevelt, he had been President William Howard Taft's secretary of war and an artillery colonel in World War I, and he had served as governor-general of the Philippines. He spoke of the "joy of war" and at times, said Hoover, was "more of a warrior than a diplomat."

In the (1921–1933) Republican era, the U.S. government was a businessman's administration. "The business of America is business," said President Coolidge, and the *Wall Street Journal* rejoiced that "Never before, here or in any other land has government been so completely fused with business." Often using businessmen to implement policy, the government raised the tariff, insisted that the Allies repay war debts, demanded an open door for U.S. trade and investments, muscled in on the oil of the Middle East, and otherwise vigorously promoted U.S. business interests throughout the world.

As secretary of commerce, Hoover had played an important role in promoting U.S. foreign trade and investments and "individualism in international economic life." In this endeavor he was joined by Andrew W. Mellon, the multimillionaire financier and manufacturer (steel, oil, coal, and aluminum) who served more than ten years (1921–1932) as secretary of the treasury.

This policy was accompanied by an upgrading of U.S. representation abroad. In 1919, Georgetown University established the first separate U.S. school of world politics. The 1924 Rogers Act merged the consular and diplomatic corps into the Foreign Service, which, in 1925, created its own Foreign Service School. Salaries and allowances for living expenses abroad rose. State Department expenditures climbed from $4.9 million in 1910 to $14 million in 1930.

International Economic Policies

Boosted by World War I, America's role in the world economy continued to expand. In 1929, America produced 46 percent of the world's industrial goods, an amount exceeding the production of the next twenty-three countries combined, and pumped 70 percent of the world's oil. Surpassing imports, U.S. exports doubled in the 1920s to $5.4 billion, the highest of any nation. Historically, America had been a debtor nation, and on the eve of World War I it owed a net $3.7 billion. During the war, foreigners sold assets in America while U.S. investments abroad rose, with the result that in 1919 foreigners owed America a net $3.7 billion. As Republican administrations slashed taxes on upper incomes, money accumulated in the hands of U.S. businessmen who eagerly sought opportunities to invest abroad, and New York displaced London as the world's chief source of capital. Total private U.S. investments overseas, only $3.5 billion in 1914, soared to $17.2 billion by 1930.

During World War I, the U.S. government had loaned allied governments $7.1 billion, plus $3.3 billion in postwar reconstruction loans, for a total of $10.4 billion. Of this, $4.3 billion had gone to England, $3.4 billion to France, and $1.6 billion to Italy. The problem of arranging repayment was difficult and controversial.

Many in the Allied countries believed that these intergovernmental debts should be canceled. The British, who had forgiven such debts after the Napoleonic wars and who had lent more than $4 billion during World War I, advocated canceling all interallied war debts. France and the others agreed. They held that the money had been spent in the common cause of defeating Germany. Furthermore, America had prospered, while they had suffered more loss of life and property, and it seemed to them unfair to ask those who had sacrificed more to pay one who had given less. "U.S." did not stand for Uncle Sam, some said, but for "Uncle Shylock." Furthermore, many believed, as the economist John Maynard Keynes wrote in *The Economic Consequences of the*

Peace, that any attempt to collect these debts would be devastating to world trade.

Americans answered that the Allies had gained territories and reparations from the war, while America got nothing. If the Allies did not pay, American taxpayers would be forced to pay the debt. Also, the loans were a business transaction, and failure to repay them would undermine the trust necessary to anyone making future international loans.

After tough negotiations, agreements were reached. The Allies agreed to repay the loans over a period of sixty-two years, while America agreed to cut the interest, which, in effect, cut the debt. From 5 percent, America lowered interest for the British to 3.3 percent, equivalent to a 30 percent cancellation; to 1.6 percent for the French, a 60 percent cut; and to 0.4 percent for Italy, an 80 percent cancellation. In effect, America canceled about half of the total debt.

Another large international debt was owed by Germany, which was assessed reparations of more than $33 billion, plus the costs of the armies of occupation. The United States refused to admit any connection between war debts and reparations, but the Allies counted on reparations to help them pay America. Germany proved to be unable to pay the amount demanded. In January 1923, after Germany defaulted, French troops occupied the Ruhr, Germany's chief industrial region, for more than a year and a half. But German workers went on strike, and France was unable to extract enough German goods to pay even the costs of the occupation. Meanwhile, the resultant loss of production so bankrupted the Germans that it reduced the value of the German mark to zero.

To relieve the situation, Secretary of State Hughes in 1924 pressured France to agree to a restudy of the reparations question by a commission headed by American banker Charles Dawes. This commission was operated, not by the U.S. government, but by private businessmen. Acceptance of its recommendations reduced Germany's reparation payment to $250 million annually until its economy could recover.

The Great Depression that began in 1929 brought another reparations crisis. A second private commission, this time headed by General Electric executive Owen D. Young, cut Germany's remaining reparations bill to $9 billion, to be paid in 59 annual installments. The Allies offered to make additional cuts if America would reduce war debts.

The payment process encountered technical difficulties. Regardless of its wealth, a nation cannot pay debts to another country with its own paper money. Americans would not accept French francs, for example, but demanded U.S. dollars. To acquire the needed dollars, France had to ship either gold or French goods to America. Americans preferred gold, but the world's gold supply was limited, and most nations believed that it was necessary to keep large amounts of gold on hand to support the value of their paper currencies. The war debt had been created by shipment of U.S. war materials to the Allies, and to repay the debt they needed to ship goods to America. However, America's manufacturers resented imports of foreign goods that cut into their own sales.

Continuing their historic policy of maintaining high tariffs, Republican administrations in the 1920s twice raised the level of U.S. tariffs, even though this seemed to contradict their professed dedication to free enterprise and economic individualism. In 1922, they enacted the Fordney-McCumber Tariff, which raised average tariffs on industrial goods to 33 percent, a new twentieth-century high. Congress followed this, in June 1930, with the Hawley-Smoot Tariff, which raised average tariffs to 59 percent. A thousand economists vainly petitioned Hoover to veto this bill, saying that it would raise consumer prices, hurt exports, and make it harder for foreigners to pay their debts to America.

Nevertheless, between 1924 and 1931, the Allies paid the United States $2.6 billion. What made this possible? The answer was that in these years Americans loaned Germans $2.5 billion, while Germany paid the Allies $2.8 billion in reparations. Thus, U.S. loans provided Germans with the dollars they needed to pay reparations, which, in turn, provided the Allies with dollars to pay war debts. After the Great Depression hit, Americans drastically cut their foreign lending and investing, whereupon international payments almost ceased.

Some people suggested that Britain could pay its debt by ceding Canada to the United States, and, in 1929, Hoover offered to cancel the debt in return for Bermuda, Belize, and Trinidad. However, this would require the consent of the peoples concerned.

At a meeting at Lausanne, Switzerland, in 1932, the Allies offered to cancel 90 percent of Germany's reparations if the United States would cancel the same percentage of Allied debts to America. Congress refused. Instead, Congress, by the 1934 Johnson Act, forbade new loans to any nation in default.

U.S. imports dropped from $4.4 billion in 1929 to $1.3 billion in 1932, while U.S. exports plunged from $5.2 billion to $1.6 billion.

It cannot be said that the U.S. government, despite its access to experts, handled the war debt problem intelligently. The futile attempt to collect the debt poisoned international relations and depressed the market for U.S. exports. However, Americans learned from the experience. In World War II, they refused to make large loans to their allies; instead, they practically gave them the supplies.

Disengagement from Europe

In the 1920s, America retreated from the level of participation in European affairs it had assumed during the war. "No entangling alliances" had been America's historic policy, a policy based on the assumption that America's vital security interests were confined to the Western Hemisphere and that no likely political development in Europe could seriously threaten America's existence. Disgusted with the results of its departure from this policy in World War I, many Americans applauded America's rejection of the League and the French alliance.

Despite Harding's pronouncement that the League was "deceased," it was inaugurated on January 1, 1920, and by the end of that year forty-eight nations had joined. For nine months, Washington did not reply to its communications and protested against putting preexisting international agencies, such as those dealing with drugs and health, under its jurisdiction. By 1922, however, no longer able to ignore the fact that the League was conducting important business, America was secretly sending observers to Geneva. Soon they became spokesmen for U.S. views on such matters as health, prostitution, and the arms trade, and by 1931, the United States was participating in League discussions of political issues.

Associated with the League was the World Court (the Permanent Court of International Justice), membership in which was open to non-League members. Elected by the League for nine-year terms, its fifteen judges were empowered to make judgments on disputes that nations voluntarily submitted to it. The court also rendered advisory opinions on questions submitted by the League.

Such a court had been repeatedly proposed by Americans as early as 1899, and it well fit U.S. emphasis on the rule of law. A large majority of the American people favored joining the World Court. Both party platforms in 1924 called for entering, Elihu Root served as one of its judges, and, in January 1926, the House endorsed membership by a vote of 303–28. Presidents Harding, Coolidge, and Hoover all favored joining. Nevertheless, membership had opponents in the Senate. Some isolationists feared that it might lead to backdoor entry into the League. Others feared that the court might rule against U.S. policies on immigration, tariffs, or the Monroe Doctrine. When, in January 1926, the Senate voted to join, it did so with the proviso that the Court could not offer advisory opinion on any disputes in which the United States was involved without America's advance consent. The other members were unwilling to accept U.S. membership on this condition.

The French remained apprehensive that Germany might seek to retake Alsace-Lorraine, and they feared that they could not successfully defend themselves without British and U.S. help. Disappointed by U.S. refusal to ratify the treaty of alliance that Wilson had signed, they sought other means of drawing America into a special relationship that would improve the likelihood of U.S. help against possible German aggression.

Consequently, the French Foreign Minister, Aristide Briand, was receptive to an approach by representatives of the American peace movement who sought treaties that would outlaw war. In 1927, Columbia University professor James T. Shotwell suggested to Briand that he propose that America and France agree to renounce or "outlaw" any future war between them. Briand issued a public appeal, written by Shotwell, asking that the American people back such a treaty.

Somewhat miffed by this bypassing of the State Department, and fearing a French attempt to draw America into an alliance, Coolidge ignored Briand's message. However, as Briand expected, American peace groups put up a tremendous clamor, including a petition with 2 million signatures, for acceptance. Senator Borah suggested a way to avoid entanglement with France while pleasing peace groups, and, at his prompting, Secretary of State Kellogg proposed that the treaty be expanded to invite other nations to sign, thus converting it from an American-French pact to a universal outlawing of war. Briand did not like the change but could think of no graceful way to reject it.

The Kellogg-Briand Pact, or Paris Peace Pact, was signed in August 1928. In it the signatories agreed to "condemn recourse to war" for the solution of international controversies, renounce war "as an instrument of national policy," and settle all of their disputes by "pacific means." After attaching reservations that exempted the Monroe Doctrine and self-defense, the Senate approved the pact in January 1929 by a vote of 85 to 1. Eventually, sixty-three nations signed it, many with reservations.

The Kellogg-Briand Pact outlawed war, but it did not remove any of the underlying causes of war, nor did it provide an alternative means of settling disputes. Thus, it was little more than an "international kiss" that America accepted largely as a means of fending off a more compromising French kiss (within a month, the Senate appropriated funds to construct fifteen additional heavy cruisers). Its principal effect was to contribute to a tendency by nations to fight wars without declaring war, which incidentally made it easier to stop fighting without a formal peace treaty.

The Red Scare

During the 1921–1933 Republican era, U.S. relations with the Soviet Union were a complex mixture of interventionism and isolationism. After the 1917 Bolshevik Revolution and Russia's surrender to Germany, the Communists (Reds) were challenged in civil war by anti-Communist (White) armies. Wilson and the Allies had sent troops into both Archangel and Vladivostok (see chapter 2). Wilson had ordered the U.S. troops not to intervene in the civil war, but they helped the Whites indirectly. In his Fourteen Points, Wilson called for allowing the Russians to determine their own political destiny, but he refused to recognize the Bolshevik regime as the legal government of Russia. By 1921, the Reds had defeated the Whites, after which foreign troops withdrew.

The Republicans seemed to be even more hostile to the Bolshevik regime. The Bolsheviks had seized about $336 million of U.S.-owned property, and they also refused to pay the $107 million owed American holders of tsarist bonds. Communist parties appeared in other nations, and, in 1919, the Bolsheviks organized the Third International (Comintern), a Moscow-headquartered organization of the world's Communist parties that was dedicated to spreading communism. Lenin sent advisers and financial aid to foreign Communist parties. These moves greatly alarmed the world's capitalists and democrats, and set off a semihysterical "red scare" in America. Fearful that Communist parties in America, though tiny, might, through "infiltration" and "subversion," seize control of America and destroy its way of life, some states banned organizations that advocated forcible overthrow of government, mobs destroyed socialist newspaper offices, the federal government made mass arrests and deported aliens, and patriotic groups purged suspect teachers and censored libraries.

Unlike most governments, Washington refused to establish diplomatic relations with Moscow. There would be no recognition, said Secretary of State Stimson, until the Soviets "ceased to agitate for the overthrow of American institutions." Also, America excluded Russia from the 1921–1922 international Washington Conference on East Asia (discussed later in this chapter).

On the other hand, Washington put pressure on Japan to withdraw its troops from Siberia. Also, when Russia experienced a terrible famine in 1921, Herbert Hoover took the lead in a relief effort that shipped $60 million in food and may have saved as many as 11 million lives. In addition to humanitarian reasons, he hoped that this effort would help wean Russians from Bolshevism.

Despite their antipathy, U.S. businessmen quickly seized upon opportunities to do business with Soviet Communists. Leading businessmen, notably Henry Ford, E. H. Harriman, and Armand Hammer, and corporations, including International Harvester, General Electric, Du Pont, and General Motors, sought contracts with them. By 1930, about a thousand U.S. engineers were in Russia, and U.S.-Russian trade had reached $95 million, double the 1914 level. "If you want to hang some capitalists," Lenin reputedly said, "advertise, and they'll submit competitive bids on the rope."

Disarmament

The Republican presidents of the 1921–1933 era promoted disarmament with considerable success. After the defeat of Germany, America, protected by oceans and blessed with weak neighbors, did not seem to need large military forces. Moreover, the Republicans were determined to cut taxes on upper incomes, and their commitment to balanced budgets required them first to cut government spending.

A naval race was then in progress. Proposing that America build the world's largest navy, Wilson had secured congressional approval for construction of enough new battleships and cruisers to build a U.S. navy more powerful than Britain's. In March 1921, the British, who had a policy of keeping their navy at least as large as the next two, announced a major construction program. Meanwhile, Japan embarked on a program of building its navy to equal any in the world. Harding favored naval expansion, but Congress failed to appropriate the required money. This raised the possibility that America might lose the naval race.

A December 1920 Senate resolution called for America, Britain, and Japan to hold an arms limitation conference. The British suggested that it be broadened to include consideration of international problems of the Far East. Accepting this proposal, Hughes issued invitations to Britain, Japan, China, France, Italy, Belgium, the Netherlands, and Portugal, all of whom had Far Eastern interests, to assemble in Washington in December 1921. The Soviet Union protested its exclusion.

Three treaties emerged from the Washington Conference. The two that concern East Asia's political problems are discussed in the next part of this chapter. This section focuses on naval disarmament.

When Hughes opened the conference, the delegates expected platitudes and words of welcome. They were jolted when they realized that he was proposing specific naval cuts of astonishing magnitude. He actually recommended that the great naval powers destroy more than half of their large warships, more naval tonnage, said one commentator, than "all the admirals of the world have sunk in a cycle of centuries." His dramatic speech, a worldwide sensation, captured the public's imagination and stimulated demand in America and abroad for its implementation.

In the Five-Power Treaty (1922), the principal naval powers agreed to build no additional capital ships (battleships and battle cruisers of more than 10,000 tons) for ten years. Furthermore, they agreed to destroy many already built or under construction—a total of thirty U.S. ships totaling 846,000 tons, thirty-six British ships totaling 583,000 tons, and thirty-six Japanese ships totaling 449,000 tons. They would retain only 500,000 tons each for America and Britain, and 300,000 tons for Japan. Italy and France would be limited to 167,000 tons each. Furthermore, no battleship could be larger than 35,000 tons or carry larger than sixteen-inch bore guns.

The Japanese were reluctant to accept naval inferiority, and their newspapers and mass meetings demanded equality. The Americans and the British pointed out that, unlike Japan, they had security problems in more than one ocean. In the end, the Japanese were induced to sign the treaty by joint U.S. and British pressure, sweetened by promises to refrain from further fortifying U.S. and British islands in the western Pacific. This conceded to Japan control of its home waters.

Outraged by being assigned an inferior status, the French signed the treaty reluctantly and only after rejecting any limits on the tonnage of submarines or ships smaller than 10,000 tons. The British, more gracefully than many expected, conceded that the era of their undisputed naval supremacy had ended.

History contains few examples of negotiated disarmament. How did the Washington Conference succeed when so many other attempts had failed? First, it would be difficult for any of the five to cheat. One cannot hide a battleship. Second, because ships are roughly equivalent to each other, it was not necessary to negotiate equivalencies between different weapons (such as how many troops equal a battleship), complex problems that professional military leaders, who lose from disarmament, seldom succeed in solving. Third, the agreement represented a joint effort by the United States and Britain to force Japan to accept naval inferiority.

The Five-Power Treaty covered only capital (larger than 10,000 tons) ships. A naval race in smaller craft continued, in which America fell behind because Congress failed to appropriate enough money. In 1927, in an attempt to put a cap on the number of smaller ships, Coolidge invited the five signatories to a conference at Geneva. France and Italy refused to attend. At the conference, the principal controversy arose between America, which wanted to build 10,000-ton cruisers, and England, which wanted a larger number of 7,500-ton cruisers to police her farflung empire. Shipbuilders sent agents to block agreement, naval officers wrangled on details, and the conference adjourned without result. Someone quipped that experts should be on tap, but never on top. In early 1929, Congress approved construction of fifteen more 10,000-ton cruisers.

President Hoover sought disarmament, both to save money and to combat militarism and war. The alternative, he said, was "suspicion, hate, ill-will, and ultimate disaster." In preliminary negotiations, he and England's new prime minister, Ramsay MacDonald, agreed on equality, and Britain issued a call for a new naval disarmament conference to meet in London in 1930. Japan, France, and Italy attended, and Hoover sent an able delegation, including Secretary of State Stimson and two senators. They took care to keep negotiations in the hands of politicians, not experts.

The 1930 London Naval Treaty extended the holiday on building capital ships an additional five years. It also required further destruction—of five British ships, three U.S. ships, and one Japanese ship. It placed an upper limit on smaller vessels, but in a ratio, 10-10-7, slightly more favorable to Japan, and gave Japan equality in submarines. The conferees also outlawed unrestricted submarine warfare.

Demanding guarantees of support against possible new German aggression, and resenting being put on a level with Italy in cruisers, France refused to sign the new pact. Japan's admirals protested, and the Japanese military, resenting another loss to civilians, assassinated the premier. Nevertheless, the London Conference was a success, and the Senate ratified the treaty by a vote of 58 to 9.

The success, however, was temporary. In 1931, a crisis flared (discussed later in this chapter) when the Japanese seized Manchuria. Resenting League condemnation of this action, Japan withdrew from the League and, in 1934, gave the required two-year notice of withdrawal from naval limitation agreements. By 1936, a new naval race was under way.

These naval agreements were later criticized as conceding too much to Japan. However, without them the United States might not have spent enough to preserve its 5–3 lead over Japan. America did not even build up to the permitted limits. The naval agreements saved billions of dollars and eased international tensions for nearly sixteen years.

The Versailles Treaty had promised that disarming Germany was only the first step toward general reduction of land, as well as naval, armaments. Preliminary discussions went slowly, however, and not until 1932 did a world disarmament conference of fifty-nine nations meet at Geneva. President Hoover's proposal to abolish all offensive weapons and reduce other weapons by a third was backed by Germany, Russia, and Italy. France, however, insisted that it could disarm only after other international arrangements had been made to protect it from Germany. While the conference was in session, Franklin D. Roosevelt replaced Hoover in the White House. He endorsed Hoover's plan and also proposed that all nations sign a nonaggression pact and agree to keep their troops within their own borders.

The Germans offered to accept any level of disarmament that France also accepted, but France refused to agree to German equality. In October 1933, Adolf Hitler, who had come to power in January, withdrew Germany from both the disarmament conference and the League. The conference dissolved in futility, and, in the aftermath, all leading nations raised arms spending.

Asian Political Settlements at the Washington Conference

In 1919, Japan had sent seventy-two thousand troops and the United States had sent ten thousand troops into Russia's Siberia. One U.S. aim was to prevent Japan from annexing Soviet territory. When Japanese troops remained after America's April 1920 withdrawal, Secretary of State Hughes warned Japan that the United States would not consent to violation of Russia's "territorial integrity."

Friction between Japan and America also arose over the island of Yap, a German possession that had been acquired by Japan. All trans-Pacific cables crossed this island, and Americans wanted to keep it out of Japan's control. When Japan resisted, the United States threatened to withhold recognition of Japan's right to any German islands.

At Britain's suggestion, America had broadened the 1922 Washington disarmament conference to include discussion of East Asian political issues. Fearing a U.S.-British combination against them, the Japanese were reluctant to attend and did so only after getting Hughes's assurance that he would be neutral on Japanese-Chinese conflicts and would not challenge past Japanese gains in China.

Americans abominated the Anglo-Japanese alliance. It had been formed in 1902 to promote British-Japanese cooperation against Russian expansion, but Americans feared that it might be used against them. When he once mentioned this treaty to the U.S. secretary of state, said the British ambassador, he "had never heard anything like Mr. Hughes's excited tirade outside of a madhouse." Canadians disliked it because they feared that it might draw them into a war with the United States. At the Washington Conference, the Anglo-Japanese alliance was disposed of by having America and France join Britain and Japan in a Four-Power Treaty, transforming the alliance into a mere agreement to respect one another's Far Eastern possessions. It did not obligate them to defend each other.

In a great gain for China and for U.S. diplomacy, all the nations at the Washington Conference signed the Nine-Power Treaty, agreeing to respect the Open Door in China. They promised not only to give equal trade privileges within their spheres but to uphold the "sovereignty, the independence, and the territorial and administrative integrity of China." This treaty was a significant accomplishment. For years, with British support, America had insisted that other nations follow this policy, but this treaty was the first formal international affirmation of the Open Door. It was primarily intended to put a curb on Japan's encroachments, and much pressure was required to get Japan to sign it. However, it did not require surrender of rights previously obtained, and it contained no provision for enforcement.

In a statement to the conference, Japan announced that it had withdrawn most of the more objectionable Twenty-One Demands (see chapter 2). Japan also announced that it had no designs on Soviet territory. The last Japanese troops left Siberia by November 1922 and northern Sakhalin in 1925.

Regarding Yap, Europeans supported Japan against America. Nevertheless, Japan agreed to allow Americans to maintain a cable station there. In return, Washington recognized Japan's mandate over former German Pacific islands which Japan agreed to keep unfortified and open to U.S. trade and missionary activities.

In a February 1922 treaty with China, Japan agreed to withdraw its troops from the Shantung Peninsula, and to sell to China control of Shantung's principal railroad, which meant transferring military and economic control to China. However, Japan retained economic interests and influence there.

Although U.S. support had enabled the Chinese to make significant gains—including a nine-power pledge against further encroachments, withdrawal of Japan from Shantung, and cancellation of some of the Twenty-One Demands—the Chinese were bitterly disappointed. They had hoped that the multipower conference would concede them control over their tariffs, put an end to extraterritoriality, and remove all foreign troops from their soil.

The U.S. Senate approved the Nine-Power (Open Door) Pact unanimously, the Five-Power naval disarmament Pact with only one dissenting vote, and the Four-Power Pact dissolving the Anglo-Japanese alliance with four votes to spare after attaching a reservation that America assumed no obligation to defend the other signers.

The American humorist Will Rogers once said that America never lost a war and never won a conference, but that certainly was not true of the 1922 Washington Conference (see Fig. 3.1.). Hughes had achieved all of his major aims: naval disarmament, naval parity with England, naval superiority to Japan, affirmation of the Open Door, withdrawal of Japan from Shantung, cancellation of the more drastic Twenty-one Demands, dissolution of the Anglo-Japanese alliance, removal of Japanese troops from Siberia, and U.S. use of Yap. These stunning diplomatic triumphs helped put Hughes in the front rank of U.S. secretaries of state and make the otherwise inept Harding administration an outstanding success in foreign affairs.

The period following the Washington Conference was one of friendly relations between America and Japan. Many Americans regarded Japan as a natural ally against Communist Russia and Chinese revolutionaries. But the relationship was marred by the U.S. Immigration Act of 1924. Putting an upper limit of 150,000 on non–Western Hemisphere immigration, it assigned each nation an immigration quota based on the 1890 proportion of Americans descended from immigrants from that nation. Although this would give Japan an annual quota of only 250, a special provision barred admission of any person who was ineligible for citizenship, and earlier laws had made immigrants from the Far East ineligible for citizenship.

The sensitive Japanese were deeply offended by the insult implicit in this proposal. Fearful of its effect on relations, Secretary of State Hughes asked

Figure 3.1 French Foreign Minister Aristide Briand and U.S. Secretary of State Charles Evans Hughes at the 1921–1922 Washington Conference. National Archives.

the Japanese ambassador to make a statement explaining Japan's concern. The ambassador, unfortunately, used the expression "grave consequences," which caused some congressmen, who misinterpreted it as a threat, to vote for the law in defiance. Japan proclaimed the day on which it took effect a "National Humiliation Day," and a protesting student committed suicide on the steps of the U.S. embassy in Tokyo. This law, said Hughes regretfully, had "undone the work of the Washington Conference and implanted the seeds of antagonism."

The Rise of Chinese Nationalism

Meanwhile, China was undergoing revolutionary changes. By Western standards, the Chinese, although proud of their culture, traditionally had little feeling of nationalism. However, the experience of being defeated, dominated, exploited, and humiliated by foreigners stimulated patriotism, and a growing number of Chinese, including many students who had received Western educations, came to believe that China should reform and modernize and thereby acquire the strength with which to cast off foreign rule. They sought to abolish the "unequal treaties" through which Western nations and Japan had forced China to concede the right to fix Chinese tariffs, station warships on Chinese rivers, keep troops in China, enjoy immunity from Chinese law, and dominate huge areas as "spheres of influence." The most prominent of these modernizing nationalists was the Western-educated Dr. Sun Yat-sen.

The necessary first step, Sun believed, was to free China from the rule of the decadent Manchu dynasty. In 1911, the Chinese overthrew the Manchus, but power devolved not on Sun, but on the commander of the most modern army, Yuan Shih-kai, who sought to make himself emperor. After Yuan died in 1916, the central government declined, and more power was assumed by regional military commanders, called "warlords," some of whom ruled entire provinces or groups of provinces. In shifting alliances, warlords made war on each other and vied to control the remaining shell of central government at Peking. Foreigners, including the Japanese, found that this internal disunity facilitated their encroachments.

In alliance with a local warlord, Sun Yat-sen established a regime at Canton in south China and sought foreign help to extend his rule over all of China. Only Soviet Russia responded. In 1921, Russia advised the small Chinese Communist party to merge with Sun's political party, the Kuomintang, and sent political and military advisers to reorganize it and help train a party army. When Sun died in 1925, leadership was assumed by his top military man, the young Chiang Kai-shek, who, in 1926, felt strong enough to launch a campaign, the "northern expedition," against warlords to unite China. By early 1927, the campaign was nearing success. At this time, Chiang split with the Communists and attempted to exterminate them, but some of them escaped and established a regime in a remote section of south China. In December 1928, Manchuria's warlord announced that he had joined the Kuomintang, nominally completing China's reunification.

The victorious revolutionaries bitterly resented China's long humiliation at the hands of foreigners. China was the colony of all nations, Sun Yat-sen had said, and the Chinese had become the "slaves" of all. Chiang Kai-shek repudiated all previous treaties.

America had not responded to Sun Yat-sen's pleas for help, and few Americans understood events in China, but many were inclined to favor Chiang's reassertions of sovereignty, and many were pleased by Chiang's purge of Communists. Chiang further pleased Americans by converting to Christianity and marrying Christian, American-educated Meiling Soong. In 1928, America became the first nation to sign a treaty returning to China control of its tariffs. U.S.-Chinese trade rose from $50 million in 1914 to $190 million in 1930, but U.S. trade and investments in China still did not exceed 3 percent of total U.S. foreign trade and investments.

The Manchurian Crisis

The progress toward the modernization and unification of China endangered the special concessions foreigners had extorted from China. The Japanese particularly felt threatened by these developments.

With the nation's industrialization, Japan's population had risen by 1931 to 65 million people in an area the size of California, making the Japanese more dependent on foreign food, raw materials, and markets. The usual response of industrializing nations to increasing dependence on foreign supplies was to build military forces to protect access to vital goods and markets. Theoretically, Japan might have followed a policy of inoffensiveness, counting on the economic interests of other countries to keep it supplied, but no major industrializing nation had yet tried that option. Some of Japan's civilian leaders, saying that Japan was a latecomer and that it was too dangerous to attempt imperialistic expansion in a world already dominated by great powers, wanted to try a peaceful approach, but most considered enlarging the navy and army to be more realistic.

Manchuria, to the northeast of China proper and as large as Germany and France combined, not overpopulated and a source of food, coal, and iron, was particularly important to Japan's economy, and, after Japan's victory over Russia in 1905, many Japanese moved there. Later, Japanese influence increasingly penetrated north China. However, the rise of Chinese nationalism threatened these gains.

The Japanese constitution, like that of Germany, did not give the civilian government control of the armed forces which, instead, constituted a coequal branch of government under the emperor. Acceptance by Japan of the settlements arranged at the Washington Conference represented a victory of civilians over the military. However, following outbreaks of fighting between Chinese and Japanese in China in 1927 and 1929, Japanese troops landed in Shantung. The Chinese retaliated with boycotts of Japanese goods, a damaging weapon against Japan.

At this time, Chiang Kai-shek was redoubling his efforts to restore Chinese control of Manchuria, the northern part of which was dominated by Russia, while the southern part was under strong Japanese influence. Victory over Russia in 1905 had given Japan the upper hand, Manchuria held more than half of Japan's foreign investments, and the United States had recognized Japanese rights there.

In 1929, Chiang attempted to seize from Russia control of the Chinese Eastern Railway, which was the key to northeast Manchuria. Reinforcing their troops, the Soviets, after battles, forced Chiang to retreat. Many Americans sympathized with Russia which was defending rights legalized by treaty with China.

Chiang also challenged Japanese power in southern Manchuria. In violation of existing treaties, he built new railroads to compete with Japanese-controlled railroads, encouraged ethnic Chinese to move into Manchuria, and attempted to halt the leasing of land to Japanese settlers.

In September 1931, casting off the restraints of Japan's civilian government, Japan's Manchurian army launched an offensive to complete its subjugation of Manchuria. In February 1932, Japan proclaimed that Manchuria was an independent nation, renamed it Manchukuo, and installed the last Manchu emperor of China as its puppet ruler.

In response to Japan's aggression, China appealed to America and the League for help. Meeting promptly, the League Council called on both sides to withdraw their troops to their previous positions. Instead, the Japanese army made further advances. America sent a representative to sit with the League Council and, when the League appointed a five-man commission, the Lytton Commission, to investigate the situation, the United States assigned General Frank R. McCoy to serve on it. Thus, America moved into full cooperation with the League.

Secretary of State Henry L. Stimson was strongly pro-Chinese. The issue in Manchuria, he said, was between two "theories of civilization and economic methods." He sent Japan a strong reminder of its obligations under the 1922 Nine-Power Treaty, which had promised an Open Door. Unable to restrain its military, the Japanese government resigned in December 1931. Stimson proposed that the United States impose economic sanctions, cutting off trade and loans to Japan. While refusing to permit action that might lead to war, President Hoover, wary of Stimson's "combat psychology," promised limited cooperation if England and France imposed sanctions, which both declined to do.

Many in Britain, France, and the United States valued Japan as a barrier to Communist expansion. Telling his cabinet that Japan faced danger from "a Bolshevik Russia to the north and a possible Bolshevik China," Hoover rejected a Soviet proposal for a joint stand against Japan.

Nevertheless, in January 1932, at Hoover's suggestion, Stimson, in notes to Japan and China, wrote that America would not acquiesce in any arrangement that injured U.S. treaty rights, the integrity of China, or the Open Door, and would not recognize "any situation, treaty, or agreement" that might be "brought about by means contrary to the covenants and obligations of the Pact of Paris." Most Americans approved of this nonrecognition "Stimson Doctrine," but not of any use of force to back it. Britain and France refused to take a similarly strong stand against Japan's seizure of Manchuria, but in March 1932 the League Assembly endorsed nonrecognition.

Less than two weeks after Stimson's note, the Japanese launched a large attack in Shanghai (China's New York City). The attack was intended not to seize territory but to force the Chinese to abandon their boycott of Japanese goods. The Chinese put up unexpectedly strong resistance, but after Japanese shelling and bombing had killed thousands of Chinese, the Chinese army retreated. This Japanese action inflamed anti-Japanese sentiment in America, and both the United States and Britain sent naval and troop reinforcements to Shanghai. But Stimson failed to get either a joint U.S.-British protest or economic sanctions.

In February 1932, in a public statement, Stimson said that Japan's aggressions had freed America from arms restrictions. This was an implied threat to enlarge the U.S. navy and/or to fortify America's Pacific islands.

The Lytton Commission issued its report in September 1932. It concluded that China had threatened Japan's legitimate interests in Manchuria, but that the Japanese military had aggressively overreacted. Denouncing Manchukuo as a puppet regime, it called for a new Manchurian government and new Sino-Japanese treaties that would maintain Chinese sovereignty but protect legitimate Japanese economic interests. The League adopted this report, and America announced its "substantial accord." Highly offended, Japan charged that other nations dominated parts of China and that what the Japanese were doing in Manchuria was not substantially different from what France was doing in Indochina and the United States in Latin America. Japan withdrew from the League.

Later, many Americans would regret that Washington had not taken a stronger stand against Japan in 1931–1932, when its aggression might have been stopped short of major war. Inhibiting America's response were its insistence on privileges of its own in China and the value that some Americans put on Japan as a barrier to Bolshevism. Nevertheless, America's stand was bolder than that of either Britain or France.

In this major test, the peace machinery laboriously constructed after World War I—the League of Nations, the Four-Power Pact, the Nine-Power Treaty, and the Paris Peace Pact—all proved inadequate to check aggression.

Relations with Latin America

The 1921–1933 Republican era saw no relaxation of the U.S. policy of hegemony (preponderant influence or authority) in the Western Hemisphere. With the encouragement and protection of the U.S. government, U.S. investors enlarged their role in Latin America's economy. Direct U.S. investments in Latin America, especially in electric power, railroads, bananas, sugar, and mining, nearly tripled from $1.3 billion in 1914 to $3.5 billion in 1929. This was about a third of U.S. total direct foreign investments. In the same period, annual U.S. exports to Latin America tripled to $1 billion, while the United States received, for example, 68 percent of Cuba's exports and 96 percent of Nicaragua's exports. Washington continued to bristle at any signs of influence from outside the hemisphere, particularly any connection between Latin American revolutionaries and world communism.

The Caribbean area contained a number of small, extremely poor nations. Their populations were small—in 1921 Nicaragua contained 600,000 people. Their mostly agricultural and extractive economic and social systems were characterized by great extremes of wealth and poverty, and their politics were turbulent and often violent. Conservative parties defended the interests of the wealthy, while liberal parties sought reforms beneficial to the poor, who included many native Americans. With little experience in democracy, they held elections that were seldom free or fair, and losers sometimes rose in violent rebellion.

Frequent fighting endangered the lives and property of resident foreigners, and the U.S. Navy patrolled coastal waters and sometimes landed troops to protect the lives and property of U.S. citizens. Also, to reduce the level of violence, U.S. officials in some countries took over the collection of their principal tax, the import duty, so as to remove one financial incentive to revolution. The United States also helped conduct elections, refused to recognize some governments that achieved power through violence, and sought to replace armies, which were often the instruments of particular parties, with nonpartisan police forces that were trained, and sometimes officered, by U.S. personnel.

In the 1904 Roosevelt Corollary to the Monroe Doctrine, the United States had claimed the right to intervene in (invade) Latin American nations. Between 1900 and 1930, on about thirty occasions, Washington sent troops into Latin American, particularly Caribbean countries. Bitterly resenting these actions, most Latin Americans regarded the United States, not Europe, as the major threat to their freedom and independence. Intervention, said one foreign minister, was the "curse of America." Repeatedly, they urged Washington to agree that no nation had a right to invade another.

In 1920, the United States held protectorates over Cuba, Panama, Nicaragua, Haiti, and the Dominican Republic (see Fig. 3.2). U.S. naval officers governed Haiti and the Dominican Republic, and Washington exercised some control over the financial policies of about half of Latin America's nations.

The businessmen who ran the U.S. government during the 1920s continued to intervene. "The person and property of a citizen are part of the general domain of the nation even when abroad," said Coolidge. However, they made some changes. They put less emphasis than Wilson on championing the common man and more on defending U.S. property interests, even when that meant supporting undemocratic elements. Also, finding that sending troops was expensive and sometimes counterproductive, Washington sought alternate ways of promoting U.S. interests. In an attempt to improve relations, Harding paid $25 million to Colombia in compensation for the U.S. role in depriving it of Panama, and, in 1924, President Coolidge withdrew U.S. Marines from the Dominican Republic.

Intervention in Nicaragua

By 1925, Nicaragua's debts to U.S. banks had been paid, and Adolfo Diaz, whom Americans had installed as president in 1911, and his conservative successors, whom U.S. Marines helped keep in power, seemed to be firmly in control. In August 1925, Coolidge withdrew U.S. marines from Nicaragua where they had been since 1911.

After the marines left, however, unrestrained competition betwen conservatives and liberals for the presidency produced renewed violence. With U.S. support, Diaz reassumed power, but liberal Dr. Juan B. Sacasa, a former vice president, headed a rival government that refused to submit to Diaz. Fighting continued, with Sacasa receiving support and arms from Mexico and Diaz receiving loans from U.S. banks.

In December 1926, charging, on flimsy evidence, that Communists in Mexico were behind the trouble in Nicaragua, Coolidge sent five thousand U.S. troops to support the conservative Diaz. Because he acted without a congressional declaration of war, some called this invasion Coolidge's "personal war," but, citing "obligations flowing from the investments" and the need to exclude foreign influences and to save lives, Coolidge maintained that it was merely a police action. "We are not making war on Nicaragua any more than a policeman on the beat is making war on passersby."

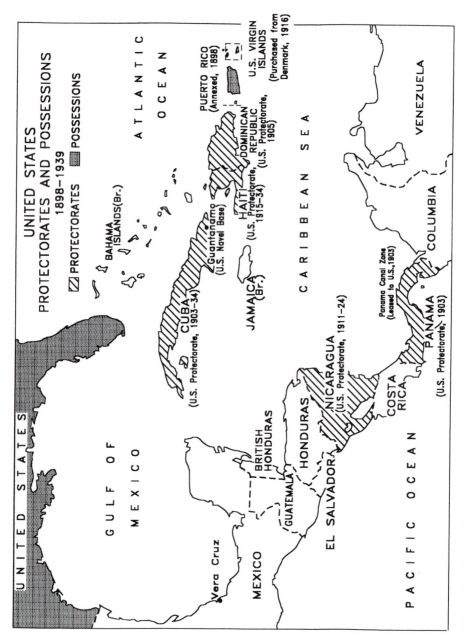

Figure 3.2 United States Protectorates and Possessions, 1898–1939.

In April 1927, in a conciliatory move, Coolidge sent his Amherst classmate Henry L. Stimson to seek a settlement. Stimson proposed an open and honest election conducted by U.S. marines. In the meantime, he arranged for an interim coalition government under Diaz, U.S. command of a nonpartisan national guard, and surrender of weapons by both sides. The 1928 election was conducted, and ballots counted, by U.S. marines. To prevent double voting, the marines required voters to dip their fingers in Mercurochrome. Apparently the election was honest, for it resulted in the victory of the liberal Jose Moncado over the pro-U.S. conservative. In the ensuing 1932 election, also supervised by marines, Diaz was defeated by the liberal Juan Sacasa, whom Washington had debarred from the presidency in 1926.

Nevertheless, one liberal leader, Cesar Augusto Sandino, refused to accept the U.S.-arranged settlement, and for three years he waged guerrilla warfare against 5,500 U.S. marines. To many, he became a symbol of resistance to Yankee imperialism. After the marines left in 1933, Sandino, as he had promised, ceased resistance and entered into talks with the government, whereupon he was murdered by the Nicaraguan National Guard.

By this time, the U.S.-trained and -armed National Guard had become the most powerful political force in the country. In 1933 its commander, Anastasio Somoza, seized control of the government. His regime favored foreign investors but became infamous for its cruel repression and the concentration of much of the country's wealth in the hands of his family. His son would be overthrown in 1979 by rebels who called themselves Sandinistas.

Stormy Relations with Mexico

Relations with Mexico also remained uneasy. By World War I, 40 percent of Mexico's farmland and 60 percent of its oil reserves had been acquired by U.S. investors. However, the 1917 Mexican constitution provided that all subsoil minerals belonged to the Mexican people. Seizing many large estates, the government distributed land to peasants or put it in collective farms. It promised to pay for seized lands, but U.S. investors complained that payments were inadequate. The Mexican government also took land owned by the Catholic Church and sought to wrest control of education from the Church.

Washington refused to recognize President Alvaro Obregon, who seized power in 1920, because he refused to sign a treaty confirming the ownership by U.S. investors of oil lands. But, with the help of the U.S. banking leader Thomas W. Lamont, Obregon was persuaded to allow foreign investors to keep title to oil lands acquired prior to 1917 if they had performed some "positive act" of development on them. Resuming diplomatic relations, Washington even sold Obregon arms while denying them to rebels.

Plutarco Calles, Mexico's president from 1924 to 1928, was more radical. His seizures of Catholic property and the transfer of church schools to the government provoked a church strike during which no mass was held for three years. He also set a fifty-year limit on mineral rights on lands acquired before 1917. Furthermore, he backed Nicaragua's liberal Sacasa regime.

U.S. oil companies and many Catholics and conservatives urged that the United States invade Mexico to overthrow its government. A business journal charged that the Calles regime was "directed from and dominated by Soviet Russia." In January 1927, Kellogg sent the Senate a memo titled "Bolshevik Aims and Policies in Mexico and Latin America," in which he charged that Russia was seeking footholds in Latin America and that Mexico was the center of Bolshevik activities. The Mexicans, he charged, were creating a "Bolshevik hegemony intervening between the United States and the Panama Canal." This sounded like war talk, and newspapers reported that invasion was near.

But opposition developed. The *New York Post*, then edited by the distinguished political commentator Walter Lippmann, exposed and denounced the plan to invade. The Federal Council of Churches and other organizations condemned it, and the Senate unanimously urged arbitration. Any plan to invade was abandoned.

In September 1927, turning negotiations over to the businessmen who had investments in Mexico, Coolidge appointed Dwight W. Morrow, a leading banker, as ambassador to Mexico. His only instructions, Coolidge told him, were "to keep us out of war with Mexico."

Morrow proved to be an able negotiator. Establishing good personal relations with Calles and bringing in the hero Charles A. Lindburgh on a goodwill visit, Morrow mediated a settlement between the Mexican government and the Catholic Church. Also, he got Calles to drop the fifty-year limit on ownership of oil lands. So much did this improve relations that, in 1929, the United States sent Calles arms to help him suppress rebels.

A Good Neighbor?

As time neared for the January 1928 Sixth Conference of American States in Havana, the United States faced rising opposition among Latin Americans. U.S. troops remained in Nicaragua, and Washington had threatened war with Mexico. To meet the expected criticism, Coolidge went personally to open the conference and appointed former Secretary of State Hughes to head the U.S. delegation.

As expected, Latin Americans, who almost unanimously opposed Washington's practice of invading their countries, introduced a resolution outlawing it: "No state has the right to intervene in the internal affairs of another." Hughes defended intervention as a temporary measure required by anarchy to save lives. With some difficulty, and the aid of several nations then occupied by or heavily dependent on the United States, he secured postponement of a vote on the resolution to the next conference.

Shortly after his election as president in 1928, Herbert Hoover made a ten-week goodwill tour of Latin America. The United States, he said, wanted to be a good neighbor, and he opposed intervention. In his inaugural address, he

Figure 3.3 President Calvin Coolidge and Herbert Hoover at Hoover's 1929 inauguration. Brown Brothers.

added that America had "no desire for territorial expansion, for economic or other domination of other people"—which to many Latin Americans was welcome news.

In 1930, the State Department published the Clark Memorandum, written in 1928 by Undersecretary J. Rueben Clark, which said that the right to intervene was not a part of the Monroe Doctrine. Since the Clark Memorandum did not renounce the right to intervene, its significance was not apparent unless one remembered that most Americans regarded the Monroe Doctrine as sacred and unalterable. Thus, Washington was saying that it no longer considered the right to intervene to be unalterable.

In line with its deemphasis of intervention, Washington returned to the practice of recognizing governments established by revolutionaries as soon as they secured firm control of their countries. Despite a wave of Latin American revolutions and repudiations of debts, Hoover refrained from intervening, and he withdrew the remaining U.S. marines from Nicaragua.

Much of the goodwill engendered by this soft-pedaling of intervention was lost during the Great Depression, when Washington dealt a heavy blow to Latin American economies by raising U.S. tariffs to new highs.

The businessmen's administrations of the 1920s followed an isolationist policy toward Europe. Rejecting U.S. membership in the League of Nations, they practiced economic nationalism. However, they were active in promoting the worldwide expansion of U.S. investments, and they were not isolationist regarding East Asia or Latin America. They called an international conference to deal with East Asian questions, secured international endorsement of the Open Door for China, and cooperated with the League of Nations in opposing Japan's seizure of Manchuria. While continuing the policy of dominating a number of Latin American countries, they took some steps toward deemphasizing intervention. Meanwhile, a great new threat arose in Europe.

4 From Isolation to Involvement

Roosevelt Organizes His Administration

After a landslide victory over Hoover, in an election decided by the Great Depression, Governor Franklin D. Roosevelt of New York became president in March 1933. A distant cousin of Theodore Roosevelt, educated at Harvard and at Columbia Law School, he was a master politician with a genial personality that charmed the voters and helped to draw able men into his service.

Roosevelt was more experienced in foreign affairs than most entering presidents. In his eight years as Wilson's assistant secretary of the navy, he had played a leading role in U.S. interventions in Latin America, and had advocated U.S. entry into World War I. As the Democratic candidate for vice president in 1920, he had campaigned for U.S. membership in the League of Nations but, for political reasons, dropped that advocacy in his 1932 presidential campaign. Thus, his record was that of a militarist and an imperialist with a touch of Wilsonian idealism.

For secretary of state, Roosevelt appointed sixty-two-year-old Cordell Hull, a fine-looking, hot-tempered former Tennessee judge and senator. Hull was a traditional Democrat who had fought for lower tariffs, and who had many friends in Congress. But he had little foreign affairs experience, and his chief interest in the job was the opportunity it gave him to promote international trade. He was to hold the office longer than any previous person, during a period of revolutionary change in U.S. foreign relations.

Roosevelt was not concerned about Hull's lack of foreign policy expertise because he intended to keep control of foreign policy in his own hands. He often conducted foreign relations from the White House through special emissaries and sometimes neglected to inform Hull of important foreign policy matters. Hull once referred to him as "that man across the street who never tells me anything." Of course, this magnified the importance of Roosevelt's other foreign policy advisers, among the more prominent of whom were Harry Hopkins, a former social worker; the elegant career diplomat Sumner Welles, who became undersecretary of state; and William C. Bullitt, who became the first U.S. ambassador to the Soviet Union. All had colorful personalities and shared Roosevelt's spirit of adventure.

Efforts to Restore World Trade

The Great Depression reached its nadir in the month Roosevelt took office. The Depression, which had begun in 1929, cut American industrial production by half and raised the unemployment rate to more than 25 percent. For a time, Roosevelt was necessarily preoccupied with taking emergency measures to counteract its effects. In foreign policy, he was particularly eager to restore foreign markets for U.S. products.

The Hoover administration had enacted the 1930 Smoot-Hawley Tariff, which raised the average U.S. import tax to more than 50 percent, an historic high. Other countries retaliated by raising their tariffs. As the depression spread abroad, world trade dropped by more than half. From 1929 to 1932, U.S. exports plunged from $5.2 billion to $1.6 billion. Meanwhile, nations competitively devalued their money (that is, reduced its value in gold and, therefore, in foreign money) in efforts to raise exports by making them cheaper to foreigners and to reduce imports by raising the prices of foreign goods. International loans, debt payments, and investments plunged.

Hoping to achieve international cooperation to solve these problems, sixty-four nations met at the London Economic Conference in June 1933. They sought to stabilize the values of world currencies, renew international payments and loans, and restore world trade. Roosevelt refused to consider reducing debts owed by foreign governments to America, but, appointing a delegation headed by former Democratic presidential nominee James M. Cox and Secretary of State Cordell Hull, he endorsed currency stabilization and agreed to discuss other issues. But, while the conference was in session, Roosevelt became convinced that America must have inflation to reduce the burden of debt in America and that, therefore, he must devalue the dollar. A message from him rejecting stabilization of currencies torpedoed the London Economic Conference. International economic cooperation thus succumbed to economic nationalism.

On the other hand, Roosevelt took the lead in reducing tariffs. However, instead of unilaterally cutting America's tariff, he employed a technique that enabled him to secure reductions in other nation's tariffs as well. In June 1934, Congress enacted the Reciprocal Trade Agreement Act, which authorized the president to negotiate treaties to cut U.S. tariffs on specific items by as much as 50 percent in return for reciprocal cuts by other nations in their tariffs on U.S. products.

Secretary of State Hull enthusiastically threw himself into this work. He believed that international trade was the "greatest civilizer and peacemaker in the experience of the human race" and that a freer flow of goods would raise worldwide living standards, "thereby eliminating the economic dissatisfaction that breeds war." He soon negotiated twenty-nine reciprocal trade treaties. In 1945, Congress would authorize further cuts of as much as 50 percent from the 1945 tariff rates. Between 1934 and 1947 the average tax on imports fell from 47 to 13 percent. Furthermore, because most nations had "most-favored-nation" trade agreements that guaranteed to each any reduction given to any other nation, the agreements produced a worldwide lowering of tariffs. He also secured establishment of the Export-Import Bank to lend foreigners money with which to buy U.S.-made goods. International trade soared, and U.S. merchandise exports jumped from $1.6 billion in 1932 to $3.2 billion in 1939.

The Good Neighbor Policy

Roosevelt's first major initiative in foreign political affairs was the "Good Neighbor Policy." In his inaugural address, he promised to "dedicate this nation to the policy of the good neighbor," a term that came to be applied to his relations with Latin America.

Latin Americans were demanding, with growing heat, that the United States renounce its practice of invading their countries. Presidents Coolidge and, particularly, Hoover had made some concessions to this sentiment but had fended off demands to renounce all right to intervene.

Roosevelt was ready to go further. Democrats had been somewhat less inclined than Republicans to send troops to protect the property of U.S. corporations abroad, and, in a 1928 article, Roosevelt had called for an end to unilateral "intervention by us in the internal affairs of other nations." Also, U.S. invasions were antagonizing Latin American nationalists to the point that they were threatening to destroy U.S.-owned property and boycott U.S. goods. This, and the Depression, cut Latin American purchases from the United States by three-fourths. Also, the growing hostility of Latin Americans raised the danger that they might invite Tokyo or Berlin to help defend them against Washington.

At the 1933 Seventh Inter-American Conference at Montevideo, Secretary of State Hull, to the surprise of most Latin Americans, agreed to support Argentina's anti- intervention resolution: "No state has the right to intervene in the internal or external affairs of another." Roosevelt announced that "the definite policy of the United States from now on is one opposed to armed intervention." In the future, he promised, Washington would recognize de facto (revolutionary) governments. Latin Americans were ecstatic.

Nevertheless, some of them continued to worry that a future U.S. administration might renew intervention. At the 1936 Inter-American Conference in Buenos Aires, they persuaded Washington to add the phrases "directly or indirectly" and "for whatever reason" to the nonintervention pledge.

A test of the Good Neighbor Policy came quickly in Cuba. To help end a long period of uprising and repression, Roosevelt, through Ambassador Sumner Welles, helped pressure Cuba's dictator, Geraldo Machado, to resign in August 1933. Months of violent disorder followed as Cuban factions struggled for power. Refusing to recognize the army-installed liberal, Dr. Ramon Grau Martin, who suspended payments on U.S. bank-supplied loans and expropriated some U.S.-owned sugar plantations, and whom Welles called a Communist, Roosevelt ordered U.S. warships into Cuban waters, but he did not land troops. In January 1934, the Cuban army, led by Sergeant Fulgencio Batista, replaced Grau with conservative Carlos Mendieta, whom Roosevelt quickly recognized.

When, a few months later, Roosevelt signed a treaty with Cuba canceling the Platt Amendment, which had given the United States the right to send troops into Cuba, Cubans celebrated with a three-day festival. Also, Washington cut the tariff on Cuban sugar, and trade doubled.

In 1934, the United States withdrew its marines from Haiti and renounced any further right to send troops there. Washington also renounced the right to intervene in the Dominican Republic. By 1935, no U.S. troops remained in any Latin American country except on U.S. bases in Panama and Cuba. However, Washington retained control of the finances of Haiti and the Dominican Republic until 1941.

In 1936, the United States acted to satisfy certain grievances of Panama. Washington was paying rent on the Panama Canal in devalued dollars that were worth only 49 percent of their pre 1935 value, and it now agreed to restore the payment to its former level. Also, in a new treaty, Washington surrendered the right to invade Panama, and promised to consult its government on measures to defend the canal. But the Senate delayed approval of this treaty until 1939, when Panama agreed that in emergencies the United States might take defense measures without consultation.

The most severe tests of the Good Neighbor Policy came in Mexico. Despite the 1911 revolution, wealth remained very concentrated in Mexico, with the rich usually in alliance with the church and foreign investors. In 1934, the very liberal, or leftist, President Lazaro Cardenas took office. He stepped up expropriation (seizure of property with compensation to the owner) of large land holdings for distribution among landless peasants, fostered labor unions, and sought to transfer control of education from the Catholic Church to the government. Some U.S. landowners and Catholics, calling Cardenas a Communist, asked Washington to intervene.

In 1938, after foreign-owned oil companies refused to give oil workers a government-recommended raise, the Mexican government expropriated foreign-owned refineries and oil lands. Britain broke diplomatic relations, and U.S. oil companies and conservative U.S. newspapers demanded that the United States invade Mexico. But Roosevelt and his genial ambassador, Josephus Daniels, had some sympathy for Cardenas's efforts to help the poor, and Mexicans warned that invasion might force them into the arms of the Germans and the Japanese. Rejecting invasion, Roosevelt shifted the principal burden of negotiating a settlement onto the oil companies themselves. In 1941, Mexico agreed to pay the companies $42 million for the oil properties and also to pay $40 million to former owners of expropriated land and other properties. To facilitate the deal, Washington agreed to buy Mexican silver, lend Mexico money for road construction, and negotiate tariff reductions. This settlement facilitated a renewal of U.S. investments and a period of cordial U.S.-Mexican relations.

The improved relations produced by the Good Neighbor Policy not only promoted trade—U.S. exports to Latin America soared from $244 million in 1933 to $642 million in 1938, when about half of Latin America's trade was with the United States—it also enabled Washington to draw Latin Americans into arrangements designed to exclude German and Japanese influence from the Western Hemisphere.

Some Latin American countries contained large numbers of people of Italian or German origin, and the trade of these countries with Germany and Italy was rising, causing Washington some anxiety. Roosevelt attended the Inter-American Conference at Buenos Aires in 1936 and secured adoption of the Declaration of Inter-American Solidarity, which provided for consultation among Western Hemisphere nations in the event of any threat from outside the hemisphere. This agreement enlisted Latin America's assistance in enforcing the Monroe Doctrine. In September 1939, after World War II began, the foreign ministers of the nations of the Americas, meeting at Panama, agreed to deny use of their territory as bases by either side. A second meeting of foreign ministers in June 1940, the month when France surrendered to Germany, adopted the Act of Havana, refusing to allow France's Latin American colonies to be occupied by Axis powers, and designating any attack on any American nation as aggression against all.

Recognizing the Soviet Union

The Roosevelt administration discontinued the existing U.S. policy of trying to isolate the Soviet Union. Charging that the Communist government was dictatorial, failed to pay Russia's debts, and supported revolutions abroad, Washington had refused to recognize it as Russia's legal government. Of course, this implied a hope that the Russian people would overthrow it. However, a growing number of U.S. business leaders favored relations, and most Europeans regarded nonrecognition as absurd. Roosevelt was eager to increase exports to Russia, and he also told advisers that it might be useful in the future to confer with the Soviets about the rising menace of Japan. For its part, Moscow sought economic aid, and cooperation against Japan and Germany.

In November 1933, Roosevelt invited Soviet Foreign Minister Maxim Litvinov to the United States, where he was feted by top capitalists at New York's Waldorf Astoria Hotel. In personal meetings, he and Roosevelt quickly agreed that neither country would conduct propaganda in the other's country or work to overthrow its government and that Americans residing in Russia would be given religious freedom and due process. The issue of whether the Communist government would repay debts incurred by the tsars was more difficult, but the two agreed to future negotiations on such matters. Extending official recognition, Roosevelt chose William C. Bullitt to be America's first ambassador to the Soviet Union.

The results of recognition were disappointing. After the 1934 Johnson Act forbade new loans to nations that were behind in debt payments, the Soviets lost interest in making part payments on the tsar's debts. Trade between the two countries actually declined. Moreover, the U.S. Communist party remained active, which Americans considered a violation of the agreement. Meanwhile,

Stalin conducted bloody purges in Russia. Bullitt left Moscow in 1936, an embittered enemy of the Soviet Union.

Freeing the Philippines

Desire to avoid involvement in future wars contributed to America's decision to give the Philippines independence. Filipinos had continued to resist U.S. rule, and maintaining sufficient U.S. army and naval forces to defend the islands was expensive. Also, of course, possessing the Philippines added to the difficulty of staying out of major wars in East Asia. Although Theodore Roosevelt had taken the lead in acquiring the islands, he had later concluded that they were America's "Achilles heel."

A number of U.S. economic interests demanded that the Philippines be freed. U.S. producers of sugar, cotton, dairy products, and lumber resented the competition from tariff-free imports of these goods from the Philippines. Apparently, America found it more difficult than had England to make imperialism pay.

In 1932, over Hoover's veto, Congress had passed the Hawes-Cutting Act providing for Philippine independence. The Philippines rejected the offer, partly because it did not promise continued immigration or low tariffs and partly because it preserved U.S. military control of the islands. Meeting most of these objections, the 1934 Tydings-McDuffie Act provided for continued tariff and immigration concessions and for further negotiations concerning U.S. military bases. America promised to grant independence in stages over a ten-year period (World War II delayed independence until July 4, 1946).

The Rising Threat of New World War

Roosevelt took office in March 1933, less than two months after Adolf Hitler had become chancellor of Germany. Hitler had come to power on a program calling for rearmament and expansion. This development in Europe's greatest industrial power, following the rise of aggressive regimes in Italy and Japan, gave the international situation an air of rising menace. Predictions of a new world war were common.

Many Americans hoped that the United States would stay out of any coming war. Many of those who had entered World War I with high hopes, inspired by Wilson's statements that the war was being fought for peace and democracy, were disillusioned when victory was followed by a harsh peace, communism, and fascism. Others were disappointed that America received no territorial or material gain for its expenditure of blood and treasure, and little gratitude from the Allies it had saved. Cynicism was reinforced by the 1934–1936 revelations, by a Senate investigating committee, the Nye Committee, of huge profits reaped by bankers and arms manufacturers from the war, and by revisionist historians who concluded that Germany was not solely responsible for World War I and that America had entered the war, not because it was attacked, but as a result of propaganda, the efforts of bankers and arms manufacturers ("merchants of death"), and Wilson's errors.

On the other hand, the perception of rising threats from overseas caused many other Americans to question isolationism's feasibility. Terrible dangers seemed to emanate from the Soviet Union, Germany, Italy, and Japan.

In 1924, when Lenin died, leadership of the Communists had been assumed by Josef Stalin. In a 1928 speech, Stalin had said that again and again Russia had been defeated by invaders because of its backwardness and that it would probably be defeated again if it did not quickly modernize and industrialize. In a series of five-year plans, he launched a crash program of industrialization that required large imports of Western machinery. To pay for such technology, he exported food, and, in the ensuing food shortage, millions of Russians starved. At terrible cost, his program succeeded in its main aim, and, by 1940, the Soviet Union was the world's second largest producer of manufactured goods.

Meanwhile, Communist parties based on the Soviet model appeared in most of the world's nations, and they formed a worldwide organization, the Third International, or Comintern, with headquarters in Moscow. Many alarmed capitalists and democrats feared that the Comintern was an instrument of Soviet foreign policy through which it sought universal dominion. Hence, even though the Soviet Union did not send troops abroad, it was regarded as a menacing aggressor.

Also, the governments of Japan, Italy, and Germany were bitterly dissatisfied with the status quo and made no secret of their determination to change it—by war if necessary. Moreover, their rising industries gave them power with which to implement their ambitions. These three threats of aggression were eventually to combine, but they were quite separate in origin.

The Japanese, driven largely by their perception of a need to secure raw materials and markets for their growing industry, sought to bring much of China under their control. In 1931, Japan completed its occupation of Manchuria, withdrew from the League of Nations, and stepped up its economic and political penetration of north China. In 1935, Tokyo announced that it had assumed responsibility for "peace and order in East Asia," an attempt to establish its own Monroe Doctrine in "adjacent" areas. By 1937, Japan's continued encroachments on China produced full-scale war. As the most powerful nation in East Asia, Japan was increasingly perceived by Americans as a threat to U.S. interests.

Italy had fought on the winning side in World War I, but many Italians felt defeated. They had lost their major battles and had gained little at the peace conference. Italy's economy was in shambles, and communism was mushrooming—half of Italy's city halls flew the red flag.

This situation distressed many Italians, particularly patriotic young veterans who formed clubs (*fasci*) to combat communism and to restore Italy's national power. They were led by Benito Mussolini (see Fig. 4.1), a former Socialist party leader who had broken with that party to advocate Italy's entrance

Figure 4.1 Italy's dictator, Benito Mussolini, and Germany's dictator, Adolf Hitler. Their aggression alarmed most Americans. Brown Brothers.

into World War I. Thus, instead of an internationalist socialist who sought worldwide association of working people, he was a nationalist socialist who regarded socialism as a means of increasing his nation's power.

In the struggle between Communists and Fascists, involving much street fighting, the Fascists won, and, in 1923, Mussolini successfully demanded dictatorial power. In office, he permitted only one political party, extended government controls, and raised economic production. He also increased military spending and proclaimed an ambitious foreign policy of taking control of the Mediterranean and restoring the glories of the Roman Empire.

To the north of Italy, an even greater threat arose in the form of a newly autocratic and militarized Germany. In October 1918, the Germans had overthrown the kaiser and formed a democratic government, the Weimar Republic, which had a short and troubled history. At the peace conference, the Allies stripped Germany of all colonies and an eighth of its European territory and ordered it to pay reparations. The terms of the treaty heavily burdened Germany's economy, and poor economic conditions contributed to the growth of antidemocratic parties, particularly the Communists and the Nazis. The worldwide depression that spread to Germany in 1930 so crippled the republic as to raise the question of which party would displace the democracy—the Communists or the Nazis.

The Nazis (National Socialists) were led by Adolf Hitler, an ethnic German born in Austria. An aspiring artist who quit school at age fifteen, he became a fanatical nationalist. At first he was attracted by the militant tactics of Communists, but he was horrified when he discovered that they sought to abolish nations. The need, he concluded, was for a movement that used the same tactics, but in the service of the nation. Moving to Germany, he volunteered to fight in World War I, in which he won medals for heroism. Germany's defeat plunged him into despair, and he resolved to devote the rest of his life to restoring Germany to its former greatness.

Maintaining that Germany could not survive under the conditions imposed by the Versailles Treaty, Hitler called on Germans to rearm and to compel the Allies to return the territories they had taken. All personal and class interests, he insisted, must be subordinated to the national interest. He outlined a program of suppressing Communists, expelling citizens who were not ethnic Germans, uniting all German-inhabited lands, and annexing additional territory, including part of Russia, to give the nation more living room (Germany had 70 million people in an area two-thirds the size of Texas).

When the worldwide depression spread to Germany, the Nazis, in the 1932 elections, garnered more votes than any other party, and, in January 1933, Hitler became chancellor. Expulsion of Communists and Socialists from the Reichstag (the German parliament) gave the Nazis the majority they needed to vote Hitler dictatorial power. He provided efficient government, built superhighways and public buildings, and brought Germany out of the depression. He also stripped ethnic minorities of their citizenship.

In 1936, Hitler formed an alliance with Italy that commentators called the "Rome-Berlin Axis," hence the term "Axis powers." In November, Germany signed an Anti-Comintern Pact with Japan, which Italy joined in 1937, thus creating a "Berlin-Rome-Tokyo Axis."

By the 1930s, the world's industrial nations seemed to be divided into two groups—the "haves" and the "have-nots." The British Empire, the French Empire, the Soviet Union, and the United States possessed large land areas with ample farmland, raw materials, and access to trade. Germany, Italy, and Japan were convinced that they had less than their fair share of these necessities. The two camps had contrasting world outlooks. The have nations sought to preserve the status quo. Hence, they were nonaggressive and peace loving. On the other hand, convinced that the haves would never share their possessions peacefully, the have-nots built up large armies for the purpose of forcing a redistribution—they were aggressive and warlike.

Each side had an exceedingly unfavorable view of the other. The have nations condemned war, particularly aggressive war, as immoral and called the have-nots criminals who were plotting murderous attacks on peaceful neighbors to rob them. The have-nots regarded the haves as retired robbers who asked to be left undisturbed in their enjoyment of the loot—Mussolini asked to be shown "father Adam's will" that left the world for the exclusive enjoyment of Englishmen, Frenchmen, and Americans.

Beginning in 1931, when Japan seized Manchuria, the have-nots repeatedly committed aggressions. In 1935, Italy invaded Ethiopia. In 1936, the Fascist

General Francisco Franco, backed by Hitler and Mussolini, launched an uprising against Spain's elected government. In 1937, Japan invaded China. In March 1938, Germany annexed Austria. In October 1938, Hitler seized the ethnically German Sudetenland area of Czechoslovakia. In April 1939, Italy took Albania. On September 1, with the avowed intent of recovering German-inhabited areas that the Versailles Treaty had given Poland, Hitler invaded Poland and thereby set off World War II.

"Appeasement"

A question much debated at the time, and by historians later, was why the have nations were so slow in calling a halt to Axis aggression. Possessed of more of the elements of national power, the haves could have checked the aggression at less cost had they committed forces before the Axis made large gains. The answer most commonly given is that the haves were following a policy of "appeasement"—that, lacking courage to fight, they allowed aggressors to take territory in the hope that this would satisfy them and make them less aggressive. From this experience, Allied statesmen and historians drew a lesson—that appeasement leads to war and that, therefore, aggression must be resisted with full force from its inception.

Some of the events of the 1930s, however, do not fit this explanation. For example, in 1935, when Italy invaded Ethiopia, Britain sought to block oil shipments to Italy, but France refused to cooperate. Also, in 1935, England signed a treaty with Hitler accepting German rearmament on the condition that he limit the size of his navy to no more than one-third that of Britain's navy. When Hitler sent German troops into the Rhineland, France wanted to resist, but England held back. These do not appear to be simple cases of reluctant caving in to aggressors.

In 1936, General Francisco Franco, backed by wealthy businessmen, led the Spanish army in rebellion against the liberal democratic government of Spain. Fearful of the Spanish Communists and Russians who backed the Spanish government, England, France, and America stopped arms shipments to both sides. Because only the government had a legal right to import arms, this was an unneutral act that helped Franco, who received arms from Hitler and troops from Mussolini. Three thousand Americans volunteered to fight for the Spanish government, but it succumbed in 1939. This put a junior partner of Hitler and Mussolini in control of Spain.

Thus, the policies followed by the haves were more complex than simple appeasement. Some have nations were enemies of other have nations. The revival of German power, for example, eased British fears that France or Russia might dominate Europe. The Soviets charged that Western policy was dominated by anticommunism and that, because Hitler and Mussolini were anti-Communist, England and France allowed them to build up their power to counterbalance or destroy the Soviet Union.

World War

Eventually the haves did call a halt to Axis aggression. Why? Influencing the British was a belated recognition that the growing German air force was giving Germany, despite its naval inferiority, the power to disrupt England's vital ocean trade. In March 1939, when Hitler seized most of the remainder of Czechoslovakia, Britain, reversing its policy, offered the nations abutting Germany a virtual blank check—if they found it necessary to fight Germany to preserve their independence, London would immediately come to their aid.

Britain then sought to form an anti-German alliance with the Soviet Union. Although the Soviets had long sought such cooperation with the democracies, they were wary. They seemed to fear that England's secret policy was to encourage Russia and Germany to destroy each other while it stood aside. They asked if England would allow Russia to move troops into Estonia, Latvia, and Lithuania to strengthen Soviet defenses and how many troops England would send to help Russia if Hitler attacked. Convinced that the Soviets had no choice but to accept an alliance on any terms, the British refused to give permission to occupy the Baltic states or to promise any specific number of British troops.

On August 23, 1939, to the astonishment of the world, Germany and Russia signed the Molotov-Ribbentrop Pact, a promise that neither country would attack the other for at least five years. Secretly, they also agreed to divide Poland. Few had dreamed that the world's two leading ideological enemies and military rivals could come to terms. This treaty freed Hitler to invade Poland without having to fight both Russia and the Western Allies simultaneously. When Germany invaded on September 1, Britain and France declared war.

From the Soviet point of view, England and France had created a Frankenstein's monster—Hitler—in the hope that he would invade Russia and destroy Communism. But in the Molotov-Ribbentrop Pact, the Soviets had turned the monster around and sent it crashing back against its creators.

Both Axis and Allies had underestimated the willingness of the other to risk world war. Hitler had said: "While England may talk big . . . she is sure not to resort to armed intervention." British Prime Minister Neville Chamberlain had said: "Hitler is highly intelligent and therefore would not be prepared to wage a world war." Both were wrong.

The Neutrality Acts

Americans were interested spectators of the drama being played out in Europe. Although increasingly disturbed by the aggressions of Italy and Germany, most still wanted to stay out of Europe's wars. According to a 1939 Gallup Poll, two-thirds thought U.S. entry into World War I had been a mistake, and many of them vowed "Never again."

President Roosevelt did not share these isolationist views. Instead, he seemed to have concluded early in his administration that Axis moves threatened U.S. interests and that America should resist them. However, nonintervention sentiment was so strong that he found it politically necessary to soft-pedal his views. Thus, U.S. foreign policy was heavily influenced by popular desire to stay out of war. In 1935, much to Roosevelt's disgust, Congress even defeated his attempt to join the World Court.

The clearest expression of antiwar sentiment was enactment of the neutrality acts. In three principal laws, passed between August 1935 and May 1937, Congress made it illegal, in the event of war abroad, for any U.S. ship to enter a war zone or for any American to sell arms to any belligerent, travel on its ships, or lend it money. Further, the laws empowered the president to put the sale of other goods on a "cash-and-carry" basis—that is, to require the purchasing nation first to pay for them and then to carry them away in its own ships so that no U.S. property or lives would be at risk.

Clearly, these neutrality acts were attempts to block any repetition of the events believed to have propelled the United States into World War I. They showed distrust of the discretion of the president, and they surrendered "freedom of the seas" rights for which Americans had previously fought. Objecting, Roosevelt wanted the ban to apply only to loans and arms sales to aggressors—which, of course, would have converted them into unneutrality acts. He lost this fight, and antiwar sentiment was so strong that he found it politically necessary to sign the neutrality acts. However, in 1938, Roosevelt secured defeat of a proposed Ludlow Amendment to the Constitution to require a popular vote before America could go to war. Congressional efforts to legislate neutrality could not be effective, he said, because success in staying out of war would depend on the wisdom and the day-to-day decisions of the president and the secretary of state.

Resistance to Axis Aggression

Although hoping to stay out of the threatening war, Americans were not indifferent to its outcome. Most were repulsed by the undemocratic governments of Japan, Italy, and Germany and by their violations of human rights, their anti-Semitism, and their militarism. U.S. businessmen disliked Axis economic controls—their socialism. Americans also sensed that Germany and Japan were the most powerful nations in Europe and East Asia and that, if they continued to expand, they could threaten U.S. security. Consequently, most Americans favored both staying out of the war and helping the democracies—and they did not seem aware that these two policies might be incompatible. In the early 1930s, most attached greater importance to staying out of war, but gradually many shifted to giving higher priority to helping the Allies.

The neutrality acts required Roosevelt to enforce them whenever a war broke out abroad. But after the signing of the Kellogg-Briand Pact (1928), declarations of war had gone out of style; instead, nations fought without declaring war. In such cases, the president had the power to decide whether or not to recognize an outbreak of fighting as a war. Roosevelt used this authority to favor the Allies.

In 1935, when Italy, without declaring war, invaded Ethiopia, Roosevelt designated that action a war, thereby stopping loans and arms sales to both Italy and Ethiopia. Because isolated Ethiopia could not import arms, the only effect was to deny arms to Italy. (The League imposed an arms embargo, but Mussolini threatened to declare war on any nation that stopped selling oil to Italy. None did.) On the other hand, Roosevelt did not recognize Japan's 1937 invasion of China as a war. Because Japan was already heavily armed, but China badly needed to buy arms, an arms embargo would hurt China more than Japan. U.S. manufacturers continued to sell arms to both sides.

Attempts to Stop Japan

Roosevelt took an increasingly overt stand against Japan's expansion. Continuing Hoover's policy of refusing to recognize Japan's control of Manchuria, he demanded an open door there for U.S. trade and investments, and he protested Japan's encroachments on U.S. treaty rights in China. Securing a doubling of appropriations for the navy, he raised the number of U.S. marines stationed in China.

In his October 1937, "quarantine speech," Roosevelt called for coordinated international action against aggression. An "epidemic" of international lawlessness, he said, was spreading, and "the very foundations of civilization are seriously threatened." The world community, he continued, should impose a "quarantine" to protect the community against its spread. He did not say exactly what he meant by quarantine; secretly he was considering a joint British-American embargo on Japan. However, reaction to his speech at home and abroad did not encourage him to propose strong action. Although U.S. public opinion opposed Japan's actions by 59 to 1, a large majority also opposed risking war with Japan, and a January 1938 poll showed that 70 percent of Americans favored withdrawing completely from the Far East. Also, 63 percent of congressmen opposed stopping sales of U.S. goods to Japan. Neither the British nor the French would join in strong action unless America promised to protect their East Asian possessions, and British Prime Minister Neville Chamberlain dismissed Roosevelt's quarantine speech as the "utterings of a harebrained statesman." It was "terrible," said Roosevelt, "to look over your shoulder when you are trying to lead to find no one there."

In October 1937, America joined the League in condemning Japan for violating the Nine-Power Treaty and the Paris Peace Pact. Nevertheless, at the November 1937 nineteen-nation Brussels Conference, called by the League to consider Japan's violations, only Russia sought real reprisals. The United States declined to support economic sanctions, and the conference adjourned in futility.

In December 1937, the Japanese bombed and sank a U.S. gunboat, the *Panay*, and three tankers it was escorting up the Yangtze River to take aviation gasoline to the Chinese. Two Americans were killed. This sinking was apparently an unauthorized action by a local commander, and, quickly apologizing, the Japanese government offered to pay $2.2 million in damages, while Japanese civilians collected additional funds to compensate victims.

Partly to increase the effectiveness of U.S. resistance to Japan, Roosevelt, in 1938, secured a billion-dollar appropriation to construct two new aircraft carriers and to double the number of naval aircraft. Also, he transferred the Pacific fleet from its base in California to Hawaii, thus moving it two thousand miles closer to Japan.

When the Japanese bombed Chinese cities, Americans were horrified (see Fig. 4.2). Bombing civilians was not then a common practice, and many Americans thought that it proved that the Japanese were demonic. In July 1938, Roosevelt asked U.S. airplane manufacturers, in a "moral embargo," to refuse to sell planes to any nation that bombed civilians.

In November 1938, America protested that the Japanese had closed the door in Manchuria to U.S. trade and investments. The Japanese replied that an anti-Communist "New Order" had arisen in East Asia, bringing political, economic,

Figure 4.2 In 1937 Americans were horrified by reports, including the picture of a crying Chinese child survivor, that the Japanese were bombing Chinese civilians. Roosevelt banned further sales of warplanes to nations that bombed civilians. National Archives.

and cultural "coordination between Japan, Manchukuo, and China" and that, therefore, old principles no longer applied.

To provide China with the foreign exchange it needed to import arms, America, in December 1938, extended to China a $25-million loan, the first of a series of loans. Russia, fearful of possible invasion by Japan, furnished much more aid to China.

In January 1939, stepping up the pressure, America gave Japan notice of termination of the U.S.-Japanese trade treaty; after the required six-months notice period, America would be legally free to stop trade with Japan. This was a serious threat, because Japan's economy depended on trade, and 40 percent of its trade was with America. Some U.S. economists maintained that a U.S. trade stoppage could bring Japan to its knees within six months.

Many Americans were deeply offended by Japan's aggression. Years of missionary and educational activities had given Americans an emotional interest in China, and they were proud of their Open Door Policy of favoring China's independence. Nevertheless, Japan's actions did not seem to pose a major threat to vital U.S. interests. Only one-fifth of U.S. trade was with East Asia, and U.S. trade with China was only one-third as large as U.S. trade with Japan. Moreover, Japan was much less powerful than the United States. Consequently, East Asian interests seemed to many Americans to be insufficiently important to justify going to war. Germany, however, posed a graver menace.

Rising Opposition to Germany

Europe contained an unequaled concentration of modern industry that had given its nations the power to make conquests throughout the world. Germany's industrial production had surpassed that of England to become the second highest in the world. If Germany continued to expand, it might become strong enough to dominate all Europe and thereby grow powerful enough to endanger America. "The control of all Europe by a single, aggressive, unfriendly power," a future secretary of state would say, "would constitute an intolerable threat to the security of the United States."

In March 1938, Hitler annexed ethnically German Austria. Later in 1938, Hitler threatened to send his armies into the Sudetenland, the German-inhabited part of Czechoslovakia. The Czechs prepared to defend their territory. Because the Czechs had alliances with Britain, France, and Russia, Germany's invasion could precipitate World War II. Roosevelt joined in pleas to Hitler's ally, Mussolini, to persuade Hitler to attend a conference at Munich. Russia was not invited but signaled that it would fight to save Czechoslovakia if England and France did. Privately, Roosevelt told Britain that America could not help. On September 30, England and France agreed to allow Hitler to occupy part of Czechoslovakia in return for his promise to respect the remainder of its territory. Returning to London, British Prime Minister Neville Chamberlain claimed that he had brought "peace in our times." Actually, he had postponed war for only a year. The Munich Conference became a symbol of appeasement. From the Soviet point of view, it constituted permission by Western capitalists to allow Hitler to expand to the east, thereby increasing the menace to Russia.

Meanwhile, Americans strongly denounced Hitler. He could "scarcely believe," said Roosevelt, that Hitler's persecution of the Jews could "occur in a Twentieth-century civilization." When a cabinet member called Hitler a "brutal dictator," the State Department rejected Hitler's demands for an apology. Both countries withdrew their ambassadors, and the Germans, convinced that America was unalterably hostile, ceased even to protest U.S. actions.

An early 1939 poll showed that Americans supported, by more than 2 to 1, giving the Allies every aid short of war. In his January 1939 State of the Union address, Roosevelt told Congress that there were many methods "short of war, but stronger and more effective than words" of opposing aggression. He sold America's most advanced bombers to France.

In March 1939, Hitler seized most of the remainder of Czechoslovakia, and, in April, Mussolini seized Albania. As usual, both announced that these were their last territorial demands. Roosevelt asked Hitler and Mussolini to sign nonaggression treaties with neighboring nations, a request they disregarded.

Many Americans became increasingly fearful that the European "haves" lacked the will to stop the headlong aggression of Germany and Italy. They also feared that Europeans were restrained from taking a stronger stand by the neutrality laws that would bar America from selling them arms in a war. If it were made clear that the United States would aid the Allies, many Americans hoped, Hitler might be deterred from risking war. In May 1939, Roosevelt asked Congress to amend the neutrality acts to allow sale of arms to belligerents on a cash-and-carry basis. In July, the Senate Foreign Relations Committee rejected the measure by a vote of 12 to 11.

In late 1939, after Hitler threatened to invade Poland if it did not return the part of Germany awarded to Poland by the Versailles Treaty, Roosevelt secretly urged the Poles to resist Hitler's demand.

On September 1, the Germans invaded Poland. Two days later England and France, who had treaties of alliance with Poland, declared war on Germany. These were stunning developments. Many people had hoped that civilization had outgrown major war. But what they had long dreaded as an unimaginable horror had become reality. World War II had begun.

In a neutrality proclamation, Roosevelt said that he hoped America would keep out of the war, and he promised that if he could prevent it, "there will be no blackout of peace in the United States." However, in contrast to President Wilson, who had asked the American people to be neutral in thought, Roosevelt said that "I cannot ask that every American remain neutral in thought as well." Actually, few Americans were neutral. A public opinion poll showed that 84 percent wanted the Allies to win, while only 2 percent wanted Germany to win. Nevertheless, only 3.3 percent favored entering the war.

Calling a special session of Congress, Roosevelt asked it to amend the neutrality acts to permit the Allies to buy U.S. arms. This, he said, would be a return to international law and would help keep America out of the war. Opponents argued that changing the rules after war had begun would be an un-neutral act that would put America on the road to war. On November 3, Congress voted to allow sale of arms on a cash-and-carry basis. Of course, this favored the Allies who controlled the seas.

The Allies imposed a naval blockade on all German-occupied territories, stopped neutral ships in international waters, and forced U.S. ships to enter British ports to be searched. They lengthened the list of contraband to include even food. America protested against these violations of international law, but took no action to stop them, although a threat to cut off arms sales might have sufficed.

The Germans, with some help from the Russians, who moved in from the east to occupy the part of Poland that Germany had conceded to them, defeated the large Polish army in only seven weeks. The campaign saw a new use of fast-moving armored columns with close air support, a strategy the press called *blitzkrieg* (lightening war). In the next six months, the war was waged in the Atlantic and in the air, but the Germans launched no additional ground campaign.

In November 1939, the attention of much of the world was diverted by a Soviet attack on Finland. The Russians had occupied half of Poland, plus Latvia, Estonia, and Lithuania. Nevertheless, their principal city and port, Leningrad, remained exposed to enemy attack. Finland's territory extended into Leningrad's suburbs, and there, on an isthmus between the Baltic Sea and Lake Ladoga, the Finns had built a powerful fortified line. Finland received military aid from Germany, which the Soviets feared. They offered to swap larger territories farther north for the isthmus, but Finland refused. When Soviet armies invaded, the Finns put up a remarkable resistance, and their exploits, particularly those of their ski troops, won worldwide acclaim, while Russia's image plunged to a new low. The League of Nations expelled the Soviet Union.

Denouncing the dreadful "rape of Finland" by an "absolute dictatorship," Roosevelt called on Americans to halt the sale of airplanes, gasoline, and war materials to Russia. A House motion to close the Moscow embassy failed by only three votes. By 61 to 39 percent, Americans opposed lending money for arms, but Washington extended to Finland a $30-million loan for nonmilitary supplies, and a private group collected "Fighting Funds for Finland." The British asked for permission to transport British troops to Finland across Norwegian territory; Norway's refusal may have saved Britain from war with Russia.

The Finns inflicted a remarkable number of casualties on the invading Soviet forces, thus renewing speculation that Stalin's execution of many top Soviet generals had weakened the Soviet military. But, sending in larger forces, the Soviets overwhelmed the Finns by March 1940.

Meanwhile, Hitler was attempting to persuade England and France to make peace. He argued that Germany had no more territorial ambitions (a promise he had broken more than once) and also that if western European nations continued to fight, they would so weaken each other as to leave Europe helpless before Communist Russia. When the British and the French refused to again reverse their policy, Hitler, angrily placing responsibility for coming disasters on England, attacked to the west.

In April 1940, in an astonishing display of military power, German troops quickly overran Denmark, Norway, Belgium, and the Netherlands, and then, on May 10, drove into France. The British army that had been sent to help the French fell back to the port of Dunkirk, where the British succeeded in evacuating 338,000 men, but not their heavy weapons. Choosing this moment to enter the war, Mussolini sent Italian troops into southern France. On June 22, France surrendered. Germany stood supreme in western Europe.

A German invasion of England was widely expected. Dismissing the government of Neville Chamberlain, who had become the symbol of appeasement, the British named Winston Churchill as their new prime minister. Churchill had headed the British navy in World War I, and in the 1930s he had demanded stronger resistance to the Axis. His mother was American, and he was much admired in America. With magnificent oratory, he rallied the British people, vowing never to surrender but to fight on the beaches and in the lanes until "the New World, with all its power and might, steps forth to the rescue and liberation of the old."

He proved to be a good prophet.

5 The United States Enters World War II

Preparation for War

Americans were stunned by Germany's quick (April-June 1940) conquest of Denmark, Norway, Belgium, and France, which gave Germany control of vast resources in western Europe, a goal that had eluded it in World War I. In many alarmed minds, this raised the question of whether any existing force could stop the Nazi war machine. Some Americans feared that Hitler might invade England, capture the French and British fleets, and invade the Western Hemisphere.

Responding vigorously to the perceived danger, Roosevelt moved rapidly to arm the United States. In May 1940, outlining how America could possibly be bombed, he called for expansion of U.S. capacity to manufacture warplanes to fifty thousand a year, construction of a navy large enough to defend both the Atlantic and the Pacific oceans simultaneously, and enactment of America's first peacetime conscription law. The draft act passed in September, and the number of personnel in the U.S. armed forces jumped from 335,000 in 1939 to 1,800,000 in 1941, while annual military spending soared from $1.4 billion to $6.3 billion.

In June 1940, Roosevelt appointed to his cabinet two leading Republicans, both ardent interventionists: former Secretary of State Henry L. Stimson as secretary of war, and Frank Knox as secretary of the navy, thus creating the kind of bipartisan coalition government usually formed only in wartime. In addition, he established new government agencies to mobilize the economy for war production.

Meanwhile, Roosevelt moved further away from neutrality. On June 10, with France collapsing, he bitterly condemned Italy's entry into the war and announced that America would "extend to the opponents of force the material resources of this nation." Americans trained Allied pilots and repaired Allied warships. Also, Roosevelt ordered that huge quantities of military equipment, including artillery, tanks, and warplanes, be transferred from U.S. arsenals to the Allies. "Scrape the bottom of the barrel," he told the armed forces, to furnish all they could spare. Because giving arms by a government to a nation at war is legally equivalent to entering the war, Roosevelt preserved technical neutrality by "selling" these arms to private companies who then passed them on to the Allies.

The Great Debate

These moves were accompanied by one of the great debates in U.S. history—on whether America should enter the war. Those who advocated all-out aid to the Allies regardless of risk of war, or who advocated entering the war, were called "interventionists." Those who wanted to stay out of the war, and who objected to what they considered steps leading to war, were called "isolationists," or, more properly because some of them were idealistic internationalists, "noninterventionists." Most prominent Americans were noninterventionists, but interventionists occupied the key posts of president, secretary of state, secretary of the treasury, secretary of war, and secretary of the navy.

In May 1940, interventionists formed the Committee to Defend America by Aiding the Allies, headed by Republican Kansas newspaper editor William Allen White. At first, this committee stressed aid short of war, but later it shifted so far toward advocacy of war that White resigned. Interventionists argued that the Axis nations were ruled by militaristic, dictatorial regimes that inflicted horrible atrocities on both enemies and their own people and sought to destroy freedom and religion, and that their victory would take Europe back into the Dark Ages. A victorious Axis could strangle America economically, or invade the Western Hemisphere, or, at least, interventionists argued, force the United States into a military buildup that would endanger U.S. freedom and democracy.

Noninterventionists included former President Herbert Hoover; prominent senators including William E. Borah, Robert M. LaFollette Jr., Robert A. Taft, Arthur Vandenberg, Hiram Johnson, and Burton K. Wheeler; historian Charles A. Beard; Socialist party leader Norman Thomas; industrialist Henry Ford; the *Chicago Tribune*; and the Hearst newspaper chain. In September 1940, they organized the America First Committee, chaired by Sears Roebuck head Robert Wood. The famous aviation hero Charles A. Lindbergh emerged from seclusion to become the most popular of the nonintervention speakers. Rejecting interventionist arguments, they maintained that the two sides were equally civilized, or uncivilized, and that religion and civilization were not at issue. Furthermore, they said, the British and the French empires were already practicing what the Axis nations sought to do—holding unwilling peoples in subjugation—and it was thus a war between rival imperialisms. They argued that war itself was destructive of democracy and civilization and that the more widely it spread, the greater would be its damage. No matter how much Axis leaders might want to conquer America, antiwar forces argued, they could not possibly do so even in the unlikely event that they conquered all Europe and Asia. The only real gainer from the war, some feared, would be Russia which would replace Germany as Europe's most powerful nation.

Before the fall of France, U.S. public opinion overwhelmingly favored the Allies, but an almost equal majority wanted to stay out of the war. After France fell, the number who believed that German victory would menace America rose from 43 percent to 69 percent.

Roosevelt, a master politician, was well aware that the American people wanted to stay out of the war and that they also wanted the Allies to win. Personally, he had early become convinced that America must prevent an Axis victory even if that required entering the war. But he was also convinced that if he openly proposed intervention, the people and Congress would reject it. Instead, he offered a program that, he claimed, would both keep the United States at peace and ensure Allied victory. The way to keep America out of war, he insisted, was to give the Allies enough aid to enable them to win without U.S. entry. Noninterventionists argued that Roosevelt was taking America closer to war, even that he secretly sought to enter the war, but most Americans backed the president.

The Election of 1940

Early in 1940, it appeared that the question of whether the United States should enter the war would be the principal issue of the coming election. The leading candidates for the Republican nomination, Robert A. Taft, Arthur H. Vandenberg, and Thomas E. Dewey, were all noninterventionists. In their national convention, the Republicans adopted an antiwar platform that called for keeping aid to the Allies within the limits of international law. Nevertheless, in an astonishing political development, an interventionalist, Wendell Willkie, a relatively unknown businessman who had until recently been a Democrat, captured the Republican nomination.

Maintaining that the great world emergency justified a departure from the no-third-term for presidents tradition, the Democrats renominated Roosevelt. Their platform favored maximum aid to the Allies, but promised not to participate in foreign wars or to send U.S. armed forces to fight in "foreign lands outside the Americas." At Roosevelt's insistence, however, they added "except in case of attack."

In the campaign, Roosevelt emphasized national defense by touring shipyards, factories, and arsenals. Democrats maintained that America should not change horses in midstream, and that Hitler hoped for Roosevelt's defeat.

On September 3, Roosevelt announced that he had transferred fifty U.S. destroyers to Britain. He did this by executive agreement, without consulting Congress. He traded them, he said, for the right to construct eight U.S. military bases on British Western Hemisphere territories from Newfoundland to Guiana. However, because America would use these bases to help the British fight German submarines, the British gained from both sides of the "trade." Roosevelt called this destroyer-base deal the "most important action in the reinforcement of our national defense that has been taken since the Louisiana Purchase." Willkie called it the "most dictatorial action ever taken by any president." It was of questionable legality under U.S. law, and obviously unneutral. Senator Gerald P. Nye said it made America "a party to the war," and Winston Churchill said that "according to all the standards of history," it would have "justified the German government in declaring war." The public approved by 62 to 38 percent.

Although he was an interventionist, Willkie, finding that he could get applause when he criticized Roosevelt's movement toward war, stepped up such criticism. "When I say [aid] short of war," he said, "I mean short of war," and he promised to avoid bringing about a situation that would make war necessary. In the polls, he closed to within four percentage points of the president.

To counteract Willkie's attacks, Roosevelt's advisers wrote a speech that Roosevelt refused to deliver because, he said, it did not represent his policy. When his advisers told him that otherwise he would lose the election, he delivered it at Boston on October 30. It contained some of his most remembered phrases: "I have said this before, but I shall say it again and again and again: Your sons are not going to be sent into any foreign wars." Willkie exclaimed: "That hypocritical son of a bitch! This is going to beat me!" On November 2, Roosevelt added: "Your president says this country is not going to war."

Roosevelt won the election, receiving 27 million votes to Willkie's 22 million. Willkie's nomination, and Roosevelt's antiwar pledges, had prevented the election from conveying a clear message on the most momentous issue of the day.

Lend-Lease

In a December 1940 radio address, Roosevelt told the American people that "our national policy is not directed toward war. Its sole purpose is to keep war away from our country and our people." But, he added, America must "become the great arsenal of democracy."

By this time, the Allies were buying so much war material as to strain their financial resources. "The moment approaches," said Churchill, "when we shall no longer be able to pay cash." To Roosevelt, it was unthinkable to allow the flow of arms to stop. In his January 1941 State of the Union address, he urged: "Let's get away from that silly, foolish, old dollar sign" and lend the Allies arms, in the same way that one would lend a neighbor a garden hose to put out a fire that might otherwise spread to one's own house. He asked Congress to authorize him to supply the Allies with weapons to be either returned or paid for with other goods after the war.

A "Lend-Lease" bill was introduced as House Resolution 1776, an "Act to Promote the Defense of the United States." It authorized the president to ship without charge weapons and goods to any country whose defense he considered "vital to the defense of the United States." Because this would be undisguised intervention in the war, the "great debate" reached a crescendo as antiwar forces made a last-ditch effort to block it. Senator Taft ridiculed the idea of lending arms, saying that it was "like lending chewing gum, you don't want it back." Senator Wheeler called it the New Deal program to "plow under every fourth American boy," which Roosevelt called the rottenest thing said in public life in his generation. Lend-Lease would keep America out of the war, Roosevelt insisted, an interpretation Churchill supported with the statement: "Give us the tools and we will finish the job."

The Gallup Poll showed that the people, by more than two to one, backed Lend-Lease. In March 1941, Congress enacted it by a vote of 60 to 31 in the

Senate and 260 to 165 in the House. The first appropriation was $7 billion; the total would eventually rise to more than $50 billion, $32 billion of which went to Britain. Its enactment clearly committed America to Allied victory. Historian Thomas A. Bailey called it an "unofficial declaration of war."

In secret meetings in January 1941, top U.S. and British military staffs worked out joint war plans. They agreed to concentrate first on defeating Germany before sending major forces against Japan. Roosevelt ordered the U.S. Navy to escort ships carrying arms to England, seized the sixty-five Axis ships in U.S. ports and transferred most of them to Britain, and began preparations to dispatch part of the U.S. Air Force to China. In June he severed remaining economic relations with Germany and Italy and forced them to close their consulates.

Aid to the Soviet Union

On June 22, 1941, to the amazement of the world, Hitler launched a massive invasion of the Soviet Union. In so doing, he brought on the two-front war that he had long warned would be disastrous for Germany. Why? Hitler had always regarded Communist Russia as the chief enemy. After the 1939 Molotov-Ribbentrop Pact, Germany had received supplies from Russia, but the two nations had clashed on Finland and in the Balkans. Moreover, in 1940, for the first time, Soviet industrial production surpassed Germany's, which meant that Russia would eventually become Europe's most powerful nation. Also, Hitler seems to have believed that the Russian people hated their Communist rulers and would greet German troops as liberators.

Americans were uncertain how to respond to this stunning development. They hated communism as well as Nazism. Senator Harry S. Truman told a reporter that "if we see that Germany is winning then we ought to help Russia and if Russia's winning we ought to help Germany, and . . . let them kill as many as possible." Roosevelt returned Soviet properties that America had seized, but for months he extended no further aid.

The British were quicker to give Russia aid. Although he had long been a leading anti-Communist, Churchill, saying that if "Hitler invaded hell, I would at least make a favorable reference to the Devil," ordered immediate assistance.

One cause of U.S. reluctance was the expectation that Soviet resistance would collapse so quickly that any arms sent would fall into German hands. The Soviet army had made a poor showing in its war against Finland. Also, American propaganda had long depicted the Soviet regime as so inept and inhuman that it was sure to fail, and had maintained that most Russians would welcome the overthrow of the Communists who had enslaved them. America's top military man, George C. Marshall, predicted that Soviet resistance would collapse within six weeks. Although the Germans drove deep into Russia, Soviet fighting proved to be much more determined than expected. In November, nearly five months after the invasion began, Congress authorized $1 billion in Lend-Lease aid to Russia, which eventually rose to $11 billion.

The Atlantic Conference

On August 9–12, 1941, Roosevelt and Churchill, with their top military leaders, met secretly on a battleship near Newfoundland. They discussed whether an invasion of Europe across the English Channel would be needed to defeat Germany, how Lend-Lease supplies should be allocated, and military plans for war with Japan.

At this Atlantic Conference, Roosevelt and Churchill issued a statement outlining their common aims, a statement known as the "Atlantic Charter." They sought, they said, to bar territorial changes not approved by the people involved, to disarm aggressors, to establish a "wider and permanent system of general security," and to ensure to all peoples the right to choose their own governments and to have equal access to foreign raw materials. They also called for freedom of the seas, improved labor standards, and, "after the final destruction of Nazi tyranny," freedom from fear and want. Churchill, who was proud of his success in winning U.S. support for Britain's war effort, called this statement of joint war aims by a belligerent and a neutral "astonishing" and a "challenge" to Germany.

Impressed that Roosevelt was "obviously determined to come in," Churchill reported to his cabinet that the president had said that he "would wage war, but not declare it, would become more and more provocative," and would do everything to "force an incident which would justify him in opening hostilities."

Naval War with Germany

It seemed to make little sense for America to give Lend-Lease arms to England only to have them sunk. In April 1941, the United States established sea and air patrols in the North Atlantic to spot German submarines. To support these patrols, U.S. forces occupied Denmark's island possession Greenland and, as early as April 10, 1941, secretly began firing on German submarines. However, German captains, under strict orders not to fire unless necessary to escape destruction, did not return fire for months.

In July, Americans took over from the British the military occupation of Iceland, also a possession of Denmark. By July 19, U.S. ships had begun convoying (protecting against German submarines) British ships as far as Iceland, with instructions to destroy hostile forces. A poll indicated that 55 percent of the American people favored convoying.

On September 4, notified by a British plane of the location of a German submarine, a U.S. destroyer, the *Greer*, gave chase. After three and a half hours of pursuit, during which a British plane dropped depth bombs, the German submarine fired a torpedo that missed. In his report to the American people, Roosevelt claimed that the Germans "fired first . . . without warning" in furtherance of a Nazi plan to attack the Western Hemisphere. On September 11, he said that he had ordered the navy to shoot on sight—which meant undisguised naval war. The public approved by 64 percent.

On October 17, Americans suffered their first casualties. Entering a battle between a British convoy and German submarines, the U.S. destroyer *Kearney* dropped depth bombs and was hit by a torpedo that killed eleven U.S. sailors. "America has been attacked," Roosevelt told the American people, by "rattlesnakes of the sea." "We have wished to avoid shooting," he added, "but the shooting has started. And history has recorded who fired the first shot." In the same speech, he charged that the Nazis had prepared a map dividing South America into "five vassal states" and that they planned to "abolish all existing religions." By November 1, America had lost eleven merchant ships, one destroyer, and ninety-five lives. On November 13, Congress voted to repeal the remaining portions of the Neutrality Acts and thereby authorize U.S. merchant ships to arm themselves and carry war supplies through war zones to British ports.

Although, under international law, the United States was then legally at war with Germany and engaged in a "shooting" naval war, many Americans continued to maintain that America should stay out of the war. In September, extension of the service of draftees beyond one year passed the Senate by only one vote. In early November, public opinion was 63 to 24 percent against declaring war. As the leader of a nation at war, Roosevelt urgently needed to find a way to unite the people behind the war.

Economic Sanctions Against Japan

After Germany's defeat of France in June 1940, the Japanese, promising to respect French sovereignty, had moved their troops into northern French Indochina (North Vietnam). It was essential, they said, to the conduct of their war against China.

In July 1940, America stopped the sale of aviation gasoline to Japan. In September, it also banned the sale of steel, scrap metal, lead, copper, aluminum, and machine tools. These actions hurt Japan's economy and intensified Japanese fears that America might impose a crippling total embargo.

In September 1940, the Axis powers—Japan, Germany, and Italy—signed the Tripartite Pact, an agreement that if one of them were attacked by a nation not then in the war, the other two would immediately come to its assistance. Apparently, the Japanese hoped that if the United States knew that going to war with Japan would also mean war with Germany, it would refrain from taking additional measures against Japan.

Instead, America accelerated its anti-Japanese measures. In October, Washington persuaded Britain to reopen the Burma Road, the chief land route for supplying arms to China. In January 1941, Washington began to implement plans to transfer U.S. Air Force pilots with planes, the "Flying Tigers," to China to fight the Japanese. After the enactment in March of the Lend-Lease Act, America extended Lend-Lease arms and supplies to China.

In April 1941, Japan signed a nonaggression treaty with the Soviet Union, which committed each to neutrality if the other were attacked. By reducing the danger of war with Russia, it improved Japan's position vis-à-vis the United States. However, it disappointed the Germans, who had hoped for Japan's help in their planned invasion of Russia, which began two months later.

Meanwhile, the Japanese made conciliatory gestures. In February 1941, Premier Fumimaro Konoye, who seemed to seek a peaceful settlement, appointed Admiral Kichisaburo Nomura, a pro-Western friend of Roosevelt, to be Japan's ambassador to Washington. In July, Konoye fired the warlike foreign minister Yosuke Matsuoka. Meanwhile, he pursued negotiations.

On July 24, 1941, however, in a fateful move, the Japanese sent their troops into southern Indochina, a move they could not justify as required to support military operations against China. Instead, it placed them closer to British and Dutch possessions in southeast Asia.

The next day, July 25, the United States froze Japan's assets. This meant that America seized for an indeterminant time all Japanese-owned property, including bank accounts, in U.S. territory. Of course, freezing assets stopped trade. Because Japan lived by trade, and 40 percent of its trade was with America, this was a crippling blow to Japan's economy. Its effect was magnified when, on the same day, the British and the Dutch also froze Japanese assets. These measures almost completely severed Japan's access to oil, which was vital to the operation of its navy, air force, mechanized divisions, and industry.

In 1940, Roosevelt had warned that stopping oil shipments would force Japan to invade the oil-rich Dutch East Indies. Japanese admirals maintained that they could not embark on a war with less than a year's supply of oil, and they had enough reserves for only eighteen months. Thus, Japan had only a few months in which to decide whether to yield to U.S. demands or to fight.

Although the U.S. government was choking Japan economically, it wished to postpone the outbreak of fighting. Shortly before the freezing of Japanese assets, Roosevelt had written: "It is terribly important for the control of the Atlantic for us to help keep peace in the Pacific. I simply have not got enough navy to go around." Navy commander Admiral Harold Stark opposed the freezing of Japan's assets. After July, wrote Secretary of State Hull, "our major objective with regard to Japan was to give ourselves more time to prepare our defenses."

In the negotiations, the Japanese sought to ascertain as soon as possible the conditions on which America would lift the embargo. At first, Americans talked in terms of general principles, but their underlying demands became more and more apparent. These were that the Japanese break their alliance with Germany and Italy, withdraw their military forces from Indochina, and withdraw from China where they had been at war for more than four years.

These demands were considerably in excess of what nations historically had been willing to concede without first being defeated in war. Nevertheless, Premier Konoye seemed to be willing to go a long way toward meeting them. He was convinced that Japan could not win a war with America. Japan's population was only half that of America's, its GNP was only 10 percent of America's, and its navy was smaller than America's. Moreover, Japan's military forces were bogged down in a war with China. Many Japanese leaders, including its naval commanders, maintained that war with America would be suicidal.

Nevertheless, many army leaders were bellicose. They particularly objected to withdrawing from China. The Japanese army had started the China war despite the opposition of Japan's civilian government and had fought in China for four years, suffering more than two million casualties. Furthermore, many Japanese assumed, perhaps mistakenly, that when Americans specified "China," they included Manchuria, where the Japanese had been since 1905. Agreement by the army to withdraw would be equivalent to admitting that it had arrogantly led the nation into disaster, and many army leaders regarded such humiliation as intolerable.

Under the Japanese constitution, the premier did not command the military forces, but Konoye developed a plan that he hoped would circumvent army obstruction, and he got the support of Emperor Hirohito for his plan. The plan was for Konoye to meet with Roosevelt to make the necessary concessions in return for a commitment by America to resume trade and assure Japan of secure access to the materials vital to its economy (a relationship between the two nations similar to that which would exist after World War II). Then, when Konoye brought the treaty back to Japan, the emperor would summon Japan's top civilian and military leaders and directly order them to carry out its terms. If thus summarily overruled by the emperor, the army could withdraw from China without confessing error. Endorsing the request for a summit, Ambassador Joseph C. Grew reported that Konoye was ready to withdraw all Japanese troops from China.

Konoye's request for a meeting arrived when Roosevelt was at the early August Atlantic Conference. At first, Roosevelt, who loved summit conferences, seemed to favor meeting Konoye, but the bitterly anti-Japanese Hull persuaded him not to meet the premier unless the Japanese would agree in advance to U.S. terms, which Konoye could not do. On October 2, Roosevelt rejected the Japanese request for a summit. This reply, wrote the historian Arthur Link, "spelled the doom not only of the projected conference, but of peace as well." On October 16, Konoye resigned and was replaced as premier by the minister of war, General Hideki Tojo.

Pearl Harbor

Many Americans assumed that replacement of Konoye by the minister of war meant that Japan had decided on war. But Tojo, also, doubted that Japan could win a war with the United States—in early October he had suggested that, if the navy would publicly state that it could not defeat America, the army might be forced to withdraw from China. The emperor appointed him on the condition that he continue negotiations.

Time was running out. With oil supplies dwindling, a September 9 imperial conference had concluded that if negotiations did not succeed, Japan would have go to war by the end of October. Later extending this deadline, the government told Ambassador Nomura that it was "absolutely necessary" to get an agreement by November 25 because afterwards "things are automatically going to happen."

In 1940, in an operation called "Magic," Americans had decoded the secret radio codes in which Tokyo communicated with its diplomats. By reading these messages, Americans learned more about Japan's diplomatic and military moves than was known to most Japanese officials. Americans knew, of course, that Japan's oil reserves were dwindling and that, consequently, Japan must give priority to a naval expedition to seize the oil-rich Dutch East Indies. If that invasion failed, Japan would soon lose its ability to wage war.

As countermeasures, the British moved important units of their fleet to Singapore to cooperate with the U.S. fleet based in Hawaii, and Americans strengthened their forces in the Philippines with additional aircraft. If the Japanese convoys descended on the Netherlands East Indies, the Allies planned for the U.S. fleet to move in from the U.S. naval base at Pearl Harbor in conjunction with a British naval movement from Singapore and, aided by Phillipine-based planes, destroy the Japanese convoys—and with them Japan's hope of continuing the war. One American admiral predicted that the war would last only seven weeks.

These preparations, however, could not be completed by Japan's November 25 deadline. U.S. aircraft carriers were still strung out across the Pacific, ferrying aircraft to Pacific islands. Army reinforcements for the Philippines were still in transit. The U.S. military asked that the diplomats postpone war for three more months.

Consequently, Hull suggested a three-month modus vivendi. Under its terms, Japan would withdraw its troops from southern Indochina, while the United States would allow Japan to import enough oil to supply its daily civilian needs as negotiations continued. Eager for America to enter the war, the British objected, and Chiang Kai-shek denounced the suggestion violently. If the embargo were relaxed, he said, the Chinese people "would consider that China had been completely sacrificed. The Chinese army will collapse . . . an unparalleled catastrophe." Roosevelt dropped the proposed modus vivendi.

The Japanese gave their diplomats five additional days, postponing the deadline from November 25 to November 30. On the evening of November 25, the president met with the "War Cabinet"—the secretary of state, the secretary of war, the secretary of the navy, and the army and navy chiefs of staff—at the White House. The president told them that America was likely to be attacked as early as Monday, December 1. "The question," wrote Secretary of War Stimson in his diary, "was how we should maneuver them into the position of firing the first shot without allowing too much danger to ourselves." One of their decisions was to instruct Hull to hand the Japanese the Note of November 26, an unyielding statement that America did not wish to continue negotiations unless Japan was ready to meet U.S. demands. It demanded that Japan:

1. Withdraw Japanese troops from Indochina
2. Pull out of China and support no government there other than that of Chiang Kai-shek
3. Disavow the Tripartite Pact
4. Sign nonaggression treaties with China, Thailand, the Netherlands, Britain, the Soviet Union, and the United States.

When Hull gave him the note, Japan's Ambassador Saburo Kurusu, reported Hull, "turned white." Kurusu said that he felt that it "meant the end" because it gave the Japanese "the alternative of surrendering to the United States or of fighting." Hull told Stimson: "I have washed my hands of it, and it is now in the hands of you and Knox, the army and navy." A message to Admiral Husband Kimmel, commander of America's Pacific fleet, read: "This dispatch is to be considered a war warning." Hull told the British to expect Japan to move "suddenly and with every element of surprise."

The Note of November 26 silenced peace advocates in Japan, and a December 1 imperial conference gave the go-ahead for war. Later, Tojo said that the Japanese, viewing the note as an "ultimatum," decided that, "rather than await extinction it were better to face death by breaking through the encircling ring to find a way for existence."

The British were fearful that the Japanese forces advancing on the East Indies might avoid contact with U.S. forces and that the Dutch and British would find themselves at war with Japan without U.S. participation. At the Atlantic Conference, Churchill had persuaded Roosevelt to warn Japan that an attack on the British or Dutch would cause America to "take steps." Now he urgently pressed for a stronger commitment. Finally, on December 3, after the cabinet unanimously assured him that Congress would support such a move, Roosevelt told the British that if the Japanese attacked them, America would immediately give "armed support." He also prepared a possible war message to Congress in which he made the case that an attack on British or Dutch possessions would justify war.

The advance of Japanese troopships toward the Dutch East Indies raised the question of how far the United States should allow Japan's convoys to go before firing on them. Americans decided that it would be too risky to allow them to proceed any farther south than the southern tip of Indochina. At that time, the president decided, he would make a personal appeal to the emperor; afterwards, when the Japanese hit Thailand or British or Dutch possessions, he would ask Congress to declare war. On December 6, when the Japanese rounded the southern tip of Indochina, Roosevelt appealed to the emperor to withdraw his troops from southern Indochina.

On December 6, Japanese embassy personnel began burning documents, an indication that war was imminent. That afternoon, the Japanese government began to radio to its Washington embassy its reply to the note of November 26. U.S. decoding machines deciphered it immediately, and by evening enough of it had been received that Roosevelt concluded: "This means war." By 3:10 A.M., December 7, more than ten hours before the attack on Pearl Harbor, Americans had decoded the last section of the message, which amounted to a declaration of war.

Tokyo ordered the Japanese ambassador to deliver the message to Hull at 1:00 P.M. Unknown to the ambassador, this would be only twenty-five minutes before the scheduled attack on the U.S. naval base at Pearl Harbor. Marshall prepared a warning to the Hawaii commanders that the Japanese were scheduled to deliver an ultimatum at 1:00 P.M. "Just what the significance of the hour set may have we do not know, but be on alert accordingly." Incredibly, instead of using the telephone, military wire, or radio, he sent this message by Western Union, and it did not arrive until seven hours after the attack.

Having destroyed their decoding machine and sent their American secretaries home, the Japanese had to use Japanese personnel to type the message and were late for their appointment. Hull kept them waiting further until 2:20. The Note of November 26, said the Japanese reply, ignored Japan's sacrifices in four years of fighting in China, menaced Japan's existence, and disparaged its honor, making it "impossible to reach an agreement through further negotiation." After pretending to read the message, Hull replied that it was "crowded with infamous falsehoods and distortions."

Americans had not been tracking the six Japanese aircraft carriers which, with escorting vessels, had set out on November 25 and moved, with their radios silent, to a spot 230 miles north of Hawaii. Their mission was to bomb the U.S. fleet before it could disrupt Japan's invasion of the East Indies. On Sunday morning, December 7, at 7:55 A.M. Hawaiian time (1:25 P.M. Washington time), the first 171 Japanese planes hit the completely surprised Americans at Pearl Harbor. In two hours of bombing and strafing, they sank two battleships, temporarily disabled six battleships, and destroyed 188 planes, causing the deaths of 2,348 Americans (see Fig. 5.1). The Japanese lost only twenty-nine planes, one submarine, five midget submarines, and fifty-five dead. They were disappointed to find no aircraft carriers, which were to be the decisive weapons in the Pacific war, and, worried about a possible counterattack from some undetected carrier, they called off a planned second-wave attack on oil storage tanks.

The attack on Pearl Harbor was a great military victory for Japan, for it immobilized America's Pacific fleet and allowed the Japanese to secure desperately needed oil. But this victory came at a terrible political cost. It united the American people in flaming anger and resolve to avenge what they saw as an unprovoked sneak attack. The isolationist Senator Burton K. Wheeler said, "There is nothing to do now but to lick hell out of them," and Lindbergh sought to join the air force. Stimson was relieved that war "had come in a way that will unite all our people," and Harry Hopkins felt that "Japan had given us an opportunity" to enter the war against Hitler. Roosevelt said that Pearl Harbor made it possible for him to send troops to Europe. The attack was a "blessing," wrote Churchill, that "brought America wholeheartedly into the war" and meant "we had won."

On December 8, Roosevelt addressed a joint session of Congress. "Yesterday, December 7, 1941—a date which will live in infamy—America was sud-

Figure 5.1 The December 1941 Japanese surprise attack on the U.S. fleet in Hawaii aroused a fierce popular demand for punishment of Japan. National Archives.

denly and deliberately attacked by naval and air forces of the Empire of Japan," an attack, he said, that was "unprovoked and dastardly." The Senate voted unanimously to declare war and, in the House, only Jennette Rankin, who had voted against entry into World War I, voted nay.

On December 11, Germany and Italy, honoring the Tripartite Pact, declared war on the United States. America had moved from unneutrality to "open acts of war against Germany," charged the German government. Roosevelt further defined the war: "The forces endeavoring to enslave the entire world are now moving toward this hemisphere. Never before has there been a greater challenge to life, liberty, and civilization." But, he said, united effort by peoples who were "determined to remain free" would "insure a world victory of the forces of justice and righteousness over the forces of savagery and barbarism."

Postmortems

Traditional historians stress that Japan's moves were so aggressive, menacing, and morally reprehensible that they gave America no choice but to actively oppose them, and also that accidents, mistakes, and misunderstandings contributed to the breakdown of negotiations.

Later, some noninterventionists, Roosevelt critics, and historians would question Roosevelt's version of the events that led to war. They maintained that Roosevelt, having failed to win popular support for war with Germany, had taken measures, particularly the freezing of Japan's assets, that were lethal to Japan and coupled them with demands that no nation could reasonably be expected to accept. Revisionist historians have speculated that Roosevelt forced Japan to fight because he knew that it would silence opponents of war, and thus bring Americans wholeheartedly into the war with Germany through the back door. Many historians came to accept at least part of this "back-door theory." The army historian Louis Morton concluded that America gave Japan "no honorable alternative" but to attack, a conclusion that the diplomatic historian Thomas A. Bailey amended to no alternative at all.

An additional theory, constructed atop the back-door theory, was advanced by America's military commanders at Hawaii, Admiral Husband E. Kimmel and General Walter C. Short, who charged that Roosevelt deliberately withheld from them information on the imminence of war to prevent them from taking defensive measures that might cause the Japanese to cancel the assault. Thus, they charged, he exposed Pearl Harbor as a sitting duck to tempt the Japanese to attack. This "sitting duck theory" is less widely accepted. Americans knew that an attack in the Far East was imminent and, in January, Ambassador Grew warned that a surprise attack on Pearl Harbor was likely, and, a few weeks before Pearl Harbor, Secretary of the Navy Frank Knox wrote Stimson that "hostilities would be initiated by a surprise attack on Pearl Harbor." Nevertheless it is possible that most officials expected the Japanese to attack other targets.

In any case, the evidence seems to indicate that Roosevelt put Japan in a position in which its leaders felt that their choice was between abject surrender and fighting. Apparently Roosevelt was not forced unwillingly into war but believed that America's interest demanded an Allied victory, even if that required U.S. participation. Further, it appears that America entered the war for reasons that pertained at least as much to Europe as to Asia.

What underlay the Roosevelt administration's perception of the Axis as intolerably threatening to U.S. interests and security? Denunciations of the Axis concentrated on the danger that its ideology and systems presented to the American way of life. There was much condemnation of dictatorship, militarism, expansionism, anti-Semitism, and socialism. Also, Germany and Japan were economic rivals and, given the high degree of government control of their economies, if victorious, they might have excluded Americans from markets in Europe and China. Possibly more basic was the U.S. fear of the effect that an Axis victory might have on the balance of power; if Germany won, it might achieve such enormous power that it could threaten U.S. interests everywhere.

In addition, many Americans, particularly idealistic intellectuals, were eager for America to play a larger role in world affairs. They were convinced that America had developed a superior form of government, culture, and economy and that, free of the ancient irrational hatreds that bedeviled the old world, it was uniquely qualified to help elevate other world areas into a new era of peace and prosperity. This, they believed, was America's great mission, and, consequently, isolationism was morally wrong. Few of them doubted that an enlarged U.S. role would be beneficial, and many were confident that defeat of the evil Axis would usher in a new and better postwar world.

Despite the cumulative appeal of these motives, a large number of Americans were never convinced that U.S. interests demanded entry into World War II and were largely unaware of the steps that led to war. A 1948 poll showed that eight of ten Americans believed that, at the time of Pearl Harbor, Roosevelt should have been trying to keep the United States out of the war.

Also, some of those who shared Roosevelt's conviction that entry into the war was essential nevertheless regretted the deviousness, misrepresentation, and manipulation of public opinion he employed. This, they feared, short-circuited democracy and set unfortunate precedents that future presidents might follow in pursuit of less defensible aims.

In any case, the great debate had been resolved. Henceforth, for better or for worse, America would participate fully in the international politics of both Europe and Asia.

6 Wartime Diplomacy

The United States at War

Modern war requires mobilization, not only of armed forces, but of civilian populations to produce quantities of arms, ammunition, food, and transportation for the armed forces. This mobilization necessitates a vast expansion of government functions, controls, and personnel. In World War II, the government assumed the power to conscript men into the armed services, allocate raw materials, convert factories to arms production, ration consumer goods, set prices, ban strikes, imprison without trial, and censor speech and press. Between 1941 and 1945, in a vast explosion of government, Washington spent twice as much money as it had spent in all of previous U.S. history.

The wartime output of the U.S. economy was impressive. Although 15 million potential members of the labor force were taken into the armed services, and much of what was produced was devoted to destruction, economic production soared from $111 billion in 1939 to $184 billion in 1944 (in constant dollars), a 72 percent rise. Industrial output doubled. Production of ships and tanks reached startling highs, and in 1944 America manufactured more than ninety-six thousand airplanes. The Axis nations could not hope to destroy more than a fraction of them—U.S. production inundated them.

The direct cost of the war was $341 billion. To raise that enormous sum, the government raised the top income tax rate to 94 percent, imposed sales taxes on nearly everything, and levied an excess profits tax. It also borrowed huge sums, partly by pressuring the public to buy war bonds, which raised the national debt from $49 billion in 1941 to $259 billion in 1945.

The Pearl Harbor attack so united the people that there seemed to be little need for the government to suppress opposition to the war. Nevertheless, Washington imposed censorship, issued a vast flood of prowar propaganda, and required aliens to keep the government apprised of their movements. Thirty alleged fascists were put on trial.

Japanese-Americans were harshly treated. Although accused of no crimes, the 110,000 who lived in West Coast states, two-thirds of whom were American citizens, were arrested and placed in "relocation centers," which some critics called "America's concentration camps" and where most were held for the duration of the war. They had to sell farms, homes, and businesses, while much of their property, including bank accounts, was seized. The American Civil Liberties Union called this "the worst single wholesale violation of civil rights of American citizens in our history." The official rationale was that they were arrested, not only because of misgivings regarding their loyalty, but also to prevent them from being mistaken for the enemy if the Japanese invaded. However, the larger number of Japanese in Hawaii were not arrested. Perhaps the imprisonment of West Coast Japanese lent plausibility to Roosevelt's charge that the Axis was moving on the Western Hemisphere and, therefore, to the sense of danger that stimulated Americans to mobilize. No Japanese-Americans were convicted of disloyalty, and two brigades of Japanese-American troops received more medals for heroism than any other brigades in the U.S. Army. Not until 1989 did Congress vote survivors partial compensation for their wartime economic losses.

In the 1944 election, the first wartime presidential election since 1864, both parties shifted to the right. After liberal Republican Wendell Willkie lost in the primaries, he was replaced as party leader by Thomas E. Dewey who, for his running mate, chose an extreme right-wing senator, John W. Bricker. The Democrats replaced liberal Vice President Henry Wallace with moderate, Harry Truman. Maintaining that Roosevelt was the world leader best qualified to win the war and the peace, Democrats nominated him for a fourth term. During the campaign, Dewey discovered that America had broken Japan's secret codes before Pearl Harbor, but he was persuaded not to use that information on the grounds that it might help Japan. However, Clare Booth Luce, the prominent wife of the publisher of *Time* and *Life*, charged that Roosevelt had "lied us into a war because he did not have the political courage to lead us into it." Roosevelt got 26 million votes to Dewey's 22 million, while several noninterventionist congressmen went down in defeat.

Military Fronts

At the outset of the war, the Axis had possessed an initial advantage because it had begun preparing for war earlier. However, as a group, the Allies had much more of the basic ingredients of power—industry, population, and resources—and, in time, they could mobilize larger and better-equipped forces. Consequently, to win, the Axis nations had to employ their initial superiority to knock out the Allies before they could fully arm or, failing that, seize enough territory and resources to enable them to withstand an Allied counteroffensive. Thus, the early part of the war saw an Axis lunge to advance as fast and as far as possible.

In the European area, Germans and Italians overran Romania, Yugoslavia, Greece, Mediterranean islands, and the north coast of Africa. After June 1941 the Germans advanced over vast stretches of the Soviet Union, an invasion to which they committed the bulk of their armed forces and in which they suffered 80 percent of their casualties. They encircled Leningrad, but could not capture it and advanced to the outskirts of Moscow before being repulsed. Their deepest penetration came in south Russia where they reached the Volga River at Stalingrad. In North Africa, Germans and Italians drove into Egypt, where the British held them short of Cairo at El Alamein. By October 1942, the Axis had reached its European theater high-water mark.

Tokyo's original plan called for seizing the Dutch East Indies, the Philippines, Malaya, Singapore, Thailand, and Burma, plus a number of islands in the western Pacific on which to build airstrips, "unsinkable aircraft carriers," to defend against the U.S. counterattack. But the unexpected extent of their success at Pearl Harbor made them so overconfident that they attempted to take southern New Guinea, the Solomon Islands, and Midway, tasks that proved, as they had originally calculated, beyond their strength. For example, in June 1942, when they moved against Midway, they lost four aircraft carriers, which broke the back of their offensive naval strength. In the summer of 1942 Americans began a counteroffensive.

In November 1942, the Allies also seized the offensive in the European theater. British tanks sent the Germans reeling in retreat from Egypt, and the first American troops landed in North Africa. Also in November, the Russians counterattacked at Stalingrad, pinched off a 350,000-man German army, and recaptured that city in February 1943. The Axis gamble on a quick knockout had failed; now the question was whether they could hold out against Allied counterattacks.

Implacably, Allied forces gathered strength and momentum. By the end of May 1943, they had killed or captured the large number of German and Italian troops in North Africa. In July they invaded Sicily, which fell in a month. In September they invaded mainland Italy. Italy quickly surrendered (September 8, 1943), but eleven German divisions continued to hold most of the country, and not until June 1944 did the Allies capture Rome. Meanwhile, in a series of great battles, the Russians expelled the Germans from the Soviet Union; in January 1944 they entered Poland.

Meanwhile, the war raged in the air and at sea. The Germans had entered the war with a large air force which they used not only to attack Allied shipping and military targets, but to bomb British cities. Technological development made German submarines dismayingly effective, and in 1942 they sank 8 million tons of Allied merchant ships, far outpacing the replacement capacity of Allied shipyards. Rapidly increasing production of submarine-hunting ships and planes, the Allies, with the help of new antisubmarine technology, including radar, sank 237 German submarines in 1943 and 241 in 1944. These successes largely defeated the submarine menace.

Although Allied propaganda denounced the Axis for slaughtering civilians, the Allies, concluding that they must fight fire with fire, soon adopted many of the practices they had condemned. Shortly after Pearl Harbor, America joined the British in enforcing the long-range blockade, including a food blockade, of German-occupied areas, and adopted "unrestricted air and submarine warfare."

With U.S. aid, the British enlarged their air force and carried the war to the Germans. By May 1942, finding daylight bombing of specific targets costly and inefficient, the British began using large numbers of bombers flying in formation, often at night, to drop bombs in a pattern designed to obliterate an entire area. Of course this produced numerous civilian casualties—a 1942 area bombing of Hamburg killed 40,000 people. At first Americans objected to "area bombing," but they later adopted it. As many as 6,000 bombers hit Europe in a single night. At the cost of 40,000 airplanes and 158,000 personnel, the Allies dropped nearly 3 million tons of bombs. Estimates of the number of civilians they killed range from 305,000 to several million. Particularly spectacular were the twenty-four-hour bombing of Dresden, Germany, in February 1945, which may have killed more than 200,000 persons, and the March 1945 fire-bomb raid on Tokyo, which ignited fifteen square miles of the city. One or the other of these raids was history's greatest man-made disaster.

On June 6, 1944, "D-Day," U.S., British, and Canadian forces landed in France, and within two weeks a million men had gone ashore. On August 25 they captured Paris. In September, Romania, Finland, and Bulgaria surrendered to the Russians, while the British recaptured Athens. A December German counterattack, the "Battle of the Bulge," delayed the U.S. advance, but, in March 1945, U.S. troops crossed the Rhine as Russians poured into eastern Germany. On April 30, Hitler committed suicide, and on May 8 German resistance ceased—five years and eight months after Germany had invaded Poland.

Meanwhile, "island-hopping" Americans, utilizing air bombardment and naval shelling followed by marine landings, advanced west across the Pacific islands. In June 1944, they captured Saipan, from which U.S. bombers could strike Tokyo. In October, U.S. forces landed in the Philippines and, in the Battle of Leyte Gulf, history's greatest naval battle, destroyed most of Japan's remaining naval strength and cut Japan's vital link with Indonesian oil fields. In April 1945 U.S. troops landed on Okinawa, less than four hundred miles southwest of Japan. On August 6 America dropped an atomic bomb on Hiroshima, on August 8 the Soviets entered the war, and on August 14 Japan surrendered.

Estimated war spending by all governments totaled $1,117 billion. Including property damage, the war cost approximately $4,000 billion. With more civilians than soldiers killed, deaths totaled more than 55 million. America suffered 405,395 battle deaths, the British 400,000, and Japan 2.5 million. Germany lost about 6 million soldiers, the Russians lost 7.5 million, and China lost 10 million.

The Holocaust

The Allies had imposed a food blockade on German-occupied Europe. Long considered illegal, a food blockade had its first impact not on enemy armed forces but on civilians, especially the poor, the elderly, and the young. Also, if the blockade succeeded in producing malnutrition, inhabitants of the blockaded enemy area who opposed the government would be among the first to suffer. The Allied food blockade did succeed in causing serious food shortages, and many thousands of Belgians, French, Greeks, Poles, Gypsies, and Jews died from starvation or from diseases worsened by malnutrition. While some Americans urged that it be relaxed to save friendly civilian populations, others argued that a food shortage would goad people into revolting against the Nazis.

The Nazis marked the Jews for special cruelty. According to Nazi dogma, German Jews constituted not only a different religious group, but a different nationality; thus, they were foreigners who could not give their first loyalty to Germany and should be removed from positions of influence in Germany's economic and political life. The 1935 Nuremberg Laws stripped Jews of all political rights. Furthermore, the Nazis argued, Jews must be removed to preserve the purity of the Aryan race. Before World War II, Nazi policy was to segregate them and expel them from Germany, but other countries would accept only a limited number. Between 1937 and 1941 America admitted only eight thousand German Jews annually.

In 1941, the Nazis began a policy, "The Final Solution," of exterminating Jews. Not only the Jews of Germany, but of Poland, the Soviet Union, and other conquered areas were put in concentration camps, including Auschwitz, Dachau, and Buchenwald, to be put to death by shooting, starvation, and gas chambers. Americans received reliable evidence of this policy by 1941. Nevertheless, between 1941 and 1945, tightening immigration controls to prevent the possible entry of spies, America admitted only 20,000 European Jews. However, in January 1944, Roosevelt established the War Refugees Board which set up refugee camps in Europe and the Middle East and helped save 200,000 Jews. Estimates of the total number killed in the Holocaust range as high as 6 million of the 10 million Jewish residents of German-occupied Europe. The Holocaust was one of history's ghastliest episodes, an instance of militaristic nationalism and racism carried to insanity.

As advancing U.S. troops came across evidence of the existence of death camps, and also saw underfed Allied prisoners of war, American hatred of Germans, long building, flared to new highs. Some German prisoners in America and Europe were deliberately underfed. To avoid the requirement that German prisoners of war in Europe be well fed, Eisenhower had them reclassified as displaced persons, and many captive Germans died.

Economic Cooperation

During the war the Allies achieved much economic cooperation. In November 1943, forty-four nations established the United Nations Relief and Reconstruction Administration (UNRRA), to which they pledged 1 percent of their national incomes, to assist peoples liberated from the Axis. By 1946 UNRRA had spent $4 billion, of which America contributed 75 percent. Half of this aid went to China, Italy, Greece, and Austria, and the other half to eastern European nations, including Poland and Russia. It provided food, medical care, and shelter until 1947, when Washington halted funding.

During the war, America continued its efforts to reduce obstacles to the worldwide flow of U.S. products and investments. For example, Americans forced the British to open their empire to U.S. goods. With almost religious fervor, Secretary of State Hull continued to pursue his goal of enlarging international trade which he regarded as the key to economic progress and international peace.

In the 1930s, competitive devaluations of national currencies had harmed international trade. Hoping to prevent a recurrence, leaders of the Allied nations decided to restore a system of fixed exchange rates to stabilize the value of each nation's money in relation to the money of other nations. They agreed to maintain the value of the U.S. dollar at $35 per ounce of gold and to fix the value of other currencies in terms of dollars, and each country promised to maintain a large reserve of gold and dollars to prevent its money from changing in value. To further stabilize national currencies and facilitate international payments, forty-four nations, meeting at Bretton Woods, New Hampshire, in July 1944, established an International Monetary Fund and provided it with $8.8 billion, of which America furnished $2.75 billion.

Also at Bretton Woods they established the International Bank for Reconstruction and Development (World Bank), which they provided with $9 billion, $3.2 billion from America. Its purpose was to lend money to nations whose economies had been devastated by the war, or that were underdeveloped, to help them lift industrial and agricultural production. The World Bank made loans to governments and also to private enterprises when repayment was guaranteed by governments. Because each member nation cast votes in the bank's governing bodies in proportion to the shares of stock it held in the bank, provision by the United States of more than one-third of the bank's capital gave it the dominant voice. The bank's headquarters was located in Washington, and its president was an American.

Charging that these institutions were designed to open the world to U.S. investments, trade, and influence, the Soviets declined to join the International Monetary Fund or the World Bank. (For further information on the operation of the World Bank see chapter 13)

The United Nations Alliance

Preserving good wartime relations among allies is usually difficult. The nations in a wartime coalition normally have differing perceptions of the war and conflicting goals. They may be enemies who have only temporarily shelved their animosities to cooperate against a greater common threat. Normally, they are haunted by fear that an ally might make a "separate peace" and secure favorable terms in return for deserting the common cause. Consequently, they deal with each other very circumspectly. Sometimes they avoid discussing issues that might divide them, and fail to make adequate preparations for postwar problems.

After the Pearl Harbor attack, representatives of the nations then at war with the Axis met in Washington and, on January 1, 1942, signed the Declaration of the United Nations. They fought, they said, in defense of life, liberty, independence, religious freedom, human rights, and justice against "savage and brutal forces seeking to subjugate the world." Pledging to devote their full resources to the war, they promised to make no separate peace and to uphold the principles of the Atlantic Charter. This alliance grew to forty-seven nations. Although one of America's most significant international pacts, it was only an executive agreement that was never submitted to the Senate.

Largely relegating the State Department to the background, Roosevelt kept control of America's wartime international relations in his own hands. Savoring the drama of high-level meetings, he had great confidence in his ability, through personal charm and geniality, to bring others into agreement.

Summit conferences were still relatively new and dramatic, and Roosevelt carried this form of diplomacy to a new high. During the war he met Britain's Prime Minister Winston Churchill six times in Washington, once in Casablanca, and twice in Quebec, and the two met once with China's President Chiang Kai-shek at Cairo. The three heads of government of Britain, the Soviet Union, and the United States assembled three times: at Teheran, Iran, in November 1943, at Yalta, in Russia, in February 1945, and at Potsdam, Germany, in July 1945.

Wartime Relations with Britain

America's wartime relations with England were close. Roosevelt and Churchill greatly admired each other and enjoyed each other's company. When in Washington, Churchill stayed in the White House. They shared a spirit of adventure, a delight in directing military affairs, and a sense of making history. Once Roosevelt told Churchill: "It's fun to be in the same century with you." Churchill had cause to be enthusiastic—he had worked long to bring America into the war and believed that U.S. entry ensured Allied victory.

The British and the Americans established a Combined Chiefs of Staff to coordinate their strategy, and a Joint Munitions Assignment Board to allocate arms and ammunition. They integrated Canadian and U.S. industrial production, while Americans built the Alcan highway through Canada to Alaska. They set up a joint British, American, and Dutch command for the Pacific theater. They agreed to give priority to defeating Germany, and also to completely crush and severely punish the Axis. By 1945, six of ten Americans favored making the alliance permanent.

But even these cordial allies had serious disputes. Americans had an anti-imperialism tradition, and Roosevelt shared the disapproval with which many American liberals viewed Britain's treatment of its subject peoples. "As a people, as a country, we're opposed to imperialism," Roosevelt told a writer. "We can't stomach it." He suggested that Britain return Hong Kong to China and concede independence to India. When he asked Churchill when he was going to apply the Atlantic Charter in these areas, Churchill replied that he had told Wendell Willkie that the Atlantic Charter already applied in the British Empire. Roosevelt retorted: "Is that what killed him?" An ardent imperialist who called Mahatma Gandhi "that nasty little native," Churchill was not amused. "I have not become the King's First Minister," he told Parliament, "to preside over the liquidation of the British Empire."

They also disagreed on when and where their armies should land in Europe. Basing the judgment on purely military considerations, Americans wanted to send troops as soon as possible across the English Channel onto the north European plain, where no major geographical obstacles lay between them and the heart of German power. Churchill, who was anxious to defend Britain's line of communication with India, avoid a repetition of England's huge World War I manpower losses, and strengthen Britain's postwar position vis-à-vis Russia, preferred to concentrate Allied operations in the Mediterranean. He wanted to retake Crete and Rhodes, force Turkey to join the war, and then invade, through Greece, the "soft underbelly of Europe." This would put British and American forces in the Balkan Peninsula in a position to hold it against possible Soviet expansion. Roosevelt, who sought to persuade his allies to forget ancient enmities, and who argued that postwar political concerns "must be definitely secondary to the primary operations of striking at the heart of Germany," worked hard for an early cross-Channel operation. Churchill delayed it until June 1944.

The British approach to Russia was in the tradition of power politics. Britain sought to reestablish its power in the Balkans, limit the destruction of Germany, and restore France in order to counterbalance Soviet power. Roosevelt, while refusing to recognize Soviet annexation of the Baltic states, envisioned a new international system in which the four great powers—America, Russia, Britain, and China—would police the world; to achieve this required winning Stalin's trust and cooperation.

The British were not impressed by American criticism of the prewar system of spheres of influence and power politics. They maintained that the Monroe Doctrine made the Western Hemisphere a U.S. sphere of influence. And, grumbled Churchill, "Is having a navy twice as strong as any other nation 'power politics' . . . is having all the gold in the world buried in a cavern 'power politics'?"

England and America differed even more in their approaches to China. The British, once dominant in central China, had lost influence there, first to the Japanese and then to the Americans, who were supplying and assisting China's military forces. Possession of Hong Kong made the British a target of Chinese nationalists, and they had no desire to see China become a major power. Americans, on the other hand, regarded China as a friend. Counting on China's support on postwar issues, Roosevelt sought to promote China to big-power status. Regarding the attempt to give weak China great-power status as "an absolute farce," Churchill worried that China might become "a faggot vote on the side of the United States in any attempt to liquidate the British Empire."

Despite these differences, Roosevelt and Churchill maintained close cooperation and cordial personal relations throughout the war.

A Troubled Friendship with China

When the United States entered the war, China was hanging on the ropes after four and a half years of Japan's onslaught. The Japanese had seized China's eastern provinces, but, refusing to surrender, Chiang Kai-shek had retreated with his government west beyond the Yangtzi River gorges to Chungking. His armies were large but poorly equipped and poorly fed, and his only land artery to the outside world was the incredibly twisting Burma Road.

The Chinese had hoped for a large inflow of U.S. weapons and supplies, and the U.S. public (by 62 to 25 percent in February 1942) favored throwing America's strength first against Japan. But the Japanese overran Burma, cutting the last sea or land route for supplying China, which restricted China to the small amount of supplies that could be flown in from India. Thus, the first effects of U.S. entry damaged China.

Americans were anxious to keep Chungking in the war. They were fond of the Methodist Chiang Kai-shek and his American-educated wife, and Chiang's resistance tied down large numbers of Japanese troops and prevented Japan from fully utilizing China's resources. Moreover, Japanese propaganda sought to depict the war as a struggle to liberate Asians from white rule, and it was important to have China on America's side to reduce that slogan's appeal. Furthermore, Americans sought a strong, united, and friendly postwar China to help prevent a post war Japanese resurgence, and to counterbalance Soviet power in East Asia.

Before Pearl Harbor, America had given China Lend-Lease aid plus planes and pilots. In February 1942, Washington gave China a $500-million loan, with no strings attached. In the same month Roosevelt sent a general, Joseph Stilwell, to command U.S. troops in the area and to serve as Chiang's chief of staff. Chiang gave Stilwell command of the Chinese army sent to help the British defend Burma. In that campaign, Stilwell, badly defeated, lost much of China's small supply of modern weapons. When Americans diverted promised warplanes from China to the Mediterranean, Chiang complained that China was not being treated as an equal.

To sustain Chinese morale, the United States and Britain renounced the sovereignty-violating special rights that they had extracted in the previous century, including extraterritoriality (exemption from Chinese law) and the right to station troops in China. America also made the Chinese eligible for immigration and for U.S. citizenship. Promising to help China recover all the territories it lost to Japan, Roosevelt insisted that Britain and Russia accord China the status of one of the "Big Four" world powers. In November 1943, he and Churchill met with Chiang at Cairo and promised an all-out effort to retake Burma and to restore China's communications with the outside world (see Fig. 6.1).

Despite the friendly feelings Roosevelt and most Americans had for China, which many Chinese reciprocated, much friction developed. The undiplomatic fifty-eight-year-old Stilwell, whose nickname was "Vinegar Joe," admired Chinese soldiers, but showed Chinese leaders little respect. Chiang blamed the Burma defeat on Stilwell's insubordination and strategic errors. Furthermore, some of his activities threatened Chiang's control. Chiang's government was a military regime held together by the personal loyalty of his military commanders, and Stilwell sought to reorganize China's armies on the U.S. model, heedless of the effect on Chiang's political power. Also, Stilwell was eager to launch offensives against the Japanese, while Chiang

Figure 6.1 In November 1943 President Franklin Roosevelt and British Prime Minister Winston Churchill met at Cairo, Egypt, with China's Generalissimo Chiang Kai-shek and his wife. The hatless general behind Roosevelt is Joseph Stilwell. National Archives.

sought to conserve military forces to sustain his postwar position against Communists, warlords, and Russians.

Chiang's obstruction of his plans infuriated Stilwell. His terms for the Generalissimo ranged from "Peanut" to "snake manure," and he made no attempt to keep his opinions secret. Controlling all Lend-Lease aid to China, Stilwell from time to time withheld supplies to pressure Chiang. Chiang hoped that America would replace Stilwell, and Roosevelt told army Chief of Staff George C. Marshall that Stilwell's approach was wrong, that Chiang could not be coerced as if he were a minor sultan. But Stilwell was Marshall's personal friend, and Marshall and Secretary of War Stimson, while urging Stilwell to be more tactful, resisted his recall.

After the loss of the Burma Road, Americans flew supplies into China from India. It was a hazardous flight over "the hump" (the Himalayas), to Kunming, and, until 1945, the tonnage carried was small. Giving priority to the European theater, the Americans and the British delayed committing troops and ships to retaking Burma, while urging Chiang to undertake that task alone.

Stilwell finally secured Chiang's consent to reinvade Burma, but only with the Chinese troops Americans had trained and equipped in India. When the invasion encountered heavy opposition, Stilwell and Roosevelt successfully demanded that Chiang send additional forces from China. In a campaign that is considered brilliant, Chinese troops led by Stilwell captured the Japanese airfield at Myitkyna in May 1944, but there his drive stalled short of reopening the road to China.

Meanwhile, Americans gave priority to General Claire Chennault's efforts to build airfields in East China and to launch an air campaign against Japanese shipping. Americans also stationed newly developed long-range B-29 superbombers in China to bomb Japan. Responding in the spring of 1944, the Japanese launched their largest land offensive of the China war and quickly overran U.S. airbases and large areas of East China.

Blaming this disaster on Chinese generals, Roosevelt demanded that Chiang turn over full command of his armies to Stilwell, a demand that Stilwell rudely presented to Chiang at a party. A poem Stilwell wrote to commemorate the occasion contained the line: "Oh the blessed pleasure, I wrecked the Peanut's face." Chiang could not consent and survive. Also, Stilwell sought to arm the Communists, which could be fatal to Chiang, and even plotted to replace Chiang. In November 1944, Chiang successfully demanded that Roosevelt recall Stilwell.

This rebuff reduced America's emotional commitment to China. Reevaluating the need for China's help, U.S. military men concluded that the U.S. advance across the Pacific was going well and that Russia's promise to enter the war with Japan reduced the need for Chinese troops to defeat the Japanese in Manchuria. To ensure Russia's entry, Roosevelt agreed to large Soviet gains in East Asia, partly at China's expense.

Although Americans had arrived in China with generally favorable attitudes toward China, many of them soon became critical, at least of Chiang's regime. They were offended by its censorship, its secret police, and its use of U.S.-furnished military equipment against Chinese Communists. They found it overstaffed, inefficient, corrupt, and callous toward the poor and troops. Some even called Chiang's regime "fascist."

Gradually, Americans grew more aware that China had two governments—the nationalist government of Chiang Kai-shek and a Communist government headed by Mao Tse-tung. In 1936, after a long civil war, Chiang's generals had forced him to stop fighting the Communists and to join with them in a united front against the Japanese. After the Japanese expelled Chiang's forces from North China, the Communists organized guerrilla resistance in the countryside behind Japanese lines and, by 1944, ruled about 75 million people. Alarmed by their expansion, Chiang, regarding their challenge, a "disease of the heart," as more dangerous than that of the Japanese, "a disease of the skin," stationed his best-armed divisions around their areas to block further expansion. Americans, who wanted to use all of China's armed men against the Japanese, urged him to come to terms with the Communists, possibly admitting them into a coalition government.

When Roosevelt sent Vice President Henry Wallace to China in the summer of 1944, Wallace successfully insisted that Chiang permit Americans to establish contact with the Chinese Communists, whose north China bases were well located for attacking Japanese. The U.S. military men who went to the Communist capital, Yenan, called themselves the "Dixie Mission" because they entered rebel territory. They, U.S. newsmen, and Foreign Service officers reported that Communist leaders were less corrupt, more modern, more democratic, and more active in fighting the Japanese than were Chiang and his regime. Also, they said, economic conditions in the north were better, and the Communist troops were better fed than Chiang's. So different was all this from Americans' preconceptions of communism that they did not regard the Chinese Reds as true Communists—Roosevelt referred to them as "so-called Communists." Ardently courting Americans, Mao promised to welcome foreign trade and investment and asked to be invited to Washington.

In an attempt to smooth relations with Chiang, Roosevelt sent a "political representative," former secretary of war Patrick Hurley, who threw himself into an attempt to arrange a settlement between Chiang and the Communists. The handsome Texan made an excellent first impression, but he was no China expert. In November 1944, he startled the Communists by making a surprise flight to Yenan, where he deboarded with a war whoop and proposed a merger plan. When the Communists suggested a coalition government, Hurley endorsed their plan. Chiang rejected coalition, but Hurley continued to give him full support. Hurley's visits to Moscow had convinced him that the Soviets did not support the Chinese Communists, and he believed that, as soon as Mao realized that fact, he would accept a subordinate position in Chiang's government.

Those most knowledgeable about China, including Foreign Service officers in China, concluded that the Chinese Communists, although genuine Communists, were also Chinese nationalists, not obedient agents of Moscow, and could be expected to act in China's national interest. They also feared that the Communists, by cutting land rents and giving land to peasants, had won so much popular support that, although poorly armed, they were sure to defeat Chiang in the event of a civil war. Consequently, they advised that America seek good relations with Mao. Also, America's military men were anxious to arm and use Communist troops against the Japanese.

But Chiang and Hurley blocked such action and, in early 1945, Hurley got the dissenting military and diplomatic officers removed from China. Meanwhile, the U.S. Navy contingent in China helped Chiang's secret services hunt down and kill Communists. The war ended amid mutual frustration.

Wartime Relations with the Soviet Union

Hostility between the United States and the Soviet Union had been exacerbated by the 1939 Molotov-Ribbentrop Pact, and by Russia's invasion of Finland. Nevertheless, during the war the two nations achieved much cooperation. Declaring a truce in their propaganda war, they gave each other favorable press treatment. The Soviets were pleased by the Allied decisions to concentrate on defeating Germany first and to completely eliminate German and Japanese military power. Signing the Declaration of the United Nations, they endorsed the principles of the Atlantic Charter and, in an attempt to ease Western fears of world revolution, dissolved the Comintern and encouraged the Communist party in the United States to dissolve itself. Withholding support from the Chinese Communists, they readily agreed to U.S. predominance in China for both the war and the postwar periods.

The U.S. press cited the heroic resistance of Soviet soldiers and civilians to German invaders, Russia's help to America in the American Revolution, War of 1812, and Civil War, and the similarities between the historic drive of the Russians to the east and that of the Americans to the west. *Life* magazine reported that Russians "look like Americans, dress like Americans, and think like Americans." Films such as *Mission to Moscow* depicted Soviet leaders as estimable gentlemen, and Roosevelt termed his relations with Stalin "friendly." America's $10 billion in Lend-Lease aid to Russia, including 18,000 airplanes and 10,000 tanks, equaled nearly 10 percent of Soviet war production.

Nevertheless, old fears and conflicts of interest were merely submerged, and they sometimes resurfaced. Because of horrendous losses to German submarines, shipments of Lend-Lease supplies to the Soviet Union were twice suspended. Some supplies were sent through remote Vladivostok, but that was like supplying Washington through Alaska. The Soviets complained of delays, while Americans, in turn, felt that they received inadequate gratitude for aid, and were offended by Soviet secrecy and refusal to allow U.S. planes to use Soviet airfields. Americans shared atomic secrets with Britain, but not with Russia. The U.S. ambassador called it a "strange alliance."

The most serious friction occured over whether to expand the fighting to a "second front." In history's most powerful invasion, the Germans and their allies sent an incredible 185 divisions into the Soviet Union, and for most of the war the Nazis kept about 80 percent of their army there. They destroyed half of Russia's buildings and killed about 20 million Russians. Frantically the Soviets urged their allies to land troops in Western Europe, a "second front," to draw off some German forces, and the Allied delay in doing so made the Soviets paranoid. Convinced that the West had sought to use Germany and Japan to destroy communism, many Soviets feared that the capitalist nations had not completely abandoned that policy. Their fears were reinforced by statements such as that by Senator Harry Truman that America ought to help the Nazis and Communists kill as many of each other as possible, and by columnist Drew Pearson that State Department policy was to bleed Russia white.

Actually, America's leaders sought early formation of a second front. They maintained that making military decisions on the basis of politics instead of purely military considerations could prolong the war and cost American lives. A landing in northern Europe, they believed, made military sense. The English Channel was narrow, and England was the world's best base for an amphibious operation that would put Anglo-American forces on the great European plain with no natural barriers between them and Berlin.

In May 1942, fearing that Russia might collapse or make a separate peace, Roosevelt told Molotov that he expected to launch a second front in 1942. But, adamantly opposed to an early landing in France, the British insisted that priority be given to operations in the Mediterranean area. U.S. military leaders considered it unpardonable to divert military resources to an indecisive arena, and General Dwight D. Eisenhower warned that giving in to Churchill on this point could cause Russia to surrender, which would be "the blackest day in history."

Roosevelt seemed to believe that Germany and Japan would continue for the foreseeable future to be the main threats to peace. Therefore, he saw the problem of preventing a third world war as the problem of denying Germany and Japan any opportunity to renew aggression. He foresaw a period after the war when the four great powers—the United States, the Soviet Union, Britain, and China—would act as world policemen. If the Big Four could continue to cooperate, he said, no aggressor could start a new war. This made it essential to cultivate cooperation between America and the Soviet Union and to perpetuate the wartime alliance into the postwar period. This would require the West to show consideration for Soviet security needs. If the world were to be run by four big policemen, presumably each would be the top cop in its immediate neighborhood.

Roosevelt and Churchill early sought a Big Three summit with Stalin, but Stalin delayed, citing his need to direct the war personally and also suggesting that the Allies first establish a second front. When he finally accepted, he insisted that they meet him in nearby Iran. When they gathered at Teheran in late November 1943, personal relations among the three leaders were cordial. Roosevelt stayed at the Soviet embassy and, while rejecting private meetings with Churchill to avoid suspicions that they were collaborating against Russia, sought private meetings with Stalin, whom he found "altogether quite impressive." He even suggested that the two of them cooperate against French and British imperialists. The three set a date—May 1944—for an Anglo-American landing in France, Stalin repeated his promise to enter the war against Japan, and Roosevelt offered to help Russia secure access to a naval base and a warm-water port in Manchuria.

Roosevelt expounded on his idea of "four policemen" for the postwar world—America would police North and South America and the Pacific, China the Asian mainland, Britain Western Europe, and the Soviet Union East Europe. Agreeing, Churchill said that wars were started by "hungry" nations, and it would be wise to put "the leading nations in the world in the position of rich, happy men." "We leave here friends in fact, in spirit, and in purpose," read the official statement, and Roosevelt reported to Congress that "we are going to get along well with him [Stalin] and the Russian people—very well indeed."

The Big Three met again, this time in southern Russia, at Yalta on the Black Sea, from February 4 to 11, 1945. With Poland and Romania liberated by advancing Soviet armies and Soviet forces sweeping through Czechoslovakia and Hungary and driving to within forty miles of Berlin, there was urgent need for decisions concerning peace terms and the postwar world. At the Yalta Conference, the Big Three reached more important agreements than at any other wartime conference (see Fig. 6.2).

Roosevelt and Churchill were anxious for the Soviets to enter the war against Japan. Wildly overestimating Japan's strength, U.S. military leaders pre-

Figure 6.2 The February 1945 Big Three conference at Yalta in southern Russia was the war's most important summit conference. Behind Prime Minister Churchill, President Roosevelt, and Premier Josef Stalin stand Britain's Foreign Minister Anthony Eden, U.S. Secretary of State Edward Stettinius, and Russia's Foreign Minister Vyacheslav Molotov.

dicted that defeating Japan would require eighteen months of additional fighting after the defeat of Germany. With China apparently unable to defeat Japanese forces, Russia's help would be needed to overcome the enormously powerful Kwantung army believed to be in Manchuria. Furthermore, if the Soviets remained out of this war, in a reversal of "bleeding white," they could pursue their goals in Europe while American and British forces remained enmeshed in East Asia.

To induce Russia to fight Japan, Roosevelt made his proffers of rewards more explicit. He offered to cooperate in legalizing Russia's annexation of Outer Mongolia, southern Sakhalin, and the Kurile Islands and its control of the Manchurian port of Dairen and a naval base at Port Arthur, and to support joint Soviet-Chinese control of connecting railroads through Manchuria. This secret agreement would restore Russia almost to the position it had held before the Russo-Japanese War of 1904–1905. In return, the Soviets promised to enter the war with Japan within three months after Germany collapsed, to respect China's sovereignty in Manchuria, and to refrain from aiding the Chinese Communists against Chiang. The Chinese were not informed of these arrangements until months later.

The Big Three also grappled with issues involving the postwar control of East Europe, which Churchill called "the most urgent reason for the Yalta Conference." Poland consumed more time than any other subject. Shortly after the 1939 outbreak of war, Russia had annexed the half of prewar Poland that Russia had held before World War I, an expansion Americans were slow to accept. Moreover, Roosevelt refused to recognize Soviet annexation of the Baltic states of Estonia, Latvia, and Lithuania. The British advised that this Soviet expansion was irreversible and should, however reluctantly, be conceded. Roosevelt maintained that, at the least, plebecites should be held. At Teheran, Stalin had told Roosevelt that the Baltic states had voted to join the Soviet Union, a statement Roosevelt did not believe.

The historic corridor for invasions of Russia, Poland was a matter of "life and death for the Soviet Union," said Stalin. At Yalta, the Big Three tacitly accepted Soviet annexation of nearly half of prewar Poland and compensated Poland by giving it large areas of Germany, thus "pushing Poland across the map." But this left unsettled the question of who would govern Poland. In September 1939, when both Germany and Russia had invaded, the Polish government had fled to London to become a government in exile. Churchill arranged a reconciliation between this London government and Russia, but in 1943, when the Polish government demanded an explanation of the Soviet massacre of ten thousand Polish officers, Russia broke diplomatic relations. Collecting some Polish leaders who would serve as his puppets, Stalin set up a rival Polish government at Lublin. With Soviet troops already occupying most of Poland, Roosevelt conceded that Russia had a right to insist on a friendly government in Poland, and he and Churchill reluctantly agreed to acknowledge the Lublin government on the condition that it give some cabinet posts to persons from the London government and hold "free and unfettered elections." This, Roosevelt told a military adviser, was the best he could do for Poland at the time.

As Soviet troops drove the Germans from other nations in east Europe, the British and the Americans grew more anxious to prevent Soviet armies from imposing communism there. At Yalta, they secured adoption of the "Declaration on Liberated Europe," an agreement on procedures for establishing new governments in liberated countries. The agreement called for the creation of governments in accord with the principles of the Atlantic Charter and with "mutual consultations" among the Allies. The first step, it specified, would be to form a provisional government comprising representatives of all anti-Nazi political parties. This government would hold elections, in which all antifascist parties could participate, to choose a permanent government. This seemed to be democratic, but actually an election that excludes any element is not truly democratic, and the declaration allowed Communists to decide which political groups were antifascist. Bitter disputes lay ahead.

At Yalta, the Big Three also made important decisions concerning the United Nations and the treatment of Germany, both of which are discussed later in this chapter.

At the time, leading Americans regarded the Yalta conference as a great success. Harry Hopkins, a Roosevelt adviser at Yalta, wrote that the Soviets had been "reasonable and farseeing" and that "we really believed in our hearts that this was the dawn of the new day we had been praying for." Triumphantly, Roosevelt reported to Congress that the conference marked the beginning of a new age. *Time* magazine called it a "New Dawn" of civilization. Later, as the Cold War developed, the Yalta Conference would be the subject of much controversy. Charges would be made that Churchill and Roosevelt had unnecessarily made concessions to Stalin and thereby ill served America's national interest and strengthened world communism. Roosevelt's defenders replied that, with Soviet armies occupying eastern Europe, the agreements were the best that could be expected, and were counterbalanced by major U.S. gains in securing elections and commitments by Russia to fight Japan and support Chiang Kai-shek.

However, it may have been a mistake to offer the Soviets such huge gains in East Asia to induce them to enter the war with Japan. British Foreign Minister Anthony Eden considered it an error to offer Russia anything to enter a war it was already determined to enter. Also, Russia's military help was not needed. Instead of the estimated eighteen months after Germany's surrender, the Japanese continued fighting for only three months. Also, Chiang's interests might have been better served by keeping the Soviets out of Manchuria. Indeed, a few days before Soviet entry, Truman would express a desire to keep the Soviets out of the Japanese war.

Ideological Compromises with France and Spain

After France surrendered in June 1940, the Germans took control of about half of France, including Paris, but allowed the French to govern southwestern France with a capital at Vichy under the presidency of the aging World War I hero Marshall Henri Petain. The premier was Pierre Laval, who was regarded in the West as a Fascist. The Vichy government remained technically neutral, kept control of the French overseas empire, and withheld the French navy from the Germans.

Despite its ideological distaste for Vichy, Washington recognized the new government and, in July 1942, sent Admiral William D. Leahy as the U.S. ambassador. Americans traded with Vichy and agreed not to seize control of France's Western Hemisphere colonies.

Roosevelt had developed an intense dislike of France. Attributing its quick surrender to degeneracy, he said that it should be punished for collaborating with Germany. Refusing to consider France one of the big powers, he maintained that it should be disarmed and forbidden to reoccupy Indochina. No Frenchman over forty, he told Stalin, should ever again be allowed to hold office.

After Germany defeated France, General Charles de Gaulle had fled to London and, although not France's top military commander, proclaimed himself to be the leader of the "Free French," the French government in exile. In a remarkable performance characterized by sheer gall, he gathered followers and, conducting himself with haughty grandeur, insisted that the Allies treat him as if he were a great power. Both Churchill and Roosevelt heartily disliked him—Churchill said that De Gaulle imagined that he was Joan of Arc. Nevertheless, they gave him some aid.

In November 1942, U.S. and British troops landed in Morocco and Algeria, France's North African colonies. Vichy French troops resisted the landings. Nevertheless, on November 11, the Germans began occupying the part of France governed by Vichy, whereupon Vichy ordered the French fleet sunk rather than allow it to fall into German hands. When Vice Premier Jean Darlan, who was then in Algeria, offered to order French resistance to cease if the Allies would allow him to govern the African colonies, the Allies accepted his offer. The Allies' embarrassment at dealing with him was soon relieved when a young Frenchman assassinated him, following which General Charles de Gaulle elbowed himself into the position of the chief French authority in North Africa. After the 1944 Allied recapture of Paris, the Allies accepted De Gaulle's Free French as France's provisional government.

Relations with Spain presented America with another dilemma requiring some compromise of anti-fascist principle. General Franco, who had seized power with the help of Hitler and Mussolini, was a fascist, and he sent Spanish troops to assist Hitler's invasion of the Soviet Union. Hitler urged him to enter the war, but Franco, arguing that Spain was exhausted by civil war, said that he would need large shipments of German arms and supplies before he could fight.

Obviously, it was to America's interest to keep Spain out of the war. America, in March 1942, renewed trade and sent a distinguished Catholic historian, Carlton J. H. Hayes, as ambassador. To deny Hitler Spain's strategic ores, Americans bought them at prices higher than Hitler could pay. Nevertheless, in November 1942, when U.S. troops landed in North Africa, U.S. commanders positioned large forces to guard against a possible Spanish intervention, which did not occur. As Germany and Japan neared defeat, Franco became more cooperative. America rejected Russia's proposal that the Allies overthrow him, but did not seek Spain's admission to the United Nations.

Wartime Relations with Latin America

Roosevelt's Good Neighbor Policy paid big dividends. U.S. wartime relations with Latin American nations were remarkably friendly, and most Latin American nations supported the war. Shortly after Pearl Harbor, their foreign ministers, meeting in Rio de Janeiro, Brazil, declared that aggression against one of them would be considered aggression against all. All but Argentina broke diplomatic relations with the Axis, and nine declared war, though only Brazil and Mexico sent combat troops. Washington, in turn, gave Lend-Lease aid to all but Argentina; of the $450 million in aid, 80 percent went to Brazil. Some countries received U.S. loans to build war industries.

The big exception was Argentina. Then the wealthiest and most advanced of the Latin American countries, Argentina had many citizens of Italian origin. Located in the temperate zone, it produced many of the same products as the United States, making it an economic competitor, and most of Argentina's trade was with Europe. Argentineans resented U.S. import restrictions on their wheat and beef and also U.S. support for their rival, Brazil.

Argentina's government was a military dictatorship, and, although its military leaders had much sympathy for the fascists, the country remained officially neutral for most of the war. The United States withdrew its ambassador, froze Argentinean gold stocks, and forbade U.S. ships to carry Argentinean products.

In March 1945, as Germany collapsed, the Argentineans declared war on the Axis and made some reforms designed to free themselves from the stigma of fascism. In response, Washington lifted economic sanctions and resumed diplomatic relations. Much to Russia's disgust, the United States, at the insistence of other Latin American countries, won membership for Argentina in the United Nations.

Creating the United Nations Organization

By the time America entered World War II, most Americans were convinced that they had erred in refusing to join the League of Nations. If it were inevitable that America would be drawn into future European and Asian wars, then the only hope of staying out of future wars lay in joining with other nations to prevent war. In June 1943, the Senate overwhelmingly approved the Fulbright Resolution calling for U.S. membership in an international organization "with power adequate to establish and to maintain a just and lasting peace."

Churchill favored an international organization. Also, at a 1943 Big Three foreign ministers conference, Hull secured Stalin's endorsement.

In a number of pronouncements, Americans set forth their aspirations for the postwar world. In January 1941, Roosevelt said that America sought "Four Freedoms": freedom of speech, freedom of religion, freedom from want, and freedom from fear. In the August 1941 Atlantic Charter, he and Churchill advocated restricting territorial changes to those desired by their inhabitants, allowing all people to choose their form of government, and giving all nations equal access to trade and raw materials. This charter was later endorsed by the nations that signed the Declaration of the United Nations, but the British exempted their empire and the Soviets specified that principles must be adapted to the peculiarities of different countries.

Roosevelt and Hull grew euphoric about their vision of a new world order. In 1943, Hull told the American people that there would "no longer be need for spheres of influence, for alliances, for balance of power, or any other of the special arrangements through which, in the unhappy past, the nations strove to safeguard their security or to promote their interests." In March 1945, Roosevelt added that the Yalta Conference spelled "the end of the system of unilateral action and exclusive alliances and spheres of influence and balances of power and all the other expedients which have been tried for centuries—and have failed." Instead, "we propose to substitute for all these a universal organization in which all peace-loving nations will finally have a chance to join."

The League of Nations, though still extant, had faded into the background, and the Allies decided to dissociate themselves from its record of failure and make a fresh start. A four-power conference at the Dumbarton Oaks estate in Washington in fall 1944 drafted a new preliminary charter, or constitution, which was printed and given wide circulation.

At Yalta, the United States and Russia agreed that the big powers should have the power to veto any important action by the proposed Security Council, but the Russians accepted America's proposal that the veto not apply to discussion. The Soviets also agreed that all nations at war with the Axis on March 1, 1945, could be admitted. This allowed Washington to bring in some Latin American countries.

Proceedings were climaxed by a conference of two hundred delegates from fifty nations at San Francisco, held April 25–June 26, 1945. America took elaborate care to avoid repeating the mistakes that had contributed to the Senate's rejection of the League. Efforts were made to consult as many groups as possible, and the nine-member U.S. delegation included senators, three Republicans, and a woman.

A number of controversies developed at San Francisco. Truman had urged the Soviets to show that they considered the conference important by sending Foreign Minister Molotov. Once there, Molotov championed Soviet interests so vigorously that many Americans regretted the invitation. The Soviets secured three votes in the General Assembly, one each for the Russian, Byelorussian, and Ukrainian Republics, but America did not act on Russia's offer to support three votes for the United States. America succeeded in exempting domestic matters, such as immigration or tariff policies, from UN jurisdiction, and also in securing acceptance of the right of "collective self-defense," which allowed a military alliance among Western Hemisphere nations. Small nations resented the Big Four monopoly over important political decisions, but failed to get either limits on the veto power or a practical method of amending the charter.

The UN is made up of several bodies. The Security Council, comprised of representatives of five permanent members, the United States, Britain, France, Russia, and China, together with six other nations elected for short terms, was given jurisdiction over political questions. The General Assembly, in which each member has one vote, was authorized to make recommendations primarily on economic and social matters. An International Court of Justice adjudicates legal questions that nations choose to submit to it. An Economic and Social Council coordinates special agencies, some of which, such as the International Labor Organization and the International Monetary Fund, antedate the UN. The UN is financed by contributions from members assessed according to a formula that takes account not only of population but production and ability to pay.

Remembering the Senate's rejection of the League, the drafters gave the UN less power than had been given the League. It contained no provision making it a defensive alliance, as the League had been. Furthermore, unlike the League, the UN allowed the Big Five to veto Security Council action against themselves. In theory, it had been possible for the League to take action against a great power; it was not possible for the UN to do so.

The United States was among the first nations to join. In Senate Foreign Relations Committee hearings, a few opponents testified that it was un-American or unconstitutional or that it did too little for racial equality. Nonetheless, in five days the committee approved membership with only the veteran Senator Hiram Johnson, who had fought membership in the League, opposing. In the Senate chamber, so little opposition was expressed that one senator asked opponents to speak out so that he could debate them. The isolationist leader Burton K. Wheeler said that, because the UN was so powerless as to be little more than a "declaration of pious intentions," he would vote for it. With only two opposing votes, America joined in July 1945, a month before the end of the war with Japan. With public opinion so favorable, an opportunity may have been missed to secure U.S. membership in an international organization as strong as the League.

Imposing Peace on Italy

Italy's resistance collapsed nearly two years before the surrender of Germany. On July 25, 1943, with Allied troops invading Sicily, Mussolini's opponents forced him to resign, and King Victor Emmanuel appointed as premier Marshal Pietro Badoglio, who, on September 3, signed surrender terms. Overall control of Italy was assumed by an Allied Advisory Council composed of U.S. and British representatives—the Soviets were excluded, although they were fighting some 300,000 Italian troops in Russia. On October 13, switching sides, Italy declared war on Germany. Washington resumed diplomatic relations with Italy, but Americans were undecided over whether to treat Italy as a defeated enemy or an ally. The British and the Russians favored allowing the king to remain, but, in 1944, Americans forced his abdication.

The Soviets protested that they were excluded from decisions regarding Italy's postwar government. In August 1943, Stalin complained to Roosevelt that "the United States and Britain reached agreement between themselves while the U.S.S.R. is informed . . . as a third party," which "cannot be tolerated." This exclusion set an unfortunate precedent for procedures later followed by the Soviets in forming new governments in East European nations liberated by their troops. In the peace treaty, signed in 1947, Italy was stripped of its colonies and the city of Trieste and was forced to pay $350 million in reparations to Russia, Yugoslavia, Greece, Albania, and Ethiopia. Only Italy's quick surrender saved it from harsher punishment. Germany and Japan would not be as fortunate.

Unconditional Surrender

Many Americans had no clear ideas about what territorial or political settlements they sought in Europe and Asia. A late 1942 poll revealed that four out of ten could not say what America was fighting for; according to a 1948 poll, an overwhelming majority believed that America had no positive goals sufficient to have justified entry into the war. Most Americans assumed that they were fighting only because America had been attacked and that, therefore, the main purpose of the war was to defeat the attackers and ensure that they could not renew their aggression.

Roosevelt's war aims seem to have been only slightly more complex. He wanted the United States to assume a larger role in world affairs, and he was concious of the importance of controlling the industrial areas of Europe and Asia. But, like most Americans, he appeared to attribute World War II to the evil in the German and the Japanese characters and to believe that if those two countries were throughly defeated, purged of their evil ideology, and deprived of war-making capacity, the world could live at peace. Thus, his major aims were to destroy enemy power and to guard against divisions among the Allies that might allow the enemy to make a comeback. He did not seem to anticipate that America and Russia would be the postwar era's chief antagonists.

When Roosevelt and Churchill met at Casablanca, Morocco, in January 1943, the Axis offensive had stalled and the Allies had begun counteroffensives in North Africa and at Stalingrad. They invited Stalin to meet with them, but Stalin, citing the need for him to direct Soviet military efforts, declined. Roosevelt suspected that his real reason was anger at the delay in opening a second front in Europe. Churchill and Roosevelt devoted most time to planning future military operations in North Africa, Sicily, and Italy.

Near the end of the conference, in a joint statement, Roosevelt and Churchill announced that they would "compel the unconditional surrender of the Axis." This demand for unconditional surrender was highly unusual. Ordinarily nations at war specify territorial and political terms that the enemy must accept in return for a cease-fire. In World War I, President Wilson had announced his terms, the Fourteen Points, which seemed so fair to many Germans that it undermined their willingness to continue fighting. In contrast, Roosevelt and Churchill demanded that the Axis nations lay down their arms before being told what would be done to them.

What were Roosevelt's and Churchill's motives for demanding unconditional surrender? Roosevelt said it was a sudden impulse, and Churchill maintained that he had not been informed of the demand in advance. Actually, historians have discovered that Roosevelt had decided on it before the conference and had so informed Churchill. In the background was Hitler's claim that the Germans had not really been defeated in World War I, but had been tricked into surrendering by an offer of generous terms, only to be forced to sign a harsh treaty that violated those terms. Also, years of war propaganda and mutual killing had intensified hatred of Germany and convinced many in the Allied nations that Germans were inherently evil and the cause of all modern wars. Many argued that it had been a mistake to allow them to surrender in World War I before destroying their armies and occupying their territory. Furthermore, demanding unconditional surrender might reassure Russia that its Western allies would not make a separate peace, and postpone possible conflicts among the Allies over peace terms that might, by splitting the Allies, allow Germany to escape complete defeat.

At the November 1943 Teheran Conference, Stalin, who had earlier secretly ordered the execution of 10,000 Polish officers, proposed a toast to the death of 50,000 German officers after the war. When Churchill protested against executing prisoners, Roosevelt, perhaps in jest, suggested reducing the number to 49,000.

The demand for unconditional surrender had important effects. Undermining peace forces in the Axis countries, it strengthened the political grip of Hitler, Mussolini, and Japanese militarists. It enabled Hitler's propagandists to depict Allied war aims as so draconian that they gave Germans no alternative but to continue fighting. General Dwight D. Eisenhower concluded that it "persuaded the Germans to fight on longer" and possibly lengthened the war by a year and a half. Moreover, to obtain unconditional surrender would require such complete destruction of two of Eurasia's three major powers as to leave the Soviet Union as Eurasia's dominant power. No other wartime decision made a greater contribution to Soviet postwar superiority.

But, at the time, the policy had few critics. Stalin had not been consulted, and, although pleased by the prospect of destruction of two dangerous enemies, he said that it tended to unite the German people behind the war and asked that specific peace terms be announced to make it possible to end the war sooner. Senator Burton K. Wheeler called unconditional surrender "brutal and asinine," and a few right-wing groups worried that it would facilitate Soviet expansion. But 81 percent of the American public favored unconditional surrender.

The Morgenthau Plan

In October 1943, the State Department completed a draft of a plan for postwar Germany. It called for detaching Austria and East Prussia; disarming Germany;

destroying Nazism; restoring freedom of religion, speech, and political activity; punishing Germans for war crimes; and extracting reparations in goods and manpower.

Secretary of the Treasury Henry Morgenthau, a friend whom Roosevelt consulted on many matters, was dissatisfied with this State Department plan. He pointed out that after World War I Germany had been disarmed, revolutionized, partitioned, and forced to pay reparations, but all of these measures had not prevented it from rearming, reuniting, and launching a new war. Morgenthau understood that the key to national power is industry, and he argued that, to prevent a revival of German power, the Allies must completely remove or destroy German industry.

Roosevelt fully shared Morgenthau's hatred of Germans. "We have to get tough," he told Morgenthau, "and I mean the German people and not just the Nazis." He added that "we either have to castrate the German people or you have got to treat them in such a manner so that they can't go on reproducing people who want to continue the way they have in the past." If they were starving, he said, they could be fed from U.S. army soup kitchens. Easily persuaded to adopt Morgenthau's plan, he took Morgenthau to the September 1944 Quebec conference with Churchill. Churchill later wrote that he "violently opposed" the Morgenthau Plan, which made him angrier than he had ever been in his life. England's economy was interdependent with Germany's, and the plan he said, would, leave England, "chained to a corpse." But Roosevelt and Morgenthau persisted. With the British Empire nearly bankrupt, Churchill wanted Roosevelt to continue supplying arms while England began reconverting its industry to civilian production, and he also urgently needed a large loan. Morgenthau got Churchill's signature, and Churchill got arms and $6.5 billion. Roosevelt and Churchill announced that they had adopted the Morgenthau Plan, "looking forward to converting Germany into a country primarily agricultural and pastoral in its character."

In his 1945 New Years' speech, Hitler charged that the Morgenthau Plan meant "starvation of our masses," and Nazi propaganda denounced it as a "satanic plan of annihilation." Objecting to it, Secretary of State Hull and Secretary of War Stimson said that Germany's industry produced not only for Germany but for all of Europe. Some media opposition appeared. One observer wrote that Germany had 70 million people in a territory only two-thirds the size of Texas with farms that could feed fewer than half of them, so the Morgenthau Plan would mean starvation or deportation of more than half of Germany's people. Roosevelt said that "no one wants to make Germany a wholly agricultural nation," and some historians maintain that the plan was soon quietly dropped. However, drastic reduction of Germany's industry remained Allied policy.

When the Big Three met at Yalta, on February 4–11, 1945, Germany was near collapse, and final decisions on postwar arrangements were necessary. The big three discussed "disarmament, demilitarization, and the dismemberment of Germany." They agreed to give the northern half of East Prussia to Russia and other large German territories to Poland, but Churchill blocked further partition. They also agreed to destroy arms, aircraft, and shipbuilding industries and to remove other industry (Russia suggested 80 percent), "chiefly for the purpose of destroying the war potential." On reparations, Roosevelt tentatively agreed to a total of $20 billion, including "reparations in kind" (e.g., goods, machinery), with half to go to Russia.

Also at Yalta, the Big Three agreed that Soviet armies would occupy 40 percent of Germany and that British and American troops would share the other 60 percent. Russia accepted Churchill's demand that France be included among the occupying powers, but only if the French zone were carved out of the British and American zones. Because Germany would be governed by a four-power Allied Control Council in Berlin, which city was deep within the Soviet zone, British and American troops were allowed to occupy the western half of Berlin.

By the time that the Big Three met at Potsdam in July, two months after Germany's collapse, Roosevelt had died and been succeeded by Harry S Truman. Defeated in an election in mid-conference, Churchill was forced to depart, to be replaced by the new prime minister, Clement Attlee. The new Big Three agreed that each occupying power would take reparations from its zone, and the Western Allies promised to ship to Russia one-fourth of the factories they dismantled. However, retreating somewhat from the Morgenthau Plan, they agreed to allow Germany to retain enough industry to provide its people with a standard of living "not exceeding the standards of living of European countries."

Defeated Germany was in wretched condition. After years of Allied bombardment and blockade, many supplies, including food, were critically short. As the Allies advanced, battles for Germany's cities spread the world's most extensive ruins. The occupying armies preempted much of the remaining supplies, food, and buildings. The Allies divided German naval and merchant ships equally among the Big Three. They took large quantities of gold and coal, and Russia transported many Germans to Soviet areas to serve as unpaid labor. Americans captured more scientists, including the rocket expert Werner von Braun, and seized approximately $10 billion in scientific and technological know-how and patents.

Crushing Japan

Most Americans harbored even more hatred for Japan than for Germany. They saw the attack on Pearl Harbor as treacherous and unprovoked, and they considered the refusal of Japanese troops to surrender, their suicide attacks, and their "emperor worship" to be grotesque. They received many reports of Japanese atrocities and abuse of U.S. prisoners. For some Americans, hatred was intensified by racism, and popular comics and films depicted the Japanese as even less human than the Germans.

Unconditional surrender and deindustrialization policies that had been adopted regarding Germany also applied to Japan. The Allies agreed to strip Japan of past conquests, return Manchuria, Taiwan, and the Pescadores to

Figure 6.3 The 1945 death of Roosevelt, and the defeat of Churchill's party in an election, produced a different "Big Three"—President Harry Truman, Prime Minister Clement Attlee, and Josef Stalin—at the July 1945 Potsdam Conference. National Archives.

China, make Korea independent, and give the southern half of Sakhalin and the Kurile Islands to Russia.

Early in the war, many Japanese, including some military leaders, had formed a peace faction that was headed by former premiers. By February 1945, the emperor had made known his support for peace groups, and in April 1945, after the invasion of Okinawa, an advocate of peace, Kantaro Suzuki, became premier. The emperor ordered him to end the war, which, in the prevailing circumstances, could only mean surrender.

Suzuki's efforts to surrender were complicated by danger that the Japanese military might revolt if he agreed to surrender unconditionally. Most Japanese insisted at least on assurances that Japan could retain the emperor. The American belief that the Japanese worshiped the emperor was exaggerated, but the Japanese did revere him as the symbol of the nation and the center of the customs and relationships that held it together. Many Japanese feared that removing him would open the door to communism.

Seeking help in arranging peace, the Japanese, on July 13, asked for permission to send former premier Konoye to Moscow to request Soviet mediation. Emperor Hirohito told him "to secure peace at any price." To circumvent military opposition, they planned, said Konoye, "to wire the terms agreed upon [in Moscow] to the Emperor for action," whereupon the emperor would order all Japanese to accept them. But the Russians, whom the alliance had offered large territorial gains to enter the war, did not want the war to end before they had a chance to collect. At the Potsdam Conference, which opened on July 17, Stalin told Truman that he would refuse to mediate, for which Truman thanked him.

Some Americans, including former Ambassador to Japan Joseph C. Grew and Secretary of War Henry L. Stimson, wanted to allow the Japanese to keep the emperor. Not only would this speed Japan's surrender, they argued, but only the emperor could end military resistance and secure postwar compliance with U.S.-imposed reforms. Grew later maintained that, had the Allies announced that they would allow the emperor to remain, Japan would have surrendered before the dropping of the atomic bomb or Russia's entry into the Pacific war. Churchill expressed regret that demanding unconditional surrender was imposing a tremendous cost in lives. But Truman and the new secretary of state, James F. Byrnes, less knowledgeable about East Asia and influenced by Hull's opposition, resisted. On the day that the Potsdam Conference opened, Truman learned that the first test of the atomic bomb, (July 16), had succeeded, whereupon Stimson and the Joint Chiefs advised him to postpone any offer concerning the emperor until after an atomic bomb had been used.

On July 26, the United States and Britain issued the "Potsdam Declaration." It reiterated the Allies' intention to disarm Japan, strip it of all conquests, punish war criminals, and eliminate war potential, but said that Japan would not be "enslaved" or "destroyed as a nation" and might keep enough industry to pay reparations. Warning the Japanese that they must surrender or face "utter devastation," it promised a government "established in accordance with the freely expressed will of the Japanese people," but made no promise concerning the emperor.

Japan's situation was desperate. Its navy and merchant marine were gone, foreign trade was severed, stocks of oil and food exhausted, Okinawa lost, and its air force was too weak to defend its cities against massive bombing. A majority of the Japanese cabinet wanted to surrender, but they needed to persuade the army leaders. When newsmen questioned him about the Potsdam Declaration, Suzuki gave a reply that could be interpreted as saying either that he had "no comment" or that the Japanese would "ignore" it. Choosing the latter meaning, Americans interpreted it as rejecting their offer.

On August 6, the United States dropped an atomic bomb on Hiroshima, a city of 250,000 people with few military targets, which had been spared previous bombing to preserve it as a demonstration site for the new weapon. The bomb leveled 4.4 square miles of the center of the city and 81 percent of its buildings (see Fig. 6.5). The number killed was enormous—General Douglas MacArthur's headquarters put it at 78,000, but the Japanese Welfare Ministry estimated that 260,000 died immediately or within a few months, and another 163,000 were either missing or died later of injuries or radiation. Among those killed were hundreds of U.S. citizens and twenty-three U.S. prisoners of war. Calling it the "greatest thing in history," a jubilant Truman said that "he had never been happier about any announcement he had ever made." On August

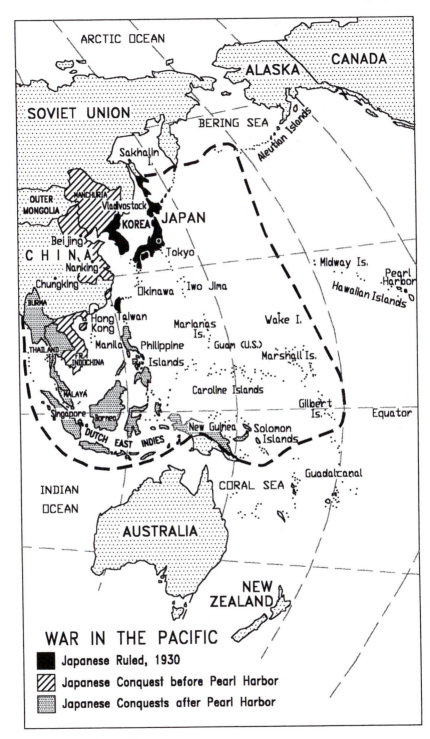

Figure 6.4 War in the Pacific.

8, Russia, moving up the date a week, entered the war. On August 9, a U.S. plane dropped an atomic bomb on Nagasaki, the center of Christianity in Japan, killing about 140,000 people.

Telling his cabinet that "the thought of wiping out another hundred thousand people was too horrible," Truman canceled plans to drop a third atomic bomb. However, conventional bombing continued to escalate—more bombs would be dropped on the last day of fighting than any other day of the war.

On August 10, after Emperor Hirohito broke precedent by personally intervening to break a cabinet deadlock, Japan offered to accept the Potsdam Declaration on the sole condition that the status of the emperor not be changed. Reversing its position, America then agreed to allow them to retain the emperor. Again the emperor intervened to obtain surrender. "The situation today," he said, "calls upon us to bear the unbearable." He and all members of the Imperial Conference wept, and the minister of war and about a thousand military officers committed suicide. The war ended on August 14, and surrender documents were signed on September 2 aboard a U.S. battleship.

Figure 6.5 The world was horrified that such massive destruction in Hiroshima could be produced by a single bomb. Some modern hydrogen bombs are a thousand times more powerful. National Archives.

The need to use the atomic bomb has been much debated. Truman and Stimson maintained that if it had not been used America would have had to invade Japan, with the loss of many American (Truman mentioned 500,000) and Japanese lives. A military estimate put the costs of planned invasions at 50,000 U.S. lives.

However, many others maintained that an invasion was not necessary to force Japan's surrender. At Potsdam, General Eisenhower argued that the Japanese were on the verge of surrender and that the bomb was not needed "to save American lives." U.S. naval commanders also said that invasion was not necessary, that with Japan's overseas trade blocked and U.S. battleships shelling Japan with "complete impunity," it had no option but surrender. General Douglas MacArthur said that his staff was "unanimous in believing that Japan was on the point of collapse and surrender," and Air Force General Curtis LeMay said that "Japan was finished" long before the atomic bombing. The postwar U.S. Strategic Bombing Survey concluded that Japan would have surrendered before the scheduled U.S. invasion even if Russia had not entered the war and no atom bomb had been dropped.

The morality of the atomic bombing was much debated. Many Americans, like Truman, rejoiced at its use, and some even wanted to delay accepting Japan's surrender until more were dropped. But others regretted that it targeted civilians. It made Americans, the *New York Times* columnist Hanson Baldwin wrote, "the inheritors to the mantle of Ghengis Khan," and Pope Paul VI later called it an "infernal massacre" and an "outrage against civilization." But wartime propaganda and casualties had convinced many Americans that the Japanese deserved extreme punishment, and racial differences made it easier to dehumanize them. "When you have to deal with a beast," Truman said, "you have to treat him as a beast." According to a poll, 13 percent of Americans favored exterminating the Japanese.

Relations with Russia may also have figured in America's decision to drop the bomb. America had offered an enormous bribe to induce Soviet entry into the war with Japan, but, after the successful July 16 atomic bomb test, Churchill reported that he and the president no longer felt that they needed Soviet help to compel Japan to surrender. Dropping of the bomb might end the war quickly enough to limit Soviet expansion in East Asia. Also, use of the atomic bomb strengthened America's hand in its intensifying diplomatic contest with the Soviets. Secretary of State Byrnes had predicted that a demonstration of the bomb's power would make Russia more manageable. It might enable America, he told Truman, to dictate its own terms. At Potsdam, after Truman learned of the successful test, Churchill wrote, "he was a changed man. He told the Russians just where they got off and generally bossed the whole meeting."

In addition, the atom bomb's apparent success in hastening Japan's surrender made the spending of $2.5 billion on constructing atomic bombs appear to be a wise use of wartime resources.

Hardly anyone at the time, other than a few scientists, argued against using the bomb. In war, nations usually hit each other with every weapon they have. Conventional bombing and the food blockade had already caused more civilian deaths than the bomb would. According to Churchill "there never was a moment's discussion as to whether the atomic bomb should be used or not."

For centuries, humanitarians had endeavored to put limits on the horror of war. In the mid-nineteenth century and the early twentieth century, international conferences at Paris, the Hague, London, and Geneva had drafted agreements on "laws of war" that outlawed some weapons, including poison gas, underwater mines, and bombs dropped from the air, required humane treatment of prisoners, and attempted to restrict the killing to men in uniform. In 1915, condemning German submarine warfare, Wilson had demanded respect for "the sacred immunities of non-combatants." Many had been shocked and sickened in 1937 when the Fascists began bombing cities in Spain, which President Roosevelt called "inhuman barbarism." Picasso's painting, "Guernica," dramatized this revulsion. And Japan's 1937 bombing of Chinese cities convinced many Americans that the Japanese were subhuman.

But in World War II all such restraints were abandoned. Not only the Japanese and Germans targeted civilians. The Allied bombing of Dresden and Tokyo killed hundreds of thousands of civilians. Before Hiroshima, America had destroyed 70 percent of the heart of Japan's largest cities. Dropping the atomic bomb differed mainly in that the damage was done, not by many bombs, but by one.

The attempt to mitigate the savagery of war, to secure a code of "civilized warfare," had collapsed. In World War II both sides engaged in wholesale slaughter of women and children. Mankind had apparently returned, said Admiral Leahy, to "an ethical standard common to barbarians." Secretary of State William Jennings Bryan had once said that he was not swayed by atrocity stories because "war itself is atrocity."

Mobilizing its vast economic resources, the United States made an enormous military contribution to Allied victory. Wartime cooperation between America and Britain was close, but they disagreed on imperialism, on the status of China, and on the timing of a second front. Americans sought to give China great-power status and to restore the territories it had lost to Japan but were displeased that Chiang did not join with the Chinese Communists in an all-out war effort.

Hostility among Americans toward Russia had been high. Americans were slow to extend aid and the Soviets bitterly denounced Allied delays in establishing a second front. However, the Allies did agree to concentrate on Germany first and to crush German power totally, and summit meetings at Tehran and Yalta were cordial. Seeking Soviet postwar cooperation against any revival of Axis power, Roosevelt made extensive concessions to secure Soviet entry into the war against Japan. Influenced by wartime propaganda, the Allies resolved to completely crush Germany, Italy, and Japan.

Axis power was destroyed but, contrary to expectations, this did not bring a stable or peaceful world. Subject peoples in Europe's empires demanded independence, civil war flared in China, and the Soviets and the West struggled for control of East Europe. Russia, Europe's strongest power, and a greatly strengthened America had become the chief players on the world scene.

7 Onset of the Cold War

A Change of Leadership

The last year of World War II saw major changes in the leading actors on the international stage. In April 1945 Mussolini was executed, Hitler committed suicide, and Roosevelt died of a brain hemorrhage. In July, loss of an election forced Churchill out of office. Of the top leaders, only Stalin remained in power at the war's end.

Roosevelt's death was a great shock. An often cited reason for his nomination for a fourth term had been that his qualifications and experience in foreign affairs were so superlative as to make him the ideal man to guarantee that America won not only the war but the peace. The shock was magnified when Americans examined his successor, Harry S Truman, a frightened man with thick glasses who read his speeches abominably and who had neither a college education nor experience in foreign affairs. The British ambassador called him a "mediocrity." He had been vice president for only four months, Roosevelt had not kept him informed of major developments, and his foreign policy views seemed little more sophisticated than those of a typical man in the street. He admitted that he "was not a deep thinker." He was described as a provincial nationalist, brash, outspoken, and assertive, who saw issues in black and white.

Thus, the death of Roosevelt brought a sharp change in the character of America's foreign policy leadership. More anti-Nazi than anti-Communist, Roosevelt had led America into war against Germany in alliance with the Soviet Union, thereby saving Communist Russia from defeat. The greatest postwar menace to U.S. security, he held, would be the danger of a revival of German power and aggression, and to avert that possibility he sought to preserve the wartime alliance with Russia as one of the four major powers that would share responsibility for preserving peace in the postwar era. He had accepted Soviet annexation of half of prewar Poland and suggested Soviet dominance in Outer Mongolia, Manchuria, Sakhalin, and the Kurile Islands. Nevertheless, as the defeat of Germany neared, problems among the Allies came to the fore, and Roosevelt might have been less conciliatory toward Russia had he lived longer. In early April, he exclaimed to an aide, "We can't do business with Stalin. He has broken every one of the promises he made at Yalta." Truman, more extreme in his anticommunism than Roosevelt, was less willing to concede the Soviets any sphere of influence beyond their own borders.

In late November 1944, Cordell Hull had resigned because of ill health and was replaced by Undersecretary of State Edward R. Stettinius, a former corporation executive. In July 1945 Truman replaced Stettinius with James F.

Byrnes, who had been governor of South Carolina, a U.S. senator, a Supreme Court justice, and Roosevelt's director of war mobilization. His qualifications and his standing in the party surpassed Truman's, and his nomination for vice president in 1944 had been blocked only by the labor unions, which considered him too conservative. Truman appointed him less because of his foreign policy experience, which was slight, than because he needed his political support.

Finding it difficult to defer to Truman, Byrnes conducted himself almost as if he were president for foreign affairs. He gave Truman an ultimatum to fire a member of his cabinet, and did not keep Truman fully informed of his negotiations, on which he once made a radio report before reporting to the president. Also, while Byrnes sought to negotiate with the Soviets, Truman, growing more unyielding, criticized what he called Byrnes's "appeasement policy" and told him he was "tired of babying the Soviets."

Truman fired Byrnes in January 1947 and replaced him with General George C. Marshall. Marshall's background was military, but as chief of staff in World War II he had dealt with thorny political problems, and he had served as presidential representative in China in a vain attempt to avert a civil war. Nevertheless, when asked how he liked being secretary of state, he replied that in the army he was the boss because he knew more than anyone else, but in the State Department everyone knew more than he did. However, he was served by capable men, knew how to take advice, and served ably until January 1949.

Figure 7.1 An officer delivers the Japanese surrender document to the President. With Truman are Secretary of the Navy James Forrestal, Secretary of War Henry L. Stimson, Chief of Staff George Marshall, Admiral William Leahy, and Acting Secretary of State Dean Acheson. National Archives.

His successor in office would be a former undersecretary of state, Dean G. Acheson. Educated at Harvard and at Yale Law School, the elegant and witty Acheson had a reputation as an intellectual, and he played a major role in the formulation of basic postwar foreign policy.

Winding Down World War II: Occupation of Germany

As Germany collapsed, Hitler, his propaganda minister, Joseph Goebbels, and the head of the secret police, Heinrich Himmler, committed suicide. But the second-highest-ranking Nazi, Hermann Goering, and twenty-two other top leaders were put on trial for war crimes by a special four-power military court at Nuremberg, Germany, November 1945 until October 1946. America's Attorney General, Francis Biddle, resigned to serve as a judge, and Supreme Court Justice Robert H. Jackson became chief prosecutor. The Allies charged the twenty-three Nazis with plotting agressive war and violating the laws of war and humanity. They acquitted three, gave long prison terms to eight, and sentenced eleven to die. Of these, Goering committed suicide; ten were hanged. Other courts punished several hundred thousand lesser figures.

The Allies expressed the hope that these trials would expand international law and serve as a ghastly deterrent to future aggression and atrocities. Critics of the trials argued that the Allies had committed similar acts, that the trials were conducted on the basis of "laws" formulated after the war (an *ex post facto* procedure forbidden in the U.S. Constitution), and that they punished military men for obeying orders. Also, some feared that they might perpetuate a "conspiracy myth" of the origins of war that would distract attention from more basic causes. Churchill concluded that the main precedent they set was that "the leaders of a nation defeated in war shall be executed by the victors."

In efforts to "denazify" Germany, the Allies barred former members of the Nazi party from holding any government position in postwar Germany and from holding private jobs other than manual labor. Purging many teachers, they rewrote textbooks.

Despite heavy bombing and battle damage, German industry was still 80–85 percent intact when Allied troops entered Germany. Banning all manufacturing of aluminum, tractors, machine tools, synthetic gasoline, and synthetic rubber, the Allies dynamited many factories and dismantled and shipped out many others, primarily to Russia. In 1946, Germany's industrial output was only 34 percent of its 1936 level. As late as October 1947, the Allies earmarked 168 additional factories for removal.

The areas of Germany awarded to Poland (see Fig. 7.2) contained 10 to 12 million Germans. The Poles ordered them to leave. Czechoslovakia and Hungary also expelled Germans. Some were moved on trucks and flat cars; others walked. Little was done to provide them with the necessities of life in Germany's remaining territory. The result, wrote Churchill, was "tragedy on a prodigious scale."

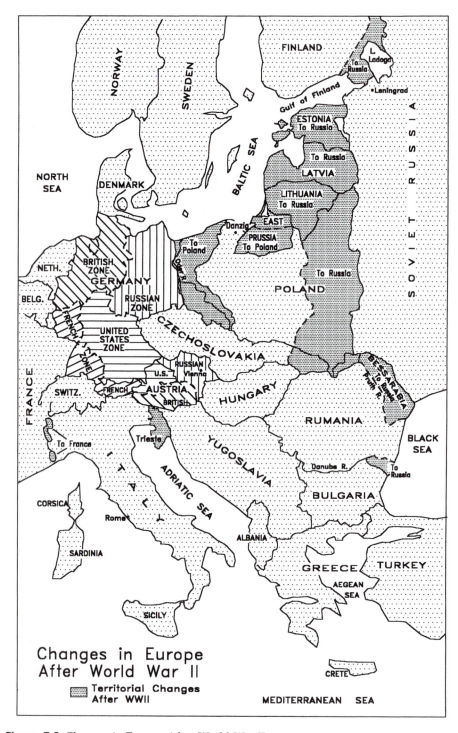

Figure 7.2 Changes in Europe After World War II.

The combined result of bombing, blockade, invasion, postwar demolition, and deportation severely reduced German living standards. Banning relief agencies, such as the Red Cross, from operating in Germany, Americans seized the remaining food stocks and allotted Germans a food ration of 1,500 calories a day, a goal not always met. Newspapers carried pictures of German women straining dishwater from U.S. army mess halls for food particles. The Swiss Red Cross reported that all children under the age of two were threatened with death and that the tuberculosis rate in Berlin had risen several thousand percent. In January 1946, Senator Kenneth Wherry said that the Allies were "subjecting millions to mass starvation."

These policies continued for more than two years. Gradually, however, Americans came to realize that Germany's industry was also Europe's industry, that its destruction hurt all Europe, and the resultant economic suffering contributed to the growth of Communist parties. Some came to believe that, although in the past Germany had been the major menace, Communist Russia posed a greater future challenge, and that someday America might need German help to block Communist expansion.

U.S. occupation policies proved to be extremely costly, both politically and economically. Destroying Germany created a power vacuum, while shipping German factories to Russia strengthened a potential enemy. Moreover, Americans then felt a need to spend billions of dollars to supply Europe with goods, such as steel, that Germany could no longer provide. Later, they would spend additional billions to rebuild the German industry they had destroyed.

Causes of the Cold War

Although widely used, the term "Cold War" lacks precision. Historians generally use it to refer to the years when international politics was dominated by a two-sided conflict between the United States and the Soviet Union. Such overwhelming force did these two superpowers command that most other nations were drawn into alignment with one or the other. Some mark the beginning at 1945 or earlier, others at 1947. It lasted more than forty years. As late as 1990 America and the Soviet Union remained the world's two leading antagonists, but the 1991 fragmentation of the Soviet Union ended the Cold War.

Curiously, if one views the entire span of U.S. history, Russia, among the major powers, had been America's best "friend." Russia favored U.S. independence, gave America support in the War of 1812, favored preservation of the union in the Civil War, and was America's ally in both world wars.

This "friendship" was not produced by a common ideology. For most of the period, Russia was a conservative counterrevolutionary nation, while the United States, originating in revolution, backed revolutions abroad. After the 1917 Bolshevik revolution, the two nations switched sides, with Russia assuming the radical and America the conservative position.

The principal cause of friendship between nations is the presence of a powerful common enemy that poses a greater threat to each of them than they do to each other—"the enemy of my enemy is my friend." In the nineteenth century, the common enemy was Britain, then the world's greatest power. After Britain's relative decline, both America and Russia felt endangered by the rising power of Germany and Japan.

What caused the Cold War? One cause was the decline of the reason for Soviet-American friendship—the power of Britain, Germany, and Japan. After World War II, Britain was bankrupt, and Germany and Japan lay in ruins.

Second, moving into the resulting power vacuums, the two nations expanded into contact, hence into conflict. The Soviets annexed the Baltic states, parts of Finland, Poland, Romania, and East Prussia, though they did not reannex all the territory Russia had held before World War I. They also installed puppet or friendly governments in Poland, East Germany, Romania, Bulgaria, Hungary, and Albania. In East Asia they acquired southern Sakhalin and the Kurile Islands and took control of ports and railroads in Manchuria.

The United States also expanded. The war had brought an enormous shift of power in favor of America. While devastating Europe and East Asia, the war more than doubled U.S. industrial production. The United States emerged from the war with a huge fleet and air force, a monopoly on atomic weapons, two-thirds of the world's gold, and a presence in areas formerly dominated by European and Japanese empires. Britain's ambassador reported that "by contrast with the exhausted and devastated countries of western Europe, the United States sees itself, as a result of the war, endowed with colossal productive and fighting capacity." America acquired, as UN trusteeships, the far-flung, formerly Japanese-held Mariana, Marshall, and Caroline islands, and assumed control of part of Germany and all of Japan. Before World War II, the U.S. Navy had been based in Hawaii and in the Chesapeake Bay, and America's small army was entirely within U.S. borders. After the war, America stationed its largest fleet in the Mediterranean and its second largest in East Asian waters, and it maintained military forces in England, France, North Africa, Turkey, Saudi Arabia, Pakistan, Taiwan, Korea, and other countries. Soon America would expand its alliances to embrace forty-five nations and give foreign aid to many more. This mutual expansion brought Russia and America into widespread contact and friction.

Third, basic Soviet foreign policies clashed with basic U.S. foreign policies. Americans usually perceived certain kinds of developments in Europe as unfavorable to their interests. When a powerful nation seized territory from a neighbor, Americans usually disapproved. Often they expressed their objections in terms of ideals—condemning aggression or the aggressor's ideology—but moral sensitivities frequently coincided with basic security interests. As long as Europe remained divided, Europe's nations would require most of their military forces to stand guard against each other, leaving less force available to challenge U.S. interests in the Western Hemisphere or other areas. But a united Europe might be more of a threat. Almost instinctively, Americans felt that expansion by Europe's most powerful nation raised the possibility that it might come to dominate all Europe and, therefore, endanger America, a fear sometimes expressed in charges that the aggressor nation sought to conquer the world.

The Soviet Union had a different set of concerns. Originating on the great European Plain, an area with few natural barriers to serve as defenses, Russia had a long history of suffering from invasions. The German assault in World War I had killed 10 million Russians, and Hitler's invasion, twenty-seven years later, had killed 20 million. Many Russians feared a possible new attack. They feared that the West was hostile to Communism and that Germany and Poland might seek to recover lost territories. Many of them maintained that their national security required them to annex additional territories or, at the least, to ensure that adjoining nations had governments that were not hostile to them.

Nations seek secure access to the ocean, the principal highway for modern commerce. Russia's few ports are not secure. Ships from the Black Sea need Turkey's permission to pass through the Dardanelles into the Mediterranean, and Britain's and Egypt's consent to exit from the Mediterranean at Gibraltar or Suez. Ships sailing from St. Petersburg, Russia's main port, must run a gauntlet past Germany, Scandinavia, and England to enter the Atlantic. Historically, this isolation had been a terrible military handicap, as demonstrated by the difficulty Americans encountered in transporting Lend-Lease supplies into Russia. Consequently, security needs had long driven Russians to seek control of the Dardanelles and, beyond that, a share in the control of the Mediterranean. Such Soviet efforts collided with the security needs of other nations and with U.S. opposition to any nation dominating Europe.

In addition to the destruction of common enemies, expansion into contact, and the clash of basic foreign policies, the Cold War seemed to result from a "law," of the prevailing system of competition-within-anarchy among sovereign states that an area's two most powerful nations automatically are that area's leading enemies. The Soviet Union and the United States were not only the most powerful presences in Europe; they were the two greatest military powers in the world. No other nation posed as great a danger to America as Russia, and no nation posed as great a military threat to Russia as America. Thus, for each, security meant primarily protection from the other.

Consequently, it was to be expected that the two superpowers would be leading antagonists.

This would have been true even if the two nations had shared a common ideology, but their dedication to conflicting ideologies intensified the hostility. Under its ruling Communist party, the Soviet Union espoused an ideology that, if it became prevalent, would destroy the power and privileges of America's upper-income groups, while America believed in an ideology that would put an end to the privileges of Russia's governing elite. Alarmed U.S. ideologists conceived of all Communists everywhere as solidly united (monolithic) under Kremlin direction and fanatically dedicated to conquering the world for communism. For their part, Soviet ideologists maintained that the world's capitalists sought to destroy communism everywhere. Each ideology did have dedicated adherents who felt a moral obligation to save or liberate the world's people from "enslavement" by the other. Each viewed any gain by the opposing ideology anywhere, no matter how otherwise insignificant, as magnifying the menace to its own system.

Furthermore, Americans eagerly sought opportunities to sell U.S. products overseas and to invest abroad. America's 1947 exports, totaling $14 billion, constituted a third of total world exports. Trade and investment were not only profitable, but were considered essential to U.S. prosperity and power. Seeking an "open door," Americans maintained that free enterprise was a prerequisite to world prosperity and peace. Consequently, Americans favored foreign governments that most freely permitted imports and foreign investments, and they objected to governments that exercised strong controls over their economies.

Many Americans regarded the Cold War as a unique phenomenon thrust upon America by Soviet fanaticism and intransigence and by its aggressive drive for world conquest. Actually, intense international rivalry was the norm, and the nearest approximation to peace that some world areas had achieved. The Cold War seemed unique to Americans because they had been absorbed in relations with Western Hemisphere nations that were not very threatening to them. In a sense, America was now joining the game of cold war politics that had long prevailed in much of the world.

Each side exaggerated the extent of the other's aggressive intent. Any move that one side considered a small step toward reducing its insecurity was seen by the other as a step toward implementing a master plan for world conquest. The result was a long and costly struggle that harmed both.

Cold War in Europe

Americans perceived the Soviet Union as terribly powerful and menacing. Its enormous victorious armies were equipped with awesome numbers of tanks and artillery, and other European nations possessed no force capable of withstanding them. Also, Soviet ideology threatened to win converts and enlist agents everywhere. Consequently, many Americans felt seriously endangered.

Few Americans sufficiently understood the elements of national power to appreciate fully the degree to which U.S. strength exceeded that of the Soviet Union. The United States had a more defensible homeland and more powerful allies. America's navy and air force were larger than those of the rest of the world combined, and only America had atomic weapons. Even before the war, Russia's GNP had been only a fraction of America's, and the war had destroyed much of its economy, while U.S. industrial production had doubled. By war's end America was producing half of the world's industrial goods, held two-thirds of its gold, and enjoyed the world's highest standard of living. This prosperity added to the worldwide appeal of America's ideology.

Nevertheless, as Germany neared collapse, Western alarm about Soviet intentions rose. The advance of Communist armies into central Europe, which U.S. Ambassador to Russia W. Averell Harriman called a "barbarian invasion," disturbed many. Churchill urged that America and Britain disregard previous agreements and send their troops as far east as possible to form a new front against Russia's "onward sweep."

Citing the need to restore Russia's economy, Stalin, in January 1945, asked Washington for a $6-billion loan, a request he later reduced to $1 billion. The State Department recommended that it be granted only if Russia opened its territory to U.S. goods and investments, a condition unacceptable to the Soviets. On the day that Germany surrendered, Truman ordered a sudden halt of Lend-Lease to Russia—some ships then en route were ordered to return—which Stalin called "brutal." Truman resumed shipment of the goods needed by Russia for war with Japan.

As the defeat of Germany neared, acrimonious disputes had arisen concerning the political fate of nations in East Europe then being liberated by Soviet troops. Their prewar governments had been anti-Communist, and some had joined Hitler in his assault on Russia.

Britain had long had a sphere of influence in the Balkan Peninsula extending north from Greece into Yugoslavia and Hungary. Now Soviet leaders, preoccupied with security, Harriman reported, sought "puppet regimes in all contiguous countries" to give them a "period of freedom from danger" during which to rebuild their economy. Churchill had proposed dividing the Balkans between British and Soviet spheres, and, in Moscow in October 1944, in a private meeting with Stalin, he secured a deal. In return for Stalin's agreement to concede to Britain 90 percent preponderance in Greece and equal influence in Yugoslavia, he agreed to allow Russia 90 percent preponderance in Romania and 75 percent control in Bulgaria and Hungary. They should not call this "dividing into spheres," Churchill cautioned Stalin, for fear of shocking Americans. When Americans expressed disapproval of such "power politics" and "spheres of influence," the British retorted that America showed no willingness to forgo a sphere in the Western Hemisphere.

At the Yalta Conference, in February 1945, discussion of East Europe consumed more time than any other question. The Big Three agreed to establish a Polish interim government "broadly representative of all democratic elements." However, by agreeing that it would be created by adding "democratic leaders" to the Soviet-organized Lublin-based government, the Allies conceded that Lublin Poles would constitute its core. Some Poles returned from London to Poland to join the new government, but, when it became clear that they would be allowed only subordinate positions, some of them resigned in protest.

Hull and Roosevelt had publicly deplored the continuation of spheres of influence. However, State Department experts cautioned that "spheres of influence do in fact exist and will probably continue to do so for some time . . . in view of the actual Eastern European sphere and the Western Hemisphere bloc." In 1945 Secretary of War Henry L. Stimson expressed regret that some Americans were "anxious to hang onto exaggerated views of the Monroe Doctrine and at the same time butt into every question that comes up in Central Europe." Diplomat George F. Kennan, who otherwise favored resisting Soviet expansion, advised that the United States should concede the Soviets a sphere in East Europe.

Nevertheless, most of the early Cold War disputes concerned America's challenge to Russia's claim to an East European sphere. When the Soviets moved to establish a Communist government in Poland, Truman was indignant. He demanded free elections and, in April 1945, so harshly scolded Soviet Foreign Minister Molotov for what he charged were Soviet violations of agreements that Molotov protested that never before had he been talked to like that. Stalin seemed to consider Poland so vital to Soviet security that he was determined to control it, whatever the cost to good relations with the West. "Throughout history," said Stalin, "Poland has been the corridor for attack" on Russia, and it was a matter "of life or death." Stalin could not understand, Ambassador Harriman reported from Moscow, why America would want to interfere with Soviet policy there unless it had some "ulterior motive." At the July 1945 Potsdam Conference, Stalin admitted that "any freely elected government would be anti-Soviet" and added, "That we cannot permit." Truman recognized the new, Communist-dominated Polish government in July 1945.

The Soviets made some conciliatory gestures. They allowed the Communists to lose elections in 1945 in Hungary, a former Axis ally, and in the Soviet zone of Austria. In December 1945, at America's request, they admitted more non-Communists to the Romanian and the Bulgarian regimes, and they withdrew Soviet troops from Czechoslovakia. After May 1946 elections, Czechoslovakia formed a coalition government under the presidency of a non-Communist, Eduard Benes, who made the pro-Western Jan Masaryk foreign minister and gave Communists only nine of the twenty-six top posts.

In Romania, which had been a German ally, the Soviets imposed a Communist government. Bulgaria contained a large number of Communists who assumed power with little Soviet help. A spring 1947 coup imposed a Communist government on Hungary.

When the British and the Americans denounced the Soviets for imposing Communist governments in East Europe, the Soviets replied that the Allies had similarly installed anti-Communist regimes in Italy, Greece, and Japan. Cynically, Stalin concluded that wherever Soviet troops went pro-Communist governments would appear, and, wherever British and American troops went, anti-Communist governments would appear.

Bitter wrangling characterized the meetings of the foreign ministers of Britain, America, France, and Russia in London (September-October 1945) and in Moscow (December 1945). The Soviets, said Secretary of State Byrnes, were "stubborn, obstinate," and "they don't scare." Nevertheless, at a peace conference in Paris (April–October 1946), twenty-one nations agreed on treaties with East European nations. The treaty with Hungary recognized its Soviet–dominated government and required it to pay $300 million in reparations. Romania was required to cede Bessarabia to the Soviet Union and to pay reparations of $300 million. In signing these treaties, America seemed to concede that it lacked the means to reverse Soviet control in East Europe.

Meanwhile, friction flared over Iran. In 1941, to facilitate transportation of war supplies to Russia, British and U.S. troops had occupied southern Iran, while the Russians occupied northern Iran. All the occupiers took some advantage of the occupation. Americans pressed for rights to extract Iranian oil, while the Soviets assisted the pro-Communist Tudah party and backed a secession movement in Azerbaijan, which province had been a tsarist sphere of influence.

The Allies had agreed to withdraw from Iran within six months after the end of the war, and the Americans and British did so by March 1946. When Soviet troops remained after the deadline, Iran appealed to the UN Security Council for help. Russia boycotted UN discussions. Truman saw this as part of a "giant pincers movement" into the Middle East. However, after Iran granted Azerbaijan some autonomy and agreed to give the Soviets oil rights in north Iran, the Soviets withdrew their troops in May. Then, Iran reneged on its promises regarding oil, while Americans helped Iran suppress unrest in Azerbaijan. Thus, a nation on Russia's border passed into the West's economic and political orbit, a stinging defeat for the Soviets.

As the Germans had withdrawn from Greece in October 1944, the British landed troops there and restored King George II, an extreme conservative of German origin. His government which, according to a U.S. official, was "incredibly weak, stupid, and venal," was unacceptable to the liberal and left-wing guerrillas, EAM-ELAS, who had led Greek armed resistance to the German occupation. Despite Roosevelt's opposition to killing anti-Nazi guerrillas, British troops helped the king suppress them. Stalin, keeping his promise to Churchill to stay out of Greek affairs, gave EAM-ELAS no aid. However, Communist Yugoslavia, which rejected Soviet control, did help the Greek guerrillas, and major fighting continued until 1949.

Clashes also occurred in the United Nations. Each side vetoed admission of the other's friends. The UN charter called for a UN police force. America wanted to provide airplanes and let the Russians furnish the foot soldiers, but the Soviets insisted that both furnish equal and identical contingents. Also, in the "Baruch Plan," the United States offered to destroy its atomic weapons and put atomic development under international supervision if a reliable inspection system were first established to prevent any country from manufacturing such weapons, but the Soviets insisted that all bombs be destroyed before they would open their territory to inspection. Commanding an overwhelming majority in the Security Council, Britain and America could have secured UN backing on these issues had Russia not exercised its veto, and they denounced Russia for its frequent use of the veto.

The Truman Doctrine

The bitterly anti-Communist Truman did not share Roosevelt's vision of a shared hegemony with Russia. Friction with Stalin deepened his hostility. At the Potsdam Conference in July 1945, when Stalin refused to put the Danube River under international control, Truman concluded that "the Russians were planning world conquest." In a January 1, 1946 letter to Byrnes, he called Soviet actions in Poland a "high-handed outrage," charged that Russia was planning to invade Turkey, and said that he was "tired of babying the Soviets" who should be "faced with an iron fist and strong language."

On his part, in a February 1946 pre-election speech to the Soviet people, Stalin referred to the inevitable clash of communism and capitalism and called for a new series of five-year plans to strengthen the Soviet Union. Although this was a repetition of long-held Soviet doctrine, *Time* called it a "warlike pronouncement."

Asked for an analysis of Stalin's speech, the chargé d'affaires in the Moscow embassy, George F. Kennan, a Princeton-educated State Department–trained expert on Russia, on February 22, 1946, sent a long, widely read telegram. He wrote that Russia, with an "instinctive . . . sense of insecurity," a fear of "capitalist encirclement," and a "neurotic view of world affairs," was "committed fanatically to the belief that with the United States there can be no permanent modus vivendi" (live-and-let-live). Consequently, America, he wrote, must oppose Soviet expansion all around its borders. Although Kennan believed this could be accomplished without war, this telegram, he later ruefully admitted, was an overstatement that appeared to be "designed to arouse the citizenry to the dangers of a Communist conspiracy."

In March 1946, Truman sat on the stage at Fulton, Missouri, while Winston Churchill charged that the Russians had lowered an "iron curtain" across Europe and, while not wanting war, sought "the indefinite expansion of their power and doctrines." Churchill called for an anti-Soviet "fraternal association" of English-speaking nations for the coming "trial of strength." Stalin termed this speech a "call to war with the Soviet Union." Harvard students chanted, "Winnie, Winnie, go away. GI Joe is home to stay."

Figure 7.3 George F. Kennan. As a member of the U.S. embassy in Moscow and, later, director of the State Department Policy Planning Staff, he was a leading architect of America's Cold War policy of which he later became a leading critic. National Archives.

In November 1946, at Foreign Minister Molotov's request, Soviet Ambassador to America Nikolai Novikov prepared a long telegram on U.S. foreign policy. It was almost a mirror image of the U.S. view of the Soviets. Striving for "world supremacy," Novikov reported, America would use its economic power to "infiltrate" the economies of other countries and was even seeking to dislodge Soviet influence from countries that adjoined Russia. It had raised expenditures on its army and navy "colossally" to thirteen times the 1938 levels and, establishing bases thousands of miles from its shores, was seeking to subdue China and to prepare Germany and Japan for use in a war against the Soviet Union, which "in the eyes of American imperialists is the main obstacle in the path of the United States to world domination."

The decline of Britain's power presented a crisis. In the nineteenth century, the British Empire covered one-fourth of the world's surface, and its navy dominated the world's oceans. This was made possible by the superior strength Britain derived from its lead in industrial production—in 1850 it produced about half of the world's manufactured goods. In later years, although victorious in war, Britain's industrial growth rate lagged behind that of the United States, Germany, Japan, and Russia. Furthermore, England's enormous military spending during the two world wars forced it to sell overseas properties that had been producing billions of dollars of annual income. Its colonies increasingly resisted its control, partly because England was no longer the sole source of cheap manufactured goods. After long struggles, India achieved independence in 1947 and Burma in 1948. Britain had lost much of its ability to project power abroad.

For more than a hundred years, Britain and Russia had been great antagonists. The sea-based British Empire and its allies had surrounded the backward Russian bear, holding it back from the sea. Now that the power of Germany and Japan was destroyed, how long could the declining British Empire continue to check Soviet expansion? Apparently, it could do so only with U.S. support. In early 1946, England asked Washington for a multibillion-dollar loan.

The question of whether to extend this loan was much debated in Congress. Opponents argued that Britain had defaulted on its World War I debt and was imperialist, socialist, and too bankrupt to be salvaged—that it would be pouring money down a rat hole. The loan's advocates argued mainly that it was essential to enable Britain to stop the advance of communism. Many recognized that it would be a major turning point in U.S. policy, the adoption of a kind of Lend-Lease against communism. In mid-1946, on the condition that England open its empire to U.S. trade, Congress, by a narrow margin, voted to lend it $3.75 billion.

In a September 1946 speech, Secretary of Commerce and former Vice President Henry Wallace, the most liberal member of the administration, while criticizing Russia's repression, argued against a policy of getting tough and said America must "get out of eastern Europe." Protesting that this speech undercut his negotiations, Byrnes threatened to resign unless Truman fired Wallace. Although Truman had given Wallace permission to make the speech, he called him one of "the Reds, phonies, and 'parlor pinks'" and fired him.

The midterm congressional election in November 1946 went badly for Truman. Republicans captured both the Senate and the House, and Truman's popular approval sank to 32 percent. His domestic program was stymied, and he seemed to be destined to be a short-term president. His only hope of winning popular support was through dramatic accomplishment in foreign affairs. In January 1947, he fired Byrnes for what he said was insubordination and insufficient anti-Soviet toughness, and replaced him as secretary of state with General George C. Marshall.

The Dardanelles Strait, the outlet from the Black Sea to the Mediterranean, is to Russians the world's most important waterway. Large rivers flow south through Russia to the Black Sea, making the Dardanelles the natural avenue for much of its trade. In both World War I and World War II, Turkey had blocked supplies and arms from reaching Russia. Turkey's control of the Dardanelles, said Stalin, gave it "a hand on Russia's throat," and he asked what would the United States do if some Latin American country had the power to close the Panama Canal? At Yalta and at Potsdam, America and Britain had promised to support Russia's demand for a share in control of the strait, but, in 1946, Truman changed his mind. In August, when Stalin put pressure on Turkey, Truman, saying, "We might as well find out whether the Russians [are] bent on world conquest now," moved an aircraft carrier to the eastern Mediterranean. With firm U.S. backing, Turkey resisted, and the Soviets relaxed their pressure.

By this time, England was saying that loans would not suffice to give it the strength needed to block Soviet expansion. America, it said, must itself take over part of the load. In February 1947, Britain notified Washington that it could no longer finance the Greek king's fight against leftist guerrillas or Turkey's resistance to Soviet pressure. This could mean the collapse of the anti-Soviet line at its very center, at the Dardanelles.

The British threat to pull out of Greece and Turkey presented Washington with a major crisis. Should America permit these barriers to Soviet expansion to collapse, or should it step into the gap? For weeks Truman consulted with military and congressional leaders. Americans would "not take world leadership," said Assistant Secretary of State Will Clayton, unless they were "shocked into doing so." With the aid of Undersecretary of State Dean Acheson, Truman argued that if allowed to spread, communism would engulf all Europe, Africa, and Asia. To win popular backing, Senator Arthur Vandenberg advised, Truman should stress the danger of Communist conquest of the world and "scare hell out of the American people."

On March 12, 1947, Truman made a momentous address. "Every nation," he said, "must choose between alternative ways of life"—that of "free people" or of "terror and oppression." Aid to Greece, he said, was vital to Greece's survival as a free nation. Also, America's national security was at stake: the imposition of totalitarian regimes on free people "by direct or indirect aggression, undermines the foundations of international peace and hence the security of the United States." Consequently, he concluded in a statement that became known as the Truman Doctrine, "it must be the policy of the United States to support free peoples who are resisting attempted subjugation by armed minorities or by outside pressures."

The Truman Doctrine meant reversal of America's former isolationism in favor of a policy of active economic and military combat against communism throughout the world. To *Time* magazine, "it sounded almost like a declaration of war."

Truman's speech set off a brisk debate. One supporter, Senator Arthur Vandenburg, warned of a Communist "chain reaction around the world which could very easily leave us isolated in a Communist-dominated earth." In a July 1947 article in *Foreign Affairs*, under the pen name "X," George F. Kennan argued that Soviet expansion would stop only where it met "unanswerable force" and that the Soviets must be "contained by the adroit and vigilant application of counterforce at a series of constantly shifting geographical and political points." In the long run, he hoped, such "containment" would eventually result in "either the breakup or gradual mellowing of Soviet power."

An opponent, Senator Robert Taft, charged that once again Britain was asking the United States to pull its chestnuts out of the fire. Other opponents objected that the Truman Doctrine bypassed the UN, and that the Greeks and Turks, far from being "free peoples," were under corrupt and brutal dictatorships. Another opponent, Walter Lippmann, the most respected columnist of the day, called for a cooling of the rhetoric. Russia, he said, was not about to invade Western Europe, and its foreign policy seemed to be motivated more by its historic search for security than by ideology. Some world areas were vital to U.S. security, he wrote, while others were not, and embarking on an unlimited worldwide ideological crusade would militarize U.S. foreign policy, ally America with corrupt dictatorships, erode U.S. democracy, and drain America's resources in a perpetual "Cold War." Kennan later maintained that he had favored checking communism primarily by political and economic measures, but that Truman, in "grandiose language," had called for a worldwide military crusade. Other critics argued that the Soviet Union's gradual recovery from World War II would narrow America's margin of superiority, making it ever more difficult to maintain sufficient counterforce at every point around the Soviet Union. Some maintained that, regardless of how hard the Russians might try, they could not possibly secure control of all of Europe and Asia.

By May 1947, after a two-month debate, the Senate (67–23) and the House (287–107) voted to furnish Greece with $300 million in economic aid, and Turkey with $100 million in military aid. These appropriations were only the down payment; enforcing the Truman Doctrine would eventually cost trillions of dollars.

The Truman Doctrine's declaration of a cold war on communism, wrote Senator J. William Fulbright, became "the guiding spirit of U.S. foreign policy." Interpreting international politics as a struggle between freedom and dictatorship, it accentuated the trend toward attributing conflicts anywhere, not to local causes, but to the machinations of a worldwide, Kremlin-directed conspiracy.

In July 1947, to strengthen the handling of international relations, Congress passed the National Security Act, which created a separate air force and grouped it and the former War Department and the Navy Department into a Department of Defense. It created a new National Security Council, consisting of the president, the vicepresident, the secretary of state, and the secretary of defense, to advise the president. It also established the Central Intelligence Agency (CIA) to handle espionage and "covert action," such as undermining hostile foreign governments.

The most unusual feature of the Truman Doctrine was that it proposed to defend "free people" not only against invasion by foreigners but also against "armed minorities" of their own people. Heretofore, interference in another country's civil wars had been considered contrary to international law. In the nineteenth century, America, championing the common man against the rich and privileged, had welcomed nearly all revolutions, but now that America had become wealthy and Communist Russia was backing revolutions, America would oppose most revolutions.

The Marshall Plan

Economic distress seemed to make Western Europe more vulnerable to communism. The war had devastated Europe's economy, and, after the war, America had destroyed and dismantled many additional German factories. Europe, said Churchill, had become "a rubble heap, a charnel house, a breeding ground of pestilence and hate." Some Europeans attributed these economic woes to the failure of capitalism and sought cures in alternate economic systems. Communist parties in Italy and France became the largest parties in those countries, where they and their allies won nearly 40 percent of the vote. "The seeds of totalitarian regimes," said Truman, "are nurtured by misery and want." Furthermore, economic weakness deprived Western Europe of its ability to finance defense forces sufficient to halt a possible advance by Soviet armies. No force existed in Europe, it was said, strong enough to bar a possible Soviet advance to the Pyrenees.

The State Department Policy Planning Board, chaired by George F. Kennan, concluded that the situation demanded large-scale U.S. aid to help restore Europe's economy, check the growth of Communist parties, and enable Europe to strengthen its military forces. In a June 5, 1947 speech at Harvard University, Secretary of State Marshall set forth what came to be called the "Marshall Plan." Speaking of "economic, social, and political deterioration" in Europe, and asserting that America must help ensure the "survival of social conditions in which freedom could flourish," he made a dramatic offer: if the leaders of Europe's nations would meet and draw up an economic recovery plan that included mutual assistance and then give the United States a statement of what aid they needed to implement it, he said, America would help.

Marshall's invitation did not specifically exclude Communist nations, some of which, notably Poland and Czechoslovakia, wanted to participate. In June

1947, Molotov came to Paris for three days of discussions with the foreign ministers of France and Britain, but the Soviets would accept neither the required degree of economic cooperation with other countries nor U.S. participation in their economic planning. After Molotov's proposal that each nation prepare a separate plan was rejected, he charged that the Marshall Plan would split Europe, revive the threat of German domination, and promote U.S. imperialism. Stalin called it an effort "to form a Western bloc and isolate the Soviet Union."

Responding with remarkable alacrity, sixteen non-Communist nations, excluding Germany and Spain, met in Paris from July to September 1947 and drafted a comprehensive four-year plan to achieve economic recovery by 1951. Aid needed from the United States, they said, totaled $22 billion.

The Truman administration decided to give Europe $17 billion over a four-and-a-half year period. In December 1947, Truman asked Congress to appropriate $6.8 billion as the first installment.

A formidable array of groups favored the Marshall Plan (European Recovery Program). Government officials told congressional committees that it would promote U.S. trade and give Europeans the means with which to protect access to Middle East oil. Humanitarian and liberal groups supported it because it meant help for Europe's suffering poor. The National Association of Manufacturers, the American Federation of Labor, and many farmers realized that it would increase exports of U.S. products. Even isolationist Senator Robert A. Taft backed it. Unless it passed, proponents argued, there would be great danger of a war, which, U.S. commander in Germany General Lucius Clay warned in March 1948, might come "with dramatic suddenness." The U.S. ambassador to Italy warned that Communists might win the coming elections.

Congressional approval of the Marshall Plan was stimulated by the 1948 coup in Czechoslovakia. For a time after the war, the Czechs had enjoyed a freely elected government. However, in February 1948, at Soviet urging, Czechoslovakian Communists seized complete control, and Foreign Minister Jan Masaryk either jumped or was pushed from a window to his death. Saying that this "sent a shock throughout the civilized world," Truman warned of a "growing menace . . . to the very survival of freedom." That month, Congress voted, by 69–17 in the Senate and 318–75 in the House, an initial $5.9 billion to finance the Marshall Plan.

Of course, Germany's economy was at the heart of Europe's economy. America's decision to include Germany among the seventeen nations receiving aid marked a complete reversal of the Morgenthau Plan.

Over the four and a half years of the Marshall Plan, America gave more than 1 percent of its GNP in aid, a total of $13.5 billion by June 1952. England received $3.2 billion, France $2.7 billion, Italy $1.5 billion, and Germany $1.4 billion. Calling the Marshall Plan "a lifeline to sinking men," Britain's Foreign Secretary Ernest Bevin said it was generosity "beyond belief."

The plan was extremely successful. By 1952, West Europe's GNP was up 32 percent, and its industrial production was up 40 percent above prewar levels. Votes received by Communist parties fell. The requirement that nations help each other gave impetus to mutual reduction of tariffs and other economic coordination. Meanwhile, avoiding the expected postwar recession, the U.S. economy boomed.

U.S. aid to Europe continued after 1952, but it shifted from economic to military aid. Already by 1952, 80 percent of the aid was for military purposes.

In response to the Marshall Plan, the Soviets drew the Communist-controlled nations of East Europe closer together. In September 1947, they adopted the Warsaw Plan, designed to integrate their economies, and in October they revived the Communist International, in a much attenuated form, as the Communist Information Bureau (Cominform). Tightening its grip on Hungary, Russia added treaties of alliance with Bulgaria, Finland, and Rumania to those they had already signed with Poland, Czechoslovakia, and Yugoslavia.

Cold War in Germany

Meanwhile, East and West clashed in Germany. The area of Germany that had been designated for occupation by the Soviets included 40 percent of Germany's territory and 33 percent of its productive resources. Americans occupied the southwestern sector, and the British occupied the northwest. Someone quipped that Russia got the agriculture, Britain the industry, and America the scenery. When France demanded a role in the occupation, the Americans and British assigned France parts of the U.S. and British zones.

Although divided for administrative purposes, with each zone commander controlling local affairs, on larger, particularly economic matters Germany was supposed to be governed as a unit by an Allied Control Council at Berlin. Comprised of the top military commanders of the four occupying armies, the Allied Control Council could make decisions only by unanimous vote, which required far more harmony than the nations could maintain. Nevertheless, it worked for a time. The genial General Eisenhower and the Soviet hero Marshall G. K. Zhukov became friends. Early difficulties resulted mostly from French obstruction of any move to revive Germany.

Each of the occupying powers printed occupation money which it forced the Germans to accept in exchange for whatever Allied personnel wanted to buy. Soon both the Western Allies and the Soviets were complaining that excessive purchases by the other were stripping Germany. Personal clashes, sometimes fatal, occurred between individual soldiers of the different powers. Part of the factories shipped from Western zones to the Soviets were supposed to be paid for in food, but in May 1946, with each side accusing the other of defaulting on promised deliveries, the Western Allies stopped shipping factories, and the Russians halted food deliveries.

Having suffered such enormous destruction at the hands of the Germans and harboring great fear of Germany, the Soviets wanted to keep Germany disarmed and neutralized. In the West, on the other hand, the assumption that Germany was the main threat to peace was gradually being replaced by fear that Russia was more dangerous. If this were true, restoring Germany could strengthen West Europe's defenses against the Soviets. In September 1946, at Stuttgart, Secretary of State Byrnes said that the occupation zones must be economically united and German industrial production allowed to recover sufficiently to pay reparations and the cost of essential imports. They would consent, the Soviets replied, if payment of the agreed-upon $10 billion in reparations were guaranteed.

In June 1948, after adopting the Marshall Plan, the Western powers issued a new currency, in effect separating their zones economically from the Soviet zone, and then severed political ties as well. Despite Soviet protests, America, France, and Britain merged their zones, and announced that they would transfer control of Germany's internal affairs to a new government to be established at Bonn.

The Soviets protested that formation of a German government without their participation would violate the Potsdam Agreements which gave the Western Allies permission to occupy West Berlin. Furthermore, if Germany were not to be governed from Berlin, they said, there was no further point to an Allied presence there. Demanding that the West withdraw troops from Berlin, the Soviets, in June 1948, stopped all Western traffic over roads through their zone to Berlin, thus instituting the "Berlin Blockade."

West Berlin, with a population of 2 million, lay 125 miles inside the Soviet occupation zone. If war came, Western troops there would have to surrender or be annihilated. Holding the city was enormously expensive, but to retreat under pressure, some Westerners feared, might encourage Soviet aggression elsewhere. Furthermore, as the historic capital city, Berlin was the symbol of the reunion desired by all Germans, and having sole possession of it might give the Soviets an advantage in dealing with Germans.

The Berlin Blockade was an electrifying crisis that raised the danger of war. Saying that if Berlin were lost, "communism will run rampant," General Lucius Clay, the commander of U.S. troops in Europe, advocated sending U.S. tanks to force their way over Soviet-controlled roads. Instead, Truman mobilized large numbers of aircraft to fly supplies into West Berlin in the largest airlift yet seen. On one day 1,400 planes landed with more than 13,000 tons, more than had been brought in over the roads before the blockade. Also, the Allies imposed a counterblockade on the Soviet zone.

The North Atlantic Treaty Organization

In times of crisis, said a top Truman adviser, Clark Clifford, "the American citizen tends to back up his president." Tension engendered by the Berlin Blockade contributed to Truman's surprising upset victory over Thomas E. Dewey in the 1948 election.

The Berlin Blockade also further consolidated the unity of the two opposing Cold War camps. In June 1948, Senator Vandenberg's resolution favoring U.S. membership in a defensive alliance passed the Senate by a vote of 64–4. By this time, most Americans were convinced that isolationism had failed, that

America would be drawn into any future general war, and that, consequently, America should play an active role in preventing war in Europe.

In April 1949 twelve nations joined together into the North Atlantic Treaty Organization (NATO), a military alliance of the United States, Canada, Britain, France, Italy, Norway, Denmark, Iceland, Belgium, the Netherlands, Luxemburg, and Portugal. (Greece and Turkey would join in 1952, and West Germany in 1955). In June the Senate approved overwhelmingly. Each nation promised to regard an attack on any member nation as an attack on itsself and to respond "as it deems necessary." Each put a part of its military forces under unified NATO commands, the most important of which was the Supreme Headquarters of the Allied Powers in Europe (SHAPE), whose first commander was General Eisenhower. Overall direction was exercised by a North Atlantic Council comprised of the foreign, defense, and finance ministers of all member nations. Thus, NATO institutionalized a continued U.S. role in Europe's defense, and fulfilled a long-standing British and French ambition to commit the new world to the maintenance of a favorable balance of power in the old. Someone quipped that NATO "kept the Soviets out, America in, and the Germans down." The first U.S. treaty of alliance since the 1778 alliance with France, it formally reversed America's earlier policy of isolationism. Realizing that the Berlin Blockade was both ineffective and counterproductive, the Soviets called it off in May 1949.

In September 1949, the German Federal Republic (the Bonn Republic, or West Germany), containing some 50 million people, was established. It was given authority over German domestic affairs, but Allied military occupation continued, and it was not permitted to rearm. Halting the dismantling of factories, Americans gave West Germany Marshall Plan aid to rebuild industry. It soon experienced remarkable economic growth.

The Russians retaliated in October 1949 by turning the Soviet occupation zone into the East Democratic Republic. Governed by a coalition of Communists and socialists, it divided big estates among small farmers and assumed government ownership of most industries. East Germany's population was relatively small, 17 million in 1985, but it became the Soviet bloc's second largest industrial producer.

Both the Soviet Union and the United States demobilized much of their armed forces after World War II. By 1949 Russia had cut its forces from 11.5 million to fewer than 3 million. Truman slashed military spending from $46 billion in 1946 to $13 billion in 1949. However, he maintained spending for the air force and for atomic bombs, on which America relied to deter the Soviets from using their ground superiority to overrun West Europe.

Developments in 1949 undermined America's sense of security. In August 1949, the Soviets exploded an atomic device. Also, the Chinese Communists, completing their rout of Chiang Kai-shek in December, took control of the world's most populous nation. The realization that 450 million more people had fallen under Communist rule was, to many Americans, a great shock that deepened their fear that America was endangered by aggressively expanding "world Communism."

The Red Scare: "McCarthyism"

America's leaders had long taken Communist professions of desire to spread communism very seriously. In the early 1920s, fear of Communist subversion had flared into a "Red Scare," resulting in purging libraries and firing teachers (see chapter 3). In the 1930s, the House established an Un-American Activities Committee that devoted most of its efforts to investigating U.S. Communists. Most Americans had never met a Communist and were ready to believe the worst of them. Meeting little contradiction, anti-Communist charges fed and enlarged upon each other. In the minds of many Americans , a picture formed of Communists as ruthless fanatics, tightly united (monolithic), and perversely dedicated to conquering the world, imposing stifling dictatorial controls on all aspects of life, and destroying religion. Moreover, utilizing mysterious methods of "infiltration" and "subversion," they possessed superhuman power, it was feared, to take control of any organization or country that they penetrated. When the leading Communist nation emerged as America's chief rival for world power, anti-Communist propaganda flared to new intensity. George Kennan wrote that Americans possessed an "image of the totally inhuman and totally malevolent adversary" and "considered any questioning of that image to be an act of treason."

The attorney general drew up a list of 168 organizations, many with high-sounding names, that he branded as fronts behind which Communists carried out their evil designs. Many feared that Communists had also penetrated the top levels of U.S. government, schools, and media and were thus in a position to betray America to the Soviet Union. Such fears were reinforced by the revelation, in 1946, that some atomic scientists had passed atomic secrets to Russia. Some feared that U.S. foreign policy was being subverted by officials who were secretly Communists, and many demanded that the government ferret out and expel Communists from positions in government, defense industries, education, and the news media. In 1947, Truman ordered an investigation of the loyalty of government employees which, conducted with little protection against false conviction, resulted in more than two thousand resignations or firings.

Some Americans, apparently motivated by Communist ideology, did assist the Soviets. In March 1948, Whittaker Chambers, a senior editor of *Time* magazine, accused Alger Hiss, head of the Carnegie Foundation and a former high State Department official, of having been a Communist in the 1930s and of passing secret government documents to Moscow. When Hiss denied these charges before a congressional committee, a young congressman, Richard Nixon, persisted in pressing the investigation. Eventually, Hiss was convicted of lying when he denied knowing Chambers, and most Americans assumed that this meant that he was also guilty of spying. Also, in March 1950, a British court convicted the physicist Klaus Fuchs of passing atomic secrets to the Soviets. In 1951, after a similar conviction, American scientists Julius and Ethel Rosenberg were executed.

In January 1950, a young Republican senator from Wisconsin, Joseph McCarthy, deciding that the best way to win reelection and national prominence was to ride the wave of anti-Communism, charged that he had a list of 205 dues-paying Communists who were employed in the State Department. His accusation captured headlines throughout the country, put him at the forefront of anti-Communism, and produced high public opinion ratings and large financial contributions to his campaign. He failed to produce his list, but when a Senate committee chaired by the conservative Senator Millard Tydings concluded that his charges were "a fraud and a hoax," McCarthy helped defeat Tydings in his bid for reelection. McCarthy continued to get headlines with new charges that numerous Hollywood script writers, college professors, media reporters, and even U.S. army officers were Communists. His allegations stimulated a kind of reign of terror, which became known as "McCarthyism," that cost many Americans their jobs and careers.

In 1950, Congress enacted the McCarren Internal Security Act, which required all Communist organizations to register with the government, barred Communists from holding jobs in defense plants or traveling abroad, prohibited anyone who had ever been a Communist from entering the United States, and authorized deportation of aliens who had ever been Communists. Truman, saying that America should not adopt the worst practices of the dictators, vetoed the bill, but Congress passed it over his veto. In 1951, McCarthy got the China expert John Carter Vincent fired from the State Department and accused General George Marshall of a "conspiracy so immense and infamy so black as to dwarf any previous such venture in the history of man."

One effect of the "red scare" was to create a political climate that seemed to require foreign party officials, if they wanted to remain in leadership positions, to take the toughest possible stand against Communists. It also aroused popular demand for the government to act as if the anti-Communist propaganda were literally true. Such a political climate made it dangerous for government official to oppose military measures against Communists, to advocate negotiations or compromises with them, or to do anything that could make them vulnerable to charges that they were soft on Communism. Furthermore, it put a premium on being the first to detect Communist plots behind reform or revolutionary movements abroad. This added to a tendency to attribute disturbances in any country, not to internal problems, but to evil machanizations by the Kremlin, which many foreigners considered an element of unreality in U.S. foreign policy.

NSC-68

In early 1950, Truman asked the State and Defense departments to make a thorough "overall review and reassessment of American foreign defense policy" in the light of the "loss of China" and the "Soviet mastery of atomic energy" and to recommend what America should do in response to the changed world situation. In April, led by Paul Nitze, chairman of the Policy Planning Staff, the panel completed a document, entitled "National Security Council-68." Summarizing the ideas that had developed among Cold Warriors, it maintained that the Soviet Union, "animated by a new fanatic faith, antithetical to our own," sought "to impose its absolute authority over the rest of the world." It "combined the ideology of Communist doctrine and the power of the Russian state into an aggressive expansionist drive, which found its chief opponent and, therefore, target in the antithetical ideas and power of our own county." This situation demanded, it concluded, a "bold and massive program of rebuilding the West's defenses" to meet "each fresh challenge promptly and unequivocally" and to "foster the seeds of destruction within the Soviet system." For this purpose, it said, America should spend 20 percent of its GNP, four times the existing level, on its armed forces.

State Department experts on the Soviet Union, including Kennan, objected that NSC-68 overstated both Communist unity and Soviet aggressiveness. In their analysis, the Soviets were concerned primarily with protecting the sphere they had already obtained and were aware that a general war would be fatal to Russia. Kennan rejected the assumption that fruitful negotiations with the Soviets were not possible until after years of military buildup. But in September 1950, after North Korea had invaded South Korea, Truman adopted NSC-68 as official policy. Stepping up military spending, Washington resolved to allow no additional country to fall to Communism, a vast expansion of America's security zone. In November 1952, America exploded the first hydrogen bomb—which had an explosive force a thousand times that of the Hiroshima bomb.

To increase Allied military strength in West Europe, the United States, rejecting Soviet proposals to reunite and neutralize Germany, sought to rearm West Germany. With memories of Germany's invasions still vivid, France and other countries objected. If they did not consent, Eisenhower's Secretary of State John Foster Dulles warned, America might be forced into an "agonizing reappraisal" of its policy of defending Europe. Eventually, in late 1954, France consented, but on conditions that Germany be restricted to twelve divisions, denied long-range missiles and atomic, chemical, and bacteriological weapons, and integrate its forces into those of NATO. Also, America promised to keep six divisions, and the British four divisions, in Europe.

Although nearer to Russia, West Europeans seemed to be less fearful than Americans of Russia's power. Washington urged them to create ninety-six divisions, but they were reluctant to raise military spending and, as late as 1974, still had fewer than thirty divisions.

In 1955, the Soviets drew their seven satellites—Poland, Czechoslovakia, East Germany, Hungary, Romania, Bulgaria, and Albania—into a military alliance called the Warsaw Pact.

At a later time, historians, with the advantage of hindsight, would see less danger of Soviet aggression than did America's leaders at the time. The Soviet Union had suffered terribly from the massive German invasion, and its industry, transportation, and housing were in shambles. As late as 1950, its industrial production was less than one-fourth of America's, and the economic inferiority of the Warsaw Pact nations to the NATO nations was even more pronounced. Despite its larger army, the Soviets lacked the military superiority essential to successful aggression. No matter how badly the Russians might want to expand, it would have been foolhardy at the time for them to seriously risk war with the West.

The Soviet documents that became available to Western scholars after the end of the Cold War shed much new light on the origins and conduct of the early Cold War. In general, they show that Stalin was painfully aware of the changed distribution of power resulting from the devastation of the Soviet Union and the explosive growth of the United States. He knew that only Americans had atomic bombs. The documents show that some Soviet government leaders were ideological Communists who operated on the theory that conflict with capitalists was inevitable, and that some men on both sides in the Cold War resembled the propaganda caricatures of ideological fanatics that each drew of the other. For example, while translating a conversation between Soviet Foreign Minister Vyacheslav Molotov and U.S. Secretary of State John Foster Dulles, the Soviet ambassador to America, Anatoly Dobrynin, got the impression that it was a dialogue of the deaf *and* the blind and that "it was obvious that as long as they and people like them were endowed with power the Cold War would never end." Nevertheless, Soviet leaders were frightened by the possibility of war with America and eager to avoid it. While seeking to capitalize on local opportunities to promote communism and improve national security, they sought to moderate their actions, and the actions of Communists in other East Europe nations, to minimize provocations of America. Except for part of East Prussia, the Soviets annexed no territory that had not been part of Russia's pre–World War I empire, and did not even recover all of the territories that Russia had lost in World War I.

Later, finding U.S. rhetoric about the magnitude of the Soviet menace overblown, some historians searched for other motivations for U.S. Cold War policies. Some maintained that America's foreign policy leaders believed that they could get public support for high military spending only if they described it as necessary to defend freedom and religion against atheistic communism, rather than as an effort to preserve a balance of power. Some scholars charged that Americans were driven by the desire to open the world to U.S. trade and investments—a kind of "Open Door Imperialism." Others pointed out that exaggerating the menace of Communist world conquest provided justification for America to expand—that overstating the menace of Communist conquest served to justify as defensive movements of U.S. troops into other continents that otherwise might have appeared to be aggressive. It was the Communist menace, wrote Kennan, that convinced Americans of the necessity of "pulling themselves together and accepting the responsibilities of moral and political leadership that history plainly intended them to bear."[1]

---

[1] The most basic difference among the historians who have written extensively on the origins of the Cold War is between those who conclude that it arose primarily from aggression by Stalin and those who see it as an outgrowth of U.S. expansion. The first group, called "orthodox" or "postrevisionist," include Herbert Feis, Arthur Schlesinger Jr., and John Gaddis. Most of these, however, see Stalin's aggression not as part of a master plan to conquer the world for communism but as a search for national security and aggrandizement. Others, "revisionists," conclude that the Cold War arose primarily from U.S. expansionism driven by the desire to secure oil and raw materials for itself and its allies and to promote foreign trade and investments, as well as worldwide free enterprise. Notable among these "revisionist" historians are William A. Williams, Gabriel Kolko, Lloyd C. Gardner, and Walter LaFeber. Others, including Melvyn P. Leffler, see as the primary force behind U.S. expansion the search for greater national security.

8 Cold and Hot War in East Asia

The "Loss of China"

At the end of World War II, China was so divided that to many it appeared to be less a nation than a mere geographical expression. Japanese troops still occupied large areas in the north and east, and Soviet troops held Manchuria. Chiang Kai-shek's forces had advanced little beyond their south-central redoubt, while Chinese Communists ruled more than a hundred million people, nearly one-fourth of China's population, in north and east China.

Communist-ruled areas lay close to China's big cities—Shanghai, Peking, and Tianjin—and the Reds seemed well positioned to capture them, along with their huge stores of Japanese weapons. This could make the Communists too strong for Chiang to defeat. "It was perfectly clear to us," President Truman wrote later, "that if we told the Japanese to lay down their arms immediately and march to the seaboard, the entire country would be taken over by the Communists."

To avert a Communist victory, the United States intervened in China's semi-suspended civil war. Ordering Japanese troops to surrender only to Chiang's forces and to defend their positions against any other forces who tried to capture them, America made the Japanese instant allies against the Communists. America used "the enemy as a garrison," Truman explained. Also, U.S. Marines landed in north China to keep ports and railroads out of Communist hands, while other American forces rushed large numbers of Chiang's troops, by air and sea, to Japanese-held areas. With this help, Chiang secured possession of the north China cities and most Japanese arms.

Chiang's troops had more difficulty in Manchuria, the provinces to the northeast of China's Great Wall. Pouring into Manchuria on August 9, 1945, Soviet armies, encountering little Japanese resistance, advanced rapidly. In the August 14 Sino-Soviet Treaty, the Soviets promised to give no aid to the Chinese Communists and to turn over the government of Manchuria to Chiang's officials. However, while General Albert Wedemeyer delayed moving Chiang's troops to Manchuria until Wedemeyer could provide winter uniforms, Chinese Reds infiltrated troops into Manchuria, where they managed, with Soviet connivance, to capture Japanese arms and take control of some areas.

America sought a strong China, united under a friendly government, to help prevent a revival of Japanese power, check possible Soviet expansion, and provide a growing market for U.S. goods. Consequently, they sought to avert escalation into all out civil war in China.

U.S. Ambassador Patrick J. Hurley had long believed that when the Communists realized that the Soviet Union would not help them in a civil war they would enter a coalition government under Chiang's leadership. He was delighted when, in the August 14 Sino-Soviet Treaty, the Russians promised that any aid they gave to China would go entirely to Chiang. Flying to Yenan, he personally escorted Mao to Chungking to negotiate with Chiang while Hurley returned to vacation in America (see Fig. 8.1). In six weeks of negotiations, Chiang and Mao came to agreement on some matters, but not on Chiang's demand that the Communists surrender control of their areas and armies as a precondition to Chiang's allowing them to share power. The Communists feared that if they laid down their arms before a coalition government took control, they would be massacred. "Negotiating with the Communists for their armies," admitted Chiang, was "like negotiating with a tiger for its skin."

Meanwhile, as Chiang's forces pushed into Manchuria and the Communists enlarged their areas in north China, the number of armed clashes multiplied. Having failed to arrive at an agreement, Mao returned to Yenan. In Washington, a distressed Hurley called a press conference and stormily resigned,

Figure 8.1 Seeking to get Communist leader Mao Tse-tung to enter a coalition government with Chiang Kai-shek, U.S. Ambassador to China Patrick Hurley flew to the Communist capital, Yenan, and triumphantly escorted a nervous Mao to Chungking to negotiate with Chiang. National Archives.

wildly blaming the collapse of his mission on interference by pro-Communist State Department officials.

To replace Hurley, President Truman appointed General George C. Marshall as special presidential emissary to China. Considered the architect of Allied victory, Marshall enjoyed enormous prestige. Truman instructed him to try to stop the fighting and to bring the Communists into Chiang's government. In the meantime, Marshall was told, he should continue to aid Chiang even if Chiang blocked any agreement.

Building on the progress already made by the Chinese, Marshall quickly scored a number of remarkable successes. In January 1946, he secured a cease-fire. Chiang agreed to move no more troops into north China, except Manchuria, and the fighting almost stopped. Also, the two sides agreed to cut the number of government divisions to fifty and of Communist divisions to ten, and to integrate gradually these two forces under Chiang's command.

Marshall also got a political agreement to merge the Kuomintang, Chiang's political party, and the Communist governments and to make preparations for adopting a new constitution. The two sides further agreed to give all citizens democratic rights and to pursue liberal policies.

But then events took a turn for the worse. When evidence mounted that a large section of the Kuomintang would refuse to abide by the agreements, the Communists demanded more proof of Kuomintang sincerity before carrying out their part of the bargain. Meanwhile, the two sides continued their race to occupy territories vacated by the Japanese, and new fighting erupted. In April, violating the cease-fire, the Communists seized Changchun, Manchuria's capital. In May, over Marshall's objections, Chiang launched an offensive that recaptured that city. Marshall got a new cease-fire, but it proved to be short.

Marshall considered the Communists, who were confident that they could win elections, to be more willing to transfer the contest from the military to the political sphere than was Chiang, who preferred to rely on his larger and better equipped armed forces. In July, Chiang launched large-scale military offensives that, he told Marshall, would crush the Communists in a few months. This meant all-out civil war. Rebuking "selfish" and "extremist" elements on both sides, Truman suspended new aid to Chiang and in January 1947, Marshall returned to America.

At the outset of the renewed civil war, the Kuomintang appeared to be much more powerful than the Communists. Its combat troops outnumbered the Communist troops by 5 to 1, and it had a monopoly on airplanes, tanks, ships, and heavy artillery. Some of its divisions were well trained and equipped by Americans. The Kuomintang also had large reserves of foreign exchange and better access to arms from abroad. Advancing on all fronts, its armies captured the Communist capital, Yenan, in March 1947.

Nevertheless, Chiang's Nationalists lost the war. The reasons for their defeat have been much debated. Chiang attributed it to his mistake in putting his best troops into Manchuria where the Communists could isolate them, his acceptance of cease-fires that interrupted his advance, and to the effectiveness of Communist infiltration and propaganda. Some ascribed the Kuomintang loss to insufficient U.S. aid. Basically, the Nationalists had less popular support. Consequently, Chiang's advancing troops found themselves in the role of an occupying enemy force instead of that of a liberating army. He had to assign many troops to guard captured cities and railroads, which left fewer troops available for further offensives, while peasant support enabled Communist forces to move quickly through the countryside to surround individual Kuomintang brigades. Also, Communist troops had high fighting morale, while many Kuomintang soldiers fought poorly or defected.

The Kuomintang was further handicapped by continued economic disruption. Deportation, at U.S. insistence, of Japanese civilians deprived China of trained technicians and industrial leaders, while U.S. destruction and dismantling of Japanese factories disabled the economy of Japan, China's principal trading partner. Also, the Russians looted machinery from Japanese-built factories in Manchuria as reparations. China's 1947 production was only half its prewar level.

Increasingly, Kuomintang armies were forced to abandon the countryside and withdraw within walled cities. Distressed by his military failures, Chiang, in September 1947, wrote that the Communists had "proved themselves abler and more devoted, and that without reform and rejuvenation the Kuomintang was doomed to extinction."

Alarmed that Chiang might lose, Truman, in July 1947, sent General Wedemeyer to China to study the situation. The general and his aides traveled and gathered information throughout the country. When, knowing that he was a friend, Kuomintang leaders sought his views, he told its assembled officials that he had found the government to be corrupt, overstaffed, and incompetent and that it abused peasants, acted more like a looting conqueror than a liberator, and looked for salvation to foreign aid rather than to its own efforts. In his report to Washington, he said that additional aid would be useless unless the Kuomintang reformed. He recommended that America first force the Kuomintang to make essential reforms and then give it massive assistance, including ten thousand U.S. officers to command its troops. Even then, he concluded, Manchuria would fall to the Communists unless it were put under international trusteeship.

Washington did not implement Wedemeyer's recommendations, nor did it make them public. All previous U.S. efforts to pressure the Kuomintang to make basic reforms had failed. Also, his proposal that America, in conjunction with other countries, take over Manchuria might not win support in America or abroad.

In July 1947, the Truman administration resumed aid to Chiang, which, according to administration figures, would total about $2 billion after Japan's surrender. Other nations furnished an additional quarter of a billion dollars. Critics charged that the amount was actually less and that much of the aid was not timely or in the kind of weapons and ammunition that were most critically needed.

In Manchuria, the Communists, taking control of the countryside, forced Chiang's troops into cities where they could be supplied only by air. Realizing the great importance of Manchuria, which contained three-fourths of China's industry, Chiang resisted U.S. advice to withdraw. In late 1948, when his armies finally attempted to break out, the Communists captured them and their vast stocks of U.S.-supplied arms.

Armed with U.S.-made weapons, the Communists then poured out of Manchuria into north China. In the battle of Huschow-Penpu, the largest of the war, they destroyed most of Chiang's best armies, whereupon Chiang's remaining troops seemed to lose the will to fight. In January 1949, the Communists captured Peking and, in April, they crossed the Yangtze River into south China. Chiang was doomed.

In August 1949, the U.S. government published a "White Paper," a collection of documents designed to prove that the imminent loss of China to the Communists was not America's fault. It maintained that the Kuomintang lost because it was inept, corrupt, and blind to the need for reform. No battle was lost because of a shortage of arms or ammunition, it said, and nothing that America could have done would have changed the result. Nevertheless, unconvinced critics stepped up their charges that Communist sympathizers had undermined U.S. support for Chiang. At the time, however, almost no one advocated going as far as sending U.S. troops to save him.

On October 1, 1949, Mao proclaimed the establishment of a new socialist state, the People's Republic of China.

In December 1949, with his surviving forces, money, and art treasures, Chiang retreated from mainland China to the large island of Taiwan. U.S. intelligence predicted that the Communists would soon take Taiwan, and, in January 1950, Truman announced that America had no intention of defending Taiwan or giving Chiang further military aid.

The conduct of the Soviets regarding China's civil war was puzzling. Despite their desire to spread communism, they contributed little to the Communist victory. They allowed Japanese arms to fall into Communist hands in Manchuria and delayed Chiang's movement of troops to Manchuria, but they made no detectable shipments of Soviet arms to the Chinese Reds. Instead, the victorious Communists were armed largely with U.S.- made weapons that they captured from Chiang. In 1946, Stalin had advised Mao against fighting Chiang and, even after a Communist victory seemed certain, advised an enraged Mao to halt his troops at the Yangtze and negotiate a peace, perhaps on the basis of a divided China.

Perhaps the Russians gave higher priority to their national interests than to spreading communism. The Soviet representative in Yenan, Petr Vladimirov, regarded Mao not as a true international (i.e., loyal to Moscow) Communist, but as a Chinese nationalist who sought good relations with America to reduce his dependence on Moscow. If China remained under Kuomintang rule, the Soviets could better justify holding Manchurian ports and railroads than it could if China had a Communist government. Also, the Russians may have believed that their national security would be better served by having a weak and divided China, rather than one that was powerful and united on their border.

After prolonged negotiation and hard bargaining, Stalin and Mao signed a treaty in February 1950 that made them allies against Japan or any nation allied with Japan. Amid much acrimony, Mao persuaded Russia to withdraw from Port Arthur and to surrender control of Manchuria's railroads.

China's adoption of communism profoundly shocked Americans. It more than doubled the number of people living under communism to one-third of the world's population. Most Americans assumed that China's Communist leaders were little more than Soviet puppets which, in American minds, greatly magnified the danger of Communist conquest of the world.

The question of what enabled the Communists to win in China was hotly debated for years by politicians and scholars, who arrived at consensus on few points. The Nationalists began the war with much greater military power and received much more foreign aid. However, because the Nationalists were allied to landlords, while Communists reduced rents and gave land to poor peasants, the Communists won the support of many of the peasants who constituted 80 percent of China's population. Also, almost all foreign observers who visited Communist areas reported that the Communists were less corrupt and more democratic than the Kuomintang.

Could more U.S. aid have saved Chiang? Most U.S. China experts and military analysts in China believed that, short of sending U.S. troops, no amount of aid could have produced victory unless the Kuomintang reformed, and few considered it capable of real reform. A government dependent on landlords, for example, could scarcely distribute their land to peasants. If this was true, the only feasible means of averting Communist rule was a coalition government. Hurley and Marshall attempted to negotiate a coalition but failed.

Nevertheless, conservative critics continued to insist that more aid would have saved Chiang, and many Republicans charged that pro-Communists in the Truman administration, betraying America, had delivered China to the Communists. In the era of McCarthyism, these attacks were politically damaging and resulted in the firing of most of the Foreign Service officers who had reported that Chiang could not win. Not until the Vietnam War did many Americans realize how difficult it was for foreigners to ensure the survival of a government that lacked popular support. "Any war, once lost in the social and political fields," Chiang wrote later, "cannot be retrieved by the military."

Britain and most other countries soon recognized the new Communist government. America did not. The Truman administration was under heavy fire for "losing China," and popular demand for a tougher anti-Communist stand was high. However, Secretary of State Dean Acheson, who had replaced Marshall, knew that China and Russia had a history of territorial disputes, and he believed that nationalism would ultimately cause the Chinese Communists to break with the Soviet Union if Americans did not "deflect from the Russians to ourselves the . . . hatred of the Chinese population which must develop." But, any possibility that America might recognize China's Communist government faded when America and China entered the Korean War. In early 1951, Assistant Secretary of State Dean Rusk charged that the Peking regime was a

Soviet puppet—it "is not the government of China. It does not pass the first test. It is not Chinese."

Later, political scientist John Spanier would conclude that "failure to establish normal relations with China, a country that might have been strongly attracted to a U.S.-Chinese policy of containment of the Soviet Union, was a strategic error of the first dimension."

The Revival of Japan

After Japan's surrender, U.S. troops occupied Japan, and General Douglas MacArthur, as Supreme Commander for the Allied Powers, took charge of governing Japan. One of his first acts was to order the emperor to announce by radio that he was not God. The embarrassed emperor, who had never claimed to be God, did broadcast a repudiation of the "false conception that the emperor is divine." The mass hysteria and suicide that many Americans expected to follow did not occur.

General MacArthur was a man of monumental ego, majestic language, and regal demeanor who, some felt, fit well into the Japanese scene. Bowing Japanese lined the streets over which he traveled, he censored newspapers, and his headquarters issued orders on all subjects. "The emperor wants to become a Christian," he once told a reporter, "but I don't think I can allow it." Some Americans called him a "Yankee Emperor." The Allies established an advisory Four Power Control Council, and a Far Eastern Commission, with representatives of all the nations that had waged war on Japan, but MacArthur ignored both. With Soviet troops excluded from the occupation, Moscow complained that it had no influence on policies regarding Japan.

The Allies stripped Japan of all the territories it had conquered, and made Okinawa and Japan's Pacific Islands, U.S. trusteeships. They rounded up the more than 5 million Japanese who had moved to its overseas possessions, particularly Korea, and returned them to Japan. They tried twenty-eight high officials for war crimes, found all guilty, and executed, among others, two former premiers, including Tojo. Ensuing trials resulted in about 700 executions and 3,000 imprisonments.

Seizing overseas Japanese-owned property as reparations, the Allies destroyed war industries and dismantled other factories to take as reparations. Japan's 1946 industrial production fell to only one-seventh its 1941 level, and its GNP dropped to only $1.3 billion, or $19 per capita. An article in the *New York Times Magazine* predicted that, stripped of its territorial possessions and industry, Japan could no longer support its 70 million people and that therefore its population would gradually fall to about 35 million, mostly through deaths from influenza and other diseases.

MacArthur's headquarters wrote a new constitution that deprived the emperor of his already scant political power, strengthened parliamentary government, guaranteed democratic rights, including academic freedom, and gave women the right to vote. Also, requiring Japan to "forever renounce war as a sovereign right of the nation," it specified that "land, sea, and air forces, as well as other war potential, will never be maintained," thus making Japan history's first officially pacifist nation.

Regarding Japan's industrialists and big landlords as enemies, Americans sought to destroy their power. A tax of up to 90 percent on capital forced the larger corporations to sell most of their assets, an effective method of "trust-busting." Seizing large landholdings and giving land to small farmers, Americans reduced farm tenancy from 50 percent to 10 percent, perhaps the lowest rate in any non-Communist country. They also imposed high graduated income and inheritance taxes, fostered labor unions, and attempted to ensure equal rights for women and universal access to education. All this added up, MacArthur told the U.S. Congress, to the "greatest reformation recorded in modern history." Historian Arthur Link concluded that MacArthur sought to create "a new and better America in the far Pacific."

General MacArthur was convinced of the primary importance of his theater of operations. "Europe is a dying system," he said. "The lands touching the Pacific with their billions of inhabitants will determine the course of history in the next ten thousand years."

Punishment of Japan eased sooner than punishment of Germany. MacArthur was treated with the respect he felt he deserved, and his hatred of the Japanese abated. He developed a sense of responsibility for them and was soon referring to them as "my little people." Also, Americans began to realize that a revived Japan was needed to check Soviet and Chinese Communist power. The phase of radical reform ended by 1948, followed by a "reverse course" that shifted emphasis to economic recovery. After MacArthur stopped exporting Japanese factories, industrial production recovered to more than half its prewar level—GNP in 1950 was $132 per capita—and MacArthur bombarded Washington for relief supplies. After June 1950, the Korean War proved a powerful stimulus to Japan's economy. By 1951, U.S. support for Japan, including military purchases, totaled an incredible $12 billion.

U.S. postwar policies regarding Japan had some unexpected effects. The creation of a temporary power vacuum in East Asia, the transfer of southern Sakhalin and the Kurile Islands to Russia, and the recognition of Soviet control of Outer Mongolia, Port Arthur, Dairen, and north Manchurian railroads greatly strengthened Russia's position in East Asia. The expulsion of Japanese civilians deprived Korea, China, and other areas of business leaders and technicians, while destruction of Japan's industry reduced East Asia's production and trade. The resulting economic distress caused many Asians to turn to communism. It cost America heavily to destroy Japanese industry, combat resultant Communist expansion, supply what Japan had formerly produced, and then rebuild its industry.

Normally, one would expect a people to resent changes imposed on them by an enemy, as the U.S. South had resented reforms imposed by the North during Reconstruction, and to abolish them at the first opportunity. Instead, after the Japanese recovered control of their government, they kept the U.S.-imposed reforms; in 1999 they still retained the "MacArthur Constitution." Because they had already decided to Westernize, and because many resented the role of their military in taking them into a disastrous war, MacArthur had driven them in the direction they wanted to go.

Also, MacArthur's redistribution of wealth and income raised the buying power of Japan's needy, thereby enlarging its domestic market and providing a powerful stimulus for economic expansion.

When Americans disarmed Japan and took over its government, they necessarily inherited responsibility for defending Japan. In treaties signed in 1951, that restored to the Japanese control of their domestic affairs, America got Japan to agree to build a "self-defense" force and accept U.S. military bases. Also Japan's economic and security needs influenced U.S. decisions to intervene in Korea and Southeast Asia.

The Korean War

On June 25, 1950, troops from Communist North Korea drove across the thirty-eighth parallel into non-Communist South Korea, thus escalating the Cold War into a hot war and raising the question of whether it would flare into a general conflagration.

Korea, a rugged six hundred-mile-long peninsula, had in 1950 a population of between 30 and 40 million. Nominally, it had been a part of the Chinese empire before 1895, when Japan expelled the Chinese. Russia competed with Japan for control of it until 1905, when Japan defeated and expelled the Russians. In World War II, the Allies decided to give Korea its independence. Soviet troops reached Korea a month before U.S. troops, but, at U.S. request, restricted their occupation to the half of Korea north of the thirty-eighth parallel.

Americans and Russians could not agree on the composition of a provisional government to conduct elections, and much bloody fighting erupted between right-wing and left-wing Koreans. In 1948, Americans established a government in the south headed by the right-wing Syngman Rhee, an ardent nationalist and a Princeton Ph.D. who had long lived in America. In North Korea the Soviets installed Kim Il Sung, a Communist. Each ruler imposed harsh dictatorship, and each claimed to head the rightful government of all Korea.

For a time it appeared that the big powers were disengaging from Korea. The Soviets withdrew the last of their troops by December 1948. Calling Korea of "little strategic value" and a costly military liability, the U.S. Joint Chiefs of Staff withdrew U.S. troops by June 1949. In a speech in January 1950, Secretary of State Dean Acheson included Japan, but not Korea and Taiwan, in America's "defense perimeter." Nations outside that perimeter, he said, must rely for defense primarily on their own efforts and on the UN.

Americans feared that Syngman Rhee, whom a presidential envoy once described as "a zealous, irrational, and illogical fanatic" and who had a large army and talked belligerently of uniting Korea, might start a war. In October 1949 he said that his army could capture North Korea's capital in three days;

in February 1950 he promised that the hour of reunification was fast approaching. An alarmed America stopped sending him offensive weapons.

Why did the North Koreans attack in June 1950? Until historians gain access to more Soviet and Chinese documents, the answer must remain tentative. Believing that world communism was monolithic, Americans assumed that the North Koreans acted on Moscow's orders. But some historians have questioned that theory. Nearly all Koreans wanted to unite their country, and Kim may have independently decided that the time was ripe.

However, it seems unlikely that either North or South Korea could have afforded to attack against the opposition of its big power backer, and North Korea was a Soviet satellite, whose army was trained and supplied by the Soviet Union. In early 1950, Kim twice went to Moscow, where he persuaded the Russians to allow him to attack, but not to promise to rescue him if he faced defeat. (In 1955, a Soviet premier would tell the Politburo: "We started the Korean War.") Russia's aid would be limited, Stalin told him, even if America intervened.

Why would the Soviets consent to a North Korean attack at this time? Perhaps they simply saw a chance to add South Korea to the Communist camp. From the statement by Acheson, and also from MacArthur's statement that he opposed a land war in Asia, they may have concluded that America would not send troops. Also, convinced that many South Koreans would welcome his troops as liberators from the oppressive Rhee regime, Kim assured Stalin that he could win a quick victory within a month, before America could enter.

Stalin insisted that Kim stop by Peking and get Mao aboard. Mao could hardly refuse. Kim had sent up to 150,000 troops to help Mao unite China; furthermore, as Stalin's successor later wrote, "no real Communist would have tried to dissuade Kim Il Sung from his compelling desire to liberate South Korea.

However, some suspected a hidden Soviet motive. At the time, Mao was massing his troops on the South China coast to invade Taiwan. America had withdrawn support from Chiang and had made it clear that it would not block a Communist invasion of Taiwan. Most observers expected the Reds to overrun Taiwan easily—Acheson told U.S. senators that its fall was inevitable. Taiwan would have been as significant a gain as South Korea for world Communism.

However, Stalin may have viewed the prospect of a Communist seizure of Taiwan with mixed feelings. The Soviets seemed to be less convinced than the Americans that the triumph of communism in China put China firmly under Soviet control. Although the Soviet Union and Communist China (PRC) were allies, their national interests were not identical. In the past, Russia and China had clashed along their 4,500 mile border, and Russia had seized territory that the Chinese considered rightfully theirs. The chief cement of their alliance was mutual hostility to America, and Communist conquest of Taiwan would remove the Chiang regime, the existence of which had been the chief source of U.S.-China hostility. Once Taiwan were annexed, Chinese patriots might even shift their attention to defending their national interests against Russia, and losing China as an ally would be a major disaster for the Soviet Union.

As soon as it became clear that the North Korean attack was a full-scale invasion, Washington reacted almost automatically, driven by domestic political necessities as well as by foreign concerns. In April 1950, under heavy attack for the "loss of China," and amid charges that it had betrayed America, the Truman administration had resolved that it could not allow any additional country to go Communist. All assumed that Stalin had initiated the Korean invasion, and foreign policy leaders were anxious to avoid repetition of pre–World War II appeasement; "otherwise, the Soviets will keep on going and swallow up one piece of Asia after another," said Truman. Also, Washington feared that any apparent lack of will to defend a friendly country might cause other allies to lose confidence in America and seek accommodation with Communists. Consequently, there was, according to Truman, "complete, almost unspoken acceptance on the part of everyone that whatever had to be done to meet this aggression had to be done."

On the day of the attack, June 25, 1950, Truman ordered arms and equipment sent from Japan to Korea. On the next day, June 26, he sent U.S. air and naval forces into the fighting. On June 27, he ordered U.S. ground forces into the battle. This, he wrote later, was the most important decision he made as president.

Meanwhile, the UN Security Council had met on June 25. The Soviet delegate, who had been absent since January to protest the Council's refusal to transfer China's UN seat to the Communists, did not attend. In his absence, the Security Council voted 9–0 to condemn North Korea as the aggressor. Two days later, on June 27, with Yugoslavia voting against and India and Egypt abstaining, the Security Council, in its first such action, called on members to give military assistance to South Korea to "repel the armed attack." Outside the UN building, the Soviet delegate sat in a limousine with radio open awaiting an order to go in and cast a veto, but Stalin decided not to veto UN intervention.

The Republican foreign policy expert John Foster Dulles argued that the North Koreans invaded "as a part of the world strategy of international communism," and Truman said that "communism has passed beyond the use of subversion to conquer independent nations and will now use armed invasion and war." If so, attacks could be expected elsewhere. On June 27, Truman ordered the U.S. Navy to move into the Taiwan Strait to prevent a Communist invasion of Taiwan, which action the Chinese Communists called "armed aggression against Chinese territory." Truman also resumed economic and military aid to Chiang, thus reentering China's civil war. In addition, he stepped up aid to the French, who were fighting Communist-led guerrillas in Indochina, thereby deepening U.S. involvement in the war in Vietnam. If Communist aggression were "allowed to go unchallenged," he wrote later, "it would mean a third world war." On June 29, the Soviet Union called on all nations to stay out of the Korean War.

Senator Robert Taft objected to Truman's taking America to war in Korea without congressional authorization. Truman called the war a "police action."

Previous presidents had used their power as commander in chief to move U.S. forces in ways that left Congress little choice but to declare war, but no previous president had waged a major war in complete absence of a congressional declaration. It was a startling demonstration of the degree to which presidents had assumed sole control of foreign affairs.

At first, the war was overwhelmingly popular—73 percent of the public supported intervention. When Congress heard that Truman had ordered U.S. forces into combat, members stood and cheered.

The Korean War meant defense of an area that was of little direct importance to America but that was important to Japan. Earlier, when the Japanese had fought for control of Korea, the United States had denounced Japan. But after Americans assumed responsibility for defending Japan, they found themselves fighting a similar war.

Unlike World War II, the Korean War was a limited war. In June 1950, Truman defined America's war aim as the expulsion of the North Korean invaders from South Korea, but he did not call for the total destruction of enemy power. Fighting a war under such restraints would be an experience that many Americans would find frustrating.

The Security Council called on all UN members to assist South Korea, but only 16 of the UN's 60 member nations sent troops. America furnished more than a million troops, 48 percent of the total UN troops, and South Korea furnished 43 percent, while the other fifteen nations provided 9 percent. Of the casualties, Koreans suffered nearly two-thirds, America almost one-third, and all others 4 percent.

At first, North Korean troops, welcomed by many South Koreans, drove south with surprising speed, and South Korea's large and well-equipped army fought less well than expected. Quickly capturing Seoul, South Korea's capital, the invaders overran all of South Korea except for a small area around a southern port city, Pusan (see Fig. 8.2).

Put in command of UN forces, U.S. General Douglas MacArthur, on September 15, 1950, landed a large force up the west coast near Seoul at Inchon. This risky but brilliantly successful move enabled Americans to cut the communications of the North Koreans, destroy more than half of the invaders, and eject the remainder from South Korea.

By expelling North Korean forces from South Korea, the UN had won the war. However, MacArthur's stunning victory, recalled General Maxwell Taylor, had an "intoxicating effect" on U.S. leaders and encouraged them to invade North Korea. Two-thirds of the American public wanted to invade, Syngman Rhee and MacArthur strongly urged it, and the Joint Chiefs favored it. On September 27 Truman authorized MacArthur to enter North Korea and destroy North Korea's armed forces.

The Allied invasion of North Korea represented a departure from containment. It meant taking the offensive to liberate a Soviet satellite. It confronted the Chinese with the prospect of the destruction of an ally and the advance of enemy troops to China's border, the Yalu River, on which the Chinese had large

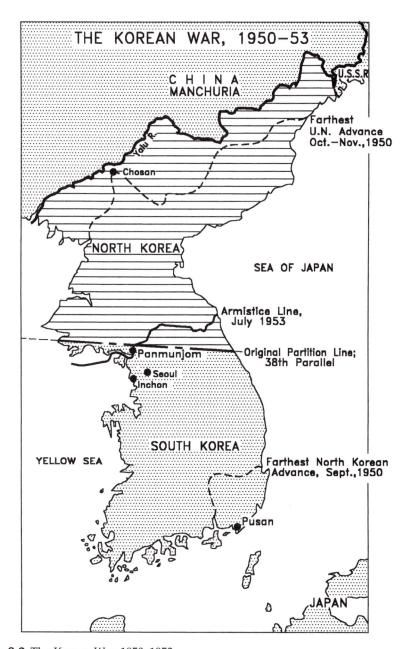

Figure 8.2 The Korean War, 1950–1953.

hydroelectric plants. In July, MacArthur had visited Chiang on Taiwan, where the two had announced that they had laid the "foundation for Sino-American military cooperation," thus making it appear that America planned to return Chiang to the mainland. On October 1, Communist China's foreign minister,

Chou En-lai, sent word through India that China would not act if South Koreans invaded North Korea but would send troops into the war if Western troops entered North Korea.

These threats did not deter Truman. Most Americans considered China, exhausted by civil war and lacking air and naval forces, to be incapable of serious fighting. Chinese intervention, said Dean Acheson, would be "sheer madness." On October 7, MacArthur sent U.S. troops into North Korea. On October 9, America secured a UN General Assembly resolution favoring elections for a "unified, independent, and democratic government," which Truman interpreted as indirect authorization to invade. He ordered MacArthur to continue his offensive even if he encountered Chinese troops. It proved to be a costly mistake.

On October 10, the Chinese announced that they would enter the war if U.S. troops continued north.

Seeking to enlarge the war, MacArthur stretched his discretionary authority to the limit. He sent planes over Chinese territory, bombed bridges between China and Korea, and, on October 9, strafed an airfield in Russia. His statements grew exceedingly bellicose, and Truman seemed to be having trouble controlling him. Worried that MacArthur's rashness might bring on World War III, the French and the British redoubled their efforts to secure a negotiated peace.

When Truman asked MacArthur to confer with him, MacArthur replied that he was too busy running the war to come to Washington, or even halfway. The president traveled to Wake Island to meet the general on October 14.

It was a curious meeting. Truman had trouble getting MacArthur to show him the respect due a commander in chief. MacArthur did not salute him. Truman brought a large staff, MacArthur almost none. Truman envisaged a long conference; MacArthur said he was too busy, and they met for less than three hours. Emphasizing that America sought to avoid reinvolvement in China's civil war, Truman told MacArthur to make no more provocative statements and to hold his air force in check. MacArthur told Truman that the war was practically won and would be over by Thanksgiving. The Chinese would not attack, he said, and if they did they would suffer "the greatest slaughter. We are no longer fearful of intervention."

Unknown to the two men, Chinese "volunteers" began crossing the Yalu River from China into North Korea that same day. On October 25–29, they inflicted a sharp defeat on the South Korean forces, apparently as a warning, but then withdrew from battle. By November 11, the Chinese admitted that they had sent volunteers, and U.S. intelligence had detected the presence of eight Chinese divisions.

Nevertheless, MacArthur continued to press for more offensive action. On November 6, Truman authorized him to continue his bombing of the Yalu River bridges. MacArthur also sought permission to pursue Chinese planes over China and to bomb Chinese airfields.

The British and the French grew increasingly insistent that Truman restrain MacArthur. They said that the general, by his aggressive moves, had derailed their efforts to open negotiations. In a new attempt, they invited China to send a delegation to the UN—it arrived in New York on November 24. That same day, saying that, if peace were to be negotiated, the talks would be handled by the military commander, MacArthur announced that he was launching an "end-the-war" offensive. Promising that it would end the war quickly enough to "have the boys home by Christmas," he sent columns of troops racing toward the Chinese border.

This November 24 offensive aroused much dismay. MacArthur's commanders opposed it as militarily unsound. The CIA had reported that as many as 200,000 Chinese troops were ready to enter the fighting, and the Joint Chiefs objected to provoking China by sending U.S. troops to its border. Europeans charged that MacArthur had launched the offensive to wreck negotiations.

Some UN troops reached the Chinese border, but they were soon in serious difficulties. On November 26, about 200,000 Chinese troops attacked, and, by November 28, they had MacArthur's forces in full retreat. Calling it an "entirely new war," MacArthur sought to bring Chiang's troops into the fighting. The Communist Chinese inflicted the worst defeat on U.S. marines that they had ever suffered and forced U.S. troops to fall back on ports for evacuation by sea.

At a press conference on November 30, Truman, calling for worldwide mobilization, suggested that he might use atomic bombs. British Prime Minister Attlee immediately flew to Washington to counsel restraint and argued that China was not a permanent Soviet satellite and that the Chinese Communists would resist Soviet control.

Expelling the Americans and the South Koreans from North Korea within two weeks, the Chinese invaded South Korea and captured Seoul in December 1950. By this time, they had the support of Soviet aircraft, which, however, operated only in rear areas. An Allied counteroffensive retook Seoul in March 1951 and pushed into North Korea, but the Allies did not again attempt to conquer all of North Korea.

Blaming his military reverses on the refusal by politicians to permit him to carry the war to China, MacArthur demanded that he be allowed to conduct all-out war. Denouncing "intolerable restrictions" that gave the enemy a "privileged sanctuary," he called for blockading and bombing China, dropping atomic bombs on North Korea and China, landing U.S. troops in China, and laying down a five-mile-wide barrier of radioactive cobalt between China and Korea. He rejected any suggestion that the Soviet Union might honor its treaty obligation to defend its Chinese ally. Unless restrictions were lifted, he said, America should withdraw. His proposals, said Truman, would involve America in war with both China and Russia, with the resultant "destruction of a good part of the world."

To increase pressure on Truman to lift restrictions, MacArthur launched a campaign of public appeals to the Republican party, Congress, and the American people. On December 5, 1950, Truman ordered him to make no more public statements and, on March 20, 1951, notified him to be particularly discreet because the president would shortly announce a peace move. On March 24, the general stated publicly that the expansion of UN military operations to China "would doom Red China" and that, if peace were to be negotiated, it would be by him. Truman called this "open defiance" that disrupted his peace move, and said later: "I was never so put out in my life." In addition, MacArthur wrote a letter to the Republican House leader Joseph Martin who, on April 5, read it in the House, saying that "if we lose the war to communism in Asia the fall of Europe is inevitable." Again, America's allies protested that a headstrong American general was attempting to drag them into world war.

For Truman, the letter to Martin was the last straw, and, on April 11, he fired MacArthur as commander of UN forces in Korea. "Good old Harry," said one British leader, "he always comes through in the end." But in America a groundswell of support for MacArthur threatened Truman's control of foreign policy. MacArthur's firing, said Senator Joe McCarthy, was the "greatest Communist victory," and Truman was "a monster conceived in the Kremlin." Republicans called for censure. According to a poll, three-fourths of Americans disapproved of Truman's conduct of the war.

Returning to America, MacArthur was greeted by enormous crowds in San Francisco and New York City, and he was invited to address a joint session of Congress. With majestic voice and high emotion, he delivered a memorable oration. On the battlefield one day, he said, he had come across a wounded soldier who asked him, "General, why must America fight with one arm tied behind its back? I could not answer." He demanded that the manacles fastened on the military by politicians be removed. He received a prolonged standing ovation, Herbert Hoover called him a "reincarnation of St. Paul," and Congressman Dewey Short said he was "God in the flesh." Then MacArthur launched a speaking tour across the country. Some feared that America's tradition of civilian control of the military would not hold.

But MacArthur had opponents. His superiority, which he made no effort to hide, aroused envy and hostility among more modestly endowed colleagues. Also, many considered his policy to be unwise. A larger war in Asia would draw U.S. resources from Europe, perhaps exposing that more vital area, and would have little allied support. The Joint Chiefs opposed it unanimously. War with China, Chief of Staff Omar Bradley told the Senate Armed Forces Committee, would be "the wrong war, at the wrong place, at the wrong time, and with the wrong enemy" and could result only in a "larger deadlock at greater expense." The Republican party invited MacArthur to address its 1952 convention, but gave its presidential nomination to one of his former aides, the genial General Dwight D. Eisenhower.

By this time the Korean War, which had developed into a military stalemate near the thirty-eighth parallel, had become highly unpopular. High costs and casualties, half-hearted support from allies, and the frustrations of fighting for limited aims embittered many Americans. Republicans began calling it "Mr. Truman's War," and Senator Robert Taft termed it an "utterly useless war." They criticized Truman both for not fighting it within sufficient vigor and for fighting it at all. A January 1951 poll showed that 66 percent of Americans favored complete withdrawal.

In June 1951, in response to a secret U.S. peace feeler, Russia's UN delegate proposed an armistice. Negotiations opened in July, but Americans found dealing with undefeated enemies difficult, and not until November 27 was agreement reached on a demarcation line between the armed forces. Negotiations dragged on for two more years while periodic outbreaks of fighting produced more casualties than had occurred before the talks began. The Communists charged that America was employing germ warfare, which America denied. Other issues were where to locate the boundary line, how and when to withdraw foreign troops, and whether to return all prisoners of war. By the spring of 1952, the two sides had settled all issues except the return of prisoners.

Americans had been delighted to learn that many of the 170,000 captured North Korean and Chinese troops did not want to return home. This, of course, was of enormous propaganda value in demonstrating the superiority of life in the free world. Also, America had a tradition of granting asylum to political refugees. Although international law required the return of all prisoners, America continued the war to defend the freedom of captured enemies not to go home.

According to Walter Lippmann, Truman was trapped in a dilemma. He was "not able to make peace, because politically he was too weak at home. He was not able to make war because the risks were too great."

The Election of 1952

With the stalemate in Korea persisting, Truman faced the decision of whether to run for reelection. He had served for almost eight years but was eligible to run again. However, a liberal in the midst of a postwar reaction, he was blamed for the stalemate in Korea, and a hostile press exaggerated the corruption in his administration. His standing in the polls fell to new lows. After he announced that he would not be a candidate, the Democrats nominated the witty intellectual governor of Illinois, Adlai E. Stevenson.

Rejecting Robert A. Taft and Thomas E. Dewey, the Republicans enlisted the popular General Dwight D. Eisenhower as their candidate. Eisenhower had led America's largest World War II military campaigns and, after the war, had served as president of Columbia University and as NATO commander. He was widely regarded as moderate on domestic issues and as internationally minded. For vice president, the Republicans nominated the young Richard Nixon, who had achieved prominence as a zealous anti-Communist. Their platform blamed the Democrats for the "loss of China" and for fighting in Korea "without will for victory." Denouncing containment as "negative, futile, and immoral" and for abandoning "countless human beings to despotism and Godless terrorism," it advocated "seizing the offensive" to liberate captive nations from communism.

In the campaign, Eisenhower said that America could "never rest until the enslaved nations of the world" had the right to "choose their own path." Nixon called Stevenson a graduate of "Acheson's Cowardly College of Communist

Containment." Particularly effective with voters was Eisenhower's promise that, as soon as he was elected, he would "go to Korea." The people gave him a smashing victory—34 million votes to Stevenson's 27 million—ending twenty years of Democratic administration.

Ending the Korean War

Peace negotiations had not succeeded by the time Truman left office in January 1953. In March 1953 Stalin died. Resolved to extricate America from the costly, stalemated war, Eisenhower employed a mixture of tough talk and concessions. In May, Secretary of State John Foster Dulles warned that America was considering using atomic weapons, and he and Eisenhower later claimed that this threat caused the North Koreans to agree to terms. However, the terms secured were far from a victor's peace. The two sides agreed to turn over all prisoners to neutral nations, and to allow both sides to interview them, after which the prisoners would tell their neutral custodians whether they wanted to return home. Bitterly objecting to ending the war short of victory, South Korea's President Syngman Rhee attempted to sabotage this agreement by releasing 27,000 prisoners. Nevertheless, the Communists kept their part of the bargain. Of North Korean and Chinese prisoners, 70,000 opted to go home, and 22,000 chose to stay in UN countries. Of the prisoners held by the Communists, 350, including 21 Americans, chose to stay with the Communists.

With this obstacle overcome, an armistice was signed on July 27, 1953, three years and a month after the war began. It gave North Koreans some territory south of the thirty-eighth parallel but gave South Korea a larger slice north of it for a net gain of about fifteen hundred square miles. The armistice also called for a conference to be held within three months to seek a political settlement, including reunification of the country, but a political agreement was not achieved.

Thus, despite much talk of rolling back communism and liberating captive peoples, Eisenhower and Dulles accepted the defeat of America's attempt to liberate North Korea. Senate Majority Leader William Knowland called the settlement "peace without honor." However, a poll indicated that the public approved of it by a margin of 88 to 12 percent.

The war further demonstrated the limits on America's ability, despite its enormous military superiority, to control events on the Asian mainland. Although China had little offensive strength, it had great defensive capacity near its borders. America handily won the first Korean War, the war to defend South Korea, but it lost the second Korean War, the war to take North Korea.

Although a relatively limited war, the Korean War had major consequences. As many as 5 million people were killed—3 million Korean civilians, 1 million Chinese soldiers, 500,000 North Korean soldiers, 100,000 South Korean soldiers, and 54,246 U.S. troops. Its direct cost to America was $22 billion. Costs to Korea, including property destruction, were incalculable. The war also elevated U.S. rearmament to a higher plateau, deepened U.S. involvement in Vietnam, saved the Chiang Kai-shek regime on Taiwan, further identified America with support of dictators, and, with $3 billion in war orders, stimulated the growth of Japan's economy.

Whether or not they had so planned it, the Soviets also benefited from the Korean War. The war diverted U.S. military resources from Europe, heightened Sino-U.S. hostility, and strengthened the Sino-Soviet alliance. Deepening China's dependence on the Soviet Union, it delayed any rapprochement between America and China that could have undermined Soviet influence in East Asia. When he learned that the Chinese were yielding to his urging that they enter the war, Stalin was deeply moved. "The Chinese," he said, "are so good!" He later urged the Chinese to prolong the war. However, the Russians paid a high price in the intensification of Cold War hostility and the quadrupling of U.S. military spending from $13 billion in 1949 to $52 billion in 1951.

In October 1953, America signed a mutual security treaty with South Korea that pledged the two countries to cooperate against any attack, thus committing America to remain on an Asian peninsula that the Joint Chiefs had pronounced a military liability. Between 1956 and 1984, U.S. aid to South Korea would total $15 billion. America also maintained troops there, forty three thousand in 1989, at an annual cost of $3.5 billion, plus the costs of the accompanying naval and air units. Despite U.S. efforts to promote democracy, dictatorship persisted, but South Korea experienced remarkable economic growth. Soon Korean products, including automobiles and computers, were competing with those of Japan in the U.S. market.

The Truman administration had seen a major revolution in America's foreign relations. With the help of Kennan, Acheson, and others, Truman, despite deficiencies in education and foreign policy experience, had laid the foundations for postwar U.S. foreign policy. There would be no return to isolationism. America switched from alliance with Russia and China against Germany and Japan to alliance with Germany and Japan against Russia and China. The Truman Doctrine and the Marshall Plan proclaimed a worldwide campaign against communism, which sometimes involved support of oppressive dictators. Multiplying defense spending to five times its postwar low, Truman made heavy commitments in Europe, the Middle East, Korea, and Vietnam. His assertive foreign policy contributed to his victory in the 1948 election, but the extreme anticommunism he helped to stimulate, and his failed attempt to take North Korea, also contributed to the ending of twenty years of Democratic rule.

9 Eisenhower and Dulles: Cold War in East Asia and Latin America

Eisenhower's Foreign Policy

Unlike many presidents, Dwight D. Eisenhower took office with broad international experience. His selection as president resulted largely from his leading role in conducting the strategy and diplomacy of World War II.

Born in 1890 in Texas, Eisenhower grew up in Kansas and graduated from West Point. He served in Panama, Europe, Africa, and the Philippines where, at the outbreak of World War II in 1939, he was an aide to General Douglas MacArthur. At age fifty, he had risen only to the rank of lieutenant colonel, but the war opened new opportunities. Chief of Staff General George Marshall appointed him to the War Plans Division and, in June 1942, passing over 366 senior officers, made him commander of U.S. forces in Europe, the war's number one combat assignment. He commanded the U.S. invasions of North Africa and Italy and, as Supreme Commander of Allied Forces in Europe, organized and led the 1944 Allied landing in France.

These duties required not only military but also diplomatic skills to deal with the conflicting demands made by the U.S., British, and French armed forces and brought him into close contact with top political leaders, including Churchill and De Gaulle. His competence, sincerity, genial manner, and friendly grin made a favorable impression. According to British General Bernard Montgomery, "he merely has to smile at you and you trust him at once." Receiving much credit for the success of military operations in North Africa, Italy, and France, he emerged as America's most popular war leader. After the war, he served successively as army chief of staff, president of Columbia University, and supreme commander of NATO forces in Europe.

After twenty years of rule by New Dealers, the Republican victory restored conservative businessmen to power. To his cabinet, Eisenhower appointed "eight millionaires and a plumber" and raised the percentage of businessmen in high offices in foreign affairs agencies from 43 percent to 76 percent. Secretary of Defense Charles E. Wilson, a former General Motors president, told Congress that he assumed that "what's good for the country is good for General Motors and vice versa."

A moderate on domestic issues, Eisenhower was an internationalist. He also fully shared the prevailing abhorrence of communism which he called "a tyranny that has brought thousands, millions of people into slave camps and is attempting to make all humankind its chattel." The contest, he said, was freedom against slavery, "light against darkness." Nevertheless, he said, he favored liberation of peoples from communism "only by peaceful means," and the only way to win World War III was to prevent it.

Eisenhower did not enter the presidency with any burning sense of mission. During the campaign he allowed Republican leaders to formulate his positions on issues and even to prevent him from defending his mentor, George Marshall, against McCarthy's accusation of treason. He conducted the presidency much as he had operated the military. Leaving day-to-day operations to subordinates, he played golf three times a week and sometimes appeared to be poorly informed on government affairs, an appearance accentuated by his verbal rambling and mangled syntax. Some thought he delegated so much power as, in effect, to make White House Chief of Staff Sherman Adams president for domestic affairs and Secretary of State John Foster Dulles president for foreign affairs. However, his relaxed manner hid passions that could boil over in awesome outbursts of anger, and Vice President Nixon found him a complex, even "devious" man who preferred to get his way by indirection.

Eisenhower's secretary of state, John Foster Dulles, a wealthy New York corporation lawyer and an experienced diplomat whose grandfather and uncle had headed the State Department, had long been regarded as the leading Republican spokesman on foreign affairs and the most likely future Republican secretary of state. The son of a Presbyterian minister, a Princeton graduate, he had studied international affairs, attended the 1919 Paris Peace Conference, become a Wall Street lawyer, and, during the war, worked with the National Council of Churches on planning for America's role in the postwar world. In 1951, Truman had assigned him to negotiate the peace treaty with Japan. "Foster has been in training for this job all his life," said Eisenhower. Contemporaries, including Soviet Premier Nikita Khrushchev, said that Eisenhower delegated management of foreign affairs to Dulles to an extraordinary degree. However, historians, including Robert Divine and Stephen Ambrose, have concluded that, although the president gave Dulles wide latitude, Dulles kept him fully informed and that Eisenhower, who shared Dulles's extreme anti-Communism, met often with foreign policy officials, made the critical decesions, overruled Dulles on some matters, and was more active in conducting foreign policy than his contemporaries believed.

Dulles's disposition was somewhat dour, and his discourse tendentious and moralistic. He was the ultimate Cold Warrior, a self-righteous, dogmatic crusader for free enterprise who interpreted the conflict between America and the Soviet Union as an apocalyptic struggle between good and evil. Emphasizing morality and religion, he insisted that America was the champion of righteousness, while Communists represented evil, and he saw nearly every political contest anywhere as an episode in this "irreconcilable" worldwide struggle. In such a conflict, he held, it was immoral to be neutral. The Republican platform plank that he wrote condemned containment as "immoral" because it "abandons countless human beings to a despotism and godless ter-

Figure 9.1 President Dwight Eisenhower and Secretary of State John Foster Dulles with South Vietnam's President Ngo Diem. Courtesy Dwight D. Eisenhower Library.

rorism." Instead, he sought "rollback" and "liberation" of peoples from communism.

Of course, Dulles was under pressure to act as if the Republican charge of insufficient vigilance against communism were true. And he had seen the ardent Cold Warrior Dean Acheson pilloried as insufficiently anti-Communist. To head the State Department personnel program, he appointed Scott McLeod, a friend of McCarthy. In his first year, in a "quiet reign of terror," McLeod fired or forced 2,200 "security risks" to resign. Dulles insisted on firing the career Foreign Service officers John P. Davis, John C. Vincent, and John Service because of their earlier criticisms of Chiang Kai-shek. He also removed George Kennan, an author of containment, who had come to believe that the Cold War was excessively militarized and to advocate mutual withdrawal of forces from Central Europe.

To head the CIA, Eisenhower appointed Dulles's younger brother, Allen Dulles, who raised the waging of secret war, or "covert action," against Communists and neutralists, particularly in less developed countries, to new highs. Empowered "to subvert, sabotage, and destroy our enemies," the CIA plotted to foment opposition to, and even to assassinate foreign leaders, including Fidel Castro of Cuba and Patrice Lumumba of the Congo, and helped to overthrow the governments of Iran and Guatemala.

Policies in East Asia

Consolidating their control of China, including semi-independent Sinkiang and Tibet, the Chinese Communists for the first time in many years brought all China, except Hong Kong and Taiwan, under one government. Most nations recognized the Communist government at Peking as the legal government of China, but the United States refused to so acknowledge it.

In Washington's view, China, long a friend of America, had betrayed that friendship and entered the Moscow-directed world conspiracy against America. China's armed forces were the most powerful in East Asia, and Americans regarded Communist China as a menace to Taiwan, South Korea, and other East Asian areas. For its part, Peking blamed America for prolonging China's civil war, attempting to conquer North Korea, protecting and arming Chiang's regime on Taiwan, blocking Peking's admission to the UN, and stationing U.S. military forces in countries near China. They charged that U.S. alliances with Japan, the Philippines, South Korea, Australia, and New Zealand were directed against them.

In addition to Taiwan, Chiang Kai-shek's nationalist regime held a number of islands close to the coast—the Tachens, Matsu, and Quemoy—which he used to interdict Communist shipping and also valued as stepping stones for his eventual return to the mainland. With U.S. aid, about $250 million annually, Chiang maintained large, modern military forces. In early 1953, Eisenhower, "unleashing" Chiang, announced that the U.S. fleet would no longer block attacks by Chiang, who thereafter occasionally bombed and raided the mainland.

In September 1954, the Chinese Communists opened up an artillery bombardment of Chiang-held offshore islands, Quemoy and Matsu, killing two Americans. This made these small islands, according to Nixon, "stakes in the 'poker game of world politics.' " The U.S. Joint Chiefs recommended using U.S. forces to defend them and also to bomb China. Calling the Communist Chinese more dangerous than Hitler, Dulles told Eisenhower that there was at least an even chance that America would have to go to war.

In December 1954, in a Treaty of Mutual Defense, Washington promised Chiang to defend Taiwan and, possibly, "other territories." However, in a move to moderate Chiang's conduct, the treaty also specified that neither he nor the United States would conduct military operations from Taiwan or reinforce the offshore islands without the consent of the other, a provision that, in effect, "releashed" Chiang. Furthermore, Americans persuaded him to withdraw from the indefensible Tachens.

In the January 1955 Formosa Resolution, Congress, with only three opposing votes in each house, authorized Eisenhower to use U.S. forces to defend Taiwan and related positions, thereby delegating in advance the power to take America into war. Sending U.S. marines to Quemoy armed with atomic-capable artillery, Eisenhower said that he knew no reason why atomic bombs should not be used. However, he ruled that America would defend these islands only if it appeared that an attack on them was preliminary to an invasion of Taiwan.

Communist bombardment tapered off, and by May 1955 the crisis had passed. When Premier Chou En-lai suggested negotiations, talks between U.S. and Chinese diplomats began in Geneva. They did not resolve the differences, but for a time transferred the dispute from armed forces to diplomacy.

In 1958, new clashes between the Nationalists and the Communists led to renewed Communist artillery bombardment of the offshore islands, primarily Quemoy, where Chiang had stationed 100,000 men, one-third of his army. Fearing that this bombardment was a prelude to an invasion of Taiwan, America assembled a large naval force. In September, Dulles implied that America would defend Quemoy with atomic bombs, while Khrushchev warned that he would consider an attack on China to be "an attack on the Soviet Union." British Prime Minister Harold MacMillan protested that these small islands were not worth taking the world to "the brink of World War III." "Who would have thought," said Mao later, that the bombardment "would stir up such an earth-shattering storm?"

However, behind a bellicose front, Washington again took moderating action. The Joint Chiefs recommended that Chiang withdraw from Quemoy and Matsu. In late September, Dulles said that if the Communists would agree to a cease-fire, America would ask Chiang to reduce his forces on Quemoy and would even promise to refrain from helping Chiang invade the mainland. Visiting Taiwan in October, Dulles secured Chiang's agreement to renounce the use of force to recover the mainland, and to withdraw some of his troops from the offshore islands. Meanwhile, the Soviets gave Mao less than total backing. In 1958, talks between Peking's and Washington's ambassadors to Poland resumed, and Peking announced that henceforth bombardment would occur only on odd-numbered days. Again tension eased.

However, the Chinese Communists continued to reject the U.S. proposal that both sides renounce the use of force in the Taiwan Strait. Insisting that Taiwan was Chinese territory and, therefore, strictly an internal affair, they continued to demand that America withdraw all troops and aid from Taiwan.

Relations with Developing Countries

With the Cold War in Europe and East Asia in apparent stalemate, the chief Cold War arena shifted to the less developed "Third World" (countries aligned with neither America nor the Soviet Union), the nonwhite countries of Southeast Asia, Latin America, and Africa. In 1949–1953 more than three-fourths of U.S. economic assistance went to Europe; in the 1953–1957 period more than three-fourths went to developing countries.

The economic, social, and political patterns prevalent in Third World countries were so different from those of North America and Europe that Americans found it difficult to understand them. By definition, a less developed country lacks industry. Most of its people, sometimes 80 percent, live by farming and mining. In such countries, ownership of agricultural land tends to concentrate in relatively few hands. Sometimes 10 percent of the farmers own 80 percent or more of the land. Consequently, the typical inhabitant is a poor farmer, or peasant, who rents the land he tills, often for half of the crop.

Most developing countries are very poor. In the 1950s the CIA listed the average per capita income in many of them as between $60 and $200 per year. Furthermore, that meager income was very unequally distributed. A small group of large landholders might be fabulously wealthy, while the mass of their countrymen were desperately poor. An estimated ten thousand people died each day of malnutrition.

Americans who visited such countries sometimes wondered how such enormous disparities could long persist. The big landlords, who collected rents and interest, usually controlled the government through a king or military dictator who protected their interests. Often they exempted themselves from taxes, thereby increasing the tax burden on the peasantry. Their sons enjoyed special privileges, such as access to education and exemption from military service. Sons of the wealthy held the top positions in the church, be it Protestant, Catholic, Moslem, or Buddhist, and the church usually supported the establishment, although lowly priests might sympathize with the peasants. This system was defended by a professional army. Foreign investors found it congenial to do business with the aristocracy, and appreciated the low property taxes and easy access to the mineral rights in vast tracts of land. Thus, the common people found themselves held in a subordinate position by a formidable combination of landlords, dictator, army, church, and foreigners.

Of course, less developed nations varied, and none exactly fit this model. Modern influences to some degree impacted all Third World nations, and all developed modern economic sectors and a small middle class. Sometimes the rising middle class joined with the peasants to overthrow the landlords and kings and to establish republics.

Meanwhile, some countries that had been conquered by whites fought for independence. World War I and World War II, by gravely weakening European nations, improved opportunities for independence movements to succeed. Nearly all the remaining colonies won independence after World War II—between 1945 and 1960 thirty-seven new nations appeared. Their leaders were ardent nationalists who sought complete freedom from foreign control and who pushed for rapid economic development of their nations. Many of them regarded themselves as champions of the common man, and only a few were deeply concerned about the Soviet-American Cold War.

The United States and the Soviet Union competed for influence in these newly independent nations. In this competition, the Soviet Union had considerable assets. An important component of Marxist-Leninist doctrine was that imperialism represented cruel exploitation by capitalists who found it necessary to sell abroad goods that their own workers were too impoverished to buy. Communists professed to oppose all imperialism and to support all fights for independence from empires. Also, Communists had lifted Russia from a semi-developed country to the world's second largest industrial producer, and they claimed that communism offered developing nations a shortcut to economic growth through government financing rather than through the slower accumulation of private capital.

Many leaders of developing nations were unwilling to rely for economic development solely on private enterprise. Such development in England and America, they believed, had been too slow. Also, relying on capitalism would prolong the period of domination of their economies by foreign investors. Instead, they favored government-led economic development, especially of basic industries. Many capitalists condemned such a government role in the economy as "socialism."

Recalling its own origins in its fight for independence from the British Empire, the United States had long championed revolutions, but its enthusiasm for them was waning. The success of the American Revolution and the system it produced made the United States rich, powerful, and protective of its wealth. Moreover, Americans had made large profitable investments in less developed nations, which gave them political influence there, and these holdings were endangered by revolutionaries who sought to free their countries from foreign exploitation and control. Anti-imperialism yielded to anti-communism; America fell increasingly into the role of the "establishment" and, wrote historian Thomas G. Paterson, became the "target rather than the model of revolution."

Nevertheless, the United States retained great assets in the competition for influence in developing nations. Its long history of supporting freedom, democracy, and the common man had made it many friends. U.S. culture had wide appeal. In 1942, after a world tour, Wendell Willkie reported an "inexhaustible reservoir of good will for the United States" among the common people of the world. Many of them sought to "Americanize" their own societies to achieve the same high standard of living, and only America was wealthy enough to give them substantial finance aid.

However, America sometimes failed to make full use of these assets. An obsessive fear of communism and of groups that received Communist support sometimes pushed America, long admired as a champion of democracy and freedom, into alliance with militarists, imperialists, oppressive landlords, feudalistic monarchies, and ruthless dictatorships that represented everything that the principles of Americanism opposed.

Eisenhower Seeks an Independent South Vietnam

The Cold War ebbed and flowed in the Third World, particularly in Southeast Asia and in Latin America, where rising nationalist revolts received Communist backing. Despite Eisenhower's insights into the nature of the problem—"nationalism is on the march," he said, "and World Communism is taking advantage of the spirit of patriotism to cause dissension in the free world"—he had little success in coping with it.

Many East Asians had been ruled by Europeans: the British in Burma, Malaysia, and Hong Kong; the Dutch in the East Indies; the French in Indochina; Americans in the Philippines; Russians in the Amur provinces; and the Portuguese in Macao. At best, rule by foreigners was exploitive. Exporting tin, rubber, spices, oil, lumber, and rice from their colonial holdings, foreigners made huge profits while most natives remained in poverty. A rising number of Asian nationalists developed a deep hatred of "imperialism," by which they meant rule of Asians by whites, and they fought to free their nations from foreign control.

Consequently, many Asians did not object in 1942 when the Japanese, using the slogan "Asia for the Asians," expelled Europeans from Asian countries. When the Japanese also proved to be abusive, however, the desire for self-government rose. Organizing independence forces, natives fought to expel the Japanese and, afterward, to prevent the return of European rule.

In line with its historic support of efforts by other peoples to win independence, America took steps to free the Philippines, advocated giving Indochina independence from France, advised the British to free India and Malaysia, and urged the Dutch to free the East Indies. However, Americans found themselves in a dilemma. Fearful of possible Soviet domination of Europe, their top priority was to draw Western European nations into an anti-Communist coalition. How could they cultivate the cooperation of these nations in Europe and, at the same time, support uprisings against them in their Asian colonies? Washington hesitated. Russia did not have this problem. All of the colonial powers were its adversaries, and any revolution against them, whether Communist or not, served its interests. Nevertheless, Soviet support for a revolution in any colony aroused U.S. fears that it might come under Communist control. Therefore, in 1949, America threw support to France's attempt to reconquer Indochina.

French Indochina was comprised of three countries: Laos, Cambodia, and Vietnam. Laos, whose 1950 population was 3 million, was landlocked and underdeveloped. Cambodia had a population of only 7 million. Vietnam, with a population of about 30 million, extended 1,000 miles north to south but only 50 to 350 miles wide, between the South China Sea and the mountains. Most of its people, concentrated in the rich deltas of the Red River in the north and the Mekong River in the south, were rice farmers, but Vietnam also exported much rubber and coffee. Its fight for independence would deeply involve the United States for decades.

Although most Vietnamese were descended from people who migrated from south China, Vietnam had a long history of fighting for independence from China. The French arrived in force in the mid-nineteenth century and consolidated their rule over Indochina in the 1880s. Acquiring large rice and rubber plantations they extracted tin, tungsten, and oil. Like other imperialists, their role was suppressive and exploitative. After nearly a hundred years of French rule, for example, Indochina had only six hundred university students, and more illiteracy than before the French conquest. Raising a third of government revenue from the sale of opium, the French bloodily suppressed rebellions.

In 1940, after France was occupied by Germany, the Japanese sent troops into Vietnam. However, they left government administration in the hands of the French until 1945, when they replaced them with a Japanese-dominated Vietnamese government headed by Emperor Bao Dai. In 1945, the Japanese, short of food, extracted so much food from Vietnam that an estimated 2 million Vietnamese starved.

Their experience under French and Japanese rule intensified the desire of Vietnamese for self-rule. In the twentieth century, their independence movements were led mostly by Vietnamese who had absorbed European culture. Of these, the Communists had a underground-type of organization that was particularly difficult for the French to eradicate. Leadership of the Vietnamese independence movement was assumed by the Communist Ho Chi Minh. Born in 1890 of upper-class parents and educated in a French school, Ho had left Vietnam as a young man and spent thirty years abroad working as a fireman on a French freighter, a laborer in America, and a cook in London. In Paris he had joined the Communist party, and in Hong Kong in 1930 he organized the Vietnamese Communist party. Returning to Vietnam in 1941, he formed a coalition of Communists and other independence forces called the Vietminh (League for Independence) to fight against the Japanese and, with some help from America's secret service, the OSS, raised an army of five thousand. After Japan surrendered, his forces moved into Hanoi, and, on September 2, 1945, with Americans at his side, he proclaimed Vietnam to be independent.

President Roosevelt had opposed returning Vietnam to France, and he suggested an international trusteeship as a preliminary to independence. But Roosevelt died in April 1945, and President Truman, fearing that support for Asian independence movements would alienate Europeans "whose help we need to balance Soviet power," ignored Ho's repeated appeals for cooperation. Instead, he told De Gaulle that America would not oppose France's return to Vietnam. The British, who occupied south Vietnam after Japan's surrender, helped the French reestablish themselves there.

The Allies assigned the Chinese to send troops into the northern half of Vietnam to accept the surrender of Japanese troops. Preferring French rule to continued Chinese occupation—"It is better to sniff French dung for a while then eat China's all our life"—Ho agreed to allow the French to return on the conditions that they send no more than fifteen thousand troops, which would withdraw within five years, give Vietnam self-government as a "free state" in the French union, and permit free elections. The French did not keep these promises. Instead, attempting to reestablish complete control, they bombarded the city of Haiphong in November 1946 and seized Hanoi, starting a long war.

Scattering Ho's poorly equipped forces, France's well-equipped armies quickly seized Vietnam's cities and communications. Together with Vietnamese troops in their hire, French forces totaled about 500,000. Nevertheless, they were unable to subdue the Vietminh who, fighting as guerrillas, held much of the countryside, particularly at night.

Claiming that they were fighting not to reconquer a colony but to save Vietnam from communism, the French restored Bao Dai as emperor in 1948. But they gave little power, and they resisted U.S. pressure to promise real independence.

Meanwhile, Americans were becoming increasingly alarmed by worldwide Communist gains. By 1949, it had become clear that the Communists would soon win the civil war in China. Under heavy attack for allowing communism to spread (some charged that Communist gains resulted from Democratic treason), the Truman administration concluded that it could not allow any additional country to fall under Communist control.

Although no one had ever considered remote Vietnam to be vital to the United States, the Joint Chiefs now warned that the fall of Indochina to the Communists would create a "Soviet position of dominance over Asia" and a "major threat to U.S. security." In May 1949, Truman made the fateful decision to support French efforts to retake Indochina, and, after the Communist invasion of South Korea in June 1950, he increased aid. By the end of his term, he had sent three hundred military advisers and $150 million to Vietnam. By 1954, when America was paying 80 percent of the costs of France's Vietnam war, total U.S. aid reached $4 billion. Meanwhile, between 1949 and 1954, the Soviets and the Chinese gave the Vietminh $400 million.

Repeatedly, Eisenhower urged the French to make a public commitment to free Vietnam. They should make it clear, he maintained, that, instead of an imperialistic war against independence, they were fighting a war between freedom and communism, thereby stripping the Vietminh of their mask of freedom fighters and casting world communism, instead of France, in the role of "outside aggressor." But the French, determined to hold on to their colony, refused.

The French won many victories, but Vietminh guerrillas continued to control two-thirds of the countryside. In an effort to tempt the Vietcong to come out and fight a large conventional battle, the French parachuted troops into an isolated inland post called Dien Bien Phu, raising the total number of troops there to twenty thousand. As they hoped, the Vietminh took the bait and gathered around, but in larger numbers than expected and with artillery they had dragged many miles through forests and over mountains. On March 13, 1954, the Vietminh launched their assault. Their artillery disabled the airstrip, and, on the third day, the French artillery commander, who had boasted that he would instantly silence any Vietminh artillery, committed suicide. Despite large manpower losses, the Vietminh, digging diagonal ditches, steadily constricted the French-held area, making resupply by parachute drop more difficult. Soon, astonishingly, it appeared that the large French force was doomed.

The prospect of such a major defeat aroused consternation in Washington. The destruction of a large French force might sufficiently discourage the French as to cause them to give up the fight. If Vietnam fell, said Eisenhower, other countries would fall in turn, like a row of dominos (the "domino theory").

France's chief of staff flew to Washington to plead for U.S. military aid. Secretary of State Dulles advocated sending both bombers and troops, and Vice President Nixon publicly suggested that America put "our boys in."

But Eisenhower, who less than a year earlier had brought the costly Korean War to an end, was reluctant. When Air Force Chief of Staff Nathan Twining proposed dropping atomic bombs around Dien Bien Phu, Eisenhower said, "We can't use those awful things against Asians for the second time." Also, Eisenhower maintained that an air strike alone would not be effective, while sending U.S. troops might be seen as a "brutal example of imperialism."

Congressional leaders advised that America should intervene only if assured of full support from its allies and if France agreed to give Vietnam independence. A poll revealed that the American people, 10 to 1, opposed sending troops. One observer wrote that "if we send armies into the war in Indochina they will go bearing the odium of white domination and, even should the result not be embroilment with China, we will find Indochina as much an albatross about our necks as have the French."

Nevertheless, Eisenhower told Dulles that he would intervene as part of an international effort if the British would also send troops. On April 5, Dulles flew to England to urge the British to do so, but Churchill refused. Foreign Secretary Anthony Eden advised that "nothing less than intervention on a Korean scale, if that, would have any effect." The situation seemed to require negotiations.

On April 26, an international conference including France, the Emperor Bao Dai, the Vietminh, Cambodia, Laos, Britain, the Soviet Union, China, and the United States assembled at Geneva to discuss Asian issues. Dulles tried to ignore the delegates from Communist China, which America did not recognize. On May 7, while this conference was in session, the French at Dien Bien Phu surrendered. On June 12, the discouraged French parliament named a new premier, Pierre Mendes-France, who promised to end the war by July 21.

In eight years of fighting, the French had killed and wounded large numbers of Vietminh, but also, had lost nearly 100,000 dead and spent more than $7 billion, nearly twice as much as they received in Marshall Plan aid. In July 1954, the French conceded Indochina independence as three nations: Vietnam, Cambodia, and Laos.

In order to separate the fighting forces, the Geneva Agreements of July 1954 provided that all of the armed forces fighting for France would withdraw into the half of Vietnam south of the seventeenth parallel, while all Vietminh forces would withdraw north of that line. Northern Vietnam would be administered by Ho Chi Minh and the south by Bao Dai. The Geneva agreements also specified that the seventeenth parallel was only a temporary military demarcation line, not a "political or territorial boundary," and that, in two years, an internationally supervised election would be held to choose a government for a united Vietnam. In the meanwhile, neither half would admit any new military forces or equipment, make any military agreement with any foreign power, or allow foreign bases.

Ho, who believed that complete victory was within his grasp and who did not trust France to permit the promised election, wanted to continue fighting. But China seemed to fear that if the French were ejected completely the Americans would replace them, or that a united Vietnam might not be China's ally. Moscow and Peking pressured Ho into accepting. Washington refused to sign the Geneva Agreements but promised not to disturb the settlement by force.

The French moved their colonial government south from Hanoi to Saigon. Along with government officials and troops went up to a million civilians who had worked, fought for, or supported the French. A smaller number of Ho Chi Minh supporters moved north of the seventeenth parallel.

Dulles was appalled by the Geneva Agreements which the National Security Council called a "disaster" and "major forward stride of Communism." Not only did they concede control of the northern half of Vietnam to Communist Ho Chih Minh, but, because most Vietnamese regarded him as their George Washington, he was widely expected to win the scheduled 1956 election and thereby also take control of the southern half of Vietnam. Although Americans had not been impressed by Japan's pre–World War II argument that it needed secure access to the resources of Southeast Asia, after Americans assumed responsibility for Japan's defense they came to believe that it was indispensable to Japan. It was, said Eisenhower, "a region that Japan must have as a trading area or Japan, in turn, will have only one place to go—that is, toward the Communist areas in order to live." If that happened, "the Pacific would become a Communist lake."

Dulles moved swiftly to block the scheduled 1956 election. Elbowing aside the French, America, in violation of the Geneva Agreements, took over the arming and financing of France's former colonial government, now located in Saigon and headed by Premier Ngo Dinh Diem, an anti-Communist Catholic Vietnamese nationalist. When skeptics expressed doubt that Americans could succeed where the French had failed, they replied, "We are not the French." With U.S. support, Diem ejected the French puppet Emperor Bao Dai and rigged an election in south Vietnam that made Diem president by a 98 percent majority of the vote. Eisenhower then promised to help him maintain the independence of South Vietnam, which, of course, cancelled the scheduled election of a government for all Vietnam. The United States was seeking to establish a separate independent nation in the south of Vietnam.

In September 1954, Dulles organized an anti-Communist Southeast Asia Treaty Organization (SEATO), enlisting Britain, France, Australia, New Zealand, the Philippines, Thailand, and Pakistan to defend the new nation, called South Vietnam. However, Indonesia, Burma, and India refused to join it.

These moves raised two questions: (1) Would the people of Vietnam, north and south, agree to the division of their country into two nations? and (2) would the people of South Vietnam allow themselves to be governed by the former French colonial regime now located in Saigon and financed and armed by the United States?

With U.S. aid, Diem moved his military forces across the countryside to secure control of South Vietnam. However, it was difficult for him to win popular support. His government was composed of northerners who had fought against independence (in terms used earlier in U.S. history, "carpetbaggers" and "Tories.") Also, he was a Catholic in a country that was mostly Buddhist. A conservative, he restored to landlords lands that the Vietminh had given to peasants, abolished democratic election of village chiefs and, violating the terms of the truce, made determined efforts to destroy or imprison all who had fought under Ho Chi Minh.

In North Vietnam, meanwhile, Ho had his hands full trying to repair the ravages of war and to restore North Vietnam's economy, and he still hoped that the election agreed upon at Geneva might be held. Therefore, he gave anti-Diem forces in South Vietnam little help. In 1959, however, he gave approval to armed resistance to Diem's regime. South Vietnamese anti-Diem fighters called themselves the Vietminh, but Ngo Diem and his American supporters called them Vietcong (Vietnamese Communists), a name that stuck.

Thus, the United States had entered Vietnam in support of an attempt by France to keep its colony, and after the failure of that effort, remained to block a nationwide election by creating an independent nation in the southern half of Vietnam. As fighting spread, Eisenhower stepped up aid to Diem. At the time, few foresaw how immensely difficult and costly this course of action would eventually prove to be.

Latin American Policy

In area, Latin America is two and a half times larger than Europe, and it contains more people than the United States. In the 1950s, about half of Latin American exports were to the United States, and about one fourth of U.S. exports went to Latin America.

In the 1950s, Latin-American economic, social, and political institutions bore little resemblance to those in the United States. In North America, the native Indians had been decimated and replaced by whites, but, in most regions of Latin America, Amerindians had not been eliminated. Peru remained 48 percent, Guatemala 54 percent, and Bolivia more than 60 percent Indian. Overall, people of mixed blood, called mestizos, were the most numerous element in the population. Partly because whites had imposed their rule through conquest, most Latin American political and social systems were undemocratic, and changes of government usually occurred as violent coups or revolutions.

Latin America was much less industrialized than the United States. Nearly half of its people were engaged in agriculture, and nearly 90 percent of its exports were of raw products of farms and mines, such as oil, coffee, bananas, sugar, copper, and tin. Its per capita income was less than 10 percent that in the United States, and this low income was very unevenly distributed. Ninety percent of the farmland was owned by fewer than 10 percent of the farmers, and 70 percent of the wealth was held by 2 percent of the people. A small upper class was wealthy, while most people lived in poverty. Half were illiterate.

Resentment by the poor of the great gap between rich and poor sometimes exploded in violence.

Over the years, U.S. capitalists invested huge sums in Latin America. U.S.-owned corporations produced 10 percent of Latin America's GDP and 50 percent of its exports. The political and economic interests of foreign investors usually coincided with the interests of the propertied upper class. For example, keeping government spending on education and public health low helped to keep taxes on property and incomes low.

The existence of oppressive regimes gave the Communists opportunities to form alliances with Latin America's poor. The resultant danger that Communists might capture control of revolutions there greatly alarmed both Latin America's wealthy class and Washington. At the April 1948 Inter-American conference at Bogota, the United States secured adoption of a resolution that "the political activity of international communism or any other totalitarian doctrine" was "incompatible with American freedom." The Declaration of Washington (1950) called for all Western Hemisphere states to cooperate to combat communism. Dulles expressed fear that Communists might take over Latin America as they had China.

Some scholars, including the president's brother, Milton Eisenhower, maintained that conditions in Latin America were so unjust that instead of allying itself with the ruling classes and repressing revolution, Washington should return to championing reform, and even revolution, and thus compete with Communists for the friendship of the poor. Eisenhower told his cabinet that, "unless we can put things in the hands of people who are starving to death, we can never lick communism." Nevertheless, in practice, he supported not reform but repression.

In Guatemala, more than half of the population was Amerindian, and 2 percent of the people owned 60 percent of the land. The huge U.S.-owned United Fruit Company held 42 percent of Guatemala's arable land. President Arbenz Guzman, elected in 1951, sought to help Guatemala's Indians and landless poor. He adopted a program of land reform and appropriated (seized with compensation) 234,000 acres of land, much of it unused, from the United Fruit Company and distributed it to landless peasants. Arbenz's cabinet and his top advisers were not Communists and only four of Guatemala's fifty-six congressmen were Marxists, but the U.S. ambassador reported that, whether or not Arbenz was a Communist, he "thought like a Communist." United Fruit warned that unless he were removed, communism would take over Central America.

In 1953, Eisenhower approved a CIA plan to overthrow Arbenz. Enlisting Guatemalans who had fled the Arbenz regime, the CIA gave them military training in Nicaragua and Honduras. At the March 1954 Caracas Conference, Washington secured OAS condemnation of "domination or control of the political institutions of any American state by the international Communist movement." Arbenz appealed to the Soviets for help and, in May 1954, he received a large shipment of arms from Czechoslovakia. In June, he proclaimed a dictatorship. "A government in which Communist influence is very strong," said

Dulles, "has come into a position to dominate militarily the Central American area."

On June 18, 1954, after an airlift of arms from the United States, several hundred CIA-trained exiles, supported by CIA-piloted warplanes, invaded Guatemala. When the Guatemalan army failed to defend Arbenz, his government collapsed within two weeks, and he fled to Czechoslovakia. Instantly recognizing the new government of Colonel Castillo Armas, Washington gave it economic aid. Executing hundreds of opponents, Castillo restored land to the United Fruit Company.

Eisenhower rejoiced at this destruction of a "beachhead of international communism." It was one of the CIA's greatest successes, and this technique would become known as the "Guatemala solution." Not everyone approved— British Prime Minister Attlee called it a "plain act of aggression," and it fanned Latin-American fears of U.S. domination.

Seeking to make Guatemala an example of the superiority of the free world over communism, Washington gave it large-scale economic aid. Nevertheless, for years Guatemala would remain the scene of oppressive rule by a right-wing military junta whose methods included assassination of opponents by "death squads." Peasant resistence continued, and by 1996 an estimated 200,000 had died. In 1996, Guatemala ranked second in the world in inequality of wealth distribution.

Latin Americans frequently displayed anti-U.S. sentiments. In April 1958, Vice President Richard Nixon was sent to attend the inauguration of a new Argentine president and to make a goodwill tour of eight Latin American countries. To many Latin Americans, he symbolized right-wing U.S. corporations which, in their view, were blocking their social and economic progress. Many Latin Americans took the opportunity to show their displeasure. In Peru, at Lima University, a mob shouted Nixon down and pelted his automobile with stones. At the Caracas, Venezuela, airport, one screaming mob showered him with spit, and another stopped his car and broke its windows. Eisenhower alerted marines for a possible rescue. Former President José Figueres of Costa Rica said that the United States, by bolstering dictators, had spat on Latin America. Attributing this hostility to Communist propaganda, Nixon urged more U.S. military aid and forcible action against Communists, but he also said that U.S. investors should avoid exploiting Latin American workers and soft-pedal their support for dictators.

In conciliatory actions in the next few years, Eisenhower visited Latin America, agreed to Latin American demands for establishment of an Inter-American development bank, and somewhat expanded U.S. aid.

Eisenhower Seeks to Overthrow Castro

The United States had long been highly interested in Cuba, a large producer of tropical products, which lay only ninety miles off Florida athwart approaches to U.S. Caribbean ports and the Panama Canal. Several American presidents, as early as Thomas Jefferson, had expressed a desire to annex it. After the 1898 Spanish-American War, Washington ruled Cuba for three years and then granted it self-government only on the condition that it accept the Platt Amendment which gave the United States rights to maintain a naval base in Cuba, to supervise Cuba's finances, and to send U.S. troops into Cuba whenever Washington considered it necessary. Not until 1934, as a part of the Good Neighbor Policy, did the United States agree to the abolition of the Platt Amendment— but it retained a naval base at Guantanamo.

By then, U.S. investors had acquired ownership of much of Cuba's economy. They owned factories, hotels, gambling casinos, and stores, 40 percent of Cuba's sugar growing land, 80 percent of its public utilities, 90 percent of its mines, 90 percent of its cattle ranches, and, with a British company, 100 percent of its oil industry. Whoever controls a nation's economy often dominates that nation's government. In 1958, the U.S. ambassador indiscreetly remarked that he was the second most important man in Cuba, sometimes "even more important than the [Cuban] president."

Cuba's president was Fulgencio Batista, a military dictator who, after ousting an elected president in 1952, followed policies acceptable to Cuba's rich elite and U.S. investors. Washington furnished him with arms and trained his military forces. Most Cubans, illiterate or semiliterate, lived in unhealthy poverty.

Among Batista's opponents was Fidel Castro, the son of a well-to-do family and a graduate of Havana University's law school, who was sent into exile after he led a failed attempt to seize guns from an army barracks with which to arm revolutionary followers. In December 1956, he returned on a ship with eighty armed companions. Alerted to their arrival, Batista set an ambush that killed or captured all but eleven of them. Among those who broke through were Castro, his brother Raul, and the Argentinean physician Che Guevera. Fleeing to the Sierra Maestra mountains, they made friends with peasants, received peasant and student recruits and, helped by favorable reports in the *New York Times*, money from Cuban exiles.

As opposition to Batista rose, the dictator responded with increasingly brutal repression which, in turn, multiplied his enemies. In March 1958, a disgusted Washington halted arms shipments to him. When Castro's forces came out of the mountains, Batista's troops were unable to defeat them. On New Years Day 1959, Batista fled, and Castro soon moved into Havana.

The group of Castro supporters who took over the Cuban government was relatively young; their average age was thirty-four, which was Castro's age. All were from the middle or upper class; all had attended universities to prepare for professions. Claiming to believe in democracy, they called for free elections. Castro had many sympathizers in the United States, Washington recognized his government within a week, and U.S. corporations helped him by making advance payments on their taxes.

Castro cut the size of the Cuban army, which had supported Batista, by one-third. For defense, he relied more on a citizen militia, which required the distribution of guns to the poor.

Castro's policies favored the poor. He cut the prices of food, rents, and utilities and opened beaches and luxury hotels to their use. Imposing an income tax on the wealthy, he raised wages and provided free medical care. Greatly increasing spending for education, he built more new classrooms than had been built in all Cuba's previous history. Of course, these policies produced a wider distribution of income.

The first foreign country Castro visited was the United States—an unofficial visit in April 1959 (see Fig. 9.2). In Washington he made a friendly speech and denied that he had any connection with Russia or that there was any Communist influence in his government. He was not invited to the White House, but Secretary of State Christian Herter invited him to dinner and Eisenhower asked Vice President Nixon to talk with him. Nixon concluded that he was not a Communist and, putting his arm around Castro, said, "We're going to work with this man." However, Nixon afterward reported that Castro was politically naive and subject to capture by Communists.

Friction soon developed. In February 1959, Castro's government had enacted a land reform program. Seizing land held by individual owners in ex-

Figure 9.2 The first foreign country Fidel Castro visited after his 1959 seizure of power was the United States, where he was invited to dinner by Secretary of State Christian Herter. National Archives.

cess of fifteen hundred acres, the government paid them the amount they had told tax collectors that it was worth. It then distributed the expropriated land to peasants, sixty-seven acres per family, to be combined into cooperative or collective farms. This program meant expropriation of $1 billion worth of land owned by U.S. citizens. Factories and apartment buildings were similarly taken over by the government.

Meanwhile many upper-class opponents of Castro fled to the United States, where their stories were sympathetically heard. The CIA reported that Communists appeared to have penetrated his movement and that, within Castro's inner group, conservative members seemed to be losing influence to leftists such as his brother Raul and Che Guevera.

In late 1959, Eisenhower gave CIA head Allen Dulles a green light to begin sabotaging Cuba's economy and to begin preliminary planning for a "Guatemala solution," an invasion by Cuban exiles to overthrow Castro.

Before he came to power, Castro had insisted that he was not a Communist, his associates did not consider him a Communist, and the Cuban Communist party did not support him. In 1958 he even received some help from the CIA. In the first year of his rule, the thrust of his policies, said U.S. Ambassador Philip Bonsal, was "exclusively nationalistic." Only after Washington began to seek his overthrow, added Bonsal, did Castro turn toward the Soviet Union. Even then, Khrushchev called him "an adventurer," not a genuine Communist.

Announcing a program of reducing Cuba's economic dependence on the United States, Castro, in February 1960, signed a trade agreement in which the Soviet Union agreed to buy 5 million tons of sugar over the next five years and to supply Cuba with oil, technicians, arms, and a $100-million loan. In March, Eisenhower gave orders to begin implementing the plan for an invasion. In May, after Cuba established diplomatic relations with Russia, Eisenhower halted all aid to Cuba.

When Soviet oil arrived in Cuba, U.S.-owned oil refineries, at Washington's request, refused to refine it. In June 1960, Castro seized the refineries. This was a fateful move, for oil companies had great political power in America. Within a week, Washington announced a halt to all imports of sugar from Cuba. Because sugar was Cuba's main export and the United States was its main market, this move threatened to cripple both Cuba's economy and Castro's rule. The United States, Eisenhower explained, would not permit the establishment in the Western Hemisphere of a "regime dominated by international communism."

In September 1960, Cuba established diplomatic relations with Communist China and appealed to the UN to stop U.S. "economic aggression." On October 12, Washington banned exports to Cuba of any goods except food and medicine. Only increased aid from Russia and China enabled Castro to survive. After Cuba ordered a reduction of the U.S. embassy staff from three hundred to eleven, Washington recalled its ambassador and, in January 1961, formally broke diplomatic relations. By the end of 1961 four-fifths of Cuba's trade was with Communist nations.

Meanwhile, the CIA recruited and armed Cuban exiles for an invasion. It trained them at bases in Louisiana, Texas, Panama, and Guatemala at a cost of $45 million, part of which was contributed by U.S. corporations. Originally scheduled for late 1960, the invasion, at the request of president-elect John F. Kennedy, was postponed until after Kennedy's inauguration.

Thus, in the Third World, Eisenhower and Dulles pursued, with mixed success, a policy of Cold War and counterrevolution. Meanwhile, dramatic developments were occurring in the Middle East and in Europe.

10 Eisenhower and Dulles: Cold War in Europe and the Middle East

Foreign Economic Policy

In the early 1930s, Republicans had been almost unanimous in opposing Roosevelt's reciprocal trade agreement program. But, by the 1950s, some of America's more powerful exporting industries, profiting from the upsurge in exports that followed tariff cuts, had begun to favor increasing imports to allow foreigners to earn dollars with which to buy U.S. products. In a reversal of the Republican party's historic position, Eisenhower secured congressional authorization to negotiate reciprocal treaties reducing U.S. tariffs as much as an additional 25 percent.

Eisenhower took other measures to raise exports. To cut enormous stocks of surplus farm products, which cost the government billions of dollars annually to store, he secured enactment of the Food for Peace program, which in ten years donated more than $12 billion in surplus farm products to needy nations. In 1959, he established the Inter-American Bank to facilitate trade among the nations of the Western Hemisphere. Between 1952 and 1960, U.S. exports doubled from $15 billion to $30 billion annually.

In this period, U.S. exports averaged several billion dollars more per year than its imports. Americans invested abroad much of the surplus foreign currency thus earned, and between 1950 and 1959 the value of U.S. private holdings overseas soared from $12 billion to $30 billion.

However, not all economic trends were favorable. The export surplus narrowed, and federal gold holdings continued their long-term decline (from $25 billion in 1945 to $10 billion in 1968). America's GNP rose at an average rate of only 2 percent during the Eisenhower years, while Soviet GNP was rising at an average rate of 6 percent a year.

Massive Retaliation

Many analysts assumed that Eisenhower, a lifelong military man, would favor high military spending. However, in the Korean War (1950–1953), military spending had quadrupled to $50.4 billion. Republicans were anxious to cut taxes, which, because they then considered budget deficits to be morally wrong, they could do only if they cut spending, and nearly 70 percent of discretionary federal spending went to the military. Republicans considered preserving U.S. military superiority to be essential, but they found the policy of containing communism, as practiced in Korea, to be too expensive. Also, convinced of an "intimate and indivisible" relationship between economic and military strength, Eisenhower feared that high arms spending might so overburden the economy that it would bankrupt the system America sought to defend or that militarizing the U.S. economy would drive us "into some kind of dictatorial government."

In an attempt to reconcile conflicting aims, the Republicans, adopting a "new look," shifted military strategy from containment to "massive retaliation." This meant relying chiefly on America's overwhelming lead in atomic bombs instead of attempting to maintain superior forces at every point around the Iron Curtain. If the Soviets committed aggression, said Dulles, Americans would not confine their response to the point of attack, but would "retaliate instantly by means and at places of our own choosing," perhaps striking at the "head of the Communist power." Instead of reserving atomic bombs as weapons of last resort, the United States would use them, Eisenhower said, "exactly as you would use a bullet or anything else." Thus, massive retaliation seemed to mean that America would draw a line and, if the Soviets stepped across that line, would immediately respond with atomic weapons, perhaps bombing Moscow. Because nuclear capability cost less than large conventional forces, this would provide "maximum effectiveness at minimum cost"—"bigger bang for the buck."

In line with this new military doctrine, Eisenhower, rejecting arguments by the Joint Chiefs for more money, substantially cut military spending from Truman's proposed $50 billion to $34 billion. He reduced army manpower from 1,553,000 to 873,000 (while three successive army chiefs of staff resigned in protest), and navy manpower from 1,245,000 to 788,000. Mothballing battleships, he concentrated on super aircraft carriers and nuclear-powered missile-carrying submarines. He upped the air force's share of the defense dollar from 34 to 50 percent. By 1959, the Strategic Air Command (SAC), the arm assigned the mission of bombing Russia, had 1800 planes, among them giant new eight-engine B-52 bombers. Meanwhile, he raised the number of U.S. nuclear weapons from 1,200 to 22,229 by 1961.

The strategy of massive retaliation had its critics. Some regretted that it seemed to call for constant brandishing of the atomic bomb and required either an all-out atomic response or none. This threat might be convincing while America held such nuclear superiority that it could destroy Russia without itself being destroyed but, as Soviet ability to retaliate rose, massive retaliation might become less credible. Few foreign leaders would believe, for example, that America would bring about its own destruction if the Soviets were to send troops into Afghanistan.

Dulles pointed out to a *Life* magazine writer that preserving peace sometimes required approaching very near to war. "The ability to get to the verge without getting into the war is the necessary art. . . . If you try to run away from it, if you are scared to go to the brink, you are lost." Dulles got away with his "brinkmanship"—Soviet Premier Nikita Khrushchev said that he knew not to push the Communists too far—but brinkmanship was a sobering reflection of how much the fate of humanity depended on avoiding miscalculation in games of "chicken."

Gradually the Soviets reduced America's once great lead in national power. Devoting more of their GNP to education and raising their industrial production more rapidly, they acquired the means with which to challenge the U.S. lead in weaponry. In 1949, they exploded an atomic bomb, four years after America. In 1953, they detonated a hydrogen bomb, only nine months after America. In October 1957, they put in orbit a space satellite, *Sputnik*, ahead of the United States which, reported the British ambassador, had an effect similar to Pearl Harbor in shaking America's "cocksureness." Demonstrating that the Russians had more advanced missile technology, it gave them an unstoppable means of delivering atomic bombs on the United States. Meanwhile, the Soviets constructed a fleet of long-range bombers, and as many submarines as America. The Ford Foundation's Gaither Report (1957) concluded that, with its GNP rising more rapidly than America's, Russia was matching U.S. spending on defense and heavy industry. Alarmed at the speed with which America's once wide lead was narrowing, Eisenhower accelerated the missile program and secured enactment of the National Defense Education Act of 1958, which raised federal spending on science, foreign language, and humanities education.

Dulles devoted much effort to building a system of alliances to block the spread of communism. America already had NATO, as well as treaties with Japan, Taiwan, the Philippines, South Korea, Australia, and New Zealand. With a zeal some called "pactomania," Dulles added new alliances. Broadening NATO to include West Germany, he agreed to give Spain's leader, Francisco Franco, aid in return for U.S. naval and air bases in Spain, backed creation of the Baghdad Pact comprised of Turkey, Pakistan, Iraq, Iran, and Britain, and formed the Southeast Asia Treaty Organization (SEATO), composed of the United States, Britain, France, Australia, New Zealand, the Philippines, Thailand, and Pakistan. By 1955, America had alliances with forty-three nations (up from zero in 1940) and maintained a million military personnel overseas.

Khrushchev's Peace Offensive

Behind the facade of implacable Cold War hostility, changes occurred. The outgunned Soviets made conciliatory gestures, the contrast between the two political and economic systems softened, rapid economic growth in other countries reduced superpower preponderance, other nations developed atomic weapons, the unity of each camp decayed, and different conflicts erupted that had little relation to the Soviet-American struggle. Under these circumstances, the Cold War occasionally thawed, until some new crisis again raised tensions.

Stalin died in March 1953. His successor, Nikita Khrushchev, who consolidated his power by 1955, is usually credited with changing Stalin's Cold War policy. Actually, after his initial postwar gains, Stalin, conscious of the inferiority of Soviet arms, had sought detente, a lessening of tensions. "Stalin never did anything that might provoke war with the United States," Khrushchev wrote later. "He knew his weakness." Although refusing to relinquish the newly created Soviet sphere in East Europe, Stalin had withdrawn from Iran, withheld aid from Greek guerrillas, advised Mao against fighting a civil war, and helped initiate Korean peace negotiations.

In personality Khrushchev appeared to be much less sinister than Stalin. A stocky, earthy, extroverted, talkative, impulsive peasant, he possessed a manner, alternately amiable and angry, more like that of a U.S. politician. A British official wondered how such a "fat, vulgar man" could head the Soviet Union. His extensive program of visits in East Europe and South Asia was characterized by boisterous informality. Nixon concluded that he had "a devastating sense of humor, agile intelligence, tenacious sense of purpose, and brutal will to power."

Khrushchev launched an energetic peace offensive. Reestablishing diplomatic relations with Yugoslavia and Greece, he somewhat relaxed the Soviet grip on its East European satellites. He gave diplomatic recognition to West Germany. In April 1955, he offered to make the Soviet Union a member of NATO. In May, he joined the West in signing a peace treaty with Austria that provided for a united, neutral, democratic Austria, which required the withdrawal of Soviet, as well as Western, troops.

Meanwhile, developments within Russia and America somewhat reduced the contrasts between the two systems. The Communist party was officially atheistic, but religion nonetheless survived. During the war, when churches supported the Soviet war effort, they were given privileges, including the right to issue religious propaganda and ring church bells. Khrushchev had denounced religious persecution as counterproductive—"it just confirms them in their superstitions." Foreign visitors were surprised to find well-attended churches, and the number of Protestants in Russia soon exceeded the pre-1917 level. While the Soviet government remained dictatorial, Khrushchev, unlike Stalin, did not execute his defeated rivals. Reining in the secret police, he opened Russia's doors to Western newsmen, cultural groups, and tourists.

In economic policy, the Soviets periodically announced reforms designed to provide more incentives, tie pay to production, and introduce some market direction. The Chinese Communists charged that they were returning to capitalism. Although still far behind, their rising educational level and standard of living seemed to be making Russians more like Western Europeans.

America preserved free enterprise but, in a long-term trend praised by some and deplored by others, increasingly put limits on economic freedom. The government intruded into business decisions affecting wages, unions, safety, reliability, environmental impact, and social desirability of business products and methods. Some economists concluded that the two economies were becoming more alike, a process they called "convergence," and that they were already more similar than serious advocates of either ideology could approve. If one best way existed of operating a complex modern industrialized economy, probably neither nation would permanently opt for a less effective way. Consequently, the future nature of the economic system, some predicted, might be dictated more by technology than by ideology.

Such developments seemed to open a possibility of lowering the level of Cold War hostility. This would be a great historic achievement for the leader who succeeded in bringing it about. For a time, that role was coveted by Winston Churchill, who, back in office as prime minister in 1953, proposed a Big Four summit. However, Dulles, maintaining that "nothing but evil can come of a meeting," "strenuously objected"—Churchill called him "a terrible handicap." Eisenhower declined to meet unless the Soviets made concessions in advance, and Churchill suffered a stroke. Perhaps Khrushchev and, later, Eisenhower, also aspired to the mantle of Cold War peacemaker.

The prospect of a reduction of tensions did not please everyone. Dulles feared that it might cause America to relax its rearmament and anti-communist effort, and thus facilitate Communist expansion. He sought to win the Cold War, not end it. In May 1955, when Khrushchev unexpectedly agreed to withdraw Soviet troops from Austria, Dulles exclaimed: "I think we've had it." When Khrushchev sought a meeting with Eisenhower, Dulles again objected. To hold a summit, he said, might cause East Europeans to lose hope that America would liberate them. Also, the Soviets were on the point of an economic breakdown, he said, and if America maintained pressure they might collapse. But Eisenhower insisted, and polls showed that eight of ten Americans favored a meeting. At least, Dulles advised, if photographed with Khrushchev, Eisenhower should maintain an "austere countenance."

In July 1955, the Big Four assembled in Geneva, Switzerland. The Soviet delegation was headed by Premier Nikolai Bulganin, but Communist party Secretary Khrushchev was the real power. Prime Minister Anthony Eden and Premier Edgar Faure represented Britain and France. The Soviets brought along Eisenhower's friend from his Berlin days, Marshall Georgi Zhukov, personal contacts were friendly and, as Dulles feared, the press soon depicted the leaders in attitudes of smiling geniality.

In discussions of Germany, the Soviets repeated their demand for a united but demilitarized and neutral Germany on the model of Austria. The West insisted that a united Germany be allowed to rearm in alliance with the West. The Soviets proposed mutual withdrawal of conventional forces, a ban on stationing nuclear weapons in Western Europe, and a halt to production of atomic weapons. Eisenhower made an "open skies" proposal that called for each to allow unlimited aerial inspection of its territory, which, Eisenhower said later, "we knew the Soviets wouldn't accept." Khrushchev objected that it would help America improve the accuracy of its targeting of Soviet installations. (The following year America began overflights of Russia in newly developed high-altitude U-2 planes.)

Khrushchev was pleased that Russians "had established ourselves as able to hold our own in the international arena," but concrete accomplishments at Geneva were limited to commitments to seek free elections in Germany and to increase cultural exchanges. Nevertheless, the conference had considerable psychological impact. Apparently indicating that neither side sought to break the stalemate in Europe by military means, it created a "spirit of Geneva," which Eisenhower described as "a new spirit of conciliation and cooperation." An August Gallup poll showed Eisenhower's approval rate at 79 percent. Dulles was bitter, and Averell Harriman worried that the West had been "psychologically disarmed."

Continuing his peace offensive, Khrushchev, in January 1956, returned the Porkala Peninsula to Finland. Also, in a secret speech in February to the Twentieth Communist Party Congress, he denounced Stalin for horrible crimes, including the murder of two-thirds of the members of the party Central Committee. Repudiating the doctrine that war between communism and capitalism was inevitable, Khrushchev called for "peaceful coexistence." Furthermore, he advocated liberalization, or "de- Stalinization" of Communist governments in East Europe. In April 1956, he abolished the Cominform, the international organization of Communist parties feared and hated in the West as designed to communize the world. In May, he announced a reduction of Soviet troops from 4 million to 2.8 million. In June, he visited Yugoslavia and signed a treaty agreeing that there were "different roads to socialism" and that it was not necessary for all Communist nations to follow the Soviet pattern, thereby conceding that foreign Communist parties were not required to submit to management from Moscow.

Disruptions in the Communist Camp

The relaxation of Cold War tensions seemed to allow supressed internal conflicts within each camp to come to the surface. They erupted first among Communist nations. In their Cold War rhetoric, anti-Communists charged that all Communists were united in a tightly disciplined conspirational world organization that obediently followed Moscow's orders. This meant that if a Communist party won power in any nation, the practical result was the same as if that nation had been conquered by Soviet troops. Thus anti-Communists credited Communist ideology with succeeding, where Christianity and Islam had failed, in creating a worldwide brotherhood that transcended selfish national interests. Actually, Communists were never that successful in elevating loyalty to communism above nationalism.

Shortly after World War II, a bitter conflict had erupted between the Soviet Union and Yugoslavia. In World War II, after Germany invaded Yugoslavia, Communist Marshal Josip Tito organized the Yugoslav resistance to German occupation forces. Because his group was more effective than a conservative rival faction, England and America gave him money and supplies. After the Germans were defeated, Tito took power without the aid of Soviet armies. Tito insisted that he was a genuine Communist, but he did not automatically follow Moscow's directions. He allowed small farmers to keep land instead of forcing them to merge it into collective farms, and he allowed factory managers some discretion in deciding what to produce. Angered, the Soviets attempted to remove him as head of the Yugoslavian government. Fighting back,

Tito executed Soviet spies caught in Yugoslavia. In 1948, the Russians expelled him from the Cominform.

Taking advantage of the opportunity afforded by the Soviet-Yugoslavian split, the Truman administration decided to help Tito preserve his independence. The advantage of subtracting his thirty divisions from the Soviet bloc was obvious, and also U.S. support for Tito might encourage other Communist nations to break with Moscow. In 1949, America extended loans to this Communist dictator, in 1950 economic grants, and in 1951 military aid. Reciprocating, Yugoslavia supported America in the UN and, in 1950, closed its border with Greece, dooming the Communist-led Greek rebels. In 1954, Yugoslavia joined an anti-Soviet alliance with Greece and Turkey. Defending U.S. aid to Tito, Eisenhower said that "to throw Tito back into the arms of Moscow would be the most tragic thing the United States could do."

Reversing Stalin's policy, Khrushchev accepted Tito's departure from the Soviet model of Communism and, in 1955 and 1956, exchanged visits with him. A worried U.S. Congress suspended further aid to Tito pending a determination by Eisenhower that Yugoslavia was still independent. After a new Yugoslavia-Soviet rupture, Congress approved additional aid, including two hundred jet planes. But again Tito mended relations with the Soviets and, sensing that Washington was about to sever aid, notified America in 1957 that Yugoslavia had no further need of help. By this time, U.S. aid to this Communist dictator had totaled nearly $3 billion—a remarkable victory of *realpolitik* (persuit of power and property) over ideology.

Khrushchev's relaxation of the Soviet grip on East European satellites was followed in several countries by nationalistic uprisings seeking greater independence. In Poland the citizens had resisted land collectivization and Soviet-style economic controls. The Polish Communist party leader Wladyslaw Gomulka, whom Stalin had imprisoned for nationalistic tendencies ("Titoism"), won his release in 1954 and regained the party leadership. In 1956, alarmed by growing Polish defiance, Khrushchev moved Soviet troops into position to occupy Poland and, on October 19, flew to Warsaw for a showdown. Gomulka distributed arms to Polish workers and warned that a forcible Soviet attempt to reverse recent changes would cause a bloodbath. Giving in, Khrushchev withdrew some Soviet troops and accepted Gomulka as Poland's Communist party chairman. Gomulka allowed Poles more freedom, released the imprisoned Cardinal Wyszenski, and maintained sufficient independence of Moscow to win U.S. economic aid.

In October 1956, an uprising in Hungary against Stalinist officials, led by Hungarian Communists posed an even greater threat to Soviet control. Student-led demonstrations demanding the withdrawal of Soviet troops were joined by workers and soldiers. Toppling Stalin's statue, the rebels killed a number of Stalinists and, on October 24, installed Imre Nagy, a national Communist and a leader of the insurrection, as premier. He admitted non-Communists to his new government.

For a time it appeared that the Soviets would yield. On October 28, they began withdrawing troops and, on October 30, calling for a "great commonwealth of socialist nations," seemed to agree to give Hungary autonomy. But they changed their minds.

We can only speculate on what caused the Soviet reversal. Their policy may have been affected by the dangerous international crisis created by Israel's October 29 invasion of Egypt (discussed later in this chapter), or by Nagy's November 1 withdrawal from the Warsaw Pact and his appeal to the UN, which raised the danger that Hungary might join the camp of Russia's enemies. On November 4, the withdrawing Soviet troops turned around and returned to Budapest to crush the uprising. Because the Hungarian Communists had threatened to join the anti-Communist camp, Russia's suppression was backed by China, Poland's Gomulka, and even Yugoslavia's Tito. In bloody battles, seven thousand Russians and thirty thousand Hungarians died. The victorious Soviets then executed Nagy.

The Eisenhower administration had proclaimed a policy of "liberation," and the Voice of America and Radio Free Europe, and some unauthorized CIA agents, had urged East Europe to assert independence. "Where are the Americans?" Hungarian fighters asked U.S. reporters. Washington denounced Russia's suppression and sent medical supplies to Hungary, but, unwilling to risk world war on this issue, it assured the Soviets that it had no intention of sending troops. This constituted a grudging recognition of a Soviet sphere of influence. "I wish there was some way of helping them," said Eisenhower, but Hungary was "as inaccessible to us as Tibet." Thus, the uprising exposed the hollowness of the policy of liberation.

Disruptions of U.S. Alliances

Conflicts also arose within America's alliances. Some governments of European nations that had once been great powers bitterly resented the degree to which they were being overshadowed by Russia and the United States. Many resented the massive invasion of American culture and the extent to which U.S. corporations were taking control of Europe's economy. Europe was "drowning in a sea of Coca-Cola," complained France's President Charles de Gaulle. Also, many Europeans scorned what they regarded as the amateurishness of America's approach to international politics and complained that America was too doctrinaire, moralistic, militaristic, rash, and obsessed with Russia. Americans complained that Europeans seemed ungrateful, inclined to appeasement, and reluctant to pay their fair share of defense costs.

U.S. relations with France were particularly strained. Americans pressed France to make reforms in its Vietnam and Algerian colonies, and even to grant them independence. Bitter clashes occurred before compromises were reached on the restoration and rearmament of Germany. In August 1954, when France flatly rejected the U.S. plan for Germany, Dulles warned that this could force Washington to make "an agonizing reappraisal" of its European policy. After additional safeguards against any renewal of German aggression including strict limits on weapons and the stationing of four British divisions in Germany were added, agreement was reached. Nevertheless, although shielded by America's nuclear umbrella, France developed its own nuclear strike force to enable it to act independently of the United States.

Although it usually agreed with U.S. policies, Britain also developed an independent nuclear force.

In 1956, the Western alliance was severely strained when the Middle East policy of Britain and France clashed with that of the United States.

Middle East Policy and the Suez Crisis

The Middle East is a large, mostly dry area with scarcely enough natural vegetation for grazing animals, and crops can be grown only with irrigation. Most of its approximately 200 million people are Moslem. Although home to Iranians, Turks, and Jews, it is preponderantly Arab. Its most populous nations (1997) are Iran (68 million), Egypt (65 million), Turkey (64 million), Iraq (22 million), Saudi Arabia (20 million), Syria (16 million), and Israel (6 million). In gross national product (1996), Turkey leads, followed by Iran, Saudi Arabia, Egypt, Israel, Syria, and Iraq.

In the nineteenth century, except for Iran, the Middle East was part of Turkey's Ottoman Empire. When this empire decayed, the British acquired dominance in Egypt, Jordan, and Iraq, while the French took control in Syria and Lebanon.

America's early contacts with the area were slight, but, in 1933, U.S. oil companies acquired concessions to drill oil wells in Saudi Arabia which, it turned out, had the world's largest pool of oil. Urging France and Britain to free their Middle Eastern colonies, America backed the establishment of Israel and gave military aid to Turkey. After 1953, when the CIA helped overthrow Iran's leftist premier, Mohammed Mossadegh, who had nationalized Iranian oil, and helped restore the young Shah Mohammed Reza Pahlavi to power, the grateful shah gave U.S. oil companies a 40 percent share in Iran's oil. In 1955, Dulles organized Turkey, Iraq, Iran, Pakistan and Britain into the anti-Soviet Baghdad Pact.

America's national interests in the Middle East seemed to require excluding Soviet power, preserving secure access to its oil, and keeping strategic trade routes open. Protection of these interests seemed to require support of Arab independence, modernization, and unity in order to strengthen Arab ability to resist Soviet expansion. However, pursuit of these policies was complicated by U.S. backing of Israel.

Palestine, an area between the Mediterranean Sea and the Jordan River that is 140 miles long and 30 to 70 miles wide, is, in the Jewish religion, the "promised land" given to Jews by God, where in ancient times they established a kingdom under David and Solomon. Most Jews were expelled by the Romans in 70 A.D., but many dreamed of returning. They called the movement to recover Palestine "Zionism." By 1939, Jews constituted 400,000 of Palestine's 1.4 million people. Jews' desire for a homeland was given added strength by Nazi Germany's slaughter of millions of European Jews.

Palestine was a British mandate, and the British made conflicting commitments to grant independence to Arabs and Jews. In the 1917 Balfour Declaration, Britain announced that it would create a Jewish homeland, but, to minimize Arab hostility, it allowed only a limited number of Jews to enter. In October 1946, Truman announced U.S. support for the formation of a Jewish state in Palestine.

When the British withdrew from Palestine in 1947, the UN recommended that Palestine be partitioned between Arabs and Jews, with Jerusalem, a holy city to both, put under international control. When the Jews proclaimed the formation of the state of Israel, America recognized the new nation within an hour, and Russia followed within three days.

Nevertheless, Palestinian Arabs continued to claim all of Palestine and, in a 1948–49 war in which they were assisted by Lebanon, Syria, Jordan, Egypt, and Iraq, sought to repossess the lands awarded to Israel. Defeating the Arabs, the Jews also annexed much additional territory, including part of Jerusalem. Egypt and Jordan assumed administration of the areas of Palestine that remained in Arab hands, and more than half a million Arab refugees from Jewish-occupied areas gathered in refugee camps, where they received UN subsistence grants.

Many Americans had strong religious and sentimental attachments to Israel. It was the most democratic nation in the area and was strongly supported by U.S. Jews, many of whom lived in politically pivotal cities such as New York. Although Israel rejected Washington's suggestions that it make concessions concerning territory and refugees, U.S. aid to Israel in the 1952–1961 period totaled $374 million. Many American Christians also viewed Israel as a "Holy Land" and wished to support it.

Meanwhile, America also struggled to preserve good relations with the Arabs. Washington paid Saudi Arabia a secret subsidy, allowed U.S. oil companies to deduct payments to Arab countries from their income taxes, extended economic and technical aid, and may even have colluded in an oil price rise to give Arabs more income.

Most Arab states were medieval monarchies, but in some of them revolutions produced modern governments. A 1952 uprising in Egypt overthrew the king and brought to power Colonel Gamal Abdel Nasser. In a program he called "Arab socialism," Nasser inaugurated land reform, adopted an income tax, nationalized banks, heavy industry, and public transportation, and raised government spending on schools and public health. In foreign affairs, he aspired to leadership of the pan-Arab cause—the movement to erase the remnants of colonialism and unite all Arab countries into one Arab nation.

Engineers recommended that Egypt build a high dam across the Nile River at Aswan. It would be expensive, $1.3 billion, but would make available sufficient irrigation water to enlarge Egypt's farm acreage by 25 percent, help control floods, and generate electricity for industry.

In February 1955, Israel made a retaliatory military raid into Egyptian-held Gaza, involving more troops and achieving deeper penetration of Egyptian territory than before. This attack revealed Egypt's weakness. Fearing future attacks, Nasser attempted to buy arms from America, but Washington, concerned with the security of Israel, refused. In September 1955, Nasser bought arms from Communist Czechoslovakia, for which he pledged much of Egypt's cotton crop. In December 1955, partly to forestall possible Soviet aid for the Aswan Dam, America made a preliminary offer to finance it with the help of Britain and the World Bank. But a series of events soon brought a rupture between America and Egypt, and also between America and its British and French allies.

In April 1956, Nasser signed an anti-Israel alliance with Saudi Arabia and Syria, and, in May, he extended diplomatic recognition to Communist China. Enraged by these moves, Dulles, in July, without consulting the British, withdrew the U.S. offer to help build the Aswan Dam. This move, which could have caused Nasser's overthrow, was applauded in America. However, Senate Foreign Affairs Committee Chairman J. William Fulbright concluded that Dulles, mistaking Nasser's nationalism for communism, had, by alienating Nasser, opened the door to Soviet influence.

Saying "let them strangle in their hatred," Nasser seized the Suez Canal and announced he would use its $25 million annual profits to finance the Aswan Dam. The canal cut through Egyptian territory but was owned primarily by British and French stockholders. Egypt's action was legal, but the canal was Britain's main trade route to its holdings in the East, "the lifeline of the British Empire," and the main avenue for moving Arab oil to the West. Also at stake was Britain's and France's prestige as world powers. Nevertheless, Eisenhower told them that he opposed the use of force against Egypt.

When their efforts to have the canal put under international control failed, the British and French entered into a secret plot with Israel. On October 29, 1956, with the aid of French air cover, Israel struck into the Egyptian-held Sinai Peninsula and, advancing rapidly, captured 6,000 Egyptian troops and most of the arms Egypt had bought from Czechoslovakia. On the pretext of preventing the fighting from closing the Suez Canal, the British and French announced that they would occupy the canal zone. On October 31, the British bombed Cairo and the canal zone and, on November 5 landed troops at the canal. Enraged Arab countries stopped oil exports, creating a severe oil shortage in the West.

Dulles had not consulted the Allies before canceling the Aswan Dam aid, and the British, French, and Israelis kept America in the dark on their plans to attack Egypt. Americans took seriously their condemnation of aggression as evil, and they also saw the British and French action as imperialist and, therefore, as giving the Soviets an opportunity to win influence among Arabs. The Israeli ambassador found Eisenhower in a "full righteous fury." Telephoning Anthony Eden, who had recently succeeded the aging Winston Churchill as British prime minister, Eisenhower gave him such a tongue-lashing that he was reduced to tears. On October 13 both Russia and America asked the UN to demand a cease-fire, which it did by a vote of 64 to 5. "There can be no peace without law," said Eisenhower in an October 31 broadcast, "and there can be no law if we were to invoke one code of international conduct for those who oppose us and another for our friends." The United States cut oil shipments and loans to Britain and France. Thus, America and Russia had united in opposition to Britain, France, and Israel. The Soviets proposed a joint U.S.-Soviet military expedition to expel the aggressors.

On November 6, unable to withstand the combined pressure of Russia and America, Israel and Britain agreed to a cease-fire. British and French troops withdrew by December 22, and the Israelis withdrew in March 1957. A UN police force moved in to occupy a buffer zone between Israel and Egypt.

This 1956 Suez crisis had significant results. It temporarily disrupted NATO. It soured U.S. relations with Israel—Eisenhower even threatened economic sanctions when Israel delayed its withdrawal. It forced Eden to resign, raised Nasser's prestige, and brought America much praise from Third World countries for taking a stand against imperialism. It revealed how far Britain and France had fallen from their former status as Middle East and world powers and the extent to which they had lost their capacity to act independently of their superpower ally, reduced British and French influence in the Middle East, and it marked the assumption of a leading Middle East role by America. "The existing vacuum in the Middle East," Eisenhower told congressional leaders, "must be filled by the United States before it is filled by Russia."

Russia received much credit from the Arabs for defending Egypt. Later the Soviets assisted Egypt in building the Aswan Dam. Through such aid to Egypt, Russia had leapfrogged the Baghdad Pact to extend its influence into the Middle East.

Eisenhower worried that the Soviet Union planned "to seize the oil, to cut the canal and the pipelines of the Middle East, and thus seriously to weaken Western civilization." In March 1957, in what became known as the Eisenhower Doctrine, he secured congressional authorization to use armed force to defend any Middle East nation against "armed aggression from any country controlled by International Communism." Dulles remarked that "gradually one part of the world after another is being brought into" America's defense system which might soon become "worldwide." When Jordan's King Hussein charged that Communist forces were trying to overthrow him, Washington sent him $3 million in aid. When a pro-Soviet coup occurred in Syria, Eisenhower rushed arms to Syria's neighbors.

The February 1958 merger of Egypt and Syria into the United Arab Republic (UAR), and the pressure they put on Lebanon and Jordan to join them, increased America's sense of danger.

In July 1958, pro-Nasser Iraqi army officers, led by General Abdul Karim Kassem, killed Iraq's king, withdrew from the Baghdad Pact (which was then renamed the Central Treaty Organization), and soon signed a treaty of alliance with the UAR. When the frightened conservative President Chamoun of Lebanon appealed for aid, Eisenhower landed 14,000 troops in Lebanon. America wanted, said Dulles, "to reassure many small nations that they could call on us in time of crisis." When Jordan appealed for aid, British paratroopers landed there. These U.S. and British moves were condemned by Arab nationalists and Third World nations, and it soon became evident that Eisenhower had overestimated the danger of a Nasser or Communist takeover. Actually, the new Iraqi regime competed with Nasser for Arab leadership, and Syria outlawed its Communist party. U.S. troops withdrew from Lebanon in October.

The Soviet Union gave Nasser economic and military aid and supplied many advisers, but dividends to the Soviets were less than hoped. While receiving Soviet aid, Nasser continued to outlaw the Communist party in Egypt, and he preserved sufficient independence to enable him later to break off his relationship with the Soviets.

A Spy Plane Disrupts a Peace Conference

In 1957, maintaining that the Cold War had been excessively militarized and that the arms race in missiles was creating new risks of accidental war, George F. Kennan proposed neutralizing Germany and withdrawing big-power forces from Central Europe. Similar suggestions were made by the respected newspaper columnist Walter Lippmann and by Poland's foreign minister. Moscow endorsed these suggestions, but Dulles rejected them.

Meanwhile Khrushchev, dismayed by rising German rearmament, sought another summit conference. Dulles strongly objected. Khrushchev applied pressure. The place where America was most vulnerable to pressure was Berlin.

The half of Berlin occupied by the Western Allies was an enclave of 2.3 million people, located 120 miles inside Communist East Germany. Seeking to make West Berlin a showcase of Western society, America and West Germany, at the cost of billions of dollars, had rebuilt the city's bombed buildings and restored its economy to give it a better appearance and a higher living standard than those of Communist East Berlin. West Berlin provided easy entrance and exit for spies, opportunities to intercept Communist communications, and radio stations for broadcasting propaganda to Communist nations. Refugees from East Germany and other Communist countries made their way into West Berlin to be flown to the West; about 300,000 annually moved through this hole in the Iron Curtain. Many of them were educated and skilled people that Communist economies could ill afford to lose.

The Soviets insisted that the West's establishment of the Bonn Republic had annulled the preoccupation agreements that gave the West permission to transport people and supplies over East German roads to West Berlin. Calling West Berlin a "bone in my throat," Khrushchev, on November 10, 1958, said that he would turn over control of East Germany's roads to East Germany unless the Allies agreed within six months to negotiate. Termination of Soviet protection of their right to use East German roads would require Western nations to negotiate with the East German government, which they did not recognize, for the use of its roads.

Although the West generally favored withdrawal of Soviet control over East European governments, it insisted that Russia continue to protect its rights in East Germany. Many Americans felt that, regardless of the legalities, the United States could not, for considerations of prestige, allow Communists to force it to withdraw from any area that it occupied. Some saw the dispute as a test of wills that put the entire U.S. position in Europe at risk. America was "solemnly committed" to holding West Berlin, Dulles said, "if need be by military force." Rather than withdraw, said the chairman of the Joint Chiefs, he was ready "to fight a general nuclear war."

The resignation of Secretary of State Dulles in April 1959, a month before his death of cancer, changed the conduct of U.S. foreign affairs. His successor, Christian Herter, lacked his expertise and authority. Eisenhower took more personal control and, more receptive than Dulles to negotiations, he was confident of his personal ability to achieve agreement. "What a splendid exit it would be for me," he said, "to end up with an agreement between East and West."

Nevertheless, Eisenhower's invitation to Khrushchev to visit America was partly accidental. A State Department official was instructed to mention it as a possibility if progress were made in negotiations at a foreign ministers conference, but the official neglected to make the suggestion conditional. The surprised Khrushchev leapt at the proposal, and his acceptance "staggered" Eisenhower. In late August, Eisenhower visited Europe to assure America's allies that he would not give away the store.

In September 1959, Khrushchev flew to America for a twelve-day visit, an event that many Americans found astounding. Over the years they had come to think of Russia's top Communist as the head of a diabolical conspiracy to enslave the world who, logically, should be shot on sight. Now he was in America as the president's guest. His presence, wrote the right-wing columnist William Buckley, "profanes the nation." Khrushchev was well aware of such sentiments. "You have heard that I have babies for breakfast," he said. "Actually, it's only scrambled eggs," and he turned around to show reporters that he had no forked tail. The short, stout, earthy, peasant politician did not well fit Americans' preconception of a demonic superman; he seemed quite human. He was wined and dined with great conviviality by high corporation and government officials. He seemed to be highly amused that top capitalist Nelson Rockefeller held so lowly a job as governor of New York. On meeting CIA head Allan Dulles, he said, "I understand we have been hiring the same people." Then he was off for a tour of America. When, in introducing him, the mayor of Los Angeles lambasted communism, Khrushchev replied that "you don't insult people who have atomic bombs." In Hollywood, he seemed to enjoy watching the filming of the movie *Can-Can*, but he could not resist the chance for propaganda: "In Russia, we prefer people's faces." When denied an opportunity to visit Disneyland, he exploded in anger. Later he admitted: "You slaves of capitalism live well."

Occasionally he revealed what seemed to be a surprising sense of inferiority. He seemed to consider it a great elevation in status to be invited to America. "We'd come a long way from the time when the United States wouldn't even grant us diplomatic recognition," he wrote. And he seemed overwhelmed when Eisenhower casually addressed him as "my friend."

On September 26–27, he conferred with Eisenhower at the presidential retreat, Camp David in Maryland. At first he was angered to discover that Eisenhower had nothing definite to propose, but they soon developed good personal relations. Khrushchev lifted the time limit on negotiations on Berlin, while Eisenhower admitted that the Berlin situation was "abnormal." Disclaiming any intent of using force, they agreed on the need for "general disarmament" and scheduled a Big Four summit conference for May 1960, to be followed by an Eisenhower visit to Russia. The media referred to a new friendliness as the "Spirit of Camp David." In January 1960, Khrushchev told the Supreme Soviet, that he would cut Russian military forces by 1.2 million men. It seemed possible that Eisenhower and Khrushchev might defuse the Berlin crisis and achieve agreements on an atomic test ban and arms limitation.

Eisenhower's self-assurance was bolstered by the warm reception he received on a trip in December 1959, to eleven nations, in the course of which huge crowds heaped adulation on him. He reported to Congress that there was worldwide "faith that America will help lead the way toward a just peace," and he persuaded the heads of government in France, Germany, and England to agree to a summit conference.

But the summit conference aborted. On May 1, just two weeks before the meeting was to convene, the Soviets shot down a U.S. spy plane thirteen hundred miles inside Russia. The plane was a CIA-operated U-2, specially developed for spying. Its light construction, long wings, and single jet engine were designed to enable it to fly at a height of thirteen miles, far higher than any other plane of the day, above the range of Soviet planes and antiaircraft missiles. Equipped with high-resolution cameras and other spy equipment, U-2s had begun overflying the Soviet Union in mid-1956. Well aware of them, the Soviets had made desperate efforts to shoot them down. Eisenhower had suspended their flights before Khrushchev's visit to America, but he yielded to CIA urging that the plane be allowed a last reading on Soviet missiles before an arms agreement was reached. The May 1 flight was a nine-hour flight from Pakistan to Norway across the heart of Russia. It revealed that the Soviets had only four intercontinental ballistic missiles (ICBMs). How the Soviets hit the plane is not clear; perhaps their missiles had improved, or perhaps engine trouble forced the plane to a lower altitude. When the pilot, Francis Gary Powers, failed to follow his instructions to destroy the plane or commit suicide, the Soviets captured him and much equipment.

On May 3, Washington announced that a "high-altitude weather plane" was missing. On May 5, Khrushchev claimed that a spy plane had been shot down. The State Department denied spying: "There was absolutely no deliberate attempt to violate Soviet air space . . . there never has been." Then, on May 6, Khrushchev displayed to the news media the wrecked plane, its intelligence-gathering equipment, and Powers.

This flight put Khrushchev in a bind. For years he had worked to secure a summit conference, but to meet Eisenhower now, and thereby to appear to tolerate America's flights over the Soviet Union would be unacceptable to Soviet nationalists and military leaders. However, if Eisenhower would deny personal responsibility, Khrushchev could still meet with him. Khrushchev offered him an excuse: "I am prepared to grant that the president had no knowledge of a plane being dispatched to the Soviet Union," and he blamed the overflight, instead, on "aggressive circles" who were trying to "torpedo the Paris summit."

For a time it appeared that this formula might save the summit. Allen Dulles advised Eisenhower to blame the flight on the C.I.A. On May 7, the State Department admitted that a plane had flown over Soviet territory, but insisted that "insofar as the authorities in Washington are concerned, there was no authorization."

However, former President Truman wrote that for Eisenhower "to admit that he doesn't know what is going on" would put him in a "ridiculous position." Earlier press comment that Eisenhower had seemed uninformed about what the government was doing made his administration particularly sensitive to such criticism, and the requirements of domestic politics seem to demand that he accept responsibility.

Reversing itself on May 9, the State Department said that Eisenhower had authorized the flight. Although still claiming, falsely, that "specific missions have not been subject to presidential authorization," it said that Eisenhower had issued directives to gather intelligence information "by every possible means," including "penetration." Soviet "excessive secrecy" made such measures necessary to guard against surprise attack. This seemed to be claiming that America had a right to violate Soviet territory. One reporter concluded that Washington had "spied, denied, lied, and defied." Presidential assumption of personal responsibility for spying, wrote political scientist John Spanier, was "unprecedented in the history of espionage," and the implication that the flights would continue was a challenge to the Soviet Union's sovereign rights.

Khrushchev seemed stunned. It put him "in a terrible spot," he told the American ambassador on May 9. "I was horrified to learn that the president had endorsed the acts," he added on May 11. If Eisenhower claimed that he had personally sent these planes over Russia, Khrushchev needed an apology and a promise that they would not continue. He arrived in Paris on May 14 for the scheduled May 16 summit conference, evidently in the hope that Eisenhower would suggest a private meeting. On the advice of Secretary of State Herter that Khrushchev would interpret such a suggestion as a sign of weakness, Eisenhower did not propose a meeting. Khrushchev was accompanied by Soviet Defense Minister Marshall Malinovsky, who stuck to him "like a leech," apparently to guard against concessions unacceptable to the military. Shortly before 1:00 A.M. on May 16, Americans called a worldwide military alert that sent B-52 bombers aloft on the first stage of bombing runs on Russia. Lippmann called the timing of the alert even worse than the timing of the U-2 flight.

The Big Four met at 11:00 A.M. on May 16 in what Khrushchev insisted on calling not the summit conference but a preliminary meeting. Premier Charles de Gaulle represented France and Prime Minister Harold Macmillan represented England. In an emotional forty-five minute speech, Khrushchev denounced the overflight. When he said, "As God is my witness, I come with clean hands and a pure soul," Eisenhower "almost choked." Replying that the flights "were suspended," Eisenhower promised that they would not be resumed. Khrushchev asked for an apology: "Please understand that our internal politics requires this. It is a matter of honor." Eisenhower refused to apologize.

The second meeting was scheduled for 3:00 P.M. on May 17. Khrushchev telephoned and said he would come if the participants agreed to call it a preliminary meeting or if America would apologize. Accepting neither condition, the three adjourned the conference. At a press conference that evening, Khrushchev displayed raging anger, but issued no new ultimatum (see Fig. 10.1).

Many observers felt that the Eisenhower administration had fumbled. British newspapers carried comments as "trigger-happy" Americans "made fools of themselves." Prime Minister Macmillan was horrified by Eisenhower's acceptance of personal responsibility for the flight. Customarily, nations handle such incidents differently. In 1940, when a German spy plane had crashed deep inside Russia and the Russians angrily demanded disavowal and apology, the Germans had replied that they regretted the incident and had taken

Figure 10.1 At a news conference, Soviet Premier Nikita Khrushchev, flanked by Foreign Minister Andrei Gromyko and Defense Minister Rodion Malinovsky, expresses his anger at Eisenhower's refusal to apologize for sending a U-2 spy plane over the Soviet Union. National Archives.

steps to prevent a repetition. No doubt the Germans meant that they regretted getting caught, but the Russians, if they wanted to, could consider the note an apology. Senator John F. Kennedy said that Eisenhower should have "expressed regrets." Calling Eisenhower a "fishy friend" of little ability and saying that it was "dangerous for a man like that to run a nation," Krushchev withdrew the invitation to him to visit Russia. Rioting in Japan against renewal of the U.S.-Japanese treaty also forced the Japanese government to withdraw its invitation to Eisenhower to visit Japan.

Both Eisenhower and Khrushchev had sought to improve relations, and they had made a promising beginning. Failure, wrote the *New York Times* columnist James Reston, was caused by "whims of personal pride and caprice." Eisenhower's assumption of personal responsibility and his refusal to express regret for the flight had put Khrushchev in a position where he could not attend the conference without appearing to acquiesce in the violation of Soviet airspace. It was a dramatic example of how peace could be disrupted by internal politics, accident, and pride.

Some observers feared that the summit conference had been deliberately torpedoed by elements opposed to relaxation of tensions. Russia was beginning to install ICBMS, an unstoppable means of delivering hydrogen bombs on America, and 1960 might be the last year in which America could destroy Russia without itself suffering unacceptable damage. If an eventual U.S.-Soviet war were inevitable, which many believed, then logic demanded that it be fought while America could still win without self-destructing. Otherwise, America might be forced to stand by helplessly while the Soviets took over the world by subversion and infiltration. Opposing detente were elements in the armed forces, intelligence agencies, and defense industries. Could such forces, critics asked, have arranged the May 1 U-2 flight, even sabotaged the U-2, to torpedo the summit conference?

Khrushchev later wrote that disruption of the 1960 Paris summit greatly weakened his political position in Russia and undermined his attempts to cut military spending and to improve relations with the West. Never again, he wrote, was he able to gain full control of the government.

Eisenhower later told an adviser that his main effort in the final two years of his presidency was to achieve an agreement that would end the Cold War. He believed he was making much progress, he said, until "the stupid U-2 mess had ruined all his efforts."

Eisenhower's Legacy

The eight years of Eisenhower's administration ended in January 1961. Denouncing containment, his administration had called for liberating nations from communism, but no rollback had occurred. Instead, Communists acquired new clients in Egypt and Cuba and made gains in Indochina. Eisenhower negotiated an end to the Korean War (which he considered his greatest achievement), met with Khrushchev, refused to send U.S. forces into Vietnam, and suspended atomic testing, but he also deepened U.S. involvement in the Middle East and set in motion an invasion of Cuba. "I had longed to give the United States and the world a lasting peace," he said, but "was able only to contribute to a stalemate."

To the surprise of many, Eisenhower had held down military spending. "Every gun that is made, every warship launched, every rocket fired," he said, "signifies, in the final sense, a theft from those who hunger and are not fed, those who are cold and not clothed." Militarization, he feared, "would either drive us into war—or into some form of dictatorial government." He felt that he had succeeded in controlling military spending only because his military experience enabled him to know when the demands of the army, navy, and air force were excessive, and he worried that his successors might lack the military expertise required to resist their demands. "God help the nation," he exclaimed, "when it has a president who doesn't know as much about the military as I do." Nevertheless, military spending remained at more than double the pre–Korean War level, and the stockpile of nuclear weapons multiplied nineteen times. In his farewell address, he warned that America was developing an extremely powerful "military-industrial complex" that must be strictly controlled if America was to avoid bankruptcy and if traditional American government were to be preserved.

Having a profound long-range impact on America's international position was the slowness of economic growth during the Eisenhower administration. The GNP increased an average of only 2 percent annually, while more rapid growth abroad narrowed America's relative superiority in national strength.

11 Kennedy's Foreign Policy

The Election of 1960

As the 1960 election approached, public opinion polls revealed that foreign affairs was the public's number one concern.

As their presidential candidate, the Republicans nominated Vice President Richard Nixon. His previous political campaigns had been characterized by attacks on his opponents as Communist sympathizers, and he had won national prominence by pressing the espionage case against Alger Hiss. Memorable incidents of his eight years as vice president were his confrontations with hostile crowds on a Latin American trip and with Khrushchev over whether a U.S. exhibit in Moscow actually represented a typical worker's kitchen. A hard-liner in foreign affairs, he had urged Eisenhower to send troops into Vietnam and Cuba.

When Adlai Stevenson, twice the Democratic nominee for president, showed little enthusiasm for a third try, the Democrats, passing over Senate majority leader Lyndon Johnson of Texas, nominated young (43) Senator John F. Kennedy of Massachusetts. Born into a wealthy, politically active Catholic family, he had graduated from Harvard, fought in World War II, and served as secretary to his father when he was ambassador to London. He had published a book, *Why England Slept*, which was critical of England's delay in fighting German aggression. A second book, *Profiles in Courage*, praising political leaders who had taken unpopular stands, won him a Pulitzer Prize. In fourteen years in Congress, he had been strongly anti-Communist, denounced Truman's "loss of China," refrained from criticizing Senator Joe McCarthy, and consistently voted for higher defense spending.

Both Nixon and Kennedy were dedicated Cold Warriors and each sought to appear more anti-Communist than the other. The world issue, said Kennedy, was "freedom under God versus ruthless godless tyranny." He charged that America had lost ground and prestige during the Eisenhower administration and that the Soviets were narrowing the U.S. economic lead: "It's time America started moving again." He accused the administration of allowing the Soviets to get ahead in installing ICBMS, creating a "missile gap." Condemning Eisenhower for insufficient vigor in fighting the Cold War in the Third World and for allowing Cuba to become a "Communist satellite," he called for strengthening Cuban forces in exile who sought to overthrow Castro.

Although the Eisenhower administration was then engaged in secret preparation for an invasion of Cuba by Cuban exiles, Nixon denounced Kennedy's
statements on Cuba as "dangerously irresponsible" and contrary to five treaties
and the UN Charter. A move to overthrow Castro, he said, would alienate U.S.
friends in Latin America and be "an open invitation" for Khrushchev to enter
Latin America. On the other hand, Nixon charged that Kennedy favored giving Matsu and Quemoy to the Communists. In November, Kennedy won with
only 49.7 percent of the vote.

Kennedy Organizes His Administration

Many Americans wanted Kennedy to appoint Adlai Stevenson as secretary of
state. Instead, naming Stevenson to the relatively powerless post of ambassador
to the UN, he chose Rockefeller Foundation head Dean Rusk, a Georgian who
had been a Rhodes Scholar, intelligence officer, political science professor, and
assistant secretary of state for East Asian affairs (see Fig. 11.1). Except for his
ideological anticommunism, the quiet, genial, unflappable Rusk had a reputation for seldom revealing his position on issues, and he was everyone's second

Figure 11.1 President John Kennedy with Secretary of State Dean Rusk and Secretary
of Defense Robert McNamara. National Archives.

choice for secretary of state. He had recently published an article maintaining that the president must conduct foreign policy personally.

To the post of White House security adviser, Kennedy appointed McGeorge Bundy, a World War II intelligence officer and former Harvard dean. For secretary of defense, he named Harvard business administration professor and president of Ford Motors Robert Strange McNamara. Kennedy's younger brother, Robert F. Kennedy, whom he made attorney general, also advised him on foreign affairs.

Kennedy made C. Douglas Dillon, the head of a leading Wall Street investment firm who had been Eisenhower's undersecretary of state, his secretary of the Treasury. Dillon and Kennedy continued the vigorous promotion of U.S. worldwide economic expansion, including the sale of U.S.-manufactured arms abroad. America must maintain an export surplus, said Kennedy, to finance its "overseas military commitments." In 1962, Congress authorized them to negotiate new reciprocal trade treaties reducing U.S. tariffs as much as 50 percent, and they negotiated a new "Kennedy Round" of tariff reduction that cut world tariffs on industrial goods an average of 35 percent.

Kennedy kept the right-wing Communist hunter J. Edgar Hoover as head of the FBI and Allan Dulles as head of the CIA, moves eminently pleasing to hard-line anti-Communists. As aides, Kennedy's appointees brought in promising veterans and university graduates, "whiz kids," whom one reporter called "the best and the brightest."

The president's elegant wife, Jacqueline, also played a prominent role. She attracted so much favorable attention abroad that, in Paris, Kennedy introduced himself with: "I am the man who accompanied Jacqueline Kennedy to Paris." (See Fig. 11.2.) She later made highly successful visits to the heads of governments of India, Pakistan, and Cambodia.

Kennedy brought new excitement into the presidency. The youngest man ever elected, he was rich, dynamic, intellectual, handsome, witty, and determined to "get America moving again." Calling him "incandescent," Dean Rusk said that he "was on fire, and he set people around him on fire." Some presidents are father figures; Kennedy was America's leading man.

In a stirring inaugural address, in January 1961, Kennedy proclaimed that "a new generation of Americans . . . tempered by war" and unwilling to permit a worldwide loss of human rights had come to power, and, he said, "We shall pay any price, bear any burden, meet any hardship, support any friend, oppose any foe, to assure the survival and success of liberty." To some this seemed to be a replay of Truman's proclamation of worldwide cold war.

An inauguration-day message from Nikita Khrushchev expressed hope for "a fundamental improvement in relations" that "step by step" could "remove existing suspicion and distrust and cultivate seeds of friendship and practical cooperation." Khrushchev released two crewmen from a U.S. plane shot down the previous year over Russia, thereby removing, said Kennedy, an obstacle to improvement of relations. He later told Kennedy that he had delayed this release until after the election to help Kennedy defeat "that son-of-a-bitch Richard Nixon."

Figure 11.2 Kennedy with his wife Jackie and President Charles de Gaulle in France. On this visit, Jackie received such extensive media coverage that Kennedy introduced himself to one audience by saying, "I am the man who accompanied Jackie to Paris." National Archives.

But Kennedy was not ready for detente. In his January 30 State of the Union address, he said that America must never be lulled into believing that either the Soviet Union or China had "yielded its ambitions for world domination." "Each day we draw nearer the hour of maximum danger." In September, he added that the enemy was "the Communist system itself—implacable, insatiable, unceasing in its drive for world domination," creating a "struggle for supremacy" between "freedom under God versus ruthless, godless tyranny."

Military Policy

In the presidential campaign, Kennedy had accused the Eisenhower administration of allowing Russia to achieve superiority in atomic missiles, a "missile gap." Actually, Defense Secretary McNamara found, the "gap" was in America's favor. In addition to numerous intermediate-range missiles near Soviet borders, America had seventy intercontinental ballistic missiles (ICBMS) to Russia's four.

In his inaugural address, Kennedy said that "only when our arms are sufficient beyond doubt can we be certain beyond doubt that they will never be employed." Lifting a three-year-old ban on atmospheric atomic testing, he boosted the number of U.S. ICBMS to 424, and accelerated construction of Polaris nuclear-powered missile-carrying submarines. When a Rand Corporation study concluded that a missile attack on America could kill as many as 80 percent of its people, he sponsored a massive bomb shelter program.

Kennedy deemphasized Eisenhower's "massive retaliation" doctrine in favor of a policy of strengthening the nation's capacity to fight wars with conventional arms. He feared that the Soviets would utilize "indirect nonovert aggression, intimidation, subversion, internal revolution" to achieve "the steady erosion of the free world through limited wars," and he wanted a "wider choice than humiliation or all-out nuclear action." By mid-1963 he had upped the number of combat-ready army divisions by 45 percent.

Kennedy was particularly interested in developing special forces to fight Communist-backed "wars of national liberation" in the countryside or jungles of developing nations. Among these special forces was the Green Berets, a highly trained outfit with advanced-technology equipment, to fight guerrillas on their own grounds. He raised the manpower of such units by 600 percent. Overall, Kennedy upped military spending from $43 billion in 1960 to $56 billion in 1963. It was the greatest peacetime military buildup to that date in U.S. history. Much of this power was projected abroad: in 1963 America had 1.3 million military-related personnel overseas and 275 major bases in 31 nations, and it was training the troops of 72 countries.

The Alliance for Progress

Kennedy was much concerned with the contest between the United States and the Soviet Union for influence among the developing countries, which he called "the great battleground for the defense and expansion of freedom today." He showed more awareness, however, than had Dulles that revolutions had indigenous causes that required local solutions. Saying that this struggle could not be won by military force alone and that supporting oppressive governments handicapped America in competing for friendship, he put more emphasis on promoting political, economic, and social reform as a means of combating communism. "If a free society cannot help the many who are poor," he said, "it cannot save the few who are rich."

In March 1961, Kennedy established the Peace Corps, and made his brother-in-law, Sargent Shriver, its first director. "A pool of trained American men and women sent overseas for the United States government to help foreign countries meet their urgent needs for trained manpower," it attracted idealistic, mostly young, people to work overseas for two years at low pay. Soon 15,000 volunteers were working in fifty-two countries of Latin America, Africa, and Asia. Most of them were teaching English, but many also worked in community development, living among village people and helping them meet their needs for better schools, recreational areas, or sanitation. Some were medical assistants, and a few were agricultural experts. Their goals were to alleviate poverty and to promote development. They won friends for

America and also helped to educate Americans on the problems of low-income countries.

Less than 6 percent of U.S. foreign aid had gone to Latin America in the past. On March 13, 1961, calling together Latin American ambassadors to the United States, Kennedy proposed an ambitious program of economic development for Latin America, coupled with social and political reform, which he called the Alliance for Progress. Describing the prevailing "ignorance, despair" and "daily degradations of hunger and poverty," he said that it was the duty of Western Hemisphere leaders to demonstrate that "man's unsatisfied aspirations for economic progress and social justice can best be achieved by free men working within a framework of democratic institutions." He called for investment in Latin America in ten years of $100 billion, of which $20 billion would come from abroad, half from the United States. But money alone would not suffice, he insisted, democratization and land and tax reforms were also essential "so that all, and not just a privileged few, share in the fruits of growth."

In an address in May to Congress, he returned to this theme. "No amount of arms and armies," he said, could stabilize governments that were unwilling to make social and economic reforms. Military assistance could not help nations "whose social injustice and economic chaos invite insurgency." He would not find it easy, however, to implement these ideals in practice.

The Bay of Pigs Invasion

When Kennedy took office, his most urgent problem was how to handle the already scheduled invasion of Cuba.

A decision on the Cuban invasion could not be postponed. Castro was scheduled to receive jet fighters from Russia in mid-May 1961, and Guatemala's president was insisting that the exile army leave his territory by the end of May. The exiles were armed, trained, and determined to go, and it would not be easy to disband them. The project had acquired too much momentum to be easily canceled, especially since cancellation would require Kennedy and his inexperienced intellectuals to overrule the veteran military intelligence experts of the Joint Chiefs of Staff and the CIA, who assured him that the prospects of success were good.

Within the administration, Secretary of State Rusk, Secretary of Defense McNamara, and National Security Adviser Bundy favored the invasion. However, a White House aide, historian Arthur M. Schlesinger Jr., called it a "terrible idea" that would dissipate international goodwill and give the new administration a "malevolent image." Former Secretary of State Dean Acheson termed it "wild" and "disastrous." Saying that the invasion would show "hypocrisy and cynicism," Senate Foreign Relations Chairman J. William Fulbright said that the Castro regime was only a "thorn in the flesh," not "a dagger in the heart." But Kennedy feared that canceling the invasion would make him appear weak. At the decisive conference, a general said: "We've got to have a showdown with communism in the Western Hemisphere sooner or later. Let her rip!"

Eisenhower and the military leaders considered air cover essential to the mission's success. However, Kennedy, saying that bombing Cuba would be too damaging to America's world relations, ruled that U.S. forces could not participate. Though disappointed, the Cuban leaders unanimously favored going ahead, as did the Joint Chiefs. At his April 12 press conference, the day before the invading force sailed, Kennedy publicly ruled out intervention by U.S. forces and said that this was understood by anti-Castro exiles. Nevertheless, CIA head Allen Dulles and some of the exiles believed that, in a crunch, Washington would do whatever was necessary to prevent the mission's failure.

Cuban exiles had formed two main groups, one composed of conservatives who wanted to transfer land back from peasants to landlords, and the other of liberals, including some former Castro supporters, who favored allowing peasants to keep land. The liberals had a larger underground organization within Cuba, but the CIA, which kept tight control of the operation, favored the conservatives and did not even inform the liberals of the date of the invasion.

The site chosen was the Bay of Pigs on Cuba's southern coast, ninety miles southwest of Havana. There, a ten-square-mile strip of solid ground was surrounded by impassible swamps with only three or four built-up highways, or "causeways," connecting it with the rest of Cuba. It resembled an island on which the invaders might hope to establish a base from which to expand, with the help of Cuban uprisings, to take all Cuba. In retrospect, it is difficult to understand how fewer than 1,500 exiles were expected to accomplish so much. Washington estimated that Castro had 40,000 of his own troops plus 10,000 Soviet troops (actually, he had 270,000 armed Cuban troops and 40,000 Soviet troops). The chairman of the Joint Chiefs said that the exiles were expected only to reinforce anti-Castro guerrillas, and Rusk said that their main aim was to spark an uprising. Many U.S. officials maintained that communism was so unpopular that most Cubans would greet the exiles as liberators and that many Castro troops would defect.

Preparation of the invasion was a poorly kept secret. As early as November 1960, *Nation* magazine and Miami newspapers were reporting on the recruiting of exiles and their training in camps in Guatemala. Castro, who had spies in these camps, repeatedly issued charges that an invasion was imminent. Two weeks before the invasion, the administration called in media representatives and briefed them on its plans.

On April 13, the invading force sailed from Nicaragua—three cargo ships, two submarine chasers, two landing craft, and converted yachts—escorted by two U.S. destroyers. Their equipment included five tanks, armored trucks, dozens of artillery pieces, and antitank bazookas. The landing force, 1,453 men, was composed mostly of the sons of well-to-do Cuban whites.

On April 15, in an effort to destroy Castro's small air force, eight B-26 bombers, flown by U.S. pilots, struck Cuban airfields. They scored hits on fuel dumps and some planes, but failed to destroy Castro's four jet fighters. In an attempt to disguise their origins, a shot-up bomber with Cuban insignia was flown from Nicaragua to Miami where its Cuban pilot told the press that part of Cuba's air force had rebelled and bombed its own airfields. In the UN, Adlai Stevenson, who had not been informed, passionately maintained that the bombers were Cuban. But this cover story deceived few foreigners, and so great was the international outcry against U.S. bombing of Cuba that Kennedy called off a scheduled second air strike.

Shortly after midnight on April 17, the exile force landed at the Bay of Pigs. Quickly seizing the narrow strip of land, the exiles launched raids inland. The CIA's Radio Swan proclaimed that "Cuban patriots in the cities and in the hills began the battle to liberate our homeland." But, with ample forewarning, Castro had arrested many of his opponents, and the Cuban people did not rise in support of their liberators.

Khrushchev, on April 18, promised to give Castro "all necessary assistance in beating back the armed attack." Kennedy replied that America would protect the Western Hemisphere against outside intervention.

Most foreign reaction was unfavorable. England and France gave no support. Neutral nations were critical. Brazil and Argentina opposed the invasion, and Mexico condemned it as "intervention." Protest riots occurred throughout Latin America.

The exiles were supported by nine U.S.-supplied bombers plus fighter planes with U.S. pilots, but their bases were in Nicaragua, a six-hour flight away. They lost ten planes, while Castro lost only one. Also, Castro's planes sank five rebel ships which held much equipment. Furthermore, the exiles had no answer to Castro's long-range artillery. By the second day, they were falling back on their beachhead. A contingency plan to escape to the mountains proved impractical, they could not get through the swamps.

With the exiles failing, conferences in Washington on April 18 and 19 agonized over whether to send in U.S. forces. A majority of the Joint Chiefs favored sending them, and the CIA wanted, at least, to send planes. But Rusk and Kennedy's White House staff objected. Open use of U.S. forces could bring Soviet retaliation elsewhere, perhaps in Berlin. In a compromise, they sent U.S. planes from an aircraft carrier for one hour to provide cover for resupply ships and for exile bombers to strike Castro's air force. But, because of time zone confusion, the exiles' bombers arrived early, and two were shot down, one by a U.S. plane. Later, U.S. ships moved in to evacuate a few survivors.

By 5:30 P.M., April 19, less than three days after the landing, the invasion collapsed. Of the exiles, 114 died, nearly 1,200 surrendered, and only 180 escaped. Castro lost 150 dead. Four U.S. pilots were killed. Calling it a "colossal mistake," a despondent Kennedy exclaimed: "All my life I've known better than to depend on the experts. How could I have been so stupid, to let them go ahead." He soon fired CIA head Allan Dulles.

Many Americans continued to insist that the entire operation had been conducted solely by Cuban exiles. But the evidence of U.S. involvement was so overwhelming that the pretense could not be sustained. On April 23, 1961, Kennedy publicly accepted full responsibility. Rallying around the president, the American people endorsed the invasion by 83 to 5 percent, and popular approval of his conduct of the presidency soared to 82 percent, a new high. "The worse I do," he said, "the more popular I get."

Republican leaders, including Barry Goldwater, Richard Nixon, and Nelson Rockefeller, denounced Kennedy for not giving the exiles more help. Leading Democratic senators Wayne Morse, Hubert Humphrey, and J. William Fulbright called the invasion a mistake. Columnist Walter Lippmann concluded that the failure was bad, but success would have been worse.

The Bay of Pigs invasion harmed the United States. According to a *New York Times* columnist, it made the United States look "like fools to our friends, rascals to our enemies, and incompetents to the rest." It violated international law, U.S. law, the UN Charter, and more than thirty treaties committing Washington to nonintervention. Casting Castro in the role of defender of Latin American independence, it increased his popularity in Latin America, strengthened his hold on Cuba, and dramatized his need for Soviet protection. In July 1961, he signed an alliance with the Soviet Union, and in December he declared himself a Communist. Two years later Washington suffered the additional humiliation of having to pay Castro $50 million in goods to ransom Bay of Pigs prisoners.

Kennedy's Cold War rhetoric remained at a high emotional pitch. On April 20, charging that the Communists were using nuclear armaments as a shield behind which to employ subversion and infiltration in villages all over the world, he said he was determined to ensure the success of America's system regardless of cost or peril in "a relentless struggle in every corner of the globe." It was, he said, "a time of peace and peril which knows no precedent in history."

The disaster undermined Kennedy's confidence in the Pentagon and the CIA. If the invasion had not occurred, he said later, he might have followed their advice to send U.S. troops into Laos, with perhaps more disastrous results (see discussion later in this chapter).

The Vienna Conference and the Berlin Crisis

Retaining his eagerness for a summit conference, Khrushchev suggested that he and Kennedy first meet for an informal exchange of views. In June 1961, against Rusk's advice, Kennedy met Khrushchev in Vienna for two days for the announced purpose of discussing a possible nuclear test ban, the status of Berlin, and the conflict in Laos.

Kennedy told Khrushchev that the two nations should avoid allowing direct confrontations to develop to the point where neither side could back down. But it was a turbulent meeting. When they discussed underdeveloped nations, Kennedy said that America would resist their entering the Communist camp. Khrushchev, picturing Russia as the champion of freedom over feudalism, defended the right of suppressed people to rebel against undemocratic and reactionary governments. Saying that the Soviets could not be expected to help preserve capitalism and colonialism, he asserted that he would continue to support "wars of national liberation." Their one agreement was to seek a peaceful neutralization of Laos.

On Berlin, Khrushchev was bellicose. Unless they reached agreement on Germany, he threatened, he would in six months sign a treaty with East Germany giving control of Berlin to the Germans, and Russia would no longer guarantee Western access across East German territory. Kennedy insisted that America must remain in Berlin to demonstrate that its commitments were reliable. When he warned that any undermining of U.S. occupation rights would have serious consequences, Khrushchev replied: "I want peace, but if you want war, that is your problem." He was going to turn over the access routes to East Germany, Khrushchev said, and if the West violated East German territory "there would be war." Kennedy replied, "It's going to be a very cold winter." This was the harshest language yet used at a big power summit—Rusk called it a "brutal" exchange.

Inexperienced at summit diplomacy, Kennedy was not fully prepared, and, although he had forcibly stated his position, he and his advisers felt that he had not conducted himself creditably. Khrushchev later wrote that he felt sorry for the young president. Consequently, Kennedy felt a need to do something more to demonstrate his strength and determination. "We will never do anything with these people now," he told newspaper columnist James Reston, "unless we make our power credible." Unlike Khrushchev's first two meetings with Eisenhower, which improved the atmosphere, the Vienna meeting exacerbated the conflict.

Calling West Berlin "the great testing place of Western courage and will," Kennedy said that America must stay "to maintain the confidence of other free peoples in our word and resolve." Khrushchev might regard any reluctance to wage nuclear war over Berlin, Kennedy told a reporter, as lack of nerve. Any interference with America's obligation to preserve the freedom of West Berlin, Kennedy wrote Khrushchev, would "endanger the lives and well-being of millions of people." Sending 45,000 more troops to Europe, Kennedy asked Congress for a $3.2 billion increase in defense spending and for $207 million to construct fallout shelters for civilians, and he called up 250,000 reserves into active service. Never had tension over Berlin been higher.

On August 13, 1961, in a move totally unexpected in the West, the Soviets suddenly began building a twenty-eight-mile-long wall to separate the Communist-governed half of Berlin from West Berlin. This wall solved many of the Soviets' problems, such as halting the exodus (more than 2 million since 1949) of skilled workers, spies, and refugees from the East to the West. For the West it furnished good propaganda—Communists were forced to build a wall to keep their people in. However, it added to the costs and reduced the benefits to America of holding West Berlin. In October Khrushchev called off his deadline, and the tension ceased, but Kennedy remained defiant. When he visited Berlin in June 1963, he told the crowd: "Ich bin ein Berliner." The crowd cheered even though, in German idiom, his words meant "I am a doughnut."

His experiences with Cuba and Khrushchev impacted, in differing ways, the policies Kennedy adopted toward far-off Southeast Asia.

Intervention in Laos

Laos is the smallest and least developed of the three states that constituted French Indochina. A mountainous, forested, landlocked kingdom, smaller than Oregon, Laos in 1960 had a population of only 3 million. Most Laotians were engaged in simple agriculture, primarily rice growing, and, as late as 1977, their average annual income was only $90.

The politics of Laos was dominated by Prince Souvanna Phouma, the premier in the royal government, and his rival and half brother, Prince Souphanouvong, who headed the Pathet Lao, a coalition of Communist and nationalistic forces that had fought for independence. At the time of France's surrender in 1954, the Pathet Lao controlled the two northern provinces of Laos. Prince Souvanna Phouma, whose government controlled most of the country, followed a policy of neutralism, taking sides with neither the West nor the Communist countries, but he accepted economic and military aid from America, including complete financing of his 25,000-man army. In 1957, in an attempt at national reconciliation, he formed a coalition government in which he gave cabinet posts to two Pathet Lao leaders, including Prince Souphanouvong.

In 1958, in an effort to make Laos more reliably anti-Communist, the CIA helped right-wing generals overthrow Souvanna Phouma. "The Americans say I am a Communist," said Phouoma. "This is heartbreaking . . . I am looking for a way to keep Laos non-Communist." His overthrow sparked renewed civil war in which the Soviets gave aid to the Pathet Lao. To defend the government, Americans recruited Montagnard tribesmen, imported Thai troops, and furnished arms and supplies worth $300 million by 1961, more aid per capita than was given to any other country. Nevertheless, the Communists made gains.

On the map, it is difficult to see the relationship of Laos to U.S. security. But to dedicated Cold Warriors, every area was vital. Eisenhower, who regarded Laos as the key to all Southeast Asia, had told Kennedy that the Laos "mess" was the most difficult problem he was leaving to him, and he suggested that Kennedy send in 250,000 U.S. troops and threaten to bomb China or Russia if they interfered.

Denouncing what he called attacks on Laos by "externally supported Communists," Kennedy enlarged U.S. forces in the area but, after the Bay of Pigs, resisted pressure to land U.S. troops. At their 1961 Vienna meeting, Khrushchev offered to support a cease-fire and neutralization. In July 1962 a multination Geneva Conference agreed to restore Souvanna Phouma as head of a new coalition cabinet that contained four Communists, withdraw foreign forces, and allow the Communists to keep the territory they had gained in the fighting. Thus, a U.S. attempt to replace a neutralist government with a right-wing one had backfired and left the Communists in a strengthened position.

Kennedy Enlarges America's Commitment in Vietnam

Both presidents Truman and Eisenhower had assisted France's attempts to reconquer her Indochina colonies. After France admitted defeat in 1954, Eisenhower had arranged for South Vietnam to declare independence from Communist-controlled North Vietnam, and had promised its president, Ngo Dinh Diem, to help him preserve independence.

For a time it appeared that Diem might succeed. Although French educated, he was an ardent nationalist who had resisted French rule. His was an able family, and he made his brother Nhu head of the secret police and another brother head of the Catholic Church. With U.S. aid, he suppressed armed criminal and religious groups and moved his troops out to take control of the countryside. Violating the Geneva armistice, he hunted down and killed members of the Vietminh who had fought under Ho Chi Minh.

Nevertheless, it was difficult for Diem to win the support of the South Vietnamese people. Most of his government officials and military commanders had served the French, and many Vietnamese hated them as American revolutionaries had hated Tories. Also, because most of his government officials, and 80 percent of Saigon businessmen, were from North Vietnam, many South Vietnamese regarded them as carpetbaggers. Diem was Catholic, while most Vietnamese were Buddhists. Furthermore, he was heavily dependent on foreign support—America paid 80 percent of his bills—and thus suspected of being a puppet of imperialists. Diem admitted that the "best nationalists went to the other side."

Diem's ties were with the tiny minority of Vietnamese who were rich. Returning to landlords lands that the Vietminh had given to peasants, he even used troops to collect rents. In his efforts to gain control of the villages, he abolished the traditional election of village chiefs, whom he replaced with his appointees. In sum, Diem was a foreign-imposed Tory carpetbagger and pro-landlord dictator.

Seeking to help Diem win popular support, Americans urged him to make reforms. At U.S. urging, he enacted a land reform law that restricted rent to 25 percent of a farmer's crop and set an upper limit of 284 acres on individual ownership of rice land, and he distributed about a million acres, most of it taken from the French, to about 300,000 landless peasants. But this left most rich landlords undisturbed, and he forced peasants to pay heavily for the land they received. Wealth distribution remained extremely unequal.

Despite Diem's continuing attacks, the South Vietnamese Vietminh, on advice from Ho Chi Minh, generally refrained from fighting back. Still hoping that the election promised for 1956 might be held, Ho was absorbed in the problems of repairing the ravages of war and establishing communism in North Vietnam. Also, unknown to Americans at the time, the Chinese opposed any renewal of the fighting. They were not as convinced as Americans were that a Communist takeover of South Vietnam would bring all of Vietnam under Chinese control. Instead, they seemed to feel that China's national security would be better served by having a weak and divided, rather than strong and united, nation on their border. However, in 1959, after much urging by southern Vietminh, Ho gave his consent to the renewal of armed resistance. It began in the Mekong Delta, south of Saigon, and often took the form of assassination of Diem-appointed village chiefs and attacks on military outposts to capture weapons.

In December 1960, anti-Diem forces formed a political organization, the National Liberation Front (NLF), a coalition of Communist and other groups. Its chairman, Nguyen Huu Tho, a French-educated Saigon lawyer, was not a Communist, and its platform called for internationally supervised elections, land reform, private property, free enterprise, free speech and religion, and increased spending on education and social security. A surprised U.S. politician exclaimed: "You could run for Congress on a platform like that." At first, 90 percent of the NLF's financing came from mostly capitalist elements in South Vietnam.

The NLF's fighting forces called themselves the Vietminh (League for Independence), but Diem and Americans called them the Vietcong (Vietnamese Communists).

When Kennedy took office in February 1961, the Vietcong numbered fewer than 10,000. Nevertheless, U.S. military men told the new president that Diem controlled only 40 percent of the countryside. A believer in monolithic communism and the domino theory, Kennedy was determined to prevent "the onrushing tide of communism from engulfing all Asia." He had supported Dulles's cancellation of the Geneva-scheduled election, and efforts to build a separate nation in South Vietnam. He feared that the war in Vietnam represented a testing ground of a new technique of Communist aggression—the "national liberation war"—and "if we don't break it here we shall have to face it again in Thailand, Venezuela, elsewhere." After his humiliation at the Bay of Pigs and his disturbing meeting with Khrushchev, he concluded that "we have a problem in making our power credible and Vietnam is the place."

Some advisers warned Kennedy against committing U.S. power to Vietnam. General Douglas MacArthur, who had experience in such matters, told him that America could not win a war on the mainland of Asia. General Charles de Gaulle warned that "the more you become involved out there against communism, the more the Communists will appear as the champions of national independence" and "you will, step by step, be sucked into a bottomless military and political quagmire." The real solution, De Gaulle said, was to give the Vietnamese the aid they needed to escape from the poverty and humiliation that led to totalitarian regimes.

On the other hand, the U.S. National Security Council recommended that America "create in that country a viable and increasingly democratic society," and the Joint Chiefs wanted to send 200,000 U.S. troops. On returning from a May 1961 visit to Vietnam, Vice President Lyndon Johnson, praising Diem as an Asian Winston Churchill, reported that unless the war in Vietnam were won, America must "surrender the Pacific." Surprisingly, although Diem sought more U.S. arms, technicians, and economic aid, he did not want U.S. troops. That, he said, would identify him too closely with a foreign government and handicap him in competing for the support of patriots. However, said General Maxwell Taylor, "we eventually broke down his resistance" to accepting troops.

Kennedy significantly deepened U.S. involvement in Vietnam. When Eisenhower left office, America had 785 advisers in Vietnam, the number permitted by the 1954 Geneva Agreements. Kennedy raised the number of advisers and troops to 16,700. This decision to break the Geneva Agreement's limit on foreign troops, recalled Rusk later, was Kennedy's "most important decision."

In attempts at "pacification" by winning "hearts and minds," Americans built roads, schools, and houses, assisted agriculture, and provided medical care. Embarking on these tasks in an enthusiastic and optimistic spirit, they expressed great confidence in their ability to succeed where France had failed. Their motives were purer, they said, their know-how superior, and their resources greater.

Tripling military aid, the Kennedy administration sent U.S. Green Berets, devised improved techniques of antiguerrilla warfare, and piloted large numbers of helicopters to help Diem trap and destroy elusive guerrillas. The number of Americans killed in Vietnam rose from 109 in 1961 to 489 in 1962. In an attempt to isolate the Vietcong from other South Vietnamese, Diem forced 7 million peasants to relocate into seven thousand fenced and fortified "strategic hamlets." Nevertheless, the number of Vietcong rose from 12,000 in 1961 to 88,000 in 1963.

Increasingly, Americans blamed Diem for the elusiveness of victory. W. Averell Harriman and others in the State Department advised that the war could not be won without social reforms and wider income distribution, but the conservative Diem resisted reforms. Moreover, a Catholic, he got into a religious fight with Buddhists who made up 70 percent of the population. In May 1963, when Buddhists rioted to protest his refusal to allow them to fly the Buddhist flag, Diem's troops fired on them. When a series of Buddhist monks protested by burning themselves to death, Americans were horrified, a feeling not eased when Diem's sister-in-law, Madame Nhu, calling it a "Monk barbeque," said, "Let them burn, and we shall clap our hands." On August 20 Diem suspended all civil liberties. Moreover, Americans discovered that Diem had secretly opened negotiations with the North Vietnamese, thus raising the possibility of peace on terms that Americans opposed.

Kennedy decided to get rid of Diem. On August 29, the U.S. ambassador to Saigon, Henry Cabot Lodge Jr., reported that he had begun an effort to "overthrow the Diem government." He and the C.I.A. encouraged a group of Diem's generals to oust him, which they did on November 1, 1963. When, contrary to expectations, the generals killed Diem, Kennedy was much depressed.

Losing confidence in America's ability to win in Vietnam, Kennedy told his advisers that he hoped to negotiate a settlement after the 1964 election and withdraw all U.S. troops in 1965. His assistant secretary of state for Far Eastern affairs, Roger Hillsman, later wrote that Kennedy secretly ordered the number of U.S. advisers there reduced by one thousand, and Defense Secretary McNamara and presidential adviser Arthur Schlesinger Jr. said that they were convinced that Kennedy intended to withdraw. Whether or not this was firm policy cannot be known. On November 22, Kennedy was assassinated.

The Cuban Missile Crisis

After the Bay of Pigs fiasco, U.S.-Cuban relations remained tense. Many Americans were outraged when Castro took Cuba into the Soviet camp. Cuban-U.S. relations had long been so close that Americans felt as if the United States had been betrayed by a member of the family—and communism only ninety miles off U.S. shores seemed intolerable. Continuing to train Cuban exiles in military tactics, Kennedy ruled out negotiations with Castro "as long as Cuba makes itself a willing accomplice to the Communist objectives in this hemisphere." All U.S. trade with Cuba ceased, and in September 1961, Congress banned aid to any country that aided Cuba. In January 1962, Washington got Cuba expelled from the Organization of American States (Argentina, Brazil, Chile, and Mexico, representing three-fourths of Latin America's population, abstained).

Setting up "Operation Mongoose" with a $50 million annual budget under the direction of Robert Kennedy, the president ordered the group to conduct a secret war against Castro. The CIA sent in teams to sabotage Cuba's economy and concocted at least eight plots to assassinate Castro, one of them utilizing the Mafia. And the United States conducted large military landing maneuvers on Carribean islands.

With Washington apparently bent on his destruction, Castro's chances of holding power seemed to depend on getting aid from Moscow. When it had appeared that the Communists might seek to replace him as Cuba's president, Castro, in December 1961, reversing his previous stand, announced: "I am a Marxist-Leninist and will be until I die." Moscow sent arms, technicians, and more than forty thousand Soviet troops to bolster him against "aggressive imperialist quarters." But the more he turned to Communists for protection, the more hostile the U.S. grew, and the continued U.S. threat made his position seem extremely precarious.

Castro's anxiety was shared in Moscow. The Soviets considered it important to protect fellow Communists, and they feared that America intended to invade Cuba (later McNamara conceded that available evidence justified that Soviet fear, but insisted that actually Washington did not intend to invade).

Also, while America had many means of delivering atomic bombs on Russia, including via Jupiter missiles then being installed in Turkey, the Soviets had few vehicles that could reach the United States. Unlike Americans, they had no missile bases outside their borders. They had 300 atomic warheads (to America's 5,000) and many short-range and medium-range missiles, but only a few (probably no more than twenty) ICBMS. Khrushchev decided to place seventy-two medium- and intermediate-range missiles in Cuba, where their one- to two-thousand-mile reach would extend to much of the United States. This, he wrote later, would confront Americans "with more than words" and give them "a little of their own medicine."

Although this deployment would improve Russia's relative strategic position by tripling the number of Soviet land-based missiles that could reach the United States, America would still enjoy vastly superior capacity to bomb Russia. McNamara believed that America was not "under any greater threat from the Soviet Union's power, taken in totality, after this than before" (counting submarines and airplane-based missiles, America could quickly hit Russia with 2,000 nuclear bombs, and the Soviets could not hit America with more than 300). However, their emplacement in Cuba would appear to the world as a Soviet victory and, once in place, might rule out any U.S. invasion of Cuba.

The Soviets made great efforts to keep their move secret, but, in July 1962, Americans detected an increase in the number of Soviet ships sailing to Cuba, and of Soviet personnel in Cuba. On August 22, the CIA informed Kennedy of possible launching pad construction, after which he ordered that he be briefed daily. On September 1 Republican Senator Kenneth Keating, on the basis of information from Cuban refugees, began making public charges that the Soviets were introducing intermediate-range missiles. On September 4, Kennedy warned the Soviets that America would not permit installation in Cuba of surface-to-surface missiles.

The Soviets responded with a mixture of defiance and denials. Maintaining that Cuba had a sovereign right to purchase arms abroad and that Cuba's friends had a right to send them, they announced on September 2 that, because of threats from "aggressive imperialist quarters," they were sending Cuba armaments and "specialists." On September 11 they said that the whole world knew that America had "ringed the Soviet Union and other socialist countries with bases" and added that, if normal relations were restored between Washington and Havana, Cuba would not need to strengthen its defenses. On October 18 Soviet Ambassador to the United States Anatoly Dobrynin assured Kennedy that the cargo arriving in Cuba was for defensive purposes only. (This was not exactly lying. All nations insist, and may believe, that all of their weapons are intended only for defense.) A U.S. attack on Cuba, Khrushchev warned, would mean war with the Soviet Union.

On October 3, Congress authorized the president to use force to prevent creation in Cuba of "an externally supported military capability endangering the security of the United States." On October 14, a U-2 plane got clear photographs of a ground-to-ground missile launching pad under construction and of a missile nearby.

Kennedy did not immediately challenge the Russians. Instead, pretending to be unaware of the missile sites, on October 16, he secretly set up a special Executive Committee to help him plan a course of action in the ten days before the missiles would become operational. This EX COMM consisted of about sixteen members, including Rusk, McNamara, Douglas Dillon, Bundy, Robert Kennedy, George Ball, Theodore Sorensen, Paul Nitze, the Joint Chiefs, General Maxwell Taylor, CIA Director John McCone, and, occasionally, Vice President Johnson, Adlai Stevenson, and Dean Acheson. It was in almost constant session. At times the president met with the committee; at other times, he did not, giving them greater freedom of discussion.

From the first they all agreed that America could not allow the Soviets to install the missiles. "The 1930s," said Kennedy, "taught us a clear lesson: aggressive conduct, if allowed to go unchecked and unchallenged, ultimately leads to war." Although, as McNamara argued, the missiles did not deprive America of its overwhelming nuclear superiority, their installation would appear to the world to be a major setback, and failure to stop it would be a disastrous blow to U.S. prestige, alliances, and world leadership. Furthermore, failure to act would hurt the administration politically, and a mid-term congressional election was only three weeks away. If he did not act, said Kennedy, he would be impeached.

The normal approach would be to call in the Soviet ambassador and demand that the missiles be withdrawn. Advocating a diplomatic solution, Adlai Stevenson suggested that America offer to withdraw U.S. missiles from Turkey in exchange. But there was little sentiment among other EX COMM members for a diplomatic approach, and Kennedy did not raise the subject in his prescheduled meeting on October 16 with Soviet Foreign Minister Andrei Gromyko. Instead, most favored military action. The Joint Chiefs, supported by Acheson and Fulbright, favored bombing the launching sites. However, this would kill Russians, and the air force could not guarantee total success. The Joint Chiefs advocated in addition a massive invasion. If America took that course, Kennedy predicted, the Soviets might bomb U.S. missiles in Turkey or seize West Berlin.

Other members of the committee were more cautious. If they unnecessarily started a war, said Undersecretary of State George Ball, they would carry "the mark of Cain" on their brows for the rest of their lives. Ball and Robert Kennedy said that, without betraying American ideals, America could not launch a Pearl Harbor–type surprise attack. Instead, McNamara, Robert Kennedy, and Ball advocated clamping a blockade on Cuba, halting further shipment of missiles. This would not in itself start a war, could leave the Soviets room to back down, and, if it did not work, would leave open other options. Eventually, this became the EX COMM's recommendation.

Time was running short. Quickly consulting U.S. allies, Kennedy got the support not only of Europeans but of Latin Americans.

At 7:00 P.M. on October 22, Kennedy made a dramatic televised appearance. Denouncing the Soviet move as a "clandestine, reckless and provocative" threat to world peace, he said it could not be accepted "if our courage and our commitments are ever to be trusted again by either friend or foe." Warning that he would regard the launching of any nuclear missile from Cuba against any Western Hemisphere nation "as an attack by the Soviet Union on the United States requiring a full retaliatory response upon the Soviet Union," he announced that he was imposing a blockade on "all offensive military equipment" and demanded "prompt dismantling and withdrawal" of all ground-to-ground missiles.

Kennedy's position was contrary to international law and to the historic U.S. position on freedom of the seas. Also, rather than a diplomatic approach, he had opted for a public showdown and was demanding that Khrushchev make a humiliating public surrender. Never before had the two superpowers seemed so close to nuclear holocaust.

In an outburst of patriotism, the U.S. public enthusiastically backed the president. Also, endorsing the blockade almost unanimously, the OAS council demanded that Russia withdraw offensive weapons and called on members to resist their placement in Cuba by "all necessary means, including the use of force." America's NATO allies were similarly supportive.

Denouncing the blockade as an illegal aggression, Khrushchev, on October 24, accused Kennedy of pushing mankind "toward the abyss of a world missile-nuclear war." When he asked Kennedy for a summit conference, Kennedy replied that he would not meet until after the Soviets dismantled the missiles.

More than a hundred U.S. warships moved into position 500 miles out from Cuba to intercept the twenty-five Soviet vessels then en route. Soviet submarines were nearby. McNamara had announced that America would not hesitate to sink Soviet arms-carrying ships that attempted to run the quarantine, but Kennedy ordered U.S. ships to fire only on their rudders, or to drop small depth bombs if Soviet submarines refused to surface. A large U.S. invasion force assembled in Florida. Openly calling a full airborne alert, the Strategic Air Command (SAC) sent hundreds of B-52s aloft with hydrogen bombs. U.S. bombing and invasion of Cuba was scheduled for October 30. "A smell of scorching," Khrushchev later wrote, "hung in the air."

On October 25, Soviet ships and an escorting submarine approaching Cuba stopped, and some turned back toward Russia. The two sides had been "eyeball to eyeball," said Rusk, and the other side just "blinked." However, twenty missiles and sixty-eight nuclear warheads had already arrived, the Soviets were rushing to complete their launching sites, and Soviet commanders of the 43,000 Soviet troops in Cuba had ninety-eight tactical atomic warheads for possible use against a U.S. invasion. On October 27, in this tense atmosphere, an American U-2 spy plane strayed into Russia, and a Soviet officer (against Khrushchev's wishes) shot down a U-2 over Cuba with a surface-to-air (SAM) missile. Many people, said Robert Kennedy, were "spoiling for a fight." War could come through whim or miscalculation, McGeorge Bundy later recalled, and events were threatening to slip out of control.

Castro spent the night of October 26 in a bomb shelter, but Khrushchev did not put his forces on alert. From Moscow, Ambassador Averell Harriman, telephoning that Khrushchev was desperately seeking a peaceful solution and practically "begging our help to get him off the hook," recommended some concession "to give him an out." At 9:00 P.M. on October 26, a long, rambling, personal letter from Khrushchev came over the cable. It was a conciliatory appeal to Kennedy's humanity. "If you have not lost your self-control," Khrushchev wrote, we "ought not now to pull on the ends of the rope in which you have tied the knot of war." For "if war should break out it would not be in our power to stop it. . . . Only lunatics or suicides, who themselves want to perish and to destroy the whole world before they die, could do this." All he wanted, he insisted, was to protect Cuba from invasion, and if Kennedy would make a public pledge that the United States would not invade Cuba, he would withdraw the missiles.

The following morning, Saturday, October 27, a second letter was broadcast on Radio Moscow, one that was more formal and impersonal and that probably reflected the views of Khrushchev's military advisers. It offered to remove the missiles, but only if America removed its missiles from Turkey. Most of Kennedy's advisers opposed a deal because they feared that withdrawing missiles under Soviet pressure would damage U.S. prestige and might be seen as "selling out" a NATO ally. But Kennedy asked whether America would be justified in going to war if it could secure removal of Soviet missiles from Cuba in exchange for removal of U.S. missiles from Turkey.

A majority of the EX COMM, including the Joint Chiefs and the CIA head, now advocated bombing the missile installations. But, accepting Bundy's and Robert Kennedy's proposal to ignore the second letter and to reply only to the first, the president wrote Khrushchev that if Moscow removed the missiles, America would promise not to invade. This, wrote Rusk, proved to be "the key that defused the crisis."

In addition, in a secret meeting that evening, Robert Kennedy told Soviet Ambassador Dobrynin that, although it could not be a part of a publicly announced deal, U.S. missiles would soon be removed from Turkey and Italy. Robert Kennedy also told Dobrynin that if the president did not have a reply by the next day, he would take military action. (President Kennedy had another offer in reserve—to have UN Secretary General U Thant propose a mutual withdrawal of missiles from Cuba and Turkey, which he would accept).

Khrushchev's reply was broadcast over Radio Moscow on Sunday morning, October 28. In return for assurances that America would not invade Cuba, he agreed to withdraw the missiles, dismantle the launching structures, withdraw thirty long-range bombers and Soviet troops from Cuba, and accept UN inspection. He did not mention U.S. missiles in Turkey. Thus, the thirteen-day crises ended. Kennedy had apparently achieved a spectacular victory in the big power facedown.

Not all members of EX COMM were happy. Some opposed making any deal; they were confident that America's military superiority was so great that Russia had no choice but to concede whatever America demanded. Air Force General Curtis LeMay said that they should "attack Monday in any case." The military, said Kennedy, "are mad."

Castro was enraged. Passionately denouncing the deal, he refused to allow UN inspectors on Cuban soil. The crisis dramatically reduced his influence in Latin America.

Kennedy had estimated the chances that the Soviets would not yield as "somewhere between one-in-three and even," and the Pentagon had estimated that a nuclear exchange would kill 110 million Americans. In what Rusk called "the most dangerous crisis the world has ever seen" and the historian Stephen Ambrose called "the most serious crisis in the history of mankind," Kennedy had won his gamble. In a test of wills, a game of "chicken," he had demonstrated that he was more willing than Khrushchev to go to war. As his standing in the Gallup Poll soared to a new high, he was widely applauded for his skillful use of power. His success reinforced the faith of many in the efficacy of military force in combating communism.

However, some State Department officials, columnist Walter Lippmann, U.S. Ambassador John Kenneth Galbraith, and historians have criticized Kennedy's handling of the dispute. Questioning his broadcasting of an ultimatum before presenting demands through diplomatic channels, thereby making it more difficult for Khrushchev to back down, some have speculated that he did so to improve Democratic chances in the upcoming congressional election. Some Europeans were shaken by the extent to which their fate had been determined by others, how close they had come to extermination without representation, and some questioned whether the missiles were sufficiently important to justify taking the world to the brink of war. The world, some said, had been brought close to atomic destruction over a matter of appearance or prestige.

Kennedy did not crow over his victory, and he ordered members of his administration to refrain from doing so. He expressed fear that people might conclude that all America had to do in dealing with the Soviets was to be tough. Facilitating the victory, he said, were the facts that it occurred in an area where the U.S. had military superiority and Soviet security was not directly threatened, and that the Soviet position could not be plausibly defended before world opinion.

Khrushchev bragged that he had saved Cuba, and he had, in fact, achieved two objectives: Cuba was not invaded and the Jupiter missiles were removed from Turkey within six months. Rusk called surviving the crisis "a triumph of both American and Soviet diplomacy." But, in the eyes of the world, Khrushchev had suffered humiliation. Only a few peace groups gave him more credit than Kennedy for avoiding war. The Chinese criticized him both for rashness in installing the missiles and for weakness in capitulating to a "paper tiger." Replying that the so-called paper tiger had atomic teeth, Khrushchev accused the Chinese of wanting Russia and America to destroy each other, leaving China the dominant world power.

The missile crisis stimulated Soviet military spending. Military inferiority had weakened Khrushchev's hand in the confrontation. "The Soviet Union," the Soviet deputy foreign minister told a Kennedy adviser, "is not going to find itself in a position like this ever again." In 1964, Khrushchev was forced from power and replaced by the more militant Leonid Brezhnev, who conducted a sustained buildup. In six years Russia had 860 ICBMs plus 120 submarine-launched missiles capable of reaching America, dwarfing the number of missiles removed from Cuba.

Efforts to Relax Tensions

The Cuban missile crisis seemed to have a sobering effect on both sides. In a direct confrontation, the superpowers had nearly unleashed the horrors of atomic war. Both emerged somewhat shaken by the experience and determined to prevent superpower confrontation from reaching that point again. In June 1963 they installed a teletype "hotline" to permit instantaneous communication in a future crisis between Washington and the Kremlin.

In a June speech at American University, Kennedy seemed to make a significant change of approach. Americans, he said, must reexamine their attitudes. It was necessary, he said, "not to see only a distorted and desperate view of the other side, not to see conflict as inevitable, accommodation as impossible, and communication as nothing more than an exchange of threats." No social system, he said, was "so evil that its people must be considered as lacking in virtue." War would destroy "all we have built, all we have worked for," and the massive sums spent on weapons could be better spent to combat ignorance, poverty, and disease. Consequently, he concluded, people must break the "vicious and dangerous cycle in which suspicion on one side breeds suspicion on the other and new weapons beget counterweapons." Khrushchev called this speech "the greatest speech made by an American president since Roosevelt."

In his October 26, 1962, letter to Kennedy, Khrushchev had condemned the arms race: "Armaments bring only disasters. When one accumulates them, this damages the economy, and if one puts them to use, then they destroy people on both sides." Environmentalists expressed increasing concern at the rise in background radiation caused by atomic tests. In August 1963, after a public initiative by Khrushchev, the two superpowers signed their first significant arms control pact, a treaty agreeing to conduct no more atomic tests in the air, under water, or in outer space. The Joint Chiefs feared that it might produce "euphoria" and reduce vigilance, but McNamara said that it would retard Soviet progress and prolong U.S. superiority. The Senate approved it by a vote of 80 to 19, and eventually more than a hundred nations signed it. Kennedy called it "a step toward reason" and considered it his proudest achievement.

In October 1963 the United States agreed to sell $250 million in wheat to Russia.

Some of Kennedy's admirers insist that, if he had not been assassinated in November 1963, he would have moved foreign policy further in the direction of detente. The Soviet ambassador believed that he was moving toward "a more active and conciliatory policy." When he learned of Kennedy's passing, Khrushchev wept. His death, Khrushchev wrote, was "a great loss" because he was "gifted with the ability to resolve international conflicts by negotiation" and was "a real statesman." If he had lived, Khrushchev wrote, Soviet-American relations would have been "much better."

In general, Kennedy's foreign policy was hard-line anti-Communism. Rejecting the movement toward detente of Eisenhower's last years, he returned to confrontation and Cold War rhetoric that would have pleased John Foster Dulles. His policy, concluded *The Wall Street Journal* was long on vigor, eloquence, and brilliance, but short on restraint, thoughtfulness, and common sense. One history of his foreign policy is entitled *Cold War and Counterrevolution*. Many of his admirers insist that he was too intelligent to persist long in this policy. Those who believe that he would have moved toward detente cite his emphasis on the need for reform in the developing world, his acceptance of a compromise settlement in Laos, his American University speech, and his expressions of desire to withdraw troops from Vietnam. But he had no more time.

12 The Lyndon Johnson Administration

The Johnson Style

The assassination, on November 22, 1963, of John Kennedy brought to the presidency fifty-five-year-old Vice President Lyndon Baines Johnson of Texas. In contrast to the Ivy League Kennedy, Johnson seemed to be a product of the cowboy West. Associates described him as crude, arrogant, egotistical, grasping, devious, and overbearing. A graduate of a Texas teachers college, he had been an assistant to a congressman and, during the New Deal, a relief administrator before winning election to Congress. After buying a television station, he acquired riches and a large Texas ranch, to which he invited guests to shoot fenced deer from the window of a Cadillac. His dynamic one-on-one persuasiveness and his knowledge of politics made him an effective congressional leader, and his presidential administration was one of the great eras of American humanitarian reform. However, his education and experience were mainly in domestic politics, and his discussion of foreign affairs was characterized by overblown rhetoric, emphasis on military preparations, and references to the Alamo and Munich. He fully subscribed to the Cold War view that all Communists were united in an evil plot to enslave mankind, and he believed that it was vital to block Communist aggression everywhere to prevent another world war. Soviet Ambassador Anatoly Dobrynin found him "visibly bored" by diplomatic topics.

Johnson asked Kennedy's Secretary of State Dean Rusk, Secretary of Defense Robert McNamara, and National Security Adviser McGeorge Bundy to stay on in his administration (see Fig. 12.1). Not until 1966 did he replace Bundy with the more hawkish Walt Rostow.

Johnson's presidency lasted five years and two months. His overshadowing international problem was the Vietnam War, but he was also actively involved with Latin America and the Middle East. In all three areas he continued and enlarged the policies of his predecessors but added a distinctive Johnson touch.

Flare-up in Panama

In relations with Latin America, Johnson put less emphasis than Kennedy on promoting reform and more on preserving stability. Putting conservative

Figure 12.1 President Lyndon Johnson meeting with Ambassador to South Vietnam Henry Cabot Lodge Jr., Secretary of State Dean Rusk, Secretary of State Robert McNamara, and Undersecretary of State George Ball. National Archives.

Thomas Mann in charge of Latin American affairs, he gave priority to protecting U.S. economic and security interests, even when that meant supporting reactionary oligarchies and military dictators. Stepping up U.S. training of Latin American police and armed forces, he cut off aid to the leftist president of Brazil, Joao Goulart, and encouraged the military to remove him, after which it installed a brutally repressive military dictatorship. When Peru's civilian government threatened to seize properties owned by Standard Oil, he halted aid to Peru.

Johnson's first crisis flared in Panama. Resenting the degree of U.S. control, Panamanians argued that they got less than their fair share of profits from the Panama Canal and suspected that the United States intended to annex the Canal Zone. Consequently, in January 1964, the illegal raising of a U.S. flag by U.S. students at a Canal Zone high school sparked several days of Panamanian rioting, which left four U.S. soldiers and twenty Panamanian civilians dead.

Panama broke diplomatic relations with the United States. When Johnson telephoned, Panama's president demanded revision of the treaties governing U.S. rights. Johnson agreed to open negotiations, which were still in process when he left office in 1969.

Intervention in the Dominican Republic

When Johnson took office, a crisis was smouldering in the Dominican Republic, the white-ruled nation that shares the island of Santo Domingo with black-ruled Haiti. The Dominican Republic had been a U.S. protectorate until freed in the early 1930s under the Good Neighbor Policy, leaving it under the rule of a U.S.-installed dictator, Rafael Trujillo, to whom Washington continued to give aid. Corrupt and bloody, Trujillo may have killed as many as twelve thousand of his opponents during his thirty-year rule, some of them on U.S. territory, before he was assassinated in 1961.

Seeking a more democratic government, Kennedy had pressured Trujillo's sons to depart, poured in aid, and helped secure election, in 1962, of Juan Bosch, a non-Communist leftist writer, as president. After attending his inauguration, Vice President Johnson had reported that Bosch was intelligent and idealistic but lacked strength and concrete plans. Undersecretary of State George Ball called him a "muddle-headed, anti-American pedant." As Bosch attempted to make social reforms, he was overthrown in September 1963 by the military which replaced him with Donald Reid, a member of the rich oligarchy. Refusing to recognize Reid, Kennedy cut off aid. Reversing Kennedy's policy, Johnson in December 1963 renewed diplomatic relations and aid.

On April 24, 1965, young army officers staged an uprising and demanded the restoration of Bosch as president. Passing out guns to thousands of civilians, and supported by liberals and leftists, they seized part of the capital city. Reid resigned, and pro-Bosch forces took over the presidential palace. But the anti-Bosch bulk of the army bombed the presidential palace and attempted to recapture the city. Approximately thirteen hundred persons died in inconclusive fighting. With more than a thousand U.S. citizens trapped in hotels, Johnson landed 500 U.S. marines to safeguard their withdrawal. Although a violation of nonintervention, this protective action had wide support.

However, Johnson then went further and interfered in the Dominican Republic's politics. The country's fewer than 4,000 Communists were split into three Communist parties—one pro-Soviet, one pro-Chinese, and one pro-Castro. Nevertheless, the U.S. ambassador expressed fear that power would be seized by groups "identified with the Communist party." Despite Rusk's doubts that the country's small number of Communists could play a decisive role, Johnson concluded that "the Communist leadership had the keys to what Lenin once called 'the commanding heights' of power." In an April 28 television address, he said that fifty "identified and prominent Communist and Castroite leaders" were among the rebels. "I am not going to sit here in this rocking chair," he told an adviser, "and let Communism take over another country in the Western Hemisphere."

Most informed U.S. and foreign observers denied that Communists controlled the rebels. When reporters checked Johnson's list of fifty Communists, they discovered that some of them were in prison, others were outside the country, and some were right-wingers.

On April 29, without OAS approval, Johnson sent in 22,000 U.S. troops who, with the loss of twenty-six killed and thirty wounded, helped conservative generals suppress the pro-Bosch forces. This action violated the OAS and UN charters and many U.S. treaties.

Defending his action, Johnson charged that "what began as a popular democratic revolution, committed to democracy and social justice . . . was taken over and really seized and placed into the hands of a band of Communist conspirators." And, enunciating what some called the "Johnson Doctrine," he said that "American nations cannot, must not, and will not permit the establishment of another Communist government in the Western Hemisphere."

Johnson's intervention produced a wave of protest in Latin America, Europe, and the United States. Most Latin Americans, said Robert Kennedy, did not agree that the revolt was Communist-inspired or that Johnson had a right to intervene without consulting the OAS. The intervention, said Senator Fulbright, alienated Latin American young people and reformers, preserved the power of a reactionary military oligarchy, and made the United States appear to be the enemy of social justice. "The slightest suspicion of Communist support," he said, "seems to be enough to discredit a reform in North American eyes and to drive U.S. policy makers into the stifling embrace of the generals and oligarchs" who "use the term Communist very loosely . . . to scare the United States into supporting their selfish and discredited aims." "Thus was a democratic revolution," said Bosch, "smashed by the leading democracy of the world."

In May, Johnson persuaded the OAS to send a five-nation Inter-American Peace Force to replace some of the U.S. troops in the Dominican Republic. In June 1966, a moderate rightist, Joaquin Balaguer, was elected president, defeating Bosch. Thus, the United States emerged from the involvement with minimum damage except to its reputation for favoring reform and nonintervention.

Implementing the Alliance for Progress

The ten-year Alliance for Progress had been inaugurated by Kennedy, but its implementation occurred chiefly in the Johnson administration. Accepting Kennedy's proposals, Latin Americans set ten-year goals of 2.5 percent annual per capita production growth, more democracy, wider land ownership, higher wages, improved education and health, tariff reduction, and more equitable distribution of income. This, U.S. experts estimated, would require $20 billion in outside capital, half from the United States, of which private investors would supply $3 billion. Each Latin American nation prepared a comprehensive plan for economic development and then submitted requests for aid for specific projects.

The Alliance had some successes. Alliance funds built new roads, schools, homes, water systems, hospitals, and sewage systems, trained teachers, and fought disease. The U.S. Food for Peace program provided surplus U.S. food for free lunches for 8 million school children, improving both their diet and their school attendance. Fourteen nations began land reforms, and eleven undertook tax reform. Furthermore, growing industry facilitated the growth of labor unions and of the middle class—both of which supported reforms.

Some reductions were made in trade barriers. The Central American common market, organized in 1960, eliminated nearly all tariffs among the small Central American countries. A large Latin American Free Trade Association, which included Mexico and all of South America except Bolivia, set a goal of abolishing all tariffs between its members.

The United States had generated high hopes, but made a relatively small net contribution. In the first eight years of the Alliance, Americans drew from Latin America $2 billion more in corporate profits than they gave, loaned, or invested there. Latin America's foreign debts doubled to $20 billion, on which annual interest payments amounted to more than a third of its exports.

Less interested than Kennedy in promoting reform and democracy, Johnson was more receptive to military dictatorship. In 1964, he cooperated in a seizure of power by Brazil's military. Between 1960 and 1970, thirteen civilian governments were displaced by military rule, and, by 1970, three-fourths of Latin Americans lived under military government.

Congress forbade the use of any U.S. funds to finance land redistribution. With only Venezuela and Chile actually implementing significant land reform, the number of landless peasants in Latin America rose. Food production and school enrollment lagged behind population growth, and the housing shortage worsened. Income distribution did not become more equal, and the rapid population rise held per capita growth to 1.5 percent, below that of the previous decade.

The Alliance for Progress had begun as an attempt to induce Latin America's ruling classes to allow more democracy, to divide huge estates, and to provide more education and health care—to relinquish some of their privileges and to share their wealth with their less fortunate countrymen. Such a voluntary peaceful social revolution led by a privileged social class against itself would be, said Senator Hubert Humphrey, "unique in history." Kennedy had planned it as an effective answer to communism. It did not happen.

Johnson and the Soviet Union

Johnson sought to improve relations with the Soviet Union. While demonstrating that aggression would not succeed, he wrote, he hoped to create a climate in which East and West "could begin cooperating to find solutions to their worst problems." Attempting to "sweep away small irritants one by one," he decided to avoid harsh epithets such as "ruthless totalitarianism." He saw no contradiction between fighting Communists in Latin America and Asia and negotiating and trading with them in Europe.

In this policy, he wrote, he was aided by an easing of the McCarthy-era tendency to see "Communist conspiracy" in every foreign policy question. The air, he wrote, became "somewhat less charged with blind anti-Communist sentiment," and the break between Russia and China helped people realize that the "Communist world was not a tightly disciplined monolith." Furthermore, Americans had grown more confident that they could preserve their technological and economic lead.

In October 1964, Khrushchev was replaced by Leonid Brezhnev as party chairman and Aleksei Kosygin as premier, but the dour and wily Andrei Gromyko, whose main concern was to keep the U.S.-Soviet conflict from escalating into war, remained as foreign minister.

Johnson made some progress in improving relations. He negotiated a civil aviation agreement that established regular airline flights between New York and Moscow. He secured a consular convention providing for the opening of more U.S. consulates in Russia and more Soviet consulates in America. He also sought to remove America's special restrictions on trade with Russia. In this he was backed by a resolution of the U.S. Chamber of Commerce, a stronghold of big business, favoring increased trade with Communist countries. Nevertheless, he failed to persuade Congress to enact his proposal, which, he wrote, fell victim to the war in Vietnam.

Shortly after the 1967 Six-Day War (discussed later in this chapter), Kosygin attended the UN session in New York primarily to champion the Arab cause. Americans suggested a meeting with Johnson, but, in the highly charged atmosphere, Kosygin did not want to meet in the White House or on a military base. Johnson arranged to meet him on June 23 on a college campus in Glassboro, New Jersey, a small town halfway between Washington and New York, for two days of talks. It was a curious meeting. The two were friendly, but could find little common ground. McNamara, who accompanied Johnson, argued that Russia should not install antiballistic missiles around Moscow because, if it did, America would build even more offensive missiles to overwhelm them. Kosygin, livid, protested that defensive weapons were moral, but offensive weapons were immoral. Johnson sought to begin negotiations on reducing strategic arms, but Kosygin was preoccupied with securing Israeli withdrawal from the lands they had just seized. He accused America of protecting Israeli aggression. When Johnson sought Soviet help in arranging a negotiated Vietnam settlement, Kosygin replied that the Vietnam War had given China "a chance to raise its head with consequent great danger for the peace of the entire world" and that peace would require U.S. withdrawal. In two days of discussion, they made little progress on major issues.

Later, in July 1968, Johnson secured a treaty on nonproliferation of nuclear weapons that was signed by America, Russia, Britain, and more than fifty other nations. All agreed that nations that did not already have nuclear weapons would not acquire them and that all would share in the peaceful benefits of atomic power. Johnson called this "the most important international agreement since the beginning of the nuclear age."

Johnson sought to ease the arms race "so that public funds could be spent on vital needs of people instead of the military." By 1967, the United States had 1,054 ICBMS, and the Soviets almost 900. Competitive arming, he wrote Kosygin in January 1967, incurred "colossal costs without substantially enhancing the security" of either. In July 1968, Johnson secured Soviet agreement to open discussions on reducing long-range missiles and antiballistic missiles, and the Soviets invited Johnson to visit Moscow, but these plans were derailed when, on August 21, the Soviets sent troops into Czechoslovakia to suppress a liberalization of that nation's Communist government.

By this time, both Johnson and Brezhnev had enforced "doctrines"—Johnson that the United States had a right to invade Latin American countries to prevent them from becoming Communist, and Brezhnev that Russia had a right to invade East European Communist countries to prevent them from abandoning Communism.

The Six-Day War

In the Middle East, Arab governments had wrested control of their oil resources from British, French, and U.S. oil companies and, in 1959, enlisting Venezuela, formed the Organization of Petroleum Exporting Countries (OPEC) to control production and prices. Oil prices soared. These developments increased the financial and military strength of Arab nations. In 1964, Palestinian Arabs established the Palestine Liberation Organization (PLO) which denied that Jews had a right to establish a state in Palestine. The Soviets supplied Egypt, Syria, and Iraq with modern weapons.

In May 1967, alarmed by reports that Israel was preparing to attack Syria, Egypt forced the UN to withdraw its troops that separated Egyptian and Israeli armed forces. Also, Egypt blocked Israel's trade through the Gulf of Aqaba to the Red Sea. Johnson failed in his attempt to organize an international effort to lift this blockade.

Russia urged Egyptian President Nasser not to strike the first blow, and urged Johnson to restrain Israel. Johnson asked Israel not to go to war, but said he would not block them as Eisenhower had done in 1956. "Don't make war," French President Charles de Gaulle warned Israel, for that would "cause the Soviet Union to penetrate more deeply into the Middle East," and would so strengthen Palestinian nationalism that "you will never get rid of it."

Nevertheless, responding to the blockade and to what they regarded as a growing military threat, the Israelis, on June 5, 1967, without declaring war, launched a massive surprise air attack on Egypt, Jordan, Syria, and Iraq. It destroyed most of their warplanes on the ground. This attack shocked and angered Secretary of State Rusk. However, accepting the Israeli view that it was defensive, much of the Western press applauded its stunning success. Commenting on the contrast between international reaction to Israel's surprise air attack and to Japan's surprise attack on Pearl Harbor, a bemused Japanese newspaper concluded that no consensus existed on what objective criteria made a particular military action defensive or offensive.

In the first use of the telephone "hot line," Soviet Premier Kosygin assured Johnson that Russia would not intervene in the war if America did not inter-

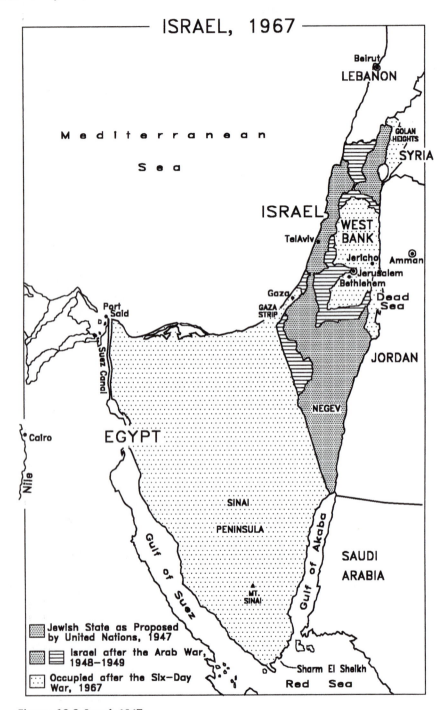

Figure 12.2 Israel, 1967.

vene. Surprised to discover that the hot line ended at the Pentagon, Johnson quickly arranged to extend it to the White House.

Ensuing Israeli land victories were almost equally spectacular. In a "Six-Day War," the Israeli army decisively defeated the armies of Egypt, Syria, and Jordan and captured the Golan Heights from Syria, East Jerusalem and the West Bank from Jordan, and the Gaza Strip and the Sinai Peninsula from Egypt.

The Soviets proposed a cease-fire which, with U.S. support, the UN endorsed on June 6. On the morning of June 10, calling Johnson on the hot line, Kosygin told him that continued Israeli advances in defiance of the cease-fire threatened "grave catastrophe" and that, if they continued, Russia would take "necessary action, including military." Opposing Soviet military intervention, Johnson ordered the Sixth Fleet to the Syrian coast. Tension rose. Later that day, however, Israel accepted the cease-fire.

The Six-Day War further damaged U.S.-Arab relations. Because Washington had armed and financed Israel, America received part of the blame for the attack. As Arab mobs staged anti-U.S. demonstrations, Arab nations seized U.S.-owned property and halted the shipment of oil to America. Seven of them broke diplomatic relations. The war strengthened Soviet claims to be the champion of Arabs against Western imperialism spearheaded by Israel. After the war, more Arabs turned to Russia for aid and received large shipments of arms, accompanied by thousands of Soviet technicians and advisers.

UN Security Council Resolution 242, adopted on November 1967, proposed a three-point peace program: (1) withdrawal of Israeli forces from territories occupied in the Six-Day War, (2) Arab recognition of Israel and its right to its prewar territories (see Fig. 12.2), and (3) a "just settlement of the refugee problem." Arab leaders, however, were unwilling to admit that Israel had any right even to its pre-1967 territories, while the Israelis were unwilling to withdraw from the additional territories they had taken. These newly occupied lands contained a million Arabs and were so indisputably Arab that Israel did not incorporate them, but called them "occupied territories." This occupation created additional refugees, stimulated Arab nationalism, and strengthened the PLO. For years, Americans had assured Arabs that Israel posed no aggressive threat, and Rusk bitterly opposed Israel's retention of indisputably Arab lands. America was committed to defend Israel's existence, another American secretary of state would say, but not Israel's conquests.

Violent clashes between Israel and Egypt and Syria continued. Palestinian terrorists hijacked Israeli airplanes and conducted murderous raids on Israelis in other parts of the world. Israelis struck back with raids, including bombing flights deep inside Jordan, Lebanon, and Syria, often with high civilian casualties. Meanwhile, with Soviet help, Arab states rebuilt their armed forces.

Johnson Escalates the Vietnam War

As vice president, Johnson had fully supported Kennedy's Vietnam intervention and escalation of the war. Losing Vietnam, he told Henry Cabot Lodge on

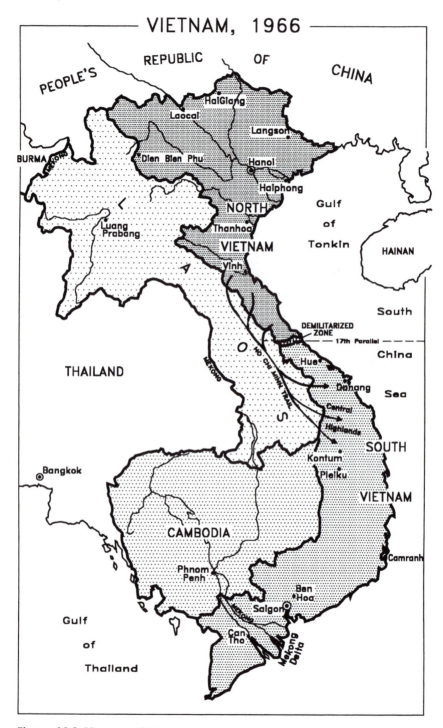

Figure 12.3 Vietnam, 1966.

the day of Kennedy's funeral, would ruin him politically: "I am not going to be the president who saw Southeast Asia go the way China went." During Johnson's administration, U.S. involvement in Vietnam flared into a major war that eventually consumed his administration and forced him from the presidency.

In Johnson's view, the Vietnam War presented him with an unpleasant dilemma. If he waged it vigorously, the expense would starve his "Great Society" program of domestic reform. But "losing another country to Communism," Johnson feared, would arouse so much popular denunciation that his administration would be destroyed. While Vice President Hubert Humphrey urged immediate withdrawal, Rusk argued that Vietnam was "of great strategic importance" and that its loss would cause "a basic shift in the global balance of power." Without additional U.S. troops, the Saigon government might not survive, but sending large numbers of troops into the country might make Saigon appear to be a puppet of white imperialists. It seemed to Johnson that his best choice was to continue the Kennedy policy in the hope that it would at least avert catastrophe.

The enormous U.S. effort to construct a viable independent nation in South Vietnam had not succeeded. Johnson put less emphasis on reforms designed to win popular support and more on military measures. Giving the military command to General William Westmoreland, an experienced paratroop commander, he replaced Lodge as ambassador with General Maxwell Taylor. He also transferred control of "pacification" programs designed to win the "hearts and minds" of South Vietnamese villagers to the military. "If you get them by the balls," Johnson said, "their hearts and minds will follow." However, his buildup of U.S. troops was slow—from Kennedy's 16,700 to only 23,000 by the end of his first year.

As their 1964 presidential candidate, the Republicans nominated an extreme right-wing hawk, Senator Barry Goldwater. Charging that Johnson was not fighting to win, Goldwater called for removing restraints on the military and allowing them to take whatever actions they considered necessary, such as bombing North Vietnam, regardless of any international complications.

By comparison, Johnson's campaign statements on Vietnam seemed relatively moderate. He was not going to send American boys nine or ten thousand miles, he said, to do fighting that Asian boys ought to do for themselves, and he was not going to get America bogged down in a land war in Asia.

Nevertheless, during the campaign, Johnson sought congressional authorization to make war on North Vietnam. He presented his request after North Vietnamese boats, on August 1 and 4, 1964, attacked U.S. destroyers in the Gulf of Tonkin near North Vietnam's coastline. When Johnson retaliated by bombing North Vietnam, his public approval rating shot up from 42 percent to 72 percent. He asked Congress to authorize him to take "all necessary measures to repel any armed attack" against U.S. forces and to "prevent further aggression." Critics later charged that this "Tonkin Gulf Resolution" had been prepared weeks in advance, that the U.S. destroyers were supporting South Vietnamese raids on North Vietnam, and that the reported second attack probably never occurred. However, on August 7, with only Democrats Wayne Morse and Ernest Gruening voting "no," Congress granted the requested powers. Johnson would subsequently cite the Tonkin Gulf Resolution as equivalent to a declaration of war that authorized him to expand military operations against North Vietnam as he saw fit.

Saigon's military situation continued to deteriorate. The Vietcong steadily rose in number from 12,000 in 1961, 88,000 in 1963, 116,000 in 1965, and 221,000 in 1966. They took control of much of the countryside, leaving scarcely half of the population under Saigon's control.

Americans insisted that the fighting resulted from aggression by Communist North Vietnam which, in turn, they charged, was the agent of Communist Russia and China. America's own statistics, however, did not support that claim. In 1961, 90 percent of the Vietcong were native South Vietnamese and were armed chiefly with weapons captured from Diem's armed forces. Not until 1964 did substantial numbers of North Vietnamese troops enter South Vietnam.

Despite stepped-up U.S. aid and bombing, the war went badly. Although much larger and immensely better armed than the Communists, the Army of South Vietnam (ARVN) could not suppress the Vietcong guerrillas. Its morale was so low that in 1965 desertions reached an incredible 113,000, and the Vietcong seemed to be poised to launch an offensive from the mountains that could cut South Vietnam in two. "To take no positive action now is to accept defeat in the fairly near future," warned Ambassador Taylor in January 1965. After a February trip, Bundy added, "without new U.S. action defeat appears inevitable."

In February 1965, Soviet Premier Aleksei Kosygin, accompanied by his air force chief, visited North Vietnam's's capital, Hanoi. Having removed Khrushchev from power, speculated Johnson, the new Soviet leaders were reversing Khrushchev's policy of "relative inaction" and were moving in "to share credit for the anticipated victory." After a Vietcong attack, on February 6, on a U.S. base at Pleiku destroyed seven U.S. airplanes and killed nine Americans, Johnson ordered immediate reprisal raids on North Vietnam. Kosygin was embittered that this raid occurred while he was in Hanoi.

Later in February, Johnson moved from retaliatory raids into a sustained bombing campaign, code-named "Rolling Thunder." Three months of heavy bombing, Bundy predicted would cause Hanoi to seek peace. Personally selecting the targets, Johnson followed a strategy of escalating the bombing gradually to maximize pressure on North Vietnam to call off the war in order to save its remaining assets. When Hanoi did not surrender, the bombing became heavier and less discriminate until North Vietnam, despite its scarcity of targets, became history's most heavily bombed country. In the year and a half from mid-1965 to the end of 1967, Americans dropped more bombs on Vietnam than the Allies dropped on Europe during all of World War II.

This bombing was costly to Americans. The Soviets supplied North Vietnam with sophisticated anti-aircraft weapons, and by 1968 America had lost 918 planes, valued at $6 billion. The bombing cost America nearly ten dollars for each one dollar of damage it inflicted on the enemy. Also, the heavy bombing of a small, underdeveloped country aroused worldwide condemnation. Likening U.S. actions to Nazi atrocities, Sweden's premier, Olaf Palme, gave "humanitarian" aid to North Vietnam.

It became increasingly clear that Saigon had little popular support and that its military force, the ARVN, despite its larger size and better equipment, could not defeat the Vietcong. Moreover, in early 1965, wrote Johnson, complete North Vietnamese fighting units began arriving in the south. Although ARVN forces still outnumbered Communist forces by 570,000 to 137,000, new reports indicated that Saigon could be saved only if America sent large numbers of U.S. combat troops.

In March 1965, Johnson landed two marine battalions, 3,500 men, thereby raising U.S. military personnel in Vietnam to 27,000. When the situation continued to deteriorate, he sent additional U.S. forces, raising the total to 180,000 by the end of 1965, 380,000 by the end of 1966, and 500,000 by the end of 1967 (they would peak out at 542,000 in February, 1969). In addition, he enlarged the U.S.-trained and -armed Saigon military force to nearly 800,000 men.

The Saigon governments that followed Diem, nine different ones within sixteen months, seemed to lack Diem's patriotism and efficiency. Despairing of finding competent civilian leadership, Washington in 1965 turned over the government to the military, to General Nguyen Van Thieu and the flamboyant air marshal Nguyen Cao Ky, both of whom had fought for France (see Fig. 12.4). This, said Bundy, was "scraping the bottom of the barrel."

Figure 12.4 President Johnson with South Vietnamese President Nguyen Thieu and Premier Nguyen Ky. National Archives.

In July 1965, Johnson resolved to commit as many U.S. bombers and troops as necessary to prevent an enemy victory. Deploying more than 3,000 helicopters, and huge B-52 bombers, which dropped explosives, phosphorus bombs, and napalm, Americans lavishly applied artillery and automatic fire. By 1971, America had expended 26 billion pounds of explosives, more than a thousand pounds per inhabitant and twice as much as was used in all of World War II. To deny Vietcong guerrillas cover and food, Americans sprayed one-eighth of South Vietnam with defoliants, and leveled forests with huge bulldozers. They removed the population from large areas and designated them "free-fire zones," subject to random bombing and shelling. A fourth of the population became refugees. A U.S.-directed "Phoenix" program assassinated Vietcong leaders. In "search-and-destroy" missions, South Vietnamese and U.S. troops swept repeatedly across the countryside, rolling up a huge "body count" of real and suspected Vietcong.

In addition to the sustained bombing campaign, "Rolling Thunder," in North Vietnam, Johnson stepped up the bombing in South Vietnam. In all, America would drop 8 million tons of bombs on Vietnam—four times as much as had been dropped in World War II.

Of course, these measures inadvertently killed large numbers of civilians, thus alienating much of the population whose support was vital to U.S. success. According to Roger Hillsman, every time Americans bombed a village they created ten new Communists for every one they killed.

Americans were confident that no military force that a small underdeveloped country could field could long withstand such overwhelming military power. Vietcong forces numbered fewer than 300,000 lightly armed men and, as predicted, they suffered high casualties and won no sizable battles. Amazingly, however, they continued to exist, even to expand, a fact Americans found inexplicable. The accumulated total of Americans killed in Vietnam rose to 6,000 in 1966, 9,400 in 1967, and 15,600 in 1968.

America obtained support for the war from Korea and Thailand, both of whom sent troops for which America paid large sums. Australia and New Zealand also sent a few troops. Taiwan and Australia willingly, and Japan somewhat reluctantly, allowed Americans to use bases on their soil.

Hawks versus Doves

Meanwhile, the international outcry against America's war in Vietnam rose. Church leaders, including the Pope and the World Council of Churches, denounced it, as did the governments of Sweden, Canada, and the nonaligned nations. UN Secretary General U Thant demanded a halt. Prime Minister Indira Ghandi of India asked if Americans would so heavily bomb civilians if they were Europeans. President De Gaulle of France called it a "detestable war." Never before had America been so widely and emotionally condemned.

Opposition within America also grew. Leading scholars, including Hans Morgenthau, Arthur Schlesinger Jr., George F. Kennan, and Henry Steele Commager, argued that the war resulted from an excessive enlargement of what Washington regarded as America's sphere of vital interests and from misdiagnosis of the cause of the conflict. Lavish application of firepower in support of undemocratic governments, they maintained, was not an effective means of defending democracy, and persisting in it would harm America. By 1965, college students were holding prolonged "teach-ins," with many speakers, to educate themselves and others on the issues. Celebrities, including Martin Luther King Jr., Dr. Benjamin Spock, Jane Fonda, Bob Dylan, and Joan Baez, campaigned against the war. In Congress, Senators Wayne Morse and Ernest Gruening were joined in opposition by leading senators, including George McGovern, Senate Majority Leader Mike Mansfield, Senate Foreign Relations chairman J. William Fulbright, Frank Church, and, in 1966, Robert Kennedy (see Fig. 12.5). They were backed by the *New York Times*, the *Washington Post*, George F. Kennan, and Walter Lippmann.

America had no national interest to defend in Vietnam, Mike Mansfield told Johnson in February 1964, and the war would be "an indecisive, bloody and costly military involvement" that would require constant escalation to

Figure 12.5 Four prominent opponents of America's war in Vietnam: Senators J. William Fulbright, Mike Mansfield, Frank Church, and Wayne Morse with a picture of an earlier noninterventionist senator, William Borah. Boise State University Library.

stave off defeat. Vice President Hubert Humphrey continued to express private misgivings. Some generals, including former Marine Corps commander General David M. Shoup and former Korean War commander General Matthew B. Ridgway, turned critical of the war.

Johnson maintained that America was in Vietnam to defend a free nation against outside aggression by international Communism, and Rusk denied that the conflict was in any sense a civil war. According to a U.S. White Paper, "a Communist government has set out deliberately to conquer a sovereign people in a neighboring state," and "we learned from Hitler at Munich that success only feeds the appetite of aggression." Unless America defeated this aggression, hawks argued, America's allies would lose faith in its willingness to keep its commitments to defend them (and faith in the integrity of U.S. commitments, wrote Rusk, "was the principal pillar of peace in the world"), wars of national liberation would break out elsewhere, China would become more aggressive, additional Asian countries would fall to Communists like a row of dominos, and America would lose control of the Pacific. If America failed to "stop the Reds in South Vietnam," said Johnson, "tomorrow they will be in Hawaii, and next they will be in San Francisco."

America had the responsibility to fight communism in Vietnam, Johnson maintained, because only America had the required power. And, he said, America's power was "greater than the combined might of all the nations, in all the world, in all the history of this planet." But "if we are driven from the field in Vietnam," said Johnson, "then no nation can ever again have the same confidence in American promises," and that would "open the path to World War III." Also, he was confidant that America could win. It should not be difficult to defend South Vietnam against invasion by North Vietnam, which was no larger or better armed. Johnson's position had the support of former presidents Truman and Eisenhower and of former Republican presidential candidates Thomas E. Dewey, Richard Nixon, and Barry Goldwater.

However, a growing number of Americans rejected the hawk view. Opponents maintained that Vietnam was not two nations but one. They said that the war had begun not with an invasion from North Vietnam, but as an uprising in the southern part of South Vietnam, and that most of the Vietcong were native South Vietnamese. And, according to Pentagon figures, only 7.5 percent of them were Communists. The Vietcong had less outside funding and arms than did Saigon, and the only foreign troops engaged were on the U.S. side. Furthermore, an aggressor can conquer hostile territory only by having superior force, and the Vietcong were less numerous and less well-armed than Saigon. Thus, they concluded, America's war was not against invading foreigners, but against Vietnamese, most of whom were native South Vietnamese.

The Vietnamese began the war, critics said, as a struggle against French control and were continuing it against U.S. control; thus it was basically a fight by nationalists for independence from foreign domination. Wars for national liberation long antedated Communism, they said—the American Revolution was such a war. Also the Vietcong sought land reform and other measures helpful to the poor who constituted the vast majority of Vietnam's people, while

Saigon favored the minority who were rich. The fact that the Vietcong fought as guerrillas, who could not long survive without aid from civilians, and had higher morale indicated that they had both more popular support and faith in their cause than did Saigon's troops.

Also, rejecting the domino theory, opponents of the war maintained that, as demonstrated by Germany, Italy, Turkey, and Iran, nations did not automatically go Communist when an adjacent country became Communist. They further denied that a Vietcong victory would give China control of the Pacific. The Vietnamese would not accept Chinese domination, they said, and China had little navy or other means of projecting military power far beyond its borders.

Critics maintained that America had first intervened in Vietnam in support of French imperialism and remained to prevent the election that the Geneva Conference had scheduled to choose a government for all Vietnam. Thus, it was basically a fight to prevent the Vietnamese from exercising their democratic right to choose their own government. "The underlying cause of the war," the North Vietnamese maintained, "was the American imposition of a stooge administration on the Vietnamese people."

In addition, critics maintained, the war mired U.S. military and economic strength in an indecisive war, depleted U.S. reserves of gold and foreign exchange, reduced its ability to give foreign aid, alienated friends, and damaged U.S. economic production, education, and internal unity—all of which were important to long-term national power. Furthermore, critics argued, the war was harming America's image by making America appear imperialistic and inhuman. In May 1967, McNamara wrote that "the picture of the world's greatest superpower killing or seriously injuring a thousand noncombatants a week, while trying to pound a tiny backward nation into submission on an issue whose merits are hotly disputed, is not a pretty one."

To many Americans, the Vietnam effort seemed increasingly irrational, an irrationality compounded of anti-Communism, ignorance of Asia and international relations, and arrogance of power. "A feeling is widely and strongly held," wrote Assistant Secretary of Defense John McNaughton, "that 'the Establishment' is out of its mind . . . that we are trying to impose some U.S. image on distant peoples we cannot understand, and that we are carrying the thing to absurd lengths."

The antiwar movement gained strength and momentum. Antiwar hecklers, chanting "Hey, hey, LBJ! How many kids did you kill today?" became so numerous as to prevent Johnson from making public speeches except on military bases. Secretary of Defense Robert McNamara, once so enthusiastic a warrior that many called it "McNamara's War," concluded that no amount of military force could produce a victory, and turned so dovish in 1967 that Johnson transferred him to the presidency of the World Bank.

Critics demanded that Johnson seek a negotiated settlement, but Johnson was leery of negotiations. He frequently offered to negotiate with Russia, China, or North Vietnam, which, if they accepted, would thereby confess to his charge that they were responsible for the war, but he refused to negotiate with the Vietcong. To do so would be a tacit admission that the real enemy was Vietnamese and that America was intervening in a civil war.

Johnson also opposed allowing Vietnam to become a nonaligned nation. Neutralization, he said, "would only be another name for a Communist takeover." It would, he argued, be surrender on the installment plan, allowing South Vietnam to be taken over through Communist subversion. Thus, said one official, "the very word 'negotiations' was anathema to the administration."

Nevertheless, Johnson conducted peace offensives—often and loudly. In April 1965, he offered $1 billion in economic aid to develop the Mekong River valley. In December 1966, he ordered a bombing pause that lasted thirty-seven days, during which, in a diplomatic spectacular, he sent Vice President Hubert Humphrey, Arthur Goldberg, and Averell Harriman to visit forty capitals. In September 1967, he offered to halt the bombing in return for productive discussions. But his offers applied only to "governments," which excluded negotiations with the principal enemy, the Vietcong. Thus, critics charged, the primary purpose of his offers was to blunt opposition to the war and to provide justification for escalating it.

Tet

In 1967, America seemed to be winning the war. More weapons were being captured from the Communists than were lost to them, and four Vietcong were being killed for every government soldier lost. The number of South Vietnamese under Communist control dropped by a million to 2.4 million. In November, General Westmoreland announced, "We are winning." He had "never been more encouraged," he claimed, the number of Vietcong had declined, and "the end begins to come into view." In June 1967, Johnson claimed that South Vietnam was "nearly all secure." Against this background, the "Tet Offensive" of January 1968 came as a rude shock.

In late 1967, North Vietnamese troops and the Vietcong launched an attack on Khe Sanh near the Laotian border. Regarding this as an attempt by the Communists to repeat their Dien Bien Phu success, Americans bombed the area heavily and sent in "large numbers of troops, killing many of the enemy."

The major holiday, Tet, fell on January 30 and many ARVN went home for the holiday. Unreported by the peasants, the Vietcong moved large forces toward urban areas and achieved complete surprise with massive simultaneous attacks that hit five of South Vietnam's six major cities, thirty-three of its forty-four provincial capitals, and sixty-four district capitals. About 7,500 Vietcong seized the central walled citadel of the ancient capital city of Hue and held it for three weeks. Fifteen Vietcong even penetrated the grounds of the U.S. embassy in Saigon. These attacks set back pacification projects and freed thousands of prisoners. In all, the Vietcong killed nearly 4,000 Americans and 5,000 ARVN.

Despite its startling initial successes, the Tet offensive proved a military disaster for the Vietcong. It exposed their secret organizations and membership. They failed to capture radio stations, and the population did not rise in their support. In the assault against superior U.S. weapons, perhaps 58,000 Vietcong died. Westmoreland hailed the fighting as a U.S. victory, and the Vietcong's "last gasp." Ironically, the death of so many South Vietnamese fighters gave North Vietnam more influence over the war in South Vietnam.

Nevertheless, Tet had great psychological impact on Americans. News media carried pictures of ruined cities, and the statement of an American commander that it was "necessary to destroy the town to save it" (see Fig. 12.6). It proved the falsity of administration statements that the war was almost won. Robert Kennedy said that it showed that total victory was not in sight and was "probably beyond our grasp." In August, Johnson, who had long postponed asking for a tax increase, was forced to request a 10 percent income tax surcharge to help pay for the war. Public opinion polls showed that 78 percent of Americans believed that America was making no progress, that a majority believed that entering the war had been a mistake, and that public approval of the war was down to only 26 percent. The respected television news anchorman Walter Cronkite concluded that America was "mired in a stalemate," and *Newsweek* editorialized that "more of the same" was "intolerable."

Figure 12.6 The shooting of a prisoner by South Vietnam's National Police Chief Nguyen Loan reminded many Americans that the conduct of the war by our allies included actions that, if committed by an enemy, would be regarded as atrocities. AP/Wide World Photos.

Antiwar forces sought to block renomination of Johnson by the 1968 Democratic presidential nominating convention. Organizing the "Coalition for an Alternative to Johnson," the progressive leader Allard K. Lowenstein tried hard to get Robert Kennedy to enter the race. When his entreaties failed, he turned to the less-well-known Senator Eugene McCarthy. Droves of students turned out to campaign for McCarthy, who in the New Hampshire Democratic primary on March 12 got 42 percent of the vote, a major setback for Johnson. On March 16, Robert Kennedy announced that he was a candidate. Polls indicated that Johnson would lose the upcoming Wisconsin primary.

When asked how many more troops he needed, General Westmoreland requested 208,000, in addition to the 550,000 already in Vietnam. Sending so many troops would require additional tax hikes and a call-up of the reserves—both unpopular moves. Reviewing Vietnam policy, Johnson's new Secretary of Defense Clark Clifford, a hawk with ties to America's top financial leaders, was shocked to discover that the Pentagon could not tell him how it planned to win the war. Also, he concluded that the war was primarily a civil war, not a war against world communism. For advice, he summoned a council of the "Wise Men," a top-level group that included Dean Acheson, George Ball, McGeorge Bundy, Douglas Dillon, Henry Cabot Lodge, Omar Bradley, Matthew Ridgway, and Maxwell Taylor. After inconclusive talk, the best advice they could offer, by a vote of six to four, was to disengage from a war that was "not only endless but hopeless." Disgustedly, Johnson exclaimed, "the establishment bastards have bailed out."

Deciding not to send additional troops, Johnson ordered Westmoreland home to become army chief of staff. In a March 31 televised address, Johnson astounded the nation. In the interest of getting peace negotiations started, he said, he was restricting the bombing of North Vietnam to a few miles north of the seventeenth parallel. Furthermore, to take his peace efforts out of politics, he said that he would not seek, and would not accept, the Democratic nomination for another term as president.

Nevertheless, peace talks were slow in starting. Not until May 3 did the two sides agree on Paris as the meeting place. The North Vietnamese wanted the Vietcong, which Washington insisted were merely North Vietnamese puppets, to be represented at the conference, while Washington wanted the Saigon government, which the North Vietnamese said existed only as a U.S. puppet, to be represented. Eventually, each side accepted the presence of the "puppet" of the other, but claimed that they were merely members of the other side's delegation. W. Averell Harriman headed the U.S. delegation which had its first contacts with the North Vietnamese in Paris on May 10.

In February 1967, Ho Chi Minh had written to Johnson that "only after the unconditional stopping of the bombing" could conversations begin. The Vietnamese people, he said, would never "agree to talks under the menace of bombs." Both McNamara and Bundy considered the bombing of North Vietnam to be ineffective. Nevertheless, Johnson intensified the war. In 1968 he tripled the number of B-52 bombing missions. The search-and-destroy sweeps in March and April were the largest yet. Raising the ARVN's manpower to

850,000 and assigning major forces to controlling the countryside, President Thieu more than recovered the territories lost in the Tet Offensive. America was not going to be defeated, said Johnson, "by a "raggedy-ass little fourth-rate country."

The Election of 1968

The Vietnam War was a leading issue in 1968 presidential politics. McCarthy and Kennedy were both antiwar, but their followers, many of whom were idealists who scorned compromises essential to coalition building, fought each other bitterly. McCarthy had strong appeal to liberal intellectuals, but Kennedy, with more connections to party leaders, had a better, if slim, chance of nomination. Kennedy won most of the primaries, but, on June 5, he was assassinated by an Arab nationalist. Many of his followers then shifted to McCarthy, but Johnson backed Vice President Hubert Humphrey, and an incumbent president ordinarily controls his party's convention.

The 1968 Democratic National Convention, held in Chicago, was one of the more dramatic conventions in U.S. history. Seeking to influence its proceedings, thousands of student and other antiwar activists converged on the city. When they occupied parks and held rallies without permits, the police charged and clubbed them, the students fought back, and national television carried scenes of violent clashes. The police behaved with so little restraint that a later investigation found them guilty of a "police riot."

President Johnson planned to announce on August 22, four days before the convention, that he was going to Russia for a summit conference and then to hold a big birthday party in Chicago, attended by many celebrities. Some suspected that he sought to orchestrate a last-minute effort to stampede the convention into renominating him. However, on August 20 the Soviets sent troops into Czechoslovakia, which ruled out a summit conference. In addition, in Chicago, antiwar demonstrations became so uncontrollable that Chicago's Mayor Richard Daley asked Johnson not to come to the convention.

In the convention, antiwar delegates proposed that America unconditionally halt the bombing of North Vietnam in order to facilitate peace talks. Despite rumors that Humphrey supported this plank (he did), Johnson, from Washington, mobilized the votes to defeat it. Humphrey won the nomination over McCarthy by a wide margin. In the Republican convention, Richard Nixon, beating back a challenge from California's governor, Ronald Reagan, won the nomination.

As the campaign opened, public opinion polls showed Nixon ahead by twenty percentage points. Also, Johnson, who may have considered Nixon more committed than Humphrey to continuing the war, seemed to give Humphrey less than total support. When Humphrey suggested that some troops would be withdrawn, Johnson shot down the suggestion, a blow from which, wrote Humphrey, he "never really recovered." In a speech, on September 30, Humphrey said that if he were president, he would stop all bombing of North Vietnam, but not until October 31, only a few days before the voting, did Johnson announce a bombing halt. The Saigon government, knowing that to start negotiations would help Humphrey win votes, refused to agree to arrangements for getting peace talks started.

Humphrey made late gains, but Nixon, who claimed to have an undisclosed plan to "end the war and win the peace," won by seven-tenths of a percent. However 12.5 percent of the electorate voted for the hawkish third-party ticket of George Wallace and General Curtis Le May.

In domestic affairs, Johnson's political abilities enabled him to secure enactment of a remarkable program of "Great Society" reforms, which brought more benefits to low-income groups than had any administration since that of Franklin D. Roosevelt. But in foreign affairs, Johnson's belief that that allowing communist-backed groups to make gains would be fatal both to world peace and his political fortunes led him to favor stability over reform. He intervened in support of the right wing in Brazil and in the Dominican Republic, and involved America more deeply in the Vietnam War. In so doing, he put America in opposition not only to Communists, but also to forces that advocated national independence and the kind of reforms that he was implementing in America. In the process, he undermined his Great Society reforms, spent much of America's foreign exchange and gold, increased inflation and the national debt, and weakened America's ability to project power abroad.

Johnson wrote later that the "frustrations and genuine anguish" of his last year in office sometimes made him feel that he was "living in a continuous nightmare." Most observers agree that his otherwise promising administration had been ruined by the Vietnam War. Now it was Nixon's turn.

13 Nixon and Detente

Personnel and Policies

Richard Nixon had earned a law degree from Duke University, served in World War II, and won election in 1946 to Congress from California. His political campaigns had been characterized by militant attacks on his opponents as Communist sympathizers, and he won national prominence by pressing charges that a State Department official, Alger Hiss, had spied for the Communists. He had often echoed the theory that world communism was monolithic, totally evil, and bent on world conquest. Attacking the Democrats for permitting the "loss of China," Nixon backed MacArthur's efforts to enlarge the Korean War and, as early as 1954, urged sending U.S. troops into Vietnam.

Although a popular speaker, Nixon, unlike many politicians, did not have an outgoing, genial personality. His associates found him a loner, insecure, secretive, suspicious, devious, and adept at misrepresentation. His national security adviser described him as "withdrawn, lonely, and tormented" and "a very odd man, an unpleasant man," who "really dislikes people" and whose greatest dread was to be considered weak.

For the position of White House national security adviser, Nixon selected Henry Kissinger. Born in Germany, Kissinger had come to America in 1938, served in the armed forces, and won a scholarship to Harvard, where he later taught as a professor. Although he had voted against Nixon, he quickly accepted the job. He spoke with a European accent, dated glamorous women, and got favorable press notices for wit and brilliance. Like Nixon, he was insecure, conspiratorial, and egotistical. He once indiscreetly compared himself to a "cowboy leading the caravan alone," a "romantic, surprising character." However, he was less ideology-driven than Dulles. Nixon wrote of him that he was "difficult," "devious," and "some say obnoxious," but "a terrific negotiator." His cultivation of the press, and his diplomatic accomplishments, would take him to the top of the list of those whom Americans most admired.

For secretary of state, Nixon picked William P. Rogers, an attorney and a close friend who had been attorney general in the Eisenhower administration but who had little experience in foreign affairs. "No secretary of state is really important," Nixon said, "the president makes foreign policy." Expecting Rogers to keep the State Department occupied with lesser matters while Nixon and Kissinger handled major problems, Nixon left Rogers out of some important decisions and did not always keep him informed. In 1973, Nixon replaced him with Kissinger, who also retained his job as national security adviser.

Nixon and Kissinger were more experienced and knowledgeable about foreign affairs than most holders of their offices, and they brought unusual sophistication to the conduct of U.S. foreign policy. Taking a less apocalyptic view of world affairs, they showed more recognition of the changing distribution of world power, including the relative decline of America's once overshadowing preponderance, and the need to keep foreign commitments within the nation's capacity. No nation could have "absolute security," said Kissinger, because that would produce "absolute insecurity for all the others." They leaned toward traditional balance-of-power politics and, as conservatives, assigned high value to preserving order and stability. Nonetheless, they were as unrelenting as their predecessors in opposing any expansion of communism. According to banker David Rockefeller, Nixon seemed "obsessed by the idea of a global contest with the Russians" who were challenging him "in all conceivable ways."

For a time after World War II, America had possessed the capacity to destroy Soviet cities without sacrificing its own, but by the time of Nixon's presidency the multiplication of long-range atomic-armed Soviet missiles had reduced the available options to coexistence or coextermination. It was a new and uncomfortable experience, said Kissinger, and it put new limits on the extent to which America could impose its will, and on the effectiveness of threats to use nuclear weapons.

While retaining his career-long obsession with fighting communism, Nixon introduced more civility into U.S. relations with the Soviet Union and with the People's Republic of China (PRC). He and Kissinger sought areas in which they could negotiate agreements on particular issues and, while continuing to compete, achieve limited cooperation. "After a period of confrontation," he said in his inaugural address, "we are entering an era of negotiation" to "reduce the burden of arms, to strengthen the structure of peace." Nixon called his policy "detente," an easing of tension. By this he meant not an end to the Cold War, for detente was a strategy for conducting relations with an adversary, but a moderation of its intensity.

The Soviet Communist party head, Leonid Brezhnev, held similar views. Detente meant, he said, "normal, equal relations between states," including a readiness to resolve disputes by peaceful means and respect for each other's "legitimate interests."

However, Nixon also followed a policy of "linkage"—making U.S. concessions in one area, such as trade or disarmament, conditional on Soviet concessions in other areas, such as reining in client states, including North Vietnam. By utilizing rewards as well as penalties to modify Soviet behavior, he sought to create a situation in which, as Kissinger said, the Soviets would "lose by confrontation."

In 1969, the United States had 302 major military bases abroad. Nixon cut U.S. armed forces from 3.5 million in 1968 to 2.3 million in 1973 and ended the draft. Lowering the nation's preparedness goal from being prepared to fight two and one-half wars (two big wars and one small war simultaneously) to being prepared to fight one and one-half wars, he withdrew 500,000 U.S. troops from South Vietnam, 20,000 from South Korea, 12,000 from Japan and 16,000 from Thailand. However, keeping military spending high, he greatly raised the number of U.S. missiles, and increased the sale of arms abroad.

Opening Relations with Communist China

Nixon had a long record of intense hostility to Communist China. During the Korean War, he had endorsed MacArthur's proposal to blockade and bomb the PRC, and he later backed Dulles's threats to use force in the Taiwan crises. More than half of Americans, polls indicated, regarded Red China as the world's most dangerous nation, and many, including Rusk, considered the Vietnam War to be a war to block Chinese aggression. In July 1969 Nixon called China "the greatest threat to the peace of the world." Nevertheless, reversing his previous position, he opened relations with Beijing (Peking).

Disputes had disrupted China's alliance with Russia. Before the twentieth century, expanding east, the Russians had compelled China to sign "unequal treaties" and to surrender territories, including Outer Mongolia and the Amur Provinces, where Russia built its Vladivostok naval base. In 1921, the Soviets had helped to organize the Chinese Communist party, but, as the threat from Germany and Japan grew, the Soviets, giving priority to Russia's security, extended much military aid to Chiang Kai-shek while giving Chinese Communists little help in their long, bloody struggle with Chiang.

Moscow suspected that the Chinese Communist party (CCP) head, Mao Tse-tung, was primarily a Chinese nationalist, rather than an international Communist. When, disregarding Soviet advice, he fought a war with Chiang (1946–1949), the Soviets gave him little aid and even advised him to stop short of conquering south China. Possibly they preferred a divided China rather than a united China on their border and feared that Mao might ask them to return territories that Russia had taken from China. After Mao's 1949 victory over Chiang, Mao demanded, and got, Russia's surrender of the special privileges it had won in Manchuria. Stalin extended economic aid, but in the form of loans, and refused to share the technology for producing atomic weapons.

When China went to war with Americans in Korea, Russia gave China much military and technological assistance, but the end of that war brought renewed tension between them. Soviet leaders criticized the radicalism of Mao's "Great Leap Forward" and his rural communes. For his part, maintaining that the Chinese form of communism was a better model for developing countries, Mao sponsored new Communist parties in developing nations that competed with those backed by the Soviets. In 1960, in an open break, the Soviets abruptly canceled their construction projects in China and withdrew their technicians and plans, sabotaging China's economy. The Chinese denounced Russia's 1968 invasion of Czechoslovakia and, in a 1969 border dispute, attacked Soviet troops. The Soviets quadrupled their military forces stationed near China. In 1969, the Soviets even asked Western diplomats how they would react if Russia were to bomb China's emerging nuclear facilities.

So ingrained was their belief that world communism was monolithic that many Americans were slow to recognize that China and Russia had split. The two were merely arguing over how to bury capitalists, said one State Department official. But much of the world regarded America's policy of excluding the PRC from the UN as irrational, and every year this exclusion won fewer votes in the General Assembly.

In 1969, Nixon directed Kissinger to reassess U.S. China policy. Establishing relations with mainland China could increase trade and improve America's reputation for political realism. Also, he hoped to induce the PRC to cut its aid to North Vietnam. Moreover, the growing Sino-Soviet hostility had finally persuaded him that world communism was not monolithic. "International Communist unity has been shattered," he said. "Once a unified bloc, its solidarity has been broken by the powerful forces of nationalism. . . . The Marxist dream of international Communist unity has disintegrated." If so, the United States and China had a mutual interest in checking Soviet power.

In 1969, Nixon eased trade and travel restrictions and halted spy flights over the PRC. China's leaders also sought improved relations, and, in January 1970, America's and China's ambassadors to Poland resumed the conversations that Beijing (Peking) had broken off two years earlier. In December, Mao told the journalist Edgar Snow that he would welcome a visit by Nixon. In a speech, in February 1971, Nixon suggested that it would be desirable to draw the People's Republic into a "constructive relationship with the world community." When, in April, the Chinese invited a U.S. ping-pong team to China, Premier Chou En-lai greeted it with: "You have opened a new page in the relations of the Chinese and American people . . . a beginning again of our friendship." Nixon lifted the embargo on trade with China.

On July 9, 1971, while on a trip to Pakistan, Kissinger secretly flew to Beijing to make arrangements for a Nixon visit. Enthralled by Chou En-lai (a "great man") and Mao, and by the Chinese in general, he gave the Chinese secret information on Soviet military activities and satellite pictures of Soviet military installations near China's border; he even promised to keep the Chinese informed of any negotiations with the Soviets concerning China.

On July 15, 1971, Nixon announced that, to seek "normalization of relations," he would go to China. This was a stunning development. A presidential visit to a government that America did not recognize was unprecedented. Feeling betrayed, Chiang Kai-shek protested, the Japanese were shocked that they had not been consulted, and Moscow, "surprised and confused," warned against any attempt to use China to pressure the Soviet Union. However, England and France hailed the visit as a victory for realism, and Americans were generally supportive.

In August 1971, with U.S. backing, the UN admitted the People's Republic of China and gave it China's seat in the Security Council. America proposed a "two-Chinas solution"—allowing the Republic of China (Taiwan) to retain a seat in the General Assembly. But, by a vote of 76 to 35, the General Assembly simply transferred China's membership to Beijing—in effect expelling Taiwan.

This defeat, and the "undisguised glee" with which many UN members greeted it, contributed to a decline of U.S. support for the UN.

On February 17, 1972, with a group of forty officials, including Kissinger and Rogers, plus nearly ninety reporters, Nixon flew to Beijing, the first visit to China by an incumbent U.S. president. His initial reception seemed a bit cool—Chou En-lai met him at the airport, but there were no welcoming crowds. However, the atmosphere soon warmed. After meeting for more than an hour with the seventy-eight-year-old Mao (see Fig. 13.1), Nixon was entertained at a huge banquet in the Great Hall of the People. A Chinese military band played "America the Beautiful" and "Home on the Range," while television recorded numerous toasts to good relations and scenes of mutual cordiality. "Our two peoples," Nixon told the Chinese, "hold the future of the world in our hands," a statement that may have caused some unease among the Russians, the French, and the British.

Taken to see the Great Wall, Nixon pronounced it a "great wall" and added that "we do not want walls of any kind between peoples."

In the "Shanghai Communiqué," the two sides announced that they had agreed to move toward normalizing relations and expanding trade and cultural interchanges, and they expressed their opposition to any country's attempt to achieve "hegemony," China's code word for Soviet domination of East Asia (see Fig. 13.2). However, Beijing insisted that it would continue to support "the struggle of all oppressed peoples." On what China called the "cru-

Figure 13.1 Nixon, in February 1972, meets with Chinese Communist party Chairman Mao Tse-tung in Beijing. AP/World Wide Photos.

Figure 13.2 Secretary of State William Rogers and Nixon confer with China's Premier Chou En-lai. National Archives.

cial question," they agreed that all Chinese considered Taiwan a part of China. Setting an "ultimate objective" of withdrawing U.S. troops from Taiwan, Nixon promised to make reductions "as the tension in the area diminishes" but said that America "expected" relations between the two Chinas to be adjusted by peaceful means. The Chinese insisted that their relations with Taiwan were an internal matter to be settled without outside interference.

Calling this visit the "week that changed the world," Nixon would later list it first among the accomplishments of his presidency. Only he could have accomplished it, he said, which is probably true because politically it could have been done at the time only by one whose anticommunism was so extreme that it could not be questioned.

Major differences remained, but limited Sino-American cooperation developed. Study and trade delegations exchanged visits. Americans stepped up their investments in China, and each country's press became less hostile toward the other. In the 1971 war between Bangladesh and Pakistan, both countries leaned toward Pakistan: "We can't allow a friend of ours and China's," explained Kissinger, "to get screwed in a conflict with a friend of Russia's." They supported the same rebel groups in Africa against Soviet-backed groups. China bought U.S. passenger jets and grain, and two-way trade jumped from $5 million in 1971 to $900 million in 1973. In 1973, they exchanged diplomatic missions, but short of full diplomatic relations.

Regarding the Soviet Union as their most dangerous enemy, the Chinese said that they wanted Europe and NATO to be both economically and militarily strong. Also, they wanted America to keep large military forces in East Asia and to help Pakistan resist Soviet expansion. Only half jokingly, Kissinger called China "one of our stronger NATO allies."

This new relationship gave America more diplomatic flexibility. For years Washington had insisted that the Beijing government was an extension of the Soviet Union, and U.S. pressure on both had helped keep them together. Now, in "triangular diplomacy," America could cooperate with either, as political interest dictated, independent of, and even against, the other.

The Search for Detente with the Soviet Union

Nixon's visit to China had stunned Soviet leaders, but, despite it, or because of it, they soon invited him to visit Moscow. For years the Soviets had been pressing a peace offensive aimed at securing formal Western acceptance of their World War II gains. Also they sought to head off a possible U.S.-Chinese alliance and to obtain greater access to U.S. trade and technology.

The Soviets had greatly narrowed America's margin of military superiority. America had sufficient striking power, with 4,200 nuclear warheads and numerous missiles and bombers, to destroy every target in Russia several times over. However, by 1970, the Soviets had 1,300 ICBMs, which meant that America could no longer hope, even by striking first, to knock out enough of Russia's forces to prevent a Soviet counterattack sufficient to devastate America. Thus, the situation had become one of mutual assured destruction (MAD).

Although many in the West feared that the Soviets had obtained parity, not until the 1980s, despite their rapid arms buildup, would their total military strength approach, but still not equal, that of America. However, Russia had achieved second-strike capability; that is, it had sufficient missiles to ensure that enough would survive a U.S. first strike to inflict unacceptable damage on America. They were as emphatic as Americans on the necessity of avoiding nuclear war. "To count on victory in a nuclear war," Brezhnev told the 1981 Party Congress, was "dangerous madness."

Late in 1970, Americans discovered that the Soviets were building a base for their submarines at Cuba's Cienfuegos Bay. Nixon said publicly that America viewed this development with the "utmost seriousness," and Kissinger used stronger terms to the Soviet ambassador. On October 6, backing down, the Soviet ambassador, Anatoly Dobrynin, told Kissinger that the base would not be constructed. Already the White House had assured the Soviets that Nixon would honor Kennedy's pledge not to invade Cuba. The crisis passed.

While not renewing Dulles's call for "rollback" or "liberation" of East European satellites, Nixon was unwilling to concede them to Soviet control. Despite Soviet displeasure and suspicion, he visited Bucharest in 1969, Belgrade in 1970, and Warsaw in 1972. In Romania, in July 1972, Secretary of State Rogers said that all nations were "equally sovereign and equally independent and have an equal right to run their own affairs free of outside interference." Nixon told Congress that America considered the countries of Eastern Europe to be "sovereign, not as parts of a monolith."

Despite a flare-up of war in Vietnam, which almost caused Moscow to cancel the invitation, Nixon, accompanied by Kissinger and Rogers, went to Moscow in May 1972, the first presidential visit since 1945 (see Fig. 13.3). When he told his hosts that his reputation was that of "a very hard-line, Cold War–oriented anti-Communist," they said "Yes, we know!" Nevertheless, said Nixon, he believed that they could "live and work together." Received cordially, he remained in Russia for eight days and was allowed to address the Russian people on television. The two sides agreed to cooperate in space exploration, enlarge trade, work for "peaceful coexistence," and to prevent regional conflicts (such as Vietnam) from disrupting superpower detente.

In 1966, Russia had begun deploying around Moscow antiballistic missiles (ABMs) designed to destroy incoming hostile missiles. America was also developing ABMs. This raised the danger that one side might come to believe that its defense was sufficiently effective to allow it to destroy the other without itself being destroyed. By 1972 both nations had "overkill" (more missiles than there were suitable targets). Russia had nearly 1,500 ICBMs on launching pads, and America had 1,000. Moreover, America had learned how to install

Figure 13.3 Kissinger and Nixon are cordially received in Moscow by Chairman Leonid Brezhnev and Premier Alexsey Kosygin. National Archives.

multiple (three to ten) independently targeted re-entry vehicles (MIRVs) on ICBMs.

The major accomplishment of the 1972 Moscow summit was the Strategic Arms Limitation Treaty (SALT), for which preparatory talks had begun during the Johnson administration. The two agreed to limit ABMs to two one-hundred-missile clusters, each designed to protect their respective capitals and ICBM launching sites. This would leave the bulk of the population exposed to destruction.

They also agreed to freeze further construction of offensive missiles for five years and to limit ICBMs to 1,410 land-based and 950 submarine-launched missiles for the Soviets and 1,000 land-based and 710 submarine-based missiles for the United States, and they halted construction of new missile-launching submarines. Russia had larger missiles that carried bigger bombs, but America's missiles carried more than twice as many warheads, and Nixon refused to accept limits on loading missiles with multiple warheads. Thus, SALT did not reduce the level of armaments or halt the multiplication of warheads, but it did set a precedent for agreed-upon limitations on weaponry.

Nixon had expressed his willingness to concede the Soviets "parity" in strategic weapons, but the SALT treaty set no limits on strategic (long-range) bombers, of which America had 450 to Russia's 150. Nor did it restrict cruise missiles (small, pilotless, low-flying, bomb-carrying jet planes). Furthermore, because America had stationed many intermediate and short-range missiles close to Russia, America retained a huge lead (5,700 to 2,500) in ability to deliver atomic bombs. Furthermore, no limits were placed on the number of missiles possessed by America's allies.

Also at the 1972 summit, the United States and the Soviet Union, agreeing that there was no alternative to peaceful coexistence, signed a document entitled "Basic Principles of Mutual Relations." It pledged them to seek normal relations based on equality and noninterference in each other's internal affairs, to avoid military confrontations, to respect each other's security interests, and to renounce any "special rights or advantages in world affairs." Attaching little importance to this document, Nixon dismissed it as an aspiration. The Soviets, however, regarded it as the summit's most important accomplishment, the first commitment by the United States, in "international juridical form," to peaceful coexistence, and acceptance of the Soviet Union's entitlement to "equal security." The summit indicated U.S. recognition, the *Washington Post* observed, that the Soviet Union had achieved international and "psychological parity."

Nixon and Brezhnev further agreed on rules of naval conflict designed to prevent unnecessary friction between their navies, and to cooperate in launching a joint space flight. They also agreed to take joint measures to protect the environment and to exchange information on science and health. The Soviets agreed to pay $722 million to settle their Lend-Lease debt and reaffirmed the 1962 agreement on Cuba. Brezhnev presented Nixon with a hydrofoil boat, and Nixon gave Brezhnev a Cadillac.

Nixon was elated. "Let us seize the moment," he said on his return to Washington, "so that our children and the world's children live free of the fears and free of the hatreds that have been the lot of mankind throughout the centuries." Brezhnev concluded that "you can do business with Nixon." The Senate approved both the SALT and the ABM treaties by a vote of 88 to 2.

Other Soviet-American agreements followed. Earlier in 1972, the two countries had agreed to ban bacteriorological weapons. In July 1972, the two sides agreed to purchase by the Soviets of at least $750 million in U.S. grain annually for the next three years. America extended new credits to Russia. U.S. exports to the Soviet Union rose by 1976 to $2.3 billion.

Nevertheless, detente had its opponents. Former California governor Ronald Reagan called it a combination of containment and appeasement. In 1974, Congress enacted the Jackson-Vanik amendment, which denied the Soviets normal trade privileges until they permitted the free emigration of Jews. The Soviets responded by cutting the number of Jews allowed to emigrate by 40 percent.

On June 18, 1973, Brezhnev arrived in Washington for a second summit conference. His ceremonial reception on the lawn of the White House was a proud moment for the Soviets, to whom it symbolized acceptance as an equal by the world's greatest power. He and Nixon also conversed at Camp David and at Nixon's summer home at San Clemente, California.

Figure 13.4 Nixon and Kissinger had a frequently genial relationship with the able Soviet ambassador Anatoly Dobrynin. National Archives.

Brezhnev showed the most interest in discussing the Middle East. Saying that his Arab allies were difficult to control and that there was imminent danger of war unless America and Russia jointly took the initiative in arranging a diplomatic settlement, he proposed that Israel return the territories seized in 1967 in return for U.S. and Soviet guarantees of its pre-1967 borders. Confident that the Arabs would not attack because Israel had military superiority, Nixon preferred not to deal with the Soviets on Middle East matters. (Actually, an Arab attack was then only four months away.)

The Soviets seemed to be much alarmed by China. In early 1973, when Kissinger was in Moscow to arrange for Brezhnev to visit Washington, Brezhnev had told him that the Chinese were barbarians and that, now that they were producing atomic weapons, something must be done about them. Complaining of China's "perfidious attempts to bring about a clash between the Soviet Union and the United States," Brezhnev urged Nixon not to sign any military agreement with China.

Nixon and Brezhnev signed the Agreement on the Prevention of Nuclear War, which provided for immediate consultations if a threat of nuclear war arose. They also signed a number of agreements to expand cultural exchanges and trade. Because America relied on atomic weapons to deter the large Soviet army from invading western Europe, Nixon rejected a Soviet proposal that neither be the first to use nuclear weapons.

On June 27, 1974, Nixon traveled again to the Soviet Union to meet with Brezhnev. Other than helping to make summit conferences a regular feature of superpower relations, this meeting accomplished little. By this time Nixon was under heavy fire at home for abusing presidential power, in the so-called Watergate Affair, which in five weeks would force him to resign the presidency. One wag wondered if he would seek political asylum in Russia. Public approval for Nixon's foreign policy was still at 54 percent, but critics of detente were gathering strength—liberals who denounced Soviet violations of civil rights, rightists who opposed any concessions, military personnel who feared arms reductions, and others who feared that the superpowers might limit Israel's freedom of action. "Activities of the anti-detente forces," wrote Nixon, "reached almost fever pitch just as I was getting ready to leave for the Soviet Union."

Nixon and Brezhnev were unable to agree on the number of ICBMs that could be MIRVed, but they placed additional restrictions on atomic tests. Nixon rejected Brezhnev's proposal that America and Russia sign a nonaggression treaty to prevent China from embroiling them in war.

The 1973 Arab-Israeli War

In the Middle East, meanwhile, armed clashes between Israel and Arabs continued. Palestinian terrorists hijacked Israeli airplanes and conducted murderous raids on Israeli interests in other parts of the world. Israelis retaliated by bombing Palestinian camps in Jordan, Lebanon, and Syria and by making commando raids and bombing missions into Egypt, often with high civilian casualties. America continued to arm Israel, while the Soviets sent 20,000 advisers to Egypt, armed Egypt and Syria, and even supplied Soviet fighter pilots to help protect Egyptian cities. Americans helped to arrange a cease-fire in 1970, but the agreement was often violated.

Arabs and Israelis remained far apart on proposed peace terms. In return for recognition, the Israelis were willing to withdraw from some of the territories they had occupied in 1967, but they seemed determined to retain at least Jerusalem, the Golan Heights (formerly part of Syria), and Sharm el Sheikh, the port city that commands the entrance to the Gulf of Aqaba. Softening their previous stand, Arabs seemed to be ready to recognize Israel's right to exist in Palestine, but only if Israel returned all the lands it had seized in 1967. The continued stalemate was more galling to the Arabs than to the Israelis because Israel held the disputed area, and the Suez Canal was closed.

In a fateful new development, Israel began settling Jews in some of the occupied territories, which seemed to demonstrate Israel's intention to keep them permanently. This further enraged Arabs, who considered them to be rightfully Arab.

In 1972, Brezhnev, seeking to preserve detente, rejected Egypt's request for additional offensive weapons. Losing hope for Soviet backing in a war, Egypt expelled all Soviet advisers, a stunning blow to Soviet influence in the Middle East. Egyptians hoped that Washington would reward their break with the Soviets by pressuring Israel to return Arab lands. Instead, in an election year, America sent Israel more warplanes. Egypt then sought economic and military support from other Arab countries to prepare for war to regain lost territories.

Urging Egypt not to go to war, Brezhnev vainly attempted to persuade Nixon to agree to a joint U.S-Soviet attempt to arrange a peaceful settlement.

In a surprise attack on October 6, 1973, during Israel's Yom Kippur holiday, Egyptian forces crossed the Suez Canal and drove back Israeli troops, while Syrian troops overran the Golan Heights. Soviet-supplied SAM missiles downed many Israeli planes. Never before had the Arabs demonstrated such military power. Israel put its nuclear weapons on alert. Recovering quickly, however, the Israelis repulsed the Syrians and engaged the Egyptians in history's second greatest tank battle, in which Israel lost more than 500 and the Arabs 1,800 tanks. To replace the enormous amounts of lost equipment, America and Russia airlifted more than $2 billion each in arms and ammunition to their respective clients. Launching a counteroffensive on October 15, Israeli troops broke through Egyptian lines and crossed the Suez Canal.

On October 20, Kissinger flew to Moscow where he and Brezhnev agreed on terms to end the fighting, which the UN Security Council endorsed on October 22. It called for an immediate cease-fire in place and for implementation of UN resolution 242, requiring Israel to withdraw from Arab lands in return for Arab agreement to a peace settlement. Although Israel accepted this proposal, Israeli troops continued to advance, isolating the 25,000-man Egyptian Third Army in the desert with little food and water. Soviet efforts to save this army led to the most dangerous Soviet-American confrontation since 1962.

In response to Egyptian President Anwar el-Sadat's request for joint intervention to enforce the cease-fire, the Soviets, on October 24, demanded that the superpowers immediately send troops to separate the combatants. If Washington refused, they hinted, they might act alone. The Nixon administration, in what Kissinger called a "deliberate overreaction," put U.S. armed forces on a worldwide atomic alert. "We were determined to resist by force if necessary," wrote Kissinger, the entry of Soviet troops into the Middle East under any pretext. At the same time, by threatening to cut off arms shipments, Kissinger induced Israel to release its stranglehold on the Egyptian army.

Although this 1973 October War was an Israeli victory, it produced some shocks. The Arabs' unexpected unity and proficiency with modern weapons put Israel's security in doubt. Also, Israel received little international support. Twenty black African countries broke diplomatic relations with Israel, and all NATO nations except Portugal refused to allow Americans to use their territories to airlift arms to Israel. Demonstrating a new-found ability to act jointly to use oil as a weapon, the Arabs halted the sale of oil to America until March 1974, producing severe gasoline shortages. Furthermore, they raised the price of oil from $2.60 to $10 per barrel, which brought an enormous additional flow of money to Arabs from Europe, Japan, and America.

In the next two years, in a strenuous effort to arrange a Middle East peace settlement without Soviet participation, Kissinger spent much time flying from one Middle East capital to another—"shuttle diplomacy." He threatened to cut aid to Israel if it refused to compromise, and promised to give aid to Arabs if they would compromise. He persuaded the Arabs to lift their oil embargo, and Syria and Israel to allow UN forces to occupy a buffer zone between their armies. In 1973, America and Egypt renewed diplomatic relations, and in 1974 America resumed giving aid to Egypt. In September 1974, Kissinger persuaded Israel to withdraw its troops from the Suez Canal and to allow the canal to reopen in exchange for Egypt's agreement to allow Israeli goods to pass through the canal. In 1975, after promising substantial aid to Israel and Egypt, Kissinger got Israel's commitment to eventual return of part of the Sinai.

Meanwhile, Washington promised Israel that it would never negotiate with the PLO unless the PLO first recognized the right of Israel to exist as a nation. But the fundamental problems defied Kissinger's and Nixon's negotiating skills. The Middle East remained in a state of continuing war crisis.

Strains within NATO

To promote harmony within the NATO alliance and reassure Europeans that America's rapprochement with the Soviet Union and China did not mean deemphasis of relations with Europe, Nixon proclaimed 1973 to be the "Year of Europe." The Europeans did not appreciate having a special year devoted to them, and the term was soon dropped. Instead, 1973 brought serious strains to the alliance.

Despite development by France and Britain of separate atomic striking forces, Europe remained heavily dependent on America for defense. Providing a nuclear umbrella, America stationed U.S. forces in Germany as a "trip wire" to bring America into war if the Soviet army were to invade. Of course, Europeans were concerned that so much of their defense was under foreign control, and they were painfully aware that Europe would be World War III's principal battlefield. They also feared that America's inexperience and rashness might unnecessarily precipitate war, or that the United States might go to war over Far Eastern or Latin American issues that were not of vital concern to them. Furthermore, as Russia acquired sufficient missiles to destroy America, they wondered if America would really come to their aid if doing so meant suicide. Many of them sought independently to improve their relations with Russia. Americans, in turn, criticized Europeans for not paying more of the cost of their defense, and for not giving Washington full support in its disputes with Communists outside Europe.

The October 1973 Arab-Israeli war produced severe strains within the alliance. Most Europeans maintained that America gave Israel excessive support, and they criticized Israel for refusing to withdraw from occupied Arab lands. They considered good relations with the Arabs, on whom they depended for 80 percent of their oil supply, essential. They were angered when Washington called a worldwide atomic alert without consulting them. Much to Washington's disgust, all NATO allies except Portugal refused to allow U.S. planes to use their airports or even to overfly their territory to resupply Israel; Greece and Turkey permitted Soviet, but not U.S., overflights.

Although most Europeans fully approved of detente, they refused to impose trade sanctions on the Soviets to support the policy of linkage.

An important initiative to reduce Cold War tensions was taken by the Germans. West Germany's chancellor, the Social Democrat (i.e., socialist) Willy Brandt, had won fame when mayor of Berlin by his defiance of the Russians. Nevertheless, he sought to settle some long-festering disputes. In August 1970, he signed an agreement with East Germany to renounce war, to enlarge trade, and to respect the existing boundaries in Europe, including those between the two Germanys, thus indefinitely postponing German reunification, and in September 1971 he established diplomatic relations with East Germany. While not fully appreciating Brandt's "Ostpolitik" policies, Nixon also opened diplomatic contacts with East Germany, and, in 1973, the UN admitted the two Germanys to membership. In 1975, Brandt signed a treaty accepting Poland's annexation of formerly German territory. Brandt received the Nobel Peace Prize.

Continuing Cold War in Latin America

Detente did not extend to Soviet-American rivalry in Third World countries. The Soviets continued to supply aid to Communist and independence movements in Southeast Asia, Africa, Latin America, and the Middle East, while the

United States militantly fought any possible extension of Communist influence in these areas.

Chile, a narrow twenty-six-hundred-mile-long country of 10 million people, is one of Latin America's most developed nations, with above-average income, education, and life expectancy. Civilian rule and democracy seemed to be deeply rooted there. The U.S. role in Chile was also large. U.S. companies, particularly Anaconda Copper, owned almost all of the nation's copper mines, which furnished 80 percent of its export earnings, and, by 1970, direct U.S. investments in Chile totaled about $758 million.

Chile's Socialist party was headed by the charismatic Dr. Salvador Allende, an economics professor, who became a serious contender in the 1964 presidential election. One of the planks in his platform called for nationalization (seizure with compensation) of U.S.-owned mines. The CIA secretly contributed about $3 million to his opponents.

Allende lost the election to the leader of the Christian Democratic party, Edwardo Frei. Hoping to prevent Allende's support from growing, Frei adopted liberal reforms, and the United States gave more aid per capita to Chile than any other Latin American country. But the constitution forbade Frei to run for a second term.

In 1970, Allende, recruiting the small Chilean Communist party and other groups into a coalition with his Socialist party, ran again. Nixon told the CIA to spend up to $10 million to defeat him, but Allende won the most votes (37 percent) in a three-man race. An attempt by Nixon to arrange a military coup before he took office failed. Thus, for the first time in Latin America, a Marxist came to power by democratic election.

Allende preserved civil liberties. He did not imprison opponents, outlaw opposing political parties, or suppress freedom of speech. In 1971, promising to pay compensation, he nationalized the Chilean property of two major U.S. companies, Anaconda Copper and International Telegraph and Telephone. In the 1972 congressional election he raised his supporters' share of the popular vote to 43 percent.

Nixon, who had long denounced the Democrats for allowing communism to establish a base in the Western Hemisphere, was enraged. The people had no right to elect a Communist, said Kissinger—"I don't see why we have to let a country go Marxist just because its people are irresponsible." Seeing Allende, in Kissinger's words, as "a challenge to our national interests," Washington sought to overthrow him. Secretly, the CIA subsidized his opponents, promoted strikes and demonstrations, and obstructed Chile's access to copper markets and foreign loans. Copper production fell, with devastating impact on Chile's economy, and many shortages developed. The Soviets failed to provide the large sums Allende needed to surmount these difficulties.

In September 1973, the Chilean military, with U.S. cooperation, attacked the presidential palace and killed Allende and many of his supporters. The military then imposed an iron-fisted repressive military dictatorship under General Augusto Pinochet. Pinochet compensated Anaconda for its properties, restored free enterprise, lowered the tariff to 10 percent, and cut taxes on corporations and upper incomes.

Unlike Allende, Pinochet restricted freedom of speech, outlawed opposition groups, executed two thousand opponents, and sent many others into exile. Evidence of large-scale torture and executions by his brutal dictatorship brought condemnation by nearly all international human rights organizations, the OAS, and the UN. When U.S. congressional investigations in 1973–1974 revealed the involvement of U.S. corporations and the CIA in overthrowing Allende, many Americans were shocked. According to a 1974 Harris Poll, 60 percent believed that these actions had been wrong. In April 1976, citing human rights violations, Washington suspended arms sales to Chile. When Allende's former foreign minister and an American companion were killed by a car bomb in Washington, D. C., Washington attributed the murders to Pinochet's secret police.

Most Latin Americans resented U.S. interference in their internal politics. In 1974, when Mexico submitted a "Proposed Charter of Economic Rights and Duties of Nations" recognizing the right of any nation to nationalize foreign-owned properties, the UN General Assembly adopted it by a vote of 120 to 6. In 1975, over U.S. opposition, the OAS ended its blockade of Cuba.

Nixon's Economic Policies

Nixon vigorously promoted America's worldwide commercial interests, but with mixed success. Aware of the crucial role of economic growth rates on relative world power, Nixon, in 1971, said that the "five great economic superpowers [the United States, the Soviet Union, Western Europe, Japan, and China] will determine the economic future," and, "because economic power will be the key to other kinds of power," they would also determine "the future of the world."

By 1976, more than a hundred nations had joined the World Bank. Because each member nation cast votes in its governing bodies in proportion to the shares of stock it held in the bank, provision of approximately one-third of its capital gave the United States the dominant voice. The bank was headquartered in Washington, and its president was always an American. The World Bank's capital was expanded to nearly $30 billion, and the total of its loans was much higher. Approximately a third of its loans, extended for an average of twenty years, were made to finance expansion of electric power production, and another third went to improve transportation—railroads, roads, ports, and pipelines. The bank operated at a profit, which was added to its capital.

Under U.S. leadership, the World Bank sought to promote free enterprise and international trade. By making loans conditional on adoption of financial practices the bank considered sound, it exerted great influence on world economies. As a condition of obtaining loans, it might require nations, for example, to reduce deficits and inflation, protect foreign investment, and repay international loans. It provided economic training to government officials of developing countries and sometimes worked with them to prepare acceptable economic plans. All of which, of course, helped to make the world more hospitable to U.S. trade and investments.

Facilitated by a reduction in trade barriers under the Reciprocal Trade Agreement program and the General Agreement on Trade and Tariffs (GATT), international trade soared. Between 1970 and 1978, U.S. exports quadrupled, from $27.5 billion to $121 billion, and by 1978 the output of one of every nine U.S. manufacturing workers and one-fourth of U.S. farmland was sold abroad. Meanwhile, U.S. direct foreign investments (U.S.-owned properties, not loans) rose from $76 billion in 1970 to $150 billion in 1977. Some large U.S. corporations earned more than half of their profits overseas.

However, foreign sales to America rose even more rapidly. Japanese and German industries grew more competitive, America found it necessary to import more oil at higher prices, and military spending abroad, particularly for the Vietnam War, soared. In 1971, for the first time since 1894, purchases of foreign goods by Americans exceeded foreign sales. As receipts of U.S. dollars by foreigners rose faster than their purchases from America, they traded some of their surplus dollars for U.S. gold, reducing America's gold reserves, which by 1971 had shrunk to $10 billion. Meanwhile, foreign holdings of U.S. dollars soared from $78 billion in 1969 to $373 billion in 1977.

In 1971, Nixon devalued the dollar (i.e., reduced its worth in gold). He called the agreement in which America's allies accepted this devaluation the "greatest monetary agreement in the history of the world." In 1973, he devalued the dollar a second time. Then, abandoning the policy of exchanging dollars for foreign currencies at fixed rates, he allowed the dollar to "float," letting its value be determined by supply and demand. This brought to an end the Bretton Woods system of fixed international monetary exchange which had prevailed since World War II.

These moves had the effect of raising the prices Americans paid for foreign goods and cutting the prices of U.S. goods to foreigners. This, it was hoped, would stimulate U.S. production by reducing imports and increasing exports, but it also adversely affected America's standard of living. Nixon also cut foreign aid. These measures seemed to be an admission that the U.S. economy had lost its former overwhelming predominance. Most other nations had higher growth rates. America still produced about one-third of the world's goods and services, but this share was down from the half that the U.S. had produced in 1948.

14 Cold War Continued: Nixon and Ford Policies in Africa and Vietnam

Relations with Africa: Struggles for Independence and Unity, and Cold War

The U.S. relationship with Africa had developed slowly, but, by the Nixon administration, Africa had become an area of considerable concern. Four times the size of the United States and rich in resources, Africa is the ancestral home of 25 million Americans. The area near the Mediterranean, north of the Sahara Desert, is populated mostly by Arabic people and has close relation with Europe. The larger area south of the wide Sahara is peopled mostly by blacks. Although sub-Saharan Africa contains large, modern cities, most of it is less developed, and millions of its people live as subsistence farmers under primitive conditions. Seventy percent are illiterate.

Attracted by its natural resources, Europeans, by the end of the nineteenth century, had conquered nearly all of Africa. Britain and France got the larger shares, but Belgium took the huge Congo area. Germany, Italy, Portugal, and Spain also claimed colonies. Ethiopia preserved its independence except for a brief occupation by Italy in the 1930s.

South Africa and Egypt won at least nominal independence shortly after World War I. Following World War II, forty-two more African countries achieved independence. In some cases this required long and bloody fighting, in others little more than riots and protests.

During World War II, announcing that America sought self-determination for all, Secretary of State Hull asked the colonial powers to "fix, at the earliest practicable moment, dates upon which the colonial people would be accorded the status of full independence." Also, Americans helped create the UN Trusteeship Council to give subject peoples opportunities to redress grievances against empires. As the Cold War developed, the need to support European allies, and the fear that wars for independence might open the door to communism, weakened U.S. support of independence movements. Nevertheless, establishing a Bureau of African Affairs in the State Department, America promptly opened embassies in the new nations.

The achievement of nationhood confronted Africa with new problems. The continent had few college graduates and little experience in self-government. Most new countries adopted democratic constitutions, but their new governing elites sometimes proved as exploitative as the whites they replaced, and most of the new states fell under military dictatorships. In some places, European-drawn colonial boundaries, now national borders, split tribal homelands. Within nations, hostilities among tribes sometimes erupted in destructive civil wars. Dependent on the export of raw materials whose selling prices fluctuated, most nation's went deeply into debt. Industrialization was slow, and 85 percent of Africans remained engaged in agriculture. The world's highest population growth helped hold per capita income to less than 5 percent of America's.

Many African students attended U.S. universities, while U.S. missionaries, the Peace Corps, and businesses were active in Africa. However, Africa accounted for only 3 percent of U.S. foreign trade and 4 percent of its foreign investments. Not until 1970 did a U.S. secretary of state visit black Africa.

The throwing off of colonial rule did not put an end to European influence and power in Africa. The new nations depended on Europe for trade and aid, and Europeans continued to own and operate much of their economies. Also, 6 million people of European descent lived in sub-Saharan Africa. Africans fought bitterly to erase the remnants of colonial rule. They particularly resented Portugal's persistence in holding on to its colonies, and the attempts by white minorities to continue to rule black majorities in southern Africa.

In 1961, blacks in the Portuguese colony of Angola began a guerrilla war for independence. Portugal was a U.S. ally in NATO, and America continued to supply it with aid and weapons on the condition that they not be used in Africa, a restriction that could not be enforced. This compromise satisfied no one. The Kenyan leader, Tom Mboya, said that Africans felt a sense of "puzzled disappointment" that America's actual policy did not measure up to its reputation for supporting freedom and independence.

The Congo, a richly endowed area one-third the size of America, was ruled and exploited by Belgium. In 1960, unable to suppress riots and disorders in the colony, Belgium suddenly set the Congo free before the blacks there had a chance to organize a national government to preserve order.

The Congo's richest province was Katanga in the south, where most Belgians lived and where a huge European- and American-owned mining corporation operated enormously profitable diamond and copper mines. Katanga's black governor, Moise Tshombe, allied himself with foreign investors and sought to make Katanga a separate nation, which would make it easier for foreign investors to keep the mines. Staffing his government with whites, he hired mercenary white troops and invited Belgian troops to return. If successful, Katanga's succession would impoverish the rest of the Congo.

The Congo's first prime minister, Patrice Lumumba, fought to retain Katanga. He visited America, but Washington refused to help him. When he sought Communist help, he was dismissed as premier and, in 1961, with CIA involvement, killed by pro-Tshombe forces.

Continuing the fight to recover Katanga, the Congolese government appealed to the UN to send troops to restore order and to force the Belgians to withdraw. In response, the UN sent a police force that America supported in the belief that the UN was "the only instrument by which the end of the Western system of colonialism can be prevented from opening up doors to the new imperialism of the East." Under the command of Secretary General Dag Hammarskjold, it held the country together, forced Tshombe to go into exile, and slowly restored order.

In 1964, however, with the backing of Belgians and Americans, Tshombe returned to the Congo as prime minister. In November, U.S. airplanes dropped Belgian paratroopers to help him seize the city of Stanleyville and rescue whites from the threat of mob violence there. Condemning this action, Africans said it showed a willingness to sacrifice black lives to save white lives, and was an act of support for Tshombe, whom most Africans regarded as an agent of imperialism.

In 1965, General Joseph D. Mobutu, commander of the Congolese army, seized power; by 1969, he had suppressed armed resistance by followers of both Lumumba and Tshombe. In 1970, he changed the country's name to Zaire.

U.S. involvement in Zaire aroused much ill will in Africa. The United States favored unity and helped to preserve it. But a fear of potential Communist influence caused Americans to oppose Lumumba and to support Tshombe, whom most Africans regarded as a Belgian puppet. By accepting Mobutu, America partly recouped some of its popularity, although his government proved to be repressive and corrupt.

In some African countries, the achievement of independence did not mean transfer of power to blacks. Instead, white settlers preserved white rule. The largest of the white-ruled counties was the Republic of South Africa. Of its nearly 30 million population (1970), 70 percent were black, 18 percent white, 9 percent of mixed blood, and 3 percent Asian. In this richest nation on the continent, the per capita income of whites was higher than the average income of Americans, but black income averaged only 7.4 percent of that of whites.

The South African government enforced a policy of "apartheid," strict separation of the races designed to maintain the supremacy and purity of the white race. Forbidding intermarriage, apartheid attempted to confine permanent black residence to "homelands" that contained only 14 percent of the country, and, in the area reserved to whites, treated blacks as aliens. To blacks, such repressive white rule was intolerable, and many Africans dedicated themselves to overthrowing it. The UN repeatedly censured South Africa for violating the Charter's pledge to respect human rights "without distinction as to race, sex, language, or religion." South Africans replied that their distinctions were based not on race but on nationality.

Many Americans deplored South Africa's racism, but its government was anti-Communist and welcomed U.S. investments. For years the United States refused to vote against South Africa in the UN, but after 1960 it voted with the majority to denounce apartheid and to deny South Africa arms. America refused, however, to break diplomatic relations. Meanwhile, U.S. investments there rose by 1980 to more than $2 billion, 40 percent of all U.S. investments in sub-Saharan Africa. This policy injured U.S. relations with black Africa and, to some degree, with anti-imperialist nations in Asia and Latin America. In 1965

Martin Luther King Jr. denounced America's "massive support" for "this monstrous government with its grim war on its own black people." U.S. college students demonstrated to demand that universities withdraw investments from South Africa.

Deciding to free its colony of Rhodesia, Britain began preparing its blacks for self-government. In 1965, however, white settlers, who made up only 4 percent of Rhodesia's 7 million population, illegally declared Rhodesia to be independent under white rule. Denouncing this action by a "racist settler minority," the UN called on all members to impose economic sanctions.

America broke diplomatic relations with Rhodesia, but vetoed a 1970 Security Council resolution calling on Britain to use force to remove the illegal government. "Although we abhor the racial policies of the white regime," said President Nixon, "we cannot agree that progressive change in southern Africa is furthered by force." In 1972, America resumed buying Rhodesian chrome in violation of the UN embargo.

Rhodesian blacks resorted to guerrilla warfare. The fact that the black guerrilla leader, Robert Mugabe, was an avowed Marxist who received arms from Communist countries made it difficult for Americans to support him. In 1976, Kissinger conferred with the Rhodesian premier, Ian Smith, in an attempt to arrange peaceful transition to majority rule. Smith agreed to a gradual transfer of power over a two-year period, but delayed implementing his promise.

Communist propaganda sought to convince Africans that America favored imperialism and white supremacy and that only Communists could be relied upon to help Africa win true independence. By backing guerrilla fighters against white rule, and advertising communism as a short cut to economic development, they won considerable popularity. Most black African governments called themselves socialist.

However, most Africans seemed to be more interested in independence than in the Cold War. They took aid from Communist nations, but resented any foreign interference in their affairs. They expelled Chinese Communists from Burundi, the Central African Republic, Dahomey, and Tunisia, and overthrew left-wing governments in Ghana and Mali. Apparently, acceptance of aid from Communists did not mean that they were ready to enter the Communist camp.

When Portugal finally conceded independence to its African possessions in 1975, a bitter civil war erupted between tribally based black groups seeking control of Angola. The Soviet Union backed a Marxist group, MPLA (Popular Movement for the Liberation of Angola), which controlled the capital city. Communist China supported the anti-Soviet FNLA (Front for the National Liberation of Angola); thus, both sides in the war were "Communist-backed." America supported the FNLA. However, when South Africa sent troops to help the FNLA, Nigeria and other African states indignantly threw their support to the MPLA. The U.S. State Department advised that the situation in Angola was so complicated and uncontrollable that, if the United States sought a test of strength with the Soviet Union, it should pick a more favorable location.

The MPLA defeated the FLNA, but was unable to pacify the country. A third group, UNITA (National Union for the Total Independence of Angola), emerged as the leading opposition force and received South African, Chinese, and U.S. support. (If you are confused by all this then you have correctly understood the situation.) When South African troops drove deeply into Angola, fifteen thousand of Castro's soldiers entered Angola to fight for the MPLA. Bitterly resenting this Cuban intervention, America increased its aid to UNITA. With memories of military involvement in Vietnam still fresh, Congress, in January 1976, voted to halt all U.S. military aid to Angola.

The principal African criticism of U.S. policy was that, in its effort to limit the spread of communism, America, sometimes in league with racist South Africa, supported forces that were fighting against freedom and independence. UN Secretary General U Thant called it strange that descendants of "those who started it all at Lexington and Concord" should find it so difficult to sympathize with the modern "heirs of 1776." To such criticism Kissinger replied: "You may be right in African terms, but I'm thinking globally." Thus, the welfare of African people took second place to big-power rivalry, and they suffered for considerations that had little relevance to Africa.

The Indian Subcontinent

Although the second most populous nation in the world (945 million in 1996), India was impoverished, poorly armed, and absorbed in the politics of the subcontinent, and did not play a leading role in the international politics of the Cold War.

To outsiders, India seemed to be a welter of numerous ethnic groups who spoke more than a thousand languages, and were sharply split along lines of caste and religion. In ancient times, many ethnic groups had settled there, the largest of which, Indo Europeans, were related to the people of Europe. In religion, about 80 percent of its people are Hindus. About twelve hundred years ago, India was conquered by Moslems, who, in the eighteenth century, were conquered by the British. India won its independence soon after the end of World War II when it split into two nations, a Hindu nation called India, and a Moslem nation called Pakistan.

At the beginning of the Cold War, India and China, huge developing nations, each had per capita incomes of approximately $50 annually. China fell under the rule of Communists, but India maintained free and democratic government. Many Americans hoped that India would prove to be more successful than China and thus demonstrate that a free society was superior to communism in producing economic growth in underdeveloped countries. Between 1947 and 1987 America gave India approximately $10 billion in grants and loans, half of which was in the form of surplus food. Other non-Communist countries gave a total of $6.5 billion.

India's economic condition improved. The rise in GNP averaged 3.6 percent annually from 1965 to 1980. However, its high birth rate, which added 13 million people per year, held its annual per capita GNP rise to 1.3 percent, and more than half of its people existed on less than $1 per day.

India's most prominent role in international affairs was as a leader of the nonaligned nations that refused to take sides in the Cold War. Indian leaders, particularly the revered non-violent independence leader Mohandas Ghandi, and its first prime minister, Jawaharlal Nehru (1947–1964) were widely respected not only as political but as moral and spiritual leaders. They were frequently critical of America's foreign policies, particularly of its war in Vietnam.

The most serious of U.S. problems with India grew out of U.S. shipment of arms to Pakistan. Unlike India, Pakistan took America's side in the Cold War, and became its ally in both SEATO and CENTO. America responded with large-scale economic and military aid. However, in 1962, when India became engaged in a border war with China, America also shipped large quantities of arms to India.

India and Pakistan fought two wars (1948 and 1965) for possession of the province of Kashmir. Also, India's support for the 1971 fight by East Pakistan to secede and to become the new nation of Bangladesh caused a third war between India and Pakistan. America supported Pakistan; the Soviet Union supported India. As a result, in 1972 India signed a twenty-year treaty of peace, friendship and cooperation with the Soviet Union in which each agreed to give no assistance to any other nation "that engaged in armed conflict" with the other. The Soviet Union displaced America as India's leading trading partner.

Nixon and Vietnam

When Richard Nixon became president, America had been involved in Vietnam for twenty years as a supporter of, first, the French and, later, Saigon. America had 541,500 troops in that distant country, and 31,000 Americans had died there, nearly 15,000 of them in 1968. By the end of his first year in office, 1969, the total number of American battle deaths rose above 40,000. By then, the direct cost of action in Vietnam was running at $30 billion annually.

Nixon had been one of the first to urge that America send troops into Vietnam, and he had supported every subsequent escalation of U.S. involvement. This gave him a deep emotional commitment to the war.

Perceiving the war as an attempt by North Vietnam to conquer South Vietnam, Kissinger, also, had favored sending U.S. combat troops. However, he subsequently became convinced that the war was draining America's strength and must be ended. Because it could not be won by military action, Kissinger concluded, ending it required the formulation of a better political program for South Vietnam, coupled with negotiations to allow the United States to withdraw militarily without undermining the credibility of its commitments to other allies.

Pressures to end the war were rising. Leading political figures, some of whom had formerly supported the war, including Senator Fulbright, Republican Senator Jacob Javits, and former Vice President Hubert Humphrey, grew more vehement in denouncing it, and former Secretary of Defense Clark Clifford called for withdrawing all U.S. troops. Student protests spread from the large universities to small, conservative colleges. October 1969 "Moratorium" demonstrations brought out 4 million people in two hundred cities, and, on November 15, approximately 250,000 people demonstrated in Washington.

Nixon and Kissinger wanted to end the war. "I'm not going to end up like L.B.J., holed up in the White House afraid to show my face in the street," Nixon said. However, "we would destroy ourselves," he added, "if we pulled out in a way that wasn't really honorable." By "honorable" he meant, at a minimum, preserving an independent, non-Communist government in South Vietnam. By this time, Kissinger explained later, the reliability of America's commitments was at stake. Saying that America could not "simply walk away," but must end the war in a way that maintained faith in America's "strength and purpose," he expressed regret that some Americans "failed to understand the need for additional sacrifice for something so elusive as honorable withdrawal." Such understanding was particularly difficult for the parents of sons who died in the prolonged effort to make a withdrawal honorable.

One possible option was to try to win the war early in the administration, the "honeymoon period," through all-out escalation. A study group concluded that all-out military action would not produce a victory, and that at least eight years would be required to get control of all South Vietnam. Nevertheless, Kissinger later wrote that he and Nixon could have ended the war if they had "bombed the hell out of them the minute they took office," and Nixon wrote that his failure to do so was his greatest mistake as president.

Opposition was approaching the point at which Congress might cut off funds for the war. Thus, Nixon had a great need to reduce opposition to the war to allow him to continue it long enough to arrange "honorable withdrawal." The method he chose was "Vietnamization." Forced to give up the attempt to overwhelm the enemy with U.S. troops, he sought to enlarge and equip South Vietnam's army to the point that it could take over more of the fighting and thereby allow a slow reduction of U.S. forces. Someone called this "changing the color of the corpses." Cutting the number of Americans drafted and killed, Nixon hoped, would reduce opposition to the war—troop withdrawals, he predicted, would "drop a bombshell on the gathering spring storm of antiwar protest." However, some generals condemned it as "surrender on the installment plan."

In July 1969, on Guam, Nixon set forth the policy that came to be known as the "Nixon Doctrine." The United States, he said, could no longer "undertake all the defense of the free nations of the world." Consequently, while continuing to provide those resisting Communist aggression with a "nuclear shield" and economic and military aid, America would no longer send U.S. troops. Nations under attack must themselves provide the manpower. America, said Defense Secretary Melvin Laird, would "no longer try to play policeman to the world." Of course, this constituted recognition that America's power had limits. Johnson had halted escalation; Nixon began deescalation. Furthermore, in the future, he said, "we must avoid that kind of policy that will make countries in Asia so dependent on us that we are dragged into conflicts such as the one that we have in Vietnam." The public approved of the Nixon Doctrine by 77 to 6 percent.

However, South Vietnam's President Thieu warned that it would be many years before Saigon acquired sufficient strength to survive without the protection of U.S. troops.

"Deescalation," Nixon hoped, would enable him to resist pressures to end the war. He promised to withdraw more troops as progress in negotiations, reductions in enemy activities, or improvements in Saigon's army made it possible. On November 3, 1969, saying that to abandon America's Saigon allies "would risk a massacre that would shock and dismay everyone in the world who values human life," he appealed to America's "great silent majority" to show that they backed him and not the antiwar protesters. "North Vietnam cannot defeat or humiliate the United States. Only Americans can do that." The ensuing groundswell of support caused Nixon to exclaim: "We've got the bastards on the run."

Nixon also hoped that he could, through "linkage," induce Russia and China to drop their support of North Vietnam. He was confident that if Russia put pressure on North Vietnam, Hanoi would end the war. If the Soviets helped, Nixon told them, America would grant them trade concessions. Warning Soviet Ambassador Dobrynin that "settlement in Vietnam was the key to everything," Kissinger postponed discussing other matters. Actually, both Russia and China did pressure Hanoi to compromise, but their control of the North Vietnamese was not as complete as Americans imagined.

Nixon redoubled U.S. efforts to win a quick military victory. In March 1969, he began "secretly" bombing Vietcong bases in Cambodia. At the same time, he enlarged the bombing of North Vietnam. That little "fourth-rate power," said Kissinger, "must have a breaking point." So massive did these bombing campaigns become that they made Nixon, in the words of the *Washington Post*, "the greatest bomber of all time." Nixon also enlarged Saigon's forces from 850,000 to 1.1 million and improved their pay, training, and armament. Counting militia, South Vietnam's armed forces reached nearly 2 million, more than half of its able-bodied men. In troops and equipment, Saigon became the world's fourth-ranking military power.

Meanwhile, applying lessons learned from years of failure to win South Vietnamese "hearts and minds," Nixon introduced a new realism into his pacification efforts. He arranged for more troops to be stationed near villages to protect and control them, and he returned to villagers the power to elect village chiefs. Also, he had America assume the cost of a land reform program that distributed nearly 2.4 million acres of land to poor peasants. These measures seemed to bring some progress in securing the countryside and restoring production.

Also, Nixon pressed negotiations. He proposed a stand-still cease-fire, followed by a phased withdrawal of all non–South Vietnamese forces and the democratic election of a new Saigon government. However, in countries with little experience in democracy, elections are usually won by those who count the ballots. Consequently, the Vietcong insisted that Thieu and Ky must first be replaced by a coalition government formed to conduct the election. Kissinger branded this a demand that America overthrow its South Vietnamese ally and "install a Communist-dominated coalition government."

Hawks in the United States had long complained that presidentially imposed restraints prevented the military from conducting the war effectively. In particular, they argued that U.S. forces should be allowed to: (1) invade Cambodia to destroy enemy communications and sanctuaries; (2) invade Laos to cut the Ho Chi Minh trail along which supplies moved from North to South Vietnam; and (3) massively bomb North Vietnam's capital, Hanoi, and its principal harbor, Haiphong. Nixon unleashed the military to do all three.

War in Cambodia

After France's 1954 grant of independence to Cambodia, a small agricultural country of about 6.5 million people, America had given Cambodia aid and helped equip and train its army. Premier Prince Norodom Sihanouk, although anti-Communist, performed a delicate balancing act to keep his weak country out of the war. He urged America to negotiate a settlement of the Vietnam War, which, he said, was multiplying the number of Communists. Lacking the military strength to police the area of Cambodia that bordered Vietnam, he tolerated the use of this territory by North Vietnam to transport supplies into South Vietnam in return for a percentage of the arms transported, and he did not protest when, in March 1969, Nixon began a sustained bombing of this area of Cambodia.

Impatient at Sihanouk's inability to keep the Vietcong from using Cambodian territory, and hoping to receive large amounts of U.S. aid, Cambodian army leaders, led by Marshal Lon Nol, overthrew Sihanouk in March 1970. From abroad, Sihanouk, who retained much popularity among the peasants, formed an anti-Nol alliance with the Cambodian Communists (the Khmer Rouge). Lon Nol appealed to Washington for help.

On April 29, 1970, after secluding himself at Camp David for two days, Nixon, over the objections of both his secretary of defense and his secretary of state, but with Kissinger's support, sent 40,000 South Vietnamese and 20,000 U.S. troops into Cambodia. Announcing this incursion, he said that the troops would enter only border areas controlled by North Vietnam and would withdraw after completing their mission, which, he said, was "cleaning out sanctuaries" that held the "headquarters for the entire Communist military operation." This, he said, would facilitate U.S. withdrawal from Vietnam. Also, "if when the chips are down the United States acts like a pitiful helpless giant, the forces of totalitarianism and anarchy will threaten free nations and free institutions throughout the world." He concluded: "it is not our power, but our will that is being tested tonight."

Antiwar forces considered the invasion of Cambodia an outrageous violation of Nixon's announced policy of deescalation. Student protests were both more widespread (448 campuses) and even more emotional than they had been before. At Kent State University in Ohio, students burned the ROTC building. The next day, May 4, national guard troops fired into demonstrating students, killing four, including two girls, and wounding nine, some of whom were passersby. This killing set off a new wave of even more emotional protests on more campuses, and 100,000 demonstrators converged on the White House.

Although polls showed that a slight majority of Americans supported the invasion, and that most blamed the students for the Kent State killings, Nixon was shaken. That night, Nixon, unable to sleep, appeared to Kissinger to be "on the edge of a nervous breakdown." "The enormous uproar," said Kissinger, was "profoundly unnerving" and "the Executive Branch was shell-shocked." Three top members of Kissinger's staff, including Anthony Lake, and a hundred Foreign Service officers resigned in protest. In a May 8 news conference, Nixon said that he agreed "with everything they [the protestors] are trying to accomplish," and at 4:00 A.M. he walked out to the Lincoln Memorial and talked awkwardly with student demonstrators.

Other Americans rallied to Nixon's support. In May, New York City construction workers, "hard hats," violently broke up a student antiwar demonstration and held a huge rally of their own. A prowar "Honor America Day" assembly in Washington, in July, addressed by the Reverend Billy Graham and the comedian Bob Hope, drew 250,000 people.

In June, after U.S. troops returned from Cambodia, Nixon reported that they had killed 2,000 of the enemy and destroyed vast quantities of equipment. Kissinger credited this invasion with cutting enemy activity in adjoining areas of South Vietnam for the next two years. But the troops did not find the Vietcong headquarters, and they pushed some Vietcong deeper into Cambodia, where they helped Cambodia's Communist guerillas. America subsequently broadened its bombing of Cambodia, and the Soviets increased their aid to the Khmer Rouge. Thus was Cambodia swept into the war that would soon produce in Cambodia one of history's ghastliest tragedies.

In January 1971, Congress repealed the Tonkin Gulf Resolution, and barred the use of U.S. troops in either Cambodia or Laos. This was a significant reversal of previous congressional support for escalation.

Nevertheless, Nixon arranged an invasion of Laos to cut the so-called Ho Chi Minh Trail. Massive "secret" bombing had failed to stop the North Vietnamese from using the trail to transport supplies and men into South Vietnam. Circumventing congressional restrictions by employing only South Vietnamese troops supported by U.S. planes and helicopters, in February 1971, Americans airlifted two South Vietnamese divisions into Laos and, in support, dropped 48,000 tons of bombs. Americans claimed that as many as 15,000 enemy troops were killed, the supply route disrupted, and many supplies destroyed. But stopping South Vietnamese troops short of their targets, the North Vietnamese launched a counterattack that inflicted a casualty rate of 50 percent on the ARVN, and the remainder retreated in panic. Pictures of troops clinging to the skids of evacuating helicopters reinforced the impression that the invasion had been a fiasco.

Meanwhile, support in America for the war continued to slide. Late in 1970, a National Security Council study concluded that America could neither persuade nor force North Vietnam to withdraw. In April 1971, approximately 2,000 U.S. Vietnam Veterans Against the War demonstrated at the Capitol—700 of them threw away the medals they had won—and called for ending "this barbaric war." Not even right-wing hawks could dismiss these veterans as pinko hippies; they were "our boys," America's heroes. Senator George McGovern called theirs the "most effective protest to date," and President Nixon was deeply affected.

Late in April 1971 antiwar demonstrations amassed as many as 300,000 people. On May 1, the "Mayday Tribe" descended on Washington with the avowed aim of shutting down the government. With tactics that included lying down in the streets, they disrupted rush-hour traffic. Five thousand police and 41,000 federal troops summarily arrested some 12,000 of them.

In the summer of 1971, the conviction of Lieutenant William Calley on charges of leading his men in the 1968 murder of more than 300 Vietnamese at the village of My Lai reminded Americans that the U.S. war effort in Vietnam included actions that, if committed by an enemy, most Americans would regard as atrocities. Furthermore, in June, the *New York Times* began publication of the *Pentagon Papers*, a secret collection of documents that revealed that U.S. officials, including presidents, had repeatedly misled the public by claiming that they were seeking peace when their real policy was to continue or enlarge the war.

Public opinion polls taken in summer 1971 revealed that only 31 percent of Americans still supported Nixon's Vietnam policies. Of those polled, 71 percent said that sending U.S. troops to Vietnam had been a mistake, 58 percent called the war "immoral," and a majority wanted complete withdrawal even if that would result in a Communist takeover. Military leaders grew increasingly concerned about the effect of the war in undermining troop morale and discipline and the military's public image. There were increasing reports of U.S. atrocities, soaring drug use, and "fragging"—assassination by U.S. troops of officers who ordered them into battle. A growing number of business leaders concluded that it was time for America to cut its losses. Obviously, to salvage anything from the war, Nixon must negotiate.

Negotiations on Vietnam

Kissinger had opened secret conversations with North Vietnam in Paris in August 1969. His personal emotional commitment to the war was less intense than Nixon's, and he seemed to be willing to settle for a "decent interval" of perhaps two or three years between U.S. withdrawal and a Communist takeover. Nevertheless, progress was slow. Meanwhile, the North Vietnamese captured the crews of some of the U.S. planes they shot down, which, because of public anxiety to secure the captives' release, gave North Vietnam additional bargaining power. In May 1971, America proposed to withdraw all U.S. troops within six months if North Vietnam would release all prisoners. Omission of any demand for withdrawal of North Vietnamese troops from South Vietnam represented a major new concession. In their June counterproposal, the North Vietnamese insisted that America also allow a new coalition government to be formed to conduct elections.

In October 1971, Kissinger offered to force Thieu to resign one month in advance of an election conducted under international supervision if North Vietnam agreed to release U.S. prisoners. However, this would still have left Saigon officials in control of the election machinery, and Hanoi rejected the offer.

In March 1972, with U.S. troops in Vietnam down to 95,000, only 6,000 of whom were combat troops, the North Vietnamese launched a major invasion of South Vietnam with 120,000 troops supported by tanks. Their main purpose was to force the transfer of ARVN troops from the villages to the northern border in order to allow the Vietcong to disrupt pacification programs. Although ARVN resistance was surprisingly determined, the North Vietnamese overran Quang Tri, South Vietnam's northernmost province.

In response, Nixon widened the bombing of North Vietnam to include Hanoi and Haiphong. "The bastards have never been bombed like they're going to be bombed this time," he said. He also laid mines in Haiphong Harbor, thereby endangering Soviet and Chinese shipping. America held the Soviets responsible for the invasion, Kissinger told Brezhnev. Four Soviet merchantships hit mines and sank. North Vietnam suffered enormous damage, but its movement of troops and supplies into South Vietnam did not slow.

Senator Edmund Muskie charged that Nixon was "destroying land and people" and sacrificing young American lives in a war that had become "senseless and immoral." However, the stepped-up bombing, perceived as decisive presidential action, raised Nixon's ratings in the polls. Despite their protests, the Soviets did not cancel a scheduled summit conference. Moreover, Russia and China put pressure on North Vietnam to accept a compromise.

On October 11, after years of negotiations, a deal was struck in Paris by Kissinger and North Vietnam's negotiator, Le Duc Tho. It was, wrote Kissinger, the most thrilling moment of his career. The key provision was that the Vietcong would be given a share in the control of an election to be conducted by a new tripartite electoral commission composed of representatives of Saigon, the Vietcong, and neutral nations. In return, the North Vietnamese dropped their demand for prior removal of Thieu. An in-place cease-fire would leave the Vietcong in control of parts of South Vietnam, and not require withdrawal of North Vietnamese troops from South Vietnam. Within sixty days, U.S. prisoners would be returned, and all U.S. troops would withdraw. Nixon accepted this agreement on the condition that Thieu also accept it.

Enraged that he had not been consulted before the deal was concluded, Thieu balked. Kissinger spent five days in Saigon in a vain effort to bring him around. Thieu said that he did not have sufficient popular support to compete with the Vietcong in a political contest, and that the contemplated tripartite election commission would be, in effect, a coalition government. He also protested that the agreement, although it would forbid entry of new North Vietnamese forces, would leave North Vietnamese troops in the south and concede to the Vietcong possession of much of South Vietnam.

Meanwhile, a presidential campaign under way in America pitted Nixon, running for a second term, against a liberal Democrat, George McGovern, who had long opposed the war. Realizing that their bargaining power would drop after the election, the North Vietnamese published the agreed-upon terms and set an October 31 deadline for the United States to sign them. Nixon announced that he would refuse to yield to pressure, but on October 31, partly to undercut McGovern's appeal, Kissinger announced that "peace is at hand." Nixon got nearly 61 percent of the vote in November.

Seeking to induce Thieu to accept the agreement, Nixon gave him more than $1 billion in additional military supplies and also offered "absolute assurances" that, if North Vietnam violated its terms, America's reaction would be "swift and severe." In November, Kissinger got the North Vietnamese to agree to make token troop withdrawals and to accept some reduction in the political status of the Vietcong and the powers of the trilateral electoral commission. But when Kissinger insisted that the North Vietnamese accept the seventeenth parallel as a national boundary, Le Duc Tho refused. Nixon and Kissinger decided to turn from negotiations to military force.

On December 18, Nixon unleashed massive bombing, the "Christmas bombing," of North Vietnam. Ordering all available B-52 bombers to Vietnam, he told the air force that there would be no more "of this crap about the fact that we couldn't hit this target or that one." In twelve days, in the heaviest bombing of the war, U.S. planes dropped 36,000 tons of bombs, devastating Hanoi's and Haiphong's industrial, railroad, and residential areas and largest hospital and killing at least 2,200 civilians. It was, said a Kissinger aide, "calculated barbarism." Fifteen of America's giant B-52 bombers were shot down, in addition to eleven other bombers, an alarming blow to U.S. world air power. Also, nearly a hundred additional Americans joined those already in North Vietnam's prisons.

A number of considerations seem to have contributed to this massive Christmas bombing. It might cause the Russians and Chinese, said Nixon, to "think that they were dealing with a madman" and cause them to "force North Vietnam into a settlement before the world was consumed in a larger war." Also, according to Nixon officials, it was intended to "create the image of a defeated enemy crawling back to the peace table." Furthermore, by demonstrating what America would do if North Vietnam were to violate the agreements, it might help persuade Thieu to sign.

The bombing aroused angry outcries in America and the world. The *London Daily Mirror* said it made the world recoil in revulsion, and Sweden's prime minister compared it to Nazi atrocities. It made the United States, said the *Los Angeles Times*, "appear a barbarian gone mad." "Our souls have withered," editorialized the *New Yorker*, and "we are turning into monsters." Nixon's popular approval plunged to a low of 39 percent, and danger arose that the Democratic Congress might cut off funds for bombing North Vietnam.

After Hanoi offered to resume talks if the bombing stopped, Nixon called off the onslaught on December 29. A new agreement was signed on January 27 (Lyndon Johnson, who died on January 22, lived to see the abandonment of the war for which he had sacrificed his presidency). Recognizing the "unity" of Vietnam, America agreed that the seventeenth parallel was not a territorial boundary, thus forfeiting the point that had disrupted negotiations before Christmas and conceding, after all, that the war was a civil war and not a defense against international aggression. A cease-fire in place left the Vietcong and North Vietnamese in control of much of South Vietnam. America agreed to withdraw all military forces, technicians, and advisers, and to dismantle its military bases within sixty days in return for simultaneous release of all U.S. prisoners.

When Thieu objected, Americans threatened to cut off aid if he did not sign, while secretly Nixon promised Thieu "swift and retaliatory action" in "full force" if Hanoi failed to honor the agreement. However, at Thieu's insistence, they dropped the proposed election in favor of vague provisions for future political settlement and reunification. Once reunified, Vietnam could "not join any military alliance or military bloc" or permit foreign bases on its soil. These terms were little different from those agreed to in November, except that they did not require Thieu to submit to a democratic election.

In a separate, semisecret agreement, America promised to give North Vietnam $4.8 billion in reconstruction aid.

The settlement left Saigon in a weak position, with its survival in doubt despite Nixon's secret promise to reenter with "full force" if the North Vietnamese violated its terms. However, it did provide what Kissinger called a "decent interval" between U.S. withdrawal and a complete Communist takeover.

This ended America's direct participation in the fighting and brought America's longest war to an end. It had been twenty-three years since America began aiding France's effort to subdue Vietnam, and seven years since Johnson sent U.S. regiments into the war. Having failed to establish a viable independent anti-Communist nation in South Vietnam, America was forced to admit that Vietnam was not two separate nations, and to accept Communist control of much of South Vietnam. The enemy imposed this settlement on Nixon, an anti-Communist hawk. In 1973 Kissinger and Le Duc Tho won the Nobel Peace Prize for ending the war. Undersecretary of State George Ball remarked that "the Norwegians [who chose the receipients] must have a sense of humor."

During Nixon's presidency, 1969 to 1973, America had dropped nearly 4 million tons of bombs, carried the war into Cambodia and Laos, mined Haiphong harbor, and, with the South Vietnamese, killed more than 500,000 enemy fighters and a much larger number of civilians. In the same period, America's South Vietnamese allies suffered 108,000 battle deaths, while 20,543 Americans died. The agreement achieved was probably no more favorable than was available at the beginning of Nixon's term.

While withdrawing U.S. troops and halting the bombing of North Vietnam, Nixon left 9,000 U.S. advisers, transferred huge quantities of supplies to the

ARVN, and continued the secret bombing of Cambodia. Thieu, seeking to make the most of his military superiority, launched large-scale offensives against Vietcong areas in violation of the cease-fire. The North Vietnamese, possibly fearing a reversal of America's evacuation, were comparatively quiescent.

In the wake of the war, Congress moved to trim the powers of the presidency. Late in June, it voted to require an immediate halt to all U.S. military operations in or over Cambodia. Nixon vetoed this measure but was forced to accept a compromise that only delayed the cutoff date to mid-August. In November 1973, in an effort to reassert Congress's control over going to war, Congress enacted the War Powers Act, which required the president to inform Congress within forty-eight hours if he sent U.S. forces into a combat area, and specified that he could keep them there no more than ninety days unless Congress specifically authorized him to do so.

Nixon's powers were further undermined by evidence that he had been involved in illegal acts, the "Watergate Affair." In 1971, when Daniel Ellsberg had leaked the secret *Pentagon Papers* to the *New York Times*, Nixon had created a special White House unit, dubbed the "Plumbers," to plug such leaks and to conduct other secret operations. On June 17, 1972, the group was caught burglarizing the headquarters of the Democratic National Committee in the Watergate office and apartment building. Investigations produced a series of sensational revelations which the news media, never friendly to Nixon, gave full play. In an effort to divert suspicion from himself, Nixon fired his two top White House assistants, but additional disclosures indicated that he had been aware of illegal activity and had participated in its illegal coverup.

This prolonged series of dramatic developments eroded Nixon's image and power to govern. By June 1974, his public approval rating had fallen to 23 percent. On August 9, with Congress on the verge of voting to impeach him for abuse of power, obstruction of justice, and contempt of Congress, Nixon resigned the presidency, turning over the office to Vice President Gerald R. Ford. In his final address, Nixon said that "the world is a safer place today" because of his efforts to achieve detente: "This, more than anything, is what I hope will be my legacy to you."

Meanwhile, Saigon's prospects faded. The war had disrupted South Vietnam's rural economy, making refugees of one-fourth of the population, many of whom crowded into the cities. Saigon's population jumped from 300,000 to 3 million. Lacking industry, the urban economy, characterized by black marketing, war spending, prostitution, and real estate speculation, was dependent on the continued flow of money from America. As U.S. military aid fell from $2.3 billion in 1973 to $1 billion in 1974 (and to a projected $700 million for 1975), shortages occurred, corruption worsened, and unemployment and inflation soared. Military morale collapsed, and, in 1974, 240,000 ARVN soldiers deserted. Responding to Thieu's violation of the cease-fire, North Vietnam sent more troops south, and, in early 1974, the Vietcong recovered much of the territory it had lost in 1973. Vietnamese Buddhists demanded peace, and some Christian church members begged Americans not to send more aid and thereby prolong the war.

In March 1975, the Vietcong and the North Vietnamese made what they intended to be a preliminary probe in the central highlands and, with unexpected ease, quickly captured Pleiku and Kontum. Thieu decided to withdraw his forces from the highlands to more defensible areas. But the retreat of his troops quickly turned into a panic-stricken rout, and his stampeding armies and accompanying refugees spread panic before them. Defenders of the important cities of Hue and Danang fled, and in only fifty-five days the Saigon regime, for which America had sacrificed so much blood and treasure, collapsed like a house of cards. Congress rejected President Ford's request for additional military aid, but voted $300 million for humanitarian aid and evacuation costs. Blaming U.S. aid cuts, Thieu resigned on April 21.

In a vain attempt to maintain South Vietnamese morale, U.S. Ambassador Graham Martin had delayed evacuation until it was too late to take out many of the Vietnamese who had put themselves at risk by working for Americans, but ships and helicopters got out all Americans and about 150,000 Vietnamese by April 30. Those left behind bitterly fired on the last departing U.S. helicopters. Saigon surrendered on May 1. The North Vietnamese acquired vast U.S.-built military installations and at least $5 billion worth of U.S. weapons.

In Cambodia, on April 1, a month before Saigon fell, a weeping Lon Nol fled, and the Communists moved into Cambodia's capital, Phnom Penh. Laotian Communists completed their takeover of Laos in October. It had been twenty-six years since the first commitment of U.S. aid to the defense of Indochina, and twenty-one years since the Geneva agreement to unite Vietnam.

This was the most humiliating defeat in America's history, but its consequences were not as disastrous to America's vital interests as four American presidents had predicted. Tens of thousands of ARVN and Saigon officials were imprisoned in reeducation centers, but the predicted bloodbath did not occur. Communists seized Cambodia and Laos, but no other dominos fell. The Communist victory did not give China control of Vietnam; instead, Vietnamese Communists fought to expel Chinese influence from Cambodia. Russians secured use of the gigantic former U.S. naval base at Cam Ranh Bay, but the United States did not, as President Johnson had predicted, lose control of the Pacific. Nor did America's allies desert to the Communists. The loss of South Vietnam did not bring a major shift in the distribution of world power.

In the eight years that U.S. troops had participated in the fighting, America had lost 58,000 dead, 300,000 wounded, and 1,400 missing. Also, many veterans carried psychic scars. Including aid to France's effort to retake Indochina, America had spent more than $300 billion (one scholar calculated $885 billion in 1989 dollars). The war left as many as 2 million Vietnamese dead and twice as many wounded. It damaged America's image and alienated its allies. A leading U.S. diplomatic historian called it "America's most disastrous foreign policy adventure."

By 1978, polls showed that 72 percent of Americans regarded participation in the Vietnam War to have been, more than a mistake, "fundamentally wrong and immoral." Ironically, the voters did not reward those who had opposed the war but, ousting such doves as Fulbright, Church, and McGovern, twice elected Ronald Reagan, who in the 1980s still spoke of the Vietnam War as a "noble cause" and "America's finest hour," to the presidency.

For a time, the Vietnam experience seemed to make Americans somewhat less willing to send troops to fight abroad. Also, it somewhat undermined Americans' conviction that they were purer, more noble, and more humane than foreigners and that, therefore, U.S. intervention always benefited other countries.

What had gone wrong? The answers conflicted. Many hawks, and a majority of the public, remained convinced that the United States could have won the war if politicians had not restrained the military from striking quickly with full force. On the other hand, critics of the war argued that America had applied more than enough military force to win against an impoverished nation of 30 million people if the war had been politically winnable. But, they argued, U.S. troops had been sent on a mission impossible, because no amount of military force could compel the Vietnamese to accept the division of their country, or to support the Saigon regime. Even if America had sent enough U.S. troops to occupy North Vietnam (which not even most extreme hawks advocated), the United States could not have achieved peace, doves maintained, because Asians would no longer peaceably accept white rule. If so, military success could have achieved only a more costly stalemate.

Apparently Americans had misdiagnosed the problem in Vietnam. They had tried to reform a society whose language they did not speak and whose history, politics, and culture they did not understand. The means they applied seemed more than adequate—555,000 American troops backed by unlimited naval and airpower and more bombs than were dropped by both sides in World War II should have sufficed to defeat North Vietnam. They could lose militarily only if their actions were self-defeating.

Throughout, America's leaders seemed insufficiently aware of the extent to which the Vietcong were fighting, not to serve foreign Communists, but to rid themselves of foreigners and to achieve independence and self-rule. Americans could easily have defeated Communist aggression; they lost not to foreign Communists but to native nationalists. The Reverend Jesse Jackson concluded that America had fought on the "wrong side of history."

Ford's Foreign Policies

Vice President Gerald R. Ford became president on August 9, 1974, and held office until January 9, 1977, nearly two and a half years. A college football player and a law school graduate, Ford was a long-time congressman from Michigan who had risen to be House minority leader. The new president was an experienced and popular politician, and many regarded him as a welcome change from Nixon whom they had come to regard as sinister. However, he was better known for amiability than for intellect, and he had little experience in international relations. Asking Nixon's foreign policy personnel to stay, he continued Nixon's policies. In November 1975, he removed one of Kissinger's titles, that of White House national security adviser, and gave that job to Kissinger's deputy, General Brent Scowcroft. At the same time, he replaced CIA director William Colby with George Bush.

Long a hawk on Vietnam, Ford was in office when the Saigon government and the anti-Communist government of Cambodia collapsed in April 1975.

In May 1975, Communist Cambodian patrol boats seized a U.S. merchant ship, the *Mayaguez*, for allegedly violating Cambodian territorial waters and captured thirty-nine Americans. Feeling the sting of defeat in Vietnam, Ford and Kissinger took the opportunity to demonstrate that America was still ready to respond with force if challenged. Without resort to diplomacy, Ford ordered immediate military action which sank three Cambodian gun boats and bombed an air base and an oil depot. Forty-one U.S. marines who went to the rescue, unaware that Cambodians had freed the captives, were killed in an accident. Despite this loss of life, the action was widely applauded in America.

Continuing arms limitations efforts, Ford met with Brezhnev at Vladivostok on November 23, 1974. They agreed to allow each side 2,400 ICBMs and heavy bombers (at the time Russia had approximately 2,500 and America 2,100), of which 1,320 missiles might carry multiple warheads. This agreement gave the Soviets parity in these weapons but put no limits on the number of medium-range U.S. missiles based within reach of Russia. Both Ford and Brezhnev were euphoric, Kissinger called the accord a "breakthrough," and both houses of Congress voted approval. However, when experts attempted to draft an implementing treaty, disputes developed over how to count cruise missiles, Soviet Backfire bombers, and sea-launched missiles. The Ford administration ended with these issues unresolved.

In 1972, Nixon had negotiated a trade agreement granting Russia most-favored-nation status (reducing tariffs on Soviet goods to the level of tariffs on goods from other nations), and additional credit. But, in 1974, over Kissinger's opposition, Congress enacted the Jackson-Vanik amendment, which denied the Soviets equal trade privileges until they permitted free emigration of Russian Jews. Resenting what they considered to be interference in their internal affairs, the Soviets rejected the amended trade agreement and cut the number of Jews permitted to emigrate from its 1973 peak of 35,000 to 13,000 in 1975. This was a heavy blow to detente, trade, and Jews.

In July 1975, the heads of thirty-five nations, including the United States, gathered in Finland to sign the Helsinki Accords. They agreed to accept the existing national boundaries in East Europe as "inviolable," thus legitimizing Soviet World War II gains, including Soviet annexation of the Baltic states and parts of Poland, Finland, and Romania. They also pledged greater economic, scientific, and environmental cooperation and respect for certain human rights, including the rights to information, freedom of expression, family reunification, and travel. This agreement would contribute to liberalizing East European regimes. Many on both sides would later refer to the Helsinki Accords as the high point of detente.

The most serious strain on detente in the Ford administration came in Africa. Americans bitterly resented Cuba's intervention in Angola, which they blamed on Russia. Opponents of detente charged that the Soviets were taking advantage of detente to launch further aggression.

As right-wing leaders, including former Secretaries of Defense James Schlesinger and Melvin Laird and former Governor Ronald Reagan of California, stepped up their attacks on detente, Ford and Kissinger retreated from the concept. In a speech in March 1976, Ford said, "We are going to forget the use of the word detente," and he shifted his campaign slogan to "peace through strength." Kissinger changed his definition of detente from "a search for a more constructive relationship" to "prevent Soviet expansion."

To many, the most striking feature of the Nixon-Ford presidencies was the degree to which they reversed the policies Nixon had previously advocated. Power seemed to bring an instant conversion from ideologue to pragmatist, and Nixon recognized that the shifting power distribution had reduced America's ability to impose its will. Formerly a strident denouncer of anything resembling softness on communism, Nixon opened relations with the People's Republic of China and adopted a policy of detente with the Soviet Union. An ardent hawk on Vietnam, Nixon disengaged from that war.[1] Despite his long advocacy of military buildup, he signed arms limitation agreements, and reduced U.S. troop strength not only in Vietnam but in Korea and Taiwan. If Hubert Humphrey or George McGovern had been elected president, they probably could not have implemented as much of their programs—because hawks like Nixon would not have allowed it.

---

[1]The Vietnam War has produced a voluminious historical literature. Some historians conclude that the United States would have won had it gone into the war with full force and fought it without restraint. Among this group are Guenter Lewy, Harry Summers, Norman Podhoretz, and Phillip B. Davidson. Others maintain that at least equally responsible for the failure were the inadequacies of the pacification program. In this group are Cecil B. Currey, Andrew Krepinevich, and Larry E. Cable. However, most historians of the war see America's failure in Vietnam as a result of Cold War obsessions and misunderstanding of Vietnam that led Americans into making war against Vietnamese nationalists in the mistaken belief that it was defending them against foreign aggression. Among the best known of this group are David Halberstam, Theodore Draper, Arthur M. Schlesinger, Jr., Richard J. Barnet, Frances Fitzgerald, Leslie H. Gelb, George C. Herring, Paul Kattenburg, Gabriel Kolko, Lloyd C. Gardner, George McT. Kahin, John Prados, Gary Hess, and Marilyn Young.

15 The Carter Administration

The Election of 1976

As the election of 1976 approached, the Republican party, badly wounded by the Watergate scandals, was in disarray. President Ford, who had been chosen for vice president by the disgraced Nixon, hurt his popularity by pardoning Nixon for any crime Nixon might have committed. Ford beat back a challenge for the nomination by the right-wing former governor of California Ronald Reagan, but the party platform, largely reflecting the views of Reagan backers, condemned the Helsinki Agreements for accepting Communist control of East Europe, and called for increased defense spending.

Among Democrats, public opinion polls showed Senator Edward Kennedy, the younger brother of the assassinated John and Robert Kennedy, to be the favorite. But, citing responsibilities as head of a large family, he withdrew from the contest. Former Governor Jimmy Carter of Georgia, who emphasized that he had not been a part of the Washington "mess," won in the primaries and defeated Hubert Humphrey for the Democratic nomination.

In the 1976 campaign, Ford, under pressure from conservative Republicans, sounded more hawkish than Nixon. Dropping the word "detente," he emphasized anti-Communism and military strength.

Carter's position on foreign policy issues was more complex. Sometimes he took a hard line. Criticizing detente, he blamed the Republicans for allowing America's relative power to decline, accepting Soviet domination of East Europe, and selling grain to Russia. On the other hand, he called for cutting military spending and arms sales, condemned intervention in the internal affairs of other nations, including Vietnam and Chile, promised not to support oppressive dictators, and advocated withdrawing U.S. troops from Korea. Deeply religious, he wanted America, he said, to follow a "moral and ethical" foreign policy "that reflects the decency and generosity and common sense of our own people."

In a televised debate, Ford made a major fumble when he twice asserted that there was no Soviet domination of East Europe and never would be in a Ford administration.

In a close election, Carter won, but his victory may have been less the result of popular approval of his position on the issues than of popular revulsion against the Nixon scandals, and lack of confidence in Ford.

Carter Organizes His Administration

Carter had been a naval officer, a businessman, and governor of Georgia. Enrolling in the U.S. Naval Academy in 1943, he studied engineering, served on a nuclear submarine, and then resigned in 1953 to become a farmer and businessman. Entering politics, he won election to the Georgia legislature and, in 1970, the governorship, where he attracted national attention by making bold statements in favor of civil rights. He was invited to join the Trilateral Commission, a group of leading political, business, and academic persons, formed to promote better cooperation among America, Europe, and Japan, and its meetings helped educate him on international issues. As a hard-working president, he read history, studied international problems, and mastered detail. He also appointed recognized foreign policy experts to the posts of national security adviser and secretary of state.

For White House national security adviser Carter selected Zbigniew Brzezinski, the son of a Polish diplomat, who had come to America in 1953, studied at Harvard, and become a Columbia University professor. Brash and outspoken, he was an advocate of *realpolitik*, the school of thought that holds that the aim of foreign policy is to improve the nation's relative power, mainly through amoral military force. He was also a highly ideological anti-Communist; Kissinger called him "a theoretician of anticommunism." A critic of detente, he sought to combat communism everywhere, build America's military strength, loosen Russia's hold on Eastern Europe, and even break up the Soviet Union. Someone remarked that he was the first Pole in many years "in a position to stick it to the Russians."

The secretary of state was of a different mold. A soft-spoken West Virginian and a graduate of Yale Law School, Cyrus Vance had become a wealthy New York lawyer, President Kennedy's secretary of the army, and, under Johnson, diplomat and deputy secretary of defense. Vance deplored the tendency to attribute all world problems to Soviet aggression. Most Third World conflicts, he said, had deep-seated indigenous economic, social, racial, and political causes and must be dealt with "on their own terms," not as East-West issues. Military intervention, he maintained, could not permanently prevent change or sustain regimes that lacked popular support, nor were there "American solutions to every problem." He sought to continue detente and to approach problems through quiet diplomacy. The Soviet ambassador found him "highly professional, methodical, consistent," and "sociable." Brzezinski said that Vance tended to "shy away from the unavoidable ingredient of force." (See Fig. 15.1.)

As ambassador to the UN, Carter named a black man, Andrew Young of Georgia, a former preacher, congressman, and civil rights leader, who had given Carter valuable help in carrying the South in the 1976 election. In the UN, he was an active and eloquent champion of human rights and friendship with Third World nations. Carter's secretary of defense was Harold Brown, former president of the California Institute of Technology and secretary of the air force.

Figure 15.1 Carter's National Security Adviser Zbigniew Brzezinski and Secretary of State Cyrus Vance. Carter Library.

To head the CIA, Carter appointed an Annapolis classmate, Admiral Stansfield Turner, who kept CIA covert actions at a relatively low level.

Carter called for changes in U.S. foreign policy, particularly in regard to the Third World. U.S. policy, he said in May 1977, would no longer be dominated by "an inordinate fear of communism which once led us to embrace any dictator who joined us in that fear." Vietnam had demonstrated the "intellectual and moral poverty" of military intervention, and he wanted "no more Vietnams" and "no more Chiles." Instead, America would conduct a North-South dialogue in awareness that political unrest was often caused by local economic and social problems. The best way to promote freedom in the world, he said, was "to demonstrate here that our democratic system is worthy of emulation." Democratization and reform, he said, would be more effective in preventing Communist takeovers than force and suppression, and this might require concessions to nationalists who sought to reduce U.S. influence in their countries, or even recognition of left-wing governments. Americans should give more attention to world economic and social problems, promote morality in international relations, lead by example, and "replace balance of power politics with world order politics."

Like his predecessors, Carter favored reducing barriers to international trade. In July 1979, Congress approved new tariff reductions, the "Tokyo Round," negotiated by most leading trading nations in a new General Agreement on Trade and Tariffs (GATT). They cut tariffs about 30 percent.

Like Presidents Johnson and Nixon, Carter was alarmed by America's growing dependence on imported oil. "Next to preventing war," he said, achieving energy independence was "the greatest challenge that our country will face during our lifetime." He even called it the "moral equivalent of war." But feeling less urgency, Congress did not enact the measures Carter proposed.

Carter's Approach to the Soviet Union

Carter and Secretary of State Vance favored detente, which Carter defined as a mix of "competition and cooperation" and "progress toward peace." Also, he wanted to move away from obsession with the Soviet Union and pay more attention to the Third World. Nevertheless, relations with the Soviets deteriorated during his administration.

The late 1970s was a difficult time for U.S. foreign policymakers. Communists had broken through containment in Cuba and Vietnam and seemed threatening elsewhere. The defeat in Vietnam damaged America's international standing. America had lost the overshadowing preponderance of world power that it had enjoyed immediately after World War II; its share of world economic production had dropped by half, its atomic monopoly had vanished, its holdings of gold and foreign exchange had plunged, and its allies had become less dependent.

This relative decline of U.S. dominance puzzled and angered many Americans. Attributing it to detente's softening of U.S. opposition to communism, the right wing, bolstered by a postwar reaction, demanded a massive military buildup to restore America's superiority and to revive the policy of facing down Communists. Brzezinski wanted to challenge "their very existence."

At the same time the Soviets behaved as if the growth of their economy and their achievement of near-military parity entitled them to more equal consideration and an equal right to support allies on other continents. Their foreign policy grew more assertive. During the Carter administration, they seized opportunities to back revolutions in Angola, Ethiopia, and Afghanistan. Brzezinski called this a new wave of Soviet aggression across an "arc of crisis."

Carter was a hard-working, hands-on president who made strenuous efforts to remedy his deficiencies in history and international relations. However, some advisers considered him to be better at mastering the details of particular problems than at weaving all aspects together into a comprehensive world strategy. However, his approach avoided the pitfalls of judging all situations in terms of an overarching theory. The hawkish national security adviser Brzezinski and the more pacific secretary of state Vance pulled him in opposite directions. At first he seemed inclined to agree with Vance, but, as his frustrations grew, he moved toward the Brzezinski stance.

Carter continued the policy of challenging Soviet control of its East European satellites. High officials exchanged visits; Carter visited Poland. Also, he gave Hungary, Poland, and Romania most-favored-nation trading status.

Some of Carter's moves that damaged detente may not have been so intended. The degree of offense that the Soviets took at his advocacy of human rights surprised him. The Soviets regarded it as an attempt to undermine their regimes in eastern Europe and to destroy their system. "We will not tolerate interference in our internal affairs by anyone," warned Soviet President Leonid Brezhnev. Also, Carter seemed to be surprised when his attempt to change the terms of the Vladivostok arms agreement enraged the Soviets. Carter's one meeting with the Soviet leader did not come until the middle of his third year as president, and Brzezinski later considered Carter's failure to meet earlier with Brezhnev a great mistake. The Soviets regarded Carter as the most hostile U.S. president since Truman.

Friends and foes alike complained of what seemed to them to be Carter's inconsistency. After advocating reduction of arms spending, he began a rapid buildup. After promising to withdraw troops from Korea, he kept them there. After promising to reduce U.S. personnel overseas, he raised their number. After pledging to cut arms sales abroad, he raised them from $13 billion in 1977 to $17 billion in 1980. After asking the Soviets to help bring about Middle East peace, he excluded them from negotiations. Despite his call for human rights, he supplied weapons to some repressive regimes.

Chancellor Helmut Schmidt of West Germany was particularly irritated. Under Carter's urging, Schmidt, at some political cost to himself, declared himself in favor of deploying the neutron bomb, which would kill people without destroying property, only to have Carter cancel deployment. Also, Schmidt did not approve of Carter's crusading for human rights in the Soviet Union. Accusing him of formulating policy "from the pulpit," he said that Carter "knows everything and understands nothing." Once, in a "bitter" discussion, Carter recorded, Schmidt got "personally abusive."

Human Rights

Carter energetically championed human rights, by which he meant rights traditional in Western democracies, including the freedom to worship, speak, assemble, travel, emigrate, and choose an occupation, as well as freedom from slavery, torture, forced labor, arbitrary imprisonment, and discrimination based on race, sex, or religion. He sought to return the United States to the championship of democracy and freedom abroad that, with some exceptions, had characterized its foreign policy before 1945. In 1948, human rights activists, including Eleanor Roosevelt, had secured agreement by most nations to the Universal Declaration of Human Rights. Later, in the 1975 Helsinki Agreements, the signatories, including the Communist countries of East Europe, had promised to respect human rights. In 1976, Congress declared that observance of such rights by all countries was a principal U.S. goal and that America should not give aid to countries engaging in "a consistent pattern of gross violations of internationally recognized human rights."

Declaring that human rights was the "soul" of his foreign policy, Carter established a Bureau of Human Rights in the State Department, which prepared annual reports on civil liberties abroad. America's foreign policy had been "strongest and most effective," he later wrote, when emphasizing "morality and a commitment to freedom and democracy." Condemning support of "right-wing monarchs and military dictators," he maintained that promoting democracy and respect for human rights would be more effective in checking communism. "We are particularly dedicated to genuine self-determination and majority rule," he said.

Carter lifted prohibitions on travel to Cuba, North Korea, Vietnam, and Cambodia. He corresponded with prominent Soviet dissidents and sought release of Soviet "prisoners of conscience." He also halted or reduced aid to some countries that grossly violated human rights, including Argentina, Guatemala, El Salvador, Chile, Uganda, and Rhodesia, and his pressure may have influenced some nations to reduce executions, release political prisoners, and move toward democracy.

However, he did not insist on "blind" consistency in applying this policy. Giving priority to U.S. security interests, he took no official notice of human rights violations in Iran, the Philippines, South Korea, Saudi Arabia, Zaire, Indonesia, China, and, most notably, Cambodia, the world's worst violator of human rights. Some critics called Carter's policy self-righteous interference in the internal affairs of selected nations and they noted that America also had human rights deficiencies, including persistent race discrimination, the highest percentage of its population in prison, and the largest proportion of its children living in poverty of any industrialized nation.

Military Policies

As a candidate, Carter had attacked excessive military spending. As president, he canceled further construction of B-1 bombers, the expensive superbombers that many military men had come to regard as less effective than missiles. He ordered withdrawal of atomic weapons from Korea (an order the Pentagon later persuaded him to rescind) and suspended production of battlefield neutron bombs. Also, he appointed Paul C. Warnke, who believed that both superpowers already had more than enough atomic weapons, to head the Arms Control and Disarmament Agency. Because of the lobbying by weapons manufacturers and their Pentagon allies, Carter wrote later, "the purchase of unnecessary military equipment was undoubtedly the most wasteful element in American government." However, he continued development of the MX, an improved multiple-warhead mobile ICBM.

Carter gave high priority to seeking agreement on mutual nuclear arms reduction. When Brezhnev announced that the Soviet Union did not seek military superiority, Carter replied that neither did America. Calling for a halt to nuclear-weapon testing, he told Brezhnev that his goal was "to liquidate nuclear weapons completely."

In the Ford administration, a tentative agreement had been reached at the 1974 Vladivostok summit to limit to 2,400 each side's arsenal of long-range missiles, only 1,320 of which might be MIRVed (mounted with clusters of smaller, independently targeted missiles), and to limit to 308 the heavy Soviet missiles designed to carry large atomic bombs to America. Instead of seeking Senate approval of this agreement, Carter, in a dramatic gesture at the beginning of his administration, called for greater reductions. In March 1977, he sent Vance to Moscow with a proposal to reduce the number of allowed missiles to 2,000, of which only 1,200 might be MIRVed, and to cut the number of Soviet heavy missiles from 308 to 150. The surprised Soviets, perceiving that the new cuts were mainly in areas in which they were strong, and suspecting that Carter was seeking to sabotage the Vladivostok Agreement, called his proposal a "cheap and shady maneuver" and "deliberately unacceptable." Carter was shocked by the abrupt Soviet rejection.

Two years of torturous negotiations ensued before compromises were achieved. In June 1979, Carter met at Vienna with Soviet President Brezhnev. "God will not forgive us," said Brezhnev, "if we fail." When the two walked together, the aging Soviet leader steadied himself on Carter's arm and, when they parted, embraced him. In their communiqué they promised that neither would strive for military superiority, "since that can only result in dangerous instability, generating higher levels of armaments with no benefits to the security of either." Their agreement, SALT (Strategic Arms Limitations Treaty) II, set a limit of 2,250 on each side's long-range missiles and bombers, of which 1,320 missiles might be MIRVed, and kept the number of permitted heavy missiles at 308 but restricted to ten the number of independently targeted warheads each could carry. This treaty required the Soviets to scrap 250 delivery vehicles, while allowing America to add 190. Also, it gave each the right to inspect the observance of the treaty by the other.

SALT II provided for substantial parity between America and Russia in long-range delivery vehicles. However, it did not limit British and French weapons capable of bombing the Soviet Union. Nor did it count the large number of U.S. intermediate-range weapons based in Europe and elsewhere that could reach Russia. Thus, it left America with a wide margin of superiority.

The SALT II treaty was not ratified. The Senate Foreign Relations Committee approved it by a vote of 9 to 6, but when the Soviets invaded Afghanistan in 1979 Carter asked the Senate to defer action. Nevertheless, for the most part, both sides observed its terms.

When the Soviets began installing improved mobile intermediate-range three-warhead SS-20 missiles aimed at Western Europe, Carter threatened to add 572 Pershing and cruise missiles to the 7,000 U.S. nuclear weapons already in Europe. In 1980–1981 students staged huge protest demonstrations against installing additional missiles in Europe. After relations with the Soviets soured (see below), Carter began a military buildup that raised the Pentagon's budget (in 1986 dollars) from $170 billion in 1976 to $197 billion in 1981.

Improved Relations with China

Continuing Nixon's policy of seeking better relations with Communist China, Carter sent Secretary of State Vance, in August 1977, and National Security Adviser Brzezinski, in May 1978, to China. "We have been allies before," Brzezinski told Chinese leaders, and "we should cooperate again in the face of . . . the emergence of the Soviet Union as a threat." Complaining that America was too afraid of offending Moscow, Chinese leader Deng Xiaoping urged America to take a stronger anti-Soviet stance.

In December 1979 Carter established full diplomatic relations with the People's Republic of China (PRC). This required breaking diplomatic relations with America's old ally, the Republic of China, on Taiwan. The agreement contained a U.S. statement of expectation that any settlement between the two Chinas would be made "peacefully and with patience," but this was not binding on Beijing (Peking). America withdrew troops from Taiwan and reduced arms sales but maintained "cultural, commercial, and other official relations with the people of Taiwan."

Although Nixon had led in reopening relations with the PRC, conservative Republicans condemned this recognition. Senator Barry Goldwater charged that it betrayed an ally, and Ronald Reagan said it "abandoned Taiwan to the Red Chinese." Goldwater and twenty-three senators brought a legal suit that (unsuccessfully) challenged the president's right to abrogate a treaty without the Senate's consent. Nevertheless, the Senate approved recognition by 85–4, and the House concurred, 339–50.

Brzezinski found the Russians "paranoid" on the subject of China. They demanded that America sell China no weapons.

At U.S. invitation, China's leader, Deng Xiaoping, visited America in February 1979 (see Fig. 15.2). After Mao's 1976 death ended the terrorism of Mao's "Cultural Revolution," Deng had reopened China to the West and adopted some free market reforms. Finding him "small, tough, intelligent, frank, courageous, self-assured, friendly," Carter called his visit "one of the delightful experiences of my presidency." Deng echoed Brzezinski's proposal for a virtual anti-Soviet alliance. "Since the early 1970s," he said, "the United States has been

Figure 15.2 Secretary General of China's Communist Party Deng Xiaoping visits President Carter in the White House. National Archives.

on the strategic retreat. . . . We consider that the true hotbed of war is the Soviet Union. . . . The only realistic thing for us is to unite." When asked about China's emigration policy, Deng humorously offered to allow 10 million Chinese to emigrate to America. When asked about opposition in China to normalizing relations, he replied, "Serious opposition in one Chinese province—Taiwan." Over the objections of Vance, who sought to avoid offending Russia, their communiqué expressed opposition to "hegemony."

In early 1980, America gave China most-favored-nation status, a status not yet extended to Russia, thereby cutting U.S. tariffs on Chinese goods and making China eligible for loans. In a separate agreement, America agreed to accept more Chinese textiles. Also, America sold China items that could be used to strengthen China militarily, including atomic energy plants, Boeing 707 jets, radar, helicopters, and advanced electronic spying equipment, all of which it denied to Russia. U.S. corporations entered joint business ventures with Chinese, ranging from hotels to major hydroelectric projects and oil exploration. China became the fourth largest buyer of U.S. farm products. By 1981, two-way trade totaled nearly $6 billion.

Scientific and cultural exchanges expanded briskly. In 1980, more than 7,000 American officials and tourists visited China, more than 100 Chinese delegations per month visited America, and 6,000 Chinese students attended American colleges and universities. By 1981, U.S. Fulbright professors were teaching in Chinese universities.

The two countries continued to disagree on Israel and Korea, but they cooperated against Soviet interests elsewhere. The Chinese urged NATO to build up its military strength, and America to maintain strong forces in East Asia. Both nations denounced the 1979 Soviet intervention in Afghanistan, and both supplied arms to the Afghans who were fighting Soviet troops. Both supported Pol Pot's forces in Cambodia against the Soviet-backed Vietnamese invaders. They also backed identical political and military factions in Africa.

In 1980, Secretary of Defense Harold Brown visited China. When the Chinese learned that America had changed its military preparedness goal from having the ability simultaneously to fight two major wars and a minor war ("two and a half-war strategy") to being ready to fight only one and a half wars, they objected until they were told that the war canceled was war with China! Chinese hospitality was legendary, and Carter wrote that all American leaders who visited China were "completely enchanted and grateful." In 1981, America offered to sell China weapons, and the Chinese allowed Americans to install electronic sensors on their territory to gather information on the Soviet military. Secretary of State Vance said that China was "friendly" and that America's self-interest in modernizing China was "clear."

Meanwhile, Vietnam made "friendly overtures" to America, and the Chinese indicated that they would welcome an improvement in U.S.-Vietnamese relations to help detach Hanoi from the Soviet camp. Carter sent a commission, including the labor leader Leonard Woodcock and Senator Mike Mansfield, to Hanoi and also opened talks with Vietnamese diplomats in Paris. The main issues were U.S. insistence that some Americans missing in the war were still in Vietnam, and Hanoi's demand that America honor Nixon's promise to provide aid. However, progress toward better relations was disrupted in late 1977 by Vietnam's invasion of Cambodia.

Later, Carter speculated on whether it might be better automatically to open diplomatic relations with any established government, whether or not America approved of its conduct. This, at least, he wrote, "would give us a toehold in the unfriendly country and an opportunity to ease tensions, increase American influence, and promote peace." This was the policy that America had followed before 1913, and it was standard European diplomatic practice.

The massive U.S. bombing sustained by Cambodia during the Vietnam War, followed by the savage civil war there, had left Cambodia's economy ruined and its people largely dependent on U.S. rice shipments, which stopped when the Communists seized the capital in April 1975. Cambodia was a "basket case," said one U.S. diplomat, but "it was not our basket case." Under these circumstances, massive suffering by Cambodians could hardly be avoided, but the suffering was compounded by Pol Pot's vengeance on city dwellers, and his draconian efforts to quickly establish an extreme form of communism. The number of resulting deaths was frightful—as many as 2 million. Even such antiwar liberals as Senator George McGovern called for an international expedition to rescue Cambodians from Pol Pot, whom Carter called the world's worst violator of human rights.

Nevertheless, when Vietnamese troops invaded Cambodia to replace the Pol Pot regime, Cold War considerations took precedence over human rights. Because both Americans and Chinese regarded Vietnam as a Soviet satellite, they both supported the atrocious Pol Pot. His fight against the Vietnamese, said Brzezinski, was a "proxy war between China and the Soviet Union." In January 1979, after the Vietnamese captured the Cambodian capital, America tacitly supported China's three-week punitive military invasion of Vietnam. America also voted to let Pol Pot take Cambodia's seat in the UN (70 nations voted for Pol Pot, while 69 voted against him or abstained). Vance, however, protested that these moves pushed Vietnam more deeply into the Soviet camp.

Moderation Regarding Latin America

When Carter took office, trade with Latin America was running at $60 billion annually, and U.S. investments in Latin America were approaching a total of $25 billion. While welcoming the economic benefits, many Latin Americans resented the control exercised by U.S. citizens over their economics and politics. They particularly resented any intrusion by Washington into their internal political affairs, which often took the form of supporting military dictators who followed policies favorable to the rich and to foreign investors. Also, Latin Americans demanded that the United States cut tariffs, pay more for their products, and put less emphasis on backing U.S. corporations.

As a candidate, Carter had promised to treat Latin Americans as equals. "We should get away permanently," he said, "from an attitude of paternalism or punishment." Most Latin Americans, said Brzezinski, regarded the Monroe Doctrine as "presumptuous U.S. paternalism." Somewhat contradictorily, Carter interfered in Latin America in support of human rights. For example, he withdrew U.S. support from the repressive military ruler of Chile and later, in attempts to pressure their governments into respecting human rights, suspended aid to Guatemala, El Salvador, and Bolivia.

Panama presented Carter with his most excruciating Latin American problem. The increasing number of ships too large to pass through the Panama Canal had somewhat reduced its importance, but 10 percent of U.S. trade still passed through the canal, and it was the most important spot outside U.S. territory to U.S. defense. Panamanians believed that they were not getting full value from their greatest national asset, and considered U.S. rule of the Canal Zone, a ten-mile-wide strip through the center of their nation, and the special privileges accorded the large U.S. military force stationed in Panama to be violations of Panamanian sovereignty. Though Panama was small and weak, Panamanians could endanger resident U.S. citizens and sabotage the canal. Also, so much sympathy for them existed elsewhere that a forceful crackdown could harm U.S. interests throughout Latin America.

Negotiations on meeting Panama's grievances had been conducted in the Johnson and Nixon administrations. A letter signed by seven Latin American presidents asked Carter to continue negotiations. Carter gave high priority to reaching agreement.

In treaties signed in September of his first year as president (1977), Carter agreed to raise annual payments for the canal to $20 million and to relinquish the Canal Zone to Panama in the year 2000. In return, Panama agreed to a permanent U.S. right to move its warships through the canal and to "defend [the canal's] neutrality" (keep it out of the hands of a hostile third country).

This treaty was unpopular in the United States. In a public opinion poll, 46 percent opposed and only 39 percent supported it. Opposition was particularly strong among conservatives and veteran's groups, who saw it as a reduction of America's world power. They believed that the canal belonged to the United States—Ronald Reagan called it "sovereign U.S. territory"—regardless of the methods by which it had been acquired. According to one U.S. senator, "we stole it fair and square."

The fight for the treaty was prolonged. Carter was aided by former President Gerald Ford, Henry Kissinger, Averell Harriman, Senate Democratic Leader Robert Byrd, Minority Leader Howard Baker, the actor John Wayne, and the National Association of Manufacturers. After the treaty was amended to enlarge U.S. rights to defend the canal, including the "use of military force in the Republic of Panama," and to give priority to the transit of U.S. warships in emergencies, the Senate ratified it by only one vote more than needed. Foreign policy experts considered it a major accomplishment that averted future trouble, and President Carlos Andres Perez of Venezuela called it the century's "most significant advance in political affairs in the Western Hemisphere." Nevertheless, in 1978, when 13 of the senators who had voted for it stood for reelection, 7 were defeated, and 11 more supporters lost in 1980.

Carter also sought to improve relations with Cuba. A memo by Secretary of State Vance advocated moving away from "our past policy of isolation. Our boycott has proved ineffective, and there has been a decline of Cuba's export of revolution." In March 1977, Carter opened the first U.S. negotiations with Castro in sixteen years. Lifting the ban on travel to Cuba, he also suspended spy flights over Cuba. The two countries reached agreement on fishing and airplane hijackings and, in September, exchanged small groups of official representatives they called "diplomatic interest sections." Castro released 3,600 political prisoners.

But, again, Cold War developments disrupted an incipient rapprochement. In January 1977, Colonel Haile-Maryam Mengistu seized power in Ethiopia and, declaring himself a Marxist, turned to the Soviet Union for aid. After Somalia invaded Ethiopia, Cuban troops went to the support of the Ethiopian government. Offended by this enlargement of Cuba's role in Africa, Washington maintained its embargo on Cuba.

In response to Carter's denunciation of Cuba's restrictions on emigration, Castro, in the spring of 1980, announced that any Cuban who wanted to go to the United States could leave by boat from the port of Mariel. About 125,000 Cubans did so, including many released from prisons and mental hospitals. "Fidel has flushed his toilet on us," exclaimed the mayor of Miami. Many "Mariel" Cubans were soon in U.S. prisons.

Carter also faced a difficult problem of how to respond to revolution in Nicaragua, a small, poverty-stricken country of 2.5 million people. With its $900 per capita income very unevenly distributed, the country contained great extremes of wealth and poverty. Since 1936, it had been ruled by the Somozas, father and then son, who, with U.S. support, headed a corrupt and oppressive but strongly anti-Communist regime that received U.S. military aid and cooperated with U.S. operations against Guatemala (1954), Cuba (1961), and the Dominican Republic (1965). Holding power with the aid of a large National Guard infamous for bloody suppression, the Somoza family corruptly gathered much of the nation's wealth into its own hands. A guerrilla opposition, the Sandinista National Liberation Front, which included both Communists and non-Communists, received growing support from church, student, and business groups. Nearly 50,000 thousand Nicaraguans died in the fighting between the government and its opponents.

Denouncing Somoza's human rights violations, Carter, in January 1979, halted military aid and cut economic aid to Nicaragua. However, his attempts to arrange a transfer of power to non-Sandinista moderates failed. Worried about Communist and Cuban involvement, Vance proposed that the OAS send a peacekeeping force, but no Latin American country would agree to such intervention. Despite his uneasiness, Carter refrained from interfering when the Sandinistas forced Somoza to flee in July 1979.

The new Sandinista regime was headed by Daniel Ortega, who was regarded in Washington as a Communist. Nevertheless, according to the State Department, it was "a broad and popular coalition" of mostly non-Communist elements. Carter immediately recognized the new government and, to encourage moderation, persuaded Congress, in July 1980, to extend it a $76 million loan. Mexico, Venezuela, and other Latin American countries also made loans. Ortega received aid from Cuba and accepted a number of Cuban advisers, but, promising to maintain a partly capitalist economy and a multiparty system, he left 60 percent of the economy in private hands.

However, U.S.-Nicaraguan relations were complicated by a Communist-backed insurgency in nearby El Salvador. In early 1981, accusing Nicaragua of supplying the El Salvador rebels, Carter stopped aid to Nicaragua.

El Salvador was smaller in area, but more densely populated than Nicaragua. Its 5 million people had an average income of only $750, 2 percent of them owned half of the land, 80 percent of the children were undernourished, and rich landlords ruled with the aid of the armed forces and right-wing death squads that assassinated opponents. Rebels, supported by the poorer peasants, conducted a guerrilla-type resistance. Protesting against human rights violations, Carter suspended aid for a time in 1977.

In October 1979, a group of moderate military officers and civilians who hoped that more enlightened policies would undercut support for the guerrillas installed the moderate José Napoleon Duarte as president, and announced a program of land reform. Nevertheless, wealthy Salvadorans blocked reform, guerrilla resistance continued, and right-wing death squads, with the support of elements of the army, continued their killing. U.S. Ambassador Robert White called these right-wingers "one of the most out-of-control, violent, bloodthirsty groups of men in the world." In March 1980, they murdered the Catholic Archbishop Oscar Armulfo Romero, and, in December, raped and murdered four U.S. nuns. More than 13,000 died in the fighting in 1980. Because of violations of human rights, Carter again cut off aid for a time in 1980, but he resumed it in 1981.

The guerrilla insurgency received arms from Communist sources, and many Americans feared that a rebel victory would put El Salvador under Communist control. But many U.S. church groups believed that the rebellion was caused not by Communists but by local injustice. To blame it on Cuba and the Soviet Union, said Mexico's president, was "an insult to our intelligence." "It is not at all a question of Communist subversion," said France's President Francois Mitterrand, but of "the people's refusal to submit to misery and humiliation." France and Mexico backed the rebels, but Washington tried hard to block all arms shipments to them. The fighting continued.

Human Rights and Cold War in Africa

When Carter took office, the U.S. economic stake in Africa was still relatively small, but growing. Americans had invested about $4 billion in black African countries, in addition to $1.7 billion in the white-ruled Union of South Africa. Trade totaled more than $30 billion annually, and Africa, particularly Nigeria, supplied about 40 percent of U.S. oil imports. On a 1978 trip to Africa, the first by a U.S. president, Carter told a Nigerian audience that he shared with them "a commitment to an Africa that is at peace, free from colonialism, free from racism, free from military interference by outside nations."

The point man for Carter's African policy was U.S. ambassador to the UN Andrew Young. Sympathetic to black Africa's efforts to free itself from remaining imperialism, Young believed that, because of their rising nationalism, Africans would reject subjugation to any foreign power, and he had little fear that the Soviets could take control in Africa. He recognized that black Africans would accept Soviet help in fighting imperialism, and that oppressive rule by white minorities gave the Soviets opportunities to win friends, but, convinced that this problem could not be met simply by killing Communists, he sought "African solutions to African problems." He was fully supported by Secretary of State Vance who said that the best course was to "help resolve the problems which create opportunities for external aggression."

In Rhodesia, white settlers, although less than 3 percent of the population, continued to maintain white rule over the black majority. To help the British pressure the whites into allowing majority rule, Carter restored the ban on the purchase of chrome from Rhodesia. Finally yielding to the growing pressures, the whites permitted an election in 1980, which produced a black Marxist president, Robert Mugabe. This ended a long civil war. Accepting the election of Mugabe, whose country was renamed Zimbabwe, Carter extended aid. Mugabe ruled with moderation and in August 1980 was received in the White House.

In 1977, war erupted on the east coast, in the so-called "Horn" of Africa south of the Red Sea. Marxist-ruled Ethiopia was invaded by Marxist-ruled Somalia in an attempt to take the Ogaden, a desert region peopled by ethnic Somalians. Both Ethiopia and Somalia had been receiving Soviet aid, but their war forced the Soviets to choose between them. Opting to back the larger Ethiopia, Moscow sent $1 billion, a thousand advisers, and 20,000 Cuban troops. National Security Adviser Zbigniew Brzezinski was much alarmed by what he saw as further Soviet penetration of a strategically important area. Denouncing Soviet and Cuban intervention, Carter, in 1980, gave aid to Somalia, even though he considered Somalia the aggressor. The war continued.

Carter was even more critical than his predecessors of the racial policies of the white-ruled Union of South Africa. When Vice President Walter Mondale visited South Africa, he warned that apartheid might "increase Soviet influence and even racial war." Calling on U.S. corporations to withdraw their investments, Carter supported a UN arms embargo, and stopped the sale of police equipment to South Africa. He also supported the efforts of Namibia to free itself from South Africa's control. But these pressures had little immediate effect.

Interpreting the continuing war in Angola in Cold War terms, Brzezinski wanted to increase aid to UNITA, that, with U.S. and South African support, was fighting the Soviet-supported Marxist government. On the other hand, Young and Vance believed that Cuban troops served mainly to defend Angola from South Africa and that they would withdraw if South Africa withdrew its forces. However, Carter said he would refuse to recognize the government of Angola as long as Cuban troops remained.

Overall, America fared reasonably well in relations with Africa during the Carter administration. Zambia's president praised Carter for bringing "a breath of fresh air to our troubled world." Soviet influence remained largely restricted to Ethiopia and Angola. Somalia expelled the Russians and allowed Americans to establish bases there. And when Russia invaded Afghanistan in 1979, many African countries voted with America in the UN to condemn the Soviet action.

A Step Toward Peace in the Middle East

In relations with the Middle East, Carter grappled with the same dilemmas that had troubled previous presidents: (1) how to retain the friendship of Arabs while financing and arming Israel, (2) how to arm Arabs against Russia without endangering Israel, (3) how to reverse Israeli aggression while supplying it with money and arms, and (4) how to achieve self-government for Palestinians over Israeli opposition. Reiterating the pledge of previous presidents to defend Israel, Carter also asked Israel to accept UN Resolution 242 which called on Israel to return the lands taken in the 1967 war in exchange for Arab peace treaties. Calling for a "homeland" for Arab Palestinians, he objected to Israel's policy of settling Jews in the Arab lands that Israeli armies had overrun in 1967; America considered these settlements illegal, and Vance called them "obstacles to peace." Carter sold weapons, including advanced fighter planes, not only to Israel but to Egypt and Saudi Arabia.

In May 1977, Israel chose as its prime minister Menachem Begin, an extreme nationalist and former terrorist, who accelerated the program of settling Jews in the occupied territories and insisted that these settlements were permanent.

Despite advice that Middle East problems were so difficult that any attempt to arrange peace was sure to fail, Carter threw himself into an effort to achieve a settlement. First he sought to reconvene the Geneva Conference of several nations, including Russia, which had been suspended since 1973. In October 1977, Washington and Moscow jointly issued a call for it to meet, but this move was stymied by Arab demands that the Palestinian Liberation Organization (PLO) be invited and by Israel's refusal to discuss the return of occupied territories.

The impasse was broken by Egypt's Premier Anwar al-Sadat. When he and Carter met in April 1977, they established a quick rapport. "A shining light burst on the Middle East for me," Carter wrote in his memoirs, "a man who would change history and whom I would come to admire more than any other leader." Carter considered him a "close personal friend." Deciding to break away from the solid Arab anti-Israel front, Sadat, with Carter's help, secured an invitation to visit Israel, where, in November 1977, he addressed Israel's parliament. It was a sensational move. He was the first leading Arab official to accept the existence of a Jewish state in Palestine, a move that was bitterly condemned by other Arabs and the Soviets.

In Israel, Sadat admitted that the nation of Israel was an "established fact" and called for peace, but he also restated Arab demands—return of the occupied lands, Israeli negotiation with the PLO, and establishment of a Palestinian homeland. His visit received high praise in America.

After conferring separately with Begin and Sadat, Carter invited both to meet with him at his Maryland retreat, Camp David. They remained at Camp David for twelve days, from September 5 to September 17, 1978. With the aid of Vance, Brzezinski, and State Department Middle East experts, Carter made a deep study of the issues and participated fully in the discussions. "Your president is a wonderful man," said the Israeli foreign minister. "He is constantly learning . . . always writing out formulas and revising them. . . . His will not to fail is fantastic." Arguments were so heated that, after the third day, Begin and Sadat stopped meeting each other, and Carter acted as go-between. Several times it appeared that the conference had failed. Nevertheless, in the end, they signed a "General Program" as a basis for future negotiations. It called for Egypt to grant diplomatic recognition to Israel, and for Israel to give Palestinians self-government and to return the Sinai Peninsula to Egypt. Although far short of a full settlement, this was a major breakthrough and, said Carter, one of the "bright moments of human history"—"we have a chance for peace." (See Fig. 15.3.)

Figure 15.3 Egypt's President Anwar el-Sadat and Israel's Prime Minister Menachem Begin with President Carter at Camp David. National Archives.

In early 1979, after the Israeli-Egyptian negotiations stalled, Carter traveled to the Middle East and cajoled, threatened, and bribed the two into completing a treaty which was signed at the White House on March 26. It set a timetable for Israel to withdraw in stages from Egyptian territory. Inaugurating full diplomatic relations, Egypt gave Israel the right to use the Suez Canal. Carter promised $5 billion in military and economic aid to the two countries, and they arranged for a UN force and U.S. planes to monitor the border.

In the first treaty between Jews and Arabs, Egypt had recovered its lost territories, while Israel, by detaching the most powerful Arab state from the ranks of its enemies, had greatly improved its security. Without Egypt's help, other Arab countries could not soon acquire sufficient military strength to defeat Israel. Bitterly denouncing Sadat, most of them broke diplomatic and trade relations with Egypt.

Carter and Sadat said they had Begin's commitment to halt further Jewish settlement of the occupied lands, but, instead, the Israelis stepped up such settlement, thereby indicating their determination never to return the land. This enraged all Arabs, including Sadat.

U.S. involvement in the Middle East was proving to be costly. By 1981, direct U.S. military and economic aid to the region since 1945 totaled $18.5 billion.

A Flare-up in the Cold War

The Carter-Brezhnev embrace at the end of the June 1979 Vienna summit marked the high point of detente in the Carter administration. Relations worsened thereafter. In August 1979, Washington discovered a Soviet combat brigade, 2,500 troops, stationed in Cuba. Carter said that this was "not acceptable." The Soviets replied that these were training troops and that no change had occurred in their number or character since 1962. Further U.S. investigation revealed that the Soviet statement was correct—apparently the U.S. government had forgotten about them. Nevertheless, public indignation in America aroused by this acrimonious exchange delayed ratification of the SALT II treaty.

The arms race continued. The Soviets emplaced new SS-20 intermediate-range ballistic missiles (IRBMs), with three independently-targeted warheads and improved accuracy, in Eastern Europe. In response, Carter persuaded the NATO allies to accept installation of new U.S. Pershing III IRBMs capable of reaching targets in Russia. This represented a major escalation of striking power by both sides. Later, the Soviet ambassador called Russia's decision to install the SS-20s a major mistake. The Soviet military had sought to neutralize a Western advantage, but the effect, instead, was a Western deployment that worsened Soviet inferiority and costs.

In the late 1970s, it appeared to alarmists that Communists were making significant gains. In 1975, Communists completed the takeover of Vietnam, Cambodia, and Laos. In 1976, they seemed to be winning in Angola; in 1977, they supplanted the United States in Ethiopia; in 1978, Communists came to power in Afghanistan. Meanwhile, Americans were ejected from Iran.

Soviet military intervention in Afghanistan in December 1979 plunged Soviet-American relations to their lowest point in years. Afghanistan, a dry, mountainous, underdeveloped nation the size of Texas, with a population of 15 million, lies south of central Russia and also borders Iran, Pakistan, and China. It had remained neutral in the Cold War. However, in April 1978, Marxists staged a coup and installed a Communist as president. America recognized this government but, denying its request for aid, supported Islamic fundamentalists and mountain tribe leaders who rebelled against its policies of land reform, modernization, and emancipation of women. To avert the defeat of a Marxist regime in a nation on their border by U.S.-backed Islamic fundamentalists, the Soviets, in December 1979, sent 85,000 troops into Afghanistan, the first entry of Soviet troops into an area outside the Warsaw Pact. The UN Security Council condemned the Soviet action by a vote of 13 to 2.

The Soviets claimed that their troops had entered "at the request" of a friendly government, but Washington called the move an invasion. Denouncing it as immoral and a threat to the oil-rich Persian Gulf, Carter, on the hot line, told Brezhnev that it could cause a "fundamental and long-lasting" change in their relations. Publicly, he called it "a stepping stone" to possible Soviet control over much of the world's oil, a threat to America's security, and the "gravest threat to peace since World War II." It had caused a "dramatic change," he said, in his opinion concerning Russia's "ultimate goals." (Raising the specter of Communist world domination, explained Brzezinski, seemed to be a "desirable and justified simplification" to arouse popular support for Carter's policy.)

To punish the Soviets, Carter dismantled most of the cooperative arrangements that had been painfully constructed under detente. He canceled Soviet fishing rights in U.S. waters, stopped the sale of U.S. wheat and high-technology items, told the Senate to postpone indefinitely consideration of the SALT treaty, and canceled cultural exchanges, including U.S. participation in the Summer Olympic Games in Moscow. U.S.-Soviet trade plunged from $4.5 billion in 1979 to $2 billion in 1980. Also, Carter increased aid to the Afghanistan rebels, accelerated U.S. defense spending, reintroduced draft registration, shipped more arms to Pakistan, and began selling military equipment to China. Thus, the Brzezinski hard line prevailed as Carter took the most hostile anti-Soviet stand since John Foster Dulles.

Afghanistan extended to within three hundred miles of the Persian Gulf, through which passed one-third of America's, two-thirds of Western Europe's, and three-fourths of Japan's oil imports. In what came to be known as the "Carter Doctrine," the president, in a January 1980 address, proclaimed U.S. determination to keep that vital waterway out of hostile hands. "An attempt by any outside force to gain control of the Persian Gulf," he said, would be considered "an assault on the vital interests of the United States," to be "repelled by any means necessary, including military force."

America's European allies seemed much less alarmed. In their view, Carter had overreacted. They would not permit, said Germany's Chancellor Schmidt, ten years of detente and arms control to be destroyed. They sent their athletes to the Moscow Olympics and increased their trade with the Soviet Union.

The Iran Hostage Crisis

Surprisingly, foreign affairs in Carter's last year in office were dominated, not by renewed Cold War, but by a bitter dispute with Iran, long an enemy of Russia and a staunch ally of America. This was a striking example of the extent to which international relations had ceased to be bipolar. It also demonstrated the limits of U.S. power, and damaged Carter politically.

Situated between the Soviet Union and the Persian Gulf, Iran is the Middle East's most populous nation. Although Moslem, its people are not Arab and speak an Indo-European language related to the languages of Europe. Its oil production is second in the Middle East only to that of Saudi Arabia. Its government was a monarchy, but a modern one headed by Shah Mohammed Reza Pahlevi, who had inherited the throne in 1941 (see Fig. 15.4).

After World War II, the leading figure in the Iranian government had been Prime Minister Mohammed Mossadegh, a Western-educated nationalist who seized Iranian oil refineries from their British owners. In 1953, when his grow-

Figure 15.4 The Shah of Iran, here seen entertaining Nixon and his wife, was a close ally of America. National Archives.

ing power threatened the shah, the CIA helped organize strikes and demonstrations that forced Mossadegh to flee, whereupon the shah gave U.S. companies a 40 percent share in Iran's oil production.

America's desire to strengthen the nations that abutted Russia coincided with the shah's desire to make Iran a great military power. A strong pro-American Iran could help check Soviet expansion, protect the Persian Gulf, serve as a reliable source of oil, and offer a fertile field for U.S. trade and investments. Iran became America's chief partner in the region, and soon seventy thousand Americans lived in that country. The CIA helped train and arm the shah's secret police, the SAVAK, which ruthlessly suppressed opposition to the shah; according to Amnesty International no country had a worse record on human rights. Presidents Eisenhower, Nixon, Ford, and Carter gave or sold Iran practically all the weapons the shah requested; sales totaling $19.5 billion between 1972 and 1979 helped alleviate America's balance of payment problems and made Iran the region's greatest military power.

The shah was Western-educated and a modernizer. With the advice of U.S. experts, he constructed irrigation works and, in a "white revolution," carried out some land reform, promoted modern industry and education, and gave women the vote. But popular support eluded him. His introduction of Western ways offended orthodox Moslems, his expensive lifestyle and huge military spending alienated those who sought more help for the poor, and his increasingly dictatorial and corrupt government offended those who advocated democracy.

When Carter visited Iran in December 1977, he gave the shah fulsome praise. His "great leadership," said Carter, had made Iran "an island of stability" and won the "respect and admiration and love" of the Iranian people. With no other nation, said Carter, did America have a closer military relationship, and for no other leader did he have "a deeper sense of personal gratitude and personal friendship."

But the shah faced rising opposition. His opponents included fundamentalist Moslem clergy, a small Communist party, and nationalists who were offended by his close partnership with America. His leading opponent, the Ayatollah Ruhollah Khomeini, charged that "the oil revenues have at no time been spent to serve the people's interests." Instead, he said, the shah served "the interests of the oil companies, and the rich consumer countries . . . who plunder our resources, impose on us the purchase of weapons, and then set up on our lands military bases to defend these interests." Street demonstrations became increasingly violent and met increasingly bloody repression which, in turn, aroused more hatred of both shah and America—"Carter gives the guns, the shah kills the people." In August 1978 "all hell broke loose," with troops firing on demonstrators and strikes reducing oil production below even the level of Iranian consumption.

Aghast at these developments, Carter was perplexed about how to respond. He wrote that Americans "knew little" about anti-shah forces other than that they used anti-American slogans. State Department experts advised that the shah was doomed, Vance recommended that Carter negotiate a compromise political solution, and some U.S. diplomats suggested that the shah abdicate in favor of his son. On the other hand, maintaining that the shah's fall would be a political calamity, Brzezinski backed the shah's use of military force against his enemies. Carter "encouraged him to hang tough and to count on our backing." The shah declared martial law, and his troops killed many demonstrators, but, despite U.S. help, his position crumbled and, on January 15, 1979, he fled. Kissinger called U.S. failure to save him "the biggest foreign policy debacle for the United States in a generation."

On February 1, 1979, the Ayatollah Khomeini, the eighty-one-year-old leader of the fundamentalist Moslems, returned from exile to be greeted by enormous crowds. Taking no formal position in the government, he allowed a representative of the middle class, Mehdi Bazargan, to be prime minister, but throughout the country Khomeini's followers, executing opponents, emerged as the dominant group. Denouncing America as the "Great Satan," Khomeini utilized anti-Americanism against Iranian westernizers, and forced Americans to withdraw from spying stations near the Soviet border. In February 1979, Carter recognized the new government, but the Senate, in May, condemned Khomeini's execution of his foes.

When the shah fled, he went first to Egypt, then to Morocco, then to Mexico. He did not abdicate, and many Iranians, vividly remembering that in 1953, when Mossadegh threatened the shah, the CIA had restored the shah to power, feared that with U.S. support, he might attempt to return. By October 1979 he was ill with cancer and needed treatment not then available in Mexico. Brzezinski, David Rockefeller, and Kissinger urged Carter to allow him to enter a hospital in New York. Carter feared that admitting him would so agitate his enemies that it would put Americans in Iran in danger. But humanitarian considerations were compelling and, although the U.S. embassy in Teheran warned that admitting the shah would endanger Americans there, Carter, having received assurances from Prime Minister Bazargan that the embassy would be protected, gave him permission to enter the United States.

The shah entered a U.S. hospital on October 23. This, said Iran's foreign minister, was "as if Franco's Spain had offered to treat Hitler." On November 1, 3 million demonstrators marched on the U.S. embassy in Teheran. On November 4, about three thousand student followers of Khomeini stormed the U.S. embassy and seized seventy-six diplomats and military personnel. Unable to secure their release, Bazargan resigned.

Of course, this seizure violated the age-old custom of diplomatic immunity. Condemning it, both the UN and the World Court called for immediate and unconditional release. The American people were stunned by television views of huge crowds shouting their fanatical hatred of America and enraged by reports that the hostages were mistreated. And they were frustrated when the American government proved unable to free them.

For the next fourteen and a half months, Carter made freeing the hostages his top priority. Halting the importation of Iranian oil and the sale of U.S. goods to Iran, he froze more than $10 billion in Iranian funds and property, and he unsuccessfully urged U.S. allies to join the embargo. The enormous attention given to the hostages by the U.S. president and the media (ABC started a new 11:30 P.M. program, "America Held Hostage") had the unintended effect of enhancing the value to the Iranians of holding them, and the political damage to Carter of failing to free them.

At first, it was not clear what the militants wanted. Eventually, it appeared that they were demanding that America return the shah and his wealth to Iran and apologize for past U.S. interference in Iran's internal affairs. The December 1979 departure of the shah from America did not mollify them. As usual, Carter got conflicting advice. Vance, putting a high value on saving lives, advocated patient negotiations. Brzezinski, more concerned with upholding national honor and demonstrating U.S. strength, urged military action even if that risked the hostages' lives.

After long delay, Carter, in April 1980, broke diplomatic relations and secretly ordered a rescue attempt. On April 25, ninety Americans on eight U.S. helicopters and six transport planes departed for a rendezvous on an isolated Iranian desert. The plan was to transfer the men to trucks for a raid on the embassy and then to fly out the hostages. But wind-blown sand and mechanical failure disabled three of the helicopters and forced Carter to abort the mission. Eight Americans died when two planes collided on take-off.

The Iranians responded by quickly moving the hostages to scattered secret locations. Vance, who had argued that the rescue mission, even if successful, would result in the death of hostages, endanger other Americans in Iran, and worsen relations, resigned in protest, the first secretary of state since William Jennings Bryan to resign on a matter of principle. By July, public disapproval of Carter's foreign policy had reached 82 percent.

The shah died in Egypt in July 1980. On September 4, Iraq invaded Iran, increasing Iran's need for the money that America had seized. The Iranian parliament authorized negotiations and, working hard, Carter had an agreement completed before he left office in January 1981. It provided that America would release $8 billion, two-thirds of the frozen assets, while reserving one-third for possible claims for damages by U.S. corporations, in return for release of the hostages. Iran dropped its demands for the return of the shah's wealth and for an apology. On January 20, 1981, a few minutes after Carter left office, the hostages, captive for 444 days, boarded aircraft to fly out of Iran.

The crisis was over, but America had lost a powerful ally. Also, the resultant oil shortage had more than doubled the price of oil and more than doubled U.S. inflation; already high at 7 percent, it rose to 15 percent in 1979.

Other aspects of Carter's foreign policy were also widely criticized. The perception was widespread that America's power was slipping, and many put at least part of the blame on Carter. Organizing the Committee on the Present Danger, right-wingers, including many Democrats, demanded that America take a more forceful stand against its foreign enemies. In a mid-1980 poll, Americans expressed disapproval of Carter's handling of the Iran hostage crisis by a margin of 79–19, his handling of Cuban refugees by 83–16, and his overall conduct of foreign policy by 82–17 percent.

Carter had upheld traditional American democratic ideals with some effect. His dropping of the policy of automatic intervention against revolutions did much to restore America's reputation in the Third World. He could take credit for bringing about a peace treaty between Israel and Egypt, improving relations with China, and negotiating the Panama treaty and SALT II. However, some international problems remained impervious to well-intentioned idealism, and the increasingly assertive Soviets actively challenged the United States for influence in Africa and, for the first time, sent their troops into a nation outside their post–World War II sphere. Meanwhile, U.S. hard-liners maintained a drumfire of condemnation of Carter for not taking a tougher stand. Late in his administration, he shifted from agreement with Vance to support of Brzezinski's hard line; by the end of his administration, detente had been replaced by confrontation and a renewed arms race.

To some diplomatic historians, it might appear that Carter's lack of background in international politics made him underestimate the difficulty of implementing ideals within a system of amoral anarchy. But perhaps the Egyptian-Israeli agreement could have been accomplished only by someone who did not know that it could not be done. He took pride, as had Thomas Jefferson, that no American died in combat during his term. In general, his administration was marked by agreements reached rather than by enemies destroyed and was more satisfactory to those who wished America to stand for humanitarian and democratic values than to those who advocated the use of more amoral force. A poll taken in 1995 gave him an above-average rating as president.

16 Reagan: Cold War and Counterrevolution

The Election of 1980

As the election of 1980 neared, Jimmy Carter was in deep political trouble. In a time of postwar reaction, his moderately liberal principles were out of phase with the public mood. His foreign policy successes brought little popularity—many regarded the Panama treaty as a giveaway, his Camp David accord as unproductive, and his effort to free the Iranian-held hostages as inept. A July Harris Poll showed approval of his presidency at only 22 percent, the lowest level ever recorded.

Carter was challenged for the Democratic nomination by Massachusetts Senator Edward Kennedy, who, in early polls, led among Democrats by a two-to-one margin, but Kennedy was hurt in the primaries by his reputation for liberalism. Insisting that the hostage crisis required all of his time, Carter refused to debate, and he easily won renomination.

Victory in the Republican primaries went to the genial and handsome former film actor and California governor Ronald Reagan, a spokesman for right-wing positions on economic and international issues. Although his strongest opponent in the primaries, George Bush, had called his proposals "voodoo economics," Reagan chose Bush as his running mate. Denouncing detente, the platform demanded military superiority and condemned aid to any Marxist regime.

"Is the United States stronger and more respected than it was five and a half years ago?" Reagan asked. Charging that America was "in decline," Reagan promised to "make America great again," to dump the "one-sided" SALT II treaty, and to launch a massive arms buildup to reclaim military superiority. Calling the Soviet Union the cause of all of the world's unrest, he promised to impose harsher sanctions on Cuba, and to send more arms to Taiwan.

Carter charged that Reagan's positions were so bellicose that the choice before the electorate was between peace and war, but in the election, Reagan won 51 percent of the votes to Carter's 41 percent. Also defeated, as Republicans captured the Senate, were leading liberal senators George McGovern, Frank Church, and Birch Bayh. If he had bombed Teheran, Carter said later, he would have been reelected.

The Reagan Team

Reagan had majored in economics at Eureka College, played football, and worked as a sports announcer and an actor, appearing in approximately fifty films. As president of the Screen Actors Guild, he had fought Communists in that union and, as host of the General Electric television program, became a traveling spokesman for business. In 1966, he won election to the first of his two terms as governor of California, administrations notable for opposition to spending for welfare and education. A number of wealthy friends groomed him for the presidency, but he lost a 1968 bid to Nixon and a 1976 race to Ford before, at age sixty-nine, capturing the 1980 Republican nomination. With an amiable and easygoing style, he was an effective communicator who brought star quality to the role of president, but he had no experience in and, except for anticommunism, little interest in foreign affairs. Bush said that he was startled to find Reagan's thought dominated by "Hollywood cliches" and ideas garnered from his wealthy but poorly educated California friends.

For secretary of state, Reagan named General Alexander M. Haig, whom Nixon, in what he meant as a compliment, had called "the meanest, toughest S.O.B. I ever knew." Haig shared Reagan's hawkish views: "There are more important things than peace," he said. He impressed the Soviet ambassador as "a military man by information and behavior" and "confrontational." There could be no negotiations, Haig said, until the Soviets moderated their behavior and reined in their client states, such as Cuba and Libya. Claiming that he was the administration's "vicar" for foreign affairs, he was soon involved in bruising battles with all rivals, including Reagan's White House staff, for sole control of foreign policy. Reagan concluded that "he didn't want to carry out the president's foreign policy, he wanted to formulate it and carry it out himself."

In June 1982, the abrasive Haig was replaced as Secretary of State by George Shultz, a Massachusetts Institute of Technology Ph.D., an economics professor, Nixon's secretary of the treasury, and president of an international construction firm. Associates called Shultz impassive, stolid, and pragmatic. Although strongly anti-Communist, he sometimes served as a counterweight to the administration's ideological zealots, whom he called "hard-line cavemen with their muscle-bound approach to the Kremlin," by maintaining that military confrontation with communism should not preclude diplomatic negotiations.

Rejecting Henry Kissinger as tainted by detente, Reagan named Richard V. Allen, business consultant and zealous anti-communist, as White House national security adviser. But neither Allen nor his successors, William B. Clark (1981–1983), Robert McFarlane (1983–1985), Admiral John M. Poindexter (1985–1986), Frank Carlucci (1986–1987) and General Colin Powell (1987–1989), achieved the same control of foreign affairs, or publicity, previously enjoyed by Kissinger. (See Fig. 16.1.)

Secretary of Defense Caspar W. Weinberger, who had served with Reagan in California and as Nixon's budget director, proved to be the administration's

Figure 16.1 Secretary of Defense Caspar Weinberger, Secretary of State George Shultz, Attorney General Edward Meese, and Secretary of the Treasury Donald Regan in the Oval Office with President Reagan. Courtesy Ronald Reagan Library.

most extreme anti-Communist and an unceasing advocate of a major defense buildup. His mission, he said, was to "rearm America."

As ambassador to the UN, Reagan appointed Georgetown University professor Jeane J. Kirkpatrick, a defender of right-wing forces in Third World countries, and of U.S. policies against Third World criticism. Her debating style was heavy and tendentious. "Five minutes with her," said NBC television anchor Bryant Gumbel, "can seem like an eternity."

William Casey, who had served in the OSS, held high positions in the Nixon administration, and directed Reagan's 1980 campaign, was appointed to head the CIA. His anticommunism was so extreme that it aroused Shultz's concern that his ideology might distort his intelligence reports.

Political and Military Policy Shifts

At first, Reagan's foreign policy seemed strongly ideological. Rejecting detente, he charged that the Soviet Union was an "evil empire" and "the focus of evil in the modern world." "Americans," he wrote later, were defending "democracy and freedom," while the Soviets were "evil men" engaged in "immoral and unbridled expansionism." In his view the Russians had taken advantage of detente to overcome America's once great military lead and to project their power abroad in pursuit of their goal of conquering the world for communism. According to an aide, he saw "the world in black and white terms." In a 1982 speech to the British Parliament, he called for "a global campaign for freedom" that would "leave Marxism-Leninism on the ashheap of history." The Soviet ambassador found him uninterested in negotiations—preferring, instead, "recrimination conducted in public." He obsessively viewed all international events in terms of confrontation with the Soviet Union, the Soviet ambassador wrote, "restricting America's foreign policy to a gross and even primitive anti-Sovietism," and he was "unwilling to reach any agreement whatever." In his first two years he did not meet with the Soviet ambassador or any Soviet official.

Anticommunism dominated Reagan's policies regarding Third World nations. It was time, he said, to put an end to "self-doubts" and to assert America's "ideals and interests" throughout the world. Calling the Vietnam War a "noble cause," he stepped up intervention and covert action in the Third World.

Many intellectuals considered Reagan's election to be a foreign relations disaster. To them, he appeared to be uneducated and unlikely to remedy his deficiencies. They regarded his concept of an apocalyptic struggle between evil Reds and the free world as dangerously simplistic. *New York Times* columnist Anthony Lewis described his tendency to "dehumanize Russians and to treat the U.S.S.R. as an undifferentiated conspiratorial mass," as "anti-Communist zealotry carried beyond rationality." George F. Kennan called it "intellectual primitivism."

However, Reagan was popular with the electorate, many of whom, no better educated in history and world affairs than he, shared his view of world affairs. Explaining world problems in simple terms that common people could understand, Reagan assured them that America was on the side of the angels, standing tall and vigilant against the forces of evil. And, he promised, America would recover its former margin of superiority and resume its mission of reforming the world. He often seemed lazy and confused on the details of international controversies, but, poised, amiable, and consistent, he spoke with conviction and seemed to have no misgivings. Unlike Carter, he was not known for hard work, reading books, or attention to detail, and, while setting general policy, he delegated much authority. His White House chief of staff called him the "most affable and passive of presidents," and a national security adviser marveled that "he knew so little and accomplished so much." Nevertheless, his overwhelming popularity cowed his opponents and made him a strong president who dominated U.S. domestic and foreign policy to a remarkable degree.

In the first part of his administration, Reagan showed no interest in arms limitation. He enlarged the navy and the rapid deployment forces designed to act against Third World enemies. Calling for military superiority, Reagan, in history's largest peacetime military buildup, raised military spending (in constant dollars) 70 percent, from $174 billion in 1980 to nearly $300 billion in 1988.

When Reagan took office, the Soviets were installing SS-20 intermediate-range three-warhead missiles in Europe. After obtaining approval from America's European allies, Reagan announced a plan to more than match them with additional U.S. cruise missiles and Pershing II IRBMS. However, at the same time, he offered a "zero option," a proposal that both sides remove all inter-mediate-range missiles from Europe, which would require the Soviets to de-stroy 613 and America to refrain from installing 572 such missiles. As expected, this was more than the Russians were ready to concede, but it reduced Euro-pean opposition to the U.S. deployment of IRBMs.

By the 1980s, both the Americans and the Soviets had so many virtually unstoppable ballistic missiles that not even a surprise attack could deprive ei-ther of the ability to annihilate the attacker. Early in his presidency, U.S. intel-ligence informed Reagan that even a "victorious" war with Russia would leave at least 150 million Americans dead. Nevertheless, in 1981 U.S. defense forces were ordered to prepare themselves not only to deter but to "prevail" in an atomic war. In March 1983, with encouragement from physicist Edward Teller and the Joint Chiefs, Reagan called on U.S. scientists to develop a space-based defense system, which he called "Strategic Defense Initiative" (SDI) (and jour-nalists dubbed "Star Wars") of satellites armed with lasers and particle beams capable of destroying Soviet missiles in flight. If successful, such a system could restore U.S. ability to destroy Russia without itself being destroyed—the situ-ation, said Weinberger, "when we were the only nation with the nuclear weapon."

Many scientists doubted SDI's technical feasibility. Even if it could stop nearly all enemy missiles, the few that would get through could destroy much of America. Instead of a space shield, said former President Nixon, SDI would be a "space sieve." Nevertheless, the Soviets were much disturbed by the pro-posal. To them, it appeared that Reagan was designing the U.S. military to fight and win an atomic war. Also, the system could increase the incentive for both sides to make a first strike in the hope of slashing the number of en-emy missiles to the number that could be shot down by antimissile weapons. Soviet Foreign Minister Andrei Gromyko accused the president of a "patho-logical obsession with military force." Finally, SDI would be fantastically ex-pensive (by 1996, America had spent $40 billion on preinstallation prepara-tions), and, if the Soviets were forced to match it, the cost would further strain their already over-stressed economy. A 1986 Politburo resolution would de-nounce America for trying to "exhaust" the Soviet Union through economic and military pressure, and, in his 1993 memoirs, Reagan's national security adviser Robert McFarlane would write that the SDI program was adopted for the purpose of bankrupting the Soviet Union, a purpose, he said, that it achieved.

The enormous nuclear buildup by America and Russia aroused increasing protests in America and abroad. Alarmed by Reagan's apparent assumption that a nuclear war could be won, organizations, including the Roman Catholic Bishops of the United States, the World Council of Churches, SANE-FREEZE, the Union of Concerned Scientists, and the American Medical Association, stepped up their demands for restraint. In June 1982, 500,000 people assembled in New York for an antinuclear demonstration, and huge antinuclear weapon demonstrations occurred in Europe. "Cease this madness," implored George F. Kennan. A sixth of the U.S. Senate and a third of the House endorsed a nuclear freeze. But negotiations between the superpowers to control the atomic arms race stalled.

Back to Cold War

Reagan waged Cold War at high intensity. Rejecting detente, he took the offensive against Communist-affiliated groups in developing countries and he cut U.S.-Soviet trade and cultural exchanges. Also, he escalated the challenge to Soviet control in Eastern Europe. America would not accept, he said, "permanent subjugation of the people of Eastern Europe." In June 1983, Russia's President Yuri Andropov said that Reagan had brought "confrontation, unprecedented in the entire postwar period by its intensity and sharpness." Reagan's aim, he added, was "U.S. domination of the world."

In Gdansk, Poland, workers formed an unauthorized labor union, called "Solidarity," under the presidency of a personable ship worker, Lech Walesa. Calling for free elections and greater independence from Russia, Solidarity quickly mushroomed to a membership of 10 million, and its growth threatened the Communist party's monopoly of power. Reagan warned the Soviets against sending troops to crush the union. In late 1981, when Poland's Communist government imposed martial law and suppressed Solidarity's strikes and demonstrations, Reagan cut grain sales and suspended Poland's most-favored-nation trading status, but he could not persuade other Europeans countries to join him in these sanctions, most of which he lifted in 1984. Thus, Reagan was forced to concede in practice that Poland was within the Soviet sphere. However, though defeated and outlawed, Solidarity did not disappear, and Lech Walesa was visited by Pope Paul II and awarded the 1983 Nobel Peace Prize.

Meanwhile, the Soviets were building a long pipeline for transporting natural gas from Siberia to Western Europe, for which project they sought the West's latest technology and equipment. The French and the British welcomed greater access to Siberian gas to reduce their dependence on Middle East oil, but Washington, fearing that the pipeline would strengthen the Soviet Union's finances and influence in Europe, forbade Europeans to resell U.S.-made equipment or technology for use in constructing it. In 1982, the European Economic Community condemned these U.S. efforts as "unacceptable interference in EEC affairs." The pipeline, from Siberia to France, was completed in 1984.

Soviet-U.S. relations hit a new low in September 1983, when Korean Airlines Flight 007 from Alaska to Korea strayed 350 miles into Soviet territory over sensitive military installations and was shot down by a Soviet air-to-air missile, killing all 269 on board, including 60 Americans. Reagan charged that the Soviets had deliberately killed unarmed civilians in a "crime against humanity," an unspeakable "act of barbarism," and Jeane Kirkpatrick called it "deliberate murder." The Russians, in turn, accused the West of sending a civilian airliner over key defense installations to spy. Privately, Soviet Premier Yuri Andropov admitted that downing the plane was a "gross blunder." Subsequent investigations, including a 1993 UN report, revealed that the Soviets had assumed that it was a military plane, but these investigations did not clarify why the plane had flown deeply inside Russia, why it was not warned by U.S. and Japanese monitors, and why it took evasive action. The historian Raymond Garthoff concluded that to the suspicious the circumstantial evidence that the airliner was used for military reconnaissance "would seem compelling." Reagan ordered a halt to commercial flights between Russia and America. Much mutual ill will lingered.

Under William C. Casey, the CIA actively conducted covert operations in the Third World. Dropping Carter's emphasis on human rights, Reagan endorsed Kirkpatrick's distinction between "totalitarian" Communist dictatorships, which, she said, were permanent, and merely authoritarian dictatorships, which were open to U.S. investments and could possibly evolve into less oppressive regimes. Reagan backed right-wing dictators no matter how abominable their human rights violations as barriers to the establishment of left-wing regimes, and he sought to overthrow left-leaning governments.

In 1985, in what became known as the "Reagan Doctrine," the president emphasized that America would aid armed groups, "freedom fighters," in developing countries who were fighting communism. "We must not break faith," he said in his 1985 State of the Union message, "with those who are risking their lives—on every continent, from Afghanistan to Nicaragua—to defy Soviet-supported aggression. . . . Support for freedom fighters is self-defense." Enlarging the navy and the rapid deployment forces designed to fight in Third World areas, he implemented this "Reagan Doctrine" in Latin America, Africa, and South Asia.

Latin America

Increasing rapidly, Latin America's population by 1950 equaled the U.S. population. Many Latin Americans, particularly from Mexico and Central America, migrated to the United States, helping to make Hispanic Americans the most rapidly growing group in the U.S. population.

Although some Latin American nations developed modern economies, problems from their colonial past persisted. According to Assistant Secretary of State for Latin American Affairs Elliot Abrams, they were plagued by "inherited inequalities between the landed rich and the landless poor." Large shares of their economies were owned by foreigners who preempted much of the profits. Nevertheless, between 1960 and 1980, Latin America's population and per capita income both doubled. A growing middle class of businesspeople and professionals challenged dominant landlords and added to revolutionary pressures. Kennedy had emphasized the need to correct the basic problems that produced violent revolutions, but Reagan emphasized the forcible repression of Communists and their allies. Between 1980 and 1988, per capita income in Latin America fell 10 percent.

The counterrevolutionary crusade in Latin America was intensified by the conviction, in the tradition of the Monroe Doctrine, that the United States deserved to dominate the Western Hemisphere and by the fear that a "Moscow-Havana axis" might pose a threat to U.S. Caribbean trade routes and military security and thereby reduce America's ability to act boldly against Communists in other areas of the world. Failure to stop communism in central America, Reagan maintained, would destroy U.S. credibility and cause its world-wide alliances to "crumble."

Victory in Grenada

In Grenada, a small (100,000-population) Caribbean island that is nominally affiliated with Britain, Maurice Bishop, a Marxist, took power in 1979 and requested advisers from Cuba. The distaste with which the Reagan administration regarded him was increased by his construction, with the aid of Cuban technicians, of a long airstrip on which he agreed to allow the Soviets to land reconnaissance aircraft. In October 1983, Bishop was killed and replaced by a more radical Communist, General Hudson Austin. On August 25, citing concern for six hundred U.S. medical students on the island, Reagan sent in more than 6,000 U.S. troops accompanied by small forces from six Caribbean states. In the fighting, 160 Grenadians, 71 Cubans, and 40 Americans died.

Objecting, Congress immediately applied the War Powers Act, thereby restricting U.S. troop presence in Grenada to sixty days. The British were furious that the United States had invaded a member of the British Commonwealth despite British objections. The UN Security Council voted 15–1 to condemn the invasion, and the General Assembly called it, 108–9, a "flagrant violation of international law." The Good Neighbor Policy seemed abandoned.

Installing an anti-Communist government in Grenada, Washington deported the surviving Cubans, closed the Soviet embassy, canceled distribution of land to the poor, and then helped complete the airstrip to promote tourism.

Cuba

Castro's Communist regime in Cuba was abhorrent to Reagan, who saw a great threat from the "Moscow-Havana axis" to America's vital sea lanes and, also, a danger that Castro would foster revolutions in other countries to create other Cubas.

In April 1982, Washington banned travel to Cuba and imposed new restrictions on trade. In May 1985, it set up a powerful radio transmitter, "Radio Marti," to make anti-Castro broadcasts to Cuba. Relations reached a new level of incivility when Reagan called Cuba one of "a confederation of terrorist states" and Castro called Reagan a "madman, imbecile, and a bum." Nevertheless, Castro agreed to take back some of the criminal and mentally ill Cubans he had allowed to sail in 1980 from Mariel to Florida.

Intervention in El Salvador

In some Central American countries, bloody civil war between the rich and the poor had long alternately smoldered and flared. When Reagan took office, the most active armed conflicts were in El Salvador and Nicaragua. Ignoring their indigenous causes, Reagan treated these conflicts as battles in the Cold War. The rebellion in El Salvador, said the State Department, was a "textbook case of indirect armed aggression by Communist powers."

The El Salvadoran peasant-based rebel group, the National Liberation Front (NLF), received aid from Cuba and the Soviet Union, but not until 1980 did the local Communist party join the armed resistance, and no Soviet or Cuban soldiers served with rebel forces. As NLF rebels waged guerrilla war, pro-government right-wing groups operated "death squads," composed partly of police and soldiers, to assassinate leftist opponents; in 1983 they killed 5,300 people. Carter had suspended military aid to El Salvador; Reagan renewed it, sending more advisers and CIA operatives. Nonetheless, the number of rebels increased.

Reagan appointed a commission, headed by former Secretary of State Henry Kissinger, to study Central American problems. Its January 1984 report recommended enlarging U.S. military and economic support to the region to $8 billion for the next five years. It recommended doubling annual aid to El Salvador to $400 million. With U.S. financing, the Salvadoran army more than quadrupled between 1981 and 1986 reaching 54,000. By 1987, Washington had provided $2.5 billion and was financing most of El Salvador's national budget. However, Congress made continuation of aid conditional on annual State Department certification that El Salvador was curbing its violations of human rights.

In 1984, with CIA aid, a civilian reformer, University of Notre Dame graduate José Napoleon Duarte, won election as president. Duarte implemented some land reform, reduced death squad killings, and opened negotiations with the rebels. By 1987, the number of rebel troops had declined from 12,000 to 6,000. Nevertheless, peace remained elusive. U.S. aid strengthened reactionary forces, the army stifled Duarte's proposed reforms, the death squads disrupted land distribution, and gross inequities of wealth persisted. After Duarte succumbed to cancer, the 1988 elections returned the right wing to power, land reform was reversed, and the fighting continued. "As long as people lack work, roofs, and health," said a colonel, "the problem is interminable."

The civil war would continue after Reagan left office. In November 1989, government troops murdered six Jesuit priests. The *New York Times* called El Salvador's armed forces "the hemisphere's most brutal." By 1990, the war had left 70,000 dead. In the United States, dissatisfaction rose at the ineffectiveness of Washington's $4 billion in aid, while the decline of the Soviet threat reduced support for combating Central America's leftist groups. In November 1990, Congress cut military aid to El Salvador by half. With prospects for foreign aid fading, the government and the NLF signed an agreement in September 1991.

It called for removal of death squad leaders from the army and the integration of rebels into a new national police force.

In El Salvador, the United States had tried a mix of aid to the military and aid to the poor, but had been more effective in helping the rich control the poor than in alleviating the causes of discontent.

Intervention in Nicaragua

The Nicaraguan government was a broad coalition of left and moderate groups, and it tolerated some freedom of speech and political action and left 60 percent of the economy in private hands. However, the presence of Communists among the Sandinistas, the dominant faction in the government, caused Reagan to fear that Nicaragua might become a second Cuba. Some Sandinista behavior reinforced his fears. Removing leading liberals from the State Council and postponing elections, they nationalized banks and foreign trade. Also, in addition to aid from Canada, Latin-America, Western Europe, and Japan, they secured technical assistance and advisers from Cuba and aid from Moscow.

By 1981 the Reagan administration, accusing the Sandinista government of imposing "Communist totalitarian internal rule," forming close ties with Cuba and the Soviet Union, arming, and "attempting to subvert its neighbors," had resolved that Nicaragua's government must be overthrown. In May 1983, Reagan cut imports of Nicaraguan sugar, a heavy blow to its economy, and, in 1985, he imposed a complete trade embargo.

Most Americans opposed sending U.S. troops into Nicaragua, and the Joint Chiefs were reluctant to wage another unpopular war. Instead, Washington made war by proxy. Many members of Somoza's infamous National Guard and upper-class supporters had fled abroad, where they were later joined by some former members of the Sandinista regime. In August 1981, the CIA began organizing exiles into a military force, called "Contras." Financing, training, and arming them, the CIA stationed them in U.S.-built camps in neighboring Honduras, from where, in March 1983, they invaded Nicaragua. Calling them "freedom fighters," Reagan equated them to America's "founding fathers." Disagreeing, the *Boston Globe* called them "an unlikely collection of cattle rustlers, terrorists, members of a discredited dictatorship, profiteers, and mercenaries."

The Contras, who in 1986 numbered 20,000, lacked sufficient military strength or popular support to overthrow the government, but they destroyed bridges, factories, and government buildings and assassinated government officials. The CIA prepared a pamphlet instructing them in terrorism, including the murder of selected "judges . . . police and state security officials." U.S. church groups working in Nicaragua reported that the Contras committed atrocities, and Amnesty International acccused them of "routine torture and summary execution."

CIA planes airlifted supplies for the Contras into Nicaragua. Also, in 1984, CIA frogmen sowed Nicaragua's principal harbor with mines, which damaged ships and killed persons from other countries. Exposure of this CIA exploit aroused much indignation: all members of the UN Security Council, except the United States, voted to condemn it, the World Court, judging it a breach of international law, awarded Nicaragua damages, and Congress barred further use of funds to mine harbors.

Americans disagreed on whether the Sandinistas should be regarded as unredeemably Communist. Those who so considered them pointed to a statement by the head of the armed forces, Humberto Ortega, brother of President Daniel Ortega, that Sandinista ideology was Marxist, to the 3,500 technicians and advisers sent to them by Communist countries, to their nationalization of 40 percent of the economy, and to Daniel Ortega's visits to Moscow. Other Americans did not regard the Sandinistas as Moscow-dominated and said that they were following policies, including land reform and multiplied spending on education and medical care, that helped the poor majority. Their programs received much support from U.S. church and humanitarian groups, and many U.S. citizens went to Nicaragua to work in land reform and rural reconstruction programs. The Nicaraguan Communist party chairman called the Sandinistas "ideologically promiscuous." They had priests, nuns, evangelicals, and businessmen in the government, he said. "It has nothing to do with Marxism-Leninism." Ortega repeatedly visited the United States and received aid from Canada, Japan, and America's European allies.

Because an effort to overthrow Nicaragua's government would violate international law, the charters of the UN and OAS, and more than thirty U.S. treaties, Reagan needed to disguise his policy. At first he said that its purpose was only to halt arms shipments from Nicaragua to El Salvador and to secure democratic reforms. Other statements, however, indicated that he sought to destroy the regime. In a March 1986 speech, he warned that, using Nicaragua as a base, the Soviets and Cubans could dominate Central America, "threaten the Panama Canal, interdict our vital Caribbean sea lanes, and, ultimately, move against Mexico."

Some U.S. citizens charged that Reagan's Nicaragua policy was shaped less by concern for U.S. security than by ideology. With memories of the disastrous Vietnam War still fresh, a large majority of Americans opposed aiding the Contras, whom many regarded as unpopular terrorists. In December 1982, Congress adopted the Boland Amendment, which forbade the use of U.S. funds to provide military equipment or training to overthrow Nicaragua's government, and in October 1984 a second Boland Amendment banned aid to military operations in Nicaragua. To counteract this aid cut, Reagan and his aides energetically solicited funds for the Contras from other sources, despite Secretary of State Shultz's warning that to do so was an impeachable offense.

Reagan's policy got little international support. In January 1983, a conference of nonaligned nations unanimously condemned U.S. efforts to overturn Nicaragua's government. In 1986, France and other U.S. allies in Europe gave Nicaragua $100 million. In June 1986, the International Court of Justice ruled that U.S. aid to the Contras violated international law and that Washington owed Nicaragua an indemnity.

To many Latin Americans, it seemed that the devastating fighting in Central America resulted from their being caught in the crossfire of the Cold War. Criticism was particularly strong among those who had painful memories of past U.S. interventions. Resentful at not being consulted, Mexico repeatedly warned Washington not to use military force and also gave the Sandinistas $200 million in aid.

In January 1983, leaders of Mexico, Colombia, Venezuela, and Panama, meeting on an island named Contadora, issued a statement of objectives. Seeking, they said, to remove all foreign bases and troops and to establish democratic government, they urged Washington to halt aid to the Contras simultaneously with Sandinista democratization and arms reduction. This program was endorsed by Brazil, Argentina, Peru, and Uruguay, and by twelve Western European nations. Ortega offered to accept the "Contadora Process," but Washington did not.

In August 1987, the presidents of Costa Rica, Honduras, Guatemala, El Salvador, and Nicaragua, without consulting Reagan, adopted a peace program prepared by Costa Rica's President Oscar Arias Sanchez. The Arias Plan called for cease-fires between all contending forces in Central America, a halt to all outside aid to all rebel forces, refusal to allow outside forces to use any nation's territory to mount attacks, and the holding of free elections. These proposals were widely applauded and were endorsed by the U.S. Congress. Arias received the Nobel Peace Prize.

Seeing the Arias Plan as a move to undercut his policy of overthrowing Ortega, Reagan termed it "fatally flawed." Also objecting to the plan, the Contras, in December 1987, launched their biggest offensive of the war. But three developments soon made them more amenable: the Iran-Contra scandal (discussed in chapter 17) reduced private financial support, Congress refused more aid, and they suffered a disastrous military defeat that cost them their principal foothold in Nicaragua and half of their supplies.

Ortega also was under pressure. By 1988 the war had caused Nicaragua $3.5 billion in damages and, with the economy in shambles, popular dissatisfaction with his government was rising. Moreover, the Soviets cut arms and oil shipments. Allowing the opposition newspaper and the Catholic radio station to resume operations, Ortega offered to pardon Contras who laid down their arms. Agreeing to a cease-fire late in March 1988, the Sandinistas and the Contras opened negotiations.

Near the end of his administration, Reagan said that his failure to dislodge the Sandinista government was his biggest foreign policy disappointment. He put most of the blame on Congress.

President George Bush, who took office in January 1989, would change Reagan's policy. In February 1989, Bush agreed to disband the Contras in exchange for Ortega's agreement to hold elections within a year. The Soviets continued to aid Ortega, but not with arms, and urged him to conduct the February 25, 1990 election in a "free and fair" way satisfactory to Washington.

During the election campaign, Washington made lavish financial contributions to the opposition leader, Violeta Chamorro, but expected Ortega to win.

Instead, Chamorro won. The new Chamorro government allowed a Sandinista to head the military and allowed peasants to whom Sandinistas had given land to keep it. Surprisingly, it resisted pressure from Washington to drop its claim to the World Court's award of $17 million for damages resulting from U.S. support for the Contras. Bush lifted the five-year old trade embargo.

In the long effort to overthrow the Sandinistas, Washington had employed economic sanctions, CIA attacks, and a proxy war that cost the United States more than $250 million, while Nicaragua suffered more than 40,000 deaths and a 40 percent drop in GNP. Some credited U.S. policy with ousting Ortega. Others credited his replacement to the decline of foreign aid to fighters on both sides and to the determination of Central Americans to take control of their own affairs.

Chile and the Falkland Islands

One of the Reagan's first acts as president, in February 1981, was to lift the ban on exports to Chile, which Carter had imposed because of its human rights violations. But so persistent were Chile's abuses that the United States voted for a 1986 UN resolution condemning them. In 1988, Chileans voted against continuing Pinochet's dictatorship, and the December 1989 election of Patrico Aylwen brought a return to civilian government, though Pinochet retained command of the military. The new government retained Pinochet's free-market reforms, and Chile's economy continued to grow.

In March 1982, war erupted between Argentina and Britain. Argentina had a claim to the Falkland Islands, near Argentina, which were ruled by England. In late March, the Argentinans landed troops and seized the islands with little fighting. The European Economic Community and the UN Security Council demanded that they withdraw, while the OAS and the Soviet Union sided with Argentina. Breaking with Latin America, Washington backed Britain. A British naval expedition retook the islands, which resulted in great popularity in Britain for Prime Minister Margaret Thatcher, and disgrace in Argentina for its military regime, which was shortly replaced by more democratic government.

Latin America's Debt Crisis

Latin American governments tended to borrow heavily, and foreign banks were ready to lend them vast sums at high rates of interest. This money was not always invested in productive enterprises that could help them repay the debt, and some of it was corruptly squandered. In the 1970s, Latin Americans had enjoyed an impressive 40 percent rise in per capita income, but much of the expansion was financed by loans which raised their accumulated foreign debt by 1990 to a staggering $430 billion. As a result, they were forced to devote about $33 billion a year, one-third of their exports, to repaying creditors. This forced them to delay new investment in expansion and left them with less money to buy U.S. goods; after 1982 U.S. sales to Latin America fell below the level of U.S. imports from Latin America. Several nations adopted "austerity" measures designed to cut consumption and to raise exports, which depressed the already low living standards and fanned revolutionary discontent. Between 1980 and 1989 per capita income dropped by 10 percent. Many economists regarded their debt as unpayable and expected that the crisis would require both acceptance of losses by foreign banks and an increase in foreign aid.

After Reagan left office, Bush's secretary of the Treasury, Nicholas F. Brady, prepared a plan, in March 1989, to help Latin Americans pay foreign debts. This "Brady Plan" required lending banks either to cancel part of the debt or to make new loans and Latin American countries to adopt World Bank specifications on economic policy in return for additional World Bank loans. Such deals enabled Mexico and Brazil to continue making payments, but arrangements with other countries were slow to materialize.

Reagan and Africa

The Cold War also dominated Reagan's approach to Africa. He stepped up aid to UNITA, the military group that was attempting to overthrow the Marxist government of Angola. Inviting UNITA's commander, Jonas Savimbi, to the White House, Reagan provided him with advanced TOW antitank missiles and Stinger antiaircraft missiles. In supporting UNITA, America aligned itself with South Africa's white-supremacy government, Savimba's principal backer, which repeatedly sent troops into Angola in support of UNITA. Regarding South Africa's invasions as necessary to counterbalance Cuban military support for Angola's government, Washington vetoed a Security Council condemnation of these invasions. However, as opposition to backing South Africa rose, America's U.N. representative, in 1987, voted to condemn the latest South African raid.

In 1988, in a major breakthrough, U.S., South African, Angolan, and Cuban representative agreed to give Namibia independence in 1989 in return for the withdrawal of Cuba's 50,000 troops from Angola. Praising the Soviets for pressuring Cuba and Angola to be flexible, Shultz said that Moscow had been "very cooperative."

Meanwhile, Reagan resisted popular demands that he impose economic sanctions to compel South Africa to modify its racist policies. In 1981, when the UN expelled South Africa and called on all members to impose a trade embargo, Reagan said that the South African government was "reformist" and that America should back it while it tried to solve its problems. The Organization of African Unity repeatedly condemned U.S. "collusion" with South Africa, the European Economic Community imposed economic sanctions, and Canada, Sweden, and Denmark suspended trade with South Africa.

Under increasing pressures within America and abroad, Reagan gradually assumed a more critical stance. In 1985, he forbade U.S. banks to make loans to South Africa and restricted nuclear and computer sales. In 1986, he called on

South Africa to establish a timetable for ending apartheid, and he appointed a black, Edward J. Perkins, as U.S. ambassador. But Reagan vetoed a congressional ban on new U.S. investments there—which Congress then enacted over his veto.

Afghanistan

Reagan's anti-Communist crusade scored a partial success in Afghanistan. Raising aid to Muslim leaders, the *mujahedeen,* who were fighting that country's Communist regime, he provided them with Stinger missiles that could bring down Soviet aircraft. Afghanistan became the Soviet Union's Vietnam—although they sent in 115,000 troops, they could not suppress the rebels, but suffered 40,000 casualties and a ruinous economic drain. In early 1988, Soviet General Secretary Mikhail Gorbachev agreed to withdraw all Soviet troops. Nevertheless, Communists held the capital until 1992.

Dictators in the Philippines and Haiti

Reagan supported any government, regardless of how repressive, against Communist-backed rebels. Nevertheless, in some cases he was eventually persuaded that some of these dictatorships, by unpopular policies, excessive corruption, or ineptitude, were contributing to the growth of Communist-backed movements.

In the Philippines, where Americans had naval and air bases and heavy investments, America had long supported the dictator Ferdinand Marcos. In 1981, Vice President Bush told Marcos that "we love your adherence to democratic principles." However, low economic production, Marcos's excesses of corruption and oppression, and the 1983 murder of a popular rival, Benigno Aquino, fanned a growing Communist-backed guerrilla insurgency. Under U.S. prodding, Marcos agreed to elections in 1986. The opposition candidate, Aquino's widow, Corazon Aquino, had popular support, and Marcos "won" only through transparent rigging. Large-scale protest demonstrations erupted, and part of the army defected to Aquino. When it appeared that Marcos would order a bloody suppression, Reagan was persuaded to drop his support and to induce Marcos to leave Manila in February 1986 in a U.S. plane that he thought was taking him to his stronghold, but that actually took him to Hawaii. Mrs. Aquino took over the government.

Also in 1986, Reagan helped ease out Jean-Claude Duvalier, the dictator of Haiti. After advising Duvalier not to use military force against demonstrators, Americans furnished an airplane to fly him to France. In explanation, the Reagan administration declared that "the American people believe in human rights and opposing tyranny in whatever form, whether of the left or the right." This sounded like conversion to the Carter human rights policy, but it actually did not apply to situations in which overthrowing a right-wing dictator might weaken resistance to pro-Communist forces.

Harmony and Disharmony in NATO

Reagan's relations with America's NATO allies were somewhat less troubled than Carter's. At first many Europeans were alarmed by the election of one whom they feared was a trigger-happy cowboy, and they were relieved when his actions proved to be less rash than his rhetoric. They were also pleased by his emphasis on defending Europe, and by his resistance to congressional efforts to raise tariffs.

Reagan's relations were particularly close with Britain's conservative Prime Minister Margaret Thatcher, with whom he was ideologically compatible (see Fig. 16.2). She greatly appreciated his support for her recapture of the Falkland Islands, a foreign policy success that ensured her reelection. In turn, Britain, almost alone, supported Reagan's air raid on Libya (see chapter 17).

Many Europeans considered Reagan's backing of Israel to be too uncritical. Also, they were disturbed by his Strategic Defense Initiative (SDI), which they saw as better suited to protecting the United States from Soviet ICBMs than to shielding Europe from intermediate-range missiles. Many criticized his Third World policies, particularly his attempts to overthrow the government of Nicaragua.

Figure 16.2 Britain's Prime Minister Margaret Thatcher and President Reagan at an international economic conference. National Archives.

After the 1985 advent of Mikhail Gorbachev with his policies of democratic and free market reforms (see chapter 17), Gorbachev became the most popular foreigner among West Europeans, most of whom believed he was making more arms concessions and was less likely to start a war than Reagan. Gorbachev's call for creation of a "common European home" from the Atlantic to the Urals threatened to undermine the closeness between America and its NATO allies.

Declining Support for the UN

Reagan's relations with the UN were uneasy. General Assembly votes frequently went against America, particularly in regard to South Africa, the Middle East, and Third World nations.

In the UN's early years, when a majority of the members had regularly voted as America wished, popular support for the UN in America had been high. Washington referred important matters to it, and President Truman had pledged "unfaltering support."

Between 1946 and 1983, however, UN membership expanded from 51 to 158 nations. Most of the new members were newly independent former colonies. Less concerned with Cold War issues than with lingering elements of imperialism, they resented attempts by whites to retain control of non-European peoples and resources. In these changed circumstances, the United States frequently found itself in the minority. Particularly galling to Americans were the General Assembly's vote, in 1971, to deny a seat to Taiwan, the standing ovation accorded PLO chief Yasser Arafat in 1974, and its resolution, in 1975, that condemned Zionism as a "form of racism." Also, the UN repeatedly denounced U.S. support for Israeli "aggression." In 1982, on the twenty most important issues, the 101 nonaligned nations voted with the United States only 22 percent of the time.

In 1983, U.S. representative to the UN Jeane J. Kirkpatrick said that America's position in the UN had become "essentially impotent, without influence, heavily outvoted, and isolated." According to a 1983 Gallup Poll only 36 percent of Americans believed that the UN was doing a good job. Dislike was particularly strong among conservatives, who accused it of anti-American and anticapitalist bias.

However, the General Assembly sometimes voted against the Soviets. Repeatedly, it demanded that the Russians withdraw their troops from Afghanistan and that Communist Vietnam remove its troops from Cambodia. It also condemned the Soviets for shooting down Korean Airlines Flight 007.

Nixon had reduced America's contribution to UN expenses from about a third to 25 percent of its total costs. Objecting to what he considered hostility from the United Nations Educational, Scientific, and Cultural Organization (UNESCO) to a free market, and its extravagant spending, Reagan announced that America would withdraw from UNESCO unless it made major changes in policy and procedures. Reagan also withheld payment of U.S. dues, a heavy blow to the UN, which had annual expenses in 1986 of $806 million. In May 1987, facing bankruptcy, the General Assembly adopted reforms demanded by America. It cut the UN staff by 15 percent, imposed mandatory retirement at age 60, and slashed spending for travel and publications. Nevertheless, demanding further reforms, Reagan continued to withhold funds. By 1988, U.S. arrears totaled $537 million.

The second largest contribution to the UN budget was the Soviet Union's 11.8 percent. Moscow paid its regular dues, but refused to contribute to special peacekeeping forces. In 1987, reversing this policy, the Soviets agreed to pay their share of the costs of peacekeeping forces, including $197 million in arrears.

Reagan's International Economic Policies

Having criticized Carter's suspension of wheat sales to Russia, Reagan renewed the sales. Also, consistent with his party's conversion to low tariffs, he resisted, albeit unsuccessfully, congressional efforts to retaliate against other countries by restricting their exports to America. During his administration, the share of U.S. imports subject to restraints doubled. By 1989, more than two-thirds of the goods imported from Japan were subject to quotas, special tariffs, or other import barriers. Nevertheless, U.S. foreign trade continued to rise. Imports soared from $245 billion in 1980 to $530 billion in 1988. Exports rose, but less rapidly, and in 1988 America bought approximately $112 billion more in foreign goods and services than it sold abroad.

Subsidizing U.S. tobacco exports, Washington induced Japan, Taiwan, and South Korea to reduce their tariffs on tobacco. Between 1986 and 1988, U.S. cigarette exports doubled to $2.6 billion annually. Some Americans were uneasy about federal promotion of a drug that, according to the U.S. surgeon general, annually killed 450,000 Americans, and Congressman Mike Snar found it "outrageous" that the government used "taxpayers' money to promote death abroad." Some critics even charged that it made the U.S. government the world's leading drug pusher.

Reagan's presidential campaign had called for cutting taxes, particularly taxes on upper-income groups, while raising military spending. Promising to balance the budget by slashing social spending and by stimulating new investment to produce higher tax revenues, he cut the top income tax rate from 70 percent to 33 percent, and sliced $45 billion from spending for health, housing, education, and social services. Nevertheless, he was never able to submit a balanced budget to Congress. During his eight years, as president, federal budget deficits averaged $176 billion annually and the national debt soared from $800 billion to almost $3 trillion. By 1989, interest payment was absorbing $150 billion per year, 14 percent of federal spending. Of course, this restricted Washington's ability to take action in America or abroad.

Budget deficits tend to be inflationary. The burden of controlling inflation fell on the Federal Reserve Board, which fought it by keeping interest rates high. Higher interest rates made it more costly for U.S. businesses to modernize or expand and also, by raising the value of the dollar in relation to foreign currencies, raised the costs to foreigners of U.S. goods, while making imports cheaper to Americans.

During the Reagan administration, America fell from the world's leading creditor to become the world's leading debtor nation. In 1980, U.S. investments abroad had surpassed investments by foreigners in America by about $150 billion. By the end of 1988, foreign investments in America exceeded U.S. investments abroad by $500 billion. Between 1980 and 1988, direct ownership of U.S. properties and businesses by foreigners soared from $83 billion to $263 billion, while the total value of U.S. assets (including bonds) owned by foreigners nearly tripled to $1.5 trillion. The resulting higher outflow of profits and interest further drained America's financial strength.

At the same time, the production of many regions rose faster than America's. East Asia's share of world production rose to 20 percent, while America's share of total world economic production fell from about 50 percent in 1947 to about 23 percent in 1988.

Great productive and financial superiority had enabled the United States to project economic and military power to many overseas areas and to overwhelm opponents. However, military spending absorbed economic resources that might otherwise have been used to raise production. During the Reagan administration, America grew relatively stronger militarily but relatively weaker economically. Many feared that, in the long run, economic strength might be more decisive. Because of its growing national debt, international trade deficit, and unfavorable international investment balance, America would find it more difficult to finance wars abroad. After a study of the rise and fall of empires, the historian Paul Kennedy concluded that "Great powers in relative decline instinctively respond by spending more on security, thereby diverting potential resources from investment and compounding their long term dilemma."

17 Reagan: From Confrontation to Closeness

Reagan and the Middle East

Early in his administration Reagan was less critical than Carter of Israel. He defended the planting of new Jewish settlements in the occupied Arab territories and, in an April 1982 letter to Israel's Prime Minister Begin, promised to help preserve Israel's military superiority.

Nevertheless, over Israeli objections, Reagan continued to sell advanced weapons to Arabs. Saudi Arabia bought U.S. tanks, air-to-air missiles, and Airborne Warning and Control System (AWACS) planes capable of tracking all aircraft within 350 miles. Reagan also gave Egypt massive economic and military aid.

U.S.-Israel relations were soon troubled. In June 1981, when Israel, using U.S.-made jets, launched a surprise bombing attack to destroy Iraq's nuclear reactor, America introduced a resolution in the Security Council condemning Israel's action as aggression. Also, Secretary of Defense Weinberger called Israel's annexation, in December 1981, of the Golan Heights "provocative," and Reagan made the UN General Assembly vote condemning that annexation unanimous. Nevertheless, the United States continued to supply Israel with arms, and to veto Security Council resolutions denouncing Israel's treatment of the Arab residents of occupied territories. In April 1982, the General Assembly again condemned America for support of Israel.

To the north of Israel, the people of the small country of Lebanon were so bitterly divided between an impoverished Moslem majority and a relatively well-to-do Christian minority that they could not maintain effective government. Moslems were themselves split into warring factions, some allied with Syria or Iran. Fighting among these groups, each of which maintained separate armed forces, "militias," frequently disrupted Lebanon. Neighboring Syria, whose government maintained that Lebanon rightfully belonged to Syria, sent in troops "to restore order." Adding to the instability was the increasing number of Palestinian refugees who settled mostly in southern Lebanon, where they maintained separate armed forces and sometimes launched terrorist or rocket attacks against Israel, to which Israel usually retaliated by bombing their settlements. When Reagan protested an Israeli bombing of a PLO village in Lebanon, Begin reminded him of the U.S. bombing in Vietnam: "You don't have a right from a moral perspective to preach to us."

On June 6, 1982, Israel launched a large-scale invasion of Lebanon, apparently for the purpose of destroying the PLO and helping Lebanese Christians establish an effective and friendly government. Inflicting a stunning defeat on the Syrian air force, it forced Syria to sign a cease-fire on June 11. Sweeping rapidly north, Israeli troops entered the Lebanese capital, Beirut, trapping PLO forces in Moslem West Beirut.

Although Reagan asked Israel to halt the invasion, many believed that he gave it tacit support. In May, 1982, a month before the invasion, Israel's defense minister had visited Secretary of State Haig, who, by calling for "international action" to end the Lebanese civil war, had appeared to give Israel a green light. After Israel launched its attack, Haig said that it created "new and hopeful opportunities" for peace, and America vetoed UN resolutions calling on Israel to withdraw from West Beirut and all nations to halt arms sales to Israel.

However, Israeli actions soon exceeded what the Reagan administration considered acceptable, especially after Haig was replaced as secretary of state by George Shultz. When the destruction of Arab civilian lives seemed excessive, Washington suspended the sale of cluster artillery shells and expressed disapproval of Israel's bombardment of Beirut. When, violating a cease-fire, Israel launched a heavy assault on civilian areas of Beirut, which Reagan later called a "brutal" attack that "sickened me and others in the White House," the president telephoned Begin to express "outrage." By a vote of 120 to 2, the General Assembly called for sanctions against Israel.

Under pressure, Israel agreed to a cease-fire to allow the surviving PLO forces, including PLO head Yasser Arafat, to leave Beirut by sea. The United States landed 800 marines to join French and Italian troops in supervising the evacuation of more than ten thousand PLO fighters, a retreat completed by September.

On September 11, 1982, Reagan proposed that peace be negotiated on the basis of "self-government" for the 1.5 million Palestinian Arabs on the Israeli-occupied West Bank and a freeze on further Israeli settlement there in return for Arab recognition of Israel. Jordan and Egypt welcomed the proposal, and a leading U.S. Jewish organization called it "worthy of consideration." But, rejecting it, Israel announced plans for new Jewish settlements. From 1977 to 1983 the number of Jews settled on the West Bank rose from 5,000 to 30,000.

After the PLO and the international police force withdrew, Israeli forces, violating Israeli promises to Washington, seized part of Beirut, an action the Security Council condemned. Beirut contained settlements, "camps," of Palestinian refugees, and the Israelis asked Lebanese Christian militiamen, enemies of the Palestinians, to enter one of these camps in an Israeli-controlled area. Soon, reports appeared that these militiamen had killed eight hundred Palestinian civilians in what the Security Council called a "criminal massacre." Shultz was "shaken and appalled." Expressing "outrage and revulsion," Reagan demanded that Israel withdraw immediately from Beirut. Hundreds of thousands of Israelis also demonstrated against the killings, and an Israeli investigating commission called for the dismissal of top officials.

However, not even Reagan's February 1983 offer to guarantee its northern border could persuade Israel to withdraw its troops from Lebanon.

Lebanon reported that more than 19,000 Arabs had died as a result of Israel's invasion, while the Israelis lost 368 dead. Much of Beirut lay in ruins, and prospects for settlement of the Arab-Israeli conflict seemed more remote than ever. Israel gained little from its costly effort except worldwide condemnation. In August 1983 a depressed Begin announced that he would resign.

In an attempt to restore peace, U.S. marines, along with Italian and British forces, returned to Lebanon. Reagan wanted to help the government, composed of Lebanese Christians, to subdue rival fighting groups and restore order. Of course, rebel Moslem militia objected, and marines guarding the airport came under sniper fire. An April 1983 bombing of the U.S. embassy in Beirut killed sixty-three persons. In September, U.S. warships shelled positions held by the Syrians and their Lebanese allies. In October, a Moslem suicide car-bomb attack on a U.S. marine barrack killed 241 Americans. Although Reagan had insisted that America would never "be intimidated by terrorists" to "cut and run" and that keeping marines in Lebanon was "central to our credibility on a global scale," he withdrew the U.S. marines in February 1984. He later wrote that he regretted sending marines into Lebanon more than any other act of his presidency. Israel evacuated most of Lebanon by June 1985, but continued to occupy a "security zone" in southern Lebanon.

Former Presidents Carter and Ford and former Secretaries of State Cyrus Vance and Henry Kissinger called on Israel to withdraw from occupied Arab lands, but Israel continued to settle Jews there; by 1988 approximately 65,000 settlers. Reagan wrote later that he believed that peace would never come to the Middle East as long as the occupied area remained under Israel's control. Nevertheless, he increased financial and military aid to Israel. In 1985, Israel received more U.S. aid than any other nation—$3 billion—equivalent to $700 per Israeli.

In December 1987, to reinforce Arab demands that they be freed from Israeli rule, Arab residents of the West Bank and the Gaza Strip began a series of strikes and demonstrations, a prolonged uprising called the "intifadah," against continued Israeli occupation. Crowds of Arab civilians, many of them children, shouted denunciations and threw stones at patrolling Israeli troops. The Israelis, who had long followed a policy of harsh retaliation against any Arab attack, fired rubber bullets and, sometimes, real bullets, made numerous arrests, deported Arab leaders, and demolished Arab homes. Nearly every week brought reports of more deaths, which intensified both Arab nationalism and world sympathy for Arabs. Israel's actions were also condemned by many Jews in America and in protest demonstrations in Israel. By 1988 only 37 percent of Americans expressed sympathy for Israel.

Washington had promised Israel that it would have no contacts with Yasser Arafat's PLO until after it renounced terrorism and agreed that Israel had a right to exist. In 1988, when America refused to grant Arafat a visa to make a speech at the UN, the General Assembly moved to Geneva for his speech, a tremendous boost to his prestige. Arafat finally made PLO acceptance of Israel sufficiently explicit to satisfy Washington. He said that he recognized the right of Israel "to exist in peace and security." He also renounced terrorism. As a result, U.S.-PLO talks began within a week.

Meanwhile, America clashed with Libya, the Arab country adjoining Egypt, which was ruled by the eccentric Muammar al-Qaddafi. In 1981, accusing Qaddafi, whom Reagan called "the mad dog of the Middle East," of engineering international terrorism, America expelled his diplomats. In August, U.S. naval forces maneuvering off Libya's coast shot down two Libyan planes and shelled shore batteries, and, in early 1982, Reagan halted purchase of Libyan oil. In April 1986, after a bomb in a West Berlin discotheque killed a U.S. serviceman, Reagan, attributing this bombing to Qaddafi, sent fifty-five warplanes from bases in England to bomb Libya. They struck military targets and Qadhafi's living quarters, killing his daughter and wounding two of his sons. They also accidentally hit civilian areas, killing, Libya reported, thirty-seven civilians. France and Spain had refused to allow the planes to fly over their territory, and many Europeans denounced the bombing. Later investigations indicated that probably Syria, not Libya, instigated the German discotheque bombing.

The Iran-Contra Affair

Relations with Iran would draw Reagan into his most embarrassing imbroglio. Iran's 1979 seizure of the U.S. embassy in Teheran had been bitterly resented in America. Adding to the hostility was the belief that Iran encouraged terrorists in other nations to attack Americans. Pro-Iranian terrorists in Middle East countries had seized Americans, including State Department and CIA personnel, as hostages. As a result, when Iraq invaded Iran, beginning a long and destructive war (1980–1988), Americans favored Iraq. Removing Iraq from its list of countries that supported terrorism, America secretly sold Iraq arms while insisting that all nations maintain an arms embargo on Iran.

Consequently, a report, in November 1986, in a Lebanese magazine, that the United States had secretly sold arms to Iran in exchange for Iran's help in securing the release of Americans held hostage by pro-Iranian groups in Lebanon had a devastating impact on Reagan, who, condemning anyone who negotiated with terrorists, had promised that he would "never deal with terrorists."

The embarrassed Reagan administration admitted that, in May 1986, National Security Adviser Robert McFarlane had made a secret flight to Iran, but it flatly denied that he had exchanged arms for hostages. Admiral John Poindexter, who had replaced McFarlane as national security adviser, said that as long as Iran advocated terrorism, America would maintain an arms embargo, and Reagan insisted that his "policy of not making concessions to terrorism" remained intact.

When evidence multiplied that Washington had, in fact, sold arms to Iran, Reagan acknowledged that arms shipments had been made, but, he insisted, only for the purpose of establishing contacts with moderate Iranian groups. In a November 13 speech, he again claimed that "we did not, repeat, did not trade weapons or anything else for hostages—nor will we." He also said, "We got our hostages back—three of them."

Many criticized the sale of arms to Iran. The Democratic Senate leader Robert Byrd called it "shocking," and right-wing Republican Senator Barry Goldwater called it a "dreadful mistake." Breaking ranks with Reagan, Secretary of Defense Weinberger and Secretary of State Shultz let it be known that they had opposed the deal. "Some of us are like a shovel brigade that follows a parade down Main Street cleaning up," said White House Chief of Staff Donald Regan, and "here we go again."

Equally embarrassing was the subsequent revelation that money obtained from the sale to Iran was secretly used to buy weapons for the Nicaraguan Contras after Congress had cut off funds for arming them. On November 25, Attorney General Edwin Meese, preempting imminent newspaper revelations, announced that he had discovered evidence that $10–30 million had been so diverted. This, said Republican Senate Leader Robert Dole, was a "bizarre twist."

Claiming that he had not been informed of the diversion of funds, Reagan fired Poindexter and his aide, marine Lieutenant Colonel Oliver North, who had handled the Iran-Contra operation. The next day he appointed a high-level investigative commission, composed of former Texas Republican Senator John Tower, former National Security Adviser Brent Scowcroft, and former Secretary of State Edmund Muskie.

Most Americans did not believe Reagan's denial. For years, quipped House speaker Tip O'Neill, critics had charged that Reagan did not know what was going on in the White House, but then, when he admitted it, they accused him of lying. Polls showed popular approval of the president dropping from 67 to 46 percent.

The February 1987 Tower Commission report concluded that laws had been broken. Reagan, Senator Tower told the press, "clearly didn't understand . . . what was happening." In March, Reagan admitted that the arms sale to Iran had "deteriorated" into an arms-for-hostages deal. Later, however, he returned to denying it. To Reagan, a bemused Shultz concluded, "reality was different."

From May to August 1987, Congress conducted televised hearings on the Iran-Contra affair. Representatives who had voted to halt aid to the Contras expressed outrage that Reagan had defied the decision, but Oliver North, who, under Poindexter and CIA director William Casey, had run the operation, was unrepentant. While acknowledging that he had lied to Congress and destroyed evidence, he maintained that he had been implementing the president's policy, had made full reports, had received enthusiastic CIA cooperation, and that giving the Contras money received from sale of arms to Iran was a "neat idea." He won much popular approval, and Reagan called him a "national hero." McFarlane, who attempted suicide the day before he appeared before the Tower Commission, testified that he had kept Reagan informed and, for political reasons, had destroyed a document that proved that Reagan knew of arms sales. North later wrote that Reagan "knew everything."

The evidence that gradually came to light revealed that the Reagan administration had, in fact, arranged a secret sale of arms to Iran in exchange for hostages. According to Weinberger's memo on a White House meeting of January 7, 1986, the president had decided to accept an Iranian offer to free five U.S. hostages in return for the sale of missiles. In May 1986, McFarlane and North had flown secretly to Teheran, carrying arms, gift pistols, a cake, a Bible, and poison for suicide if taken captive, and they had spent several days negotiating with Iranian officials for the release of hostages. Three hostages were then freed by pro-Iranian groups in Lebanon (who took three additional Americans hostage).

Meanwhile, in 1984, after Congress had forbidden the use of U.S. funds to provide arms to the Contras, Reagan had told his staff to secure alternative funds "any way you can." White House officials secretly solicited money from oil-rich Arabs and from nations that received U.S. aid. Saudi Arabia gave $25.5 million, the Sultan of Brunei $10 million, and Taiwan and South Korea furnished additional millions. Also, North, with an occasional assist from the president, collected more than $10 million from U.S. businesses.

Arms sales to Iran were handled by private businessmen, organized as "the enterprise." Paying the Pentagon less than their true value for the weapons, they then sold them to Iran for a huge profit. These businessmen took commissions of $4.4 million and gave North spending money plus $214,000. They hid other sums in secret accounts in Swiss banks. Of the $16 million of profits, less than $4 million reached the Contras. Financially, said Shultz, America "got taken to the cleaners."

The operation was illegal. U.S. law forbade export of arms to any country that supported terrorism. Also, proceeds from the sale of government arms legally belong to the government. Thus, the White House had circumvented Congress's authority to appropriate U.S. funds. Furthermore, requesting gifts from recipients of U.S. aid could be considered as soliciting illegal kickbacks. A Senate committee concluded that the Reagan administration was guilty of "dishonesty" and "deception and disdain for the law." Committee chairman Daniel K. Inouye called it a "chilling story."

The sale strengthened the war effort of Iran, which received 2,008 TOW missiles plus parts for antiaircraft missiles. It also damaged the credibility of America's campaign against terrorism.

In March 1988, a grand jury indicted North, Poindexter, and two others on charges of conspiring to defraud the government and to illegally supply the Contras. North and Poindexter were convicted, but, in 1991, their convictions were reversed on the grounds that Congress had given them immunity to criminal prosecution to induce them to testify before congressional committees. In all, eleven members of the Reagan administration either pled guilty or were convicted of crimes in the Iran-Contra affair. Historian Walter LaFeber concluded that the Iran-Contra affair revealed "an inept imperial executive out of control."

Crisis in the Persian Gulf

Tiny Kuwait, located at the head of the Persian Gulf adjoining Iraq and Saudi Arabia, exported enormous amounts of oil and enjoyed one of the world's highest per capita incomes. When Kuwait assisted Iraq in its war with Iran, the Iranians proclaimed a blockade of Kuwait and fired on ships carrying Kuwaiti oil. In 1987, the Soviets loaned Kuwait three tankers, and offered to help protect Kuwaiti ships. To forestall such a projection of Soviet influence into the Persian Gulf, Washington offered to allow Kuwait to fly the U.S. flag on its tankers, thus bringing them under U.S. protection. To escort them, America sent more warships to the Persian Gulf.

Denouncing America for enlarging its naval presence in the Gulf, Iran mined international waters, damaging several U.S. ships. In October 1987, after Iranian missiles struck a Kuwait tanker that was flying an American flag, Americans shelled Iran's oil-loading facilities, and extended protection to all neutral shipping. Tension with Iran approached the point of war.

In July 1988, the overly tense crew of a U.S. ship illegally sailing in Iranian territorial waters mistakenly shot down an Iranian civilian airliner, killing all 290 aboard. Reagan expressed "deep regret." The horror of the incident reminded all of the danger that an accident could produce war. Iranians stopped mining the sea, the United States withdrew some ships, oil tanker traffic resumed, and the crisis passed.

The clash with Iran was a curious episode. It meant undermining an enemy of the Soviet Union, a country that was the strongest southern barrier to Soviet expansion. An assistant defense secretary said, "We can't stand to see Iraq defeated" by Iran, but Henry Kissinger wrote that "America can have no conceivable interest in a victory by either side." Moreover, he added, "fundamentally, there are few nations in the world with less reason to quarrel and more compatible interests than Iran and the United States."

Japan: A Protégé Grows Up

The "MacArthur constitution" imposed by the United States on Japan after World War II made it unconstitutional for Japan to maintain military forces or even to fight in self-defense. Responsibility for defending Japan was assumed by the United States. Maintaining large naval forces in East Asian waters, America stationed U.S. troops (63,000 in 1988) in Japan. America's war in Korea was partly motivated by Japan's security needs, as was the conflict in Vietnam and the defense of the Persian Gulf.

In return, Japan usually followed America's lead in international relations and gave the United States dependable support in the Cold War. A senior Japanese diplomat told Americans that Japan was "the best, most obedient ally you have."

At U.S. urging, the Japanese, stretching and reinterpreting the MacArthur constitution, built sizable armed forces. Although they held defense spending below 1 percent of GNP (one-sixth of the U.S. level), that sum, as their economy expanded, rose by 1988 to $40 billion, higher than Britain's defense budget ($36 billion), making Japan the world's third-ranking military power. Closely coordinating its defense plans with America, Japan expanded the mission of its forces from temporary resistance in the home islands to defending sea lanes a thousand miles out to sea.

Japan's economy continued its rapid growth, rising at an average annual rate of 6 percent between 1960 and 1988. Its per capita GNP soared from $17 in 1946 to $13,000 (compared to America's $18,000) in 1987, surpassing that of several West European nations. At the outbreak of World War II, its GNP had been only 10 percent of America's; by 1988, it was nearly 50 percent and was challenging Russia's GNP for the world's second highest.

Some of those who sought to explain how Japan achieved such rapid growth pointed to MacArthur's land reform, trust-busting, and progressive taxation which redistributed wealth and enlarged consumer buying power. In 1986, Japan's income tax ran as high as 84 percent (compared with America's 33 percent). Other factors were the willingness of the Japanese to work longer for less pay, their greater propensity to save and invest, the family-type relations between management and workers, business's willingness to postpone immediate profits to capture a larger market share, their higher teacher salaries and longer school terms, and their comparatively low military spending.

Much cultural exchange occurred. In 1988, 20,000 Japanese students were studying in America, almost 2,000 U.S. students were enrolled in Japan, and 2.25 million Japanese tourists and delegates visited America.

Some friction developed. U.S. forces in Japan committed crimes, and occupied scarce land. The Japanese sought to exclude atomic weapons, which they abhorred, a wish Americans did not always respect. Some Japanese so strongly opposed the Vietnam War that they advocated that Japan develop atomic weapons to enable it to pursue an independent foreign policy. Americans pressured Japan to assume a larger share of its own defense costs by enlarging its armed forces and to raise its share of the costs of maintaining U.S. forces in Japan from the existing 44 percent.

However, the greatest friction occurred over trade. Between 1981 and 1988, two-way trade between the United States and Japan more than doubled, to $120 billion annually. America sold more to Japan than to any other country except Canada, and Japan was the largest buyer of U.S. farm products. But Japan's sales to America rose even faster. In quality and price, Japanese-made radios, TVs, and other electronics bested all competitors, and Japanese cars reputedly had better "fit and finish" and required fewer repairs. Also, Japan's retail marketing system was difficult for Americans to penetrate, and the Japanese forbade or restricted importation of rice, beef, oranges, and some other goods. In 1988, Japan sold $89.8 billion to the United States while buying only $37.7 billion from America.

Under pressure from U.S. industries to protect them against what they called unfair competition, Washington pressured Japan into imposing "voluntary" quotas on the quantities of automobiles, steel, and many other products that it sold in America. Also, Washington put heavy pressure on Japan to import more U.S. goods.

Reagan visited Tokyo in 1983, and the Japanese prime minister made several visits to the United States. Ongoing negotiations on trade issues resulted in Japanese concessions without satisfying Americans. Some economists calculated that removal of all Japanese obstacles to U.S. sales would narrow the trade gap no more than 10 percent. The real causes of the imbalance, they maintained, were U.S. policies, including the huge federal deficit, which caused unfavorable U.S. trade balances with many countries.

Japan cut tariffs on some U.S. products and removed restrictions on imports of beef and oranges, but not on rice. Also, it took steps to increase Japanese consumption in order to raise the share of Japanese products sold at home and to make Japan a better market for foreign products. Japan's imports rose rapidly, and half of these were manufactured goods. In 1988 U.S. sales to Japan soared 34 percent. Nevertheless, Japan's excess of exports to America over imports from America ($52.1 billion in 1988) accounted for nearly 40 percent of America's global trade deficit.

The Japanese used dollars earned in this trade to buy U.S. government bonds and to build and buy factories, hotels, office buildings, corporations, and other properties in the United States. In 1988, total Japanese direct investment in America, $33 billion, still trailed that of the British ($75 billion) and the Netherlands ($47 billion) but was rising rapidly. Also, the Japanese held some $160 billion in U.S. bonds and stocks. Some Americans worried that the Japanese were "buying America." Its huge reserves of gold and foreign currencies gave Japan power that could be exerted around the world. In 1988, 60 percent of Americans said that they were more apprehensive about the economic threat from Japan than about the military threat from the Soviet Union.

Reagan and China

In the 1980 campaign, Reagan had pledged to transfer recognition back to the Republic of China, and, after his inauguration, he increased arms sales to Taiwan. Nevertheless, he soon showed unexpected readiness to cooperate with Communist China. This represented a departure from the ideological purity of his position that all Communists were evil agents of Moscow.

Within six months of Reagan's inauguration, Secretary of State Haig, putting *realpolitik* above ideology, said that better relations with Communist China were "imperative in view of the Soviet threat." On a visit to China, Haig told the Chinese that "our objectives in practically every part of the world are similar if not identical." In June 1981, Reagan lifted curbs on trade and, in September, he signed a cultural exchange pact that soon had American professors teaching history, government, and law in Chinese universities. By 1988 about 50,000 Chinese students were enrolled in America. Incredibly, Reagan even began selling arms to the world's largest Communist dictatorship.

In April 1984, Reagan went to China, his first visit to a Communist country. When shown a Chinese commune, once condemned in the West as communism at its worst, he exclaimed: "I think it's wonderful." He allowed U.S. companies to construct nuclear power plants in China and expressed hope that this "new friendship of ours will mature and prosper." Fending off this embrace, the Chinese insisted that they remained independent of both superpowers.

Meanwhile, tension between the Communist mainland and Taiwan eased. The Communists promised to allow Taiwan to maintain its separate political and economic system, and even armed forces, if it would accept reunification. Taiwan's prime minister said that someday reunification might be possible if Communist reforms continued to narrow the differences between their systems. In 1988, the Taiwanese lifted their long-standing ban on travel to the mainland. Trade between the two Chinas through Hong Kong rose by 1987 to $1.3 billion, and Taiwanese investments on the mainland soared by 1993 to $10 billion.

:   In the 1980s, China underwent a remarkable transformation. Deng Xiaoping made sweeping reforms. Under a new "responsibility system," he allowed farmers to rent land in exchange for selling a fixed quantity of their crops to the state and permitted them to sell any additional production on the open market for profit. Agricultural production soared, farm income doubled, and China achieved self-sufficiency in food. Cutting China's army from 5 million to 3.5 million, Deng converted many military factories to civilian production. He also slashed the size of China's huge bureaucracy, lightening that heavy burden on the economy. He introduced reforms to allow market forces to influence production and required factories to make a profit—a little capitalism, he said, would not hurt China. By 1988, 20 million private businesses employed nearly 30 million people and handled 15 percent of retail sales. Also, he invited foreign capitalists to open businesses. Meanwhile, by restricting families to one child each, China cut its annual population growth more than half from 2.4 percent in 1979 to 1.1 percent in 1987.

Under these reforms, China achieved prodigious economic growth. From 1979 through 1988, the GNP rose an average of 9 percent a year, the highest for any large nation, doubling per capita income.

America and China cooperated against Russia in East Asia and other areas. They demanded that Soviet-backed Vietnam withdraw its troops from Cambodia, and both assisted Cambodian guerrillas, including the infamous Khmer Rouge, who were fighting the Vietnamese. They helped rebels against the Soviet-sponsored government in Afghanistan and backed identical factions in Africa, usually in opposition to Soviet-backed groups. Furthermore, the Chinese refrained from giving aid to Communist groups in Thailand, the Philippines, Malaysia, and Indonesia.

However, the Chinese deplored what they considered to be America's excessive commitment to Israel, which, they maintained, drove Arabs into the Soviet camp. Also, they said, U.S. support for reactionary governments in Africa and Latin America, including El Salvador and Nicaragua, created allies for

Moscow. On the other hand, when the Chinese sold advanced missiles to Iran, America retaliated by halting the sale of some advanced technology to China. But Sino-American cooperation far outweighed these disputes, and, in the 1980s, relations between them were friendly to the point of cordiality.

From Animosity to "Closeness"

Although Reagan had waged Cold War against Russia more intensely than anyone since Dulles, the last final years of his administration saw a remarkable thawing of relations. This relaxation of tensions occurred amid changes in Russia, in the international power distribution, and in Reagan.

In the years after World War II, the Soviet economy had grown faster than America's, raising Soviet GNP from about 20 percent to more than 50 percent of America's. But problems, including the allocation of 15 percent of its GNP (twice America's share) to the military; a bloated bureaucracy; aid to Marxist governments in Cuba, Vietnam, Angola, Ethiopia, and Afghanistan; a low birth rate; excessive alcoholism, smoking, and absenteeism; poor industrial quality control; and lagging technology slowed Soviet growth to an average of only 2 percent between 1976 and 1985, well below that of America. Reagan wrote that "in arming themselves to the teeth," they aggravated their "desperate economic problems." These difficulties reduced the appeal of Communist ideology, both within Russia and abroad.

Furthermore, the overshadowing dominance that the United States and the Soviet Union had once had over world affairs by virtue of their major shares of world production was ebbing as several other nations achieved more rapid economic growth than either superpower. As allies of each superpower asserted their independence, both camps fragmented. In the changed international power distribution, conflicts erupted, such as those between Israel and Syria, and Iran and Iraq, that were unrelated to the Cold War. America found itself embroiled with nations, such as Iran, that were also enemies of Russia, while becoming a near-ally of the world's largest Communist dictatorship, the People's Republic of China.

By 1984, Reagan's statements on the Soviet Union had grown less hostile. "The fact that neither of us likes the other's system is no reason to refuse to talk," he said. And, he added, America's military buildup had put America in such a position of strength that it was ready for constructive negotiations.

Meanwhile, Leonid Brezhnev, who had presided over the Soviet Union for nearly twenty years, died. He was followed in late 1982 by Yuri Andropov, who launched a new peace offensive and arms limitation effort, but who himself died after only fifteen months in office. In February 1984, he was succeeded by Konstantin Chernenko who lived only until March 1985. His death brought to power Mikhail S. Gorbachev, fifty-four, an ardent reformer.

Determined to shake Russia out of its economic stagnation, Gorbachev declared war on alcoholism, absenteeism, and corruption. Young people, he told a Soviet audience, should get off alcohol and back to church. Calling for the introduction of elements of democracy and free enterprise, he advocated "glasnost" (openness), by which he meant freedom of information and debate in government decision making, and "perestroika," or reconstruction of Russia's economic and political system. He sought to reduce the size of the bureaucracy and to relax its controls in order to give individual enterprises more freedom to compete for profits. He also proposed that the state rent out farmland for private farming and encourage individuals to operate small businesses and to practice crafts for profit. He encouraged foreign corporations to establish enterprises in the Soviet Union.

Apparently, Gorbachev believed that the principal obstacle to fundamental economic reform was the selfish desire of the vast entrenched bureaucracy, including that of the Communist party, to hold onto power. In order to break its monopoly, he moved to introduce more democracy. In a 1988 speech, he proposed that Communists introduce "democracy and self-government into all spheres of life," emphasize freedom of speech and religion, respect "spiritual-mindedness," and strictly guarantee the rights of citizens. Many students of Russia found the degree and speed of his proposals breathtaking.

Desire to revive Russia's stagnant economy increased Gorbachev's desire to reduce international tensions and arms spending. The arms race had proved to be ruinously costly. "We need a lasting peace," he told British Prime Minister Margaret Thatcher, "to concentrate on developing our society and improving the life of the Soviet people." Renouncing the quest for military superiority, he advocated respect for the security needs of both superpowers. "It is vital," he told a Communist party meeting, "that all should feel equally secure." He proposed total abolition of nuclear weapons. Also, he sought to reduce the economic drain of subsidizing foreign revolutionary movements. While not renouncing support for wars of national liberation, he said that Russia would not initiate them: "It is inadmissible and futile," he told the Twenty Seventh Communist Party Congress, "to encourage revolutions from abroad."

However, he expressed doubt that Reagan would respond favorably to his peace initiatives. "Your president couldn't make peace if he wanted to," he said. "He's a prisoner of the military-industrial complex."

In April 1985, Gorbachev announced that Russia would halt nuclear testing and deployment of intermediate-range missiles. He allowed Soviet-bloc countries to develop close economic relations with the European Economic Community (EEC). In July, he removed the dour Andrei Gromyko as foreign minister and replaced him with the genial and flexible Eduard Shevardnadze.

Gorbachev's reforms made the idea of improving relations more acceptable to Reagan. In October 1985, calling for a "fresh start" in U.S.-Soviet relations, Reagan told his cabinet to suspend the use of terms such as "evil empire."

For nearly five years, longer than any president since Truman, Reagan had avoided a summit conference, but in November 1985, he met Gorbachev in Geneva. He hoped, he told the American people, to "begin a dialogue for peace." The exchange of views between the world's top communist and the world's top anti-communist was frank, and sometimes heated. To Gorbachev,

Reagan was stubborn and contradictory, "not simply a conservative, but a political dinosaur." When Reagan criticized Soviet violations of human rights, Gorbachev spoke of hunger, unemployment, poor health care, and race discrimination in America. Each blamed the other for the arms race. Gorbachev charged that America's military-industrial complex fattened its profits by inducing anti-Soviet paranoia and that some Americans planned to escalate the arms race to "break down the Soviet economy." Their most heated exchanges came over the issue of weapons in space. Refusing to believe Reagan's promise to share SDI ("Star Wars") technology, Gorbachev charged that it would launch a new arms race. When Reagan told him that stationing large numbers of Soviet advisers in Nicaragua was "intolerable," Gorbachev replied that Russia was "helping people achieve freedom," while America was trying to "export counterrevolution."

Nevertheless, the meeting had some positive results. As the "human factor" came into play, they showed some desire to better understand each other. Forced to listen to hours of defense of the Communist position on the issues, Reagan realized that "potentially fatal" "myths and misconceptions" existed on "both sides of the iron curtain." Appearing to enjoy each other's company, each concluded that he could do business with the other. They agreed that "nuclear war cannot be won and must never be fought," that neither would "seek military superiority," that they would seek a reduction of strategic nuclear weapons, negotiate on troop reduction, and renew cultural exchanges. Gorbachev considered the meeting a breakthrough. When they were photographed shaking hands, Reagan quipped: "I bet the hard-liners in both our countries are bleeding." Reagan, calling it a "fresh start," gave an enthusiastic report on the meeting to Congress, and his ratings in the polls hit a high of 84 percent.

In a January 1986 speech, Gorbachev, accepting Reagan's "zero option" for intermediate-range missiles in Europe, proposed a nuclear test ban and the abolition of all nuclear weapons by the year 2000, and he offered to allow Western inspection of sites in the Soviet Union. He also proposed drastic cuts in conventional armaments. In February, he told the Communist Party Congress that the need was for "constructive, creative interaction among states and peoples on the scale of the entire world," and he called for "creation of a comprehensive system of international security."

On October 10, 1986, at Gorbachev's request that they accelerate progress on arms control, the two met at Reykjavik, Iceland. They continued frank exchanges on human rights and regional conflicts. Gorbachev proposed that they cut by half the number of strategic (long-range) nuclear weapons in each of the three main groups: submarine-launched missiles and long-range bombers, of which America had more, and intercontinental missiles, in which Russia was superior. Also, they agreed to total elimination within ten years of all Soviet and U.S. intermediate-range missiles in Europe (the "zero option.") Reagan proposed that they eliminate all ballastic missiles, and Gorbachev proposed eliminating all nuclear weapons, to which Reagan replied "that suits me fine." For a moment the world seemed close to agreement on nuclear disarmament, a prospect that Shultz called "breathtaking." But then, when an elated Reagan thought they had agreed on everything, Gorbachev insisted that all depended "on your giving up SDI." Enraged, Reagan "blew my top" and "walked out on Gorbachev." The tentative agreement to eliminate long-range missiles died in the debacle. SDI was proving to be expensive. (See Fig. 17.1.)

In December 1987, after Gorbachev agreed to negotiate on reducing intermediate missiles regardless of whether America abandoned SDI, he visited Washington for a summit conference. Calling for a world "which is democratic and free, with equality for all and with every nation enjoying the right to its own social choice without outside interference," he made a favorable public impression. He stopped his car to shake hands with a Washington crowd and, at a White House banquet attended by David Rockefeller, Henry Kissinger, Joe DiMaggio, Billy Graham, and Mary Lou Retton, sang along with Van Cliburn's rendition of "Moscow Nights." In a public opinion poll, 59 percent gave him a favorable rating , only 4 percent below Reagan. Someone suggested that he run for U.S. president, but he replied that he had a job. He was the first Soviet leader, said Reagan, who did not espouse "the Marxian theory of one-world Communist state." Establishing a personal relationship Reagan called "very close to friendship," he and Reagan called each other "Ron" and "Mikhail."

At this Washington summit, the two leaders signed the Intermediate-Range Nuclear Forces Treaty. They agreed to the "zero option," to remove all intermediate-range (300 to 3,400 miles) nuclear missiles from Europe, and Gorbachev agreed to destroy Soviet SS-20 missiles in Asia as well. This INF treaty required Russia to destroy 1,846 and America to destroy 846 missiles. Reagan, who, said Gorbachev had discovered a Russian saying that he quoted at every meeting—"trust but verify"—secured provisions that allowed each side to inspect the other's launching sites. Reagan insisted that the treaty be signed at precisely 1:45 on December 8, which, unknown at the time, had been chosen as a propitious time by Nancy Reagan's astrologer. The Senate approved by the accord by a vote of 93 to 5. The last of these missiles was destroyed in May 1991.

Figure 17.1 President Ronald Reagan and Soviet President Mikhail Gorbachev unhappily leaving their failed October 1986 Reykjavik summit conference. Courtesy Ronald Reagan Library.

Nothing is more difficult to negotiate than an arms reduction agreement. The earlier SALT treaties had set upper limits on future missile construction, but INF was the first ratified pact that required both sides actually to reduce the number of missiles. It affected only about 5 percent of the superpowers' nuclear arsenals, but it was a historic breakthrough that set a precedent for possible greater future reductions. In his diary, Reagan wrote this was "the best summit we've ever had."

Returning Gorbachev's visit, Reagan went to Moscow in May 1988 for his fourth summit in two and a half years, more than had been held by any previous president. Concrete accomplishments were slight (expanded student exchanges, fishing rights, space cooperation), but as theater the conference was spectacular. In his welcoming statement, Gorbachev said that long-held dislikes and stereotypes had abated. The seventy-seven-year-old president may have nodded off at a speech, and some of his anecdotes seemed unrelated to the issue, but he delivered his prepared speeches with surprising elan. He met with dissidents and the Patriarch, and took full advantage of his opportunities to lecture the Russians on human rights and the virtues of free enterprise and democracy. Making it clear that he favored Gorbachev's reforms, Reagan told students at Moscow University that they lived in an "exciting, hopeful time" when "the first breath of freedom stirs the air." Reagan seemed surprised that the ordinary citizens with whom he talked were "indistinguishable from people I had seen all my life on countless streets in America." He no longer believed, he said, that the Soviet Union was "an evil empire." He and Gorbachev shook hands with a crowd on Red Square (accompanied by a U.S. secret serviceman carrying the small black bag, known as the "football," that could send the signal to launch an atomic attack on Russia) (See Fig. 17.2). In his parting remarks, he told Gorbachev that "we think of you as friends." Gorbachev said that "we've come a long way" but that "more could have been achieved." In England, Reagan said that "all of this is a cause for shaking the head in wonder. Imagine the president of the United States and the general secretary of the Soviet Union walking together in Red Square talking about a growing personal friendship . . . realizing how much our people have in common."

The Senate had rushed approval of the INF treaty so that the leaders could sign the final version, but other concrete accomplishments at the Moscow summit were slight. The two leaders agreed to give each other twenty-four-hour notice of future missile tests and to exchange a thousand students annually. Reagan resisted Gorbachev's attempts to include in the final communique the phrase "peaceful coexistence," which right-wing Republicans had long excoriated.

In a December 7 speech to the UN, Gorbachev, saying that foreign policy should not be driven by ideology, advocated "freedom of choice" for all nations. He announced that he would unilaterally cut Soviet armed forces by 500,000 men (20 percent) and reduce Soviet forces in Eastern Europe and the European part of Russia by 10,000 tanks, and 800 aircraft, thereby assuming a strictly defensive stance. The U.S. press praised his "vision" and "boldness." In 1989 he withdrew the last Soviet troops from Afghanistan. The Soviet navy

Figure 17.2 Gorbachev and Reagan take a friendly walk on Red Square. AP/World Wide Photos.

withdrew its ballistic submarine patrols from near the U.S. coast and stopped visiting the Caribbean. Gorbachev also cut aid to the Sandinistas in Nicaragua and sought removal of Cuban troops from Angola.

Nearly all of the agreements that had been reached represented Soviet acceptance of U.S. positions. "We are going to do a terrible thing to you," said Georgi Arbatov, director of the Soviet Institute For The Study of America. "We are going to deprive you of an enemy."

In his January 1989 presidential farewell address, Reagan concluded that America had "forged a satisfying new closeness with the Soviet Union," and, he added "I want the new closeness to continue."

The Election of 1988

As the election of 1988 approached, the Republicans seemed to have the advantage. Despite his difficulties, Reagan's popularity remained high, and the economy continued to prosper. The nomination of Vice President George Bush was a foregone conclusion.

A full field of Democrats, but not the top stars, Massachusetts Senator Teddy Kennedy or New York Governor Mario Cuomo, competed in the primaries for the Democratic nomination. The early leader, Senator Gary Hart, was knocked out by a sex scandal. The victor was Governor Michael Dukakis of Massachusetts, whose chief advantage was the remarkable economic advances made by Massachusetts while he was governor.

The Republican campaign was most remembered for its efforts to depict Dukakis as softer on crime and less patriotic than Bush. Also, Bush played on the popular perception that the Republicans were more in favor of a strong defense. In the primary fight, Dukakis had opposed military aid to the Contras, advocated tougher measures against apartheid in South Africa, and criticized Reagan's Strategic Defense Initiative. However, foreign policy issues were not emphasized in the televised debates. Indicating a greater preference for military solutions, Bush attributed Russia's consent to arms control to Reagan's military buildup. Dukakis seemed to be more in favor of negotiations. One factor that kept Dukakis from emphasizing foreign policy was the fact that Bush was far more experienced in that field.

Bush won election by an impressive margin, but the Democrats retained control of both houses of Congress.

A remarkable aspect of Reagan's presidency, as of Nixon's, was the degree to which he reversed policies he had advocated before taking office. Both had been zealous and unyielding in their anticommuism but, as president, Nixon had espoused detente, and Reagan, even more extreme in his anticommunism, had signed the most significant arms limitation treaty to date and moved beyond detente to "closeness."

Reagan's administration could boast major gains. He had widened America's margin of military superiority. Top officials claimed that his military buildup and his hard line had forced the Communists to retreat and to make ruinous attempts to match arms spending. During his administration, the Soviets relaxed their grip on Eastern Europe, withdrew troops from Afghanistan, and moved toward free enterprise and democracy. "Countries across the globe," Reagan said in his farewell speech, "are turning to free markets." But, with the exception of the overturn of a Communist government in tiny Grenada, his record in promoting counterrevolution in the Third World was dismal. Despite the expenditures of enormous sums and the infliction of high casualties (the worst in Central America's history), he had not overturned the Sandinistas in Nicaragua or suppressed the rebels in El Salvador. His intervention in the Middle East was a tragic fiasco, and his attempt to secure the release of hostages by selling arms to Iran was a scandal.

Also, in his eight years, the economic and educational foundations of U.S. power had continued to erode as America lost some of its lead in economic production, accumulated a debilitating budget deficit, and moved from the position of the world's leading creditor to that of its leading debtor.

18 President Bush and the End of the Cold War

Bush Organizes His Administration

Few entering presidents were better trained for the job than George Bush. Born in 1924 into a wealthy New England family, son of a U.S. senator, he had been a World War II navy fighter pilot and later moved to Texas, where he headed an oil drilling firm. In 1966 he won election to the first of two terms in Congress. After he lost a bid for a Senate seat, Nixon and Ford appointed him successively ambassador to the UN, first chief of the U.S. liaison office in China (1974–1975), and director of the CIA. As Reagan's vice president, he had traveled widely and developed an extensive acquaintance with world leaders. Foreign affairs was his preferred field of operation.

For secretary of state, Bush chose a fellow Texan, James A. Baker III, a corporation lawyer who had been Reagan's chief of staff, secretary of the Treasury, and chairman of Bush's 1980 presidential campaign. For national security adviser, he named former Air Force General Brent Scowcroft, who held a doctorate in international relations from Columbia University and had served on Kissinger's staff and as Ford's national security adviser.

Baker had little foreign policy experience, but he later wrote that Bush gave him "wide latitude" in conducting foreign affairs and that, in contrast to the Nixon administration, the State Department, not the National Security Council, played the leading role. Also, Baker wrote, although Scowcroft was sometimes more "cautious" and was "more of a Cold Warrior," there was much less infighting in the Bush administration than in the Reagan administration.

As vice president, Bush had loyally backed Reagan's foreign policies, though observers described him as more cautious and less ideology-driven than Reagan. His subservience and his preppie manner had exposed him to the charge that he was a "wimp," an impression he seemed anxious to combat. He might turn out to be a Teddy Roosevelt, he had told reporters. "When people hit the booth, well, then they think: 'Hey, when the chips are down, this guy can defend us and what we stand for.'" Kennedy's inaugural speech promising a worldwide fight for freedom, he said, expressed the "policies and principles" he would follow.

Military Policy

When Bush took office in January 1989, America had a wide margin of military superiority. The CIA had reduced its estimate of the annual rise of Soviet military spending from 5 percent to only 2 percent, and its estimate of total Soviet arms spending to 9 percent of GNP. In May 1989, for the first time, the Soviets announced specific defense budget figures—77.3 billion rubles, less than half the U.S. level.

Reagan had raised military funding to 6.5 percent of GNP and had proposed additional annual increases of two percent above inflation. Bush, however, asked only for increases that matched inflation. In November 1989, Congress voted $305 billion for defense. America was then maintaining 530,000 soldiers and 65,000 sailors abroad.

Gorbachev's perestroika policy, withdrawal of Soviet troops from Afghanistan (February 1989), armed force reductions, and freeing of Soviet satellites (disscused in the next section) seemed to remove the menace that the U.S. armed forces were designed to combat. With the Warsaw Pact's threat "largely broken," said former defense secretary James Schlesinger, America should cut the number of its troops in Europe from 305,000 to 50,000. Former defense secretary Robert McNamara advocated slashing total defense spending by half. Nevertheless, Bush's second defense budget called for a real decrease of only 2.6 percent, to $295 billion, and he later requested $291 billion for 1993 (Congress appropriated $277 billion).

Changes in the Soviet Union

In the Soviet Union, movement toward democracy and a free market, the liberation of the empire, and improving relations with the West accelerated.

Despite years of Communist rule, about half of the Soviet people still professed a religious affiliation. "We need spiritual values," said Gorbachev, and "the moral values that the religious embodied for centuries can help in the work of renewal of our country." From mid-1988 through 1989, seventeen hundred churches opened.

In February 1990, the Soviet Communist party voted to surrender its monopoly of political power and to transfer power to an elected president. A new party constitution endorsed "individual property, including ownership of the means of production." In March, the Communists voted to allow individuals to own small factories and to hire workers.

However, the performance of the Soviet economy under perestroika was disappointing. Growth slowed to only 1.4 percent in 1989, and production fell in 1990 by 13 percent and in 1991 by 17 percent. The movement to democracy made it impossible for the government to impose changes by decree, and democracy was too new for elected delegates to have developed much sense of responsibility. For example, despite a deepening deficit, they voted down Gorbachev's attempt to raise taxes on tobacco and alcohol.

The Soviet Union was not a unitary national state but heir to the Russian empire, acquired through hundreds of years of Russian conquests, and it contained more than a hundred ethnic groups. Russians made up scarcely more than half of the population. Communists had reorganized the empire along ethnic lines as fifteen republics, of which the Russian Republic was by far the largest. Each republic also contained minorities. As Moscow's central control weakened, some republics and minorities declared independence, and fighting among them erupted.

Lithuania, Estonia, and Latvia had been independent between the two world wars. In 1991, Lithuania's Communist party declared its independence of the Soviet Communist party. Latvia and Estonia, at a slower pace, also moved toward independence. Gorbachev, saying that secession posed "enormous danger" and threatened the success of his democratic reforms, imposed economic sanctions. Bush warned him against forcible suppression.

Gorbachev's problems seemed overwhelming. "Some people are beginning to panic," he said in June 1990. "They shout about anarchy; they predict chaos, war, total ruin."

Liberation of Eastern Europe

The Cold War had begun with Western resistance to Soviet control of nations in East Europe (see Fig. 18.1). In early 1989, Gorbachev began withdrawing Soviet tanks and troops from East Europe, and he watched in apparent approval as countries there moved from hard-line Communist rule toward liberal Communist or non-Communist regimes. In June 1989, calling the changes there "inspiring," Gorbachev renounced any claim to a right to intervene in East European nations, thus repudiating the Brezhnev Doctrine and replacing it, said a high official, with the "Sinatra Doctrine"—they could do it "their way."

In April 1989, the Polish government, which had adopted a form of perestroika, legalized the non-Communist labor organization Solidarity, led by Lech Walesa, and allowed it to participate in drafting a new constitution. By June, Solidarity had won elections and control of a coalition government. In October, the new Polish government announced a program of rapid conversion to a market economy. In Hungary, in 1989, the Communist party adopted glasnost, opened its borders, repudiated Marxism, changed its name to the Socialist party, and agreed to a March 1990 election, which it lost to non-Communists. Bulgaria's Communist party dismissed the Stalinist dictator in November 1989, and, in August 1990, parliament elected a non-Communist president. In Czechoslovakia, in December 1989, soon after parliament abolished the Communist party's right to a "leading role," anti-Communist writer Vaclav Havel won the presidency.

This overthrow of hard-line Communists was accomplished with little bloodshed except in Romania, where Nicholas Ceausescu ruled with the aid of a large secret police force. The Soviets supported the December 1989 uprising,

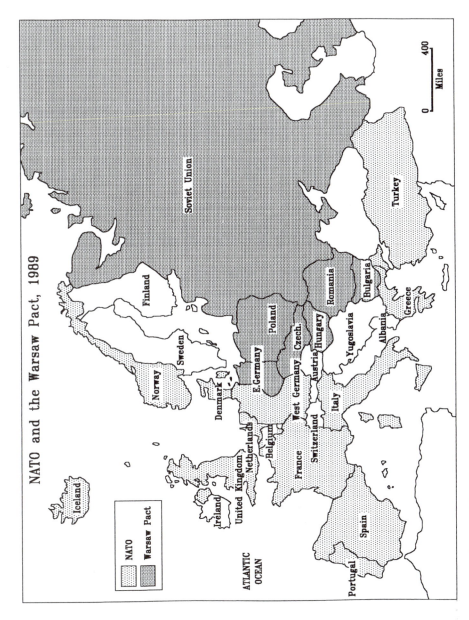

Figure 18.1 NATO and the Warsaw Pact.

and victorious revolutionaries executed Ceausescu. Visiting Soviet Foreign Minister Shevardnadze called the new atmosphere "absolutely purifying."

East Germany, the most prosperous country of the Soviet bloc, had long been ruled by a hard-line Communist, Eric Honecker, who resisted Gorbachev's advice to reform. When huge crowds demonstrated for democracy, and the security chief refused to fire on them, Honecker resigned in October 1989. On November 9, East Germany opened the Berlin Wall, long the world-famous symbol of Cold War oppression, which celebrating crowds quickly demolished.

Freeing Eastern Europe from Communist dictatorship did not immediately produce as many benefits as had been hoped. The sudden movement toward free enterprise required painful adjustments, which were accompanied by falling production, unemployment, shortages, and skyrocketing prices. In a December 1989 speech to the U.S. Congress, Walesa said that East Europe needed $10 billion in aid. Twenty-four Western nations created a $1 billion aid fund.

Dobrynin wrote that Gorbachev "never foresaw that the whole of Eastern Europe would fly out of the Soviet orbit within months." This sudden evaporation of Soviet control astounded the West, which hastened to extend aid and trade to the new East European regimes. Abandonment by Russia of the "effort to control Eastern Europe by force," said Jeane Kirkpatrick, "marks the end of the Cold War."

Unification of Germany

Western Europe continued its slow move toward economic union. After long discussion, European Economic Community (EEC) nations resolved to adopt a common currency and to abolish remaining barriers to the free movement of people and goods among them by 1999. In May 1990, at the initiative of Chancellor Kohl and President Mitterrand, they also reaffirmed a goal of "political union" and adoption of a common foreign and defense policy, but achievement of political unification did not appear to be near.

Germany, however, did achieve political unification. Nearly all Germans wanted reunion, but it was opposed by some other Europeans who remembered Germany's past aggression. Nevertheless, in December 1989, the EEC approved German "unity through self-determination." The Soviets, who had long argued that the neutralization of Germany was vital to Soviet security, offered to approve only on the condition either that Germany not join NATO or that Germany join both NATO and the Warsaw Pact. "Having East Germany leave the Warsaw Pact," said a foreign ministry official, "means we've lost the Cold War. Okay. We can accept that, although it's not so easy." But if a united Germany joined NATO, Russians would feel that they had "lost World War II."

Retreating on this issue as on others, Gorbachev, in a July 1990 meeting with Chancellor Kohl, consented to Germany's both reuniting and joining NATO. In return, Kohl pledged that Germany would acquire no atomic, biological, or chemical weapons, cut its armed forces from 590,000 to 370,000, ban foreign troops from its soil, give Russia $25 billion in aid and loans, and pay the cost of troop removal. Baker was surprised that they had reached agreement so quickly. This is a "fantastic result," said Kohl. And, he added, "it is a dream come true to see German unity and European unity taking place together."

A treaty, signed in September 1990 by the two German governments, the Soviet Union, the United States, Britain, and France, provided that Americans and Soviets would withdraw their troops from Germany and that Germany would never seek to recover territory lost to Poland and Russia. The German issue, which had been at the heart of much of the Cold War, was at last resolved. "We have closed the book on World War II," said Shevardnazdze, "and started a new age."

Unification made Germany Western Europe's largest nation, with a population of 79 million and a GNP of $1,100 billion (compared to France's $840 billion and Britain's $818 billion.) However, it had less territory than it had in 1937, its GNP was scarcely more than half Japan's, and its 1.4 birthrate (per woman) was far below the 2.1 replacement level. Moreover, Europe's movement toward economic unification eliminated any pressure for Germany to go to war to secure access to raw materials and markets.

For years, America had extended a nuclear umbrella over Europe and stationed large military forces there. But the military need seemed to have vanished; it was hard to imagine the disintegrating Warsaw Pact attacking any Western nation. In July 1990, British Prime Minister Thatcher announced that she would slash British troop strength by a fourth. Nevertheless, both Thatcher and Kohl expressed a desire that America stay in Europe. And Bush asserted that America "should remain a European power."

At a July 1990 NATO summit, NATO proposed that it and the Warsaw Pact jointly declare that "we are no longer adversaries," thus formally ending the Cold War.

Summit Conferences

In May 1989, Bush had said it was time to move beyond containment and to "seek the integration of the Soviet Union into the community of nations . . . it is time for peace." In October, saying that America wanted perestroika to succeed, Baker offered to send advisers and technical aid to help the Soviets reform their economy. George Arbatov rejoiced that the United States had "stopped economic warfare against the Soviet Union."

Gorbachev sought an early meeting with Bush, but the president held aloof. To some, the president seemed little more than a spectator of the momentous events. Finally, at the urging of Lech Walesa and others who wanted to strengthen Gorbachev politically, Bush agreed to meet the Russian leader. What changed his mind, he said, was "consultation with our allies, the rapidity of change in East Europe . . . and this concept that I just didn't want to . . . miss something." The time set was December 2–3, 1989.

On his way to the summit, Gorbachev stopped in Italy to accept an invitation to an audience with the Pope, the first such visit by a top Soviet official.

Claiming that the Soviets allowed freedom of religion, he said that they now realized that they needed not just democracy but also morality and "such universal, eternal values as goodness, mercy, mutual aid." The two agreed to establish permanent official relations.

Bush had proposed that he and Gorbachev meet on ships off the coast of Malta. The sea was too rough to allow the planned alternation between their two warships, so a reduced number of sessions was held on board a cruise ship that the Soviets had brought to serve as their hotel. The two sides sat across from each other at a narrow table. "If we run out of arguments," quipped Gorbachev, "we can kick each other." Bush asked Gorbachev to break economic relations with Cuba, and Gorbachev chided Bush for continuing U.S. intervention, such as in Panama (discussed later in this chapter), at a time when the Soviets had halted arms shipments to Nicaragua and withdrawn military forces from eastern Europe. Nevertheless, negotiations were friendly. Bush assured Gorbachev that Washington favored his reforms and planned to give the Soviets most-favored-nation trade status. They agreed to work to reduce conventional arms in Europe and to speed up negotiations on reducing long-range atomic weapons. Gorbachev said that "we don't consider you an enemy anymore" and that he wanted America to keep troops in Europe to help control the Germans. One participant said there was a "wonderful feeling in the room, almost a glow."

The leaders issued no formal communique, but held an unprecedented joint news conference in which they agreed that the Cold War should be abandoned. Bush was effusive: "We stand at the threshold of a brand-new era."

Gorbachev became immensely popular in the West. A 1989 poll showed that 90 percent of West Germans trusted him, compared to only 58 per cent who trusted Bush. In 1990, *Time* named him "man of the decade." A "dynamo," a "genius," and a "world-class leader," *Time* effused, he had "transformed the world" and inspired "awe" and "admiration." George F. Kennan called him "a miracle." In 1990, Gorbachev was awarded the Nobel Peace Prize.

In May 1990, Gorbachev flew to Washington for a four-day summit. He was greeted by large and friendly crowds, and, as on his previous trip, he plunged into crowds to shake hands. He urged businessmen to increase their investments in Russia. His meeting with Congressmen was characterized by good-natured banter. "Why did you let your administration intervene in Panama if you love freedom so much?" he asked, and he chided them for giving China most-favored-nation status after the Tiananmen Square killing (see below).

Gorbachev and Bush, continuing negotiations at Camp David, agreed to reduce long-range nuclear weapons by 50 percent, to halt production of chemical weapons, and to eliminate 80–90 percent of poison gas stockpiles. (See Fig. 18.2.) They agreed on terms for the reunification of Germany. They also agreed to increase trade, expand exchanges of university students, and conduct a joint relief operation in Ethiopia. Back home, Gorbachev told his colleagues that he no longer felt "any more danger from Washington."

Gorbachev badly wanted a trade agreement to assist the Soviet economy and, he repeatedly told Bush, to give him and his reforms a boost at home. He

Figure 18.2 Secretary of State James Baker, Mrs. George Bush, President Bush, Mrs. Raisa Gorbachev, President Gorbachev, Soviet Ambassador Eduard Shevardnadze, and National Security Adviser Brent Scowcroft at Camp David. Bush Presidential Library.

relaxed restrictions on the emigration of Jews (from 900 in 1987, the number of emigrés rose to more than 60,000 in 1989). However, Bush made most-favored-nation status conditional on the Soviets enacting liberal emigration laws, which did not happen until 1991, too late to help Gorbachev.

At Bush's request, the two met for a third time, in September 1990, at Helsinki, Finland. Bush arranged this meeting to demonstrate their unity on the Iraq crisis. This was something new—a Soviet-American summit convened to demonstrate unity.

In July 1991, Bush flew to Moscow for yet another summit. In a Strategic Arms Reduction Treaty (START I), Bush and Gorbachev agreed to lower the number of nuclear warheads from 30,000 to 8,600 for each side, and the number of strategic (long-range) delivery vehicles to 1,600 each. This cut their respective nuclear arsenals by half. "Thank God," said Gorbachev, "that we stopped this." In September, Bush announced that America would remove all tactical nuclear missiles and artillery shells from Europe. Also, they agreed to remove short-range nuclear missiles from warships. In October, Gorbachev promised to deactivate 503 intercontinental missiles, and in November he offered to open Soviet territory to aerial inspection. This was a long-dreamed-of achievement, but it was overshadowed by even more astounding developments.

The Cold War Victory

The long series of Soviet-American agreements came as the result not of mutual concessions, but of Soviet acceptance of U.S. positions. By 1990, the Soviets had moved their political and economic system toward democracy and free enterprise, liberated East Europe, and dropped their challenge to America for influence in the Third World.

Underlying these changes was the failure of the Soviet economy to remain competitive. Earlier it had narrowed America's economic lead and created successful atomic and space programs. But in the 1970s and 1980s its bureaucracy, grown bloated (18 million people), privileged, and unresponsive, proved incapable of keeping up in technology. Also, its military buildup and aid provided to Marxist regimes abroad proved to be ruinous economic drains. Its standard of living remained low—for example, 30 percent of its houses had no running water. America widened its production lead, Japan lifted its per capita GNP to more that double Russia's, while China's GNP rose at triple the Soviet rate. The Soviet economy was losing the ability to sustain competition.

The first requirement, Gorbachev decided, was to break the power of the bureaucracy by instituting democracy. He won political victories over hard-line Communists, but this did not raise production. Instead, it weakened central economic control before the appearance of an alternative economy to replace it. The resulting drop in economic output put additional pressure on him to reduce Russia's expensive foreign commitments.

Abandoning its worldwide challenge to America, the Soviet Union withdrew its troops from Afghanistan, stopped supplying arms to rebels in Central America, had Cuba withdraw its troops from Angola and Ethiopia, and got Vietnam to pull its troops out of Cambodia. In June 1991, the Warsaw Pact dissolved. Gorbachev even sought to make the Soviet Union America's ally. "We want to enter NATO," he told Baker.

The West had also won a striking ideological victory. Not only Russia, but countries in Latin America, Africa, and East Asia now moved toward democracy and market economies. A proposed Soviet economic plan conceded that history had not yet invented a means superior to the free market for raising production.

So complete was the victory that some warned against excessive gloating. "The West," said a high Soviet Foreign Ministry official, "must not rub our noses too much in our defeat." Gorbachev wrote that "rejection of confrontation and hostility has made us all winners."

Some wondered if the Soviet threat had ever really been as menacing as it had been pictured in the West. Policy had been dominated, said George Kennan, by "unreal and exaggerated estimates of the intentions and strength of the other party." *Time* editor Strobe Talbott wrote, January 1, 1990, that Western policy had been based on "grotesque exaggeration."

In 1991, in yet another startling development, the Soviet Union dissolved. Trying to hold the country together, Gorbachev, in January, called for a referendum on preserving the union, but six republics—Armenia, Estonia, Georgia,

Latvia, Lithuania, and Moldavia—refused to participate. In the March 1991 vote in the other republics, 77 percent favored unity and, in June, Gorbachev and the leaders of six republics signed a new union treaty. However, in June, Boris Yeltsin, an advocate of rapid reform and Russian independence, was elected president of the republic of Russia.

Seeking to halt the dissolution of the union, hard-line Communist leaders attempted to dismiss Gorbachev and reassert central control. In August 1991, confining Gorbachev to his Black Sea vacation dacha, they announced that power had been transferred to the vice president. However, eluding arrest, Boris Yeltsin, who sought to make Russia independent, barricaded himself in the Russian parliament building, and a crowd of citizens gathered to help protect him. Soviet troops approached but did not attack, and some troops defected to Yeltsin. Apparently reluctant to shed blood and unsure of popular support, the leaders of the coup gave up. Saying that "everything I have worked for is being destroyed," one of them committed suicide.

The result of the coup's collapse, however, was not to restore power to Gorbachev but to transfer it to Yeltsin, who had broken with Gorbachev and the Communist party. Yeltsin seized the property of the Communist party and banned any further activity by it. The name of the city of Leningrad was changed back to St. Petersburg, and the red flag was hauled down from the Kremlin. On December 25, 1991, leaders of eleven republics declared that the Soviet Union no longer existed. The newly independent republics created a powerless "Commonwealth of Independent States," but Estonia, Latvia, Lithuania, and Georgia rejected even this loose association. These developments eliminated the Soviet Union and Gorbachev's job.

Curiously, Bush did not promote the fragmentation of the old Cold War enemy. Instead, while warning against the use of force to suppress the movement toward independence, he urged Estonia, Latvia, and Lithuania to go slowly in asserting independence, and, returning from the July 1991 Moscow summit, he made a speech to the Ukrainian parliament favoring that state's continued union with Russia. He feared that disruption would derail Gorbachev's reforms and complicate the problem of controlling the Soviet Union's nuclear weapons.

Under Yeltsin's leadership, Russia declared its independence, speeded up its movement toward a free market, and raised the prices it charged other republics for oil. However, Russia's budget deficit and inflation continued to soar, and economic production dropped an additional 20 percent in 1992.

The newly independent nations immediately began quarreling over the terms of the divorce, such as which would control what part of the armed forces. Also, each contained sizable ethnic minorities, and fights for territory erupted between these groups. Wondering foreign observers asked how far such disintegration would go.

The end of the Cold War ended the superpower practice of conducting proxy wars in developing countries as the Russians withdrew their support of overseas Marxist groups. The violence of some of these wars, including those in Angola, Cambodia, Nicaragua, and El Salvador, abated, and progress was made toward peaceful settlements.

In his February 1992 State of the Union address, Bush proposed additional cuts in strategic warheads and bombs to 4,700 for America and 4,400 for the former Soviet Union. At the UN, Boris Yeltsin proposed cutting the number to 2,500 each. "From now on," said Yeltsin, "we do not consider ourselves to be potential enemies." In the 1992 START II treaty, the two leaders agreed to reduce the number of nuclear weapons to 3,500 each.

International Economic Policy

America conducted more international trade than any other nation, but had an unfavorable merchandise trade balance (1990) of $101 billion. Even including service and investment income, Americans paid foreigners $78 billion more than foreigners paid Americans.

A Bush administration document eloquently restated the case for free trade: competition, it said, was the "life blood of a healthy world economy," and, even if imports hurt some industries, the resultant shift of labor and capital to more profitable businesses would improve the national well-being. Furthermore, it added, raising barriers to imports had the effect of cutting exports because it denied foreigners opportunities to earn the dollars needed to buy U.S. goods. The solution to America's trade problems, it concluded, was to produce more, consume less, upgrade education, and cut the federal deficit.

Bush vigorously promoted U.S. exports. Accusing Japan, Brazil, and India of unfairly discriminating against U.S. goods, he pressured them to buy more from America. He also continued to subsidize exports of tobacco.

In August 1992, the United States, Mexico, and Canada completed an agreement to remove all trade barriers between them within fifteen years. This would create a North America Free Trade Area (NAFTA) larger than the European Economic Community and, its advocates predicted, stimulate economic development and raise the living standards of all three countries.

Americans had long taken pride in the generosity of their foreign aid. In 1990, new grants and loans totaled nearly $17 billion. However, in amount U.S. aid was less than that provided by Japan, and as a percent of GNP it was the lowest of any industrialized democracy. Two-thirds of America's aid went to five countries: Israel ($3 billion), Egypt ($2.1 billion), the Philippines ($.6 billion), Turkey ($.6 billion), and Pakistan ($.5 billion), mostly for military purposes.

As East European nations discarded communism, they solicited economic aid to help them finance free market reforms. America joined a twenty-four-nation plan to give aid, and, in 1990, Congress voted $532 million for Poland and Hungary. In 1991, Congress voted to extend most-favored-nation trade status to the Commonwealth of Independent States (the former Soviet Union) and provided $500 million to help the Russians destroy their stockpile of nuclear weapons. However, the huge U.S. budget deficit restricted the amount of U.S.

funds available, and other nations complained that Washington was not bearing its fair share of the load.

Japan: Competitive Ally

Between 1960 and 1989 Japan's economic production grew twice as fast as America's. The CIA's *World Factbook* listed Japan's 1990 GNP at $2.1 trillion, compared to the Soviet Union's $2.7 trillion and America's $5.5 trillion. By 1992, Japan's GNP ranked second in the world. Japan's surplus of exports over imports was $100 billion in 1991, and, home of the world's ten largest banks, Japan had become the world's biggest lender and foreign aid donor.

As compared to Americans, the Japanese had higher wages, lower executive salaries, better public education, and a more equal distribution of income. U.S. labor productivity, however, remained higher, and total U.S. exports exceeded Japan's.

In attempts to narrow the gap between what Americans imported from Japan and what they sold to Japan ($41 billion in 1991), Americans urged the Japanese to raise government spending on public works, reduce the work week to five days, dissolve monopolistic corporations, and allow big department stores, which might carry U.S. goods, more freedom to compete with small shops that did not. The Japanese, in turn, advised Americans to raise the tax on gasoline to cut oil imports, upgrade schools, spend more on scientific research, cut executive pay, raise income taxes, and balance the federal budget.

The Japanese frequently made concessions. In 1989, U.S. sales to Japan soared 18 percent, to surpass U.S. exports to Germany, France, and Italy combined. In 1990, the Japanese began giving large tax credits to companies that raised imports of manufactured goods. In 1992, they massively increased government spending on public works. Their imports from America almost doubled in ten years; by 1992 they imported $394 per capita of U.S. goods, while Americans imported only $360 per capita from Japan.

Increasingly, also, the Japanese placed factories in America, where they provided jobs for U.S. workers. By 1992, approximately 600,000 Americans worked for Japanese companies. Most of the Honda automobiles sold in America were made in America, and the Japanese even exported some of their U.S.-made cars to Japan. U.S. corporations successfully penetrated the Japanese market; the largest restaurant chain in Japan was MacDonald's. Nevertheless, the trade gap persisted.

In 1988, at $39 billion, Japan's military spending was surpassed only by Russia's $119 billion and America's $290 billion. Japan also paid America $3 billion annually for half of the cost of maintaining sixty thousand U.S. troops in Japan. Still, Americans continued to press Japan to raise its military spending.

In the 1990-91 Persian Gulf crisis, Japan gave America full diplomatic support, plus $13 billion in financial backing, which required Japan to raise taxes. Expressing little appreciation, American slightingly referred to "checkbook diplomacy" and criticized Japan for not sending troops (which the "MacArthur Constitution" forbade).

Bush planned a trip to Japan but, under fire for devoting too little attention to the U.S. economic recession, he postponed it to January 1992. Then, billing the trip as a trade promotion venture, he took with him the chairmen of America's large automobile companies, a gesture that did not please the Japanese. The emperor and his son defeated Bush and Baker at tennis, after which, at a dinner, Prime Minister Kiichi Miyazawa fed Bush raw fish. Fainting, Bush vomited in the prime minister's lap. Although he secured Japan's agreement to double its purchases of U.S. automobile parts, the *New York Times* called the trip a "fiasco," and columnist George Will termed it "the worst foreign trip in the history of presidential travel."

The close U.S.-Japanese partnership that had developed after World War II had provided Japan with security and enabled the Japanese to concentrate on economic advance. Also, America's policy of promoting international trade had helped the Japanese to integrate their economy with the world economy. But if a trade war developed, the threat existed that Tokyo might be forced to form an East Asian trading bloc, and that U.S.-Japanese relations might revert to the rivalry that had existed before World War II.

Friction with China

When Bush took over the White House in early 1989, U.S.-Chinese relations were at a high point. China was helping Washington deal with North Korea, Americans were pleased by China's free market reforms, and trade and cultural exchanges were booming. Bush, who had represented the United States in China 1974–1976, had friendly personal relations with China's leaders. Prospects for continued cooperation were excellent.

China had achieved remarkable advances in the 1980s. With the campaign against religion abating, temples and churches reopened, and the number of Christians rose above that of the pre-Communist era. Foreign study and travel soared, and military spending dropped by more than half. Economic reforms allowed private enterprises to flourish. By 1992, the share of industrial goods produced by government-owned factories had fallen below half of total output.

Concentrating on reforms that directly raised production, and testing them in one province before applying them nationwide, China, unlike East Europe, made the difficult transition from socialism toward a free market without loss of production. Instead, between 1979 and 1992, rising at an average annual rate of 9 percent, its per capita income more than doubled. This meant an enormous elevation of the quality of life of hundreds of millions.

Nevertheless, many Chinese were dissatisfied. Expectations, fed by increased contacts with the West, raced ahead of performance. Prices rose, and uneven distribution of the new economic gains aroused jealousy and suspicion that government officials were corruptly enriching themselves. Many sought democracy. Feeling particularly shortchanged, students and professors hoped to wrest from China's aging bureaucracy leadership of the modernization movement of which they considered themselves to be the natural vanguard.

On April 15, 1989, after the deposed Communist party chairman Hu Yaobang, whom students considered an advocate of desired reforms, died, a crowd of 100,000 mourners gathered on Beijing's Tiananmen Square in front of the Great Hall of the People, China's capitol. Speakers attacked the Communist leadership and demanded reform. On April 24, students began a continuous occupation of the square. On May 17, more than a million demonstrated there, and similar protests occurred in twenty other cities. Much of the world was impressed with the idealism of the students and the civilized conduct of both demonstrators and government.

Had the demonstrators stopped there, the effect might have been to accelerate reforms. But the movement escalated from a demand for reform to an attempt to seize power. Demands arose for the removal of party leaders, and some protesters sought the overthrow of Communist rule. Alarming many Communists, these developments strengthened the hands of party leaders who wanted to suppress the demonstrators.

On May 20, Premier Li Peng imposed martial law and ordered demonstrators to disperse. Refusing to do so, they erected a "Goddess of Democracy" statue and repulsed the unarmed troops who sought to remove them. On June 4, using tanks, armed troops launched an all-out assault that killed hundreds while clearing the square. Watching on television, the world was appalled.

Premier Li concluded that the students "had good reason to protest," but that their protests had escalated into an attempt to overthrow the government, which could not be forgiven. It was a "counterrevolutionary rebellion," said Deng Xiaoping, an attempt to overthrow the Communist party.

The immediate results were calamitous. The government disbanded many student and worker organizations, closed schools, and executed or imprisoned demonstration leaders. Tourism and foreign investment plummeted, and economic growth stalled.

Overwhelmingly, Americans sympathized with the demonstrators. Baker told the Chinese ambassador that "the actions of your government cast a serious pall over our relations." America and other countries imposed sanctions, including suspension of sales of military equipment, and broke off high-level government contacts. However, refusing to go as far as many Americans demanded, Bush did not withdraw China's most-favored-nation status. Maintaining that no government would have tolerated such disruptions, Henry Kissinger called it "entirely a domestic matter" that should not disrupt Sino-American relations. In July, Bush secretly sent Scowcroft to Beijing.

Gradually, China returned to more normal conditions. The government lifted martial law by March 1990 and released many prisoners. Economic reform continued, and by 1991 economic growth had recovered to 6 percent.

Gorbachev's visit to China, on May 15, 1989, had coincided with the Tiananmen protests, and he had expressed sympathy with the protestors. Economic change was impossible, he said, without political change, and all Communist countries were moving "toward greater freedom of expression, democracy, and individual rights." Nevertheless, the two countries increased their economic and scientific cooperation, and Gorbachev cut the number of Soviet troops in East Asia by 200,000 (leaving 500,000). In a switch, China extended credits to the Soviets to buy Chinese goods.

In addition to human rights, Americans were concerned about China's weapon sales to Pakistan, Syria, Iran, and Libya, and its assistance to Pakistan and Iran in the construction of atomic power plants. When Baker visited Beijing in November 1991, the Chinese defended their crackdown on opposition as necessary to avert the kind of disruption that had devastated the quality of life in the Soviet Union and Yugoslavia, and they complained about being excluded from the GATT trading system and from the Middle East conference at Madrid (see below.)

As America eased sanctions, U.S.-Chinese trade rose from $2.3 billion in 1979 to $33 billion in 1992. In earlier years, U.S. exports to China had greatly exceeded imports, but in 1992 Americans exported $7.5 billion in goods to China, while China sold more than $25.5 billion to Americans.

Invasion of Panama

The end of the Cold War did not end U.S. military interventions, but other motives displaced anticommunism. Humanitarian Americans were appalled by atrocities and starvation resulting from civil wars, and they sought to promote democracy, free enterprise, and human rights abroad. Also, Washington was eager to protect access to key resources such as oil, and apprehensive about possible new threats to U.S. interests by aggressive regional powers. Furthermore, interventionists argued that America was morally obligated to intervene because only America had the military power to do so effectively. In the Bush administration, non–Cold War interventions occurred in Central America, Africa, and the Middle East.

By the 1990s, world production and sale of illegal drugs totaled $100 billion a year. Latin American countries produced or transshipped 80–90 percent of the cocaine and marijuana that entered the United States. Although the United States spent billions helping Latin Americans fight drug dealers and on attempts to interdict drugs bound for U.S. territory, drugs remained in plentiful supply. Apparently, as long as Americans were willing to pay billions for drugs, the drugs would be supplied.

In Panama, when army commander General Manuel Antonia Noriega, who had been trained in a U.S.-operated military school and had been on the CIA payroll, had seized power in 1986, Washington had cooperated with him. He helped Reagan catch drug dealers and arm and train the Contras. However, in 1987, he was indicted by a U.S. court on evidence that he had engaged in the international drug trade, and, in April 1988, Reagan imposed economic sanctions, including freezing Panama's assets and withholding canal toll revenues, that badly hurt Panama's economy. Although the OAS condemned Noriega,

Latin American countries did not support the sanctions, and, in May 1988, thirteen Caribbean nations called for an end to U.S. intervention in Panama.

Under crippling sanctions, Noriega agreed to a May 1989 internationally supervised election. However, when it appeared that the opposition was winning, Noriega seized the ballot boxes and proclaimed his candidate the victor. Foreign observers, including Jimmy Carter, called this a fraud and estimated that Noriega had actually lost by a margin of 3 to 1. Rejecting Baker's recommendation that he offer to drop drug charges against Noriega if he would agree to leave Panama, Bush demanded that he resign and sent 11,000 U.S. troops to Panama to reinforce the 13,000 already there.

On December 16, Panamanian soldiers stopped a car occupied by off-duty U.S. soldiers and, when they attempted to escape, killed one of them. On December 20, 1989, citing need to protect U.S. lives, halt the drug traffic, and bring Noriega to justice, Bush ordered 27,000 troops to invade Panama. This was the first U.S. intervention unrelated to the Cold War in many years. At a time when the Soviets were repudiating the Brezhnev Doctrine, it appeared that Bush was reviving the Roosevelt Corollary.

Bush launched the invasion, "Operation Just Cause," with little prior consultation. He maintained that he did not need congressional approval. "I have an obligation as president," he told reporters, "to conduct the foreign policy of this country the way I see fit."

Panamanian resistance collapsed quickly. U.S. forces lost only 26 killed, but between 300 and 700 (Noriega partisans said 7,000) Panamanians died, and property losses totaled an estimated $1 billion. Capturing Noriega, Americans took him to Miami for trial, thereby putting another country's leader on trial for violating U.S. laws. In 1992, Noriega was sentenced to a long prison term.

Britain, Japan, Canada, and West Germany seemed to support the invasion. But Russia called it illegal, and China expressed opposition to military intervention "under any pretext." Latin Americans denounced it, Peru's president called it a "criminal act," and the OAS, in its first formal censure of the United States, voted 20 to 1 to "deeply deplore" it. The UN, by a vote of 75 to 20 in the General Assembly and 10 to 1 in the Security Council, also condemned the invasion.

Nevertheless, Bush's popularity with the U.S. public soared, demonstrating anew that presidential military action could be of great political value. He was no longer called a wimp. In Panama, the drug traffic rose.

Faltering Steps Toward Arab-Israeli Agreement

America remained deeply involved in the Middle East, even though Baker regarded it as "a pitfall to be avoided," where Americans expended "an inordinate amount of time and effort" with "few prospects for success."

In October 1989, Lebanon's warring factions agreed on a new constitution in which the dominant Christian minority conceded some power to the Muslim majority. Denouncing this settlement, the right-wing Christian General Michel Aoun attempted to drive Syria from Lebanon. After the Iraq crisis (see next section) caused America to seek Syria's support against Iraq, America stood aside while Syrian troops crushed Aoun. Thus, the long U.S. and Israeli effort to preserve Christian supremacy and expel Syria from Lebanon collapsed.

Bush continued to give Israel large-scale aid while urging it to grant more rights to the residents of the Arab lands that its troops had occupied. He continued America's policy of exhorting Israel to stop planting Jewish settlements in the occupied territories and to return these lands to the Arabs in exchange for peace treaties. "Lay aside, once and for all, the unrealistic vision of a greater Israel," Baker told Israel's leaders in May 1989. "Forswear annexation. Stop settlement." But Prime Minister Yitzhak Shamir replied that he would continue to settle Jews in occupied lands, and would never agree to creation of a Palestinian state. By 1991, Jewish settlers made up 123,000 of the West Bank and Gaza's 1.8 million population. Nevertheless, U.S. aid to Israel, a total of $77 billion since 1967, continued in 1992 at the rate of $4.7 billion a year, more than $1,000 per Israeli citizen.

In April 1991, America and the Soviet Union agreed to cosponsor a Middle East peace conference. In October, a conference opened in Madrid, attended by representatives of Israel, Egypt, Syria, Lebanon, Jordan, and the Palestinians of Israeli-occupied territories—an historic first meeting of all parties to the conflict except the PLO. Also present were Bush, Gorbachev, and representatives of the UN and the European Community. The sessions were stormy and brief. "Those whom the Gods would destroy," Irving Kristol had observed, "they first tempt to resolve the Arab-Israeli conflict." However, in June 1992, the Israelis voted the unyielding Shamir out of power in favor of the Labor Party's Shimon Perez, who favored trading land for peace. U.S. Jewish organizations urged Israel to accept a compromise, and Perez slowed Jewish settlement in Arab areas.

The Gulf War

On August 2, 1990, Iraq invaded Kuwait (see Fig. 18.3).

Both Iraq (population 19 million) and Kuwait (population 2 million) were Arab and Muslim. In 1932, Britain had given Iraq independence, but it held Kuwait, which Iraqis considered part of Iraq, until 1961. Refusing to recognize Kuwait's independence, Iraq made repeated attempts to occupy it. Kuwait partly blocked Iraq's outlet to the Persian Gulf (Saddam demanded a territorial adjustment), and its rich oil deposits gave it a larger per capita income ($14,000 to Iraq's $2,000). Also, Iraq accused Kuwait of overproducing oil, and thereby driving down the price that Iraq could get for its oil, and also slant-drilling under their border to steal Iraqi oil.

Iraq's President, Saddam Hussein, had a well-deserved reputation as a murderous dictator. However, he was, in the Arab context, a modernizer. He improved housing, built roads, doubled average food consumption, cut illiter-

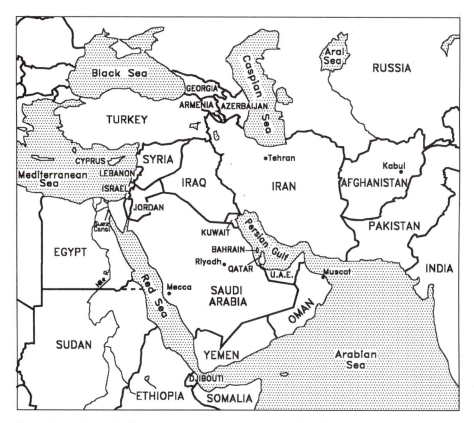

Figure 18.3 The Middle East.

acy, and guaranteed equal pay for women. The Soviets helped train and equip his military forces. Americans favored Saddam in his war against Iran (1980–1988) and valued him as a counterbalance to Iran and Syria, both of which America accused of aggression and terrorism. In early 1990, an assistant secretary of state called him "a force of moderation." Washington continued to give him aid and secret intelligence up to a month before he invaded Kuwait.

On July 25, 1990, as Saddam moved troops into position to invade Kuwait, he summoned U.S. Ambassador April Glaspie for a meeting. Although urging a peaceful settlement of the issues (see above) she, as instructed by the State Department, told him that America had little interest in Arab border disputes. According to a senior U.S. diplomat, this statement, by indicating that America would not fight for Kuwait, had the effect of giving Saddam a green light.

Invading Kuwait with massive force on August 2, Saddam quickly overran light Kuwaiti resistance. This seizure doubled Saddam's control of known world oil reserves to 19 percent. He was known to favor unification of all Arabs, and he invaded, he said, in the name of all "zealous Arabs who believe in the Arab nation." Some feared that he might also invade Saudi Arabia.

Bush reacted strongly. A *Newsweek* reporter found him "invigorated by the crisis and appearing to relish" handling it. "Our jobs, our way of life, our own freedom and the freedom of friendly countries around the world," Bush said, would suffer if Saddam controlled the world's great oil reserves. Comparing him to Hitler, Bush warned against appeasement. "This aggression," he asserted, is "a test of our mettle" and "will not stand."

Telephoning national leaders, and sending Baker to visit leaders in twenty countries, Bush lined up a coalition to oppose Iraq. He had much bargaining power. The end of the Cold War had left America as the world's unrivaled superpower, and "everyone," wrote Baker, "wanted to get closer to the United States." Although Iraq had long been a Soviet client, the Soviets and Cuba joined in a Security Council vote condemning Iraq's invasion. On August 6, the UN Security Council, including China, voted to impose a mandatory world embargo.

On August 7, Bush ordered U.S. military forces to Saudi Arabia to protect that country, he said, from possible attack. Muslim Egypt, Syria, Morocco, Pakistan, and Bangladesh, as well as Britain and France, also sent troops. Canada, Greece, Italy, the Netherlands, Spain, and Belgium sent ships to help enforce the blockade, and several other nations gave money. A total of forty-eight nations helped in some way.

Time magazine called the near unanimity Bush had achieved "astonishing," and his handling of the crisis "masterly . . . even brilliant." Commending his "enormous sophistication and skill," Kissinger said that success would make Bush "the dominant world leader."

Iraq seemed to be an ideal place to test the effectiveness of the economic sanctions that many had long hoped could prove an alternative to war. It had little industry and produced only a fourth of the food it consumed, and thus was heavily dependent on imports paid for by sales of oil. In December 1990, the CIA reported that the UN-imposed embargo had blocked 90 percent of Iraq's imports and 97 percent of its exports.

Meanwhile, in a massive sea and air lift, Bush moved 250,000 U.S. military personnel to Saudi Arabia and the Persian Gulf. Polls showed that 68 percent of Americans favored sending troops.

However, Saddam had much support among Arabs. The region's great oil reserves were situated in countries that contained only 10 percent of the Arab population, whose rulers enjoyed fabulous wealth while most Arabs lived in poverty. Calling on all Arabs to spurn "oil emirs," Saddam demanded a wider distribution of oil profits. Also, many of those who wanted to unite all Arabs considered his armed forces, the most powerful in the Arab world, to be the only ones capable of withstanding Israel's military. Saddam received PLO support, and pro-Saddam demonstrations occurred in several Arab countries.

U.S. military leaders, including Chief of Staff Colin Powell (the first African American to hold the top military position), and Commander of U.S. Forces in the Persian Gulf H. Norman Schwarzkopf, favored waiting for the embargo to take effect. So did the Soviet Union, Egypt, Italy, Germany, France, Argentina, Turkey, and China, two former chairmen of the Joint Chiefs of Staff, seven former secretaries of defense, and former President Jimmy Carter. But Baker argued that the coalition could not be held together long enough for sanctions to be effective, and Bush pressed for early military action.

He was determined, Bush said, to see that the invader withdrew from Kuwait "with no compromises of any kind whatsoever." Saying that "I have resolved all moral questions in my mind" and that "this is black and white, good versus evil," he dismissed Saddam's offer of concessions as a "cruel hoax." In February 1991, Brzezinski wrote that Bush seemed to be "dedicated to the prevention of a diplomatic solution."

However, the international consensus Bush had achieved was for defending Saudi Arabia and embargoing Iraq, not for invading Iraq. Although Iraq had been a Soviet client, Russia was united with America, said Gorbachev, "in the belief that Iraq's aggression must not be tolerated." U.S. officials praised Soviet cooperation. But the Soviets did not favor military action. Instead, they favored political measures, and they suggested a multination conference to consider all Middle East problems. Gorbachev regretted that some were "thirsting for blood."

At first, Bush emphasized the need to prevent Saddam from controlling so much of the world's oil supply that he could raise the price of oil. But many critics rejected this as an acceptable reason for war. "No blood for oil" chanted antiwar demonstrators. The loss of oil exports from Iraq and Kuwait raised world oil prices from $18 to above $40 per barrel, but other oil-producing countries quickly restored world production to precrisis levels, and the price dropped.

Bush also insisted that America was in the Gulf to champion the principle that aggression must be punished: "We are ready to use force," he said, "to defend a new order emerging among the nations of the world." "The world's key task," he told the UN on October 2, 1990, was "to demonstrate that aggression will not be tolerated." Some critics asked if this was a new "Bush Doctrine." Also, many foreigners regarded America's record on aggression as insufficiently pure to justify his stance. For example, UN majorities had condemned invasions by Reagan and Bush of Grenada, Nicaragua, and Panama as aggression.

Bush also charged that Iraq constituted a "strategic threat" and a "worldwide threat to democracy." Critics charged that these words much exaggerated any threat to worldwide democracy posed by a small developing nation.

In some earlier wars, America had defended freedom and democracy, but Kuwait and Saudi Arabia were feudalistic monarchies. Also within the anti-Iraq coalition were Syria and Iran, both of which America had denounced as terroristic states. The fact that the enemy was not communism, Brzezinski argued, removed any reason for U.S. intervention, and many critics, including the *New York Times*, Senate Armed Forces Committee chairman Sam Nunn, and leading news magazines, maintained that Bush had not made a convincing case for war.

Nearly all mainline churches opposed war, as did the World Council of Churches. Also many students demonstrated against going to war. Polls indicated that 80 percent of Americans wanted to delay military action to ascertain if the blockade would be effective.

In October, Saddam offered to withdraw from Kuwait in return for two small islands and Kuwait's share of a disputed oil field, a deal that Saudi Arabia had earlier suggested. Bush, however, said he would not negotiate until Iraq withdrew unconditionally. Also, America obtained UN resolutions demanding that Saddam restore Kuwait's former government and pay reparations. Calling these terms "unconditional surrender," Saddam said that if his only choice was between fighting and humiliation, he would fight.

In November 1990, Bush gave orders to double the U.S. forces in the gulf area to more than 500,000, to provide an "offensive option." On November visits, Baker got Shevardnadze to say that Russia would not "rule out the use of force," and China agreed that it would not veto it in the UN. On November 29, the UN, by a vote of 12 to 2, with Cuba and Yemen voting against and China abstaining, authorized the use of force if Iraq did not withdraw from Kuwait by January 15, 1991.

Many feared that Bush intended to go to war without a congressional declaration. While not dropping his claim that he had to power to do so, Bush, after soundings convinced him he could win, requested a congressional resolution authorizing military action. Congress, on January 12, 1991, by a vote of 52 to 47 in the Senate and 250 to 183 in the House, authorized war. Voting against it were 224 Democrats and 5 Republicans.

Redoubling his peace efforts, Gorbachev got Saddam to announce his willingness to withdraw from Kuwait. Nevertheless, on January 16, America and coalition forces unleashed history's heaviest sustained bombing. According to Jimmy Carter, "there was never any good-faith talks," but "we attacked Iraq without them." Calling the attack horrible, Gorbachev pled in vain for a pause to allow Soviet diplomacy to arrange for an Iraqi withdrawal.

Maintaining that the bombing and the embargo were sufficient to accomplish the allies' objectives, many Americans and nearly all the allied governments sought to avoid the additional carnage of ground fighting. But Bush gave Iraq an ultimatum demanding withdrawal from Kuwait City within forty-eight hours and from Kuwait within a week, beginning no later than February 23. On February 21, Gorbachev telephoned Bush that he believed that he had secured Iraqi agreement to withdraw within twenty-one days.

Rejecting these terms, Bush ordered coalition troops to invade, which they did at dawn on February 24. Again, the public rallied around the flag. On February 15, only 8 percent had favored a ground invasion, but in a poll taken shortly after the attack 75 percent said that Bush had been right to invade.

By this time, America had more than 540,000 military personnel in the area. Bush also secured troops from coalition partners: from Saudi Arabia, 118,000, from Britain, 43,000; from Egypt, 40,000; from France, 16,000; and from Syria, 15,000; plus smaller numbers from Pakistan, Kuwait, Bangladesh, Gulf sheikdoms, and Morocco. Some nations made large financial contributions—Saudi

Arabia gave $17 billion; Kuwait $16 billion; Japan $13 billion; Germany $7 billion, and others for a total of $54 billion—which paid at least 90 percent of the war's cost.

The ground war proved as one-sided as the air war. Allied forces destroyed more than 80 percent of Iraq's tanks. On February 25, Baghdad radio announced that Saddam had ordered his army to withdraw from Kuwait. After six weeks of round-the-clock bombardment, front-line troops emerged dazed from bunkers to kiss the hands of their captors. With allied troops pouring into Iraq, and complete destruction of Saddam's forces imminent, Bush suddenly, after 100 hours, halted the invasion. Schwarzkopf expressed disappointment that Bush did not allow him to finish the annihilation, and many were surprised at his sudden reversal. The explanation was complex.

Bush did not seek complete destruction of Iraq's military forces because that would have benefited Iran and Syria, neither of which America wanted to strengthen. He wanted to leave Iraq with sufficient forces to preserve its independence and unity. Also, drawing a lesson from the Vietnam War, and assuming that Saddam's defeat would cause his overthrow, he did not want to get bogged down in Iraq's internal affairs. He wanted to finish the job quickly and get out—"do it, do it right, get gone." Furthermore, television coverage of the bombing of fleeing Iraqis was making the fighting appear like wanton slaughter.

The victory made most Americans as ecstatic as if they had defeated a major power. They rejoiced at the technical superiority of U.S. weapons, the one-sidedness of the casualities—only 343 coalition forces, 266 of whom were Americans, killed, compared to 100,000 to 150,000 Iraqi military (Schwarzkopf's estimates), plus perhaps 20,000 Iraqi civilians. The war, Bush said, had reestablished America's "credibility." Opinion polls showed public approval of Bush's conduct of the presidency at an astonishing 90 percent. "By God," said Bush, "we've kicked the Vietnam syndrome [reluctance to intervene] once and for all."

The war had destroyed $100 billion of Iraqi property. Effects of the bombing, a UN commission sent to survey civilian damages reported, were "near apocalyptic." Water could not be purified, hospitals could not operate, and supplies of food were so reduced that Iraq faced "epidemic and famine." The commission recommended massive relief and an immediate end to the food embargo.

Nevertheless, Bush said that the embargo would continue until Baghdad met all UN conditions—recognition of Kuwait's borders, destruction of all nuclear, chemical, and biological weapons, and cooperation with UN inspection to prevent their future production. Also, Bush added, the Iraqis must overthrow Saddam.

Emboldened by Bush's incitement to overthrow Saddam, Saddam's opponents, principally Shiite Muslims in southern Iraq and ethnic minority Kurds in the north, rose in rebellion. But Iraq's surviving army crushed first the Shiites and then the Kurds. An estimated 20,000 died in this civil war. When thousands of Kurds, who fled into the mountains, were faced with starvation, Bush sent 20,000 U.S. troops into northern Iraq to establish a "safe area" for Kurds.

By weakening their enemy, the war benefited Iran, Saudi Arabia, Syria, and Israel. Iran regained all the territory seized by Iraq in their recent war, while Syria consolidated its grip on Lebanon. Among the big losers were Palestinian Arabs. As the war distracted world attention from the intifadeh, the Israelis stepped up the planting of Jewish settlements in Arab territories. Also, because the PLO sided with Saddam, Saudi Arabia and other gulf states cut off financial subsidies to the Palestinians, and America broke off talks with the PLO.

The U.S. victory was not universally admired. Gorbachev continued to maintain that Saddam could have been forced to withdraw without military action, and he speculated that the real reason that Bush chose the military option was because a political settlement would raise Soviet prestige and Bush wanted to destroy Saddam's regime. Some were appalled at the magnitude of the destruction of life and property. Bangladesh's foreign minister deplored the world's most powerful nation "pounding people who are weak and vulnerable," and Sudan's government called it a "hideous, bloody massacre." Nearly unanimously, delegates at the World Council of Churches branded the war "disproportionate" and "unjust." This dismay was deepened when Bush insisted on continuing economic sanctions after the war's end. An investigating physician's committee predicted that the blockade would cause the death of 170,000 infants in a year.

Bush also intervened in Somalia, but, because the consequences of that intervention were dealt with mostly by President Clinton, discussion of it is reserved for chapter 19.

Enormous changes in the world scene, chief of which was the dissolution of the Soviet Union, occurred during the Bush administration. Bush continued Reagan's policy of accepting a partnership with Gorbachev and, later, with Yeltsin. He resisted the popular demand to impose harsh sanctions on China, and continued to pressure Japan to import more U.S. goods. His reputed expertise in foreign affairs and his emphasis on rejecting diplomacy in favor of military action were most evidenced in his invasions of Panama and Iraq.

19 President Clinton and Post–Cold War Complexities

The Election of 1992

The Gulf War raised President Bush's public approval rating to an unprecedented 90 percent, and he was almost automatically renominated by his party. The Democrats nominated William Clinton, age forty six, a graduate of Yale Law School, Rhodes Scholar, and five-term governor of Arkansas. Foreign policy played only a minor role in the political campaign. Clinton criticized Bush for discouraging Ukraine from asserting its independence and for "coddling" right-wing dictators, but he did not challenge his intervention in Bosnia, Iraq, or Somalia. Instead, Clinton promised to do more to defend the Bosnian Muslims. Both pledged to promote democracy and free markets abroad. The high popular approval Bush had gained by the victory over Iraq did not last, and Clinton won the election with 43.2 percent to Bush's 37.7 percent, while a third-party candidate, Ross Perot, got 19 percent.

The Clinton Team

Bush had regarded himself as a foreign policy president, but Clinton's experience and interests were chiefly in domestic affairs, to which he hoped to devote his major attention. His exposure to foreign policy, he said, "was largely through international economic issues," and "foreign policy is not what I came here to do." However, he had majored in international affairs at Georgetown and served for a time as a student intern on the staff of Senate Foreign Affairs Committee chairman J. William Fulbright. When a Rhodes Scholar, he had joined student demonstrations against the Vietnam War. In his inaugural address, he said: "There is no longer division between what is foreign and what is domestic—the world economy, the world environment, the AIDS crisis, the world arms race—they affect us all." By 1994 foreign affairs was absorbing half of presidential time.

As secretary of state Clinton named sixty-seven-year-old Warren Christopher, a graduate of Stanford Law School, an experienced foreign affairs official who had served as Deputy Secretary of State in the Carter Administration and who had negotiated the release of U.S. hostages held by Iran. In manner, he was cautious and professorial.

National Security Adviser Anthony Lake had graduated from Harvard and Cambridge and earned a Ph.D. in international relations at Princeton. After becoming a Foreign Service officer, he had served on Kissinger's White House staff, from which he had resigned in protest against the 1970 invasion of Cambodia, and he later served in Carter's State Department. In his view, the national security adviser should be not a spokesman but "strictly an inside operator" as adviser and agent of the president. He favored the use of U.S. power to promote peace, but was determined to avoid misuse of that power as in Vietnam.

As ambassador to the UN, Clinton appointed Madeleine Albright. The daughter of a Czech diplomat, a Columbia Ph.D., and a Georgetown University professor of international relations, she had served on Brzezinski's staff in the Carter Administration. Vocal and outgoing, she was an ardent champion of U.S. interests and of the UN. She was the first women to hold the position of secretary of state.

This post–Cold War administration needed to reexamine U.S. foreign policy. Public support for an active world role seemed to be ebbing. Polls indicated that between 1990 and 1995 the percentage who considered it very important to defend America's allies fell from 61 to 41, and the percentage who advocated defending weak nations against aggression fell from 57 to 24. Support for defense of human rights dropped to 24 percent and for raising living standards in underdeveloped countries to 19 percent. Between 1984 and 1996 Congress cut U.S. international affairs spending from $38 billion to $19 billion.

In his election campaign, Clinton had promised to work for "a world of security, freedom, democracy, free markets, and growth." In July 1994, Lake said that U.S. policy was "to consolidate the victory of democracy and open markets" and to defend "the tolerant society." Consequently, America's enemies, he said, were "regional rogue states like Iran, Iraq, and Libya." If so, continued U.S. intervention would be necessary. Despite America's Cold War victory, there would be only limited military demobilization.

Clinton was under pressure to favor the military. Political opponents had attacked him for avoiding service in Vietnam and for demonstrating against the Vietnam War. Enormous economic interests, particularly in key states like California, depended on continued high military spending. Also, Clinton's efforts to end discrimination against homosexuals in the military antagonized the armed forces. Senator Jesse Helms of North Carolina, who would become chairman of the Senate Foreign Affairs Committee, called Clinton unfit to be commander in chief and said that he would need a bodyguard if he visited a military base.

Clinton made some reductions in the size of the armed services. Total troop strength fell 30 percent between 1990 and 1995, and total military spending ebbed from $304 billion in 1989 to $278 billion in 1995. However, this level overshadowed 1994 military spending of $49 billion by Japan, $36 billion by France, $35 billion by Germany, and $29 billion by Russia. U.S. military spending roughly equaled that of the rest of the world combined, and in 1994 U.S. troops were still stationed in approximately 100 countries, including 102,000 in Germany, 45,000 in Japan, 40,000 in the Persian Gulf, 37,000 in South Korea, 18,500 in Haiti, and 15,000 in Britain. Partly concealed in the budget was spending on espionage agencies, including the National Security Agency, the CIA, and the Defense Intelligence Agency, of more than $36 billion annually.

During the campaign, Clinton had promised to cut sales of U.S. weapons abroad. Instead, they soared from 13 percent of the world total in 1986 to 70 percent in 1994. For the years 1990–1993, the major sales were to Saudi Arabia ($30 billion), Taiwan ($8 billion), Egypt ($4 billion), Kuwait ($4 billion), and South Korea ($4 billion). Clinton took a militant stand on crises in Somalia, the former Yugoslavia, Iraq, North Korea, and Haiti.

Clinton's Economic Policy

Economics, said Christopher, was "at the top of our foreign policy agenda." Clinton fully subscribed to the prevailing view that U.S. economic health demanded growing access to world markets, which required a more open world economy. Seeking "to expand and strengthen the world's community of market-based economies," he achieved some remarkable successes in reducing barriers to world trade.

In November 1993, Clinton secured congressional approval of the North American Free Trade Agreement (NAFTA), initiated in the Bush Administration, which provided for gradual abolition of trade barriers among Canada, the United States, and Mexico. This created a free-trade zone containing 370 million people with a gross domestic product of $6.5 trillion. In NAFTA's first year, 1994, U.S. trade with Mexico rose more than 20 percent, lifting Mexico above Japan as the second largest buyer of U.S. exports.

Another great success was achieved in 1994 with the conclusion, after years of international negotiations, of the "Uruguay Round" trade agreement, in which the United States and more than a hundred other countries agreed to slash tariffs by an average of 38 percent. Even more significant, they agreed to abolish all import quotas, replacing them with gradually declining tariffs. They also reached agreements in areas impervious to all previous attempts at reduction, including agriculture, services (such as banking), and patents. It was the largest international tariff reduction yet. To supervise compliance with the rules, they created a new World Trade Organization. However, national subsidies to civil aircraft, financial services, shipping, steel, and telecommunications continued.

By this time, most Americans were convinced that free trade served America's interests. In December 1994, obtaining the backing of former Presidents Gerald Ford and Jimmy Carter and of Senate Republican leader Bob Dole, Clinton secured Senate approval of these tariff cuts by a vote of 68 to 24. An upsurge of world trade seemed to be in prospect. Also, between 1985 and 1993, U.S. investments in Latin America tripled, and in East Asia they quintupled. Exports rose from 25 percent of America's GDP in 1992 to 30 percent in 1996, when 11.6 million Americans were producing for export.

Relations with the Peoples of the Former Soviet Union

Russia and the other republics that had composed the Soviet Union, including Ukraine, Belarus, Georgia, and Kazakhstan, all declared independence (see Fig. 19.1). Russia was left with a population of only 150 million, including regional ethnic minorities that also sought self-government. An independence movement in Chechnia produced a bloody civil war, in which 100,000 died, and left it substantially independent.

Repudiating communism, Russia and the other states adopted varying degrees of free-market reform. However, these changes did not immediately bring the expected gains. Instead, economic production continued to fall dismayingly. From 1992 to 1996 industrial production fell by more than half. Also, the changeover was accompanied by upsurges of corruption, tax evasion, crime, and violence. Apparently, the Russians had opened the economy to free enterprise with insufficient awareness of the myriad regulatory laws and agencies free enterprise nations had developed over the years to protect the public interest against private greed. A tiny minority of Russians got rich, but millions were impoverished. According to a UNICEF report issued in 1994, this produced "a deterioriation of unparalleled proportions in human welfare," multiplying by ten the number of Russian families living in poverty, disrupting health care, worsening the rates of malnutrition, alcohol use, and suicide, and shortening life expectancy. In 1996, the director of the Institute for Economic Analysis reported that "this country has gone through terrible, almost unimaginable agony." By 1995 Russia's GDP was below that of China, Japan, Germany, or India. Slowing the economic slide to 6 percent in 1996 was hailed as progress.

Also, freeing themselves from Russian domination and achieving self-rule did not bring the expected benefits to the newly independent nations. Instead, severed from the larger Russian economy, they suffered economic losses even more severe than those of Russia, and their living standards plunged faster and farther. In a 1994 poll, 65 percent said that life had been better under communism.

In these circumstances, popular pressures developed to slow the pace of reform and to restore some of the unity among the former Soviet republics. Clinton did not oppose attempts to restore cooperation. Ukraine and Belarus elected pro-Russian presidents. In mid-1993 most of the former Soviet republics agreed to reunite their economies.

To advise him on Russian affairs, Clinton enlisted his fellow Rhodes Scholar and Oxford housemate Strobe Talbott, a *Time Magazine* columnist. Talbott advised him to maintain a close relationship with Boris Yeltsin, who, he said, personified reform, and to provide financial support for his reforms. Clinton wrote Yeltsin often and during his first administration met with him in ten summit conferences (see Fig. 19.2). These summits, characterized by effusive geniality, did not entail the high drama of the Cold War conferences upon which hinged war or peace, but important work was done. In January 1993 they signed START II, which, together with the 1991 START I treaty, meant a two-thirds cut in to-

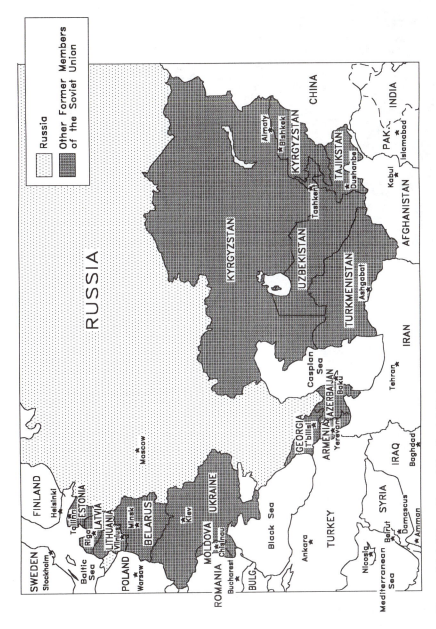

Figure 19.1 Disruption of the Soviet Union.

Figure 19.2 Russia's President Boris Yeltsin at the White House with President William Clinton in 1994. Official White House photograph.

tal long-range nuclear weapons. Dropping its worldwide challenges to U.S. influence, Russia suspended aid to Cuba. "We are no longer enemies," said Yeltsin, "but partners." America even provided moderate amounts of economic aid to Russia—from 1993 to 1996, a total of $4.5 billion.

Of course, Russian and U.S. interests sometimes clashed. When fighting erupted in the territory of the former Yugoslavia (see next section), Clinton championed the Bosnian Muslims, while Yeltsin showed sympathy for the Bosnian Serbs. Also, Russia wanted U.S.-imposed sanctions on Iraq lifted so that Iraq could repay its debt to Russia. Russia did not object to its former East European satellites joining with NATO in a "Partnership for Peace," which Russia itself joined, but it strenuously objected to making them full members of the historically anti-Russian NATO military alliance. Protesting that no one nation should presume to control the entire world, Yeltsin warned of the danger of the development of a "Cold Peace." Americans, in turn, objected to Russia's sale of nuclear reactors to Iran, and to the harshness of Moscow's military suppression of an independence movement in Chechnya. "The honeymoon," said Russia's Foreign Minister Andrei V. Kozyrev in March 1995, "has come to an end."

The most serious U.S.-Russian friction arose over the issue of expanding NATO to the east to include formerly Communist nations. NATO had been formed as an anti-Russian alliance, and the move to extend it to Russia's borders seemed to Russia to be hostile and aggressive. Some Western experts also opposed such expansion. They did not consider further anti-Russian security measures to be needed. In February 1997, George F. Kennan wrote that it "would be the most fateful error of American policy in the entire post-cold-war era," a "challenge" that would restore the Cold War atmosphere and cause Russia to take defensive measures. In the future, some critics warned, the European Union, not Russia, would prove to be America's chief European rival. The Russian parliament delayed ratification of the START II treaty, which, by abolishing multiwarhead ICBMs, required Russians to give up their most economical and effective anti-U.S. weapon. Nevertheless, in July 1997, NATO admitted Poland, Hungary, and the Czech Republic, which meant that their military forces would be reequipped, expanded, and integrated into NATO forces. More such expansions seemed probable.

As their military security on their European front deteriorated, the Russians mended their relations with China. Cutting the number of troops it had stationed in the Far East, Russia agreed to lend China $2.5 billion to construct a nuclear power plant, sold it advanced fighter planes, and agreed to hold summit conferences twice yearly. Trade between the two jumped from $1.5 billion in 1995 to $7 billion in 1996. At an April 1997 summit conference, President Boris Yeltsin of Russia and President Jiang Zemin of China called for a "multipolar world," stated that "no country should seek hegemony, practice power politics, or monopolize international affairs," and formed a "strategic partnership" against any who sought to "push the world toward a unipolar order." Any further chilling of U.S.-Russian relations would probably produce closer Chinese-Russian cooperation.

Tragedy in the Former Yugoslavia

Clinton inherited two U.S. interventions in progress: in Somalia and in the former Yugoslavia. In addition, in his first year, he intervened in Haiti. These interventions were not designed to combat communism or to deal with military or economic menaces. Instead, they seemed to represent primarily a championing of humanitarianism and U.S. values—against starvation, ethnic attrocities, and military despotism.

Europe's Balkan Peninsula contains a number of ethnic groups that have for centuries struggled with each other for territory. The largest of these groups is the Slavs, but the Slavs themselves are subdivided into Serbs, Croats, and Slovenes. Most of them profess Christianity, but Croats and Slovenes are predominantly Catholic, while the Serbs are Eastern Orthodox. Also, under Turkish rule many Slavs had become Muslims. This welter of struggling ethnic and religious groups made the Balkans "the powder keg of Europe," where, in 1914, a conflict exploded into World War I.

After World War I, Serbia, Croatia, Bosnia, Slovenia, and Montenegro joined in a federation under the name Yugoslavia, the land of the southern Slavs. The largest group, the Serbs, made up about 40 percent of the population. In World War II, when Yugoslavia was invaded by the Germans, many Croats allied with the Germans against other Yugoslavians. The Communists, under Josip Tito, who led resistance to the German occupation, became the postwar government. Conceding much local self-government, the government of Yugoslavia restrained ethnic conflicts and generated a fair amount of prosperity. This facilitated ethnic dispersion and intermixing.

However, the weakening of Yugoslavia's Communist government after Tito's 1980 death and the end of the Cold War provided opportunities for elements within each ethnic group that, unable or unwilling to give loyalty to Yugoslavia, preferred to form independent nations. The C.I.A. predicted that such attempts would produce bloody ethnic wars, and Washington advocated continued unity but opposed the use of force to preserve it. In the summer of 1991, Slovenia, Croatia, Macedonia, and Bosnia each declared independence, leaving Serbia and Montenegro in a rump Federal Republic. This breakup was encouraged by some foreigners who preferred to have a weak rather than a strong neighbor or who sought alliances with particular ethnic groups. Germany favored and quickly recognized the independence of Slovenia and Croatia. In 1992, the independence of the four states was recognized by the European Community and by America.

Rival ethnic elements were not neatly separated by the borders of the new nations, each of which contained large minorities. The population of Muslim-ruled Bosnia was only 44 percent Muslim, while 31 percent of it was made up of Serbs who, resenting Muslim rule, demanded self-government for their part of Bosnia. A large area of Croatia, also, was inhabited by Serbs. Furthermore, part of Bosnia was peopled by Croats, who composed 17 percent of the population and who declared independence of the Bosnian government.

It is difficult for ethnic groups to settle disputes without violence when they are not under a common government. The government of Yugoslavia had constituted the peace machinery for the area. Predictably, its destruction was followed by fighting. Bosnian Serbs, achieving military superiority, seized about half of Bosnia; Croats seized nearly a third. Seeking to preserve Bosnia's territorial unity, Muslims fought back. Each group attempted "ethnic cleansing" of its area—expelling or killing people of other ethnic groups.

In an attempt to limit the fighting, the UN imposed an arms embargo, sent in a peacekeeping force, and banned the flight of warplanes over Bosnia. The Bush administration sympathized with the Bosnian Muslims, but did not take strong action in their behalf. By the end of 1992, fighting had claimed 150,000 lives.

In the 1992 presidential campaign, Clinton criticized Bush for not doing more to help the Muslims. However, after Clinton inherited what Christopher called this "problem from hell," the European Community rejected his proposals for joint military intervention. However, because Serbia was believed to be supporting the fighting by fellow Serbs in Bosnia and Croatia, the UN imposed sanctions on Serbia. In February 1994, by threatening to bomb them, Clinton forced the Bosnian Serbs to pull their artillery back from Sarajevo, and vigorous U.S. bombing in September 1995 forced the Bosnian Serbs to retreat from some conquered territories.

After a ceasefire was achieved, a peace conference met in Dayton, Ohio, in November 1995. The Dayton Accords preserved nominal unity, but in effect partitioned Bosnia along ethnic lines. America contributed troops to a 53,000-man NATO-led force assigned to police the ceasefire and oversee implementation of the Dayton Accords. A nationwide election was held in September 1996, but the elected government was unable to function, and the country was governed as three separate areas.

It was difficult to see that U.S. national interests were at stake in Yugoslavia, and the intervention seemed primarily motivated by a desire to limit the suffering. However, it also appeared that Americans had not understood the complexities of the situation. In seeking to preserve the unity of Bosnia, Americans were opposing those who sought to restore the unity of all of former Yugoslavia. The settlement achieved was far short of the unified Bosnia that America had sought. Also, it appeared that if foreign troops withdrew, fighting would resume.

After World War I, President Woodrow Wilson had championed "self-determination," by which he meant allowing each people, if it so voted, to form its own separate nation. At the time, this policy was widely praised as idealistic and democratic, but, in practice, it did not prove to be a path to peace. In 1994, UN Secretary General Boutros Boutros-Ghali argued that the doctrine was seriously flawed. "If each minority will ask for self-determination," he said, "we may have 500 to 1000 countries, and that is not in the interests of peace or economic development." Instead, it would be a regression toward tribalism. An increasingly interdependent world demands not more fragmentation but greater unity and cooperation.

Success and Failure in Africa

America had long urged the minority white government of South Africa to grant democratic rights to South Africa's black majority. In 1989, F. W. De Klerk, who was receptive to reform, became president. In September 1993, South Africa's parliament voted to allow blacks to participate in the government, whereupon the foremost black leader, Nelson Mandela, asked the UN to remove all remaining economic sanctions. Mandela won election as president in April 1994, and, in June, South Africa was readmitted to the UN. Mandela and DeKlerk received the Nobel Peace Prize.

In Angola, the United States had been heavily involved in the long and bloody civil war between the Soviet-backed government headed by Jose Dos Santos, and the U.S.- and South Africa–backed rebel force, UNITA, headed by Jonas Savimbi. The Bush administration had helped to arrange an election, which UNITA lost. Refusing to accept electoral defeat, Savimbi resumed fighting, and, by early 1993, he controlled about half of the country. Clinton recognized the elected government, thereby reversing America's policy of favoring

UNITA. Fighting continued despite the presence of a six thousand-man UN peacekeeping force. In 1995 President Dos Santos said that there was "no ideological reason to have a war," and a *New York Times* columnist concluded that the war in Angola was Africa's "most senseless" and "stupidest" war, an appalling hangover from the defunct Cold War. In August 1997, the Security Council, by a vote of 15 to 0, adopted a joint U.S.-Russian resolution to impose sanctions on areas under UNITA control.

Intervention in Somalia

Somalia, an elongated arid coastal country of 8 million people on the eastern Horn of Africa, won independence from Britain and Italy by 1960. General Muhammad Said Barre took over as dictator in 1969. A Marxist, Said received Soviet aid, but when larger Ethiopia, with which nation Somalia was at war, also came under Marxist rule, the Soviet Union, in 1977, switched its support to Ethiopia. Allowing America to establish military bases in Somalia, Said received nearly $1 billion over a decade in U.S. economic and military aid. Thus, the Cold War rivals supplied Somalians with extraordinary numbers of weapons.

Tribal groups resisted Said's rule and, in January 1991, after America cut aid, forced him into exile. America seemed indifferent. "There are no geopolitical stakes" in "the Horn of Africa any more," said a State Department official. Unable to form a central government, revolutionaries continued to fight among themselves. Meanwhile, a drought, together with the widespread fighting, brought malnutrition to 70 percent of the people, nearly a million of whom sought help in squalid relief camps. In two years, more than 300,000 died.

The United States and the UN were slow to respond. America's national interest did not appear to be involved. However, as U.S. news media depicted horrible scenes of dying children, more Americans demanded action to rescue the starving. In April 1992, the Senate called for "active U.S. initiatives." Under rising pressure, Bush, in July, ordered a military airlift of food and, in August, flew in a small UN peacekeeping force to guard the delivery of supplies.

When this proved to be inadequate to prevent seizure of food by armed bands, U.S. armed forces landed in Somalia in December 1992. By January, more than 38,000 foreign troops, 28,000 of whom were Americans, were there. *Time* called it "the most unalloyed, most unprecedented example of humanitarian intervention in memory, perhaps in history."

Bush said that the intervention was intended only to get food to the starving and that most U.S. troops would be out by the time he left office. However, some observers maintained, in Somalia control of food automatically meant political power, and protecting its distribution through areas disputed by fighting factions would draw America into Somalian politics. Furthermore, critics feared that furnishing food would be only a Band-Aid unless a government were established that could end the bloody chaos. Consequently, they said,

America should prepare a political, as well as humanitarian, program for Somalia.

Clinton, who assumed office in January 1993, continued Bush's Somalian policy. As foreign troops got food to the relief camps, and rains ended the drought, starvation fell to pre-crisis levels. Transferring control of the operation to the UN, Clinton withdrew most U.S. troops. In July, 14,000 UN troops remained, only 4,000 of whom were American.

Nevertheless, U.S. involvement deepened. By May 1993, fifteen UN troops had died. Expanding its mission, the UN attempted to disarm some of the armed bands. The U.S. Ambassador to the UN, Madeleine Albright, redefined the mission as "an unprecedented enterprise aimed at nothing less than the restoration of an entire country." This required subduing groups that disrupted the peace. In June, twenty-four UN soldiers were killed, for which the forces of warlord Mohammed Farah Aidid were blamed. In July, UN helicopters attacked Aidid's headquarters, killing fifty-four persons, and the UN offered a $25,000 reward for his capture. An October U.S. attack on Aidid headquarters went awry, resulting in the death of eighteen U.S. soldiers, some of whose bodies were dragged through the streets.

For many Americans, this was more than enough, and criticism of the intervention soared. Backing down from "nation building," Clinton concluded that "it is not our job to rebuild Somalia's society." Suspending the attempt to arrest Aidid, he withdrew all U.S. troops by April 1994.

The Somalia mission cost the lives of forty-four Americans and a hundred other peacekeepers, plus a much larger number of Somalians, and $2 billion. It failed to restore order. Nevertheless, it may have saved as many as 250,000 Somalians from starvation.

Interventions in Latin America

In December 1994, at the first summit of Western Hemisphere nations in nearly three decades, representatives of thirty-three nations agreed to seek free trade among themselves by 2002; between 1988 and 1992 U.S. exports to Latin America had already doubled.

For Cuba, the end of the Cold War was a disaster. The U.S. embargo had forced Cuba's economy into dependence on Communist countries which provided almost three-fourths of its imports. Soviet aid, estimated at more than $5 billion annually, had partly counterbalanced the U.S. embargo and enabled Cubans to continue enjoying one of the higher living standards in Latin America, while its relatively equitable distribution of wealth and extensive free public education and health care had improved living conditions among the poor. However, after the end of the Cold War and the collapse of the Russian economy, Soviet aid almost stopped, and between 1989 and 1994 Cuba's GNP dropped 40 percent. Employment, health care, and the standard of living all plummeted.

The end of Soviet aid seemed to improve the chances that the U.S. embargo could finally achieve its goal of inflicting so much suffering on the Cuban people that they would overthrow Castro. Clinton extended the embargo to include food and medicine.

As one result, more Cubans sought to flee Cuba. Washington had long followed a policy of welcoming Cubans who wanted to escape communism for freedom. Now, finding it difficult to feed its people, Castro's government allowed 32,000 of them to set to sea in makeshift boats and rafts for Florida.

So massive did this movement become that the United States reversed its open-arms policy and moved to intercept incoming Cubans at sea. Seizing thousands of them and holding them in temporary shelters at camps at Guantanamo Bay and in Panama, Washington opened negotiations with Castro. In an agreement in September 1994, the United States agreed to raise the legal quota of Cuban immigrants to twenty thousand annually, and Castro promised to stop illegal emigration. In 1995, Castro agreed to the return of the Cubans intercepted at sea.

U.S. sanctions on Cuba came under increasing criticism. How could Washington, some asked, continue to embargo trade with Cuba while granting most-favored-nation trading status to China, the world's largest Communist dictatorship? Critics argued that twenty-three years had demonstrated that the embargo was a blunt instrument that hurt the Cuban people without removing Castro. Some observers maintained that, by enabling Castro to blame the U.S. for his economic problems, it gave him an alibi for his own economic failures, allowed him to pose as more concerned than the United States for the welfare of ordinary Cubans, and rallied patriotic Cubans to his side and thus had the unintended effect of helping him stay in power. Also, his successful defiance made him a hero in the eyes of many Latin Americans who resented U.S. intervention. In 1993, thirteen Caribbean nations signed an economic cooperation agreement with Cuba; in 1994, the Canadian government ended its ban on aid to Cuba, and Pope Paul II called for an end to the isolation of the Cuban people. In an editorial titled "Why Punish the Cuban People?" the *New York Times* concluded that Castro posed no threat to the United States and that getting rid of him was "a job for the Cuban people," not the U.S. government. Repeatedly, the UN General Assembly voted to condemn the U.S. embargo— by a vote of 101 to 2 in 1994, and of 117 to 3 in 1995.

Adapting to the end of the Cold War, Castro deemphasized support for revolutionary movements abroad and adopted some free-market reforms and elements of democracy such as municipal elections. He encouraged foreign investments, which reached a total of $5 billion by 1995, and promoted tourism, which attracted nearly a million foreign visitors in 1996, lifting tourism above sugar as Cuba's leading earner of foreign exchange. Reversing its disastrous drop, economic production rose by 2.5 percent in 1995 and by 8 percent in 1996. Increasingly, U.S. businessmen expressed resentment that they were denied access to Cuba's market.

In 1996 relations between the United States and Cuba took a turn for the worse. A Miami-based Cuban exile group, Brothers to the Rescue, had been flying planes over Cuba, and, in February, Castro's air force shot down one of them near Cuba's coast. Calling this act "appalling," Clinton signed the Helms-Burton bill, making the embargo permanent and imposing penalties on foreign companies that profited from properties that the Cubans had seized from U.S. investors. Canada, Mexico, and America's NATO allies bitterly protested this U.S. action. However, in 1997, in a break in the policy of isolation, Clinton gave U.S. news organizations permission to open offices in Cuba and allowed Cuban exiles to go to Cuba for a visit by the Pope.

Intervention in Haiti

Haiti, which shares the island of Santo Domingo with the Dominican Republic, is Latin America's most poverty-stricken nation. Fewer than half of its densely packed 7 million people (as of 1997) are literate. After years of misrule, Jean-Bertrand Aristide, a Catholic priest sympathetic to the poor, was elected president in December 1990. However, he was detested by the rich and, after only nine months, was overthrown by the army which established a military dictatorship under General Raoul Cedras. In an attempt to force Cedras to allow Aristide to resume the presidency, the United States and the UN clamped an economic blockade on Haiti which drove average annual income down from $350 to $200. Tens of thousands of Haitians fled in small boats toward Florida: many of them perished or were forcibly returned.

Clinton secured the first ever UN authorization to use military force to restore a democratically elected leader. On September 15, citing "brutal atrocities" and the need to promote democracy and "uphold the reliability of our commitment," he ordered U.S. troops to sail for Haiti. A costly war seemed imminent. However, in an eleventh-hour peace effort, former President Jimmy Carter, accompanied by Senator Sam Nunn and General Colin Powell, flew to Haiti. They persuaded Cedras to agree to resign, whereupon U.S. troops landed without opposition.

With 21,000 U.S. troops helping to preserve order, President Aristide returned in mid-October, and Haiti began a slow and painful economic recovery. *Time* magazine called the intervention "a nearly bloodless triumph." However, some were concerned that this intervention without congressional authorization further undermined Congress's ability to restrain a president from taking America to war. In March 1995, the United States turned over policing duties to the UN, but some U.S. troops remained as part of the UN force until February 1996.

Clinton's Middle East Policies

In the first two years of the Clinton administration, Israeli-Arab relations improved. Assisted by Christopher, Israel and the PLO worked out an agreement, the "Oslo Agreement," to give Palestinians self-rule in the Gaza Strip and Jericho, an agreement signed at the U.S. White House in September 1993 (see Fig. 19.3). This restoration to the Palestinians of some of the land seized by Israel in 1967 was an historic breakthrough for which Rabin and Arafat received the Nobel Peace Prize. In May 1994, Israeli troops withdrew from the Gaza Strip and Jericho, giving the Arabs in these areas self-rule. This was followed, in July 1994, by a declaration at the White House by Rabin and King Hussein of Jordan that their countries would sign a treaty of peace. As a reward, America canceled Jordan's $1 billion debt.

A second Oslo Agreement, signed in October 1995, provided for gradual Israeli withdrawal from other West Bank cities. However, in November 1995, progress toward peace was severely set back by the assassination of Prime Minister Yitzhak Rabin by a young militant who opposed his peace moves. An election, in May 1996, was won by the right-wing leader Benjamin Netanyahu. He offended Arabs by moving more Jewish settlers into the Arab sector of Jerusalem and slowed implementation of the Oslo Agreement to turn over part of the West Bank.

Calling Iraq and Iran "rogue states," America sought to prevent any expansion by either, a policy of "dual containment." Clinton fully subscribed to

Figure 19.3 In September 1993 President Clinton helped persuade Israel's Prime Minister Yitzhak Rabin and PLO Chairman Yasir Arafat to make peace on the basis of allowing Arabs gradually to assume self rule in some Arab areas occupied by Israel. Rabin was later assassinated by an Israeli opponent of this agreement. Official White House photo.

Bush's policy on Iraq. He strictly enforced UN-imposed economic sanctions and remained unsatisfied with Iraq's moves to comply with UN demands. In June 1993, on suspicion that Iraq had participated in a plot to assassinate former President Bush when he visited Kuwait, Clinton ordered a missile attack on Iraqi intelligence headquarters in Baghdad. In August, he ordered an air attack on suspected missile sites.

Reports indicated that the effects of the UN embargo on the Iraqi population were devastating. A 1995 study commissioned by the UN estimated that it had caused the deaths of more than half a million Iraqi children and had produced disease, malnutrition, and stunted development in many others. In late 1996, UNICEF reported that the food shortage was killing forty-five hundred children per month.

The question of whether sanctions should be continued was much debated. Supporters argued that Iraq had not fully complied with the UN's conditions for lifting the embargo. Instead, they said, Iraq was rebuilding its armed forces and secretly continuing development of biological weapons. Thus, the suffering, they said, was Saddam's fault for not promptly meeting UN demands.

Opponents of continuing the sanctions argued that Iraq had surrendered its claim to Kuwait by recognizing it as an independent nation, had destroyed most weapons of mass destruction, and was allowing the UN to put in place a system of inspection to prevent the manufacture of more such weapons. In 1994, the head of the UN's monitoring team reported that "cooperation is excellent." Also, they said, the United States was illegally adding a requirement that Saddam's government be overthrown. Russia's foreign minister accused America of seeking not justice but revenge. Furthermore, critics said, the starving of innocent civilians had little impact on Saddam, while any menace from Iraq had so faded as to make continued killing of civilians unnecessary. In early 1995, the UN Secretary General said that sanctions raised "the ethical question of whether suffering inflicted on vulnerable groups in the target country is a legitimate means of exerting pressure on political leaders whose behavior is unlikely to be affected by the plight of their subjects." By 1995, the countries calling for an easing of the sanctions included Russia, China, France, Turkey, Egypt, Saudi Arabia, Syria, Algeria, Morroco, Tunisia, Qatar, the United Arab Emirates, and Yemen.

Under international pressure, a proposal was made to allow Iraq to sell some oil in exchange for food. Implementation was delayed by continued U.S. objections and by Saddam's protests that the proposed terms violated Iraqi sovereignty. In late 1996, a deal was completed to allow the Iraqis to sell $2 billion worth of oil every six months, provided that the funds were kept under UN control and used to pay UN expenses and damages to victims of Iraq's aggression as well as to buy food and medicine. However, the money produced was far below Iraq's needs, and in November 1997 the *Washington Post* concluded that shortages of food and medicine continued to cause an extra million deaths, 60 percent of them children, per year.

A new crisis erupted late in 1996 over the Kurd-inhabited area of northern Iraq. After the Kurds, a non-Arab minority that inhabited northern Iraq and parts of Turkey and Iran, had launched an unsuccessful uprising against Saddam, the United States had declared the Kurdish area a "protected area" into which Saddam was forbidden to fly planes or send troops. When the Kurds split and waged a bitter war among themselves. Iran supported one faction and even sent troops into Iraq in its support. In August 1996 the other faction appealed to Saddam for help, and Saddam sent in troops that enabled it to defeat its rival. Denouncing this violation of the protected zone, the United States launched forty four cruise missiles to punish Saddam and also enlarged the no-flight zone to cover more than half of Iraq.

This incident revealed disintegration in the coalition that Bush had organized against Saddam. Turkey and Saudi Arabia refused to allow Americans to launch missiles from their territory, forcing them to fly missile-carrying bombers from Guam. Many nations, including Russia and China, condemned the missile attack.

Meanwhile, to the east, the U.S. government put Iran near the top of the list of "rogue states" that it counted as post–Cold War enemies. Americans accused Iran of developing atomic weapons, supporting terrorists, violating human rights, opposing Arab-Israeli peace, and backing militant Islamic elements. America maintained powerful naval forces in the Persian Gulf and troops in Saudi Arabia. In 1995, Clinton toughened U.S. economic sanctions against Iran. However, other nations continued to trade with and invest in Iran.

Some critics charged that America was overinvolved in the Persian Gulf—that it was spending $60 billion annually to defend a $30 billion annual oil flow that would not stop under any conceivable circumstances. Also, they said, the United States and Iran had common national interests that had once made them allies, and were more basic than matters in dispute.

Clinton and China

East Asia's rapid economic development gave it increasing weight in world affairs. Between 1960 and 1996 Asia's share of world economic production rose from 4 to 25 percent. In 1992, two-way trade between America and East Asia reached $300 billion, a third more than U.S. trade with Europe.

The most impressive economic growth occurred in China. China continued its free-market reforms—by 1994 the share of the national output produced by privately owned enterprises rose to 57 percent—and between 1978 and 1995 its GDP multiplied an incredible five times. Its 1996 GNP of $4 trillion surpassed Japan's $2.9 trillion, giving it the world's second largest economy. This was little more than half America's $7.4 trillion, but if existing growth rates continued, the World Bank predicted, by the year 2020 China's GNP would exceed America's! In 1997 growth continued at the rate of 9.5 percent.

U.S. trade with China rose briskly. America sold China machinery, aircraft, metals, and vehicles and bought from China increasing quantities of electronics, clothing, shoes, toys, and sports equipment. In 1996, America's $40 billion excess of purchases from China over sales to China was second only to its trade gap with Japan.

Friction with China occurred over U.S. objections to Chinese violations of human rights, particularly the right of Chinese to oppose their government. In June 1993, when Clinton renewed China's most-favored-nation status for one year, he specified that future renewal would depend on increased respect by China for human rights. In reply, the Chinese pointed to U.S. discrimination against ethnic minorities and women, its huge prison population, its homeless poor, and political campaign financing that amounted to "legalized bribery." Defenders of China argued that its economic growth served human rights by freeing hundreds of millions of people from the degradations of abject poverty. The China trade became too essential to the U.S. economy to abandon and, in 1994, at the insistence of many businessmen, Clinton delinked China's trade status from human rights.

Trade disputes continued. In 1995, Clinton threatened to raise tariffs on many Chinese products if China did not stop the pirating of U.S. electronic disks of music, films, and computer programs. Eager to win U.S. support for its application for membership in GATT, China closed some factories involved in the counterfeiting, destroyed many illegal disks, and pledged stricter enforcement. Also, America objected to China's sale of weapons to Pakistan, chemicals to Iraq, and atomic reactors to Iran.

In 1995, China's fear that Taiwan might, with U.S. support, declare independence was increased by a visit by Taiwan's President Lee Tenghui to America for an alumni reunion at Cornell University and by a special Senate reception for Madame Chiang Kai-shek. Beijing conducted military maneuvers, including missile firings, near Taiwan. However, after his reelection as president in China's first democratic election of a chief executive, Lee reaffirmed his commitment to eventual reunification. Meanwhile, two-way trade between Taiwan and the mainland rose to $18 billion in 1994, and Taiwanese investment on the mainland reached $30 billion by 1996.

The reversion in 1997 of Hong Kong from British rule to China, removing the main remnant of nineteenth-century imperialism in China, left reunion with Taiwan as China's main foreign policy goal. However, the Chinese seemed to prefer continuance of U.S. military predominance in East Asia to any revival of Japanese military power.

When, in October 1997, China's President Jiang Zemin visited America for a summit conference, he was given the full honors of a state visit, complete with a twenty-one-gun salute and an official White House banquet attended by Washington's political elite and top corporate executives. A history buff who quoted Jefferson and Lincoln, Jiang ignored demonstrators to tour such historical sites as Williamsburg and Independence Hall, and he also visited Drexel University, where his son had earned a Ph.D.

To offset U.S. resentment at the widening trade gap, the Chinese placed a $3 billion order, the largest ever, for U.S. airliners. Also, Jiang agreed to stop transferring atomic technology to Iran and Pakistan, thereby opening the way for U.S. manufacturers to bid on the construction of $60 billion of atomic reactors in China. In New York, Jiang visited such citadels of capitalism as the headquarters of IBM and AT&T, was dined by the wealthy at the Waldorf-Astoria Hotel, and was asked to ring the opening bell at the New York Stock Exchange, after which, to his relief, the market rose.

Because many observers had been attacking China for violating human rights, suppressing the distinctive culture of Tibet, and menacing Taiwan, Clinton had a compelling political need to show that he was not "soft" on these issues. In his joint press conferences with Jiang he bluntly condemned China's record on human rights. Differences on human rights were "profound," he said, and reluctance to tolerate political dissent" had kept China from "winning support in the rest of the world." In reply, Jiang said that circumstances in America and China were different, that in China the "right of subsistence and development is the most fundamental and most important human right," and internal stability was needed to give the people the human right to emerge from poverty. In the future, he said, China would "expand democracy, improve the legal system," and "run the country according to law."

Some Americans did not regard China's performance on human rights as all bad. In 1996 Deputy Secretary of State Strobe Talbott, agreeing that poverty was an "obstacle to freedom," had written that ordinary Chinese were "much freer today." Talbott expressed "conviction that continued economic and cultural engagement is the best way to induce democratization." In March 1997, *Time* magazine reported that "economic progress has propelled once unthinkable social changes" and that the Chinese were free to work, live, and travel where they wanted, and elect village officials, and *U.S. News & World Report* reported that China had "allowed dramatically more personal freedoms, more open debate." Jimmy Carter maintained that in China educational opportunities and membership in Christian churches had soared.

Clinton indicated that America was not backing independence movements in Taiwan or Tibet. He and Jiang agreed to set up a "hot line," a direct telephone connection, and to work toward "a constructive strategic partnership." Clinton announced that he would visit China in the second half of 1998.

Clinton and Other Asian Nations

U.S. relations with Japan remained close, but were changing. In 1997 America maintained 50,000 U.S. troops in Japan, and Japan paid 70 percent ($5 billion annually) of their costs. Americans were pleased by Japan's large grants of foreign aid, much of it to U.S. allies. Also, U.S. corporations, including MacDonald's and Apple, successfully penetrated the Japanese market. Nevertheless, America's 1996 trade deficit with Japan was nearly $50 billion.

However, predictions that Japan's economic production would overtake America's had proved to be exaggerated. Inefficiencies in its economy—notably in agriculture and marketing—held its productivity (output per worker) below America's. Cutting corporation and income taxes, it imposed a 5 percent national sales tax making its taxes less progressive. The rise of its internal market and its economic output slowed. After thirty years of average 6.5 percent expansion, its growth rate in the years 1992 to 1995 fell to only 0.6 percent. In 1997 production actually declined.

A vexing crisis with North Korea flared when that country seemed to be accumulating materials from which weapon-grade plutonium could be extracted. Secretary of Defense William Perry called the danger that North Korea could construct atomic weapons "a threat to the entire world." America threatened economic sanctions, and held joint military maneuvers with South Korea.

Under this pressure, North Korea reopened negotiations which achieved preliminary agreement in January 1994. When the death of North Korea's longtime dictator, Kim Il Sung, disrupted the deal, Jimmy Carter visited Pyongyang and got the negotiations restarted. On August 12 North Korea agreed to dismantle the two nuclear plants that produced the suspect material and to allow full inspection of all nuclear facilities in exchange for agreement by America and its allies to build new nuclear reactors of a kind that could not produce weapon-grade materials. This remarkable agreement cost more than $4 billion, to be paid mostly by Japan and South Korea. In addition, Washington promised to establish full diplomatic relations and to protect North Korea against any nuclear attack. The *New York Times* called the settlement a "resounding triumph." In June 1998, South Korea's President Kim Dae Jung asked America to end its sanctions against North Korea and seek, instead, improved economic and political "engagement."

In early 1994, Clinton lifted the nineteen-year-old economic embargo on Vietnam and, in July 1995, resumed diplomatic relations. Vietnam's 1995 per capita annual GNP was only $1,300, but it was rising at a rate of 10 percent annually. In 1995, U.S.-Vietnam trade doubled to $500 million, and U.S. investments in Vietnam rose to $1.2 billion. At last the Vietnam War seemed to be ending.

In Cambodia, America, reversing a long-held policy, withdrew support from the Khmer Rouge and even joined in UN-imposed trade sanctions against Khmer Rouge-controlled areas. The apparent dissolution of the Khmer Rouge, and the 1998 death of Pol Pot, seemed to be bringing a long tragic chapter to a close.

The "New World Order"

The end of the Cold War required major adjustments. More than a generation had lived under the threat of nuclear catastrophe, but in the 1990s, for the first time in many years, there was little threat of war between major powers.

Russia had lost the Cold War, had admitted its loss, and had withdrawn from contention. Its empire was gone, its ideology discredited, its homeland fragmented, and its economy in collapse. Between 1991 and 1996 the size of its military fell from 3.4 million to 1.3 million. By 1997 it was spending only $20 billion annually on defense. This left America as the world's only superpower.

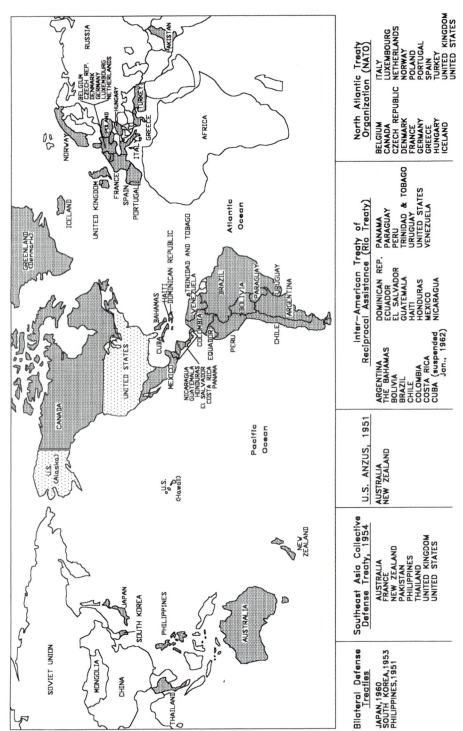

Figure 19.4 United States Collective Defense Treaties.

Never before in history had one nation achieved such worldwide military preponderance, such worldwide hegemony. In his State of the Union address, in January 1992, Bush exulted that America was the world's "sole and preeminent power" and the "undisputed leader of the age" (see Fig. 19.4). In 1996 U.S. armed forces spending was $269 billion, compared to $52 billion for Japan, $38 billion for France, $33 billion for China, $32 billion for Britain, and $32 billion for Germany.

Historically, when one nation has risen to supremacy, lesser powers have banded into alliances to oppose it. Some feared that this might happen to America and that the process would be accelerated if U.S. dominance was perceived as harmful to other world regions. They viewed rising incidents of terrorist attacks on Americans in the Middle East and elsewhere as signs of rising anti-Americanism. Hence, they were anxious to minimize the number of peoples abroad who suffered from U.S. bombing or embargos.

Also, the Cold War victory of the United States was not unqualified. U.S. military power remained unrivaled, but the nation's relative economic superiority was ebbing. During the Cold War, the U.S. share of world economic production fell from approximately 50 percent in 1947 to about 22 percent by 1997. In the 1980s, U.S. economic growth averaged only 2.6 percent annually. Moreover, America no longer had large reserves of gold and foreign exchange, nor did it enjoy the favorable balance of trade that had enabled it to finance its projection of military power throughout the world. It had ceased to be the world's leading creditor nation and become its leading debtor, with a net debt of more more $1 trillion. In 1997 it asked that its share of the UN budget be cut from the existing 25 percent to 20 percent.

In a sense, both of the superpowers lost the Cold War. The long and costly contest drained the economic strength of both. Preventing America from distinguishing between its vital interests and its secondary interests, it had led to expenditures of national treasure on areas such as Korea and Vietnam in the mistaken belief that controlling them was essential to U.S. survival. While both superpowers poured resources into armaments, other nations devoted more of their resources to economic development. America had easily financed the long Vietnam War, but it passed the hat to finance the short Gulf War. More than any other one factor, America's future relative power will depend on its performance in the worldwide competition in economic growth.

The Cold War's end brought a return from bipolarism to a more historically normal complex pattern of international rivalry. Some political scientists and historians foresaw a four-power world headed by the United States, Russia, China, and the European Union. If so, the major conflicts of each of these four might occur with its nearer neighbors, with the result that America and Russia might align against China and the EU. France's president and China's president agreed to work for a world order with "power centers beside the United States." The rise of some Third World nations, including India, added to the complexity.

It appeared that the world's second most populous nation, India, would be assuming a more active role in world politics. In 1996 its GNP was $1,493 billion, $1,580 per capita, which put its standard of living above a third of the world's nations. (This was still far below China $4,047 GNP). The average annual growth of its economy 1980 to 1996 was 5.8 percent, and for 1996 it was 7 percent. The population of its rival on the subcontinent, Pakistan, was only 134 million and its per capita GNP was only slightly higher.

In May, 1998, India set off five atomic explosions. It had produced one atomic explosion in 1974; now it seemed to be proceeding with the development of atomic weapons. Pakistan responded a few weeks later with six atomic explosions. In both countries, crowds greeted the news with street celebrations. This added number six and number seven to the number of countries that had publicly avowed atomic weapons, the "nuclear club." Strongly objecting, Clinton imposed economic sanctions on both.

However, these developments did not indicate that India, in the foreseeable future, would overtake China as the region's leading power.

Some asked whether a new center of power comparable to the pre-1991 Soviet Union would emerge in the future to challenge America's leading role. Despite Russia's possession of nuclear weapons, its economic collapse, even more than its territorial disruption, seemed to bar it from resuming such a role in the foreseeable future.

Some speculated on a possible future challenge by Japan. Japan's economic production had narrowed the U.S. economic lead, Tokyo rivaled New York as the world's financial capital, its foreign aid surpassed America's, and Japanese citizens were accumulating property throughout the world. What would be the long-term consequence of Japan's becoming an economic superpower? Historically, economic power has brought political power. Would an increasingly powerful Japan continue to defer to America in foreign policy? Some Japanese leaders saw America as in decline and occasionally spoke of assuming a leading role in East Asia's international affairs. By 1989, 60 percent of Americans regarded Japan as more of a threat than Russia.

However, Japan's population (125 million in 1994) was only half of America's. In the 1990s the growth of its economy slowed and its production fell behind that of China. Also, its small territory and its densely packed cities were extremely vulnerable to atomic attack. Moreover, Japan's economy was deeply enmeshed with that of many other nations. Possibly its self-interest demanded that it continue a policy of inoffensivism and rely on other nations' self-interest in trade to ensure continuing access to essential foreign resources and markets. As of 1998, with U.S. troops in Japan, the country was still under U.S. protection. Meanwhile, it played a major role in bringing about greater integration of the world's economy, and the consequent international interdependence could contribute to world peace.

Also mentioned as possible future great powers were the European Union, the Muslim world, and China.

Centered on Germany, the European Union had both a greater population and economic production than America. Formalized in 1991, in the Dutch city of Maastricht, the European Union by 1997 had fifteen member nations. It provided for an elected European Parliament, albeit one with little power, and a central bureaucracy. It brought continuing integration of the European economies, to the extent of adopting a common currency, the "euro," which began circulating in 1999. However, "sovereignty," the real power of decision, remained with the individual nations. Thus, despite its achievement of much economic unity, Europe's progress toward political unity was so slow as to dim the prospect that its member nations could soon construct a central government sufficiently strong to make the European Union a great world power.

The populous Muslim world extends from northwest Africa through the Middle East and southern areas of the former Soviet Union, Afghanistan, and Pakistan to Indonesia. Many Muslims dreamed of unifying many of the world's billion Muslims, and the political power of radical "Muslim fundamentalists," who sought religious rule, was rising. By 1996, they were dominant in Iran, Turkey, and Afghanistan. In May 1998 Pakistan, by a series of explosions, demonstrated that Muslims had atomic bombs. Nevertheless, Muslims remained so badly split among rival nations, branches of Islam, and rich and poor that significant unification did not seem probable.

China possessed both an enormous population and huge territory, but it was poor. However, if it could continue its remarkable economic growth of the 1980s and 1990s it would soon acquire the economic basis for great power. According to the World Bank, its 1996 GNP, $4,047 billion, exceeded Japan's $2,945 billion, and had become the world's second largest—second only to America's $7,433 billion. Consequently, as of this writing, China seemed to be the nation most likely to achieve great-power status.

The distribution of the world's wealth and population between industrialized and developing countries remained extremely unequal. The economic growth rate of high-income nations greatly exceeded that of low-income countries, while the birthrates in high-income countries plunged far below those of developing areas. Demographers predicted that whites of European extraction were destined to become a minority, even in the former Soviet Union and in North America. These developments could raise pressures to transfer a larger economic share to nonwhites and to lower the barriers to their immigration into North America and Europe.

Historically, it appears that wealth and power have usually gone to those peoples who are most successful in achieving large-scale and high-quality cooperation. In the 1990s, some regions, including the Soviet Union and Yugoslavia, fragmented and lost prosperity and power, while others, including the European Union and the North American Free Trade Association drew closer together. In China, 1.2 billion people were grouped under a common government.

Talk of "a new world order" was probably premature. Instead, there seemed to be more disorder. The ideologies of communism and anticommunism had contributed to the formation of huge coalitions in support of causes that transcended narrow ethnic loyalties. With the decay of the ideological unity, long-submerged conflicts among ethnic, religious, and nationalist groups erupted in East Europe and in the Third World, often with tragic consequences.

Some political scientists concluded that, despite the increasing globalization of the world economy, ethnic nationalism remained so strong that, in the future, more large, multiethnic nations would fragment into numbers of independent single-ethnic nations as did the Soviet Union and Yugoslavia. "The faster the world integrates," wrote historian Arthur M. Schlesinger Jr., "the more people huddle in their religious or ethnic or tribal enclaves." The only way to minimize the catastrophic effects of such disruption, they argued, was to reduce the importance of national boundaries as barriers to trade and population movement by cutting tariffs and liberalizing immigration quotas, preferably by putting trade and population movement under international control, and also to further reduce the number and frequency of wars between ethnic groups by strengthening international institutions such as the United Nations and the World Court. Humankind had had much experience in developing federalism—combining local self government with a general over all government to handle common concerns.

It was increasingly obvious that different parts of the world were becoming more interdependent and that many serious problems could no longer be solved within national borders. Proliferating telephone lines, radio and television broadcasting and the internet provided instant exhaustive worldwide communication. Between 1980 and 1996 world trade soared from an already impressive $2.5 trillion to $7 trillion, and between 1990 and 1997 direct foreign investment jumped from $24 billion to $120 billion. The flow of money across national boundaries can have enormous consequences. An influx of foreign capital contributed to producing economic booms in Latin and East Asia, and cessation of that flow contributed to an economic collapse in Latin America in the early 1980s, and in East Asia in the late 1990s. In both regions nations were forced by foreign forces beyond their control to drastically alter their economic policies.

Also, national governments found it increasingly difficult to protect their citizens from many harmful environmental effects of developments beyond their borders. Air and water pollution swept across national boundaries, ozone depletion, global warming, and epidemics of diseases such as AIDS were worldwide in their origins and effects. An atomic war anywhere would raise background radiation everywhere—a disaster no nation could excape.

Clearly, there was need for international regulatory bodies with power and financing adequate to put into effect essential controls. And obviously these bodies must represent the interests of the people being regulated.

Many hoped that the end of the Cold War would enable the United Nations to function as its creators had hoped and become more effective as a peacekeeper and peacemaker. It was increasingly active. In 1994 it fielded eighty thousand peacekeeping troops in eighteen separate operations at a cost of $3.3 billion. However, the big-power veto still restricted its competence to handle disputes among the Security Council's permanent members. Furthermore, its peace machinery was better designed to prevent aggression than to correct injustice.

Many social scientists maintained that further development of international conflict-resolving institutions, which some termed world government, was more urgent than ever. They perceived the world's increasing security needs and its environmental and economic interdependence as making such an institution indispensible, while improvements in transportation, communication, and education, and the spread of common culture, were making it possible.

Recommended Readings

Overviews

AMERICA'S RELATIONS WITH THE SOVIET UNION

Blacker, Coit D., *Reluctant Warriors: The United States, the Soviet Union and Arms Control.* 1987.

Bolkhovitinov, N. N., and Dane Hartgrove, *Russia and the United States.* 1987.

Boyle, Peter G., *American-Soviet Relations from the Russian Revolution to the Fall of Communism.* 1993.

Bradley, John, *War and Peace Since 1945.* 1989.

Brands, H. W., *The Devil We Knew: Americans and the Cold War.* 1993.

Brinkley, Douglas, *Dean Acheson: The Cold War Years, 1953–71.* 1992.

Chang, Gordon, *Friends and Enemies: The United States, China, and the Soviet Union.* 1992.

Dobrynin, Anatoly, *In Confidence.* 1995.

Froman, Michael D., *The Development of the Idea of Detente.* 1992.

Gaddis, John L., *Russia, the Soviet Union, and the United States.* 1990.

Gates, Robert M., [CIA director] *From the Shadows: The Ultimate Insider's Story of Five Presidents and How they Won the Cold War.* 1996.

——, *We Now Know: Rethinking Cold War History.* 1997.

Gartoff, Raymond L., *Detente and Confrontation: American-Soviet Relation from Nixon to Reagan.* 1985.

————, *The Great Transition: American-Soviet Relations and the End of the Cold War*. 1994.

Gromyko, Andrei, *Memoirs*. 1990.

Hill, Kenneth L., *Cold War Chronology: Soviet-American Relations, 1945–1991*. 1993.

Hyland, William, *Mortal Rivals: Superpower Relations from Nixon to Reagan*. 1987.

Judge, Edward H., and John W. Langdon, *A Hard and Bitter Peace: A Global History of the Cold War*. 1996.

Killen, Linda R., *The Soviet Union and the United States: A New Look at the Cold War*. 1988.

Koviq, Bennet, *Of Walls and Bridges: The United States and Eastern Europe*. 1991.

LaFeber, Walter, *America, Russia, and the Cold War, 1945–1992*. 7th ed. 1993.

Levering, Ralph B., *The Cold War, A Post–Cold War History*. 1994.

Libbey, James K., *American-Russian Economic Relations*. 1989.

McCormick, Thomas, *America's Half Century: U.S. Foreign Policy in the Cold War*. 1993.

Miller, Richard L., *Heritage of Fear: Illusion and Reality in the Cold War*. 1988.

Oberdofer, Don, *From the Cold War to a New Era: The United States and the Soviet Union*. 1998.

Paterson, Thomas G., *On Every Front: The Making and Unmaking of the Cold War*. 1992.

Pessen, Edward, *Losing Our Souls: The American Experience in the Cold War*. 1993.

Powaski, Ronald E., *The Cold War: The United States and the Soviet Union, 1917–1991*. 1997.

Shavit, David, *United States Relations with Russia and the Soviet Union*. 1993.

Siegel, Katherine A. S., *Loans and Legitimacy: The Evolution of Soviet-American Relations, 1919–1933*. 1996.

The United States and Europe

Barnet, Richard J., *The Alliance: America-Europe-Japan, Makers of the Postwar World*. 1987.

Bartlett, C. J., *The Special Relationship: A Political History of Anglo-American Relations Since 1945*. 1992.

Blumenthal, Henry, *Illusion and Reality in Franco-American Diplomacy, 1914–1945*. 1986.

Cogan, Charles G., *Oldest Allies, Guarded Friends: The United States and France Since 1940*. 1994.

Costigliola, Frank, *France and the United States: The Cold Alliance Since World War II*. 1992.

Hathaway, Robert M., *Great Britain and the United States: Special Relations Since World War II*. 1990.

Jonas, Manfred, *The United States and Germany: A Diplomatic History*. 2nd ed. 1994.

Kaplan, Lawrence S., *NATO and the United States: The Enduring Alliance*. 1988.

Kapstein, Ethan B., *The Insecure Alliance: Enerqy Crises and Western Politics Since 1944*. 1990.

Lees, Lorraine, *Keeping Tito Afloat: The United States, Yugoslavia, and the Cold War*. 1997.

Ninkovich, Frank, *Germany and the United States: The Transformation of the German Question Since 1945*. 2 rev. ed. 1994.

Renwick, Sir Robert, *Fighting with Allies: America and England in Peace and War*. 1996.

Smith, Joseph, *Unequal Giants: Diplomatic Relations Between the United States and Britain 1889–1930*. 1991.

The United States and the Western Hemisphere

Bothwell, Robert, *Canada and the United States: The Politics of Partnership*. 1992.

Brenner, Philip, *From Confrontation to Negotiation: U.S. Relations with Cuba*. 1988.

Chase, James, *Endless War: How We Got Involved in Central America*. 1984.

Cobbs, Elizabeth A., *The Rich Neighbor Policy: Rockefeller and Kaiser in Brazil*. 1992.

Coniff, Michael, *Panama and the United States*. 1992.

Haines, Gerald K., *The Americanization of Brazil: A Study of U.S. Cold War Diplomacy in the Third World*. 1989.

LaFeber, Walter, *Inevitable Revolutions: The United States in Central America*. 2nd ed. 1993.

Langley, Lester D., *Mexico and the United States*. 1991.

————, *The United States and the Caribbean in the Twentieth Century*. 1989.

Leacock, Ruth, *Requiem for Revolution: The United States and Brazil, 1961–1969*. 1990.

Leonard, Thomas J., *Central America and the United States: The Search for Stability*. 1991.

Lowenthal, Abraham E., *Partners in Conflict: The United States and Latin America*. 1987.

Molineu, Harold, *U.S. Policy Toward Latin America: From Regionalism to Globalism*. 1986.

Morley, Morris, *Condemned to Repetition: The United States and Nicaragua*. 1987.

————, *Imperial State and Revolution: The United States and Cuba, 1952–1985*. 1987.

Pastor, Robert A., *Whirlpool: U.S. Foreign Policy Toward Latin America and the Caribbean*. 1992.

————, and Jorge G. Castenada, *Limits to Friendship: The United States and Mexico*. 1988.

Paterson, Thomas G., *Contesting Castro: The United States and the Triumph of the Cuban Revolution*. 1994.

Perez, Louis A., Jr., *Cuba and the United States*. 1990.

Raat, W. Dirk, *Mexico and the United States*. 1992.

Smith, Gaddis, *The Last Years of the Monroe Doctrine, 1945–1993*. 1994.

Smith, Robert F. *The Caribbean World and the United States: Mixing Rum and Coca-Cola*. 1994.

Smith, Wayne S., *The Closest of Enemies: A Personal and Diplomatic Account of U.S.-Cuban Relations Since 1957*. 1987.

Szulc, Tad, *Fidel*. 1986.

Thompson, John W., and Stephen J. Randall, *Canada and the United States, Ambivalent Allies*. 1994.

Tulchin, Joseph S., *Argentina and the United States: A Conflicted Relationship*. 1990.

Weintraub, Sidney, *A Marriage of Convenience: Relations Between Mexico and the United States*. 1990.

Wood, Bryce, *The Dismantling of the Good Neighbor Policy*. 1985.

America and the Middle East

Ball, George W., and Douglas B. Ball, *The Passionate Attachment: America's Involvement with Israel, 1947 to the Present*. 1992.

Ben-Zvi, Abraham, *The United States and Israel*. 1994.

Bill, James A., *The Eagle and the Lion: The Tragedy of American-Iranian Relations*. 1988.

Brands, H. W., *Into the Labyrinth: The United States and the Middle East, 1945–1993*. 1994.

Burns, William J., *Economic Aid and American Policy Toward Egypt, 1955–1981*. 1985.

Chester, Edward A., *United States Oil Policy and Diplomacy: A Twentieth-Century Overview*. 1983.

Cottam, Richard W., *Iran and the United States: A Cold War Case Study*. 1988.

Hahn, Peter L., *The United States, Great Britain, and Egypt, 1945–1956: Strategy and Diplomacy in the Early Cold War*. 1991.

Keddie, Nikki R., *Iran, the United States, and the Soviet Union*. 1990.

Neff, Donald, *Fallen Pillars: U.S. Policy Toward Palestine and Israel Since 1945*. 1995.

Palmer, Michael A., *Guardians of the Gulf: A History of America's Expanding Role in the Persian Gulf, 1883–1991*. 1992.

Quandt, William P., *The United States and Egypt*. 1990.

Rabie, Muhammad, *The Politics of Foreign Aid: U.S. Foreign Assistance and Aid to Israel*. 1988.

Roth, Stephen J., ed., *The Impact of the Six-Day War: A Twenty-Year Assessment*. 1988.

Schoenbaum, David, *The United States and the State of Israel*. 1993.

Spiegel, Steven L., *The Other Arab-Israeli Conflict: Making America's Middle East Policy from Truman to Reagan*. 1985.

———, Mark A. Heller, and Jacob Goldberg, *The Soviet-American Competition in the Middle East*. 1988.

Taylor, Alan R., *The Superpowers and the Middle East*. 1991.

Tivnan, Edward, *The Lobby: Jewish Political Power and American Foreign Policy*. 1987.

AMERICA AND EAST ASIA

Buckley, Roger, *U.S.-Japan Alliance Diplomacy, 1945–1990*. 1992.

Chang, Gordon H., *Friendly Enemies: The United States, China and the Soviet Union, 1948–1972*. 1990.

Cohen, Warren T., *America's Response to China*. 1990.

Dudden, Arthur P., *The American Pacific: From the Old China Trade to the Present*. 1992.

Emmerson, John K., and Harrison M. Holland, *The Eagle and the Rising Sun: America and Japan in the Twentieth Century*. 1989.

Fairbank, John K., *The United States and China*. 4th ed. 1983.

Foot, Rosemary, *The Practice of Power: U.S. Relations with China Since 1949*. 1995.

Gardner, Paul F., *Shared Hopes, Separate Fears: Fifty Years of U.S.-Indonesian Relations*. 1997.

Gibney, Frank, *The Pacific Century: America and Asia in a Changing World*. 1992.

Harding, Harry, *A Fragile Relationship: The United States and China Since 1972*. 1992.

Hunt, Michael H., *The Genesis of Chinese Communist Foreign Policy*. 1996.

Iriye, Akira, *Across the Pacific: An Inner History of American-East Asian Relations*. Rev. ed. 1992.

Jiang, Arnold Xiangze, *The United States and China*. 1988.

LaFeber, Walter, *The Clash: A History of U.S.-Japan Relations.* 1997.

Liu, Ta Jen, *U.S.-Chinese Relations, 1784–1992.* 1996.

Macdonald, Douglas J., *Adventures in Chaos: American Intervention for Reform in the Third World* [China, the Philippines, and South Vietnam]. 1992.

Newman, Robert P., *Owen Lattimore and the "Loss" of China.* 1992.

Ross, Robert S., *Negotiating Cooperation: The United States and China, 1969–1989.* 1995.

Schaller, Michael, *Altered States: The United States and Japan Since the Occupation.* 1997.

———, *Douglas MacArthur: The Far Eastern General.* 1989.

———, *The United States and China in the Twentieth Century.* 2nd ed. 1990.

Wested, Odd Arne, *Cold War and Revolution: Soviet-American Rivalry and the Origins of the Chinese Civil War.* 1993.

Wolport, Stanley, *Roots of Confrontation in South Asia: Afghanistan, Pakistan, India, and the Superpowers.* 1982.

Zhai, Qiang, *The Dragon, the Lion, and the Eagle: Chinese-British-American Relations, 1949–1958.* 1994.

AMERICA IN VIETNAM

Baritz, Loren, *Backfire: A History of How American Culture Led Us into Vietnam and Made Us Fight the Way We Did.* 1985.

Berman, William C., *William Fulbright and the Vietnam War.* 1988.

Guidak, Ilya V., *The Soviet Union and the Vietnam War.* 1996.

Hannah, Norman B., *The Key to Failure: Laos and the Vietnam War.* 1987.

Herring, George C., Jr., *America's Longest War: The United States and Vietnam, 1950–1975.* 2nd ed. 1986.

Hess, Gary R., *Vietnam and the United States: Origins and Legacy of War.* 1990.

Kahin, George M., *Intervention: How America Became Involved in Vietnam.* 1986.

Karnow, Stanley, *Vietnam: A History.* 1991.

Kattenburg, Paul, *The Vietnam Trauma in American Foreign Policy, 1945–1975.* 1980.

Kolko, Gabriel, *Anatomy of A War: Vietnam, the United States, and the Modern Historical Experience.* 1986.

Lansdale, Edward, *In the Midst of Wars: An American's Mission to Southeast Asia.* 1991.

Palmer, Bruce, Jr., *The 25-Year War: America's Military Role in Vietnam.* 1984.

Prados, John, *The Hidden History of the Vietnam War.* 1995.

Sheehan, Neil, *A Bright Shining Lie: John Paul Vann and America in Vietnam.* 1988.

Truong, Nhu Tang, *A Vietcong Memoir.* 1985.

Young, Marilyn B., *The Vietnam Wars, 1945–1990.* 1991.

U.S. MILITARY POLICY

Andrew, Christopher, *For the President's Eyes Only: Secret Intelligence and the American Presidency from Washington to Bush.* 1994.

Bissell, Richard M., *Reflections of a Cold Warrior: From Yalta to the Bay of Pigs.* 1996.

Bundy, McGeorge, *Danger and Survival: Choices about the Bomb in the First Fifty Years.* 1988.

Buzzanco, Robert, *Masters of War: Military Dissent and Politics in the Vietnam Era.* 1996.

Chace, James, and Caleb Carr: *America Invulnerable: The Quest for Absolute Security from 1812 to Star Wars.* 1988.

Grose, Peter, *Gentleman Spy: The Life of Allen Dulles.* 1994.

Johnson, Loch K., *America's Secret Power: The CIA in a Democratic Society.* 1989.

Landau, Saul, *The Dangerous Doctrine: National Security and U.S. Foreign Policy.* 1988.

Lansdale, Edward, *The Unquiet American* [counterinsurgency in the Philippines and Vietnam]. 1989.

Morris, Charles J., *Iron Destinies, Lost Opportunities: The Arms Race Between the USA and the USSR, 1945–1987.* 1988.

Persico, Joseph E., *Casey: The Lives and Secrets of William J. Casey from the OSS to the CIA.* 1990.

Prados, John, *Presidents' Secret Wars: CIA and Pentagon Secret Operations Since World War II.* 1986.

Talbott, Strobe, *The Master of the Game: Paul Nitze and the Nuclear Peace.* 1988.

Tillema, Herbert K., *International Armed Conflict Since 1945.* 1991.

AMERICA AND INTERNATIONAL ORGANIZATION

Dunne, Michael, *The United States and the World Court.* 1988.

Finger, Seymour M., *American Ambassadors at the UN.* 1987.

Gardner, Lloyd C., *A Covenant with Power: America and World Order from Wilson to Reagan.* 1984.

Hoopes, Townsend, and Douglas Brinkley, *FDR and the Creation of the UN.* 1997.

Meisler, Stanley, *United Nations: The First Fifty Years.* 1996.

Wooley, Wesley T., *Alternatives to Anarchy: American Supernationalism Since World War II.* 1988.

AMERICA'S RELATIONS WITH THE THIRD WORLD

Brands, H. W., *India and the United States: The Cold Peace.* 1990.

———, *The Specter of Neutralism: The United States and the Emergence of the Third World.* 1990.

Duner, Bertil, *The Bear, the Cubs and the Eagle: Soviet Bloc Interventionism in the Third World and the U.S. Response.* 1987.

Feste, Karen, *Expanding the Frontiers: Superpower Intervention in the Cold War.* 1992.

Kolko, Gabriel, *Confronting the Third World: Third World United States Foreign Policy, 1945–1980.* 1988.

Korn, David A., *Ethiopia, the United States, and the Soviet Union.* 1986.

McMahon, Robert J., *The Cold War on the Periphery: The United States, India, and Pakistan.* 1994.

Other Overviews

Abramson, Rudy, *Spanning the Century: The Life and Times of W. Averell Harriman.* 1992.

Bill, James A., *George Ball: Behind the Scenes in U.S. Foreign Policy,* 1997.

Bohlen, Charles E., *Witness to History, 1929–1969.* 1975.

Brown, Seyom, *The Faces of Power: U.S. Foreign Policy from Truman to Clinton.* 2nd ed. 1994.

Callahan, David, *Dangerous Capabilities: Paul Nitze and the Cold War.* 1991.

Divine, Robert A., *Since 1945: Politics and Diplomacy in Recent American History.* 3rd ed. 1985.

Grabner, Norman A., *America as a World Power: A Realistic Appraisal from Wilson to Reagan.* 1984.

Hixon, Walter, *George F. Kennan: Cold War Iconoclast.* 1990.

Hodgson, Godfrey, *The Colonel: The Life and Wars of Henry Stimson, 1867–1950.* 1990.

Hunt, Michael H., *Ideology and U.S. Foreign Policy.* 1987.

Iriye, Akira, *The Globalizing of America, 1913–1945.* 1993.

Isaacson, Walter, and Evan Thomas, *The Wise Men: Six Friends and the World They Made.* 1986.

Kennan, George F., *Memoirs, 1925–1950.* 1967.

Mayers, David, *George Kennan and the Dilemmas of U.S. Foreign Policy.* 1988.

Morison, Elting E., *Turmoil and Tradition: A Study of the Life and Times of Henry L. Stimson.* 1960.

Prados, John, *Keepers of the Keys: A History of the National Security Council from Truman to Bush.* 1990.

Ranelagh, John, *The Agency: The Rise and Decline of the CIA.* 1986.

Smith, Tony, *America's Mission: The United States and the Struggle for Democracy in the Twentieth Century.* 1995.

Steel, Ronald, *Walter Lippmann and the American Century.* 1980.

Williams, William A., *The Tragedy of American Diplomacy.* 1988.

Wittner, Lawrence S., *Rebels Against War: The American Peace Movement, 1941–1960.* 1969.

Woods, Randall B., *Fulbright: A Biography.* 1995.

Yergin, Daniel, *The Prize: The Quest for Oil, Money, and Power.* 1991.

Chapter 1: The United States Enters World War I

Burk, Katheline, *Britain, America, and the Sinews of War, 1914–1918.* 1985.

Calhoun, Frederick S., *Power and Principle: Armed Intervention in Wilsonian Foreign Policy.* 1987.

Clements, Kendrick A., *William Jennings Bryan, Missionary Isolationist.* 1983.

Coogan, John W., *The End of Neutrality: The U.S., Britain, and Maritime Rights, 1899–1917.* 1981.

Cooper, John M., *The Vanity of Power: American Isolationism and World War I, 1914–1917.* 1969.

————, *The Warrior and the Priest: Woodrow Wilson and Theodore Roosevelt.* 1983.

Lansing, Robert, *War Memoirs of Robert Lansing, Secretary of State.* 1935.

Link, Arthur S., *Wilson the Diplomist.* 1963.

————, *Wilson: The Struggle for Neutrality, 1914–1915.* 1960.

————, *Wilson: Confusion and Crisis, 1915–1916.* 1964.

————, *Wilson: Campaigns for Progressivism and Peace.* 1965.

————, *Woodrow Wilson: Revolution, War, and Peace.* 1979.

Peterson, Horace C., and Gilbert C. Fite, *Opponents of War, 1917–1918.* 1957.

Schmitt, Bernadotte E., and Harold C. Vedeler, *The World in the Crucible, 1914–1919.* 1984.

Sharp, Allan, *The Versailles Settlement.* 1991.

Stevenson, David, *The First World War and International Politics.* 1988.

Tansill, Charles C., *America Goes to War.* 1942.

Chapter 2: World War and Peace Settlement

Ambrosius, Lloyd E., *Wilsonian Statecraft: Theory and Practice of Liberal Internationalism during World War I.* 1991.

————, *Woodrow Wilson and the American Diplomatic Tradition: The Treaty Fight in Perspective.* 1987.

Bagby, Wesley M., *Road to Normalcy: The Presidential Campaign and Election of 1920.* 1962.

Clements, Kendrick A., *The Presidency of Woodrow Wilson.* 1992.

————, *Woodrow Wilson: World Statesman.* 1987.

Ferrell, Robert H., *Woodrow Wilson and World War I, 1917–1921.* 1985.

Foglesong, David S., *America's Secret War against Bolshevism: U.S. Intervention in the Russian Civil War, 1917–1920.* 1995.

Gardner, Lloyd C., *Safe for Democracy: The American Response to Revolution, 1913–1923.* 1987.

Hoover, Herbert, *The Ordeal of Woodrow Wilson.* 1958.

Knock, Thomas, *Woodrow Wilson and the Quest for a New World Order.* 1993.

Lentin, A., *Lloyd George, Woodrow Wilson, and the Guilt of Germany.* 1985.

Lewis, N. Gordon, *Woodrow Wilson and World Politics: America's Response to War and Revolution.* 1968.

Lovin, Clifford, R., *A School for Diplomats: The Paris Peace Conference of 1919.* 1997.

Maddox, Robert J., *William E. Borah and American Foreign Policy.* 1969.

Rhodes, Benjamin D., *The Anglo-American Winter War with Russia, 1918–1919: A Diplomatic and Military Tragicomedy.* 1988.

Schaffer, Ronald, *America in the Great War.* 1991.

Schwabe, Klaus, *Woodrow Wilson, Revolutionary Germany and Peacemaking, 1918–1919: Missionary Diplomacy and the Realities of Power.* 1985.

Sharp, Allan, *The Versailles Settlement.* 1991

Walworth, Arthur, *Wilson and His Peacemakers.* 1986.

Chapter 3: Foreign Relations in the 1920s

Buckingham, Peter H., *International Normalcy: The Open Door Peace with the Former Central Powers, 1921–1929*. 1983.

Buckley, Thomas H., *The United States and the Washington Conference, 1921–1922*. 1970.

Cohen, Warren I., *Empire without Tears: America's Foreign Relations, 1921–1933*. 1987.

Costigliola, Frank, *Awkward Dominion: American Political, Economic, and Cultural Relations with Europe, 1919–1933*. 1984.

Doenecke, Justus D., *When the Wicked Rise: American Opinion-Makers and the Manchurian Crisis of 1931–1933*. 1984.

Ferrell, Robert H., *Frank B. Kellogg and Henry L. Stimson*. 1963.

Grieb, Kenneth J., *The Latin American Policy of Warren G. Harding*. 1976.

Hogan, Michael, *Informal Entente: The Private Structure of Cooperation in Anglo-American Economic Diplomacy, 1918–1928*. 1977.

Kamman, William, *A Search for Stability: United States Diplomacy Toward Nicaragua, 1925–1933*. 1968.

Kneeshaw, Stephen, *In Pursuit of Peace: The American Reaction to the Kellogg-Briand Pact, 1928–1929*. 1991.

Krenn, Michael L., *U.S. Policy Toward Economic Nationalism in Latin America, 1917–1929*. 1990.

Langley, Lester, *The Banana Wars: United States Intervention in the Caribbean 1898–1934*. 1985.

McKercher, Brian, *Anglo-American Relations in the 1920s*. 1990.

Salisbury, Richard V., *Anti-Imperialism and International Competition in Central America, 1920– 1929*. 1989.

Smith, Robert F., *The United States and Revolutionary Nationalism in Mexico, 1914–1932*. 1972.

Stimson, Henry L., and McGeorge Bundy, *On Active Service in Peace and War*. 1948.

Chapter 4: From Isolation to Involvement

Bennett, Edward M., *Franklin D. Roosevelt and the Search for Security: American-Soviet Relations, 1933–1939*. 1985.

Cole, Wayne S., *Determinism and American Foreign Relations During the Franklin D. Roosevelt Era*. 1995.

———, *Franklin Roosevelt and the Isolationists, 1932–1945*. 1984.

Dallek, Robert, *Franklin D. Roosevelt and American Foreign Policy 1932–1945*. 1995.

Farnsworth, Beatrice, *William C. Bullitt*. 1972.

Freidel, Frank, *Franklin D. Roosevelt: A Rendezvous with Destiny*. 1990.

Gellman, Irwin, *Good Neighbor Diplomacy*. 1979.

———, *Secret Affairs: Franklin Roosevelt, Cordell Hull, and Sumner Welles*. 1995.

Hull, Cordell, *The Memoirs of Cordell Hull*. Vol. 1. 1948.

Jablon, Howard, *Crossroads of Decision: The State Department and Foreign Policy 1933–1937*. 1983.

Little, Douglas, *Malevolent Neutrality: The United States, Great Britain and the Origins of the Spanish Civil War*. 1985.

Marks, Frederick W. III, *Wind over Sand: The Diplomacy of Franklin Roosevelt*. 1988.

Morris, Wayne, *Stalin's Famine and Roosevelt's Recognition of Russia*. 1994.

Offner, Arnold A., *The Origins of the Second World War: American Foreign Policy and World Politics, 1914–1941*. 1986.

Pratt, Julius W., *Cordell Hull, 1933–1944*. 2 vols. 1964.

Rock, William R., *Chamberlain and Roosevelt*. 1988.

Schmitz, David F., *The United States and Fascist Italy, 1922–1940*. 1988.

Sherwood, Robert E., *Roosevelt and Hopkins*. 1950.

Chapter 5: The United States Enters World War II

Bailey, Thomas A., and Paul B. Ryan, *Hitler vs. Roosevelt: The Undeclared Naval War*. 1979.

Barnhart, Michael A., *Japan's Attempt to Achieve Self-Sufficiency and the Origins of the Pacific War*. 1987.

Beard, Charles A., *President Roosevelt and the Coming of the War*. 1948.

Clausen, Henry C., and Bruce Lee, *Pearl Harbor: Final Judgement*. 1992.

Devine, Robert A., *The Reluctant Belligerent: American Entry into World War II*. 2nd ed. 1979.

Doenecke, Justus D., and John E. Wilz, *From Isolation to War 1931–1941*. 2nd ed. 1991.

Grew, Joseph C., *Turbulent Era: A Diplomatic Record of Forty Years, 1904–1945*. Vol 2. 1953.

Hearnden, Patrick J., *Roosevelt Confronts Hitler: America's Entry into World War II*. 1987.

Heinrichs, Waldo H., *American Ambassador: Joseph C. Grew and the Development of the American Diplomatic Tradition*. 1986.

———, *Threshold of War: Franklin D. Roosevelt and American Entry into World War II*. 1988.

Herzstein, Robert E., *Roosevelt and Hitler: Prelude to War*. 1993.

Hull, Cordell, *The Memoirs of Cordell Hull*. Vol. 2. 1948.

Iriye, Akira, *The Origins of the Second World War in Asia and the Pacific*. 1987.

Kimmel, Husband E., *Admiral Kimmel's Story*. 1955.

Langer, William L., and S. Everett Gleason, *The Undeclared War, 1940–1941*. 1953.

Prange, Gordon W., *Pearl Harbor: The Verdict of History*. 1986.

Rock, William R., *Chamberlain and Roosevelt*. 1988.

Sun, Youli, *China and the Origins of the Pacific War, 1931–1941*. 1993.

Tansill, Charles C., *Back Door to War*. 1952.

Toland, John, *Infamy: Pearl Harbor and Its Aftermath*. 1982.

Utley, Jonathan G., *Going to War, with Japan, 1937–1941*. 1985.

Wilson, Theodore A., *The First Summit: Roosevelt and Churchill At Placentia Bay, 1941*. 1991.

Chapter 6: Wartime Diplomacy

Aglion, Raoul, *Roosevelt and De Gaulle: A Personal Memoir of Allies in Conflict*. 1988.

Allen, Thomas B., *Code Named Downfall: The Secret Plan to Invade Japan—And Why Truman Dropped the Bomb*. 1995.

Alperovitz, Gar, *The Decision to Use the Atomic Bomb and the Architecture of an American Myth*. 1995.

Ambrose, Stephen E., *Eisenhower*. Vol. 1, *Soldier, General of the Army, President-Elect, 1890–1952*. 1983.

Armstrong, Anne, *Unconditional Surrender: The Impact of the Casablanca Policy on World War II*. 1961.

Bagby, Wesley M. *The Eagle-Dragon Alliance: America's Relations with China in World War II*. 1992.

Baldwin, Hanson, *Great Mistakes of the War*. 1950.

Barrett, David D., *Dixie Mission: The United States Army Observer Group in Yenan*. 1970.

Beaulac, Willard L., *Franco: Silent Ally in World War II*. 1986.

Bennett, Edward M., *Franklin D. Roosevelt and the Search for Victory: American-Soviet Relations, 1939–1945*. 1990.

Buckley, Thomas H., *American Foreign and National Security Policies, 1941–1945*. 1988.

Buhite, Russel D., *Decisions at Yalta: An Appraisal of Summit Diplomacy*. 1986.

Burns, James M. *Roosevelt: The Soldier of Freedom, 1940–1945*. 1970.

Dallek, Robert, *Franklin D. Roosevelt and American Foreign Policy, 1932–1945*. 1979.

Deane, John R., *The Strange Alliance: The Story of Our Efforts at Wartime Cooperation with the Russians*. 1947.

Dower, John W., *War Without Mercy: Race and Power in the Pacific War*. 1986.

Eastman, Lloyd E., "Nationalist China During the Sino-Japanese War, 1937–1945," *Cambridge History of China*. Vol. 13. 1986.

Eden, Anthony, *Memoirs of Anthony Eden, Earl of Avon: The Reckoning*. 1965.

Edmonds, Robin, *The Big Three: Churchill, Roosevelt and Stalin in Peace and War*. 1991.

Eisenhower, Dwight D., *Crusade in Europe*. 1948.

Eubank, Keith, *Summit at Teheran*. 1985.

Forrestal, James, *The Forrestal Diaries*. Edited by Walter Millis and E. F. Duffield. 1951.

Gardner, Lloyd C., *Spheres of Influence: The Great Powers Partition Europe, From Munich to Yalta*. 1993.

Harriman, W. Averell, and Elie Abel, *Special Envoy to Churchill and Stalin, 1941–1946*. 1975.

Herring, George C., Jr, *Aid to Russia, 1941–1946: Strategy, Diplomacy and the Origins of the Cold War*. 1973.

Hess, Gary R., *The United States at War, 1941–1945*. 1986.

Hurstfield, Julian G., *America and the French Nation, 1939–1945*. 1986.

Ienaga, Suburo, *The Pacific War: World War II and the Japanese, 1931–1945*. 1978.

Kimball, Warren F., *The Juggler: Franklin D. Roosevelt as Wartime Statesman*. 1994.

Kurzman, Dan, *Day of the Bomb: Countdown to Hiroshima*. 1986.

Langer, William L., *Our Vichy Gamble*. 1947.

Larabee, Eric, *Commander in Chief: Franklin Delano Roosevelt, His Lieutenants, and Their War*. 1987.

Leahy, William D., *I Was There: The Personal Story of the Chief of Staff of Presidents Roosevelt and Truman*. 1950.

MacArthur, Douglas, *Reminiscences*. 1964.

MacLean, Elizabeth K., *Joseph E. Davies: Envoy to the Soviets*. 1992.

Marrus, Michael R., *The Holocaust in History*. 1987.

Mayle, Paul, *The Eureka Summit* [Teheran]. 1987.

McCann, Frank D., Jr., *The Brazilian-American Alliance 1937–1945*. 1973.

McLellan, David S., *Dean Acheson: The State Department Years*. 1976.

Mee, Charles L., Jr., *Meeting at Potsdam*. 1975.

Miller, James E., *The United States and Italy, 1940–1950*. 1986.

Pogue, Forest C., *George C. Marshall*, Vol. 2: *Ordeal and Hope 1939–1942*. 1966. Vol 3: *Organizer of Victory, 1943–1945*. 1973.

Rodine, Floyd H., *Yalta*. 1974.

Sainsbury, Keith, *Churchill and Roosevelt at War*. 1994.

———, *The Turning Point: Roosevelt, Stalin, Churchill, and Chiang Kai-shek, 1943: The Moscow, Cairo, and Teheran Conferences*. 1985.

Sbrega, John J., *Anglo-American Relations and Colonialism in East Asia, 1941–1945*. 1985.

Service, John S., *Lost Chance in China: The World War II Dispatches of John S. Service*. Edited by Joseph W. Esherick. 1974.

Shogan, Robert, *Hard Bargain: How FDR Twisted Churchill's Arm, Evaded the Law, and Changed the Role of the American Presidency*. 1995.

Sigal, Leon V., *Fighting to a Finish: The Politics of War Termination in the United States and Japan*. 1988.

Smith, Bradley F., *The Shadow Warriors: O.S.S. and the Origins of the C.I.A.* 1983.

Smith, Gaddis, *American Diplomacy During the Second World War, 1941–1954*. 2nd ed. 1985.

Smith, Walter B., *My Three Years in Moscow*. 1950.

Stilwell, Joseph, *The Stilwell Papers*. Edited by Theodore White. 1948.

Stimson, Henry L., and McGeorge Bundy, *On Active Service in Peace and War*. 1949.

Takaki, Ronald, *Why America Dropped the Atomic Bomb*. 1995.

Thorne, Christopher, *Allies of a Kind: The United States, Britain, and the War against Japan, 1941–1945*. 1978.

Wainstock, Dennis D., *The Decision to Drop the Atomic Bomb*. 1996.

Wested, Arne, *Cold War and Revolution: Soviet-American Rivalry and the Origins of the Chinese Civil War, 1944–1946*. 1993.

Woods, Randall B., *The Roosevelt Foreign Policy Establishment and the Good Neighbor: The United States and Argentina, 1941–1945*. 1979.

Wyman, David S., *The Abandonment of the Jews: America and the Holocaust, 1941–1945*. 1984.

Young, Arthur N., *China and the Helping Hand, 1937–1945.* 1963.

Yu, Maochun, *OSS in China: Prelude to Cold War.* 1997.

Chapter 7: Onset of the Cold War

Acheson, Dean, *Present at the Creation: My Years in the State Department.* 1969.

Anderson, Terry H., *The United States, Great Britain, and the Cold War.* 1981.

Backer, John H., *Winds of History: The German Years of Lucius DuBignon Clay.* 1984.

Bills, Scott, *Empire and Cold War: The Roots of U.S-Third World Antagonism, 1945–1947.* 1990.

Brown, Seyom, *The Faces of Power: United States Foreign Policy from Truman to Clinton.* 2nd ed. 1983.

Byrnes, James M., *All in One Lifetime.* 1958.

Chase, James, *Acheson: The Secretary of State Who Created the American World.* 1998.

Cohen, Michael J., *Truman and Israel.* 1991.

Clymer, Kenton J., *Quest for Freedom: The United States and India's Independence.* 1994.

Deighton, Anne, *The Impossible Peace: Britain, the Division of Germany and the Origins of the Cold War.* 1990.

Desantis, Hugh, *The Diplomacy of Silence: The American Foreign Service, the Soviet Union, and the Cold War, 1933–1947.* 1980.

Donovan, Robert J., *The Marshall Plan and the Postwar Revival of Europe.* 1987.

Gaddis, John L., *The Long Peace: Inquiries into the History of the Cold War.* 1987.

Gardner, Lloyd C., *Architects of Illusion: Men and Ideas in American Foreign Policy, 1941–1949.* 1970.

Gardner, Lloyd C., Arthur M. Schlesinger Jr., and Hans Morgenthau, *The Origins of the Cold War.* 1970.

Gellmann, Barton, *Contending with Kennan.* 1984.

Gormly, James L., *From Potsdam to the Cold War: Big Three Diplomacy, 1945–1947.* 1990.

Hamby, Alonzo, *Man of the People: A Life of Harry S Truman.* 1995.

Harbutt, Fraser J., *The Iron Curtain: Churchill, America, and the Origins of the Cold War.* 1986.

Herken, Gregg, *The Winning Weapon: The Atomic Bomb in the Cold War, 1945–1950.* 1988.

Hixon, Walter, *George F. Kennan: Cold War Iconoclast.* 1989.

Hogan, Michael J., *The Marshall Plan: America, Britain, and the Reconstruction of Western Europe.* 1987.

Hoopes, Townsend, and Douglas Brinkley, *Driven Patriot: The Life and Times of James Forrestal.* 1992.

Jones, Howard, *A New Kind of War: America's Global Strategy and the Truman Doctrine in Greece.* 1989.

Kaplan, Lawrence S., *The United States and NATO: The Formative Years.* 1984.

Kuniholm, Bruce R., *The Origins of the Cold War in the Near East: Great Power Confrontation and Diplomacy in Iran, Turkey and Greece.* 1980.

Leffler, Melvyn P., *Preponderance of Power*: *National Security, the Truman Administration, and the Cold War*. 1992.

——, *The Specter of Communism*: *The United States and the Origins of the Cold War, 1917–1953*. 1994.

Lowe, Peter, *The Origins of the Cold War*. 1987.

Lukas, Richard C., *Bitter Legacy*: *Polish-American Relations in the Wake of World War II*. 1982.

Lytle, Mark H., *The Origins of the Iranian-American Alliance, 1941–1953*. 1987.

McCellan, David S., *Dean Acheson*. 1976.

McGlothlan, Ronald L., *Controlling the Waves*: *Dean Acheson and U.S. Foreign Policy in Asia*. 1993.

Messer, Robert L., *The End of an Alliance*: *James F. Byrnes, Roosevelt, Truman, and the Origins of the Cold War*. 1982.

Miller, James E., *The United States and Italy, 1940–1950*: *The Politics and Diplomacy of Stabilization*. 1986.

Miscamble, Wilson D., *George F. Kennan and the Making of American Foreign Policy, 1947–1950*. 1992.

Peterson, Edward N., *The American Occupation of Germany*: *Retreat to Victory*. 1977.

Pisani, Sallie, *The CIA and the Marshall Plan*. 1992.

Pogue, Forrest C., *George C. Marshall*: *Vol. 4, Statesman (1945–1959)*. 1987.

Pollard, Robert A., *Economic Security and the Origins of the Cold War, 1945–1950*. 1985.

Resis, Allbert, *Stalin, the Politburo, and the Onset of the Cold War*. 1988.

Schlaim, Avi, *The United States and the Berlin Blockade, 1948–1949*: *A Study in Crisis Decision-Making*. 1983.

Schwartz, Thomas A., *America's Germany*: *John J. McCloy and the Federal Republic of Germany*. 1989.

Taubman, William, *Stalin's American Policy*: *From Entente to Detente to Cold War*. 1982.

Thomas, Hugh, *Armed Truce*: *The Beginnings of the Cold War, 1945–1946*. 1987.

Truman, Harry S., *Memoirs*. 2 vols. 1956.

Wittner, Lawrence S., *American Intervention in Greece 1943–1949*. 1982.

——, *One World or None*: *A History of the World Nuclear Disarmament Through 1953*. 1993.

Woods, Randall B., and Howard Jones, *Dawning of the Cold War*: *The United States' Quest for Order*. 1991.

Yergin, Daniel, *Shattered Peace*: *The Origins of the Cold War and the National Security State*. 1977.

Chapter 8: Cold and Hot War in East Asia

Barnet, Richard J., *The Alliance*: *America-Europe-Japan, Makers of the Postwar World*. 1983.

Beale, John R., *Marshall in China*. 1970.

Bevin, Alexander, *Korea: The First War We Lost*. 1987.

Borden, William S., *The Pacific Alliance: United States Foreign Economic Policy and Japanese Trade Recovery, 1955*. 1984.

Buhite, Russel D., *Soviet-American Relations in Asia, 1945–1954*. 1982.

Chang, Gordon H., *The United States, China, and the Soviet Union*. 1990.

Chen, Jian, *China's Road to the Korean War: The Making of the Sino-American Confrontation*. 1994.

Cummings, Bruce, *The Origins of the Korean War*. Vol. 1: *Liberation and the Emergence of Separate Regimes, 1945–1947*. 1981. Vol. 2: *The Roaring of the Cataract, 1947–1950*. 1990.

Foot, Rosemary, *A Substitute for Victory: The Politics of Peacemaking at the Korean Armistice Talks*. 1990.

———, *The Wrong War: American Policy and the Dimensions of the Korean Conflict, 1950–1953*. 1985.

Gallichio, Marc S., *The Cold War Begins in Asia: American East Asian Policy and the Fall of the Japanese Empire*. 1988.

Gardner, Lloyd, *Approaching Vietnam: From World War II through Dienbienphu*. 1988.

Goncharov, Sergei N., John W. Lewis, and Xue Litai, *Uncertain Partners: Stalin, Mao and the Korean War*. 1993.

Grasso, June M., *Harry Truman's Two-China Policy, 1948–1950*. 1987.

Harding, Harry, and Yuan Ming, *Sino-Soviet Relations, 1945–1955: A Joint Reassessment of a Crucial Decade*. 1989.

Harries, Meirion, and Susan Harries, *Sheathing the Sword: The Demilitarization of Postwar Japan*. 1987.

Head, William P., *America's China Sojourn: America's Foreign Policy and Its Effect on Sino-American Relations, 1942–1948*. 1983.

Hess, Gary R., *The United States Emergence as a Southeast Asian Power, 1940–1950*. 1986.

James, D. Clayton, *The Years of MacArthur*. Vol. 3: *Triumph and Disaster, 1945–1964*. 1985.

Jian, Chen, *China's Road to the Korean War: The Making of the Sino-American Confrontation*. 1994.

Kaufman, Burton I., *The Korean War: Challenges in Crisis, Credibility, and Command*. 1986.

Lauren, Paul Gordon, ed., *The "China Hands" Legacy: Ethics and Diplomacy*. 1987.

Lee, Steven H., *Outposts of Empire: Korea, Vietnam, and the Origins of the Cold War in Asia, 1948–1954*. 1995.

MacDonald, Callum A., *Korea: The War Before Vietnam*. 1987.

Matray, James I., *The Reluctant Crusade: American Foreign Policy in Korea, 1941–1950*. 1985.

May, Gary, *China Scapegoat: The Diplomatic Ordeal of John Carter Vincent*. 1979.

McMahon, Robert J., *Colonialism and the Cold War: The United States and the Struggle for Indonesian Independence, 1945–1949*. 1981.

Rotter, Andrew J., *The Path to Vietnam: Origins of the American Commitment to Southeast Asia*. 1987.

Rovere, Richard H., and Arthur M. Schlesinger Jr., *The MacArthur Controversy and American Foreign Policy*. 1965.

Schaller, Michael, *The American Occupation of Japan: The Origins of the Cold War in Asia*. 1985.

————, *The U.S. Crusade in China, 1938–1945.* 1979.

Schonberger, Howard, *Aftermath of War: Americans and the Remaking of Japan, 1945–1952.* 1989.

Stuart, John Leighton, *Fifty Years in China.* 1954.

Stueck, William W., Jr., *The Korean War: An International History.* 1995.

————, *The Wedemeyer Mission: American Politics and Foreign Policy During the Cold War.* 1984.

Toland John, *In Mortal Combat: Korea, 1950–1953.* 1990.

Tucker, Nancy B., *Patterns in the Dust: Chinese-American Relations and the Recognition Controversy, 1949–1950.* 1985.

Wedemeyer, Albert C., *Wedemeyer Reports.* 1958.

Zhai, Qiang, *The Dragon, the Lion, and the Eagle: Chinese-British-American Relations, 1949–1958.* 1994.

Chapters 9 and 10: Eisenhower and Dulles
(For overviews of America in Vietnam, see page 408.)

Ambrose, Steven E., *Eisenhower,* Vol. II: *The President.* 1984.

Anderson, David L., *Trapped by Success: The Eisenhower Administration and Vietnam.* 1991.

Beschloss, Michael R., *Mayday: Eisenhower, Khrushchev and the U-2 Affair.* 1986.

Billings-Yun, Melanie, *Decision Against War: Eisenhower and Dien Bien Phu, 1954.* 1988.

Botti, Timothy J., *The Long Wait: The Forging of the Anglo-American Nuclear Alliance, 1945–58.* 1987.

Brands, H. W., Jr., *Cold Warriors: Eisenhower's Generation and American Foreign Policy.* 1988.

Broadwater, Jeff, *Eisenhower and the Anti-Communist Crusade.* 1992.

Cronin, Audrey Kurth, *Great Power Politics and the Struggle over Austria, 1945–1955.* 1986.

Divine, Robert A., *Eisenhower and the Cold War.* 1981.

————, *The Sputnik Challenge.* 1993.

Dockrill, Saki, *Eisenhower's New Look National Security Policy.* 1996.

Eden, Anthony, *Memoirs.* 1960.

Eisenhower, Dwight D., *Mandate for Change, 1953–1956.* 1963.

————, *Waging Peace, 1956–1961.* 1965.

Freiberger, Steven Z., *Dawn over Suez: The Rise of American Power in the Middle East, 1952–1957.* 1992.

Gardner, Lloyd C., *Approaching Vietnam: From World War II through Dienbienphu.* 1988.

Gleijeses, Piero, *Shattered Hopes: The Guatemalan Revolution and the United States, 1944–1954.* 1991.

Greenstein, Fred I., *The Hidden-Hand Presidency: Eisenhower as a Leader.* 1982.

Immerman, Richard, *The CIA in Guatemala: The Foreign Policy of Intervention.* 1982.

Kahin, George M., *Intervention: How America Became Involved in Vietnam.* 1986.

Kaufman, Burton I. *Trade and Aid: Eisenhower's Foreign Economic Policy, 1953–1961.* 1982.

Khrushchev, Nikita, *Khrushchev Remembers.* 1970.

Kyle, Keith, *Suez*. 1991.

Lytle, Mark Hamilton, *The Origins of the Iranian-American Alliance, 1941–1953*. 1987.

Marks, Frederick W., *Power and Peace: The Diplomacy of John Foster Dulles*. 1995.

Mayers, David, *Cracking the Monolith: U.S. Policy Against the Sino-Soviet Alliance, 1949–1955*. 1986.

Noble, G. Bernard, *Christian Herter*. 1970.

Pach, Chester A., Jr., and Elmo Richardson, *The Presidency of Dwight D. Eisenhower*. 1991.

Pickett, William B., *Dwight D. Eisenhower and American Power*. 1995.

Powers, Francis Gary, *Operation Overflight*. 1970.

Rabe, Stephen G., *Eisenhower and Latin America*. 1988.

Roosevelt, Kermit, *Countercoup* [CIA in Iran, 1953]. 1979.

Rostow, Walt W., *Eisenhower, Kennedy, and Foreign Aid*. 1985.

Schlesinger, Stephen, and Stephen Kinzer, *Bitter Fruit: The Untold Story of the American Coup in Guatemala*. 1982.

Stolper, Thomas E., *China, Taiwan, and the Offshore Islands*. 1985.

Taylor, Maxwell, *The Uncertain Trumphet* [a general's criticism of Eisenhower's defense policy]. 1959.

Welch, Richard E., Jr., *Response to Revolution: The United States and the Cuban Revolution, 1959–1961*. 1985.

Chapter 11: Kennedy's Foreign Policy (For overviews of America in Vietnam, see page 408.)

Berman, Larry, *Planning a Tragedy: The Americanization of the War in Vietnam*. 1982.

Beschloss, Michael R., *The Crisis Years: Kennedy and Khruschev, 1960–1963*. 1991.

Blight, James G., and David A. Welch, *On the Brink: Americans and Soviets Reexamine the Cuban Missile Crisis*. 1989.

Brugioni, Dino A., *Eyeball to Eyeball: The Inside Story of the Cuban Missile Crisis*. 1991.

Brune, Lester, *The Missile Crisis of October 1962: A Review of Issues and References*. 1985.

Bundy, McGeorge, *Danger and Survival*. 1985.

Catudal, Honore, *Kennedy and the Berlin Wall Crisis*. 1980.

Chomsky, Norm, *Rethinking Camelot: JFK, the Vietnam War, and U.S. Political Culture*. 1993.

Cohen, Warren I., *Dean Rusk*. 1980.

Divine, Robert A., *The Cuban Missile Crisis*. 2nd ed. 1988.

Galbraith, John Kenneth, *Ambassador's Journal: A Personal Account of the Kennedy Years*. 1969.

Fursenko, Aleksandr, and Timothy Naftali, *"One Hell of a Gamble": Khrushchev, Castro, and Kennedy, 1958–1964*. 1997.

Garthoff, Raymond, *Reflections on the Cuban Missile Crisis*. 2nd ed. 1989.

Hammer, Ellen J., *A Death in November* [Ngo Dinh Diem]: *America in Vietnam, 1963*. 1987.

Higgins, Trumbull, *The Perfect Failure: Kennedy Eisenhower, and the CIA at the Bay of Pigs*. 1987.

Hilsman, Roger, *To Move a Nation: The Politics of Foreign Policy in the Administration of John F. Kennedy*. 1967.

Kalb, Madeleine G., *The Congo Cables: The Cold War in Africa—From Eisenhower to Kennedy*. 1982.

Kennedy, Robert F., *The Thirteen Days: A Memoir of the Cuban Missile Crisis*. 1969.

Kern, Montague, Patricia W. Levering, and Ralph B. Levering, *The Kennedy Crisis: The Press, the Presidency, and Foreign Policy*. 1983.

Maga, Timothy P., *John F. Kennedy and the New Pacific Community*. 1990.

Mahoney, Richard D., *JFK: Ordeal in Africa*. 1983.

Martin, Edwin M., *Kennedy and Latin America*. 1994.

Martin, John B., *Adlai Stevenson and the World*. 1977.

Mayer, Frank A., *Adenauer and Kennedy: A Study in German-American Relations*. 1996.

Nathan, James A., ed., *The Cuban Missile Crisis Revisited*. 1992.

Newman, John M., *JFK and Vietnam: Deception, Intrigue, and the Struggle for Power*. 1993.

Nolting, Frederick, *From Trust to Tragedy: Kennedy's Ambassador to Diem's Vietnam*. 1988.

Parmet, Herbert S., *JFK: The Presidency of John F. Kennedy*. 1983.

Reeves, Richard, *President Kennedy*. 1993.

Rice, Gerard T., *The Bold Experiment: JFK's Peace Corps*. 1985.

Rusk, Dean, *As I Saw It*. 1990.

Rust, William J., *Kennedy in Vietnam*. 1985.

Salinger, Pierre, *P.S., A Memoir*. 1995.

Schlesinger, Arthur M., Jr., *A Thousand Days: John F. Kennedy in the White House*. 1965.

Schoenbaum, Thomas J., *Waging Peace and War: Dean Rusk in the Truman, Kennedy and Johnson Years*. 1988.

Sorensen, Theodore C., *Kennedy*. 1965.

Walton, Richard J., *Cold War and Counterrevolution: The Foreign Policy of John F. Kennedy*. 1972.

Welch, Richard E., Jr., *Response to Revolution: The United States and the Cuban Revolution, 1959–1961*. 1985.

White, Mark J., *The Cuban Missile Crisis*. 1995.

Chapter 12: The Lyndon Johnson Administration
(For overviews of America in Vietnam, see page 408.)

Berman, Larry, *Planning a Tragedy: The Americanization of the War in Vietnam*. 1982.

Bornet, Vaughn Davis, *The Presidency of Lyndon B. Johnson*. 1983.

Brands, H. W., *The Wages of Globalism: Lyndon Johnson and the Limits of American Power*. 1994.

Clifford, Clark, *Counsel for the President*. 1991.

Cohen, Warren I., *Dean Rusk*. 1980.

DiLeo, David L., *George Ball, Vietnam, and the Rethinking of Containment*. 1991.

Divine, Robert, *The Johnson Years*. 2 vols. 1987.

Draper, Theodore, *The Dominican Revolt*. 1968.

Fulbright, J. William, *The Arrogance of Power*. 1966.

Goodwin, Richard, *Remembering America*: *A Voice from the Sixties*. 1988.

Gardner, Lloyd C., *Pay Any Price*: *Lyndon Johnson and the Wars for Vietnam*. 1995.

Herring, George C., *LBJ and Vietnam*: *A Different Kind of War*. 1995.

Hoopes, Townsend, *The Limits of Intervention*: *An Inside Account of How the Johnson Policy of Escalation in Vietnam Was Reversed*. 1969.

Hunt, Michael H., *Lyndon Johnson's War*: *America's Cold War Crusade in Vietnam, 1945–1968*. 1996.

Johnson, Lyndon B., *The Vantage Point*: *Perspectives on the Presidency, 1963–1969*. 1971.

Leacock, Ruth, *Requiem for Revolution*: *The United States and Brazil, 1961–1969*. 1990.

Moise, Edwin E., *Tonkin Gulf and the Escalation of the Vietnam War*. 1996.

Scheman, Ronald, ed., *The Alliance for Progress*: *A Retrospective*. 1988.

Seaborg, Glenn T., with Benjamin S. Loeb, *Stemming the Tide*: *Arms Control in the Johnson Years*. 1987.

Shapley, Deborah, *Promise and Power*: *The Life and Times of Robert McNamara*. 1993.

Small, Melvin, *Johnson, Nixon, and the Doves*. 1988.

Spector, Ronald, *After Tet*: *The Bloodiest Year in Vietnam*. 1993.

Thompson, James C., *Rolling Thunder*: *Understanding Policy and Program Failure*. 1980.

Turner, Kathleen J., *Lyndon Johnson's Dual War*: *Vietnam and the Press*. 1985.

Vandemark, Brian, *Into the Quagmire*: *Lyndon Johnson and the Escalation of the Vietnam War*. 1991.

Westmoreland, William C., *A Soldier Reports*. 1976.

Chapters 13 and 14: Nixon and Ford

Ambrose, Stephen, *Nixon*: *The Triumph of a Politician, 1962–1972*. 1989.

Bundy, William, *A Tangled Web*: *The Making of Foreign Policy in the Nixon Presidency*. 1998.

Davis, Nathaniel, *The Last Two Years of Salvador Allende*. 1985.

Deibel, Terry L., *Presidents, Public Opinion, and Power*: *The Nixon, Carter, and Reagan Years*. 1987.

Ford, Gerald R., *A Time to Heal*: *The Autobiography of Gerald Ford*. 1979.

Fulbright, J. William, *The Crippled Giant*. 1972.

Hersh, Seymour M., *The Price of Power*: *Kissinger in the Nixon White House*. 1983.

Hung, Nguyen Tien, and Jerold Schecter, *The Palace File* [Nixon-Thieu correspondence]. 1986.

Isaacs, Arnold R., *Without Honor*: *Defeat in Vietnam and Cambodia*. 1983.

Isacson, Walter, *Kissinger*. 1992.

Joiner, Harry M., *American Foreign Policy*: *The Kissinger Era*. 1977.

Kissinger, Henry, *White House Years*. 1979.

———, *Years of Upheaval*. 1982.

Maresca, John J., *To Helsinki: The Conference on Security and Cooperation in Europe*. 1985.

Morris, Roger, *Richard Milhous Nixon*. 1989.

Nixon, Richard, *RN: The Memoirs of Richard Nixon*. 2 vol. 1978.

Rabe, Stephen G., *The Road to OPEC: United States Relations with Venezuela*. 1982.

Schurmann, Franz, *The Foreign Politics of Richard Nixon: The Grand Design*. 1987.

Shawcross, William, *Sideshow: Kissinger, Nixon and the Destruction of Cambodia*. 1979.

Small, Melvin, *Johnson, Nixon, and the Doves*. 1988.

Snepp, Frank, *Decent Interval: An Insider's Account of Saigon's Indecent End Told by the CIA's Chief Strategy Analyst in Vietnam*. 1978.

Smith, Gerard, *Doubletalk: The Story of SALT I*. 1985.

Starr, Harvey, *Henry Kissinger: Perceptions of International Politics*. 1984.

Sulzberger, C. L., *Henry Kissinger: Doctor of Diplomacy*. 1989.

———, *The World and Richard Nixon*. 1987.

Szulc, Tad, *The Illusion of Peace: Foreign Policy in the Nixon Years*. 1978.

Thornton, Richard C., *The Nixon-Kissinger Years: The Reshaping of American Foreign Policy*. 1989.

Wainstock, Dennis, *The Turning Point: The 1968 United States Presidential Campaign*. 1988.

Chapter 15: The Carter Administration

Bradsher, Henry S., *Afghanistan: Soviet Invasion and U.S. Response*. 1981.

Brzezinski, Zbigniew, *Power and Principle*. 1983.

Carter, Jimmy, *Keeping Faith*. 1982.

Drumbell, John, *The Carter Presidency*. 1993.

Halliday, Fred, *The Making of the Second Cold War*. 2nd ed. 1986.

Hargrove, Erwin C., *Jimmy Carter as President*. 1988.

Hogan, Michael, *The Panama Canal in American Politics*. 1986.

Huyser, Robert, *Mission to Tehran*. 1987.

Kaplan, Fred, *The Wizards of Armageddon*. 1991.

Kaufman, Burton I., *The Presidency of James Earl Carter, Jr*. 1995.

McLellan, David S., *Cyrus Vance*. 1985.

Moffett, George D., III, *The Limits of Victory: The Ratification of the Panama Canal Treaties*. 1985.

Muravchik, Joshua, *The Uncertain Crusade: Jimmy Carter and the Dilemmas of Human Rights Policy*. 1986.

Quandt, William B., *Camp David: Peacemaking and Politics*. 1986.

Rosati, Jerel A., *The Carter Administration's Quest for Global Community: Beliefs and Their Impact on Behavior*. 1987.

Ryan, Paul, *The Iran Rescue Mission*. 1985.

Scranton, Margaret E., *The Dynamics of Foreign Policymaking: The President, the Congress, and the Panama Canal Treaties*. 1984.

Sick, Gary, *All Fall Down: America's Tragic Encounter with Iran*. 1985.

Skidmore, David, *Reversing Course: Carter's Foreign Policy, Domestic Politics, and the Failure of Reform*. 1996

Smith, Gaddis, *Morality, Reason, and Power: American Diplomacy in the Carter Years*. 1986.

Spencer, Donald S., *The Carter Implosion: Jimmy Carter and the Amateur Style of Diplomacy*. 1988.

Strong, Robert, *Working in the World: Jimmy Carter and the Making of American Foreign Policy*. 1997.

Telhami, Shibley, *Power and Leadership: The Path to the Camp David Accords*. 1990.

Thornton, Richard C., *The Carter Years: Toward a New Global Order*. 1991.

Vance, Cyrus, *Hard Choices*. 1982.

Chapters 16 and 17: The Reagan Administration

Ball, George W., *Error and Betrayal in Lebanon: An Analysis of Israel's Invasion of Lebanon and the Implications for U.S.-Israeli Relations*. 1984.

Bialer, Seweryn, and Michael Mandelbaum, *Gorbachev's Russia and American Foreign Policy*. 1988.

Barrett, Lawrence I., *Gambling with History: Ronald Reagan in the White House*. 1983.

Blinkin, Anthony J., *Ally versus Ally: America, Europe, and the Siberian Pipeline Crisis*. 1987.

Burns, E. Bradford, *At War in Nicaragua*. 1987.

Burrowes, Reynold A., *Revolution and Rescue in Grenada*. 1988.

Calleo, David P., *Beyond American Hegemony*. 1987.

Carothers, Thomas, *In the Name of Democracy: U.S. Policy Toward Latin America in the Reagan Years*. 1991.

Cimbala, Stephen J., *The Reagan Defense Program*. 1986.

Dallek, Robert, *Ronald Reagan*. 1984.

Dallin, Alexander, *Black Box: The KAL Incident and the Superpowers*. 1985.

Destler, I. M., Leslie H. Gelb, and Anthony Lake, *Our Own Worst Enemy: The Unmaking of American Foreign Policy*. 1985.

Draper, Theodore, *A Very Thin Line: The Iran-Contra Affair*. 1991.

Drell, Sidney, et al., *The Reagan Strategic Defense Initiative*. 1985.

George, Alexander L., et al., *U.S.-Soviet Security Cooperation*. 1988.

Gutman, Roy, *Banana Diplomacy: The Making of American Policy in Nicaragua, 1981–1987*. 1988.

Haig, Alexander M., Jr., *Caveat: Realism, Reagan, and Foreign Policy*. 1984.

———, *Inner circles: How America Changed the World: A Memoir*. 1992.

Hough, Jerry, *Russia and the West: Gorbachev and the Politics of Reform*. 1988.

Johnson, Haynes, *Sleepwalking Through History*. 1991.

Kagan, Robert, *A Twilight Struggle: American Power and Nicaragua, 1977–1990*. 1996.

Langley, Lester, *Central America: The Real Stakes*. 1985.

Mandelbaum, Michael, and Strobe Talbott, *Reagan and Gorbachev*. 1987.

McFarlane, Robert, *Special Trust*. 1994.

McMahan, Jeff, *Reagan and the World*. 1986.

Menges, Constantine C., *Inside the National Security Council: The True Story of the Making and Unmaking of Reagan's Foreign Policy*. 1988.

North, Oliver, *Under Fire: An American Story*. 1991.

Oberdorfer, Don, *The Turn From the Cold War to a New Era: The United States and the Soviet Union 1983–1990*. 1991.

O'Shaughnessy, Hugh, *Grenada*. 1985.

Reagan, Ronald, *An American Life*. 1990.

Regan, Donald T., *For the Record: From Wall Street to Washington*. 1988.

Schaller, Michael, *Reckoning with Reagan: America and Its President in the 1980s*. 1992.

Schraeder, Peter J., *Intervention in the 1980s*. 1989.

Shultz, George P., *Turmoil and Triumph: My Years as Secretary of State*. 1993.

Smith, Steven K., and Douglas A. Wertman, *U.S.-Western European Relations During the Reagan Years*. 1992.

Talbott, Strobe, *The Russians and Reagan*. 1984.

Vanderlaan, Mary B., *Revolution and Foreign Policy in Nicaragua*. 1986.

Walsh, Lawrence E., *Firewall: The Iran-Contra Conspiracy and Cover-up*. 1997.

Weinberger, Casper, *Fighting for Peace: Seven Critical Years in the Pentagon*. 1990.

Wills, Garry, *Reagan's America*. 1987.

Winik, Jay, *On the Brink: The Dramatic, Behind-the-Scenes Saga of the Reagan Era and the Men and Women Who Won the Cold War*. 1996.

Woodward, Bob, *Veil: The Secret Wars of the CIA, 1981–1987*. 1987.

Chapter 18: The Bush Administration

Adams, Jan S., *A Foreign Policy in Transition: Moscow's Retreat from Central America and the Caribbean*. 1992.

Armacost, Michael H., *Friends or Rivals? The Insider's Account of U.S.-Japan Relations*. 1996.

———, *The Politics of Diplomacy: Revolution, War, and Peace, 1989–1992*. 1995.

Beschloss, Michael R., and Strobe Talbott, *At the Highest Levels: The Inside Story of the End of the Cold War*. 1993.

Brune, Lester H., *America and the Iraq Crisis, 1990–1992*. 1993.

Buckley, Kevin, *Panama: The Whole Story*. 1991.

Chace, James, *The Consequences of the Peace: The New Internationalism and American Foreign Policy*. 1992.

Clough, Michael, *Free at Last? U.S. Policy Toward Africa and the End of the Cold War*. 1992.

Freedman, Lawrence, and Efraim Karshe, *The Gulf Conflict 1990–1991: Diplomacy and War in the New World Order*. 1993.

Friedman, Norman, *Desert Victory: The War for Kuwait*. 1992.

Gaddis, John L., *The United States and the End of the Cold War: Implications, Reconsiderations, Provocations*. 1992.

Garten, Jeffery E., *A Cold Peace: America, Japan, Germany, and the Struggle for Supremacy.* 1992.

Graubard, Stephen R., *Mr. Bush's War: Adventures in the Politics of Illusion.* 1992.

Gregg, Robert W., *About Face?: The United States and the United Nations.* 1993.

Hilsman, Roger, *George Bush vs. Saddam Hussein: Military Success! Political Failure?* 1992.

Hiro, Dilip, *Desert Shield to Desert Storm: The Second Gulf War.* 1992.

Jentleson, Bruce, *With Friends Like These: Reagan, Bush, and Saddam.* 1994.

Matlock, Jack F., Jr., *Autopsy on an Empire: The American Ambassador's Account of the Collapse of the Soviet Union.* 1995.

Matthews, Ken, *The Gulf Conflict and International Relations.* 1993.

Miller, Judith, and Laurie Mylroie, *Saddam Hussein and the Crisis in the Gulf.* 1991.

Mueller, John, *Policy and Opinion in the Gulf War.* 1994.

Nixon, Richard, *Seize the Moment: America's Challenge in a One-Superpower World.* 1992.

Powell, Colin, *My American Journey.* 1995.

Ridgeway, James, ed., *The March to War* [Persian Gulf War]. 1991.

Shalom Stephen R., *Imperial Alibis: Rationalizing U.S. Intervention After the Cold War.* 1993.

Smith, Jean Edward, *George Bush's War.* 1992.

Szabo, Steven F., *The Diplomacy of German Unification.* 1992.

Treverton, Gregory F., *America, Germany, and the Future of Europe.* 1992.

Tucker, Robert W., and David C. Hendrickson, *The Imperial Temptation: The New World Order and America's Purposes.* 1992.

Woodward, Bob, *The Commanders* [decision making regarding the Persian Gulf War]. 1991.

Chapter 19: The Clinton Administration

Bert, Wayne, *The Reluctant Superpower: United States Policy in Bosnia 1991–95.* 1997.

Blood, Thomas, and Bruce Henderson, *State of the Union: A Report on President Clinton's First Four Years in Office.* 1996.

Cox, Michael, *U.S. Foreign Policy After the Cold War: Superpowers Without a Mission?* 1996.

Haass, Richard N., *The Reluctant Sheriff: The United States after the Cold War.* 1997.

Holbrooke, Richard, *"To End a War: From Sarajevo to Dayton—and Beyond.* 1998.

Kolodziej, Edward A., and Roger E. Kanet, eds., *Coping with Conflict After the Cold War.* 1996.

Mandelbaum, Michael, *The Dawn of Peace in Europe* [Clinton and post–Cold War Europe]. 1997.

Perry, William J., "Defense in an Age of Hope," *Foreign Affairs,* November/December 1996.

Ruggie, John G., *Winning the Peace: America and World Order in the New Era.* 1996.

Talbott, Strobe, "Democracy and the National Interest," *Foreign Affairs,* November/December 1996.

Walker, Martin, *The President We Deserve.* 1996.

Index